JUBILEE

One Hundred Years of the *Atlantic*

Editors and Publishers of the *Atlantic*

Editors

James Russell Lowell	1857–1861
James Thomas Fields	1861–1871
William Dean Howells	1871–1881
Thomas Bailey Aldrich	1881–1890
Horace Elisha Scudder	1890–1898
Walter Hines Page	1898–1899
Bliss Perry	1899–1909
Ellery Sedgwick	1909–1938
Edward Weeks	1938–

Publishers

Phillips, Sampson & Co.	1857–1859
Ticknor & Fields	1859–1867
Fields, Osgood & Co.	1868–1870
James R. Osgood & Co.	1871–1873
H. O. Houghton & Co.	1874–1877
Houghton, Mifflin & Co.	1880–1908
Atlantic Monthly Co.	1908–

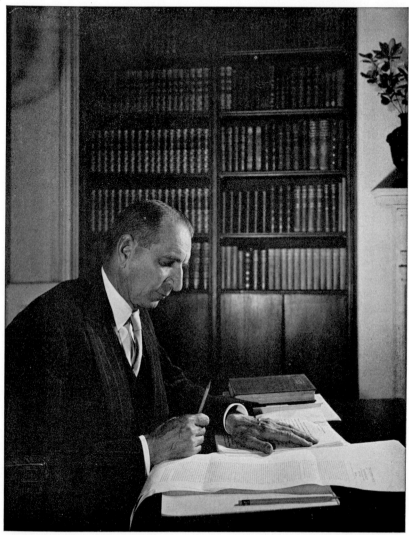

Edward Weeks, Ninth Editor of the *Atlantic*

JUBILEE

One Hundred Years of the Atlantic

Selected and Edited by

EDWARD WEEKS

and

EMILY FLINT

An Atlantic Monthly Press Book

Boston · Little, Brown and Company · Toronto

W

The editors wish to thank the following for permission to reprint the material
included in this anthology:

TRUSTEES U/WILL BROOKS ADAMS — for his "Economic Conditions for Future Defense," copyright 1903, by The Atlantic Monthly Company; and his
"A Problem in Civilization," copyright 1910, by The Atlantic Monthly Company.

DILLON ANDERSON — for his "Portrait of a Poker Player," copyright 1954, by
The Atlantic Monthly Company.

MAX ASCOLI — for his "Fascism in the Making," copyright 1933, by The Atlantic Monthly Company.

ATLANTIC MONTHLY PRESS–LITTLE, BROWN & COMPANY — for "The Glory
Hole" from Naturalist at Large, copyright 1942, 1943, by Phillips Ketchum,
Tr. u/ind. tr. made by Thomas Barbour f/b/o Mary B. Kidder, Julia A. Bar-
bour and Louisa B. Barbour, dtd. July 19, 1943. Reprinted by permission of
Mrs. Samuel H. Hallowell, Mrs. Alfred Kidder II, and Mrs. Jefferson D.
Parker, daughters of Dr. Barbour; — for "The Black Gates of Keokuk" from
A Stretch on the River, copyright 1950, by Richard P. Bissell; — for No Place
to Hide, copyright 1948, by David Bradley; — and MICHAEL JOSEPH LTD.
for "Herald Angels Miss the Boat" from Three Came Home, copyright 1946,
1947, by Agnes Newton Keith; — and MACMILLAN & CO., LTD., PEARN,
POLLINGER & HIGHAM, LTD. and ANN WATKINS, INC. for "Wilfred Owen"
from Noble Essences, copyright 1950, by Sir Osbert Sitwell; — and MICHAEL
JOSEPH LTD. for "Mickey" from The Open Heart, copyright 1946, 1947, 1948,
1949, 1950, 1951, 1952, 1953, 1954, 1955, by Edward Weeks; — for
"More Truth Than Poetry" from As I Remember Him, copyright 1939, 1940,
by Hans Zinsser.

SIR ISAIAH BERLIN — for his "Mr. Churchill," copyright 1949, by Isaiah Berlin.

BRANDT & BRANDT — for "All Around the Town," originally published in The
Atlantic Monthly, copyright, 1940, by Stephen Vincent Benét.

JOHN MASON BROWN — for his "Is This Your First Visit?" from Accustomed

Introduction

We began this book with the belief that in its first century the *Atlantic* has been a faithful and in crises an inspired reflection of our national life. We knew that the magazine had been founded at a time of great tension, when the Union was in jeopardy and passions were running high; we knew that the abolition of slavery was a driving force for our first contributors, and we had not read far in the early issues before we discovered that under this force even the most objective of them, men like Emerson and Lowell, wrote at white heat. The magazine, which grew out of the aspiration and anxieties of the 1850s, has come to contain the heartbeat and anger, the tenderness and laughter, of Americans from all quarters. Under the third editor, William Dean Howells, it made its peace with the South, and it was he also who ushered in Mark Twain and Bret Harte and the other fresh contributors from the West. Under its sixth editor, Walter Hines Page, who was a Southerner, it first predicted the emergence of the United States as a world power, and with the succession of Ellery Sedgwick in 1909 it ceased to be an exclusively New England journal; thereafter its readership has expanded with the growth of the country.

The heartbeat of a great magazine is the heartbeat of its dominant contributors, and it was our quest to find them at their vivid best. More than one hundred million words have been printed in the *Atlantic* in its twelve hundred issues, and certain things became very clear to us at the outset. First, since this was pre-eminently an American magazine, we should confine our choice as much as possible to American writers. Secondly, it did not take us long to realize that there is a vast difference between the leisurely reading of the Victorian decades and the swift nervous expectancy of today. If we were to reproduce the work of at least one hundred of our most distinguished contributors — there are actually one hundred twenty-eight of them in this volume — we would have to take the liberty of cutting. We decided that the stories and the lyrics should be reprinted verbatim, but that in some cases the longer essays, the biographical studies, and the controversial articles could be cut, to the enhanced interest of the modern reader and without grave injury to themselves. We knew that we should be criticized in some quarters for this, but we also knew that only by such editing could we hope to rescue a majority of our finest contributions from the entombment of the bound volumes of back numbers.

We hope that we have made an equally reasonable decision in the choice of our fiction. The first editors of the magazine always had one novel running serially, sometimes two. This was how we came to publish the best of the early work of Henry James and William Dean Howells, of Sarah Orne Jewett and Margaret Deland. These novels are available in book form, and no purpose would be served by reprinting episodes drawn from them at this late date. This led us to concentrate upon the short stories, particularly those by Americans. Here we were faced with a choice between the familiar *Atlantic* classics — "Marjorie Daw" by Thomas Bailey Aldrich, "A Man Without a Country" by Edward Everett Hale, and "Death on an Atoll" by James Norman Hall, to name three — which were already in anthologies, and those of more recent origin. It was our preference to look for narratives which would have a fresher appeal to contemporary readers, and whenever possible we have chosen those which exemplify the *Atlantic's* role as discoverer.

A third decision was to break away from the plodding of chronology and to group the material in a series of galaxies whose subject matter has been of vital and recurring concern to the nine editors down the decades. This arrangement permits us to place the writers of the 1950s on the same footing with those of the 1850s and to enjoy the contrast.

To Mrs. Flint, my managing editor, and myself it has been an absorbing challenge, this endeavor to edit the writing of a century. In the forewords and in the biographical notes I have tried to show the intimate relations between editor and author and between editor and reader. The process of selection was for us a humbling and enriching experience. How well these men and women wrote as they warmed up to their subjects! As we reviewed their work our thoughts went back to the letter which Charles Eliot Norton wrote from Paris in June of 1857 to his friend James Russell Lowell on hearing that Lowell was to be the first editor of the fledgling magazine.

> Of course it will succeed with you as its Editor, and with such liberal arrangements for its beginning. But such things are never permanent in our country. They burn brightly for a while, and then burn out — and some other light takes their place. It would be a great thing for us if any undertaking of this kind could live long enough to get affections and associations connected with it, whose steady glow should take the

place of, and more than supply, the shine of novelty, and the dazzle of a first go-off. I wish we had a Sylvanus Urban a hundred and fifty years old. I wish, indeed, we had anything so old in America; I would give a thousand of our new lamps for the one old, battered, but true magical light.

Anyone who gives this book a chance will perceive the "steady glow" that Norton speaks of, a steady glow rising occasionally to the fierce white light of the American character when aroused.

*　　*　　*

The *Atlantic* will always be indebted to Francis H. Underwood — "the editor who was never the editor," as Bliss Perry called him — for it was his initiative which brought the magazine to life. As early as 1853 Underwood was searching for the capital with which to found a new magazine which should "bring the literary influence of New England to aid the antislavery cause." By January 1854 he thought he had the backing he needed from J. P. Jewett, the publisher of *Uncle Tom's Cabin*. But Jewett failed, and it was not until three years later that Underwood at last succeeded in bringing together the contributors and the backers for his cherished project. They met for dinner in Boston at the Parker House on two successive afternoons, May 5 and 6, 1857; Underwood at one end of the table, Phillips of the publishing house of Phillips, Sampson & Company at the other, and between them Emerson, Longfellow, James Russell Lowell, John L. Motley (*The Rise of the Dutch Republic*), Oliver Wendell Holmes, and James Elliot Cabot, the architect. "We sat down at three P.M.," wrote Phillips, "and rose at eight. The time occupied was longer by about four hours and thirty minutes than I am in the habit of consuming in that kind of occupation, but it was the richest time intellectually by all odds that I have ever had."

Underwood had planned well, for in addition to those at the table, he had the assurance of contributions from Hawthorne, Thoreau, Whittier, Thomas Wentworth Higginson, Prescott, James Freeman Clarke, and Harriet Beecher Stowe. He knew he held a monopoly of the best writers in America, and it made him confident that he could launch an essentially American magazine, in contrast to those periodicals in New York which relied heavily on pirating or importing English authors. Finally, he was self-effacing enough to realize that Lowell's prestige would be of utmost importance to the new venture, and he had already pledged Lowell as the first editor before the dinner began. Underwood himself would serve as the "office editor" or assistant.

Under the stimulus of oysters, steak, Burgundy, and brandy, the decisions were made: the magazine would be essentially American; would be called *The Atlantic Monthly Magazine* (the suggestion came from Holmes), and each issue would be published anonymously — no contribution would be signed nor would the editor's name be printed. "The names of the contributors will be given out," said Emerson, "when the names are worth more than the articles." The contents would be devoted to "literature, art, and politics." The magazine would be the "organ of no party or clique," and its founders' unanimous and passionate belief in Abolition made no doubt that it would be controversial. The opening issue would appear in the autumn. With these resolutions Lowell and Underwood went to work.

A magazine of ideas is most in demand at a time of anxiety, and by that token the year 1857 was auspicious. Money was tight and people were worried. Abraham Lincoln was unknown outside of Illinois. There was no transatlantic cable and no telephone. "Our age is an age of daring and doing," wrote an early contributor. "The world has advanced from a speed of five miles an hour to twenty or thirty or more" (he meant, of course, by railway). Darwin's shocking book, *The Origin of Species,* was still in manuscript; not till two years later did it challenge orthodox belief. Sigmund Freud, who was to have such a profound effect on all twentieth-century writers, had just been born. Girls were at last being admitted to the Boston high schools on an equal footing with the boys. A woman teacher in those schools was paid $6.50 a month; a full professor at Harvard, such as Lowell, our first editor, received $1200 a year.

As the time approached for the calling in of the first number, Lowell decided to play it safe, and he wrote to his friend Charles Eliot Norton in·London, enclosing a bank draft and suggesting that Mr. Norton shop around for an English serial and some short stories and poems. Norton did so and brought the handwritten manuscripts back with him in his trunk. When he debarked in New York in July, Norton saw his luggage safely on the pier, but on the way to the hotel his trunk disappeared and has never been found to this day. The loss of the manuscripts so incensed the British writers that they would not come again, and thus the *Atlantic* had no choice but to be American.

*   *   *

The *Atlantic* has survived because it has changed its editors more frequently than many of its larger competitors who are no longer in the land of the living. Whenever there was a serious sag in our circulation we brought in a new editor, a younger man who gave the magazine the lift it needed. It has survived because of our predilection for American writers, and because of our good fortune and good judgment in discovering them. Boston has been our vantage point, and I think the country still respects us for the Yankee humor and integrity which flow in our veins. Our influence has been out of all proportion to our circulation. At the outset we numbered fifteen thousand readers, and it is doubtful if the subscription list was ever larger than fifty thousand in the nineteenth century. At this writing the sale of our more successful issues is in excess of a quarter of a million copies.

We have been at our best when the country was aroused, when people were eager for information and guidance and were reading conscientiously; at our second best in days of prosperity, when the editor and the nation were complacent. Our aim from the first has been to reach thinking people and to entertain them or make them think harder. We have pioneered in some fields and if we have been laggard in others, as in labor relations, it is because we have failed to persuade the union leaders to take us into their confidence. Our attention to education has been unremitting, but the articles here were addressed to a time and need, and when that was met their interest has diminished.

The editors since Reconstruction have held to the pledge that the magazine should be nonpartisan, and in election after election we have resisted the pressure of well-meaning friends who would have us become a Republican or a Democratic organ. Our refusal to do so has cost us readers and advertising. But I am sure it has increased our sense of responsibility and our value.

Our margin of profit has always been a narrow one. Any magazine that lives for a hundred years has known the high peaks and the valleys of depression. We were, I think, most vulnerable in the 1880s when the great band who had chartered us were dying or had ceased to write and when Boston was no longer the Hub. Aldrich, the editor in that period, was baffled as to where to find their successors, and each summer he went searching abroad. Today the search, as it was in the beginning, is here in this country, and it carries the Boston editor not to Concord but twenty-five thousand miles a year.

As the costs of printing rose, it became necessary to change our format. The compositors who print us have received wage increases again and again during my editorship. The soft book-paper on which we were originally printed and which could not come off the press at a rate xiv *Introduction*

faster than eight hundred impressions an hour has been exchanged for a
coated, tougher paper which comes off modern presses at eight thousand
an hour. When it became necessary to increase our circulation, we
changed, among other things, our traditional table-of-contents cover to
a pictorial cover — with the result that our newsstand sale was tripled.
It would be very pleasant to live with the spaciousness of the past, but it
is our job to serve the nervous expectancy of today.

Each *Atlantic* editor has handed on to his successor a living tradition.
The gleam of that tradition will be seen in these pages, in the communi-
cative joy of life which the most memorable of our contributors have
brought into print.

EDWARD WEEKS

Boston
July 1957

Contents

To all those who have made the *Atlantic* over the years, we dedicate this book.

We wish especially to thank these friends and associates who helped us with a task which at times seemed impossible: Richard E. Danielson, M. A. DeWolfe Howe, Ferris Greenslet, Howard Mumford Jones, Walter M. Whitehill, Ellen B. Ballou, Margaret Hackett, Donald B. Snyder, Charles W. Morton, Arthur H. Thornhill, A. Bradlee Emmons, Seymour Lawrence, Virginia Albee, Dorothy M. Burnham, Louise Desaulniers, Shirley Dunton, Priscilla H. Merritt, Mary D. Rackliffe, Nancy E. Reynolds, Nancy M. Sheehan.

We also found valuable leads and stimulus in these books: *A History of American Magazines,* Frank Luther Mott; *Fields of the Atlantic Monthly: Letters to an Editor 1861–1870,* James C. Austin; *The Road to Realism: The Early Years of William Dean Howells,* Edwin H. Cady; *The Atlantic Monthly and Its Makers,* M. A. DeWolfe Howe; *Atlantic Harvest,* edited by Ellery Sedgwick; *Letters of James Russell Lowell,* edited by Charles Eliot Norton; *Park-Street Papers,* Bliss Perry; *The Life and Letters of Walter H. Page,* Burton J. Hendrick; *The Life of Thomas Bailey Aldrich,* Ferris Greenslet; *American Life As Reflected in the Atlantic Monthly 1857–1881,* a thesis by Robert Earl Mitchell, Harvard University; *William Dean Howells As Editor of the Atlantic Monthly,* a thesis by Robert Ernest Butler, Rutgers University.

EDWARD WEEKS
EMILY FLINT

One Nation Indivisible

The Atlantic *was launched in the melancholy autumn of* 1857, *a year of financial panic with deepening anxiety here and abroad.* "It is a gloomy moment in history," *declared an editorial in* Harper's Weekly *for October,* 1857. "Not for many years — not in the lifetime of most men who read this paper — has there been so much grave and deep apprehension. In our own country there is universal commercial prostration and thousands of our poorest fellow-citizens are turned out against the approaching winter without employment. In France the political caldron seethes and bubbles with uncertainty. Russia hangs like a cloud dark and silent upon the horizon of Europe; while all the energies, resources and influences of the British Empire are sorely tried . . . in coping with the vast and deadly Indian situation, and with disturbed relations in China."

Americans were not deeply concerned in matters of foreign policy; Northerners and Southerners, what troubled them was the issue of slavery. Had we reached the end of compromise? Secession was in men's thoughts, and if attempted where would it end? These questions were bound up in the destiny of Abraham Lincoln. The selections which follow show how people reacted to him, those who saw him on the stump and those who wrote of him reflectively.

Recollections of Lincoln

by HENRY VILLARD

Henry Villard was twenty-three and still a German subject when the Staats-Zeitung of New York sent him to cover the Lincoln-Douglas debates. He had learned to speak English five years earlier and he was still somewhat unsympathetic to American humor.

FEBRUARY 1904

The first joint debate between Douglas and Lincoln which I attended (the second in the series of seven) took place on the afternoon of August 27, 1858, at Freeport, Illinois. It was the great event of the day, and attracted an immense concourse of people from all parts of the state. Douglas spoke first for an hour, followed by Lincoln for an hour and a half; upon which the former closed in another half hour. The Democratic spokesman commanded a strong, sonorous voice, a rapid, vigorous utterance, a telling play of countenance, impressive gestures, and all the other arts of the practiced speaker. As far as all external conditions were concerned, there was nothing in favor of Lincoln. He had a lean, lank, indescribably gawky figure, an odd-featured, wrinkled, inexpressive, and altogether uncomely face. He used singularly awkward, almost absurd, up-and-down and sidewise movements of his body to give emphasis to his arguments. His voice was naturally good, but he frequently raised it to an unnatural pitch. Yet the unprejudiced mind felt at once that, while there was on the one side a skillful dialectician and debater arguing a wrong and weak cause, there was on the other a thoroughly earnest and truthful man, inspired by sound convictions in consonance with the true spirit of American institutions. There was nothing in all Douglas's powerful effort that appealed to the higher instincts of human nature, while Lincoln always touched sympathetic chords. Lincoln's speech excited and sustained the enthusiasm of his audience to the end. When he had finished, two stalwart young farmers rushed on the platform, and, in spite of his remonstrances, seized and put him on their

shoulders and carried him in that uncomfortable posture for a considerable distance. It was really a ludicrous sight to see the grotesque figure
holding frantically to the heads of his supporters, with his legs dangling
from their shoulders and his pantaloons pulled up so as to expose his
underwear almost to his knees. Douglas made dexterous use of this incident in his next speech, expressing sincere regret that, against his wish,
he had used up his old friend Lincoln so completely that he had to be
carried off the stage. Lincoln retaliated by saying at the first opportunity
that he had known Judge Douglas long and well, but there was nevertheless one thing he could not say of him, and that was that the Judge always told the truth.

I was introduced to Lincoln at Freeport, and met him frequently afterwards in the course of the campaign. I must say frankly that, although
I found him most approachable, good-natured, and full of wit and humor, I could not take a real personal liking to the man, owing to an in-
born weakness for which he was even then notorious and so remained
during his great public career. He was inordinately fond of jokes, anecdotes, and stories. He loved to hear them, and still more to tell them himself out of the inexhaustible supply provided by his good memory and
his fertile fancy. There would have been no harm in this but for the fact
that, the coarser the joke, the lower the anecdote, and the more risky the
story, the more he enjoyed them, especially when they were of his own
invention. He possessed, moreover, a singular ingenuity in bringing
about occasions in conversation for indulgences of this kind. I have to
confess, too, that, aside from the prejudice against him which I felt on
this account, I shared the belief of a good many independent thinkers at
the time, including prominent leaders of the Republican party, that,
with regard to separating more effectively the antislavery Northern from
the proslavery Southern wing of the Democracy, it would have been
better if the re-election of Douglas had not been opposed.

The party warfare was hotly continued in all parts of the state from
early summer till election day in November. Besides the seven joint debates, both Douglas and Lincoln spoke scores of times separately, and
numerous other speakers from Illinois and other states contributed incessantly to the agitation. The two leaders visited almost every county in
the state. I heard four of the joint debates, and six other speeches by
Lincoln and eight by his competitor. Of course, the later efforts became
substantial repetitions of the preceding ones, and to listen to them grew
more and more tiresome to me. As I had seen something of political campaigns before, this one did not exercise the full charm of novelty upon

me. Still, even if I had been a far more callous observer, I could not have helped being struck with the efficient party organizations, the skillful tactics of the managers, the remarkable feats of popular oratory, and the earnestness and enthusiasm of the audiences I witnessed. It was a most instructive object lesson in practical party politics, and filled me with admiration for the Anglo-American method of working out popular destiny.

I firmly believe that if Stephen A. Douglas had lived, he would have had a brilliant national career. Freed by the Southern rebellion from all identification with proslavery interests, the road would have been open to the highest fame and position for which his unusual talents qualified him. As I took final leave of him and Lincoln, doubtless neither of them had any idea that within two years they would be rivals again in the presidential race. I had it from Lincoln's own lips that the United States senatorship was the greatest political height he at the time expected to climb.

He and I met accidentally, about nine o'clock on a hot, sultry evening, at a flag railroad station about twenty miles west of Springfield, on my return from a great meeting at Petersburg in Menard County. He had been driven to the station in a buggy and left there alone. I was already there. The train that we intended to take for Springfield was about due. After we waited vainly half an hour for its arrival, a thunderstorm compelled us to take refuge in an empty freight car standing on a side track, there being no buildings of any sort at the station. We squatted down on the floor of the car and fell to talking on all sorts of subjects. It was then and there he told me that, when he was clerking in a country store, his highest political ambition was to be a member of the state legislature. "Since then, of course," he said laughingly, "I have grown some, but my friends got me into *this* business [meaning the canvass]. I did not consider myself qualified for the United States Senate, and it took me a long time to persuade myself that I was. Now, to be sure," he continued, with another of his peculiar laughs, "I am convinced that I am good enough for it; but, in spite of it all, I am saying to myself every day: 'It is too big a thing for you; you will never get it.' Mary [his wife] insists, however, that I am going to be Senator and President of the United States, too." These last words he followed with a roar of laughter, with his arms around his knees, and shaking all over with mirth at his wife's ambition. "Just think," he exclaimed, "of such a sucker as me as President!"

He then fell to asking questions regarding my antecedents, and expressed some surprise at my fluent use of English after so short a residence in the United States. Next he wanted to know whether it was true that most of the educated people in Germany were "infidels." I answered that they were not openly professed infidels, but such a conclusion might be drawn from the fact that most of them were not church-goers. "I do not wonder at that," he rejoined, "my own inclination is that way." I ventured to give expression to my own disbelief in the doctrine of the Christian Church relative to the existence of God, the divinity of Christ, and immortality. This led him to put other questions to me to draw me out. He did not commit himself, but I received the impression that he was of my own way of thinking.

[In the last days of November 1860, the Associated Press sent Villard to Springfield, Illinois, to report current events by telegraph, until the departure of Lincoln for Washington. This duty brought Villard into daily relations with the President-elect, who gave him a most friendly welcome and told him to ask for information any time he wished.]

Mr. Lincoln soon found, after his election, that his modest two-story frame dwelling was altogether inadequate for the throng of local callers and of visitors from a distance, and, accordingly, he gladly availed himself of the offer of the use of the governor's room in the Capitol building. On my arrival, he had already commenced spending a good part of each day in it. He appeared daily, except Sundays, between nine and ten o'clock, and held a reception till noon, to which all comers were admitted without even the formality of first sending in cards. Whoever chose to call received the same hearty greeting. At noon, he went home to dinner and reappeared at about two. Then his correspondence was given proper attention, and visitors of distinction were seen by special appointment at either the State House or the hotel. Occasionally, but very rarely, he passed some time in his law office. In the evening, old friends called at his home for the exchange of news and political views. At times, when important news was expected, he would go to the telegraph or newspaper offices after supper, and stay there till late. Altogether, probably no other President-elect was so approachable to everybody, at least during the first weeks of my stay. But he found in the end, as was to be expected, that this popular practice involved a good deal of fatigue, and that he needed more time for himself; and the hours he gave up to the public were gradually restricted.

I was present almost daily for more or less time during his morning receptions. I generally remained a silent listener, as I could get at him at other hours when I was in need of information. It was a most interesting study to watch the manner of his intercourse with callers. As a rule, he showed remarkable tact in dealing with each of them, whether they were rough-looking Sangamon County farmers still addressing him familiarly as "Abe," sleek and pert commercial travelers, staid merchants, sharp politicians, or preachers, lawyers, or other professional men. He showed a very quick and shrewd perception of and adaptation to individual characteristics and peculiarities. He never evaded a proper question, or failed to give a fit answer.

None of his hearers enjoyed the wit — and wit was an unfailing ingredient — of his stories half as much as he did himself. It was a joy indeed to see the effect upon him. A high-pitched laughter lighted up his otherwise melancholy countenance with thorough merriment. His body shook all over with gleeful emotion, and when he felt particularly good over his performance, he followed his habit of drawing his knees, with his arms around them, up to his very face, as I had seen him do in 1858. I am sorry to state that he often allowed himself altogether too much license in the concoction of the stories.

I often availed myself of his authorization to come to him at any time for information. There were two questions in which the public, of course, felt the deepest interest, and upon which I was expected to supply light, namely, the composition of his cabinet and his views upon the secession movement that was daily growing in extent and strength. As to the former, he gave me to understand early, by indirection, that, as everybody expected, William H. Seward and S. P. Chase, his competitors for the presidential nomination, would be among his constitutional advisers. It was hardly possible for him not to recognize them, and he steadily turned a deaf ear to the remonstrances that were made against them as "extreme men" by leading politicians from the Border States, particularly from Kentucky and Missouri. As to the remaining members of his cabinet, they were definitely selected much later, and after a protracted and wearisome tussle with the delegations of various states that came to Springfield to urge the claims of their "favorite sons."

No one who heard him talk upon the other question could fail to discover his "other side," and to be impressed with his deep earnestness, his anxious contemplation of public affairs, and his thorough sense of the extraordinary responsibilities that were coming upon him. He did not hesitate to say that the Union ought to, and in his opinion would, be preserved, and to go into long arguments in support of the proposition. But he could not be got to say what he would do in the face of

Southern secession, except that as President he should be sworn to maintain the Constitution of the United States, and that he was therefore bound to fulfill that duty. I think I interpret his views up to the time of his departure for Washington correctly in saying that he had not lost faith in the preservation of peace between the North and the South, and he certainly did not dream that his principal duty would be to raise great armies and fleets, and the means to maintain them, for the suppression of the most determined and sanguinary rebellion in defense of slavery that our planet ever witnessed.

The Election in November

by JAMES RUSSELL LOWELL

James Russell Lowell, the first editor of the Atlantic, *discards its proclaimed nonpartisanship at the approach of the fateful election of 1860.*

OCTOBER 1860

The next presidential election looms always in advance, so that we seem never to have an actual Chief Magistrate, but a prospective one, looking to the chances of re-election and mingling in all the dirty intrigues of provincial politics with an unhappy talent for making them dirtier. The cheating mirage of the White House lures our public men away from present duties and obligations; and if matters go on as they have gone, we shall need a Committee of Congress to count the spoons in the public plate closet whenever a President goes out of office — with a policeman to watch every member of the Committee. We are kept normally in that most unprofitable of predicaments, a state of transition, and politicians measure their words and deeds by a standard of immediate and temporary expediency — an expediency not concerning the nation, but which, if more than merely personal, is no wider than the interests of party.

Is all this a result of the failure of democratic institutions? Rather of the fact that those institutions have never yet had a fair trial, and that for the last thirty years an abnormal element has been acting adversely with continually increasing strength. Whatever be the effect of slavery upon the states where it exists, there can be no doubt that its moral influence upon the North has been most disastrous. It has compelled our politicians into that first fatal compromise with their moral instincts and hereditary principles which makes all consequent ones easy; it has accustomed us to makeshifts instead of statesmanship, to subterfuge instead of policy, to party platforms for opinions, and to a defiance of the public sentiment of the civilized world for patriotism.

We have been asked to admit, first, that it was a necessary evil; then that it was a good both to master and slave; then that it was the cornerstone of free institutions; then that it was a system divinely instituted under the Old Law and sanctioned under the New. With a representation, three fifths of it based on the assumption that Negroes are men, the South turns upon us and insists on our acknowledging that they are things. After compelling her Northern allies to pronounce the "free and equal" clause of the preamble to the Declaration of Independence (because it stood in the way of enslaving men) a manifest absurdity, she has declared, through the Supreme Court of the United States, that Negroes are not men in the ordinary meaning of the word. To eat dirt is bad enough, but to find that we have eaten more than was necessary may chance to give us indigestion. The slaveholding interest has gone on step by step, forcing concession after concession, till it needs but little to secure it forever in the political supremacy of the country. Yield to its latest demand — let it mold the evil destiny of the Territories — and the thing is done past recall. The next presidential election is to say "Yes" or "No."

A great deal is said, to be sure, about the rights of the South; but has any such right been infringed? When a man invests money in any species of property, he assumes the risks to which it is liable. If he buy a house, it may be burned; if a ship, it may be wrecked; if a horse or an ox, it may die. Now the disadvantage of the Southern kind of property is — how shall we say it so as not to violate our constitutional obligations? — that it is exceptional. When it leaves Virginia, it is a thing; when it arrives in Boston, it becomes a man, speaks human language, appeals to the justice of the same God whom we all acknowledge, weeps at the memory of wife and children left behind — in short, hath the same organs and dimensions that a Christian hath, and is not distinguishable from ordinary Christians, except, perhaps, by a simpler and more earnest faith. There are people at the North who believe that, beside *meum* and *tuum*, there is also such a thing as *suum*; who are old-fashioned enough, or weak enough, to have their feelings touched by these things, to think that human nature is older and more sacred than any claim of property whatever, and that it has rights at least as much to be respected as any hypothetical one of our Southern brethren.

We shall continue to think the Negro a man, and on Southern evidence, too, as long as he is counted in the population represented on the floor of Congress, for three fifths of perfect manhood would be a high average even among white men; as long as he is hanged or worse, as an example and terror to others, for we do not punish one animal for the moral improvement of the rest; as long as he is considered capable of religious instruction, for we fancy the gorillas would make short work with a missionary; as long as there are fears of insurrection, for we never heard of a combined effort at revolt in a menagerie. Accordingly, we do not see how the particular right of whose infringement we hear so much is to be made safer by the election of Mr. Bell, Mr. Breckinridge, or Mr. Douglas.

We believe that the "irrepressible conflict" — for we accept Mr. Seward's much-denounced phrase in all the breadth of meaning he ever meant to give it — is to take place in the South itself; because the slave system is one of those fearful blunders in political economy which are sure, sooner or later, to work their own retribution. The inevitable tendency of slavery is to concentrate in a few hands the soil, the capital, and the power of the countries where it exists, to reduce the nonslaveholding class to a continually lower and lower level of property, intelligence, and enterprise, their increase in numbers adding much to the economical hardship of their position and nothing to their political weight in the community. There is no home encouragement of varied agriculture, for the wants of a slave population are few in number and limited in kind; none of inland trade, for that is developed only by communities of men, which is the true object of all political organizations, and which is essential to the prolonged existence of all those whose life and spirit are derived directly from the people.

No matter how enormous the wealth centered in the hands of a few, it has no longer the conservative force or the beneficent influence which it exerts when equably distributed — and even loses more of both where a system of absenteeism prevails so largely as in the South. In such communities the seeds of an "irrepressible conflict" are surely, if slowly, ripening, and signs are daily multiplying that the true peril to their social organization is looked for, less in a revolt of the owned labor than in an insurrection of intelligence in the labor that owns itself and finds itself none the richer for it. To multiply such communities is to multiply weakness.

We are persuaded that the election of Mr. Lincoln will do more than anything else to appease the excitement of the country. He has proved both his ability and his integrity; he has had experience enough in public affairs to make him a statesman, and not enough to make him a politician. That he has not had more will be no objection to him in the eyes of those who have seen the administration of the experienced public functionary whose term of office is just drawing to a close. He represents a party who know that true policy is gradual in its advances, that it is conditional and not absolute, that it must deal with facts and not with sentiments, but who know also that it is wiser to stamp out evil in the spark than to wait till there is no help but in fighting fire with fire. They are the only conservative party, because they are the only one based on an enduring principle, the only one that is not willing to pawn tomorrow for the means to gamble with today. They have no hostility to the South, but a determined one to doctrines of whose ruinous tendency every day more and more convinces them.

The encroachments of slavery upon our national policy have been like those of a glacier in a Swiss valley. Inch by inch, the huge dragon with his glittering scales and crests of ice coils itself onward, an anachronism of summer, the relic of a bygone world where such monsters swarmed. But it has its limit, the kindlier forces of nature work against it, and the silent arrows of the sun are still, as of old, fatal to the frosty Python. Geology tells us that such enormous devastators once covered the face of the earth, but the benignant sunlight of heaven touched them and they faded silently, leaving no trace but here and there the scratches of their talons and the gnawed boulders scattered where they made their lair. We have entire faith in the benignant influence of truth, the sunlight of the moral world, and believe that slavery, like other worn-out systems, will melt gradually before it. "All the earth cries out upon Truth, and the heaven blesseth it; ill works shake and tremble at it, and with it is no unrighteous thing."

The President's Proclamation

by RALPH WALDO EMERSON

A contributor from the first issue, Emerson delivered many antislavery speeches before the outbreak of the Civil War.

NOVEMBER 1862

In so many arid forms which states incrust themselves with, once in a century, if so often, a poetic act and record occur. These are the jets of thought into affairs, when, roused by danger or inspired by genius, the political leaders of the day break the else insurmountable routine of class and local legislation and take a step forward in the direction of catholic and universal interests. Every step in the history of political liberty is a sally of the human mind into the untried future, and has the interest of genius, and is fruitful in heroic anecdotes. Liberty is a slow fruit. It comes, like religion, for short periods and in rare conditions, as if awaiting a culture of the race which shall make it organic and permanent. The extreme moderation with which the President advanced to his design, his long-avowed expectant policy, as if he chose to be strictly the executive of the best public sentiment of the country, waiting only till it should be unmistakably pronounced; so fair a mind that none ever listened so patiently to such extreme varieties of opinion; so reticent that his decision has taken all parties by surprise, whilst yet it is the just sequel of his prior acts; the firm tone in which he announces it, without inflation or surplusage; all these have bespoken such favor to the act, that, great as the popularity of the President has been, we are beginning to think that we have underestimated the capacity and virtue which the Divine Providence has made an instrument of benefit so vast. He has been permitted to do more for America than any other American man. He is well entitled to the most indulgent construction. Forget all that we thought shortcomings, every mistake, every delay. In the extreme embarrassments of his part, call these endurance, wisdom, magnanimity, illuminated, as they now are, by this dazzling success.

When we consider the immense opposition that has been neutralized or converted by the progress of the war (for it is not long since the President anticipated the resignation of a large number of officers in the army, and the secession of three states, on the promulgation of this policy); when we see how the great stake which foreign nations hold in our affairs has recently brought every European power as a client into this court, and it became every day more apparent what gigantic and what remote interests were to be affected by the decision of the President, one can hardly say the deliberation was too long. Against all timorous counsels he had the courage to seize the moment; and such was his position, and such the felicity attending the action, that he has replaced government in the good graces of mankind.

It is by no means necessary that this measure should be suddenly marked by any signal results on the Negroes or on the Rebel masters. The force of the act is that it commits the country to this justice — that it compels the innumerable officers, civil, military, naval, of the Republic to range themselves on the line of this equity. It draws the fashion to this side. It is not a measure that admits of being taken back. Done, it cannot be undone by a new Administration. For slavery overpowers the disgust of the moral sentiment only through immemorial usage. It cannot be introduced as an improvement of the nineteenth century. This act means that the lives of our heroes have not been sacrificed in vain. It makes a victory of our defeats. Our hurts are healed; the health of the nation is repaired. With a victory like this, we can stand many disasters. It does not promise the redemption of the black race: that lies not with us; but it relieves it of our opposition. The President by this act has paroled all the slaves in America; they will no more fight against us; and it relieves our race once for all of its crime and false position. The first condition of success is secured in putting ourselves right. We have recovered ourselves from our false position, and planted ourselves on a law of nature.

The government has assured itself of the best constituency in the world: every spark of intellect, every virtuous feeling, every religious heart, every man of honor, every poet, every philosopher, the generosity of the cities, the health of the country, the strong arms of the mechanics, the endurance of farmers, the passionate conscience of women, the sympathy of distant nations, all rally to its support.

Abraham Lincoln

by CARL SANDBURG

American poet whose biography of Lincoln is one of the monuments of our time.

FEBRUARY 1947

The range of the personality of Abraham Lincoln ran far, identifying itself with the tumults and follies of mankind, keeping touch with multitudes and solitudes. The free-going and friendly companion is there and the man of the cloister, of the lonely corner of thought, prayer, and speculation. The man of public affairs, before a living audience announcing decisions, is there, and the solitary inquirer weaving his abstractions related to human freedom and responsibility.

Perhaps no other American held so definitely in himself both those elements — the genius of the Tragic, the spirit of the Comic. The fate of man, his burdens and crosses, the pity of circumstance, the extent of tragedy in human life, these stood forth in word shadows of the Lincoln utterance, as testamentary as the utter melancholy of his face in repose. And in contrast he came to be known nevertheless as the first authentic humorist to occupy the executive mansion in Washington, his gift of laughter and his flair for the funny being taken as a national belonging.

Though we sometimes meet the expression "a Lincolnian style," it has no strict meaning; Lincoln had many styles. It has been computed that his printed speeches and writings number 1,078,365 words. One may range through this record of utterance and find a wider variety of styles than in any other American statesman or orator. And perhaps no author of books has written and vocalized in such a diversity of speech tones directed at all manner and condition of men.

Three short pieces from his pen are kept as immemorial possessions of the American people, each keyed to a high tragic note. These are the Letter to Mrs. Bixby, the Gettysburg Address, the Second Inaugural.

The War Department records showed a Boston woman to have lost five sons in combat actions. The number was less than five, as later re-search revealed. But Lincoln spoke through her to all families that had lost a boy or man in the war. "Weak and fruitless must be any words of mine which should attempt to beguile you from the grief of a loss so overwhelming," he wrote. "But I cannot refrain from tendering to you the consolation that may be found in the thanks of the Republic they died to save." He poised his quill pen for the final sentence of the letter, he on whose initiative, action, and responsibility the war had begun and had been carried on for nearly four years, and he wrote: "I pray that our Heavenly Father may assuage the anguish of your bereavement and leave you only the cherished memory of the loved and lost, and the solemn pride that must be yours to have laid so costly a sacrifice upon the altar of freedom."

In a photographer's studio eleven days before delivering the speech at Gettysburg, Lincoln had held in his hands the lengthy address of Edward Everett, the designated orator of the day, the printed two-hour discourse covering nearly two sides of a one-sheet supplement of a Boston newspaper. To a young newspaper correspondent from Cali-fornia, Lincoln said his own speech at Gettysburg would be "short, short, short," as it proved to be, ten sentences spoken in less than five minutes. In its implicative qualities, it stands among the supreme utter-ances of democratic peoples of the world. "A new nation, conceived in liberty, and dedicated to the proposition that all men are created equal." For the perpetuation of this men were dying on battlefields, he said. And having so died, they would be forgotten men and their deaths of no use unless the living dedicated themselves to the unfinished work for which the dead had given "the last full measure of devotion."

Virtually the Gettysburg Address is one of the great American poems, having its use and acceptation far beyond American shores. It curiously incarnates the claims, assurances, and pretenses of republican institu-tions, of democratic procedure, of the rule of the people, and directly implies that popular government can come into being and can then "perish from the earth." How he would have defined "a new birth of freedom," at length, must be sought elsewhere in the body of his utter-ance. No accusations, no recriminations, no lash of invective, not even a mild outspoken reproach of the enemy. Some have detected in haunt-ing echoes of the Gettysburg Address a quiet summons to those of the South reluctant to let go of national unity: Come back into the old Union of States and let us make of it what those Virginians, Washington and Jefferson, envisioned. Apart from its immediate historic setting it is a timeless psalm in the name of those who *fight* and *do* in behalf of great human causes rather than *talk,* in a belief that men can "highly resolve" themselves and can mutually "dedicate" their lives to a cause, in a posture of oath-taking that "these dead shall not have died in vain."

As one may delve endlessly into the restless implications of the Gettysburg Address, so also one may ponder the Second Inaugural and the intricate derivations to be made from it. A cry for merciless and further war, so some took it, while others read it as a benediction, a prayer, and a fathomless hope set to music. How did the war begin? He would try to tell it in two sentences, one long and one short: "Both parties deprecated war; but one of them would make war rather than let the nation survive; and the other would accept war rather than let it perish. And the war came." The peculiar sobriety of judgments pronounced on both of the warring sections of the country has had wide discussion and keeps a permanent value: "Neither party expected for the war the magnitude or the duration which it has already attained. Neither anticipated that the cause of the conflict might cease with, or even before, the conflict itself should cease. Each looked for an easier triumph, and a result less fundamental and astounding. Both read the same Bible, and pray to the same God; and each invokes His aid against the other. It may seem strange that any men should dare to ask a just God's assistance in wringing their bread from the sweat of other men's faces; but let us judge not, that we be not judged. The prayers of both could not be answered — that of neither has been answered fully." In like pitch and key was the often quoted sentence of the First Inaugural four years earlier: "Suppose you go to war. You cannot fight always; and when, after much loss on both sides, and no gain on either, you cease fighting, the identical old questions as to terms of intercourse are again upon you."

The Bixby Letter, the Gettysburg Address, the Second Inaugural, these were widely reprinted and went to increasingly large readerships as decades passed. Yet there was another utterance of Lincoln that did not come to any immense audience until the Second World War. This consists of passages from the President's Message to Congress, December 1, 1862. In this Message, Lincoln was using to the limit his powers of persuasion to get the Congress to enact legislation enabling "compensated emancipation," the Federal government to buy the slaves and set them free. Also in this Message he presented the cause of national unity in new phases. "A nation may be said to consist of its territory, its people, and its laws. The territory is the only part which is of certain durability. 'One generation passeth away, and another generation cometh, but the earth abideth forever.' It is of the first importance to duly consider and estimate this ever enduring part. . . . Our national strife springs not from our permanent part, not from the land we inhabit. . . . Our strife pertains to ourselves — to the passing generations of men; and it can without convulsion be hushed forever with the passing of one generation."

Then, having presented his plan for compensated emancipation, he appealed for united action as between Congress and Executive. "We can succeed only by concert. It is not 'Can any of us imagine better?' but 'Can we all do better?' Object whatsoever is possible, still the question occurs, 'Can we do better?' " Then came his pleadings wherein it is seen that he was sensitively aware of how momentous was the hour and of the need for each man to make his personal record such that it would stand the scrutiny of remote generations, urging: "The dogmas of the quiet past are inadequate to the stormy present. The occasion is piled high with difficulty, and we must rise with the occasion. As our case is new, so we must think anew and act anew. We must disenthrall ourselves, and then we shall save our country."

There have been long-time students of Lincoln who place among his sublime passages the one that closed this 1862 Message: "Fellow citizens, we cannot escape history. We of this Congress and this administration will be remembered in spite of ourselves. No personal significance or insignificance can spare one or another of us. The fiery trial through which we pass will light us down, in honor or dishonor, to the latest generation. . . . We shall nobly save or meanly lose the last, best hope of earth. Other means may succeed; this could not fail. The way is plain, peaceful, generous, just — a way which, if followed, the world will forever applaud, and God must forever bless."

That the Congress paid little heed, that it balked at the legislation suggested, that it had a low or indifferent opinion of Lincoln's language and persuasions, is part of the record. That the Congress, save for a remnant of two or three members, had any dim vision that possibly eighty years later, in another national crisis of world scope, there would be global circulation of sentences from this Message of Lincoln, there is little or no indication. A grim fighting insistence was found in such lines as "The fiery trial through which we pass will light us down, in honor or dishonor, to the latest generation."

The Place of Abraham Lincoln in History

by GEORGE BANCROFT

Statesman and historian, Bancroft had been Secretary of the Navy under President Polk. He was one of those Northern abolitionists who opposed Lincoln at the outset, but the President soon won him over. This paper was written immediately after the assassination.

JUNE 1865

The funeral procession of the late President of the United States has passed through the land from Washington to his final resting place in the heart of the prairies. Along the line of more than fifteen hundred miles his remains were borne, as it were, through continued lines of the people; and the number of mourners and the sincerity and unanimity of grief were such as never before attended the obsequies of a human being; so that the terrible catastrophe of his end hardly struck more awe than the majestic sorrow of the people. The thought of the individual was effaced; and men's minds were drawn to the station which he filled, to his public career, to the principles he represented, to his martyrdom.

Why has the President been struck down, and why do the people mourn? We think we pay the best tribute to his memory, and the most fitting respect to his name, if we ask after the relation in which he stands to the history of his country and his fellow men.

Buchanan, who took the presidential chair in 1857, had no traditional party against him; he owed his nomination to confidence in his moderation and supposed love of Union. He might have united the whole North and secured a good part of the South. Constitutionally timid, on taking the oath of office he betrayed his own weakness and foreshadowed the forthcoming decision of the Supreme Court. Under the wing of the Executive, Chief Justice Taney gave his famed disquisition. The delivery of that opinion was an act of revolution. The truth of history was scorned; the voice of passion was put forward as the rule of law; doctrines were laid down which, if they are just, give a full sanction to the rebellion which ensued. The country was stung to the quick by the reckless conduct of a body which it needed to trust and which now was leading the way to the overthrow of the Constitution and the dismemberment of the Republic.

At the same time Buchanan, in selecting the members of his cabinet, chose four of the seven from among those who were prepared to sacrifice the country to the interests of slavery. In time of peace the finances were willfully ill-administered, and in the midst of wealth and credit the country was saved from bankruptcy only by the patriotism of the city of New York, against the treacherous intention of the Secretary of the Treasury. Cannon and muskets and military stores were sent in numbers where they could most surely fall into the hands of the coming rebellion; troops of the United States were placed under disloyal officers and put out of the way; the navy was scattered abroad. And then, that nothing might be wanting to increase the agony of the country, an attempt to force the institution of slavery on the people of Kansas, who refused it, received the encouragement and aid of Buchanan.

The position of Abraham Lincoln, on the day of his inauguration, was apparently one of helpless debility. A bark canoe in a tempest on mid-ocean seemed hardly less safe. The vital tradition of the country on slavery no longer had its adequate expression in either of the two great political parties, and the Supreme Court had uprooted the old landmarks and guides. The men who had chosen him President did not constitute a consolidated party and did not profess to represent either of the historic parties which had been engaged in the struggles of three quarters of a century. They were a heterogeneous body of men, of the most various political attachments in former years, and on many questions of economy held the most discordant opinions. Scarcely knowing each other, they did not form a numerical majority of the whole country, were in a minority in each branch of Congress except from the willful absence of members, and could not be sure of their own continuance as an organized body. They did not know their own position and were startled by the consequences of their success.

The new President himself was, according to his own description, a man of defective education, a lawyer by profession, knowing nothing of administration beyond having been master of a very small post office, knowing nothing of war but as a captain of volunteers in a raid against an Indian chief, repeatedly a member of the Illinois legislature, once a member of Congress. He spoke with ease and clearness, but not with eloquence. He wrote concisely and to the point, but was unskilled in the use of the pen. He had no accurate knowledge of the public defenses of the country, no exact conception of its foreign relations, no comprehensive perception of his duties. The qualities of his nature were not suited to hardy action. His temper was soft and gentle and yielding, reluctant to refuse anything that presented itself to him as an act of kindness, loving to please and willing to confide, not trained to confine acts of good will within the stern limits of duty. He was of the temperament called melancholic, scarcely concealed by an exterior of lightness of humor, having a deep and fixed seriousness, jesting lips, and wanness of heart. And this man was summoned to stand up directly against a power with which Henry Clay had never directly grappled, before which Webster at last had quailed, which no President had offended and yet successfully administered the government, to which each great political party had made concessions, to which in various measures of compromise the country had repeatedly capitulated, and with which he must now venture a struggle for the life or death of the nation.

The credit of the country had not fully recovered from the shock it had treacherously received in the former Administration. A part of the navy yards were intrusted to incompetent agents or enemies. The social spirit of the city of Washington was against him, and spies and enemies abounded in the circles of fashion. Every executive department swarmed with men of treasonable inclinations, so that it was uncertain where to rest for support. The army officers had been trained in unsound political principles. The chief of staff of the highest general officers, wearing the mask of loyalty, was a traitor at heart.

The country was ungenerous toward the Negro, who in truth was not in the least to blame, who was impatient that such a strife should have grown out of his condition and wished that he were far away. On the side of prompt decision the advantage was with the Rebels; the President sought how to avoid war without compromising his duty; and the Rebels, who knew their own purpose, won incalculable advantages by the start which they thus gained. The country stood aghast, and would not believe in the full extent of the conspiracy to shatter it in pieces; men were uncertain if there would be a great uprising of the people. The President and his cabinet were in the midst of an enemy's country and in personal danger, and at one time their connections with the North and West were cut off; and that very moment was chosen by the trusted chief of staff of the lieutenant general to go over to the enemy.

Everyone remembers how this state of suspense was terminated by the uprising of a people who now showed strength and virtues which they were hardly conscious of possessing.

In some respects Abraham Lincoln was peculiarly fitted for his task in connection with the movement of his countrymen. He was of the Northwest; and this time it was the Mississippi River, the needed outlet for the wealth of the Northwest, that did its part in asserting the necessity of Union. He was one of the mass of the people; he represented them, because he was of them; and the mass of the people, the class that lives and thrives by self-imposed labor, felt that the work which was to be done was a work of their own: the assertion of equality against the pride of oligarchy, of free labor against the lordship over slaves, of the great industrial people against all the expiring aristocracies of which any remnants had tided down from the Middle Ages. He was of a reli- gious turn of mind, without superstition, and the unbroken faith of the mass was like his own. As he went along through his difficult journey, sounding his way, he held fast by the hand of the people and "tracked its footsteps with even feet." "His pulse's beat twinned with their pulses." He committed faults, but the people were resolutely generous, magnanimous, and forgiving; and he in his turn was willing to take instructions from their wisdom.

The measure by which Abraham Lincoln takes his place, not in American history only, but in universal history, is his Proclamation of January 1, 1863, emancipating all slaves within the insurgent states. It was indeed a military necessity, and it decided the result of the war. It took from the public enemy one or two million bondmen and placed between one and two hundred thousand brave and gallant troops in arms on the side of the Union. A great deal has been said in time past of the wonderful results of the toil of the enslaved Negro in the creation of wealth by the culture of cotton; and now it is in part to the aid of the Negro in freedom that the country owes its success in its movement of regeneration — that the world of mankind owes the continuance of the United States as the example of a Republic. The death of President Lincoln sets the seal to that Proclamation, which must be maintained. It cannot but be maintained. It is the only rod that can safely carry off the thunderbolt. He came to it perhaps reluctantly; he was brought to adopt it, as it were, against his will, but compelled by inevitable necessity. He disclaimed all praise for the act, saying reverently, after it had succeeded, "The nation's condition God alone can claim."

And what a futurity is opened before the country when its institutions become homogeneous! From all the civilized world the nations will send hosts to share the wealth and glory of this people. It will receive all good ideas from abroad; and its great principles of personal equality and freedom: freedom of conscience and mind, freedom of speech and action, freedom of government through ever-renewed common consent, will undulate through the world like the rays of light and heat from the sun. With one wing touching the waters of the Atlantic and the other on the Pacific, it will grow into a greatness of which the past has no parallel; and there can be no spot in Europe or in Asia so remote or so secluded as to shut out its influence.

*   *   *

Not a few, I think, would be of the opinion that the strongly contrasted figures of Abraham Lincoln and the second Oliver Wendell Holmes were the two most creditable and encouraging embodiments which it has been the portion of the human spirit to experience in this country. Those holding that opinion would learn with the greater interest that once, in a unique and fateful moment of American history, those two met — the one a handsome towering lad in his early twenties, the other with less than a year of his course still to run — met and had salty and characteristic words with each other.

Lincoln had come from the White House to inspect the defenses, and the task of piloting him had fallen to Holmes. Lincoln wanted to know just where the enemy were, and Holmes pointed them out. The President stood up to look. Now, when standing up and supplemented by his high plug hat, Lincoln was a target of exceptional visibility. From the Rebel marksmen came a snarl of musketry fire. Grabbing the President by the arm, the young officer dragged him under cover, and afterwards, in wave upon wave of hot misgiving, was unable to forget that in doing so he had said, "Get down, you fool!"

Admittedly this was not the approved style for an officer to employ in addressing the Commander-in-Chief of the armed forces of his country. The youthful aide was the more relieved when, just as Lincoln was quitting the fort, he took the trouble to walk back. "Good-by, Colonel Holmes," he said. "I'm glad to see you know how to talk to a civilian."

From "Get Down, You Fool!" by Alexander Woollcott, February 1938

Commemoration Ode

by JAMES RUSSELL LOWELL

*Lowell's long and stirring Ode, which he delivered at the
Harvard Commencement of 1865, did not contain these lines
on Lincoln; they were written subsequently and first appeared when the poem was published in the* Atlantic.

SEPTEMBER 1865

Such was he, our Martyr-Chief,
    Whom late the Nation he had led,
    With ashes on her head,
Wept with the passion of an angry grief:
Forgive me, if from present things I turn
To speak what in my heart will beat and burn,
And hang my wreath on his world-honored urn.
    Nature, they say, doth dote,
    And cannot make a man
    Save on some worn-out plan,
    Repeating us by rote:
For him her Old World mold aside she threw,
    And, choosing sweet clay from the breast
    Of the unexhausted West,
With stuff untainted shaped a hero new,
Wise, steadfast in the strength of God, and true.
    How beautiful to see
Once more a shepherd of mankind indeed,
Who loved his charge, but never loved to lead;
One whose meek flock the people joyed to be,
    Not lured by any cheat of birth,
    But by his clear-grained human worth,
And brave old wisdom of sincerity!
    They knew that outward grace is dust;
    They could not choose but trust

In that sure-footed mind's unfaltering skill,
And supple-tempered will
That bent like perfect steel to spring again and thrust.
Nothing of Europe here,
Or, then, of Europe fronting mornward still,
Ere any names of Serf and Peer
Could Nature's equal scheme deface:
Here was a type of the true elder race,
And one of Plutarch's men talked with us face to face.
I praise him not; it were too late;
And some innative weakness there must be
In him who condescends to victory
Such as the Present gives, and cannot wait,
Safe in himself as in a fate.
So always firmly he:
He knew to bide his time,
And can his fame abide,
Still patient in his simple faith sublime,
Till the wise years decide.
Great captains, with their guns and drums,
Disturb our judgment for the hour,
But at last silence comes:
These all are gone, and, standing like a tower,
Our children shall behold his fame,
The kindly-earnest, brave, foreseeing man,
Sagacious, patient, dreading praise, not blame,
New birth of our new soil, the first American.

New England and the Hub

If Boston is a state of mind, then certainly the most sprightly of the early contributors to display the singularities of that mind was the little doctor, Oliver Wendell Holmes. His Breakfast Table papers appeared in the first twenty-six issues of the magazine without a break, first "The Autocrat," then "The Professor at the Breakfast Table." These dialogues, supposed to have taken place in a prim Boston boardinghouse, were opinionated, and disturbing in their religious views; they were clever, often amusing in their literary allusions, and again and again they reverted to the author's aggressive pride in the Hub and its standards.

The Autocrat took New England by storm. From this series and its sequel we have selected four characteristic episodes. The first describes the island of Naushon, which has been in the possession of the Forbes family since 1847, and in the last two Dr. Holmes discloses his pride in Boston and his contempt for "the mob of cities."

New Englanders have always had a keen pride of place and are rather grudging in admitting newcomers to share it with them. Thoreau in the superb passages from his essay on walking symbolizes the magnetic pull to the westward which was already drawing away many of the more eager spirits. Miss Jewett perfectly preserves the idiom which is still heard in the northern townships; Dr. Barbour reminds us of some of the amusing quiddities of ancestor worship; Arthur Pier shows us the veneration for biography and for one biographer in particular in this place of long memories; and Howard Mumford Jones expresses the skepticism of a Bostonian by adoption.

The Autocrat of the Breakfast Table

by OLIVER WENDELL HOLMES

Doctor, writer, and one of the most social of men, Oliver Wendell Holmes was a founding contributor and the one who actually gave the Atlantic its name. Indefatigable in his prose and verse, he appeared in almost every volume in the first thirty years. His characterization of Little Boston, the hunchback, with his irrepressible pride in the Hub, was one of his happiest creations.

DECEMBER 1857

Where have I been for the last three or four days? Down at the Island, deer shooting. How many did I bag? I brought home one buck shot. The Island is where? No matter. It is the most splendid domain that any man looks upon in these latitudes. Blue sea around it, and running up into its heart, so that the little boat slumbers like a baby in lap, while the tall ships are stripping naked to fight the hurricane outside, and storm-stay sails banging and flying in ribbons. Trees, in stretches of miles; beeches, oaks, most numerous — many of them hung with moss, looking like bearded Druids; some coiled in the clasp of huge, dark-stemmed grapevines. Open patches where the sun gets in and goes to sleep, and the winds come so finely sifted that they are as soft as swan's-down. Rocks scattered about, Stonehenge-like monoliths. Freshwater lakes; one of them, Mary's lake, crystal clear, full of flashing pickerel lying under the lily pads like tigers in the jungle. Six pounds of ditto one morning for breakfast. EGO *fecit*.

The divinity student looked as if he would like to question my Latin. No, sir, I said, you need not trouble yourself. There is a higher law in grammar, not to be put down by Andrews and Stoddard. Then I went on.

Such hospitality as that island has seen there has not been the like of in these our New England sovereignties. There is nothing in the shape of kindness and courtesy that can make life beautiful, which has not found its home in that ocean principality. It has welcomed all who were worthy of welcome, from the pale clergyman who came to breathe the sea air with its medicinal salt and iodine, to the great statesman who turned his back on the affairs of empire, and smoothed his Olympian forehead, and flashed his white teeth in merriment over the long table, where his wit was the keenest and his story the best.

(I don't believe any man ever talked like that in this world. I don't believe *I* talked just so; but the fact is, in reporting one's conversation, one cannot help *Blair*-ing it up more or less, ironing out crumpled paragraphs, starching limp ones, and crimping and plaiting a little sometimes; it is as natural as prinking at the looking glass.)

How can a man help writing poetry in such a place? Everybody who goes there does write poetry. In the state archives, kept in the library of the Lord of the Isle, are whole volumes of unpublished verse — some by well-known hands, and others, quite as good, by the last people you would think of as versifiers — men who could pension off all the genuine poets in the country, and buy ten acres of Boston common, if it were for sale, with what they had left. Of course I had to write my little copy of verses with the rest.

Some of you boarders ask me from time to time why I don't write a story, or a novel, or something of that kind. Instead of answering each one of you separately, I will thank you to step up into the wholesale department for a few moments, where I deal in answers by the piece and by the bale.

That every articulately speaking human being has in him stuff for *one* novel in three volumes duodecimo has long been with me a cherished belief. It has been maintained, on the other hand, that many persons cannot write more than one novel — that all after that are likely to be failures. Life is so much more tremendous a thing in its heights and depths than any transcript of it can be, that all records of human experience are as so many bound herbaria to the innumerable glowing, glistening, rustling, breathing, fragrance-laden, poison-sucking, life-giving, death-distilling leaves and flowers of the forest and the prairies. All we can do with books of human experience is to make them alive again with something borrowed from our own lives. We can make a book alive for us just in proportion to its resemblance in essence or in form to our own experience. Now an author's first novel is naturally drawn, to a great extent, from his personal experiences; that is, is a literal copy of nature under various slight disguises. But the moment the author gets out of his personality, he must have the creative power, as well as the narrative art and the sentiment, in order to tell a living story; and this is rare.

Besides, there is great danger that a man's first life story shall clean him out, so to speak, of his best thoughts. Most lives, though their stream is loaded with sand and turbid with alluvial waste, drop a few golden grains of wisdom as they flow along. Oftentimes a single cradling gets them all, and after that the poor man's labor is only rewarded by mud and worn pebbles. All which proves that I, as an individual of the human family, could write one novel or story at any rate, if I would.

Why don't I, then? Well, I am terribly afraid I should show up all my friends. I should like to know if all storytellers do not do this? Now I am afraid all my friends would not bear showing up very well; for they have an average share of the common weakness of humanity, which I am pretty certain would come out. Of all that have told stories among us there is hardly one I can recall that has not drawn too faithfully some living portrait that might better have been spared.

Sin has many tools, but a lie is the handle which fits them all.

I think, sir, said the divinity student, you must intend that for one of the sayings of the Seven Wise Men of Boston you were speaking of the other day.

The schoolmistress wanted to know how many of these sayings there were on record, and what, and by whom said.

Why, let us see, there is that one of Benjamin Franklin, "the great Bostonian," after whom this lad was named. To be sure, he said a great many wise things — and I don't feel sure he didn't borrow this — he speaks as if it were old. But then he applied it so neatly: "He that has once done you a kindness will be more ready to do you another than he whom you yourself have obliged."

To these must certainly be added that other saying of one of the wittiest of men: "Good Americans, when they die, go to Paris." The divinity student looked grave at this, but said nothing. The schoolmistress spoke out, and said she didn't think the wit meant any irreverence. It was only another way of saying that Paris is a heavenly place after New York or Boston.

A jaunty-looking person, who had come in with the young fellow they call John — evidently a stranger — said there was one more wise man's saying that he had heard; it was about our place, but he didn't know who said it. A civil curiosity was manifested by the company. I heard him distinctly whispering to the young fellow who brought him to dinner, Shall I tell it? To which the answer was, Go ahead! Well, he said, this was what I heard: "Boston State House is the hub of the solar system. You couldn't pry that out of a Boston man, if you had the tire of all creation straightened out for a crowbar."

Sir, said I, I am gratified with your remark. It expresses with pleasing vivacity that which I have sometimes heard uttered with malignant dullness. The satire of the remark is essentially true of Boston, and of all other considerable — and inconsiderable — places with which I have had the privilege of being acquainted. Cockneys think London is the only place in the world. Frenchmen — you remember the line about Paris, the Court, the World, and so forth — I recollect well, by the way, a sign in that city which ran thus: "Hôtel de l'Univers et des États Unis"; and as Paris *is* the universe to a Frenchman, of course the United States is outside of it. "See Naples and then die." It is quite as bad with smaller places. I have been about, lecturing, you know, and have found the following propositions to hold true of all of them.

1. The axis of the earth sticks out visibly through the center of each and every town or city.

2. If more than fifty years have passed since its foundation, it is affectionately styled by the inhabitants the "*good old* town of ——" (whatever its name may happen to be).

3. Every collection of its inhabitants that comes together to listen to a stranger is invariably declared to be a "remarkably intelligent audience."

4. The climate of the place is particularly favorable to longevity.

5. It contains several persons of vast talent little known to the world.

Boston is just like other places of its size; only, perhaps, considering its excellent fish market, paid fire department, superior monthly publications, and correct habit of spelling the English language, it has some right to look down on the mob of cities. I'll tell you, though, if you want to know it, what is the real offense of Boston. It drains a large watershed of its intellect, and will not itself be drained. If it would only send away its first-rate men, instead of its second-rate ones (no offense to the well-known exceptions, of which we are always proud), we should be spared such epigrammatic remarks as that which the gentleman has quoted. There can never be a real metropolis in this country until the biggest center can drain the lesser ones of their talent and wealth.

The Professor at the Breakfast Table

APRIL 1859

One of our boarders has been talking in such strong language that I am almost afraid to report it. However, as he seems to be really honest and is so very sincere in his local prejudices, I don't believe anybody will be very angry with him.

It is here, sir, right here! said the little deformed gentleman, in this old new city of Boston, this remote provincial corner of a provincial nation, that the Battle of the Standard is fighting, and was fighting before we were born, and will be fighting when we are dead and gone, please God! The battle goes on everywhere throughout civilization; but here, here, here is the broad white flag flying which proclaims, first of all, peace and good will to men, and, next to that, the absolute, unconditional spiritual liberty of each individual immortal soul. The three-hilled city against the seven-hilled city! That is it, sir, nothing less than that; and if you know what that means, I don't think you'll ask for anything more. I swear to you, sir, I believe that these two centers of civilization are just exactly the two points that close the circuit in the battery of our planetary intelligence. Why, sir, while commentators are bothering themselves with interpretation of prophecies, we have got the new heavens and the new earth over us and under us! Was there ever anything in Italy, I should like to know, like a Boston sunset?

This time there was a laugh, and the little man himself almost smiled.

Yes, Boston sunsets; perhaps they're as good in some other places, but I know 'em best here. Anyhow, the American skies are different from anything they see in the Old World. Yes, and the rocks are different, and the soil is different, and everything that comes out of the soil, from grass up to Indians, is different. And now that the provisional races are dying out —

What do you mean by *provisional* races, sir? said the divinity student, interrupting him.

Why, the aboriginal bipeds, to be sure, he answered. The red crayon sketch of humanity laid on the canvas before the colors for the real manhood were ready.

I hope they will come to something yet, said the divinity student.

Irreclaimable, sir, irreclaimable! said the little gentleman. Cheaper to breed white men than domesticate a nation of red ones. When you can get the bitter out of the partridge's thigh, you can make an enlightened commonwealth of Indians. A provisional race, sir, nothing more.

Well, sir, these races dying out, the white man has to acclimate himself. A new nursery, sir, with Lake Superior and Huron and all the rest of 'em for washbasins! A new race, and Boston is the brain of it, and has been these hundred years. That's all I claim for Boston, that it is the thinking center of the continent, and therefore of the planet.

And the grand emporium of modesty, said the divinity student, a little mischievously.

Oh, don't talk to me of modesty, answered Little Boston, I'm past that! There isn't a thing that was ever said or done in Boston, from pitching the tea overboard to the last ecclesiastical lie it tore into tatters and flung into the dock, that wasn't thought very indelicate by some fool or tyrant or bigot. No, sir, show me any other place that is, or was since the megalosaurus has died out, where wealth and social influence are so fairly divided between the stationary and the progressive classes.

We think *Baltimore* is a pretty civilized kind of a village, said the young Marylander, good-naturedly. But I suppose you can't forgive it for always keeping a little ahead of Boston in point of numbers — tell the truth now. Are we not the center of something?

Ah, indeed, to be sure you are. You are the gastronomic metropolis of the Union. Why don't you put a canvas-back duck on the top of the Washington column? Why don't you get that lady off from Battle Monument and plant a terrapin in her place? Why will you ask for other glories when you have soft crabs? No, sir, you live too well to think as hard as we do in Boston. Logic comes to us with the salt fish of Cape Ann; rhetoric is born of the beans of Beverly; but *you* — if you open your mouths to speak, Nature stops them with a fat oyster, or offers a slice of the breast of your divine bird, and silences all of your aspirations.

And what of Philadelphia? said the Marylander.

Oh, Philadelphia? Waterworks, killed by the Croton and Cochituate; Ben Franklin, borrowed from Boston; David Rittenhouse, made an orrery; Benjamin Rush, made a medical system: both interesting to antiquarians. What do we know about Philadelphia, except that the engine companies are always shooting each other?

The little gentleman was on his hobby, exalting his own city at the expense of every other place. I don't suppose he had been in either of the cities he had been talking about. I was just going to say something to sober him down, if I could, when the young Marylander spoke up.

Come now, he said, what's the use of these comparisons? Didn't I hear this gentleman saying, the other day, that every American owns all America? If you have really got more brains in Boston than other folks, as you seem to think, who hates you for it, except a pack of scribbling fools? If I like Broadway better than Washington Street, what then? I own them both, as much as anybody owns either. I am an American, and whenever I look up and see the Stars and Stripes overhead, that is home to me!

Skipper Ireson's Ride

by JOHN GREENLEAF WHITTIER

The Quaker Whittier, with his friendly persuasion, bartered with the Atlantic *for large fees more persistently than any other poet in the first decade. He wrote steadily for the magazine and not infrequently received fees of $100.*

DECEMBER 1857

Of all the rides since the birth of time,
Told in story or sung in rhyme —
On Apuleius's Golden Ass,
Or one-eyed Calendar's horse of brass,
Witch astride of a human hack,
Islam's prophet on Al-Borák —
The strangest ride that ever was sped
Was Ireson's out from Marblehead.
    Old Floyd Ireson, for his hard heart,
    Tarred and feathered and carried in a cart
    By the women of Marblehead.

Body of turkey, head of owl,
Wings adroop like a rained-on fowl,
Feathered and ruffled in every part,
Captain Ireson stood in the cart.
Scores of women, old and young,
Strong of muscle, and glib of tongue,
Pushed and pulled up the rocky lane,
Shouting and singing the shrill refrain:
  "Here's Flud Oirson, fur his horrd horrt,
  Torr'd an' futherr'd an' corr'd in a corrt
   By the women o' Morble'ead!"

Girls in bloom of cheek and lips,
Wrinkled scolds with hands on hips,
Wild-eyed, free-limbed, such as chase
Bacchus round some antique vase,
Brief of skirt, with ankles bare,
Loose of kerchief and loose of hair,
With conch shells blowing and fish horns' twang,
Over and over the Maenads sang:
  "Here's Flud Oirson, fur his horrd horrt,
  Torr'd an' futherr'd an' corr'd in a corrt
   By the women o' Morble'ead!"

Small pity for him — he sailed away
From a leaking ship in Chaleur Bay,
Sailed away from a sinking wreck,
With his own townspeople on her deck!
"Lay by! lay by!" they called to him.
Back he answered, "Sink or swim!
Brag of your catch of fish again!"
And off he sailed through the fog and rain.
  Old Floyd Ireson, for his hard heart,
  Tarred and feathered and carried in a cart
   By the women of Marblehead.

Fathoms deep in dark Chaleur
That wreck shall lie forevermore.
Mother and sister, wife and maid,
Looked from the rocks of Marblehead

Over the moaning and rainy sea,
Looked for the coming that might not be.
What did the winds and the sea birds say
Of the cruel captain who sailed away?
  Old Floyd Ireson, for his hard heart,
  Tarred and feathered and carried in a cart
  By the women of Marblehead.

Through the street, on either side,
Up flew windows, doors swung wide;
Sharp-tongued spinsters, old wives gray,
Treble lent the fish horn's bray.
Sea-worn grandsires, cripple-bound,
Hulks of old sailors run aground,
Shook head, and fist, and hat, and cane,
And cracked with curses the hoarse refrain:
  "Here's Flud Oirson, fur his horrd horrt,
  Torr'd an' futherr'd an' corr'd in a corrt
  By the women o' Morble'ead!"

Sweetly along the Salem road
Bloom of orchard and lilac showed.
Little the wicked skipper knew
Of the fields so green and the sky so blue.
Riding there in his sorry trim,
Like an Indian idol glum and grim,
Scarcely he seemed the sound to hear
Of voices shouting far and near:
  "Here's Flud Oirson, fur his horrd horrt,
  Torr'd an' futherr'd an' corr'd in a corrt
  By the women o' Morble'ead!"

"Hear me, neighbors!" at last he cried,
"What to me is this noisy ride?
What is the shame that clothes the skin,
To the nameless horror that lives within?
Waking or sleeping, I see a wreck
And hear a cry from a reeling deck!
Hate me and curse me — I only dread
The hand of God and the face of the dead!"

Said old Floyd Ireson, for his hard heart,
Tarred and feathered and carried in a cart
By the women of Marblehead.

Then the wife of the skipper lost at sea
Said, "God has touched him — why should we?"
Said an old wife mourning her only son,
"Cut the rogue's tether and let him run!"
So with soft relentings and rude excuse,
Half scorn, half pity, they cut him loose,
And gave him cloak to hide him in,
And left him alone with his shame and sin.
Poor Floyd Ireson, for his hard heart,
Tarred and feathered and carried in a cart
By the women of Marblehead.

Walking

by HENRY THOREAU

*A preacher of self-sufficiency and a prodigious walker —
he made long journeys on foot through Maine, Cape Cod,
and Canada — Henry Thoreau found transitory if not lasting satisfaction in his hut on Walden Pond and his friendship with Emerson.*

JUNE 1862

I wish to speak a word for Nature, for absolute freedom and wildness, as contrasted with a freedom and culture merely civil — to regard man as an inhabitant, or a part and parcel of Nature, rather than
a member of society. I wish to make an extreme statement, an emphatic
one, for there are enough champions of civilization: the minister, and
the school committee, and every one of you will take care of that.

I have met with but one or two persons in the course of my life who
understood the art of walking, that is, of taking walks — who had a
genius, so to speak, for sauntering: which word is beautifully derived
"from idle people who roved about the country, in the Middle Ages,

and asked charity, under pretense of going *à la Sainte Terre*," to the Holy Land, till the children exclaimed, "There goes a *Sainte-Terrer*," a saunterer, Holy-Lander. They who never go to the Holy Land in their walks, as they pretend, are indeed mere idlers and vagabonds; but they who do go there are saunterers in the good sense, such as I mean.

I think that I cannot preserve my health and spirits unless I spend four hours a day at least — and it is commonly more than that — sauntering through the woods and over the hills and fields, absolutely free from all worldly engagements. You may safely say, A penny for your thoughts, or a thousand pounds. When sometimes I am reminded that the mechanics and shopkeepers stay in their shops not only all the forenoon, but all the afternoon too, sitting with crossed legs, so many of them — as if the legs were made to sit upon, and not to stand or walk upon — I think that they deserve some credit for not having all committed suicide long ago.

No doubt temperament and, above all, age have a good deal to do with it. As a man grows older, his ability to sit still and follow indoor occupations increases. He grows vespertinal in his habits as the evening of life approaches, till at last he comes forth only just before sundown and gets all the walk that he requires in half an hour.

But the walking of which I speak has nothing in it akin to taking exercise, but is itself the enterprise and adventure of the day. If you would get exercise, go in search of the springs of life. Think of a man's swinging dumbbells for his health, when those springs are bubbling up in far-off pastures unsought by him!

Moreover, you must walk like a camel, which is said to be the only beast which ruminates when walking. When a traveler asked Wordsworth's servant to show him her master's study, she answered, "Here is his library, but his study is out of doors."

My vicinity affords many good walks; and though for so many years I have walked almost every day, and sometimes for several days together, I have not yet exhausted them. An absolutely new prospect is a great happiness, and I can still get this any afternoon. Two or three hours' walking will carry me to as strange a country as I expect ever to see. A single farmhouse which I had not seen before is sometimes as good as the dominions of the King of Dahomey. There is in fact a sort of harmony discoverable between the capabilities of the landscape within a circle of ten miles' radius, or the limits of an afternoon walk, and the threescore years and ten of human life. It will never become quite familiar to you.

I can easily walk ten, fifteen, twenty, any number of miles, commencing at my own door, without going by any house, without crossing a road except where the fox and the mink do: first along by the river, and then the brook, and then the meadow and the woodside. There are square miles in my vicinity which have no inhabitant. From many a hill I can see civilization and the abodes of man afar. The farmers and their works are scarcely more obvious than woodchucks and their burrows. Man and his affairs, church and state and school, trade and commerce, manufactures and agriculture — even politics, the most alarming of them all — I am pleased to see how little space they occupy in the landscape.

When I go out of the house for a walk, uncertain as yet whither I will bend my steps, and submit myself to my instinct to decide for me, I find, strange and whimsical as it may seem, that I finally and inevitably settle southwest, toward some particular wood or meadow or deserted pasture or hill in that direction. My needle is slow to settle, varies a few degrees and does not always point due southwest, it is true, and it has good authority for this variation, but it always settles between west and south-southwest. The future lies that way to me, and the earth seems more unexhausted and richer on that side.

Eastward I go only by force; but westward I go free. Thither no business leads me. It is hard for me to believe that I shall find fair landscapes or sufficient wildness and freedom behind the eastern horizon. I am not excited by the prospect of a walk thither; but I believe that the forest which I see in the western horizon stretches uninterruptedly toward the setting sun, and that there are no towns or cities in it of enough consequence to disturb me. Let me live where I will; on this side is the city, on that the wilderness, and ever I am leaving the city more and more and withdrawing into the wilderness. I should not lay so much stress on this fact if I did not believe that something like this is the prevailing tendency of my countrymen. I must walk toward Oregon, and not toward Europe. And that way the nation is moving, and I may say that mankind progresses from east to west.

We go eastward to realize history and study the works of art and literature, retracing the steps of the race; we go westward as into the future, with a spirit of enterpirse and adventure. The Atlantic is a Lethean stream, in our passage over which we have had an opportunity to forget the Old World and its institutions. If we do not succeed this time, there is perhaps one more chance for the race left before it arrives on the banks of the Styx, and that is in the Lethe of the Pacific, which is three times as wide.

Every sunset which I witness inspires me with the desire to go to a west as distant and as fair as that into which the sun goes down. He appears to migrate westward daily, and tempt us to follow him. He is the Great Western Pioneer whom the nations follow. We dream all night of those mountain ridges in the horizon, though they may be of vapor only, which were last gilded by his rays. The island of Atlantis, and the islands and gardens of the Hesperides, a sort of terrestrial paradise, appear to have been the Great West of the ancients, enveloped in mystery and poetry. Who has not seen in imagination, when looking into the sunset sky, the gardens of the Hesperides, and the foundation of all those fables?

Columbus felt the westward tendency more strongly than any before. He obeyed it, and found a New World for Castile and León. The herd of men in those days scented fresh pastures from afar.

> And now the sun had stretched out all the hills,
> And now was dropped into the western bay;
> At last *he* rose, and twitched his mantle blue;
> Tomorrow to fresh woods and pastures new.

Where on the globe can there be found an area of equal extent with that occupied by the bulk of our states, so fertile and so rich and varied in its productions, and at the same time so habitable by the European, as this is? Michaux, who knew but part of them, says that "the species of large trees are much more numerous in North America than in Europe; in the United States there are more than one hundred and forty species that exceed thirty feet in height; in France there are but thirty that attain this size." Later botanists more than confirm his observations. Humboldt came to America to realize his youthful dreams of a tropical vegetation, and he beheld it in its greatest perfection in the primitive forests of the Amazon, the most gigantic wilderness on the earth, which he has so eloquently described. Sir Francis Head, an English traveler and a Governor-General of Canada, tells us that "in both the northern and southern hemispheres of the New World, Nature has not only outlined her works on a larger scale, but has painted the whole picture with brighter and more costly colors than she used in delineating and in beautifying the Old World. . . . The heavens of America appear infinitely higher, the sky is bluer, the air is fresher, the cold is intenser, the moon looks larger, the stars are brighter, the thunder is louder, the lightning is vivider, the wind is stronger, the rain is heavier, the mountains are higher, the rivers longer, the forests bigger, the plains broader." This statement will do at least to set against Buffon's account of this part of the world and its productions.

To Americans I hardly need to say, "Westward the star of empire takes its way." As a true patriot, I should be ashamed to think that Adam in paradise was more favorably situated on the whole than the backwoodsman in this country.

Our sympathies in Massachusetts are not confined to New England; though we may be estranged from the South, we sympathize with the West. There is the home of the younger sons, as among the Scandinavians they took to the sea for their inheritance.

The West of which I speak is but another name for the Wild; and what I have been preparing to say is that in wildness is the preservation of the world. Every tree sends its fibers forth in search of the wild. The cities import it at any price. Men plough and sail for it. From the forest and wilderness come the tonics and barks which brace mankind. Our ancestors were savages. The story of Romulus and Remus being suckled by a wolf is not a meaningless fable. The founders of every State which has risen to eminence have drawn their nourishment and vigor from a similar wild source. It was because the children of the Empire were not suckled by the wolf that they were conquered and displaced by the children of the northern forests who were.

I believe in the forest, and in the meadow, and in the night in which the corn grows. A tanned skin is something more than respectable, and perhaps olive is a fitter color than white for a man — a denizen of the woods, "The pale white man!" I do not wonder that the African pitied him. Darwin the naturalist says, "A white man bathing by the side of a Tahitian was like a plant bleached by the gardener's art, compared with a fine, dark green one, growing vigorously in the open fields."

Ben Jonson exclaims, "How near to good is what is fair!" So I would say, How near to good is what is *wild!* Life consists with wildness. The most alive is the wildest. Not yet subdued to man, its presence refreshes him. One who pressed forward incessantly and never rested from his labors, who grew fast and made infinite demands on life, would always find himself in a new country or wilderness, and surrounded by the raw material of life. He would be climbing over the prostrate stems of primitive forest trees.

Hope and the future for me are not in lawns and cultivated fields, not in towns and cities, but in the impervious and quaking swamps.

When, formerly, I have analyzed my partiality for some farm which I had contemplated purchasing, I have frequently found that I was attracted solely by a few square rods of impermeable and unfathomable bog — a natural sink in one corner of it. That was the jewel which dazzled me. I derive more of my subsistence from the swamps which surround my native town than from the cultivated gardens in the village. When I would re-create myself, I seek the darkest wood, the thickest and most interminable and, to the citizen, most dismal swamp. I enter a swamp as a sacred place — a *sanctum sanctorum*. There is the strength, the marrow of Nature. The wildwood covers the virgin mold — and the same soil is good for men and for trees. A man's health requires as many acres of meadow to his prospect as his farm does loads of muck. There are the strong meats on which he feeds. A town is saved not more by the righteous men in it than by the woods and swamps that surround it. A township where one primitive forest waves above, while another primitive forest rots below — such a town is fitted to raise not only corn and potatoes, but poets and philosophers for the coming ages. In such a soil grew Homer and Confucius and the rest, and out of such a wilderness comes the Reformer eating locusts and wild honey.

The civilized nations — Greece, Rome, England — have been sustained by the primitive forests which anciently rotted where they stand. They survive as long as the soil is not exhausted. Alas for human culture! little is to be expected of a nation when the vegetable mold is exhausted and it is compelled to make manure of the bones of its fathers. There the poet sustains himself merely by his own superfluous fat, and the philosopher comes down on his marrowbones.

It is said to be the task of the American "to work the virgin soil," and that "agriculture here already assumes proportions unknown everywhere else." I think that the farmer displaces the Indian even because he redeems the meadow, and so makes himself stronger and in some respects more natural. I was surveying for a man the other day a single straight line one hundred and thirty-two rods long, through a swamp, at whose entrance might have been written the words which Dante read over the entrance to the infernal regions — "Leave all hope, ye that enter" — that is, of ever getting out again; where at one time I saw my employer actually up to his neck and swimming for his life in his property, though it was still winter. He had another similar swamp which I could not survey at all, because it was completely underwater, and nevertheless, with regard to a third swamp, which I did *survey* from a distance, he remarked to me, true to his instincts, that he would not part with it for any consideration on account of the mud which it contained. And that man intends to put a girdling ditch round the whole in the course of forty months, and so redeem it by the magic of his spade. The weapons with which we have gained our most important victories, which should be handed down as heirlooms from father to son, are not the sword and the lance, but the bushwhack, the turf cutter, the spade, and the bog hoe, rusted with the blood of many a meadow and begrimed with the dust of many a hard-fought field.

I took a walk on Spaulding's Farm the other afternoon. I saw the setting sun lighting up the opposite side of a stately pine wood. Its golden rays straggled into the aisles of the wood as into some noble hall. I was impressed as if some ancient and altogether admirable and shining family had settled there in that part of the land called Concord, unknown to me; to whom the sun was servant, who had not gone into society in the village, who had not been called on. I saw their park, their pleasure ground, beyond through the wood, in Spaulding's cranberry meadow. The pines furnished them with gables as they grew. Their house was not obvious to vision; the trees grew through it. I do not know whether I heard the sounds of a suppressed hilarity or not. They seemed to recline on the sunbeams. They have sons and daughters. They are quite well. The farmer's cart path, which leads directly through their hall, does not in the least put them out. They never heard of Spaulding, and do not know that he is their neighbor — notwithstanding I heard him whistle as he drove his team through the house. Nothing can equal the serenity of their lives. Their coat of arms is simply a lichen. I saw it painted on the pines and oaks. Their attics were in the tops of the trees. They are of no politics. There was no noise of labor. I did not perceive that they were weaving or spinning. Yet I did detect, when the wind lulled and hearing was done away, the finest imaginable sweet musical hum — as of a distant hive in May — which perchance was the sound of their thinking. They had no idle thoughts, and no one without could see their work, for their industry was not as in knots and excrescences embayed.

But I find it difficult to remember them. They fade irrevocably out of my mind even now while I speak and endeavor to recall them. It is only after a long and serious effort to recollect my best thoughts that I become again aware of their cohabitancy. If it were not for such families as this, I think I should move out of Concord.

We hug the earth — how rarely we mount! Methinks we might ele-
vate ourselves a little more. We might climb a tree, at least. I found my
account in climbing a tree once. It was a tall white pine, on the top of a
hill; and though I got well pitched, I was well paid for it, for I discovered new mountains in the horizon which I had never seen before — so
much more of the earth and the heavens. I might have walked about the
foot of the tree for threescore years and ten, and yet I certainly should
never have seen them. But, above all, I discovered around me — it was
near the end of June — on the ends of the topmost branches only, a
few minute and delicate red cone-like blossoms, the fertile flower of the
white pine looking heavenward. I carried straightway to the village
the topmost spire, and showed it to stranger jurymen who walked the
streets, for it was court week, and to farmers and lumber dealers and
wood choppers and hunters, and not one had ever seen the like before,
but they wondered as at a star dropped down. We see only the flowers
that are under our feet in the meadows. The pines have developed their
delicate blossoms on the highest twigs of the wood every summer for
ages, as well over the heads of Nature's red children as of her white
ones; yet scarcely a farmer or hunter in the land has ever seen them.

We had a remarkable sunset one day last November. I was walking
in a meadow, the source of a small brook, when the sun at last, just before setting after a cold gray day, reached a clear stratum in the horizon,
and the softest, brightest morning sunlight fell on the dry grass and on
the stems of the trees in the opposite horizon, and on the leaves of the
shrub oaks on the hillside, while our shadows stretched long over the
meadow eastward, as if we were the only motes in its beams. It was such
a light as we could not have imagined a moment before, and the air also
was so warm and serene that nothing was wanting to make a paradise
of that meadow. When we reflected that this was not a solitary phenomenon, never to happen again, but that it would happen forever and
ever an infinite number of evenings, and cheer and reassure the latest
child that walked there, it was more glorious still.

The sun sets on some retired meadow, where no house is visible, with
all the glory and splendor that it lavishes on cities, and, perchance, as it
has never set before; where there is but a solitary marsh hawk to have his
wings gilded by it, or only a musquash looks out from his cabin, and
there is some little black-veined brook in the midst of the marsh, just
beginning to meander, winding slowly round a decaying stump. We
walked in so pure and bright a light, gilding the withered grass and
leaves, so softly and serenely bright, I thought I had never bathed in such

a golden flood, without a ripple or a murmur to it. The west side of every wood and rising ground gleamed like the boundary of Elysium, and the sun on our backs seemed like a gentle herdsman driving us home at evening.

So we saunter toward the Holy Land, till one day the sun will shine more brightly than ever he has done, will perchance shine into our minds and hearts and light up our whole lives with a great awakening light, as warm and serene and golden as on a bankside in autumn.

The Glory Hole

from *Naturalist at Large*

by THOMAS BARBOUR

Director of the Agassiz Museum in Cambridge from 1927 to 1946, Dr. Thomas Barbour was a scientist whose knowledge of reptiles, birds, and insects was rivaled only by his delight in human nature.

NOVEMBER 1942

The man in the street has always been inclined to look down his nose at museum curators, and for as long as I have been one of them I have been pondering the reason. I think I have it. The average man doesn't like a miser and, one way or another, the curator cannot help appearing miserly. When I first took charge of a certain museum, I found one big glass jar filled with chicken heads, another with burned matches, another with old rubbers. The chicken heads were potential material for dissection, and the fact that a dollar's worth of heads filled a twenty-dollar jar never occurred to the man who ate those chickens, who was no other than Louis Agassiz himself.

The museum of which I speak at one time housed an unbelievable number of strange odds and ends accumulated through the years and saved because the old-time museum man thought it was a sin to throw anything out. I have been accused of erring in this manner myself. It is true that if you look at a thing long enough you lose perspective. Any object, no matter how revolting and loathsome, seen sufficiently often, blunts the senses, and one becomes disinclined to the effort necessary to get rid of it.

Pride of possession is a curious attribute of mankind. This was brought sharply to my mind yesterday when it occurred to me to ask myself, "Why didn't Mrs. Chase *give* her gallstones to the Peabody Museum?" Many other people had, for there were a pint or more of miscellaneous gallstones in the Peabody Museum in Salem, curiously enough in the case with an old reindeer. But these were donated gallstones; it was only Mrs. Chase's that were on loan. The answer is, Mrs. Chase's gallstones were larger than any others in the whole place and she obviously just couldn't bear to part with them permanently. I thought, Has this situation ever occurred before? And then I remembered that not long ago I was reading the last Annual Report of the Curator of the Museum of the Royal College of Surgeons in London. This venerable institution, containing much material that was priceless indeed, suffered a direct hit from a German bomb. It was almost completely destroyed, and the story of the catastrophe was told, sadly and meticulously, by its distinguished curator. But if our friend in the street were to read this report he might be inclined to laugh heretically: along with many terrific losses were listed the facts that the jar containing Napoleon's bowels was cracked and that the rib of Robert the Bruce was broken.

I have found myself justifying the preservation of objects which were inherently unpleasing to the eye by saying, "That illustrates the taxidermy of a hundred years ago." Or the preservation of a codfish pickled in alcohol by saying, "Someone may want to dissect that fish sometime," forgetting that fresh cod, infinitely preferable for dissection, are plentiful in the Boston area. And so it goes. The more I think of it, the more I believe that the average man is entirely entitled to his opinion and the average curator is a queer fish.

Now granted that the curator is a queer fish, is he a rare fish? I fear the answer today is nay. My friend Alexander Wetmore, Director of the United States National Museum, in an address at the opening of the Dyche Museum at the University of Kansas, remarks, "There are today throughout the world more than seven thousand museums, of which more than a thousand are in the United States." Every museum has at least one curator, and the breed came into being, no doubt, back in the days when the "Repositerry of Curiosity," the *Anlage* of our University Museum here at Harvard, was visited by Francis Goelet on the twenty-fifth of October, 1750. Unfortunately, Mr. Goelet does not tell us how old the museum was at that date. He does, however, tell us its treasures included "horns and bones, fishes' skins and other objects, and a piece of tanned Negro hide."

Professor John Winthrop, Hollis Professor of Mathematics and Natural Philosophy, evidently had started even at this early date to make what we call a "Glory Hole." I have had some interesting experiences cleaning out Glory Holes in Cambridge, Boston, and Salem. Only the other day I opened a parcel in Salem, the wrapping paper of which was superscribed, "Please do not disturb these shells. Caleb Cooke, February 1857." This behest had been scrupulously obeyed for eighty-five years and six months. The parcel proved to be pure gold, for the shells were collected from one of our New England rivers in which today it would be impossible to collect a single living thing, so polluted have its waters become. I hold in my hand a little vial on which is a label saying, "This vial contains two feathers of a large penguin." One wonders why these two feathers out of the tens of thousands which that penguin carried were singled out for preservation.

The only old museum I ever saw where there was no Glory Hole was the museum in Charleston, South Carolina. This venerable institution, founded in 1773, has had plenty of time to accumulate one, but the gay and carefree cavaliers of the South must have been willing to throw things away even when they became curators, while the penny-pinching men of the New England states fairly reveled in the making of Glory Holes. Certainly nothing equaling the collections of zoological atrocities once preserved in Boston, Salem, and Cambridge has ever been known in America, and probably but seldom in Europe. I remember one of my colleagues, now passed to his reward, pointing regularly to a certain cask and saying, "That's filled with the pickled heads of Chinese." Well, it was. They were garnered on the beach at San Francisco years ago after a battle, by Thomas G. Carey, no less. Now after some seventy years these heads, boiled out and the skulls bleached and cleaned, serve a useful purpose: Hooton of Harvard uses them in teaching anthropology.

Alexander Agassiz collected but one living spirula, a little squid-like mollusk whose dried shells may be found along the beaches of the tropics in countless thousands. The living spirula carried an important message, for its shell was like certain fossil shells of ages ago and gave us a clue to what the soft parts of those fossil animals were like. That spirula disappeared about forty-five years ago from the very desk at which I now sit writing these lines, and it has never been seen from that day to this.

Mr. Agassiz always said Professor E. D. Cope was unquestionably the greatest thief in the world, for the reason that he stole the largest object ever stolen. The story ran something like this: Captain Atwood of Provincetown, who did the Museum many good turns, once notified Mr. Agassiz that a strange whale had drifted ashore on the Outer Cape. Mr. Agassiz asked J. A. Allen and some students to go down and rough out the skeleton. This they did, and laid out the partially cleaned bones on a flatcar. They little dreamed that Dr. Cope from Philadelphia also had a scout on the Outer Cape, and Cope was a canny man. He went to Provincetown, hired a room in a farmhouse where he could watch proceedings, and waited until the Cambridge crew went home. Then he greased the palm of the station agent to the end that a Philadelphia way-bill instead of a Cambridge waybill was affixed to the flatcar and the whale ended up as the type of a new species which Mr. Cope described, its skeleton still being preserved at the Academy of Natural Sciences in Philadelphia. So the story runs, and I have often heard it told in the past.

I can hear the reader mildly say, "Why on earth does anyone want to be a museum curator?" This question, however, I can answer bravely and with positive assurance. To one who has by inheritance or training acquired the pack-rat instinct it is the most exciting calling in the whole world. For who, having a spark of imagination, could fail to be thrilled to hold in his hand our specimen of *Drepanis pacifica?* This was the bird from which the feathers were taken to make the royal robe of Kame-hameha the Great. The bird is extinct. Our specimen was collected by Bloxam, who sailed on the *Golden Hind* with Captain Cook. It is, more-over, the cotype of the species. Any naturalist will know what I mean.

This is how I came to think up a new kind of museum. The trustees of the Peabody Museum in Salem voted to restore East India Hall to its original monumental simplicity and to display here figureheads of ships and other objects that are best seen from a distance. The Hall for years has been filled with a jittery miscellany of zoological objects. There was a good representation of the fauna of Essex County, specimens excel-lently prepared. All else was a miscellaneous accumulation, acquired through the years from sea captains and others, of specimens which varied in quality from the utterly revolting to a few really fine things. It was easy to dispose of the repulsive material. Some of it had scientific value and the rest of it, when tossed out of a second-story window into the back yard on Charter Street in Salem, was fought for by a swarm of urchins, who carried the critters off in triumph.

The question was what to do with the few good things which did not illustrate the zoology of Essex County. These naturally presented a dilemma. I proposed discarding them all. Then one day I chanced to lunch with Gus Loring and Stephen W. Phillips, men of original mind and deep learning, who had a sentimental respect for some of the objects I proposed to discard. It was quite obvious that I could not proceed without seriously wounding feelings. I suddenly thought, "See if we can't make a human interest story out of each one; display the object with its relation to man." A sort of rough classification gradually grew on me. There was a good skylark and a good wandering albatross. Get a nightingale and set up a display. Label it "These birds have inspired great poetry." Use pictures of the poets, facsimiles of the poems, and some of the most superb verses in boldly typed labels.

What do domesticated animals teach us beside carving at table? Domestic fowl and the pigeon have been extraordinarily plastic in man's hands. Think of the contrast between a Shanghai rooster and a Seabright bantam. The Shanghai and the Langshan are the largest of the so-called Asiatic breeds of fowl, enormous creatures standing over two feet high. The breeds are now out of fashion and almost extinct. Luckily the Museum had some really historic fowls. Here was the rooster brought back over a hundred years ago, the progenitor of the stock which gave rise to the Rhode Island Red. And I found a wild jungle fowl which could be spared from the collections in Cambridge. With the help of the Essex County Agricultural School, I soon had plans for this exhibit under way.

Various species of jungle fowl, which look exactly like small game chickens found all over Southeastern Asia. When you are living in the country where they occur, you seldom see them, but their crowing at morning and evening sometimes becomes a positive nuisance. Now, conversely, although there is no reason to believe that the Aztecs did not hold the turkey in domestication for as long a time as any of the peoples of Asia had the fowl, the turkey has not proved plastic at all. Cortez sent domesticated birds which he found in Mexico back to Europe. From there they spread all over the world. They came to New England, and to this day domesticated turkeys, most of them, are hard to tell from wild birds. A few varieties have been produced, but only by the chance dropping out of elements of the normal pigmentation of the bird's plumage. In the reddish-colored turkeys, the black or the dilute black pigment — the gray — has gone and the red element alone remains. In the white turkeys all pigmentation has disappeared; albino races are always easy to produce in domestication. White rats and mice and guinea pigs come to mind, as well as leghorn fowl and fantail pigeons.

The Museum had a first-class ostrich, given it some years ago by Mrs. Stephen W. Phillips — an ostrich far too good to throw away. By good fortune, I had a sample of dried ostrich meat, one of the various kinds of biltong carried by the Boers as rations when at war or on trek. An ostrich feather fan, an old-time bonnet, and headdresses of the Nandi Masai all proved obtainable.

Think what a story you can build about the giant tortoise of the Galapagos. The old whalers called them turpin. For generations all the ships that chanced to be near the Galapagos Islands, about six hundred miles southwestward of Panama, went ashore turtling. The crews carried the beasts down to the beach, boated them to the ships, and piled them up in their empty holds. Here, being the strange creatures that they are, they survived for months without food or water. When scurvy appeared the turtles were butchered. The flesh was savory even when poorly prepared. There was enough fat in each one to shorten a mess of duff, and the water in their bladders was cool and clear. I have seen a compilation made from about thirty whalers' logs which shows that they carried off more than eleven thousand of these animals. Once they occurred in countless multitudes on no fewer than nine of the islands. Seventeen zoological species of turtles have been described. But this is not the point which we want the magnificent specimen at Salem to illustrate — rather, what turtles like this meant to seamen from the time of Dampier down to about 1867, when petroleum knocked out whale oil. Probably no fewer than half a million turpin were carried away, and now all the races of the creatures are rare or extinct.

Captain Phillips brought back from Fiji an enormous giant clam. The superb pair of matched valves are at least three feet long and weigh over a hundred pounds each. But I don't want this to be a malacological specimen. It was the terror of the pearl diver. For if a diver inadvertently thrust a hand or a foot into one of these gaping shells as it yawned open, the instant reaction was for the animal to close up, like any other clam, and the death of the diver ensued.

These giant clams were undoubtedly eaten, the meat being chopped fine and stewed. No doubt it was as good as conch, most delectable of all sea viands, unfortunately unprocurable in New England. What a dramatic underwater scene could be depicted with modern methods of creating illusions. Mold a lovely Polynesian maiden vested only with a net reticule of pearl shells tied to her waist and struggling for release from the clutch of this giant mollusk. I fear, however, that such pageantry is beyond our means — and might shock Salem, anyhow.

A Winter Courtship

by SARAH ORNE JEWETT

Fields gets the credit of discovering Sarah Orne Jewett, for he published her first story in the Atlantic *when she was twenty. She continued to write for us for the next forty years, and her stories and novels which we serialized (The Country of the Pointed Firs, Deephaven, and others) stand out as the clearest and most characteristic expression of New England.*

FEBRUARY 1889

The passenger and mail transportation between the towns of North Kilby and Sanscrit Pond was carried on by Mr. Jefferson Briley, whose two-seated covered wagon was usually much too large for the demands of business. Both the Sanscrit Pond and North Kilby people were stayers-at-home, and Mr. Briley often made his seven-mile journey in entire solitude, except for the limp leather mailbag, which he held firmly to the floor of the carriage with his heavily shod left foot. The mailbag had almost a personality to him, born of long association. Mr. Briley was a meek and timid-looking body, but he had a warlike soul and encouraged his fancies by reading awful tales of bloodshed and lawlessness in the Far West. Mindful of stage robberies and train thieves, and of express messengers who died at their posts, he was prepared for anything; and although he had trusted to his own strength and bravery these many years, he carried a heavy pistol under his front-seat cushion for better defense. This awful weapon was familiar to all his regular passengers, and was usually shown to strangers by the time two of the seven miles of Mr. Briley's route had been passed. The pistol was not loaded. Nobody (at least not Mr. Briley himself) doubted that the mere sight of such a weapon would turn the boldest adventurer aside.

Protected by such a man and such a piece of armament, one gray Friday morning in the edge of winter, Mrs. Fanny Tobin was traveling from Sanscrit Pond to North Kilby. She was an elderly and feeble-looking woman, but with a shrewd twinkle in her eyes, and she felt very anxious about her numerous pieces of baggage and her own personal safety. She was enveloped in many shawls and smaller wrappings, but they were not securely fastened, and kept getting undone and flying loose, so that the bitter December cold seemed to be picking a lock now and then and creeping in to steal away the little warmth she had. Mr. Briley was cold, too, and could only cheer himself by remembering the valor of those pony-express drivers of the prerailroad days, who had to cross the Rocky Mountains on the great California route. He spoke at length of their perils to the suffering passenger, but she felt none the warmer, and at last gave a groan of weariness.

"How fur did you say 'twas now?"

"I do' know's I said, Mis' Tobin," answered the driver, with a frosty laugh. "You see them big pines, and the side of a barn just this way with them yellow circus bills? That's my three-mile mark."

"Be we got four more to make? Oh, my laws!" mourned Mrs. Tobin. "Urge the beast, can't ye, Jeff'son? I ain't used to bein' out in such bleak weather. Seems if I couldn't git my breath. I'm all pinched up and wigglin' with shivers now. 'Tain't no use lettin' the hoss go stepaty-step, this fashion."

"Landy me!" exclaimed the affronted driver. "I don't see why folks expects me to race with the cars. Everybody that gits in wants me to run the hoss to death on the road. I make a good average o' time, and that's all I *can* do. Ef you was to go back an' forth every day but Sabbath fur eighteen years, *you'd* want to ease it all you could, and let those thrash the spokes out o' their wheels that wanted to. North Kilby, Mondays, Wednesdays, and Fridays; Sanscrit Pond, Tuesdays, Thu'sdays, an' Saturdays. Me an' the beast's done it eighteen years together, and the creatur' warn't, so to say, young when we begun it, nor I neither. I re'lly didn't know's she'd hold out till this time. There, git up, will ye, old mar'!" as the beast of burden stopped short in the road.

There was a story that Jefferson gave this faithful creature a rest three times a mile, and took four hours for the journey by himself and longer whenever he had a passenger. But in pleasant weather the road was delightful, and full of people who drove their own conveyances and liked to stop and talk. There were not many farms, and the third growth of white pines made a pleasant shade, though Jefferson liked to say that when he began to carry the mail his way lay through an open country of stumps and sparse underbrush, where the white pines nowadays completely arched the road.

They had passed the barn with circus posters, and felt colder than ever when they caught sight of the weather-beaten acrobats in their tights.

"My gorry!" exclaimed Widow Tobin, "them pore creatur's looks as cheerless as little birch trees in snowtime. I hope they dresses 'em warmer this time o' year. Now, there! look at that one jumpin' through the little hoop, will ye?"

"He couldn't git himself through there with two pair o' pants on," answered Mr. Briley. "I expect they must have to keep limber as eels. I used to think, when I was a boy, that 'twas the only thing I could ever be reconciled to do for a livin'. I set out to run away an' follow a rovin' showman once, but mother needed me to home. There warn't nobody but me an' the little gals."

"You ain't the only one that's be'n disapp'inted o' their heart's desire," said Mrs. Tobin sadly. " 'Twarn't so that I could be spared from home to learn the dressmaker's trade."

" 'Twould a come handy later on, I declare," answered the sympathetic driver, "bein's you went an' had such a passel o' gals to clothe an' feed. There, them that's livin' is all well off now, but it must ha' been some inconvenient for ye when they was small."

"Yes, Mr. Briley, but then I've had my mercies, too," said the widow somewhat grudgingly. "I take it master hard now, though, havin' to give up my own home and live round from place to place, if they be my own child'en. There was Ad'line and Susan Ellen fussin' an' bickerin' yesterday about who'd got to have me next; and, Lord be thanked, they both wanted me right off, but I hated to hear 'em talkin' of it over. I'd rather live to home, and do for myself."

"I've got consider'ble used to boardin'," said Jefferson, "sence marm died, but it made me ache 'long at the fust on't, I tell ye. Bein' on the road's I be, I couldn't do no ways at keepin' house. I should want to keep right there and see to things."

"Course you would," replied Mrs. Tobin, with a sudden inspiration of opportunity which sent a welcome glow all over her. "Course you would, Jefferson." She leaned toward the front seat. "That is to say, on-less you had jest the right one to do it for ye."

And Jefferson felt a strange glow also, and a sense of unexpected interest and enjoyment.

"See here, Sister Tobin," he exclaimed with enthusiasm. "Why can't ye take the trouble to shift seats, and come front here 'long o' me? We could put one buff'lo top o' the other — they're both wearin' thin —

and set close, and I do' know but we sh'd be more protected ag'inst the weather."

"Well, I couldn't be no colder if I was friz to death," answered the widow, with an amiable simper. "Don't ye let me delay you, nor put you out, Mr. Briley. I don't know's I'd set forth today if I'd known 'twas so cold; but I had all my bundles done up, and I ain't one that puts my hand to the plough an' looks back, 'cordin' to Scriptur'."

"You wouldn't wanted me to ride all them seven miles alone?" asked the gallant Briley sentimentally, as he lifted her down and helped her up again to the front seat. She was a few years older than he, but they had been schoolmates, and Mrs. Tobin's youthful freshness was suddenly revived to his mind's eye. She had a little farm; there was nobody left at home now but herself, and so she had broken up housekeeping for the winter. Jefferson himself had savings of no mean amount.

They tucked themselves in, and felt better for the change, but there was a sudden awkwardness between them; they had not had time to prepare for an unexpected crisis.

"They say Elder Bickers, over to East Sanscrit, 's been and got married again to a gal that's four year younger than his daughter," proclaimed Mrs. Tobin presently. "Seems to me 'twas fool's business."

"I view it so," said the stage driver. "There's goin' to be a mild open winter for that fam'ly."

"What a joker you be for a man that's had so much responsibility!" smiled Mrs. Tobin, after they had done laughing. "Ain't you never 'fraid, carryin' mail matter and such valuable stuff, that you'll be set on an' robbed, 'specially by night?"

Jefferson braced his feet against the dasher under the worn buffalo. "It is kind o' scary, or would be for some folks, but I'd like to see anybody get the better o' me. I go armed, and I don't care who knows it. Some o' them drover men that comes from Canady looks as if they didn't care what they did, but I look 'em right in the eye every time."

"Men folks is brave by natur'," said the widow admiringly. "You know how Tobin would let his fist right out at anybody that ondertook to sass him. Town-meetin' days, if he got disappointed about the way things went, he lay 'em out in win'rows; and ef he hadn't been a church member he'd been a real fightin' character. I was always 'fraid to have him roused, for all he was so willin' and meechin' to home, and set round clever as anybody. My Susan Ellen used to boss him same's the kitten, when she was four year old."

"I've got a kind of a sideways cant to my nose, that Tobin give me

when we was to school. I don't know's you ever noticed it," said
Mr. Briley. "We was scufflin', as lads will. I never bore him no kind of
a grudge. I pitied ye, when he was taken away. I re'lly did, now, Fanny.
I liked Tobin first-rate, and I liked you. I used to say you was the
han'somest girl to school."

"Lemme see your nose. 'Tis all straight, for what I know," said the
widow gently, and with a trace of coyness she gave a hasty glance. "I
don't know but what 'tis warped a little, but nothin' to speak of. You've
got real nice features, like your marm's folks."

It was becoming a sentimental occasion, and Jefferson Briley felt that
he was in for something more than he had bargained. He hurried the
faltering sorrel horse, and began to talk of the weather. It certainly did
look like snow, and he was tired bumping over the frozen road.

"I shouldn't wonder if I hired a hand here another year, and went
off out West myself to see the country."

"Why, how you talk!" answered the widow.

"Yes'm," pursued Jefferson. " 'Tis tamer here than I like, and I was
tellin' 'em yesterday I've got to know this road most too well. I'd like to
go out an' ride in the mountains with some o' them great clipper coaches,
where the driver don't know any minute but he'll be shot dead the next.
They carry an awful sight o' gold down from the mines, I expect."

"I should be scairt to death," said Mrs. Tobin. "What creatur's men-
folks be to like such things! Well, I do declare."

"Yes," explained the mild little man. "There's sights of desp-radoes
makes a han'some livin' out o' robbin' 'em clean to the bone. Your money
or your life!" and he flourished his stub of a whip over the sorrel mare.

"Landy me! you make me run all of a cold creep. Do tell somethin'
heartenin', this cold day. I shall dream bad dreams all night."

"They put on black crepe over their faces," said the driver mysteri-
ously. "Nobody knows who most on 'em be, and like as not some o' them
fellers come o' good families. They've got so they stop the cars, and go
right through 'em bold as brass. I could make your hair stand on end,
Mis' Tobin, I could *so!*"

"I hope none on 'em'll git round our way, I'm sure," said Fanny
Tobin. "I don't want to see none on 'em in their crepe bunnits comin'
after me."

"I ain't goin' to let nobody touch a hair o' your head." Mr. Briley
moved a little nearer and tucked in the buffaloes again.

"I feel considerable warm to what I did," observed the widow by way
of reward.

"There, I used to have my fears," Mr. Briley resumed, with an inward feeling that he never would get to North Kilby depot a single man. "But you see I had nobody but myself to think of. I've got cousins, as you know, but nothin' nearer, and what I've laid up would soon be parted out; and — well, I suppose some folks would think o' me if anything was to happen."

Mrs. Tobin was holding her cloud over her face — the wind was sharp on that bit of open road — but she gave an encouraging sound, between a groan and a chirp.

" 'Twouldn't be like nothin' to me not to see you drivin' by," she said, after a minute. "I shouldn't know the days o' the week. I says to Susan Ellen last week I was sure 'twas Friday, and she said no, 'twas Thursday; but next minute you druv by and headin' toward North Kilby, so we found I was right."

"I've got to be a featur' of the landscape," said Mr. Briley plaintively. "This kind o' weather the old mare and me, we wish we was done with it, and could settle down kind o' comfortable. I've been lookin' this good while, as I drove the road, and I've picked me out a piece o' land two or three times. But I can't abide the thought o' buildin' — 'twould plague me to death; and both Sister Peak to North Kilby and Mis' Deacon Ash to the Pond, they vie with one another to do well by me, fear I'll like the other stoppin'-place best."

"I shouldn't covet livin' long o' neither one o' them women," responded the passenger with some spirit. "I see some o' Mis' Peak's cookin' to a farmers' supper once, when I was visitin' Susan Ellen's folks, an' I says, 'Deliver me from sech pale-complected baked beans as them!' and she give a kind of quack. She was settin' jest at my left hand, and couldn't help hearin' me. I wouldn't have spoken if I had known, but she needn't have let on they was hers. 'I guess them beans tastes just as well as other folks',' says she, and she wouldn't never speak to me afterward."

"Do' know's I blame her," ventured Mr. Briley. "Women folks is dreadful pudjicky about their cookin'. I've always heard you was one o' the best o' cooks, Mis' Tobin. I know them doughnuts an' things you've give me in times past, when I was drivin' by. Wish I had some on 'em now. I never let on, but Mis' Ash's cookin's the best by a long chalk. Mis' Peak's handy about some things, and looks after mendin' me up."

"It doos seem as if a man o' your years and your quiet make ought to hev a home you could call your own," suggested the passenger. "I kind of hate to think o' your boardin' here and there, and one old woman mendin', and the other settin' ye down to meals that like's not don't agree with ye."

"Lor', now, Mis' Tobin, le's not fuss round no longer," said Mr. Briley impatiently. "You know you covet me same's I do you."

"I don't nuther. Don't you go an' say fo'lish things you can't stand to."

"I've been tryin' to git a chance to put in a word with you ever sence — Well, I expected you'd want to get your feelin's kind o' calloused after losin' Tobin."

"There's nobody can fill his place," said the widow.

"I do' know but I can fight for ye town-meetin' days, on a pinch," urged Jefferson boldly.

"I never see the beat o' you men fur conceit," and Mrs. Tobin laughed. "I ain't goin' to bother with ye, gone half the time as you be, an' carryin' on with your Mis' Peaks and Mis' Ashes. I dare say you've promised yourself to both on 'em twenty times."

"I hope to gracious if I ever breathe a word to none on 'em!" protested the lover. " 'Tain't for lack o' opportunities set afore me, nuther." Then Mr. Briley craftily kept silence, as if he had made a fair proposal and expected a definite reply.

The lady of his choice was, as she might have expressed it, much beat about. As she truly thought, she was getting along in years, and must put up with Jefferson all the rest of the time. It was not likely she would ever have the chance of choosing again, though she was one who liked variety. Jefferson wasn't much to look at, but he was pleasant and kind of boyish and young-feeling. "I do' know's I should do better," she said unconsciously and half aloud. "Well, yes, Jefferson, seein' it's you. But we're both on us kind of old to change our situation," and Fanny Tobin gave a gentle sigh.

"Hooray!" said Jefferson. "I was scairt you meant to keep me sufferin' here a half an hour. I declare, I'm more pleased than I calc'lated on. You tell Susan Ellen the news, won't ye? She'll be surprised to hear you've jest come on a visit. How you must ha' tugged to get them bundles ready, an' all for nothin'; but now I'll lend a hand 'bout everythin'. An' I expected till lately to die a single man!"

" 'Twould re'lly have been a shame; 'tain't natur'," said Mrs. Tobin, with confidence. "I don't see how you held out so long with bein' solitary."

"I'll hire a hand to drive for me, and we'll have a good comfortable winter, me an' you an' the old sorrel. I've been promisin' of her a rest this good while."

"Better keep her a-steppin'," urged thrifty Mrs. Fanny. "She'll stiffen up master, an' disapp'int ye, come spring."

"You'll have me, now, won't ye, sartin?" pleaded Jefferson, to make sure. "You ain't one o' them that plays with a man's feelin's. Say right out you'll have me."

"I s'pose I shall have to," said Mrs. Tobin somewhat mournfully. "I feel for Mis' Peak an' Mis' Ash, pore creatur's. I expect they'll be hard-shipped. They've always been hard-worked, an' may kind o' looked forward to a little ease. But one on 'em would be left lamentin', anyhow," and she gave a girlish laugh. An air of victory animated the frame of Mrs. Tobin. She felt but twenty-five years of age. In that moment she made plans for cutting her Briley's hair, and making him look smartened-up and ambitious. Then she wished that she knew for certain how much money he had in the bank; not that it would make any difference now. "He needn't bluster none before me," she thought gaily. "He's harmless as a fly."

"There's the big ellum past, an' we're only a third of a mile from the depot," said Mr. Briley. "Feel warmer, do ye?"

"Who'd have thought we'd done such a piece of engineerin', when we started out?" inquired the dear one of Mr. Briley's heart, as he tenderly helped her to alight at Susan Ellen's door.

"Both on us, jest the least grain," answered the lover. "Gimme a good smack, now, you clever creatur' "; and so they parted. Mr. Briley had been taken on the road in spite of his pistol.

Mark Howe of Boston

by ARTHUR STANWOOD PIER

"The Self-effacement of a Modern Biographer" might well be the subtitle of this vignette, which Arthur Stanwood Pier, editor, teacher, and author, drew of his lifelong friend, M. A. DeWolfe Howe. Mr. Howe's first contribution appeared in the Atlantic *in May 1893 and his most recent, "Books That Talk to the Blind," in December 1956.*

APRIL 1950

Speculating with a group of friends on the possibility of interplanetary travel, the late Professor Alfred North Whitehead remarked that the Earth's first visitors to Mars should be persons likely to make a good impression. "Whom would you send?" someone asked. "My first choice would be Mark Howe," replied the venerable sage.

To Mark Howe's friends, his qualifications for such a mission are obvious. His quick interest in new people and fresh points of view, his hospitality to ideas, and his courtesy should make him a welcome visitant in any sphere. In his terrestrial career his interests have led him into the field of biography, where his exploration of personalities, widely diverse, some of them eccentric, has yielded, under his sympathetic probing, a revelation of character and expression. For his success as a writer of biography he laid the foundation by what he terms his steam-shovel qualities, his persistence and thoroughness in excavating significant facts from masses of documents and letters. But to the grubbing industry of the antiquarian were added the poet's imaginative insight and the artist's skill in rounding out and lighting the portrait.

No more self-effacing biographer ever lived, nor one more industrious. His first biography, a short volume on Phillips Brooks, appeared in 1899; then came *The Life and Letters of George Bancroft, The Life and Labors of Bishop Hare,* and *The Letters of Charles Eliot Norton; Memories of a Hostess; Barrett Wendell and His Letters* (which received a Pulitzer Prize), *John Jay Chapman and His Letters, Holmes of the Breakfast-Table.*

As an undergraduate at Lehigh in the eighties he found his best friend in Richard Harding Davis. Together they wrote for the Lehigh *Burr,* and it was Howe who succeeded Davis as the managing editor. After Lehigh came two years of graduate study at Harvard; then with his M.A. degree and a letter of introduction from Professor Child he applied for a job at the *Atlantic.* Horace Scudder, the editor, had nothing to offer, but passed him along with a friendly word to the editor of the *Youth's Companion,* in whose leisurely routine Howe served for five years as one of numerous assistant editors. Scudder, however, kept him in mind and when an opening occurred in the *Atlantic* office invited him to fill it.

Howe had been assistant editor but a short time when his chief, who was planning to retire, gave him a copy of a small book he had written, in which were inscribed the words, "H. E. Scudder, to his understudy." The promise of promotion that was implied was foiled by the serious trouble that Howe began to have with his eyes. The oculist's prescriptions were of no avail; he had to give up reading, resign from the *Atlantic,* and retire to the family farm at Bristol, Rhode Island, where for the next five years he saw the world through dark glasses. He farmed and he fumed. Drastic and painful treatments slowly restored his sight. As the light came back he began to write again — poems enough to fill a slim volume and then his biography of Phillips Brooks.

On September 21, 1899, he married Fanny Quincy, the younger sister of the mayor of Boston. Her wit, her delightful humor, her judicious skepticism, were a stimulant which quickened and sharpened his work. She was herself a writer of distinction, but her essays in the *Atlantic* — " My Wife's Address-Book," "My Wife's Check-Book," "A Guilt-Edged Conscience," to name but three — were always published anonymously, as were her books, though their authorship could not long be kept secret. When any of them was praised in her presence, she would declare severely that it should no more be mentioned than if it were an illegitimate child. Upon her husband's proposal to dedicate one of his books to her, she ironically suggested the following:

> To that Daughter of Boston
> Whose censure and ridicule
> Have vastly complicated my task
> I dedicate this work
> At her own earnest request.

Fortunately the cure that Howe had undergone proved to be successful. After four years during which he devoted virtually all his spare time to the papers of George Bancroft — three enormous Saratoga trunks full of them — the monumental two-volume biography of the historian and diplomat was finished. It won for the author immediate recognition by American scholars.

Howe looks upon his biographical writings as an extension of his editorial work. His method as a biographer has been to let the subject, as far as possible, tell his own story. Most of the persons with whom he has dealt were highly articulate; in their letters they left records of their thoughts and activities, often buried under much unimportant detail. To release what was vital and interesting, to supply explanatory comment and bridge narrative gaps, called for editorial skill and wide collateral reading. Howe thinks that he may look forward to a small immortality in footnotes, for the reason that his biographies are source material for historians. The authors of books and articles relating to the Russo-Japanese War, 1904–1905, must consult his life of George von L. Meyer, who at that time was the American Ambassador at St. Petersburg. So too, those who would interpret the New England of past days are inadequately equipped for the task unless they have read Howe's books dealing with some of its eminent figures and presenting for the first time material essential to complete understanding.

In his biography of Wendell, Howe quoted his subject's opinion of a biographer's duty: "Whoever would tell the truth about any man must be in the literal sense his apologist . . . I mean that the first and perhaps the only duty of an honest biographer is, so far as may be, to set forth the man of whom he writes as that man saw himself, and to explain him on his own terms."

That theory may lead to satisfactory results when the subject is conspicuously an extrovert, who takes an objective view of himself; it cannot be successfully applied to one who, like Barrett Wendell, was introspective and given to underrating himself. In order to show Wendell in action Howe had to seek out other sources than his letters. A revealing passage, for example, is the brief report of an occurrence when Wendell, with his wife and daughter, was returning from Cambridge to Boston after witnessing a football game. "As they were boarding an electric car a man in the crowd thrust Mrs. Wendell aside and was pushing through the door when Wendell managed to arrest his progress by hooking the man's umbrella with the crook of his own walking-stick. 'Be careful, sir!' came the protest, 'you are breaking my umbrella!' 'On the contrary,' said Wendell, 'I am mending your manners.' "

The accuracy and perceptiveness of Howe's appraisal of character are nowhere better shown than in his closing words on Barrett Wendell: "Honest, pure, and original of mind; chivalrous and generous to the verge of the quixotic; given to decking serious thought in the motley of jest and caprice; but to the core of his being, faithful, and wise, and kind."

In all the biographies Howe's talent for making pictures shows attractively. *Memories of a Hostess* — his old friend Mrs. James T. Fields —is not properly a biography; it is a succession of charming scenes and sketches. One of the most delightful is the description of a dinner party at Mrs. Fields' Charles Street house in Boston at which Mrs. Julia Ward Howe, then nearly ninety years old, rose in response to her septuagenarian hostess's request and recited the "Battle Hymn of the Republic," accompanying the line ". . . be swift, my soul, to answer Him! be jubilant, my feet!" with a little clap of her hands and a decorous prancing of her feet, while from across the table Henry James gazed with rapt attention at the tiny figure. Afterwards Howe escorted her to her carriage and, having seen her comfortably bestowed, was about to bid her good night when she remarked with satisfaction, "Annie Fields has shrunk."

After Eighty

by M. A. DeWOLFE HOWE

NOVEMBER 1948

Is everything far bigger than of old,
    Far quicker and far noisier in its pace?
Or is it thus that I must now be told
    My station is a mere spectator's place?

So let it be, yet in my heart I know
    That small and slow and quiet things yet live,
And, as their gentler motions forward go,
    That from their store I still may take — and give.

New England Dilemma

by HOWARD MUMFORD JONES

Howard Mumford Jones taught at Ann Arbor, in Texas, and at Chapel Hill before his appointment as professor of English at Harvard.

APRIL 1940

What is a New England point of view? What is a New England philosophy? What is the New England way of life?

The fact that nobody can answer these questions is, of course, precisely the point. In the nineteenth century the questions would have been answerable. They included what Poe acidly summed up as Frogpondism. They meant a Protestant outlook, even if one were a member of no particular church. They meant a placid consciousness of intellectual superiority to barbarians in Broadway and the West. They meant all that is apparent in Thomas Bailey Aldrich's claim that, though he was not genuine Boston, he was Boston-plated.

Writing Bayard Taylor in 1866, Aldrich said:

> I miss my few dear friends in New York — but that is all. There is a finer intellectual atmosphere here [in Boston] than in our city. It is true, a poor literary man could not earn his salt, or more than that, out of pure literary labor in Boston: but then he couldn't do it in New York, unless he turned *journalist.* The people of Boston are full-blooded *readers,* appreciative, trained. The humblest man of letters has a position here which he doesn't have in New York. To be known as an able writer is to have the choicest society opened to you . . . here [he] is supposed necessarily to be a gentleman. In New York — he's a Bohemian! outside of his personal friends he has no standing.

This is the unadulterated snobbery of the genteel tradition, but it is snobbery concerning something real. A provincial is merely a man who is proud of belonging to a cultural tradition which he believes to be per se superior to any other cultural tradition. When a writer stands outside such a tradition and looks at it without believing in it, the result is *The Late George Apley*. When he stands inside of it and believes in it, the result is the creation of the *Atlantic Monthly* with Lowell as editor and Holmes as chief contributor. *The Late George Apley* has its chuckling excellence, but its excellence is not that of "The Autocrat of the Breakfast Table." Contemporary New Englandism is an inheritance, not a belief; a mode of behavior, not an idea.

The difference is made clear by a glance at the South. It is commonly said that in the twentieth century the South enjoys an intellectual renaissance. Though the intellectual life of the South, like the middle class, is always rising, the production of books and magazines about that region has undeniably increased. Good work has come out of various parts of that region, but a fructifying influence has poured especially from two centers — Chapel Hill, North Carolina, and Nashville, Tennessee. At the University of North Carolina, though it is possible that no one could give a definition of the Southern way of life, a group of men arose determined not merely that the Southern way of life should be improved, but also that it should be preserved. A second group arose at Vanderbilt.

In the one university, men like Howard W. Odum, Frederick H. Koch, Rupert B. Vance, Paul Green, Edgar W. Knight, E. C. Branson, L. R. Wilson, and others decided to focus the best brains they could assemble upon the problem of Southern values. The result was not only a rich historical and sociological literature; their activities also had important repercussions in imaginative writing from the Carolina folk plays to the novels of Thomas Wolfe. In the other university a group of young poets, weary of Southern sentimentalism, determined that the South was entitled to an intelligent literature. They were presently forced by the logic of their philosophy to consider the question of Southern values, and the result was the Agrarian pronouncement, *I'll Take My Stand*. One may debate endlessly the question whether the Tarheels or the Tennesseans advanced the right solution, but the point is that a solution was looked for. And that solution focuses upon the assumption that the Southern way of life is both valuable and defensible. There is no similar focus for a philosophy of value, so far as I can see, in all New England. New England is centrifugal, not centripetal.

To be sure, literature in New England now resembles the multitudinous laughter of the waves. In the summer not a country lane in Connecticut, New Hampshire, or Vermont but resounds with the click of typewriters; not a village on the coast of Rhode Island, Massachusetts, or Maine but in it novelists, poets, dramatists, critics, artists, college professors, and musicians outnumber the local population which they support. New England advertised itself as the vacation land, and all the muses moved in — from New York. But there is a difference between writing books in New England and writing New England books, and there is an even more crucial difference between describing New England and believing in it. When local color peers in at the door, regional philosophy flies out at the window. In July and August, New England is a vast antique shop rummaged for ancient articles. Admiring grandfather's clock, however, is not synonymous with that deep, unconscious act of faith which led Hawthorne to produce *Grandfather's Chair.*

New England literature has always tended to fall into two broad categories — the historical and the argumentative. The golden days of New England have always been in the past. Bradford and Winthrop lamented the degeneration which time soon wrought at Plymouth and Boston; Cotton Mather's *Magnalia* is as much a picture of the good old times as the histories of Samuel Eliot Morison; and the solemn purpose of the Connecticut Wits embalmed the Revolution in the cold coffin of epic poetry. Bryant, Longfellow, Whittier, Lowell, Holmes, Henry Adams, were all more or less reminiscent. The standard textbook phrase for the fictions of Sarah Orne Jewett, Mary E. Wilkins Freeman, and others of that generation is "chroniclers of New England decline." Tilbury Town had already been painted and analyzed by Nathaniel Hawthorne, and *Mourning Becomes Electra* was no revelation to anybody who had read *The House of the Seven Gables.*

The notion that the New England way of life has decayed is perhaps the liveliest tradition in the literary history of three centuries. But, though the complaint that New England is not what she was is perennial, the habit of looking backward engenders the habit of looking away from the present. The concept of New England as the Old Curiosity Shop comes in time to negate everything that Concord once stood for. Antiques are not culture.

It is curious how much of the organized intellectual energy of New England goes into a past which almost nobody attacks and ignores a present which almost nobody defends. The Colonial Society of Massachusetts, the Essex Historical Institute, the *New England Historical and Genealogical Register,* the American Antiquarian Society — one could add indefinitely to such a roll call. Doubtless these venerable institutions are flavorsome and valuable, but they march resolutely away from the twentieth century. I observe with interest that the Trustees of Public Reservations have just purchased the Old Manse. I am glad they will preserve the Old Manse, but who will preserve Emerson — him who wrote, "The mind of this country, taught to aim at low objects, eats upon itself. There is no work for any but the decorous and the complaisant." He also wrote, "We will speak our own minds." I think he referred to more than academic freedom.

The other side of New England letters is argumentative. Up to the World War, New England had something or other to defend. It might be Calvinism or the colonial charters, the Hartford Convention or Daniel Webster, transcendentalism or the Union, civil service reform or the Republican Party. It might even be culture. I suppose the last New Englander who really fought for culture was Charles Eliot Norton, who, though he was capable of disliking *Alice in Wonderland,* had in his quiet way a fighting philosophy. "The concern for beauty, as the highest end of work, and as the noblest expression of life, hardly exists among us," he wrote in an essay, "and forms no part of our character as a nation." This is at least perfectly definite, and he labored for twenty-three years to reform the national character by culture. We still believe in education, but who, even in New England, militantly believes in culture? The polemical strength of New England letters has vanished for the sufficient reason that New England has nothing to defend.

I suppose the two events of recent years that have most deeply stirred emotion in this region have been the Sacco-Vanzetti case and the hate-Roosevelt ground swell. In the Sacco-Vanzetti case my sympathies were with the opposition. I believe these men were innocent, and I am therefore prejudiced. But what seems to me the most disheartening thing about that tragedy is not that the men were executed, but that nobody defended the state. They died because justice and the commonwealth demanded it. No one, however, ringingly demonstrated what concept of justice and the state made this inexorable demand.

If strong conservative convictions existed, they were not adequately expressed. Conservatism usually takes refuge in silence, but Massachusetts was under attack, and who effectively defended Massachusetts?

Characteristic of certain classes and communities in New England is the strong, stubborn, covert opposition to the New Deal. But it does not take intellectual form. If President Roosevelt's policies really threaten the New England way of life, who explains or trenchantly defends what is threatened? What public man now stands for this region as Daniel Webster once stood for this region? What Congressman is essentially Yankee as John Quincy Adams was Yankee? I do not refer to his accent but to his stubborn belief in the right of petition.

Who presents a program or a policy? Is there any economic theory concerning these states which is even as articulate or as vocal as the Townsend plan? We have half a dozen governors, twelve senators, a regiment of representatives, and local leaders by the gross. Can any one of them say what he stands for and why he stands for it in terms that cut through the blurred phraseology of politics?

Of course brains are rare and statesmen do not grow on every blackberry bush, but it is felt that a whole way of life is threatened, and it would seem that six commonwealths, scores of colleges, innumerable newspapers, and a battery of magazines could produce something beyond emotionalism and platitudes. Clay and Calhoun had no doubt what New England stood for; they ran into it.

The New England way of life has been a Yankee way of life, and of course the Yankee has traditionally looked after his savings. Let us, however, broaden the perspective to include the late George Apley. The New England way was also the "Old American" way, and the "Old Americans" are now an outnumbered clan, grimly holding on to financial and social power where they can, yielding only to death and superior taxes. The social cleavage they have thus created is of course the New England tragedy. Such heroism may be magnificent, as the holding of Thermopylae was magnificent, but the Spartans yielded in the end. It took a more active strategist to rout the Persian host.

It is disheartening to trace the blindness of "Old Americans" from the mild bewilderment of Emerson and Thoreau, confronted by Irish laborers on the Fitchburg railroad, to its climactic expression in Aldrich's "Unguarded Gates," a poem which is pure snobbery in classic verse. Lovely as it is to be conscious of superior rectitude, by refusing to reinvigorate virtue from the common people the New England intellect has run thin and bloodless; and so long as it persists in regarding Irishmen, Italians, Jews, Portuguese, French Canadians, and other late arrivals as interlopers, it cannot fully renew itself on its own soil. For these are precisely the groups which are rich in the qualities the New England intellectual tradition gravely needs — earthiness, emotion, a deep sense of life, a belief that intellect is not all. Finding they are not wanted, the "immigrants" have struck back by two characteristically American attacks: they have conquered at the polls, and they are trying to conquer in the countinghouse. New England is therefore a house divided against itself. In contrast, the superior flexibility of the New Yorker has made his city, despite transient racial strains, the metropolis of the future, rich in the arts and the sciences. Mr. Apley, however, refuses to admit that a profitable amalgam of cultures can take place. After him, the deluge.

The rising culture in New England is a Catholic culture, the traditional culture of New England is a Protestant culture, but it does not follow that the twain shall never meet.

There used to be an annual conference at Williams College on international affairs. Why not an annual conference on New England affairs? We cannot reform the nation wholesale, but only piece by piece. Men who contribute money to fight injustice in California do not even contribute brain power to fight poverty in Vermont. What is done in New York and Colorado affects New England, but what is done in New England also affects Colorado and New York. We hear so much about the shrinking sides of the world that there are those who regard Connecticut as a borough of New York City. In New York, however, Boston is more remote than Hollywood. I have not heard Mayor La Guardia discuss rural slums or the decay of New England mills. I have not even read in the *Saturday Review of Literature* the pertinent question: Who are the heirs of Alcott, Emerson, Thoreau? I hear much talk of *Moby Dick,* which was written in Lenox almost a hundred years ago, but that book is supposed to prove that the universe is evil. I had thought it had something to do with the dauntless spirit of man.

Catholic or Protestant does not matter; Old American or New American does not matter; Communist or economic royalist does not matter; even George Apley does not matter. What matters is the sense of deadness and the desire of life. We have two needs in what was formerly a theocracy: conviction and application.

The cry is for a program. Programs are born, not made, is apparently the assumption, as if the Pilgrims knew precisely where they were going and what they were going to do. As a matter of history, they were tricked and deceived. Having only the pragmatic belief that they could create an economy in the wilderness, they merely began New England. We, too, live in a wilderness equally threatening, but nothing less than a declaration of bankruptcy and a total reorganization of society will satisfy us. Softly, softly. Let us take one step at a time, being, indeed, unable to walk otherwise. The calm belief that Yankee ingenuity is not confined to bolts and screws is enough for the moment. Dilemmas are not susceptible of logical resolution. An old and battered program concerns the rights of man. If we cannot agree about church and ancestry, let us at least agree that we stand where we stand. By common consent certain things are evil and remain so, among them being starvation, idleness, and disbelief.

If we must have a platform, I suggest we reinstitute the Concord school of philosophy, though there be not a transcendentalist on the faculty. Our books are disparate, atomic, descriptive. Save for Robert Frost, there is none who stands for the New England way. I read the social history of Virginia in the novels of Ellen Glasgow, but where shall I turn to read the social history of Maine, Connecticut, Rhode Island? Moving pictures in costumed prose are not what most we need. Once the Saturday Club expressed something, but what do these admirable historical novels express except an artistic arrangement of the past? Even Sam Slick and Shore Acres have vanished from the theater. Fishermen still put out of Gloucester, but it is now some decades since Kipling, a transient Englishman, wrote *Captains Courageous*. I have read no short stories about the Portuguese since Wilbur Daniel Steele. The *Yale Review* discusses everything except Connecticut, the *Atlantic Monthly* is now a national magazine.

And yet it is not magazines and reviews we need, nor yet fishermen or Portuguese or comic Yankees or farmers, but a passionate belief in values and in a way of life some centuries old. There are times when *Little Women* seems more masterly than *The Last Puritan*. Miss Alcott did what she did, and not something else. We tire of fine skepticism, and long for an affirmation, even if it concern only simple things. What shall it profit an author if he gain royalties and lose his own soul? What contract did Longfellow make, and did he bargain for the movie rights of *Hiawatha*?

To be sure, it is easy to drop into a scolding tone. To be sure, also, New England — there she stands. But how long she shall stand, or rather how long she shall stand as New England, once the home of men who believed there were eternal verities, or whether she shall stand simply as a territory belonging to the United States — this is the New England dilemma.

The West

New England and the nation were changing. "So rapid has been the development," Charles C. Coffin wrote in the Atlantic, "that maps of 1864 are obsolete in 1866." Yet there were certain undertakings so dusty and matter-of-fact that no one bothered to write about them; the Atlantic came into being only eight years after the forty-niners had begun their long haul West, but nowhere in our early issues is there any account of the prairie schooners or of such tragedies as the Donner Party encountered. What we did publish in September of 1869 was "A Lone Woman's Trip to Omaha and Beyond" by Mrs. M. E. Brown — she went by rail and doubtless by way of Dedham. The triumph of the iron horse was thought much more remarkable than the hardihood of those who went by foot.

It was William Dean Howells, the third editor, who brought the best of the Western writers, Bret Harte and Mark Twain, to the Atlantic. Bret Harte was at the height of his popularity; the Atlantic wanted exclusive rights and in the end the publishers paid him $10,000 (the equivalent I suppose of $65,000 in today's currency) for such stories and poems as he might write for their magazine in the year 1871. As a result of this bid, the highest in its early history, the Atlantic published four short stories and five poems. Meantime Mark Twain was being paid at the rate of $12 for each thousand words. Time has readjusted that evaluation.

Howells made his January issue the feature of the year and pressed Clemens for a new serial to begin in January 1875. For a time Clemens could find no fresh lead. Then, excitedly, at the close of 1874, he found the clue he needed:

> I take back the remark that I can't write for the Jan. number. For Twichell and I have had a long walk in the woods and I got to telling him about old Mississippi days of steamboating glory and grandeur as I saw them (during 5 years) from the pilot-

house. He said, "What a virgin subject to hurl into a magazine!"
I hadn't thought of that before. Would you like a series of papers
to run through 3 months or 6 or 9?

Such was the origin of "Old Times on the Mississippi," which ran
through seven issues and was eventually published in book form
as Life on the Mississippi.

Old Times on the Mississippi

by MARK TWAIN

Samuel Clemens spent his boyhood in Hannibal, Missouri, and his remembrance of "the white town, drowsing in the sunshine of a summer's morning . . . with the great Mississippi, the majestic, the magnificent Mississippi, rolling its mile-wide tide along" epitomizes for all of us the halcyon years. Actually, his life at home was none too happy, else why did he run away? Where he ran to and how he found his nom de plume, Mark Twain, are recounted in the pages which follow.

JANUARY 1875

When I was a boy, there was but one permanent ambition among my comrades in our village on the west bank of the Mississippi River. That was, to be a steamboatman. We had transient ambitions of other sorts, but they were only transient. When a circus came and went, it left us all burning to become clowns; the first Negro minstrel show that came to our section left us all suffering to try that kind of life; now and then we had a hope that if we lived and were good, God would permit us to be pirates. These ambitions faded out, each in its turn; but the ambition to be a steamboatman always remained.

Once a day a cheap, gaudy packet arrived upward from St. Louis, and another downward from Keokuk. Before these events had transpired, the day was glorious with expectancy; after they had transpired, the day was a dead and empty thing. Not only the boys, but the whole village, felt this. After all these years I can picture that old time to myself now, just as it was then: the white town, drowsing in the sunshine of a summer's morning; the streets empty, or pretty nearly so; one or two clerks sitting in front of the Water Street stores, with their splint-bottomed chairs tilted back against the wall, chins on breasts, hats slouched over their faces, asleep — with shingle shavings enough around to show what broke them down; a sow and a litter of pigs loafing along the sidewalk, doing a good business in watermelon rinds and seeds; two or three lonely little freight piles scattered about the levee; a pile of skids on the slope of the stone-paved wharf, and the fragrant town drunkard asleep in the shadow of them; two or three wood flats at the head of the wharf, but nobody to listen to the peaceful lapping of the wavelets against them; the great Mississippi, the majestic, the magnificent Mississippi, rolling its mile-wide tide along, shining in the sun; the dense forest away on the other side; the point above the town and the point below, bounding the river glimpse and turning it into a sort of sea, and withal a very still and brilliant and lonely one. Presently a film of dark smoke appears above one of those remote points; instantly a Negro drayman, famous for his quick eye and prodigious voice, lifts up the cry, "S-t-e-a-m-boat a-comin'!" and the scene changes. The town drunkard stirs, the clerks wake up, a furious clatter of drays follows, every house and store pours out a human contribution, and all in a twinkling the dead town is alive and moving. Drays, carts, men, boys, all go hurrying to a common center, the wharf.

Assembled there, the people fasten their eyes upon the coming boat as upon a wonder they are seeing for the first time. And the boat *is* rather a handsome sight, too. She is long and sharp and trim and pretty; she has two tall, fancy-topped chimneys, with a gilded device of some kind swung between them; a fanciful pilothouse, all glass and ginger-bread, perched on top of the texas deck behind them; the paddle boxes are gorgeous with a picture or with gilded rays above the boat's name; the boiler deck, the hurricane deck, and the texas deck are fenced and ornamented with clean white railings; there is a flag gallantly flying from the jack staff; the furnace doors are open and the fires glaring bravely; the upper decks are black with passengers; the captain stands by the big bell, calm, imposing, the envy of all; great volumes of the blackest smoke are rolling and tumbling out of the chimneys — a hus-banded grandeur created with a bit of pitch pine just before arriving at a town; the crew are grouped on the forecastle; the broad stage is run far out over the port bow, and an envied deck hand stands picturesquely on the end of it with a coil of rope in his hand; the pent steam is screaming through the gauge cocks; the captain lifts his hand, a bell rings, the wheels stop; then they turn back, churning the water to foam, and the steamer is at rest.

Then such a scramble as there is to get aboard, and to get ashore, and to take in freight and to discharge freight, all at one and the same time; and such a yelling and cursing as the mates facilitate it all with!

Ten minutes later the steamer is under way again, with no flag on the jack staff and no black smoke issuing from the chimneys. After ten more minutes the town is dead again, and the town drunkard asleep by the skids once more.

My father was a justice of the peace, and I supposed he possessed the power of life and death over all men and could hang anybody that offended him. This was distinction enough for me as a general thing; but the desire to be a steamboatman kept intruding, nevertheless. I first wanted to be a cabin boy, so that I could come out with a white apron on and shake a tablecloth over the side, where all my old comrades could see me; later I thought I would rather be the deck hand who stood on the end of the stage plank with the coil of rope in his hand, because he was particularly conspicuous. But these were only daydreams — they were too heavenly to be contemplated as real possibilities.

By and by one of our boys went away. He was not heard of for a long time. At last he turned up as apprentice engineer or "striker" on a steamboat. This thing shook the bottom out of all my Sunday-school teachings. That boy had been notoriously worldly, and I just the reverse; yet he was exalted to this eminence, and I left in obscurity and misery. There was nothing generous about this fellow in his greatness. He would always manage to have a rusty bolt to scrub while his boat tarried at our town, and he would sit on the inside guard and scrub it, where we could all see him and envy him and loathe him. And whenever his boat was laid up he would come home and swell around the town in his blackest and greasiest clothes, so that nobody could help remembering that he was a steamboatman; and he used all sorts of steamboat technicalities in his talk, as if he were so used to them that he forgot common people could not understand them. He would speak of the "labboard" side of a horse in an easy, natural way that would make one wish he was dead. And he was always talking about "St. Looy" like an old citizen; he would refer casually to occasions when he was "coming down Fourth Street," or when he was "passing by the Planter's House," or when there was a fire and he took a turn on the brakes of "the old Big Missouri"; and then he would go on and lie about how many towns the size of ours were burned down there that day. This fellow had money, too, and hair oil. Also an ignorant silver watch and a showy brass watch chain. He wore a leather belt and used no suspenders. If ever a youth was cordially admired and hated by his comrades, this one was. No girl could withstand his charms. He cut

out every boy in the village. When his boat blew up at last, it diffused a
tranquil contentment among us such as we had not known for months.
But when he came home the next week, alive, renowned, and appeared
in church all battered up and bandaged, a shining hero, stared at and
wondered over by everybody, it seemed to us that the partiality of
Providence for an undeserving reptile had reached a point where it was
open to criticism.

This creature's career could produce but one result, and it speedily
followed. Boy after boy managed to get on the river. The minister's son
became an engineer. The doctor's and the postmaster's sons became
"mud clerks"; the wholesale liquor dealer's son became a barkeeper on
a boat; four sons of the chief merchant and two sons of the county
judge became pilots. Pilot was the grandest position of all. The pilot,
even in those days of trivial wages, had a princely salary — from a hundred and fifty to two hundred and fifty dollars a month, and no board
to pay. Two months of his wages would pay a preacher's salary for a
year. Now some of us were left disconsolate. We could not get on the
river — at least our parents would not let us.

So by and by I ran away. I said I never would come home again till
I was a pilot and could come in glory. But somehow I could not manage it. I went meekly aboard a few of the boats that lay packed together
like sardines at the long St. Louis wharf, and very humbly inquired for
the pilots, but got only a cold shoulder and short words from mates and
clerks. I had to make the best of this sort of treatment for the time being, but I had comforting daydreams of a future when I should be a
great and honored pilot, with plenty of money, and could kill some of
these mates and clerks and pay for them.

Months afterward the hope within me struggled to a reluctant death,
and I found myself without an ambition. But I was ashamed to go
home. I was in Cincinnati, and I set to work to map out a new career.
I packed my valise and took passage on an ancient tub called the *Paul
Jones,* for New Orleans. For the sum of sixteen dollars I had the scarred
and tarnished splendors of "her" main saloon principally to myself, for
she was not a creature to attract the eye of wiser travelers.

When we presently got under way and went poking down the broad
Ohio, I became a new being, and the subject of my own admiration. I
was a traveler! A word never had tasted so good in my mouth before.
I had an exultant sense of being bound for mysterious lands and distant
climes which I never have felt in so uplifting a degree since.

We reached Louisville in time — at least the neighborhood of it. We stuck hard and fast on the rocks in the middle of the river and lay there four days. I was now beginning to feel a strong sense of being a part of the boat's family, a sort of infant son to the captain and younger brother to the officers. There is no estimating the pride I took in this grandeur, or the affection that began to swell and grow in me for those people.

What with lying on the rocks four days at Louisville, and some other delays, the poor old *Paul Jones* fooled away about two weeks in making the voyage from Cincinnati to New Orleans. This gave me a chance to get acquainted with one of the pilots, and he taught me how to steer the boat and thus made the fascination of river life more potent than ever for me. I planned a siege against my pilot, and at the end of three hard days he surrendered. He agreed to teach me the Mississippi River from New Orleans to St. Louis for five hundred dollars, payable out of the first wages I should receive after graduating. I entered upon the small enterprise of "learning" twelve or thirteen hundred miles of the great Mississippi River with the easy confidence of my time of life. If I had really known what I was about to require of my faculties, I should not have had the courage to begin. I supposed that all a pilot had to do was to keep his boat in the river, and I did not consider that that could be much of a trick, since it was so wide.

The boat backed out from New Orleans at four in the afternoon, and it was "our watch" until eight. Mr. B——, my chief, "straightened her up," plowed her along past the sterns of the other boats that lay at the levee, and then said, "Here, take her; shave those steamships as close as you'd peel an apple." I took the wheel, and my heart went down into my boots. It seemed to me that we were about to scrape the side off every ship in the line, we were so close. I held my breath and began to claw the boat away from the danger; and I had my own opinion of the pilot who had known no better than to get us into such peril, but I was too wise to express it. In half a minute I had a wide margin of safety intervening between the *Paul Jones* and the ships; and within ten seconds more I was set aside in disgrace, and Mr. B—— was going into danger again and flaying me alive with abuse of my cowardice. I was stung, but I was obliged to admire the easy confidence with which my chief loafed from side to side of his wheel and trimmed the ships so closely that disaster seemed ceaselessly imminent. When he had cooled a little he told me that the easy water was close ashore and the current outside, and therefore we must hug the bank, upstream, to get the benefit of the former, and stay well out, downstream, to take advantage of the latter. In my own mind I resolved to be a downstream pilot and leave the upstreaming to people dead to prudence.

Now and then Mr. B—— called my attention to certain things. Said he, "This is the Six-mile Point." I assented. It was pleasant enough information, but I could not see the bearing of it. I was not conscious that it was a matter of any interest to me. Another time he said, "This is Nine-mile Point." They were all about level with the water's edge; they all looked about alike to me; they were monotonously unpicturesque. I hoped Mr. B—— would change the subject. But no; he would crowd around a point, hugging the shore with affection, and then say: "The slack water ends here, abreast this bunch of China trees; now we cross over." So he crossed over. He gave me the wheel once or twice, but I had no luck. I either came near chipping off the edge of a sugar plantation or else I yawed too far from shore, and so I dropped back into disgrace again and got abused.

The watch was ended at last, and we took supper and went to bed. At midnight the glare of a lantern shone in my eyes, and the night watchman said, "Come! Turn out!"

And then he left. I could not understand this extraordinary procedure, so I presently gave up trying to, and dozed off to sleep. Pretty soon the watchman was back again, and this time he was gruff. I was annoyed. I said, "What do you want to come bothering around here in the middle of the night for? Now as like as not I'll not get to sleep again tonight."

The watchman said, "Well, if this an't good, I'm blest."

The "off watch" was just turning in, and I heard some brutal laughter from them and such remarks as "Hello, watchman! an't the new cub turned out yet? He's delicate, likely. Give him some sugar in a rag and send for the chambermaid to sing rock-a-by-baby to him."

About this time Mr. B—— appeared on the scene. Something like a minute later I was climbing the pilothouse steps with some of my clothes on and the rest in my arms. Mr. B—— was close behind, commenting. Here was something fresh — this thing of getting up in the middle of the night to go to work. It was a detail in piloting that had never occurred to me at all. I knew that boats ran all night, but somehow I had never happened to reflect that somebody had to get up out of a warm bed to run them. I began to fear that piloting was not quite so romantic as I had imagined it was; there was something very real and worklike about this new phase of it.

It was a rather dingy night, although a fair number of stars were out. The big mate was at the wheel, and he had the old tub pointed at a star and was holding her straight up the middle of the river. The shores on either hand were not much more than a mile apart, but they seemed wonderfully far away and ever so vague and indistinct. The mate said, "We've got to land at Jones's plantation, sir."

The vengeful spirit in me exulted. I said to myself, "I wish you joy of your job, Mr. B——; you'll have a good time finding Mr. Jones's plantation such a night as this; and I hope you never will find it as long as you live."

Mr. B—— said to the mate, "Upper end of the plantation, or the lower?"

"Upper."

"I can't do it. The stumps there are out of water at this stage. It's no great distance to the lower, and you'll have to get along with that."

"All right, sir. If Jones don't like it he'll have to lump it, I reckon."

And then the mate left. My exultation began to cool and my wonder to come up. Here was a man who not only proposed to find this plantation on such a night, but to find either end of it you preferred. All I desired to ask Mr. B—— was the simple question whether he was ass enough to really imagine he was going to find that plantation on a night when all plantations were exactly alike and all the same color. But I held in. I used to have fine inspirations of prudence in those days.

Presently he turned on me and said, "What's the name of the first point above New Orleans?"

I was gratified to be able to answer promptly, and I did. I said I didn't know.

"Don't *know?*"

This manner jolted me. I was down at the foot again, in a moment. But I had to say just what I had said before.

"Well, you're a smart one," said Mr. B——. "What's the name of the *next* point?"

Once more I didn't know.

"Well, this beats anything. Tell me the name of *any* point or place I told you."

I studied a while and decided that I couldn't.

"Look-a-here! What do you start out from, above Twelve-mile Point, to cross over?"

"I — I — don't know."

"What do you suppose I told you the names of those points for?"

I tremblingly considered a moment, and then the devil of temptation provoked me to say, "Well — to — to — be entertaining, I thought."

This was a red rag to the bull. He raged and stormed so (he was crossing the river at the time) that I judge it made him blind, because he ran over the steering oar of a trading scow. Of course the traders sent up a volley of red-hot profanity. Never was a man so grateful as Mr. B—— was: because he was brimful, and here were subjects who would *talk back*. He threw open a window, thrust his head out, and such an irruption followed as I never had heard before. The fainter and farther away the scowmen's curses drifted, the higher Mr. B—— lifted his voice and the weightier his adjectives grew. When he closed the window he was empty. You could have drawn a seine through his system and not caught curses enough to disturb your mother with.

Presently he said to me in the gentlest way, "My boy, you must get a little memorandum book, and every time I tell you a thing, put it down right away. There's only one way to be a pilot, and that is to get this entire river by heart. You have to know it just like A B C."

That was dismal revelation to me; for my memory was never loaded with anything but blank cartridges. However, I did not feel discouraged long. I judged that it was best to make some allowances, for doubtless Mr. B—— was "stretching." Presently he pulled a rope and struck a few strokes on the big bell. The stars were all gone now, and the night was as black as ink. I could hear the wheels churn along the bank, but I was not entirely certain that I could see the shore. The voice of the invisible watchman called up from the hurricane deck, "What's this, sir?"

"Jones's plantation."

I said to myself, "I wish I might venture to offer a small bet that it isn't." But I did not chirp. I only waited to see. Mr. B—— handled the engine bells, and in due time the boat's nose came to the land, a torch glowed from the forecastle, a man skipped ashore, a voice on the bank said, "Gimme de carpe'-bag, Mars' Jones," and the next moment we were standing up the river again, all serene. I reflected deeply awhile, and then said — but not aloud — "Well, the finding of that plantation was the luckiest accident that ever happened; but it couldn't happen again in a hundred years." And I fully believed it *was* an accident, too.

By the time we had gone seven or eight hundred miles up the river, I had learned to be a tolerably plucky upstream steersman, in daylight, and before we reached St. Louis I had made a trifle of progress in night work, but only a trifle. I had a notebook that fairly bristled with the names of towns, points, bars, islands, bends, reaches, and so forth; but the information was to be found only in the notebook — none of it was in my head. It made my heart ache to think I had only got half of the river set down; for as our watch was four hours off and four hours on, day and night, there was a long four-hour gap in my book for every time I had slept since the voyage began.

My chief was presently hired to go on a big New Orleans boat, and I packed my satchel and went with him. She was a grand affair. When I stood in her pilothouse I was so far above the water that I seemed perched on a mountain; and her decks stretched so far away, fore and aft, below me, that I wondered how I could ever have considered the little *Paul Jones* a large craft. There were other differences, too. The dingy, battered rattletrap, cramped for room; but here was a sumptuous glass temple; room enough to have a dance in; showy red and gold window curtains; an imposing sofa; leather cushions and a back to the high bench where visiting pilots sit, to spin yarns and "look at the river"; bright, fanciful "cuspadores" instead of a wooden box filled with sawdust; nice new oilcloth on the floor; a hospitable big stove for winter; a wheel as high as my head, costly with inlaid work; a wire tiller rope; bright brass knobs for the bells; and a tidy, white-aproned, black "texas tender" to bring up tarts and ices and coffee during midwatch, day and night. Now this was "something like"; and so I began to take heart once more to believe that piloting was a romantic sort of occupation after all. The moment we were under way I began to prowl about the great steamer and fill myself with joy. She was as clean and as dainty as a drawing room; when I looked down her long, gilded saloon, it was like gazing through a splendid tunnel; she had an oil picture, by some gifted sign painter, on every stateroom door; she glittered with no end of prism-fringed chandeliers; the clerk's office was elegant, the bar was marvelous, and the barkeeper had been barbered and upholstered at incredible cost. The boiler deck (that is, the second story of the boat, so to speak) was as spacious as a church, it seemed to me; so with the forecastle; and there was no pitiful handful of deck hands, firemen, and roustabouts down there, but a whole battalion of men. The fires were fiercely glaring from a long row of furnaces, and over them were eight huge boilers. This was unutterable pomp. The mighty engines — but enough of this. I had never felt so fine before. And when I found that the regiment of natty servants respectfully "sir'd" me, my satisfaction was complete.

When I returned to the pilothouse, St. Louis was gone and I was lost. Here was a piece of river which was all down in my book, but I could make neither head nor tail of it: you understand, it was turned around. I had seen it when coming upstream, but I had never faced about to see how it looked when it was behind me. My heart broke again, for it was plain that I had got to learn this troublesome river *both ways.*

The pilothouse was full of pilots, going down to "look at the river." What is called the "upper river" (the two hundred miles between St. Louis and Cairo, where the Ohio comes in) was low; and the Mississippi changes its channel so constantly that the pilots always used to find it necessary to run down to Cairo to take a fresh look when their boats were to lie in port a week; that is, when the water was at a low stage. A deal of this "looking at the river" was done by poor fellows who seldom had a berth, and whose only hope of getting one lay in their being always freshly posted and therefore ready to drop into the shoes of some reputable pilot for a single trip, on account of such pilot's sudden illness or some other necessity. And a good many of them constantly ran up and down inspecting the river, not because they ever really hoped to get a berth, but because (they being guests of the boat) it was cheaper to "look at the river" than stay ashore and pay board. In time these fellows grew dainty in their tastes, and only infested boats that had an established reputation for setting good tables. All visiting pilots were useful, for they were always ready and willing, winter or summer, night or day, to go out in the yawl and help buoy the channel or assist the boat's pilots in any way they could. They were likewise welcome because all pilots are tireless talkers when gathered together, and as they talk only about the river they are always understood and are always interesting. Your true pilot cares nothing about anything on earth but the river, and his pride in his occupation surpasses the pride of kings.

We had a fine company of these river inspectors along, this trip. There were eight or ten, and there was abundance of room for them in our guest pilothouse. Two or three of them wore polished silk hats, elaborate shirt fronts, diamond breastpins, kid gloves, and patent-leather boots. They were choice in their English, and bore themselves with a dignity proper to men of solid means and prodigious reputation as pilots. The others were more or less loosely clad, and wore upon their heads tall felt cones that were suggestive of the days of the Commonwealth.

I was a cipher in this august company and felt subdued, not to say torpid. I was not even of sufficient consequence to assist at the wheel when it was necessary to put the tiller hard down in a hurry; the guest that stood nearest did that when occasion required — and this pretty much all the time, because of the crookedness of the channel and the scant water. I stood in a corner, and the talk I listened to took the hope all out of me.

One visitor said to another, "Jim, how did you run Plum Point, coming up?"

"It was in the night, there, and I ran it the way one of the boys on the *Diana* told me; started out about fifty yards above the woodpile on the false point, and held on the cabin under Plum Point till I raised the reef — quarter less twain — then straightened up for the middle bar till I got well abreast the old one-limbed cottonwood in the bend, then got my stern on the cottonwood and head on the low place above the point, and came through a-booming — nine and a half."

"Pretty square crossing, an't it?"

"Yes, but the upper bar's working down fast."

Another pilot spoke up and said, "I had better water than that, and ran it lower down; started out from the false point — mark twain — raised the second reef abreast the big snag in the bend, and had quarter less twain."

One of the gorgeous ones remarked, "I don't want to find fault with your leadsmen, but that's a good deal of water for Plum Point, it seems to me."

There was an approving nod all around as this quiet snub dropped on the boaster and "settled" him. And so they went on talk-talk-talking. Meantime, the thing that was running in my mind was, "Now if my ears hear aright, I have not only to get the names of all the towns and islands and bends, and so on, by heart, but I must even get up a warm personal acquaintanceship with every old snag and one-limbed cottonwood and obscure woodpile that ornaments the banks of this river for twelve hundred miles; and more than that, I must actually know where these things are in the dark, unless these guests are gifted with eyes that can pierce through two miles of solid blackness; I wish the piloting business was in Jericho and I had never thought of it."

At dusk Mr. B—— tapped the big bell three times (the signal to land), and the captain emerged from his drawing room in the forward end of the texas and looked up inquiringly. Mr. B—— said, "We will lay up here all night, captain."

That was all. The boat came to shore and was tied up for the night. It seemed to me a fine thing that the pilot could do as he pleased without asking the captain's permission. I took my supper and went immediately to bed, discouraged by my day's observations and experiences. My late voyage's notebooking was but a confusion of meaningless names. It had tangled me all up in a knot every time I had looked at it in the daytime. I now hoped for respite in sleep, but no, it reveled all through my head till sunrise again, a frantic and tireless nightmare.

Next morning, I felt pretty rusty and low-spirited. We went booming along, taking a good many chances, for we were anxious to "get out of the river" (as getting to Cairo was called) before night should overtake us. But Mr. B——'s partner, the other pilot, presently grounded the boat, and we lost so much time getting her off that it was plain the darkness would overtake us a good long way above the mouth. This was a great misfortune, especially to certain of our visiting pilots, whose boats would have to wait for their return no matter how long that might be. It sobered the pilothouse talk a good deal. Coming upstream, pilots did not mind low water or any kind of darkness; nothing stopped them but fog. But downstream work was different; a boat was too nearly helpless with a stiff current pushing behind her, so it was not customary to run downstream at night in low water.

There seemed to be one small hope, however: if we could get through the intricate and dangerous Hat Island crossing before night, we could venture the rest, for we would have plainer sailing and better water. But it would be insanity to attempt Hat Island at night. So there was a deal of looking at watches all the rest of the day, and a constant ciphering upon the speed we were making. Hat Island was the eternal subject; sometimes hope was high, and sometimes we were delayed in a bad crossing and down it went again. For hours all hands lay under the burden of this suppressed excitement; it was even communicated to me, and I got to feeling so solicitous about Hat Island and under such an awful pressure of responsibility that I wished I might have five minutes on shore to draw a good, full, relieving breath and start over again. We were standing no regular watches. Each of our pilots ran such portions of the river as he had run when coming upstream, because of his greater familiarity with it; but both remained in the pilothouse constantly.

An hour before sunset Mr. B—— took the wheel and Mr. W——
stepped aside. For the next thirty minutes every man held his watch in
his hand and was restless, silent, and uneasy. At last somebody said,
with a doomful sigh, "Well, yonder's Hat Island — and we can't
make it."

All the watches closed with a snap, everybody sighed and muttered
something about its being "too bad, too bad — ah, if we could *only*
have got here half an hour sooner," and the place was thick with the
atmosphere of disappointment. Some started to go out, but loitered,
hearing no bell tap to land. The sun dipped behind the horizon, the
boat went on. Inquiring looks passed from one guest to another; and
one who had his hand on the doorknob and had turned it, waited, then
presently took away his hand and let the knob turn back again. We
bore steadily down the bend. More looks were exchanged, and nods of
surprised admiration — but no words. Insensibly the men drew together behind Mr. B—— as the sky darkened and one or two dim
stars came out. The dead silence and sense of waiting became oppressive. Mr. B—— pulled the cord, and two deep, mellow notes from the
big bell floated off on the night. Then a pause, and one more note was
struck. The watchman's voice followed, from the hurricane deck, "Labboard lead, there! Stabboard lead!"

The cries of the leadsmen began to rise out of the distance, and were
gruffly repeated by the word passers on the hurricane deck.

"M-a-r-k three! M-a-r-k three! Quarter-less-three! Half twain! Quarter
twain! M-a-r-k twain! Quarter-less — "

Mr. B—— pulled two bell ropes and was answered by faint jin-
glings far below in the engine room, and our speed slackened. The steam
began to whistle through the gauge cocks. The cries of the leadsmen
went on — and it is a weird sound, always, in the night. Every pilot
in the lot was watching, now, with fixed eyes, and talking under his
breath. Nobody was calm and easy but Mr. B——. He would put his
wheel down and stand on a spoke, and as the steamer swung into her
(to me) utterly invisible marks — for we seemed to be in the midst of
a wide and gloomy sea — he would meet and fasten her there.

Talk was going on, now, in low voices: "There; she's over the first
reef all right!"

After a pause, another subdued voice: "Her stern's coming down
just *exactly* right, by *George!* Now she's in the marks; over she goes!"

Somebody else muttered, "Oh, it was done beautiful — *beautiful!*"

Now the engines were stopped altogether, and we drifted with the current. Not that I could see the boat drift, for I could not, the stars being all gone by this time. This drifting was the dismalest work; it held one's heart still. Presently I discovered a blacker gloom than that which surrounded us. It was the head of the island. We were closing right down upon it. We entered its deeper shadow, and so imminent seemed the peril that I was likely to suffocate; and I had the strongest impulse to do something, *anything,* to save the vessel. But still Mr. B—— stood by his wheel, silent, intent as a cat, and all the pilots stood shoulder to shoulder at his back.

"She'll not make it!" somebody whispered.

The water grew shoaler and shoaler by the leadsmen's cries, till it was down to —

"Eight-and-a-half! E-i-g-h-t feet! E-i-g-h-t feet! Seven-and — "

Mr. B—— said warningly through his speaking tube to the engineer, "Stand by, now!"

"Aye-aye, sir."

"Seven-and-a-half! Seven feet! *Six*-and — "

We touched bottom! Instantly Mr. B—— set a lot of bells ringing, shouted through the tube, "*Now* let her have it — every ounce you've got!" Then to his partner, "Put her hard down! snatch her! snatch her!" The boat rasped and ground her way through the sand, hung upon the apex of disaster a single tremendous instant, and then over she went! And such a shout as went up at Mr. B——'s back never loosened the roof of a pilothouse before!

There was no more trouble after that. Mr. B—— was a hero that night; and it was some little time, too, before his exploit ceased to be talked about by rivermen.

Fully to realize the marvelous precision required in laying the great steamer in her marks in that murky waste of water, one should know that not only must she pick her intricate way through snags and blind reefs, and then shave the head of the island so closely as to brush the overhanging foliage with her stern, but at one place she must pass almost within arm's reach of a sunken and invisible wreck that would snatch the hull timbers from under her if she should strike it, and destroy a quarter of a million dollars' worth of steamboat and cargo in five minutes, and maybe a hundred and fifty human lives into the bargain.

The last remark I heard that night was a compliment to Mr. B——, uttered soliloquy and with unction by one of our guests. He said, "By the Shadow of Death, but he's a lightning pilot!"

A Boy of the Southwest

by WILLIAM DEAN HOWELLS

William Dean Howells, third editor of the Atlantic, *publicly supported his friend Mark Twain as a major novelist rather than as a comedian, and the novelist was ever grateful. After reading* Tom Sawyer, *Howells told Twain that he would gladly throw the weight of the* Atlantic *behind it: "Give me a hint when it's to be out, and I'll start the sheep to jumping in the right places." "Howells felt no scruple against this," Edwin H. Cady reminds us, "for he was convinced that he was aiding one of the greatest of Americans, 'the Lincoln of our literature.' Summing up after seventy-five years, he placed Twain at the peak of his esteem in carefully chosen words: 'If I had been witness to no other surpassing things of American growth in my fifty years of observation, I should think it glory enough to have lived in the same time and same land with the man whose name must always embody American humor to human remembrance.'"*

MAY 1876

The literature of a nation is an outcome of the national life; and to those who believe in the positive personality of a nation the study of its literature must inevitably take the form of an inquiry into the extent and fullness with which that literature embodies the purposes, aspirations, temptations, and victories of the nation. How completely has our literature mirrored both the depth and the shallowness of American life! That singular company of men and women who move across the field of Winthrop's Journal and Bradford's History leave upon the pages the enduring memorial of their nobility and their folly, their perverseness and their steadfastness, while bursts of passionate utterance disclose the repressed fervor of the life portrayed in those literary memorials. The commercial instincts of a shrewd, self-reliant, thrifty community, looking out for the main chance, were reproduced in the perspicuous, easily comprehended pages of Franklin's autobiography. Then the period of nascent force, when the country was agitated by profound questions which the conscience mooted, was openminded, stirred by the rediscovery of the Old World in travel and art, conscious of its unfolding vocation — this period was caught and contained in Hawthorne's romances, the poetry and philosophy of the transcendental school, the traditional art of Longfellow and Irving, the hopeful expansive work of Bryant and Cooper. The feverish gallop to California, an intense, confined movement, has issued in a literature of striking form, while the waves of emigration that have extended across the continent, a movement of which history will yet make great account, have found already a partial reproduction in literature.

Thomas Bailey Aldrich has studied the life of a bad boy as the pleasant reprobate led it in a quiet old New England town twenty-five or thirty years ago, where in spite of the natural outlawry of boyhood he was more or less part of a settled order of things and was hemmed in, to some measure, by the traditions of an established civilization. Samuel Clemens, on the contrary, has taken the boy of the Southwest for the hero of his new book, *The Adventures of Tom Sawyer,* and has presented him with a fidelity to circumstance which loses no charm by being realistic in the highest degree, and which gives incomparably the best picture of life in that region as yet known to fiction. The town where Tom Sawyer was born and brought up is some such idle, shabby little Mississippi River town as Mr. Clemens has so well described in his piloting reminiscences, but Tom belongs to the better sort of people in it, and has been bred to fear God and dread the Sunday school according to the strictest rite of the faiths that have characterized all the respectability of the West. His subjection in these respects does not so deeply affect his inherent tendencies but that he makes himself a beloved burden to the poor, tenderhearted old aunt who brings him up with his orphan brother and sister and struggles vainly with his manifold sins, actual and imaginary. The limitations of his transgressions are nicely and artistically traced. He is mischievous, but not vicious; he is ready for almost any depredation that involves the danger and honor of adventure, but profanity he knows may provoke a thunderbolt upon the heart of the blasphemer, and he almost never swears; he resorts to any stratagem to keep out of school, but he is not a downright liar, except upon terms of after shame and remorse that make his falsehood bitter to him. He is cruel, as all children are, but chiefly because he is ignorant; he is not mean, but there are very definite bounds to his generosity; and his courage is the Indian sort, full of prudence and mindful of retreat as one of the conditions of prolonged hostilities.

In a word, he is a boy, and merely and exactly an ordinary boy on the moral side. What makes him delightful to the reader is that on the imaginative side he is very much more, and though every boy has wild and fantastic dreams, this boy cannot rest till he has somehow realized them. Till he has actually run off with two other boys in the character of a buccaneer and lived for a week on an island in the Mississippi, he has lived in vain; and this passage is but the prelude to more thrilling adventures, in which he finds hidden treasures, traces the bandits to their cave, and is himself lost in its recesses. The local material and the incidents with which his career is worked up are excellent, and throughout there is scrupulous regard for the boy's point of view in reference to his surroundings and himself, which shows how rapidly Mr. Clemens has grown as an artist. We do not remember anything in which this propriety is violated, and its preservation adds immensely to the grown-up reader's satisfaction in the amusing and exciting story. There is a boy's love affair, but it is never treated otherwise than as a boy's love affair. When the half-breed has murdered the young doctor, Tom and his friend, Huckleberry Finn, are really, in their boyish terror and superstition, going to let the poor old town drunkard be hanged for the crime, till the terror of that becomes unendurable. The story is a wonderful study of the boy-mind, which inhabits a world quite distinct from that in which he is bodily present with his elders, and in this lies its great charm and its universality, for boy-nature, however human nature varies, is the same everywhere.

The tale is very dramatically wrought, and the subordinate characters are treated with the same graphic force that sets Tom alive before us. The worthless vagabond, Huck Finn, is entirely delightful throughout, and in his promised reform his identity is respected: he will lead a decent life in order that he may one day be thought worthy to become a member of that gang of robbers which Tom is to organize. Tom's aunt is excellent, with her kind heart's sorrow and secret pride in Tom; and so is his sister Mary, one of those good girls who are born to usefulness and charity and forbearance and unvarying rectitude. Many village people and local notables are introduced in well-conceived character; the little town lives in the reader's sense, with its religiousness, its lawlessness, its droll social distinctions, its civilization qualified by its slave-holding, and its traditions of the wilder West which has passed away. The picture will be instructive to those who have fancied the whole Southwest a sort of vast Pike County and have not conceived of a sober and serious and orderly contrast to the sort of life that has come to represent the Southwest in literature. Mr. Clemens has enforced the fact here, in a book full of entertaining character and of the greatest artistic sincerity.

How Santa Claus Came to Simpson's Bar

by BRET HARTE

When Sam Clemens, in the midst of a difficult courtship, was asked to give some personal references to his prospective father-in-law, he gave the name of Schuyler Colfax of the Pacific Coast and his secretary Frank B. Harte, editor of the Overland Monthly *"and the finest writer out there." Bret Harte, as the secretary was better known, had just published* The Luck of Roaring Camp, *and his prestige was at its peak. This friendship, as was perhaps inevitable, did not last. As Mark Twain's star rose and Harte's fell, the latter became jealous and vindictive.*

MARCH 1872

It had been raining in the valley of the Sacramento. The North Fork had overflowed its banks and Rattlesnake Creek was impassable. The few boulders that had marked the summer ford at Simpson's Crossing were obliterated by a vast sheet of water stretching to the foothills. The up stage was stopped at Grangers; the last mail had been abandoned in the *tules,* the rider swimming for his life. "An area," remarked the *Sierra Avalanche,* with pensive local pride, "as large as the State of Massachusetts is now under water."

Nor was the weather any better in the foothills. The mud lay deep on the mountain road; wagons that neither physical force nor moral objurgation could move from the evil ways into which they had fallen encumbered the track, and the way to Simpson's Bar was indicated by broken-down teams and hard swearing. And farther on, cut off and inaccessible, rained upon and bedraggled, smitten by high winds and threatened by high water, Simpson's Bar on the eve of Christmas day, 1862, clung like a swallow's nest to the rocky entablature and splintered capitals of Table Mountain, and shook in the blast.

As night shut down on the settlement, a few lights gleamed through the mist from the windows of cabins on either side of the highway now crossed and gullied by lawless streams and swept by marauding winds. Happily most of the population were gathered at Thompson's store, clustered around a red-hot stove, at which they silently spat in some accepted sense of social communion that perhaps rendered conversation unnecessary. Indeed, most methods of diversion had long since been exhausted on Simpson's Bar; high water had suspended the regular occupations on gulch and on river, and a consequent lack of money and whiskey had taken the zest from most illegitimate recreation. Even Mr. Hamlin was fain to leave the Bar with fifty dollars in his pocket — the only amount actually realized of the large sums won by him in the successful exercise of his arduous profession. "Ef I was asked," he remarked somewhat later, "ef I was asked to pint out a purty little village where a retired sport as didn't care for money could exercise hisself, frequent and lively, I'd say Simpson's Bar; but for a young man with a large family depending on his exertions, it don't pay." As Mr. Hamlin's family consisted mainly of female adults, this remark is quoted rather to show the breadth of his humor than the exact extent of his responsibilities.

Howbeit, the unconscious objects of this satire sat that evening in the listless apathy begotten of idleness and lack of excitement. Even the sudden splashing of hoofs before the door did not arouse them. Dick Bullen alone paused in the act of scraping out his pipe, and lifted his head, but no other one of the group indicated any interest in, or recognition of, the man who entered.

It was a figure familiar enough to the company, and known in Simpson's Bar as the "Old Man." A man of perhaps fifty years; grizzled and scant of hair, but still fresh and youthful of complexion. A face full of ready, but not very powerful, sympathy, with a chameleon-like aptitude for taking on the shade and color of contiguous moods and feelings. He had evidently just left some hilarious companions and did not at first notice the gravity of the group, but clapped the shoulder of the nearest man jocularly and threw himself into a vacant chair.

"Jest heard the best thing out, boys! Ye know Smiley, over yar — Jim Smiley — funniest man in the Bar? Well, Jim was jest telling the richest yarn about — "

"Smiley's a —— fool," interrupted a gloomy voice.

"A particular —— skunk," added another in sepulchral accents.

A silence followed these positive statements. The Old Man glanced quickly around the group. Then his face slowly changed. "That's so," he said reflectively, after a pause, "certingly a sort of a skunk and suthin' of a fool. In course." He was silent for a moment as in painful contemplation of the unsavoriness and folly of the unpopular Smiley. "Dismal weather, ain't it?" he added, now fully embarked on the current of prevailing sentiment. "Mighty rough papers on the boys, and no show for money this season. And tomorrow's Christmas."

There was a movement among the men at this announcement, but whether of satisfaction or disgust was not plain. "Yes," continued the Old Man in the lugubrious tone he had, within the last few moments, unconsciously adopted, "yes, Christmas, and tonight's Christmas eve. Ye see, boys, I kinder thought — that is, I sorter had an idee, jest passin' like, you know — that maybe ye'd all like to come over to my house tonight and have a sort of tear round. But I suppose, now, you wouldn't? Don't feel like it, maybe?" he added with anxious sympathy, peering into the faces of his companions.

"Well, I don't know," responded Tom Flynn with some cheerfulness. "P'r'aps we may. But how about your wife, Old Man? What does *she* say to it?"

The Old Man hesitated. His conjugal experience had not been a happy one, and the fact was known to Simpson's Bar. His first wife, a delicate, pretty little woman, had suffered keenly and secretly from the jealous suspicions of her husband, until one day he invited the whole Bar to his house to expose her infidelity. On arriving, the party found the shy, petite creature quietly engaged in her household duties and retired abashed and discomfited. But the sensitive woman did not easily recover from the shock of this extraordinary outrage. It was with difficulty she regained her equanimity sufficiently to release her lover from the closet in which he was concealed and escape with him. She left a boy of three years to comfort her bereaved husband. The Old Man's present wife had been his cook. She was large, loyal, and aggressive.

Before he could reply, Joe Dimmick suggested with great directness that it was the "Old Man's house " and that, invoking the Divine Power, if the case were his own, he would invite whom he pleased, even if in so doing he imperiled his salvation. The Powers of Evil, he further remarked, should contend against him vainly. All this delivered with a terseness and vigor lost in this necessary translation.

"In course. Certainly. Thet's it," said the Old Man with a sympathetic frown. "Thar's no trouble about *thet*. It's my own house, built every stick on it myself. Don't you be afeard o' her, boys. She *may* cut up a trifle rough, ez wimmin do, but she'll come round." Secretly the Old Man trusted to the exaltation of liquor and the power of courageous example to sustain him in such an emergency.

As yet, Dick Bullen, the oracle and leader of Simpson's Bar, had not spoken. He now took his pipe from his lips. "Old Man, how's that yer Johnny gettin' on? Seems to me he didn't look so peart last time I seed him on the bluff heavin' rocks at Chinamen. Didn't seem to take much interest in it. Thar was a gang of 'em by yar yesterday — drownded out up the river — and I kinder thought o' Johnny, and how he'd miss 'em! May be now, we'd be in the way ef he wus sick?"

The father, evidently touched not only by this pathetic picture of Johnny's deprivation, but by the considerate delicacy of the speaker, hastened to assure him that Johnny was better and that a "little fun might liven him up." Whereupon Dick arose, shook himself, and saying, "I'm ready. Lead the way, Old Man: here goes," himself led the way with a leap, a characteristic howl, and darted out into the night. As he passed through the outer room he caught up a blazing brand from the hearth. The action was repeated by the rest of the party, closely following and elbowing each other, and before the astonished proprietor of Thompson's grocery was aware of the intention of his guests, the room was deserted.

The night was pitchy dark. In the first gust of wind their temporary torches were extinguished, and only the red brands dancing and flitting in the gloom like drunken will-o'-the-wisps indicated their whereabouts. Their way led up Pine-Tree Cañon, at the head of which a broad, low, bark-thatched cabin burrowed in the mountainside. It was the home of the Old Man, and the entrance to the tunnel in which he worked when he worked at all. Here the crowd paused for a moment, out of delicate deference to their host, who came up panting in the rear.

"P'r'aps ye'd better hold on a second out yer, whilst I go in and see thet things is all right," said the Old Man, with an indifference he was far from feeling. The suggestion was graciously accepted, the door opened and closed on the host, and the crowd, leaning their backs against the wall and cowering under the eaves, waited and listened.

For a few moments there was no sound but the dripping of water from the eaves, and the stir and rustle of wrestling boughs above them. Then the men became uneasy, and whispered suggestion and suspicion passed from the one to the other. "Reckon she's caved in his head the first lick!" "Decoyed him inter the tunnel and barred him up, likely." "Got him down and sittin' on him." "Prob'ly bilin' suthin' to heave on us: stand clear the door, boys!" For just then the latch clicked, the door slowly opened, and a voice said, "Come in out o' the wet."

The voice was neither that of the Old Man nor of his wife. It was the voice of a small boy, its weak treble broken by that preternatural hoarseness which only vagabondage and the habit of premature self-assertion can give. It was the face of a small boy that looked up at theirs — a face that might have been pretty and even refined but that it was darkened by evil knowledge from within, and dirt and hard experience from without. He had a blanket around his shoulders and had evidently just risen from his bed. "Come in," he repeated, "and don't make no noise. The Old Man's in there talking to mar," he continued, pointing to an adjacent room which seemed to be a kitchen, from which the Old Man's voice came in deprecating accents. "Let me be," he added querulously to Dick Bullen, who had caught him up, blanket and all, and was affecting to toss him into the fire. "Let go o' me, you damned old fool, d'ye hear?"

Thus adjured, Dick Bullen lowered Johnny to the ground with a smothered laugh, while the men, entering quietly, ranged themselves around a long table of rough boards which occupied the center of the room. Johnny then gravely proceeded to a cupboard and brought out several articles which he deposited on the table. "Thar's whiskey. And crackers. And red herons. And cheese." He took a bite of the latter on his way to the table. "And sugar." He scooped up a mouthful en route with a small and very dirty hand. "And terbacker. Thar's dried appils too on the shelf, but I don't admire 'em. Appils is swellin'. Thar," he concluded, "now wade in, and don't be afeard. I don't mind the old woman. She don't b'long to *me.* S'long."

He had stepped to the threshold of a small room, scarcely larger than a closet, partitioned off from the main apartment and holding in its dim recess a small bed. He stood there a moment looking at the company, his bare feet peeping from the blanket, and nodded.

"Hello, Johnny! You ain't goin' to turn in agin, are ye?" said Dick.

"Yes, I are," responded Johnny, decidedly.

"Why, wot's up, old fellow?"

"I'm sick."

"How sick?"

"I've got a fevier. And childblains. And roomatiz," returned Johnny, and vanished within. After a moment's pause, he added in the dark, apparently from under the bedclothes, "and biles!"

There was an embarrassing silence. The men looked at each other, and at the fire. Even with the appetizing banquet before them, it seemed as if they might again fall into the despondency of Thompson's grocery, when the voice of the Old Man, incautiously lifted, came deprecatingly from the kitchen.

"Certainly! Thet's so. In course they is. A gang o' lazy drunken loafers, and that ar Dick Bullen's the ornariest of all. Didn't hev no more *sabe* than to come round yar with sickness in the house and no provision. Thet's what I said: 'Bullen,' sez I, 'it's crazy drunk you are, or a fool,' sez I, 'to think o' such a thing.' 'Staples,' I sez, 'be you a man, Staples, and 'spect to raise hell under my roof and invalids lyin' round?' But they would come — they would. Thet's wot you must 'spect o' such trash as lays round the Bar."

A burst of laughter from the men followed this unfortunate exposure. Whether it was overheard in the kitchen, or whether the Old Man's irate companion had just then exhausted all other modes of expressing her contemptuous indignation, I cannot say, but a back door was suddenly slammed with great violence. A moment later and the Old Man reappeared, haply unconscious of the cause of the late hilarious outburst, and smiled blandly. "The old woman thought she'd jest run over to Mrs. McFadden's for a sociable call," he explained, with jaunty indifference, as he took a seat at the board.

Oddly enough it needed this untoward incident to relieve the embarrassment that was beginning to be felt by the party, and their natural audacity returned with their host. I do not propose to record the convivialities of that evening. The inquisitive reader will accept the statement that the conversation was characterized by the same intellectual exaltation, the same cautious reverence, the same fastidious delicacy, the same rhetorical precision, and the same logical and coherent discourse somewhat later in the evening, which distinguish similar gatherings of the masculine sex in more civilized localities and under more favorable auspices. No glasses were broken in the absence of any; no liquor was spilt on floor or table in the scarcity of that article.

It was nearly midnight when the festivities were interrupted. "Hush," said Dick Bullen, holding up his hand. It was the querulous voice of Johnny from his adjacent closet: "Oh, Dad!"

The Old Man arose hurriedly and disappeared in the closet. Presently he reappeared. "His rheumatiz is coming on agin bad," he explained, "and he wants rubbin'." He lifted the demijohn of whiskey from the table and shook it. It was empty. Dick Bullen put down his tin cup with an embarrassed laugh. So did the others. The Old Man examined their contents and said hopefully, "I reckon that's enough; he don't need much. You hold on all o' you for a spell, and I'll be back." He vanished in the closet with an old flannel shirt and the whiskey. The door closed but imperfectly, and the following dialogue was distinctly audible:

"Now, sonny, whar does she ache worst?"

"Sometimes over yar and sometimes under yer; but it's most powerful from yer to yer. Rub yer, Dad."

A silence seemed to indicate a brisk rubbing. Then Johnny:

"Hevin' a good time out yer, Dad?"

"Yes, sonny."

"Tomorrer's Chrismiss — ain't it?"

"Yes, sonny. How does she feel now?"

"Better. Rub a little furder down. Wot's Chrismiss, anyway? Wot's it all about?"

"Oh, it's a day."

This exhaustive definition was apparently satisfactory, for there was a silent interval of rubbing. Presently Johnny again:

"Mar sez that everywhere else but yer everybody gives things to everybody Chrismiss, and then she jist waded inter you. She sez thar's a man they call Sandy Claus, not a white man, you know, but a kind o' Chinemin, comes down the chimbley night afore Chrismiss and gives things to chillern — boys like me. Put's 'em in their butes! Thet's what she tried to play upon me. Easy now, Pop, whar are you rubbin' to — thet's a mile from the place. She jest made that up, didn't she, jest to aggrewate me and you? Don't rub thar. . . . Why, Dad?"

In the great quiet that seemed to have fallen upon the house the sigh of the near pines and the drip of leaves without was very distinct. Johnny's voice, too, was lowered as he went on, "Don't you take on now, fur I'm gettin' all right fast. Wot's the boys doin' out thar?"

The Old Man partly opened the door and peered through. His guests were sitting there sociably enough, and there were a few silver

coins and a lean buckskin purse on the table. "Bettin' on suthin' —
some little game or 'nother. They're all right," he replied to Johnny
and recommenced his rubbing.

"I'd like to take a hand and win some money," said Johnny, reflectively, after a pause.

The Old Man glibly repeated what was evidently a familiar formula,
that if Johnny would wait until he struck it rich in the tunnel he'd have
lots of money, and so forth.

"Yes," said Johnny, "but you don't. And whether you strike it or I
win it, it's about the same. It's all luck. But it's mighty cur'o's about
Chrismiss — ain't it? Why do they call it Chrismiss?"

Perhaps from some instinctive deference to the overhearing of his
guests, or from some vague sense of incongruity, the Old Man's reply
was so low as to be inaudible beyond the room.

"Yes," said Johnny, with some slight abatement of interest, "I've
heerd o' *him* before. Thar, that'll do, Dad. I don't ache near so bad as
I did. Now wrap me tight in this yer blanket. So. Now," he added in a
muffled whisper, "sit down yer by me till I go asleep." To assure himself of obedience, he disengaged one hand from the blanket and, grasping his father's sleeve, again composed himself to rest.

For some moments the Old Man waited patiently. Then the unwonted stillness of the house excited his curiosity, and without moving
from the bed he cautiously opened the door with his disengaged hand
and looked into the main room. To his infinite surprise it was dark and
deserted. But even then a smoldering log on the hearth broke, and by
the upspringing blaze he saw the figure of Dick Bullen sitting by the dying embers.

"Hello!"

Dick started, rose, and came somewhat unsteadily toward him.

"Whar's the boys?" said the Old Man.

"Gone up the cañon on a little *pasear*. They're coming back for me
in a minit. I'm waitin' round for 'em. What are you starin' at, Old
Man?" he added with a forced laugh. "Do you think I'm drunk?"

The Old Man might have been pardoned the supposition, for Dick's
eyes were humid and his face flushed. He loitered and lounged back to
the chimney, yawned, shook himself, buttoned up his coat, and
laughed. "Liquor ain't so plenty as that, Old Man. Now don't you git
up," he continued as the Old Man made a movement to release his
sleeve from Johnny's hand. "Don't you mind manners. Sit jest whar
you be; I'm goin' in a jiffy. Thar, that's them now."

There was a low tap at the door. Dick Bullen opened it quickly, nodded good night to his host, and disappeared. The Old Man would have followed him but for the hand that still unconsciously grasped his sleeve. He could have easily disengaged it; it was small, weak, and emaciated. But perhaps because it *was* small, weak, and emaciated he changed his mind and, drawing his chair closer to the bed, rested his head upon it. In this defenseless attitude the potency of his earlier potations surprised him. The room flickered and faded before his eyes, reappeared, faded again, went out, and left him — asleep.

Meantime Dick Bullen, closing the door, confronted his companions. "Are you ready?" said Staples. "Ready," said Dick. "What's the time?" "Past twelve," was the reply. "Can you make it? It's nigh on fifty miles, the round trip hither and yon." "I reckon," returned Dick, shortly. "Whar's the mare?" "Bill and Jack's holdin' her at the crossin'." "Let 'em hold on a minit longer," said Dick.

He turned and re-entered the house softly. By the light of the guttering candle and dying fire he saw that the door of the little room was open. He stepped toward it on tiptoe and looked in. The Old Man had fallen back in his chair, snoring, his helpless feet thrust out in a line with his collapsed shoulders and his hat pulled over his eyes. Beside him, on a narrow wooden bedstead, lay Johnny, muffled tightly in a blanket that hid all save a strip of forehead and a few curls damp with perspiration. Dick Bullen made a step forward, hesitated, and glanced over his shoulder into the deserted room. Everything was quiet. With a sudden resolution he parted his huge mustaches with both hands and stooped over the sleeping boy. But even as he did so a mischievous blast swooped down the chimney, rekindled the hearth, and lit up the room with a shameless glow from which Dick fled in bashful terror.

His companions were already waiting for him at the crossing. Two of them were struggling in the darkness with some strange misshapen bulk, which as Dick came nearer took the semblance of a great yellow horse. It was the mare. She was not a pretty picture. From her Roman nose to her rising haunches, from her arched spine hidden by the stiff *machillas* of a Mexican saddle to her thick, straight, bony legs, there was not a line of equine grace. In her half-blind but wholly vicious white eyes, in her protruding underlip, in her monstrous color, there was nothing but ugliness and vice.

"Now then," said Staples, "stand cl'ar of her heels, boys, and up with you. Don't miss your first holt of her mane, and mind ye get your off stirrup *quick*. Ready!"

There was a leap, a scrambling struggle, a bound, a wild retreat of the crowd, a circle of flying hoofs, two springless leaps that jarred the earth, a rapid play and jingle of spurs, a plunge, and then the voice of Dick somewhere in the darkness, "All right!"

"Don't take the lower road back onless you're hard pushed for time! Don't hold her in downhill! We'll be at the ford at five. G'lang! Hoopa! Mula! GO!"

A splash, a spark struck from the ledge in the road, a clatter in the rocky cut beyond, and Dick was gone.

It was one o'clock, and yet he had only gained Rattlesnake Hill. For in that time Jovita had rehearsed to him all her imperfections and practiced all her vices. Thrice had she stumbled. Twice had she thrown up her Roman nose in a straight line with the reins and, resisting bit and spur, struck out madly across country. Twice had she reared and, rearing, fallen backward; and twice had the agile Dick, unharmed, regained his seat before she found her vicious legs again. And a mile beyond them, at the foot of a long hill, was Rattlesnake Creek. Dick knew that here was the crucial test of his ability to perform his enterprise, set his teeth grimly, put his knees well into her flanks, and changed his defensive tactics to brisk aggression. Bullied and maddened, Jovita began the descent of the hill. Here the artful Richard pretended to hold her in with ostentatious objurgation and well-feigned cries of alarm. It is unnecessary to add that Jovita instantly ran away. Nor need I state the time made in the descent; it is written in the chronicles of Simpson's Bar. Enough that in another moment, as it seemed to Dick, she was splashing on the overflowed banks of Rattlesnake Creek. As Dick expected, the momentum she had acquired carried her beyond the point of balking, and holding her well together for a mighty leap, they dashed into the middle of the swiftly flowing current. A few moments of kicking, wading, and swimming, and Dick drew a long breath on the opposite bank.

The road from Rattlesnake Creek to Red Mountain was tolerably level. Either the plunge in Rattlesnake Creek had dampened her baleful fire, or the art which led to it had shown her the superior wickedness of her rider, for Jovita no longer wasted her surplus energy in wanton conceits. Once she bucked, but it was from force of habit; once she shied, but it was from a new freshly painted meetinghouse at the crossing of the county road. Hollows, ditches, gravelly deposits, patches of freshly springing grasses flew from beneath her rattling hoofs. She began to smell unpleasantly, once or twice she coughed slightly, but there was no abatement of her strength or speed. By two o'clock he had passed Red Mountain and begun the descent to the plain. Ten minutes later the driver of the fast Pioneer coach was overtaken and passed by a "man on a Pinto hoss" — an event sufficiently notable for remark. At half past two Dick rose in his stirrups with a great shout. Stars were glittering through the rifted clouds, and beyond him, out of the plain, rose two spires, a flagstaff and a straggling line of black objects. Dick jingled his spurs and swung his *riata,* Jovita bounded forward, and in another moment they swept into Tuttleville and drew up before the wooden piazza of "The Hotel of All Nations."

What transpired that night at Tuttleville is not strictly a part of this record. Briefly I may state, however, that after Jovita had been handed over to a sleepy ostler, whom she at once kicked into unpleasant consciousness, Dick sallied out with the barkeeper for a tour of the sleeping town. Lights still gleamed from the few saloons and gambling houses; but, avoiding these, they stopped before several closed shops, and by persistent tapping and judicious outcry roused the proprietors from their beds and made them unbar the doors of their magazines and expose their wares. Sometimes they were met by curses, but oftener by interest and some concern in their needs, and the interview was invariably concluded by a drink. It was three o'clock before this pleasantry was given over, and with a small waterproof bag of India rubber strapped on his shoulders Dick returned to the hotel. But here he was waylaid by Beauty — Beauty opulent in charms, affluent in dress, persuasive in speech, and Spanish in accent! In vain she repeated the invitation in "Excelsior," happily scorned by all Alpine-climbing youth and rejected by this child of the Sierras — a rejection softened in this instance by a laugh and his last gold coin. And then he sprang to the saddle and dashed down the lonely street and out into the lonelier plain, where presently the lights, the black line of houses, the spires, and the flagstaff sank into the earth behind him again and were lost in the distance.

The storm had cleared away, the air was brisk and cold, the outlines of adjacent landmarks were distinct, but it was half past four before Dick reached the meetinghouse and the crossing of the county road. To avoid the rising grade he had taken a longer and more circuitous road, in whose viscid mud Jovita sank fetlock deep at every bound. It was a poor preparation for a steady ascent of five miles more; but Jovita, gathering her legs under her, took it with her usual blind, unreasoning fury, and a half hour later reached the long level that led to Rattlesnake Creek. Another half hour would bring him to the creek. He threw the reins lightly upon the neck of the mare, chirruped to her, and began to sing.

Suddenly Jovita shied with a bound that would have unseated a less practiced rider. Hanging to her rein was a figure that had leaped from the bank, and at the same time from the road before her arose a shadowy horse and rider. "Throw up your hands," commanded this second apparition, with an oath.

Dick felt the mare tremble, quiver, and apparently sink under him. He knew what it meant and was prepared.

"Stand aside, Jack Simpson, I know you, you damned thief. Let me pass or — "

He did not finish the sentence. Jovita rose straight in the air with a terrific bound, throwing the figure from her bit with a single shake of her vicious head, and charged with deadly malevolence down on the impediment before her. An oath, a pistol shot, horse and highwayman rolled over in the road, and the next moment Jovita was a hundred yards away. But the good right arm of her rider, shattered by a bullet, dropped helplessly at his side.

Without slackening his speed he shifted the reins to his left hand. But a few moments later he was obliged to halt and tighten the saddle girths that had slipped in the onset. This in his crippled condition took some time. He had no fear of pursuit, but looking up he saw that the eastern stars were already paling and that the distant peaks had lost their ghostly whiteness and now stood out blackly against a lighter sky. Day was upon him. Then, completely absorbed in a single idea, he forgot the pain of his wound and mounting again dashed on toward Rattlesnake Creek. But now Jovita's breath came broken by gasps, Dick reeled in his saddle, and brighter and brighter grew the sky.

Ride, Richard; run, Jovita; linger, O day!

For the last few rods there was a roaring in his ears. Was it exhaustion from loss of blood, or what? He was dazed and giddy as he swept down the hill, and did not recognize his surroundings. Had he taken the wrong road, or was this Rattlesnake Creek?

It was. But the bawling creek he had swum a few hours before had risen, more than doubled its volume, and now rolled a swift and resistless river between him and Rattlesnake Hill. For the first time that night Richard's heart sank within him. The river, the mountain, the quickening east swam before his eyes. He shut them to recover his self-control. In that brief interval, by some fantastic mental process, the little room at Simpson's Bar and the figures of the sleeping father and son rose upon him. He opened his eyes wildly, cast off his coat, pistol, boots, and saddle, bound his precious pack tightly to his shoulders, grasped the bare flanks of Jovita with his bared knees, and with a shout dashed into the yellow water. A cry rose from the opposite bank as the heads of a man and a horse struggled for a few moments against the battling current, and then were swept away amidst uprooted trees and whirling driftwood.

The Old Man started and woke. The fire on the hearth was dead, the candle in the outer room flickering in its socket, and somebody was rapping at the door. He opened it, but fell back with a cry before the dripping, half-naked figure that reeled against the doorpost.

"Dick?"

"Hush! Is he awake yet?"

"No — but Dick — "

"Dry up, you old fool! Get me some whiskey *quick!*" The Old Man flew and returned with an empty bottle. Dick would have sworn, but his strength was not equal to the occasion. He staggered, caught at the handle of the door, and motioned to the Old Man.

"Thar's suthin' in my pack yer for Johnny. Take it off. I can't."

The Old Man unstrapped the pack and laid it before the exhausted man.

"Open it, quick!"

He did so with trembling fingers. It contained only a few poor toys — cheap and barbaric enough, goodness knows, but bright with paint and tinsel. One of them was broken; another, I fear, was irretrievably ruined by water; and on the third — ah me! there was a cruel spot.

"It don't look like much, that's a fact," said Dick, ruefully, "but it's the best we could do. Take 'em, Old Man, and put 'em in his stocking, and tell him — tell him, you know — hold me, Old Man — " The Old Man caught at his sinking figure. "Tell him," said Dick, with a weak little laugh, "tell him Sandy Claus has come."

And even so, bedraggled, ragged, unshaven, and unshorn, with one arm hanging helplessly at his side, Santa Claus came to Simpson's Bar and fell fainting on the first threshold. The Christmas dawn came slowly after, touching the remoter peaks with the rosy warmth of ineffable love. And it looked so tenderly on Simpson's Bar that the whole mountain, as if caught in a generous action, blushed to the skies.

Owen Wister's West

Notebooks edited by FANNY KEMBLE WISTER

After his graduation from Harvard, Owen Wister, then des-
tined for the Law School, went West for his health. He
went out of curiosity, but on repeated visits he wrote down
in his notebooks the source material for a literary career.
The episode on Tisdale's ranch was so stark that at the in-
sistence of his friend Theodore Roosevelt he deleted it from
The Virginian.

MAY 1955

Owen Wister wrote *The Virginian* over fifty years ago, a romantic novel of the wild West which won instant success and skyrocketed its author to fame. Before this, cowboys had been depicted as murderous thugs. The Virginian was utterly different from the heroes of his day; besides being handsome, he was humorous and human. He got drunk, played practical jokes, and showed that you could not trifle with him. Today, in Western stories, in Western movies, and on radio and TV, the cowboy hero defends justice and his girl's honor, and shoots it out with the villain. Owen Wister created this pattern.

In 1885, when my father was twenty-five, he went to Wyoming for the first time. He sat beside the driver on the roof of a four-horse stagecoach, watching the sunrise as the bitter chill lessened. He planned to shoot big game, fish for trout, camp in unmapped territory, and see the Indians. There were a lot of expensively educated young men going West then, who were not seeking their fortunes or planning to settle, but going for adventure. They shot elk, caught rainbow trout, and returned home; but Owen Wister, struck with wonder and delight, had the eyes to see and the talent to portray the life unfolding in America.

In all, there are thirteen notebooks, comprising the record of his Western journeys from 1885 to 1900. He often spent six months at a time in Wyoming, living in U.S. Army camps as the guest of officers; observing Indians; becoming intimately acquainted with cowpunchers, cattle thieves, saloon-keepers, and prospectors; noting true incidents and reporting real conversations; making lists of words in common use that he had never heard. He ranged through the Northwest and Southwest from Oregon to Texas, but he loved Wyoming best of all, and *The Virginian* is set in Wyoming. The

Virginian is a composite character drawn from several different men my father had either seen briefly or known well.

In 1894 he met Corporal Skirdin, born in Arizona, who seemed to him a "sort of incarnation of my imaginary Virginian." Two Kansas boys he knew in New Mexico in 1894 were also a "ratification" of his imaginary character.

The source of "When you call me that, *smile!*" is found at the end of the 1894 notebook in which the Earp and Clanton feud is described.

"Card game going on — Big money — Several desperados playing — one John Lawrence among others — A player calls him a son of a b——. John Lawrence does not look as if he had heard it — Merely passes his fingers strokingly up and down his pile of chips — When hand is done, he looks across at the man and says: 'You *smile* when you call me that.' The man smiled, and all was well."

1885

July 3 — The country we're going through now was made before the good Lord discovered that variety is the spice of life. But it is beautiful. It reminds me of the northern part of Spain. The same vast stretches of barren green back to the sky line or to rising ground. We stopped at North Platte for breakfast. I paid 25 cents and ate everything I saw. Some of it was good. Just now we stopped at a station where a black pig was drinking the drops that fell from the locomotive tank, and a pile of whitened cattle bones lay nearby. Here and there, far across the level, is a little unpainted house with a shed or two and a wagon. Now either a man on horseback or a herd of cattle. We've just passed a little yelping gang of collies who raced us but got beaten. The sky — there is none. It looks really like what it scientifically is — space. The air is delicious. As if it had never been in anyone's lungs before. I like this continual passing of green void, without any growing things higher than a tuft of grass.

Friday, July 10 — Went out for the first time yesterday with my gun, and surprised myself by killing two grouse in four shots. All I need is practice, and this summer I'm going to get practice. I find riding these bronchos the easiest long-distance riding I've ever experienced. I'm afraid the creek will run dry and stop my morning baths. This country doesn't get enough water to make it a great country. They'll have to irrigate from Lake Superior or something — which they probably will if some American doesn't invent a way to pull a string and have it rain. American! There are very few of them so far in our history. Every man, woman, and cowboy I see comes from the East — and generally from New England, thank goodness. If that's the stock that is going to fill these big fields with people, our first hundred years will grow to be only the mythological beginnings in the time to come. I feel more certainly than ever that no matter how completely the East may be the headwaters from which the West has flown and is flowing, it won't be a century before the West is simply the true America, with thought, type, and life of its own kind.

July 14 — I'm a quarter of a century old today.

July 16 — Caught a gopher. Meant to tame him but he got out of his box and skedaddled. Stockings — that's the broncho that sat down with me first day — opened the gates this evening and let all the horses out into the wide, wide world. I got on another broncho, and chased them back home. An hour later I caught Stockings trying to open the gate again, and I whaled him with a rope, and then tied the gate up. Stockings is big — about 14 hands — very thick mane and topknot, and rather handsome. He's about the most knowing-looking animal I ever laid my dear eyes on. I am convinced he could speak French if he tried.

Thursday, August 6 — On Tuesday we left camp on horseback for the roundup at five minutes before seven. On the way I rode over two rattlesnakes, who played a duet with their tails, allegro energetic. The darker one got away into his hole before I could stop him, but I killed the second and handsomer of the two. After I had cut his head off it struck at me. The eye of Satan when plotting the destruction of the human race could not have been more malignant than the stare which this decapitated head gave me with its two clouded agate eyes. They had speculation in them full five minutes after the trunk was in my hands being skinned. He was four feet long, and when I put my foot on him as he was trying to get away into his hole, he felt very solid.

We reached the roundup about nine. It took place in the big plain beyond our camping ground of the first night. There were two big bodies of cattle — many hundred — and about twelve cowboys scudding around and through them, cutting out those of the V.R. brand. The mass of animals stood still for the most part, but now and then moved slowly round its own center, giving the effect of a gigantic leisurely eddy. Once or twice they broke ranks, which caused extra riding and barking and whistling from the cowboys, who flew this way and that to head them off, whirling their quirts and making sudden turns as if their ponies worked on a pivot.

When our V.R. cattle had been cut out and bunched the cowboys started the rest away over the hills. The whole mass began to move westward, creeping over the undulations in the plain — moving steadily forward as a body, and moving constantly backward and forward within its own ranks. A couple of cows would get ahead by trotting, then slow up and be overtaken by half a dozen more at different distances, while in the middle there was a constant seething to and fro. The twelve cowboys all gathered in a long line abreast behind their own cattle and drove them away in the opposite direction. Tom King, the foreman, says he likes this life and will never go East again. On Miss Irwin's inquiry whether or not he will get tired of it when he grows old, he replied that cowboys never live long enough to get old. They don't, I believe. They're a queer episode in the history of this country. Purely nomadic, and leaving no posterity, for they don't marry. I'm told they're without any moral sense whatever. Perhaps they are — but I wonder how much less they have than the poor classes in New York. On Tuesday we were six hours and more in the saddle, and I was not tired — to my satisfaction.

1891

Saturday, June 13 — At Tisdale's. I reached Casper at seven the night before last, passing desolate, deserted Fetterman and Walcott's station. Left yesterday morning at 5:30 in buggy with tough pair of little horses. Came here, 65 miles, at 7 P.M. Dreary country.

Tisdale's ranch stands where good country begins. The ranch buildings on the river make the usual flat cluster of low brown cabins and stables and corrals and fences all brown. Irrigated garden behind, irrigated area of grass in front. Ditches dry, but their carrying will start this evening when the water will get down from Willow Creek.

Thursday, June 18 — Taking the mail for the men at Tisdale's ranch. We had two extra horses with us. I rode one, leading Syd, my horse of yesterday. Tisdale led a big sorrel, an outlaw because of his bucking habits, whom he proposes to make into a team horse. We came comfortably by the Carrs' ranch on Middle Fork, passing three vultures who sat on some high bluffs with wings spread out to catch the sun. A curious sight. When we passed the last gate on the Carrs' ranch, Tisdale roped the horses we were leading pretty close together, and started to drive them in front of us. The sorrel got a little way ahead on the trail and decided he was not coming with us. So he ran up a steep sultry hill towing Sydney after him. Syd was conscientious and had no thought other than to follow the trail, but he was weak and had no other choice than to follow the sorrel. Tisdale drove his horse up after them and they turned and made for the gate we had left. Down and up, into crazy ditches of baked mud and so back to the wire fence, which stopped them. I came slowly after, not much use at this work. Then we started again, and in about 200 yards, up goes the sorrel on the other side of the steep little valley, straight among the red ridges above, dragging the harmless Syd after him.

Tisdale's horse, while he was dismounted at the gate, had put his feet inside the bridle rein as it lay along the ground, dangling from the bit. The horse was stupid about lifting his foot to free the rein. But I thought Tisdale unnecessarily violent about this. To make the horse lift his foot, he jammed his heel down on the hoof just where the hair begins, and after several kicks the rein came free, upon which he dug his heel into the other foot above the hoof, filling these actions with the language appropriate to them. Then we set after the sorrel and Syd, who were not on the trail but now climbing high among the rocks. But the sorrel soon saw the place was too steep and returned on his tracks. Then we chased them up and down, I not doing much, and Tisdale forging heavily after them, for his horse began to tire and breathed painfully. My horse was tired too, for the ground was very broken and the sun blazing down.

At length the runaways got far ahead of us, and I left Tisdale kicking and cursing his horse, who was now able to walk only. I took the high ground, pretty level and free of holes, to keep the sorrel in sight, and Tisdale kept in the trail below in the valley, his horse being too done to go uphill. I stopped and he at last came up with me. The sorrel and the kidnaped Syd were now away off, still going over the uplands at a good steady gait.

Tisdale dismounted and kicked his poor quiet beast, who stood quite patient. He kicked its ribs, its legs, its jaw, and I saw that red foam was running down its bit. I saw Tisdale was insane with rage. "I'll have to ask you to swap horses for a time," he said to me. "This ____ brute's given out on me. They'd never got away if he hadn't given out." Then he resumed his kicking the animal and jerking its head. I jumped off as soon as he said "swap," very anxious he should do so and leave his wretched horse in peace. Beyond urging him to take my horse at once, I said nothing. I felt like remonstrating, but I failed to do so. Tisdale seemed to forget about his intention of swapping. He continued to swear at his horse and kick it, and then I noticed him make several vicious grabs at its eye. Then he got into the saddle again and the brute walked slowly forward with him some twenty yards in the direction of the vanished sorrel, leaving me dismounted and watching Tisdale's heels and fists beat the horse without pause. It stood still, too weak to move, and I saw Tisdale lean forward with his arm down on its forehead. He had told me that he would kill it if he had a gun, but he hadn't.

I watched him, dazed with disgust and horror. Suddenly the horse sank, pinning him to the ground. He could not release himself, and I ran across to him and found only his leg caught. So I lifted the horse and he got his leg out. I asked him if he was hurt. He said no and got up, adding, " I've got one eye out all right." The horse turned where he lay, and I caught sight of his face, where there was no longer any left eye, but only a sinkhole of blood. I was utterly stunned and sickened at this atrocious cruelty, and walked back to my own horse and sat down, not knowing very well what I was doing. Tisdale's horse struggled to his feet and he mounted, and the animal wavered slowly away with him. Then he came back to me and asked for one of my spurs. I gave him both at once, with the idea of saving further brutality, for the spurs were not severe and all horses here answered to them from training. It turned out as I had hoped. The blinded animal walked forward without any further violence in the direction of the runaways. My first resolve was to ask for horses and quit this ranch at the earliest moment. I did not feel like eating the bread of a man whom I had seen perpetrate such a monstrous thing. I watched him grow distant, then followed him at a distance. We never saw the horses again and so we came slowly home here across 20 miles of baking desert. Now and then we crossed some gulch where Tisdale was obliged to dismount and lead his horse down and up. It was too weak to carry him through these heavy places. Once it fell in a heap as he was leading it up a steep bank. I never spoke to him, nor he to me (after the first half of our journey). At first he would turn back and make some remark, but I would answer only in monosyllables. He became silent, though I don't know whether he knew or knows what I was thinking. As we rode, I tried to think of other matters, but this damnable thing I had seen done kept burning like a blister through every thought that came to me.

Moreover, my own conduct in making no effort to prevent or stop this treatment of the horse has grown more and more discreditable to me. But the situation was a hard one. Here was I, the guest of a stranger, who had done all he could to make me at home because I had come to see his friend. He could have told me the horse was his horse, not mine, and I was riding another of his. No getting away, unless I requested to be driven the 65 miles to Casper, and then here I would have come to see Morris and gone away not seeing him — and think of an explanation!

So my worldly wisdom, for I think this is all a low argument, prevailed over the higher course.

Saturday, June 20 — I told Tisdale that if Morris did not come to-day, I should like to be sent to the railroad, if he could do so. This was arranged in a perfectly smooth manner. But today, to my great relief, Morris came, having got my letter a day late. I still find it utterly impossible to be cordial to Tisdale, or treat him in the least on the terms of before the horse incident. If he thinks anything, I imagine he sets me down as a capricious and moody crank.

Nothing disgraceful an acquaintance of mine has ever done has nauseated my soul like this. The man who cheated at cards; the man who pretended to be my sincere friend and came to my room every day and left it to blacken my character; the man who treated the Cambridge waitress in that way; none of these people's acts have had the sickening effect that the sight of that wretched fainting horse having his eye gouged out has had. I wonder if I take an exaggerated view? If any man who reads this will think I am overstrung? By God, as I rode back over those dry steep gulches, I found myself once or twice hoping the horse would fall and kill him. And I remain the moral craven who did not lift a finger or speak a word. Some confidences Otto the cook made to me today let some light in. He knows nothing about the horse, for Tisdale turned him into the pasture at once on arriving. But Otto, talking to me at this kitchen door and observing Tisdale down by the river beating a horse with a stake over the head, called my attention to it and went on to say that no one in the territory had such a name for cruelty — that the 200 or so men who had worked for Tisdale at various times all spoke of it. He then added that sometimes Tisdale gouged an animal's eye!

I was deeply astonished, of course. I begin to conclude, from five seasons of observation, that life in this negligent, irresponsible wilderness tends to turn people shiftless, incompetent, and cruel. I noticed in 1885 and I notice today a sloth, in doing anything and everything, that is born of the deceitful ease with which makeshifts answer here. Did I believe in the efficacy of prayer, I should petition to be the hand that once for all chronicled and laid bare the virtues and vices of this extraordinary phase of American social progress. Nobody has done it. Nobody has touched anywhere near it. A few have described external sights and incidents, but the grand total thing — its rise, its hysterical unreal prosperity, and its disenchanting downfall; all this and its influence on the various sorts of human character that have been subjected to it — has not been hinted at by a single writer that I, at least, have heard of. The fact is, it is quite worthy of Tolstoi or George Eliot or Dickens. Thackeray wouldn't do.

Friday, June 26 — Buffalo is a shade better in appearance than most of these towns. It stands on Clear Creek (well named) which comes pouring and sliding from the Big Horn Mountains only a short distance away. The town itself has less of that portable appearance prevailing elsewhere. The stages come in from Douglas and from Bell Fourche. Fort McKinney is two miles away to the west, almost against the mountains, whose canyons open just above it and whose snow peaks are in plain view behind the lower timbered foothills. We went up there with the doctor in the afternoon and were very cordially entertained.

Our visit to the officers started us off on a highly picturesque night, during which I was rejoiced again to encounter my friend of Riverside, Henry Smith. He is the real thing, and the only unabridged badman I have ever had a chance to know. He is originally from Texas, and pronounces Spanish very prettily. He has been "run out" of every country he has resided in. His last coup was some eighteen months ago: to persuade his friend Russell to borrow money from every man he knew to take him traveling to foreign parts on the proceeds. They disappeared suddenly. When Smith returned here this spring he had been to South America and all over Europe.

Before I forget him, I must describe Smith's appearance. A tall, long-nosed, dark fellow, with a shock of straight black hair on end all over his head. Blue overalls tucked into boots of the usual high-heeled pattern, and a slouchy waistcoat. He is so tall he bends down over almost everyone as he talks, and he has a catching but sardonic smile. His voice is unpleasant, very rasping, though not overloud. The great thing is his eyes. They are of mottled yellow, like agate or half-clear amber, large and piercing, at times burning with light. They are the very worst eyes I have ever looked at. Perfectly fearless and shrewd, and treacherous. I don't see how an eye can express all that, but it does.

I have sat and talked to Smith, or rather listened to him; he's a brilliant talker in his vagabond line, and he has found me what I set out to be in this world — a good listener. And all the while he talked I watched him as intently as I have ever studied the day before an examination, noting every turn in his speech and every lift of his hand. He is not a halfway man. Not the Bret Harte villain with the heart of a woman. Not the mixed dish of cambric tea so dear to modern novelists. He is just bad through and through, without a scruple and without an affection. His face is entirely cruel, and you hear cruelty in his voice.

How do I know all this? Because I know something of his past and present, and I have heard him speak for himself. He has attended to scores of men and women in his talk, and never to one without a corrosive sneer. When I come to my castle in Spain, my book about Wyoming, I shall strain my muscles to catch Smith. I'm getting to believe mixed characters are not the only ones in the world.

1894

Wednesday, May 23 — Deming. Some of my days at Bowie were spent in riding in company with Corporal Skirdin — or when he could not go, Private Pierce. Both have natures and histories that appeal to me strongly. Skirdin's family abandoned him when he was six, moving East from Arizona as soon as they could sell the father's property at his death. Since then Skirdin has shifted for himself, beginning when eight years old by pointing a gun at the old man with whom he lived and who beat him whenever he failed to find the horses in the morning. Skirdin left that house and the first night slept in the Pinal range — a boy of eight, possessing a pony, a gun, and a pair of trousers — in the middle of the Apache country. He's only twenty-seven now, but life has made him look thirty-five. His search and discovery of his family, a taking of many years for which he saved all his money, is deeply touching.

Skirdin is uncouth, ugly, and knows only what he has taught himself. But his talk is as simple and strong as nature and he has a most beautiful eye. The officers place a high value on him. We grew very intimate, riding about the hot hills, and our views of life were precisely similar. His native wisdom is remarkable, and now and then he says something that many a celebrity would be glad to have phrased himself. "When I've said what I've got to say to a woman, she can have as many last words as she pleases." He told us in camp the other day how he had silenced a bragging civilian who had been talking of the Texas rangers and comparing the soldiers unfavorably to them; said that he gave it to him pretty strong and straight — " And good grammar, too." This set Fowler and me laughing, whereupon Skirdin added, "Some I didn't understand myself." I parted with Skirdin with regret.

There's nothing makes this world seem so little evil as to meet good men in humbler walks of life. It has been my luck to do so often; and their sensible comments have been tonics to my cynicism when they hadn't an idea of the secret poison they were providing with an antidote.

Songs of the Cowboy

by JOHN A. LOMAX

*A Texan born on the Chisholm Trail and self-educated,
John A. Lomax came to Harvard in quest of his Ph.D. with
the earnings he had saved as a schoolteacher. He did his
graduate work under Professor George Lyman Kittredge, and
one evening when he came to call, "Kitty" heard him humming a song from the range. The professor asked if he knew
the words, and when Lomax recited them his true quest was
discovered, a quest which he wrote about in the* Atlantic *and
eventually described in his book* Adventures of a Ballad
Hunter.

MARCH 1947

When in 1908 a check for $500 came from Harvard University for
my first year as a Sheldon Fellow, I was the happiest person in the world.
Never before at one time had I owned so much money, money that
brought me both honor and responsibility. I was entirely free to spend
it in running down the words and music of cowboy songs. In a glow of
anticipation I made plans to travel throughout the cattle country.

It proved a long and hard road that I started on, as I made my way,
walking, on horseback, by buggy, by train and automobile — a tortuous
journey that has since then wound a half-million miles into every part
of the United States. Very few of my associates in the University of
Texas expressed sympathy or took the project seriously. For them this
crude product of the West had no interest, no value, no charm whatever.
Governor Jim Ferguson quoted stanzas of my cowboy songs in political
addresses to cheering crowds, and sneered at the University of Texas for
having me on its faculty, just as he sneered at a teacher of zoology, asserting repeatedly that this professor was trying to make wool grow on
the backs of armadillos and thus bring down the price of sheep! Both of
us were sorry fools to him.

It was cowboy songs I most wished, in those early days, to round up and "close herd." These I jotted down on a table in a saloon back room, scrawled on an envelope while squatting beside a campfire near a chuck wagon, or caught behind the scenes of a broncho-busting outfit or rodeo. To capture the cowboy music proved an almost impossible task. The cowboys would simply wave away the large horn I carried and refuse to sing into it. Not one song did I ever get from them except through the influence of generous amounts of whiskey, raw and straight from the bottle or jug. Once I was invited to speak at the Texas Cattlemen's Convention in San Antonio. To advertise my undertaking, I attempted to sing some of the tunes I wished to record from the trail men. My poor efforts brought only derisive whoops. One belligerent cattleman said: "I have been singin' them songs ever since I was a kid. Everybody knows them. Only a damn fool would spend his time tryin' to set 'em down. I move we adjourn." And adjourn they did, to a convenient bar.

One night in the back room of the White Elephant saloon in Fort Worth, where I had cornered a bunch of Ediphone-shy cowboy singers, a cowboy said to the crowd: "I told the professor [that's what they jokingly called me] that the Old Chisholm Trail song was as long as the trail from Texas to Montana. I can sing eighty-nine verses myself. Some of the verses would burn up his old horn, and anyhow, I'm not goin' to poke my face up to his blamed old horn and sing. The tune ain't much nohow." The tune wasn't much — but it suited the cowboy's work. He could sing it when he went dashing out to turn a runaway steer back to the herd:

> Feet in the stirrups and seat in the saddle,
> And I hung and rattled with them longhorn cattle,
> Coma-ti-yi-yippee, yippee yea, yippee yea,
> Coma-ti-yi-yippee, yippee yea.

And he could sing it with a roaring chorus as the men sat about the campfire during the long winter evenings.

"Back in the seventies," said another cowboy in the crowd, "we sang 'The Old Chisholm Trail' all the way from San Antonio to Dodge City. There was never a day that someone did not build a new verse." There is another "Chisholm Trail" tune — a quiet, jig-joggy tune — when a fellow was riding alone, scouting for drifting cattle, or riding the "line" through lonely stretches of country. I finally persuaded one of the boys to sing it. But not for my recording machine. I learned the tune and later recorded it myself for the Folk Song Archive in the Library of Congress.

Out on a busy corner near the cattle pens of the Fort Worth stockyards I had come upon a blind old man twanging his guitar while he sang doleful ditties and listened for the ring of quarters in his tin cup.

"I don't know any cowboy songs," he explained to me. "But lead me home to lunch; my wife can sing you a bookful."

The old man shuffled along beside me, clasping his guitar as I guided him over the rough places in our path. We were headed for the trees that fringed the West Fork of the Trinity River near Fort Worth. Often I stumbled, for I was carrying the heavy Edison machine.

We found the blind singer's wife out behind a covered truck, a fore-runner of the trailer, seated in front of a gaily colored tent. She wore a gypsy costume of rich brocade. She had used paint and powder with skillful discretion on a face naturally comely. While I chatted with her, the old man disappeared into the tent. In a few minutes out he came. Gone were the round, humped shoulders, the white hair, the shambling gait, the tottering figure — and the colored glasses! Before me stood a young, handsome, dark-eyed man, alert and athletic.

"We do teamwork here. My wife shakes down the saps who like to hold her hand while she reads their fortunes in the stars. All the self-righteous fools go away from my tin cup happy, marking down one more good deed on their passports to Heaven. We aim to please our customers, and I think we do." Thus the faker rambled on while a smiling Negro man served delicious food and a bottle of wine. Later on, through the long Texas afternoon, amid the cheerful talk, the fortuneteller sang the songs of the road. Her family for generations had lived as gypsies.

"This lady," said the faker, "who has joined her fortunes with mine, travels with me now from Miami, Florida, to San Diego, California. We belong to that fringe of society which takes life the easiest way. We toil not, neither do we spin." Raising a tent flap he showed me rich purple hangings, thick Persian rugs, a divan spread with soft silken covers — amazing luxury.

"With our burros, Abednego and Sennacherib, to pull our covered wagon, we travel as we like. Our rackets roll in the money."

He lay flat on his back on the mesquite grass, puffing a cigar as he gazed at the white patches of clouds that swept across the deep-blue Texas sky. And close by sat the fake gypsy lady, strumming her guitar and singing the songs that she had picked up in her wanderings.

She scorned the clumsy horn fastened to my recording machine, but I caught a few of the tunes. I remember that she sang me the first blues that I ever heard, moving me almost to tears, and a pathetic ballad of a factory girl who got splinters in her toes. Many and many another song she sang that unhappily is gone with the Texas wind. Then came four stanzas and the refrain:

> As I was walkin' one mornin' for pleasure
> I met a young cowboy all ridin' along;
> His hat was throwed back and his spurs was a-jinglin',
> As he approached me a-singin' this song:
>
> Whoopee-ti-yi-yo, git along, little dogies,
> It's your misfortune and none of my own.
> Whoopee-ti-yi-yo, git along, little dogies,
> For you know Wyoming will be your new home.

"To me," she said, "that's the loveliest of all cowboy songs. Like others, its rhythm comes from the movement of a horse. It is not the roisterous, hell-for-leather, wild gallop of 'The Old Chisholm Trail,' nor the slow easy canter of 'Good-bye, Old Paint.' You mustn't frighten the dogies. They get nervous in crowds. Lope around them gently in the darkness as you sing about punching them along to their new home in Wyoming. They'll sleep the night through and never have a bad dream."

After the refrain she would give the night herding yodel of the cowboy, born of the vast melancholy of the plains; a yodel to quiet a herd of restless cattle in the deep darkness of a rainy night, when far-off flashes of lightning and the rumble of distant thunder meant danger. While the cattle milled around and refused to lie down, close to the fringe of the circle of moving animals rode the cowboys giving this wordless cry to the cattle, like the plea of a lonesome wolf calling for his mate, like the croon of a mother trying to quiet a restless babe in the long watches of the night, like the soft moo of a cow wooing her young offspring from its hiding place to come for its milk. "Quiet, cattle, quiet. Darkness is everywhere, but we, your friends, are near. Lie down, little dogies, lie down." The yodel was persuasive, far-reaching. Even in its high notes it was soothing and tender.

As the gypsy woman, swayed by the beauty of her notes, yodeled on, the leaves of the overhanging cottonwood trees fluttered noiselessly, the katydids in the branches stopped their song and seemed to listen. In all our world there was no other sound save that beautiful voice imploring all little dogies to "lay still, little dogies, lay still."

I read through the files of Texas newspapers that printed columns of old songs, and I bedeviled librarians for possible buried treasures in frontier chronicles. In a secondhand bookstore in San Antonio I found a bat-

tered copy of *Johnson's New Comic Songs* with a San Francisco date line
of 1863. Along with the old favorites "Gentle Annie" and "Nellie Gray,"
I came on the words of "Poker Jim," "The Miner's Song," "The Dying
Californian," and other song products of the days of forty-nine.

Some months afterward I asked the Librarian of the University of California at Berkeley if he knew of other pamphlets of early frontier songs.
He had none catalogued. He then took me to the Bancroft Library and
left me to rummage in some habitually locked-up cases. I came on a stack
of dog-eared, paper-backed pamphlets tied together with an ancient cotton string. Though I lifted out the pile with care, the string crumbled
in my fingers. There they were — not a complete file of the "20,000
song books" advertised by D. E. Appleton & Co., San Francisco, but a
choice selection of early "California Songsters": *Ben Cotton's Songster,
The Sally Come Up Songster, Put's Original California Songster, Put's
Golden Songster,* and many another. I discovered that "Old Put" and a
group of men singers went from gold camp to gold camp in the early
fifties and sang to the miners. When they ran out of songs Old Put and
his like made up songs describing the life of a mining town, telling how
the Forty-niners got to California and sometimes how they got back East.
They were rough and crude creations, but among them I turned up
"Sweet Betsy from Pike" and "The Days of Forty-nine," and afterward
also discovered the tunes to which they were sung:

> Did you ever hear tell of Sweet Betsy from Pike,
> Who crossed the wide prairies with her lover Ike,
> With one yoke of cattle and one spotted hog,
> A tall Shanghai rooster and an old yaller dog?

Betsy and her man lived in the days of forty-nine:

> In the days of old when they dug out the gold,
> In the days of Forty-nine.

> There's old "Lame Jess," that hard old cuss,
> Who never would repent;
> He never missed a single meal
> Nor never paid a cent.

> But old "Lame Jess," like all the rest,
> At death he did resign,
> And in his bloom went up the flume
> In the days of Forty-nine.

Uncovering these two songs repaid me for the long trip from Texas.

Among my students in the A. and M. College of Texas was a young fellow from Denison, Texas, by the name of Harry Stephens. Harry had worked cattle in New Mexico and Arizona for three or four years; and he brought with him to college a handsome saddle, saddle blanket, bridle, spurs, and other equipment. His saddle was ornamented with silver. He didn't like the college uniform and he wasn't much interested in English literature, but he warmed up when I mentioned cowboy songs. He would stay after class and recite and sing songs to me. Now and then he would drift down to my home on Sunday and lean over the fence and sing a song to attract my attention. I never could get him farther than the gate.

Early in the spring, when the world was turning green again, Harry called on me one morning just as the bugle was blowing for the first class period. I went out to the gate on which he leaned. "Well, Professor," he said, "grass is rising — and I got to move on. I'm lonesome. I want to hear the wolves howl and the owls hoot." Twenty years went by before I saw Harry again. Meanwhile he sent me Western songs. Some I'm sure he made up; some he "doctored"; some he had taken down from the singing of others. One day I received a letter from him. He was on a ranch in southern Idaho. Enclosed were the words of what I consider the most beautiful cowboy poem in the language. The opening stanza runs:

> Oh, slow up, dogies, quit your roving around,
> You have wandered and tramped all over the ground;
> Oh, graze along, dogies, and feed kinda slow,
> And don't forever be on the go —
> Oh, move slow, dogies, move slow.
> Hi-oo, hi-oo, hi-oo-oo-oo.

Years afterward, a young woman at Flagstaff, Arizona, after one of my folk-song talks, came up and said that she knew Harry Stephens, who was then in a hospital some hundred miles away as a result of a serious accident bulldogging steers. But it was a long time before our paths crossed again.

The Black Gates of Keokuk

by RICHARD BISSELL

*A native of Dubuque, Iowa, Richard Bissell after his gradu-
ation from Harvard hankered for a stretch on the river. He
worked on the Monongahela, the Ohio, the Missouri, and the
Mississippi, first as deck hand and then as mate and pilot. His
novels,* 7½ Cents *(from which came* The Pajama Game*)
and* Say, Darling, *established his success, but his writing began, as Mark Twain's did, on the river.*

APRIL 1950

There is always some alarming or dismal feature about every job, and
in towboating on the Upper Mississippi River it is the lock at Keokuk,
Iowa. This depraved lock is too short and too deep; the lockmen are
more bored and obstructionist than any others; the extension guide walls
are floating sheer booms that disintegrate and produce lawsuits, resigna-
tions, and dementia praecox; the upper sheer fence angles off from the
direction of the lock wall causing despair and vulgar language on the
part of the deck crews; and it is always either raining or 400 degrees
Reaumur there. When the boats leave St. Paul or St. Louis the crews begin to bet and speculate as to which watch will get stuck with Keokuk
lock, and mates have been known to commit self-destruction and other
acts against nature on coming on watch and seeing the familiar contours
looming in the river ahead.

"We're it," said Joe, the Second Mate, as we foregathered at watch-
time by the engine-room door, and a beautiful zigzag of lightning suitable for framing shot down through the dark clouds hanging over the
willows on the Illinois side. The rain we had been expecting all day began to fall. In the steaming misty near distance we could see the black
gates of Keokuk lock beyond the drawbridge, and the old wooden fence
of the sheer boom floating in the water below the huge pile of concrete.

"I'm glad I greased up these oilskins," I said.

"Where's Shorty?" Joe asked.

"Back in the pigpen trying to borrow a raincoat off of Hubert," said Diamond.

The town was close over on the port side, and we were all thinking what a good evening this would be to go to a show or out to the dance hall as we looked up at the streets and houses. We would be all evening getting our barges locked through, and with the raindrops already splashing in the river, it looked as if we were in for a treatment.

Captain Sargent blew the whistle for the bridge below the lock, and after a while the big swing span commenced to wheel open, so slowly you could hardly see it move at first.

So we stood there and Sargent eased her past town and on up toward the bridge. We could see right up the main drag. This was a sad kind of evening on the boat, with the neon lights reflected on the wet street so near at hand, a few cars so close we could hear the tire noises, and a smell of pork chops in the air. A Model A came down the street and stopped, and a girl in a blue slicker got out and ran into a store.

We could see the lockmen moving around up on top of the lock, getting ready to open the lower gates — they looked about the size of window washers way up on a building. We were right in the drawbridge now, and the lights of cars waiting in line for the bridge to close, and their suggestion of dry comfort, shows, restaurants, cocktail bars, didn't cheer us up much.

The lock blew an OK whistle at us as the big lower gates, like a pair of doors to a De Mille temple, parted in the middle and very slowly began to open in the gathering gloom.

"If that don't look like the goddamn gates to hell," Joe said.

The rain came down in big drops and finally broke loose with a regular backwoods cloudburst, so we could scarcely see the gates, and Captain Sargent, four barge lengths back, could see neither the gates nor us. We were coming up dead slow.

Shorty pulled off the rake hatch cover and slid down inside, out of the rain. Joe was on the starboard corner of the lead barge looking for that floating timber sheer boom. The rain was dropping down so hard it splashed up your legs and got you wet in spite of the oilskins.

"There she is," Joe said. "Bill, run back a ways and holler at Sargent the Great and tell him he cleared the sheer fence."

I trotted back and hollered up at the Captain. He didn't hear me, so I went back further and hollered some more. Finally I went clear back to the boat and climbed up to the pilothouse and told him.

"Tell Joe to tie her off if he can, until the rain leaves off," he said.

"I could see a hell of a lot more if I was under a thousand ton of coal. I'll drop her against that wood boom, and be careful you don't tear nothing up."

I went down and the rain was harder yet, and began to blow from the east, across the water. When it first started, it came straight down, but now it was beginning to slice and slash. I ran back on the port side and got an empty vinegar jug from the stern, slid into the galley, and filled it with coffee about a third of the way. The cook was standing there clean and dry in his white clothes, smoking a cigar. "Why don't you just get a pail and bail the whole river into my galley?"

"Aw, have a heart, Harry," I said. "It's wet out there."

"Here," he said. "Put some milk in that there coffee," and he handed me a can of Carnation. "I'll leave you out a extra pie I made. Now get the hell outa my galley."

I got back in the rain again. I couldn't see much. The canvas line covers on the foredeck had blown their weights off and the coils were filled with water like little lily pools. I got back to the head of the barges all right and the tow had dropped against the floating guide fence and was still inching along upstream, but dying fast.

"If we can get two lines on her we'll stand less chance tearing up something. I'll ketch a line here and you ketch one on the quarter head, Bill, and we'll check into each other easy when she starts dropping back."

We got her tied off and a gull came and sat on top of one of the stakes they had the 40-watt bulbs strung on, and let the wind blow him around, and the rain was running off his feathers in trickles; he couldn't keep his balance — the fence was rocking back and forth — and he finally gave up and made a flop take-off and disappeared east.

"Ain't nothing much to do but set on these lines," Joe hollered. "You OK, Bill?"

"I could use a couple shots of old Peoria whiskey," I said.

"Someday I'm gonna buy me a rain outfit," Joe said.

The rain began to slack off; first we could see the big wide steps beside the lock, then the gates came into view, and the big dark lock with sheer black walls. Sargent gave a toot, meaning turn her loose, and we spun our lines off the timberheads on the fence; they lit with a splash in the river and we pulled them aboard.

"*Comin' ahead!*" Joe hollered in a voice loud enough to scare the kids clear back to Canton lock, and gave a slow drag of his arm from low down in back, up over his head, and forward, like a slow-motion baseball pitch. Sargent poured it to her and we commenced moving up.

We got in the lock, and Sargent flopped the eight barges against the wall and they slid along slow and easy, once in a while throwing up cement dust and sparks when they rubbed the wall. Cap turned the light on Joe and Joe gave him a stopping signal and we drifted for a few minutes.

"Watch your heads. Here come the lines," hollered the lockman from way up in heaven at the top of the wall and out of sight in the rain.

Diamond was back at the second coupling and I heard him holler. "OK, let her come. You can't kill me. Toss her down, old man Keokuk." Then I heard the klunk as the monkey-fist knot on the end of the heaving line hit the rake deck.

At the same time I heard another klunk, only more like bouncing a baseball on a cement sidewalk, followed by a clatter of breaking glass.

"What's that? Did Shorty drop that coffee jug? Shorty!" Joe said.

Shorty was lying down in the coal as if he wanted a nap.

"He's knocked cold," I said. "Joe, here's Shorty, out like a Monday night. He got hit with the heaving line."

Shorty was lying there in the coal with his finger still through the ring on the neck of the busted jug, and his old slouch hat had rolled off and was gathering summer rain.

"Oh, pretty mama," said Joe, coming across the deck. " That's what we need, a deck hand in the hospital."

I went over and bent the heaving line into our lock line while Joe was working on Shorty.

"All right, take it up!" I hollered up into the empty spaces, and my voice echoed back and forth in the walls of the lock. The line arose from the deck like the Hindu rope trick and traveled up and up till the eye in it disappeared over the edge of the lock wall forty feet above.

"Shorty. Shorty, you get up, hear me? Shorty, get up. Bill, this ole boy is cold," Joe said, shaking Shorty and banging him around. "Oh, oh. Feel that knob on his head. Now I got nobody to stand the head line."

About this time Shorty opened his eyes and said, "I knew that mule would git me some day."

"Ah," said Joe, "he's alive," and picking him up and shoving him across the deck he said, "Give him the line, Bill. Let's you and me go back and jackknife. Come on, kid."

Shorty was standing there with a dazed look on his face. He didn't know where he was but he laid the lock line around the center cavel, ran it over to the timberheads, and began to check her like an old master. Last I saw him he had a good strain on the line and was standing there bareheaded with the rain still coming down, rubbing that knob on his head and looking up at his line rising in the air.

Joe and I jackknifed and broke the couplings on the two outside barges and Sargent backed her out, leaving three in. We tied off on the sheer boom and sat down in the rain. Shorty and Diamond were up in the lock on the barges, locking through, and the rain was coming down steady. "Hightail it back and get us another jug of coffee," Joe said. "I'll set here and mind the lines. I can't get no wetter regardless."

I went to the stern again to hunt up another jug, and stood there for a minute and let the rain hit me from the east, and watched the cars down on the bridge, and then went into the messroom.

When I got out on the head again Joe was sitting on a timberhead and the rain was not coming down in such big drops but more concentrated, like a hotel shower. The lock gates were still shut; Shorty and Diamond were tying them off on the upper sheer boom about now; one of them would stay up there to watch the loads and the other come back to help with the second locking.

It seemed like forever waiting for them to lock through and dump the water again; from the time the gates closed until they would open again to receive the second locking it was about an hour, maybe an hour and a quarter, but try sitting still or standing with nothing to do except think about how far it is to Wabash Ave. and what's doing tonight at the Aragon Ballroom with the rain coming down your neck and trickling down your backbone so it tickles and the cuffs on your gauntlet gloves wilt and crumple and the coal paste oozes in the hole in your shoe, and your cigarette falls apart and your clothes begin to smell like an old Irish wet wash without benefit of Hilex, and after ten minutes you'd swear to God you'd been in there a week and a half. It gets tiresome.

"Well," said Joe, "it's better than farming."

"Have some coffee," I said, handing him the jug.

We didn't look very romantic, dripping like a couple of muskrats in the evening gloom, even if Joe did have a star on his cap; so unless you want to take a lot of punishment, and work an 84-hour week, just stick to that course in bookkeeping, boys, because you won't find any white whale out here, and the packet boats and the gamblers are all gone. So wipe off your chin and look serious and they'll give you a desk to sit at and show you how to work the water cooler and you can buy a blue serge suit and after a while get advanced from a single-tier letter basket to a double-decker. Well, I like to put on a new tie and go to the show on Saturday night as much as the next guy.

"This here is just a disease, this steamboating, a incurable disease," Joe said, and set the jug down on the deck at his feet. "There ain't hardly a man aboard that likes this here life, but they're all here to stay. Diamond is thinking about chickens. Shorty is moaning and complaining all the time worse than a Methodist preacher. The mess boy wishes he had never left that red clay farm. You got that St. Paul girl and all the rest of the world's troubles on your mind. Vincent ain't hardly got the brains to be unhappy but he manages it somehow. Curly wishes he was back down on the Ohio River. The cook wishes he never had quit working in that restaurant he is always raving about. And Sargent is the biggest joke of them all. He thinks he is gonna get his pile and quit.

"I seen plenty of these smart guys that is just out here to make their pile and they are getting on and off these boats like they was streetcars. They are never content again. They don't know enough to hold down a good job on the bank. Any high school kid can slide up Main Street and get a better job. Can't you see Sargent striking out for a job down home. He goes to the mill. 'Well, what can you do?' says the foreman. 'Can you run a band saw?' 'No.' 'Can you read a blueprint?' 'No.' 'Well, what can you do?' 'Well, I got Pilot's License All Tonnage from Minneapolis to Baton Rouge and Cairo to Pittsburgh and Grafton to Chicago and Prescott to Stillwater and Kansas City to the mouth and Paducah to Sheffield and the Hennepin Canal.' 'I dunno what that's all about,' says the foreman, 'but whatever it is you better go do it.' He got no more chance to retire from the river than a catfish has to get into the Knights of Columbus."

About this time the gates commenced to open and Diamond came down the steps from the lock and climbed over the fence and aboard the barges and I went back to see whether Cap was up and about. He was taking a nap on the bench in the pilothouse and I told him the gates were open, so he blew a toot to turn loose and we shoved on up and tied off three more.

Perhaps Joe was right. Steamboating is an incurable disease. And as for getting away from it, why Blackie Johnson quit the river and never did come back; of course, he finally got locked up at Stillwater and the problem of his triumphal return as Mate was no longer a problem to him or anyone else except the parole board. Then there was old Captain Lawrence Arkwright Buckingham who made more farewell appearances than Geraldine Farrar and after cussing the river in a squeaky voice and inadequate vocabulary for seventy years retired at the age of eighty-nine to a houseboat which he parked dangerously near the channel below the dam at Alma, Wis., so he could continue to lacerate his nerves with the passing of each boat.

After you have been on the river long enough to get the disease, everything looks different: Chicago is a town 200 miles east of the river. South Dakota is someplace west of Minneiska and of no interest as it hasn't even a mile of Mississippi River in the whole state. Lake Superior is an inferior watery deposit of some kind, in a general northeasterly direction from Grey Cloud Landing. And as for St. Louis, Quincy, Davenport, Moline, Rock Island, Dubuque, La Crosse, Winona — what are they? River towns, of course. Not towns — river towns. And what a difference that makes.

There isn't anything in any of these towns, but they are the most romantic and wonderful in the world because they are old Upper Mississippi River towns. Of course there's a bird in La Crosse who made a scale model of St. Patrick's Cathedral out of matchsticks, a girl down in Muscatine born without any arms who can knit with her feet, and a fellow at Winona named Trask who made two holes in one one Sunday in 1928, but those towns would be worse than Waterloo, Iowa, in spite of these local attractions, except for the big Mississippi River rolling past the door day and night.

Diamond and I stayed in the lock to ride the barges up, and Joe stayed below with the two loads left and tied them off to the boom.

The lower gates closed and there we were at the bottom of the watery pit, waiting for salvation. I was tending the lines on the forward end of the barges, and Diamond was lost down at the other end in the gloom and rain, by the lock gates. I had a lock line to the center cavel and a peg line on the quarter timberhead to keep the barge from surging.

I sang "O Sion, haste, thy mission high fulfilling, To tell to all the world that God is Light," then switched to a lighter mood with "I'll Be with You in Apple Blossom Time," and finally they started raising the water and the barges got a bit restless and began to creep up the wall.

"Hey, Diamond, think we'll get to the top by Hallowe'en?" I hollered.

"Wordely," he said, or something similar. It rattled around and bounced so off the lock walls it might have been almost anything.

We had been in here twelve years already, so it didn't much matter any more. I sang the "Freight Train Blues" for a while, and thought about whether Merle would wear the black dress, the pink sweater, or the gray suit when I met her in St. Paul, and whether I should marry her or not, and whether I would have time in St. Paul to kiss her in all the different places I wanted to. After that I returned to Keokuk lock and spat on the slimy lock wall to add to the general moisture of the evening. Modern science had raised us up about twenty feet but there was more than that left to go, and whoever made the rain had sure left the faucet on.

One of the lockmen leaned over the top of the lock wall and looked down at us. "Think it'll rain?" he hollered. A humorist.

"Hell, no," I replied. "Wrong time of year."

"Well, it's good for the corn," says the guy upstairs. "Been awful dry around here."

"—— THE CORN," Diamond hollered, making himself intelligible at last.

The lockman disappeared, his feelings hurt. I took up some slack in the lines. "By God, I believe we'll make it after all," I said to myself, because we were getting somewhere near the top now, and I could see the lights in the lock house through the rain, with the rain pouring down the windows and the lights unperturbed inside.

"Hello, you meat ball," I said *sotto voce* as the fat lock tender appeared again. "Merry Christmas, you silly bastard."

"Hey, how about hauling up some slack?" he said.

"What a capital idea, old man."

We were really at the top now, and ready for the upper gate to open. Meanwhile we had to go through the inexplicable waiting period connected with getting heavy pieces of machinery to start moving. It's always the same. You blow your whistle at the bridge tender and he comes out and waves a flag and rushes back in the control house again. What does he do in the next ten minutes? Read the instruction book on how to open bridges? Get out the dental floss and give his teeth a good going over? Finish a chapter in the Gypsy Dream Book? Finally the bridge commences to open.

Same with the locks.

"OK on the number three," says one lockman.

"OK?"

"Yeah — OK."

Five-minute lapse.

"OK then on number three."

"OK?"

"Yeah, OK."

O'Neill should get hold of some of this dialogue.

"Oh come, oh come, Emmanuel, and open those lock gates," I implored.

"How's that?" said the lockman, returning after a further exchange of OK's with the boss.

"It's a nice night for waterfowl," I said.

"I hope they enjoy it. I ain't," he replied. He was a fat goof who needed a number of pills or some Father John's medicine from his friendly naborhood druggist. Frankly, I could have used a tablespoonful of Konjola right then myself. The rain had got inside my oilskins and I was steaming inside like a baked potato. Finally I gave up in disgust and took my oilskins off.

The upper gates commenced to submerge and I took up all the slack I could get and threw on some turns; the barges started to surge for the open water, and the line squeaked and jumped; I checked easy and the barges gave up the idea and settled down. The lockman brought me the towing wire and I slipped it over the timberhead, and after another round of OK's we commenced to creep out into the pool above. The lockman was wiping his glasses and complaining and abusing the weather department and cussing the government and the state legislature — as far as he was concerned there were no prospects in sight.

"Please, Lord," I said, "bless Papa and make it rain harder. Watching this man suffer makes me forget all my sins."

"What?" he said.

"I said down on the farm they are all setting around the kitchen table listening to the radio," I said.

He said if it didn't let up raining pretty soon he was going to tell them to take the job and shove it.

Our little game with the Keokuk lock was about over. Had I met the challenge? Had I faced up to the reality of things? Had I made myself worthy of Merle, the beautiful ticket seller? Had I played the game or was I a rotter?

In short, the coal was on its way to St. Paul, but just where was I going? That was the question. Had I taken the right attitude with the lock tender? There I was and there was the coal and somewhere there was Merle, and there was nothing anybody could do about it. Should I marry her, or sell her to an agent exporting girls to Buenos Aires? I couldn't fit the pieces of the puzzle together.

In answer to my request the rain came down harder than ever.

The Civil War

"*We live on our emotions,*" *wrote Oliver Wendell Holmes,* "*as the sick man is said, in the common speech, to be nourished by his fever.*" *Readers followed the disheartening fluctuations of the Union cause in the newspapers, and in* Leslie's Illustrated Newspaper *and* Harper's Weekly. *But the conflict at no time monopolized the pages of the* Atlantic *to the extent that the world wars were to do in years to come. This was not because the* Atlantic *readers cared less; rather it seems to have been accepted by editor and reader that the* Atlantic *should be turned to for relief and that such articles and poems as we printed should be farsighted and as much as possible above the reportorial. And so they were, the best of them.*

There were two war narratives as timely as they were spectacular, and both of them too long for inclusion here. The first was of poignant interest to Bostonians; in "*My Hunt After the Captain*" (*December 1862*) *Oliver Wendell Holmes told in frustrating detail of his six-day search for his son, Captain Oliver Wendell Holmes, Jr., who had been reported wounded, perhaps fatally, in the battle of Antietam. As might be expected, the little doctor was wound up with anxiety, and he did not spare the horses either in his search or in what he wrote when he had brought the wounded captain back to Boston. The recital is highly cumulative in its effect, and in addition to its length there is another reason for not reproducing it here. This is the way Catherine Drinker Bowen puts it in her* Yankee from Olympus:

> *The most disagreeable episode of his stay at home had not been a national matter at all, but something highly personal. Proof sheets of the* Atlantic *had arrived; Wendell's father with a pleased smile had turned them over to his son. Carrying the story upstairs to his room after the family was in bed, Wendell read them, his flesh crawling. He tried to skip, tried to stop reading, but continued in horrid fascination to the end . . .* "for this our son and brother was dead and is alive again, and was lost and

is found . . . Lay him in his own bed, and let him sleep off
his aches and weariness. . . ."
   *Oh my God! thought Captain Holmes, blushing to the roots
of his hair. What if Company A should get hold of this?*

Mr. Justice Holmes could never abide that story to his dying
day, and there are contemporary readers who will agree with him.
   The second spectacular piece was "Our Visit to Richmond," by
James Roberts Gilmore, an ardent Methodist who wrote under the
pseudonym of Edmund Kirke. Gilmore and a fellow Methodist,
James F. Jaquess, parson-colonel of the "preacher's regiment," the
73rd Illinois Volunteers, won Lincoln's permission to pass through
the lines in July of 1864 to pay a personal call on Jefferson Davis,
in the belief that they could persuade the Confederate President to
agree to Peace with Union. They went as private citizens, with a
flag of truce and in an ambulance, were conducted to the Secretary
of State, Judah P. Benjamin, and were passed on by him to President Davis. Davis was obdurate. But the full account of their conversation with him and of the conditions they observed in the Confederate capital — which runs to many pages — filled the report
which they delivered to Lincoln on their return. After Lincoln had
finished reading it he asked:

   "What do you propose to do with this?"
   "Put a beginning and an end to it, sir, on my way home, and
hand it to the Tribune."
   "Can't you get it into the Atlantic Monthly?" Lincoln asked.
"It would have less of a partisan look there."

   Well, in any event, that is where it appeared, in September
1864.
   Feeling in the Atlantic office ran high against the British because of their traffic with the Confederates. "Don't let us talk or
write any longer," said Fields, wartime editor, in his letter to Longfellow of January 1, 1864, "of the vernacular spoken in treacherous Great Britain. I speak only American henceforward." But five
years later he was in London visiting Dickens. Tempers cooled
after the peace, and articles of reconciliation to and from the South
began to appear. In the years since, as attics and old desks gave up
their family letters and diaries, the Atlantic has continued to add
from both sides to the recording of that epic, the most deeply felt
in our national experience.

Chiefly About War Matters

by NATHANIEL HAWTHORNE

Nathaniel Hawthorne, in failing health, was at work on a novel when the Civil War broke out and the national anxiety brought his writing to a halt. With the aim of reviving his spirits, Fields encouraged him to visit the Capital. Hawthorne called on the President with a delegation from Massachusetts, saw McClellan in the field, and inspected the Monitor. The result was a lengthy article, from which Fields deleted the section describing Lincoln because he thought it too disrespectful. We have selected what seems to us the most prophetic episode.

JULY 1862

There is no remoteness of life and thought, no hermetically sealed seclusion, except, possibly, that of the grave, into which the disturbing influences of this war do not penetrate. Of course, the general heartquake of the country long ago knocked at my cottage door and compelled me, reluctantly, to suspend the contemplation of certain fantasies to which, according to my harmless custom, I was endeavoring to give a sufficiently lifelike aspect to admit of their figuring in a romance. So I gave myself up to reading newspapers and listening to the click of the telegraph, like other people; until, after a great many months of such pastime, it grew so abominably irksome that I determined to look a little more closely at matters with my own eyes.

Accordingly we set out — a friend and myself — toward Washington. It was a clear, frosty morning when we started. The sun shone brightly on snow-covered hills in the neighborhood of Boston, and burnished the surface of frozen ponds; and the wintry weather kept along with us while we trundled through Worcester and Springfield and all those old, familiar towns, and through the village-cities of Connecticut. But when we reached Philadelphia, the air was mild and balmy; there was but a patch or two of dingy winter here and there, and the bare, brown fields about the city were ready to be green. We had met the spring halfway in her slow progress from the South.

Beyond Philadelphia there was a much greater abundance of military people. Between Baltimore and Washington a guard seemed to hold every station along the railroad; and frequently, on the hillsides, we saw a collection of weather-beaten tents, the peaks of which, blackened with smoke, indicated that they had been made comfortable by stove heat throughout the winter. Our stopping places were thronged with soldiers, some of whom came through the cars asking for newspapers that contained accounts of the battle between the *Merrimack* and the *Monitor,* which had been fought the day before. A railway train met us, conveying a regiment out of Washington to some unknown point; and reaching the capital, we filed out of the station between lines of soldiers with shouldered muskets, putting us in mind of similar spectacles at the gates of European cities.

We were not in time to see Washington as a camp. On the very day of our arrival sixty thousand men had crossed the Potomac on their march toward Manassas; and almost with their first step into the Virginia mud, the phantasmagory of a countless host and impregnable ramparts, before which they had so long remained quiescent, dissolved quite away. The troops being gone, we had the better leisure and opportunity to look into other matters.

The waters around Fortress Monroe were thronged with a gallant array of ships of war and transports wearing the Union flag — "Old Glory," as I hear it called in these days. In pursuance of our official duty, we went on board the flagship and were shown over every part of her — and down into her depths, inspecting her gallant crew, her powerful armament, her mighty engines, and her furnaces, where the fires are always kept burning, as well at midnight as at noon, so that it would require only five minutes to put the vessel under full steam. This vigilance has been felt necessary ever since the *Merrimack* made that terrible dash from Norfolk. Splendid as she is, however, and provided with all but the very latest improvements in naval armament, the *Minnesota* belongs to a class of vessels that will be built no more, nor ever fight another battle.

On her quarter-deck, an elderly flag officer was pacing to and fro with a self-conscious dignity to which a touch of the gout or rheumatism perhaps contributed a little additional stiffness. He seemed to be a gallant gentleman, but of the old, slow, and pompous school of naval worthies, who have grown up amid rules, forms, and etiquette which were adopted full-blown from the British navy into ours, and are some-what too cumbrous for the quick spirit of today. This order of nautical heroes will probably go down, along with the ships in which they fought valorously and strutted most intolerably. How can an admiral conde-scend to go to sea in an iron pot? What space and elbowroom can be found for quarter-deck dignity in the cramped lookout of the *Monitor,* or even in the twenty-feet diameter of her cheese-box? All the pomp and splendor of naval warfare are gone by.

At no great distance from the *Minnesota* lay the strangest-looking craft I ever saw. It was a platform of iron, so nearly on a level with the water that the swash of the waves broke over it under the impulse of a very moderate breeze; and on this platform was raised a circular struc-ture, likewise of iron, and rather broad and capacious, but of no great height. It could not be called a vessel at all; it was a machine — for lack of a better similitude, it looked like a gigantic rat trap. It was ugly, questionable, suspicious, evidently mischievous — nay, I will allow my-self to call it devilish; for this was the new war fiend, destined, along with others of the same breed, to annihilate whole navies and batter down old supremacies.

Going on board, we were surprised at the extent and convenience of her interior accommodations. There is a spacious wardroom, nine or ten feet in height, besides a private cabin for the commander and sleeping accommodations on an ample scale; the whole well lighted and venti-lated, though beneath the surface of the water. Forward, or aft (for it is impossible to tell stem from stern), the crew are relatively quite as well provided for as the officers. It was like finding a palace, with all its conveniences, under the sea. The inaccessibility, the apparent impreg-nability, of this submerged iron fortress are most satisfactory; the offi-cers and crew get down through a little hole in the deck, hermetically seal themselves, and go below; and until they see fit to reappear, there would seem to be no power given to man whereby they can be brought to light. A storm of cannon shot damages them no more than a handful of dried peas. We saw the shot marks made by the great artillery of the *Merrimack* on the outer casing of the iron tower; they were about the breadth and depth of shallow saucers, almost imperceptible dents, with no corresponding bulge on the interior surface. In fact, the thing looked altogether too safe; though it may not prove quite an agreeable predica-ment to be thus boxed up in impenetrable iron with the possibility, one would imagine, of being sent to the bottom of the sea, and even there, not drowned, but stifled.

Nothing, however, can exceed the confidence of the officers in this new craft. It was pleasant to see their benign exultation in her powers of mischief, and the delight with which they exhibited the circumvolutory movements of the tower, the quick thrusting forth of the immense guns to deliver their ponderous missiles, and then the immediate recoil, and the security behind the closed portholes. Yet even this will not long be the last and most terrible improvement in the science of war. Already we hear of vessels the armament of which is to act entirely beneath the surface of the water; so that, with no other external symptoms than a great bubbling and foaming, and gush of smoke, and belch of smothered thunder out of the yeasty waves, there shall be a deadly fight going on below — and, by and by, a sucking whirlpool, as one of the ships goes down.

The *Monitor* was certainly an object of great interest; but on our way to Newport News, whither we next went, we saw a spectacle that affected us with far profounder emotion. It was the sight of the few sticks that are left of the frigate *Congress,* stranded near the shore — and still more, the masts of the *Cumberland* rising midway out of the water, with a tattered rag of a pennant fluttering from one of them. The invisible hull of the latter ship seems to be careened over, so that the three masts stand slantwise; the rigging looks quite unimpaired, except that a few ropes dangle loosely from the yards. A remnant of the dead crew still man the sunken ship, and sometimes a drowned body floats up to the surface.

That was a noble fight. When was ever a better word spoken than that of Commodore Smith, the father of the commander of the *Congress,* when he heard that his son's ship was surrendered? "Then Joe's dead!" said he; and so it proved. Nor can any warrior be more certain of enduring renown than the gallant Morris, who fought so well the final battle of the old system of naval warfare and won glory for his country and himself out of inevitable disaster and defeat. That last gun from the *Cumberland,* when her deck was half submerged, sounded the requiem of many sinking ships. Then went down all the navies of Europe and our own, *Old Ironsides* and all, and Trafalgar and a thousand other fights became only a memory, never to be acted over again; and thus our brave countrymen come last in the long procession of heroic sailors that includes Blake and Nelson, and so many mariners of England, and other mariners as brave as they, whose renown is our native inheritance.

There will be other battles, but no more such tests of seamanship and manhood as the battles of the past; and, moreover, the millennium is certainly approaching, because human strife is to be transferred from the heart and personality of man into cunning contrivances of machinery, which by and by will fight out our wars with only the clank and smash of iron, strewing the field with broken engines, but damaging nobody's little finger except by accident. Such is obviously the tendency of modern improvement.

Voluntaries

by RALPH WALDO EMERSON

Emerson contributed his war poem "Voluntaries" to the At-
lantic *in October 1863, and from it we are quoting the third stanza which, with its familiar closing lines, had such a decisive effect upon the young men who were hesitating to volunteer.*

OCTOBER 1863

> In an age of fops and toys,
> Wanting wisdom, void of right,
> Who shall nerve heroic boys
> To hazard all in Freedom's fight —
> Break sharply off their jolly games,
> Forsake their comrades gay,
> And quit proud homes and youthful dames,
> For famine, toil, and fray?
> Yet on the nimble air benign
> Speed nimbler messages,
> That waft the breath of grace divine
> To hearts in sloth and ease.
> So nigh is grandeur to our dust,
> So near is God to man,
> When Duty whispers low, *Thou must,*
> The youth replies, *I can.*

Bread and the Newspaper

by OLIVER WENDELL HOLMES

SEPTEMBER 1861

War is a very old story, but it is a new one to this generation of Americans. Our own nearest relation in the ascending line remembers the Revolution well. How should she forget it? Did she not lose her doll, which was left behind, when she was carried out of Boston, then growing uncomfortable by reason of cannon balls dropping in from the neighboring heights at all hours? War in her memory means '76. As for the brush of 1812, "we did not think much about that"; and everybody knows that the Mexican business did not concern us much, except in its political relations. No! War is a new thing to all of us who are not in the last quarter of our century. We are learning many strange matters from our fresh experience. And besides, there are new conditions of existence which make war as it is with us very different from war as it has been.

The first and obvious difference consists in the fact that the whole nation is now penetrated by the ramifications of a network of iron nerves which flash sensation and volition backward and forward to and from towns and provinces as if they were organs and limbs of a single living body. The second is the vast system of iron muscles which, as it were, moves the limbs of the mighty organism one upon another. What was the railroad force which put the Sixth Regiment in Baltimore on the 19th of April but a contraction and extension of the arm of Massachusetts with a clenched fist full of bayonets at the end of it?

This perpetual intercommunication, joined to the power of instantaneous action, keeps us always alive with excitement. It is not a breathless courier who comes back with the report from an army we have lost sight of for a month, nor a single bulletin which tells us all we are to know for a week of some great engagement, but almost hourly paragraphs, laden with truth or falsehood as the case may be, making us restless always for the last fact or rumor they are telling. And so of the movements of our armies. Tonight the stout lumbermen of Maine are encamped under their own fragrant pines. In a score or two of hours they are among the tobacco fields and the slave pens of Virginia. The war passion burned like scattered coals of fire in the households of Revolutionary times; now it rushes all through the land like a flame over the prairie. And this instant diffusion of every fact and feeling produces another singular effect in the equalizing and steadying of public opinion. We may not be able to see a month ahead of us; but as to what has passed, a week afterwards it is as thoroughly talked out and judged as it would have been in a whole season before our national nervous system was organized.

Battle Hymn of the Republic
by JULIA WARD HOWE

Mrs. Howe visited an army camp on the outskirts of Washington with the party of Governor Andrew of Massachusetts. When she retired to her tent she was too stirred to sleep; to the rhythm of "John Brown's Body" she composed her famous hymn, scribbling down the lines in the dim light. The Atlantic *paid her four dollars for her poem, and she was heartened when she saw it reprinted in newspapers and broadsides and heard it "being sung in chorus by the soldiers."*

FEBRUARY 1862

Mine eyes have seen the glory of the coming of the Lord:
He is trampling out the vintage where the grapes of wrath are stored;
He hath loosed the fateful lightning of His terrible swift sword:
       His truth is marching on.

I have seen Him in the watch-fires of a hundred circling camps;
They have builded Him an altar in the evening dews and damps;
I can read His righteous sentence by the dim and flaring lamps:
       His day is marching on.

I have read a fiery gospel writ in burnished rows of steel:
"As ye deal with my contemners, so with you my grace shall deal;
Let the Hero, born of woman, crush the serpent with his heel,
          Since God is marching on."

He has sounded forth the trumpet that shall never call retreat;
He is sifting out the hearts of men before His judgment-seat:
Oh, be swift, my soul, to answer Him! be jubilant, my feet!
          Our God is marching on.

In the beauty of the lilies Christ was born across the sea,
With a glory in his bosom that transfigures you and me:
As he died to make men holy, let us die to make men free,
          While God is marching on.

Corporal Hardy

by RICHARD ELY DANIELSON

President of The Atlantic Monthly Company from 1939 until his death on May 23, 1957, Richard Ely Danielson here recounts a story which must have seeped into his blood when he was a boy growing up in Danielson, Connecticut.

NOVEMBER 1938

In those days, during the haying season, it was my duty to keep the men in the fields supplied with sufficient cooling drink to enable them to support the heat and burden of the day. According to our established practice, this cooling drink consisted of cold water from the spring, flavored, for some obscure New England reason, with molasses, and it had to be freshly renewed every hour. We had plenty of ice in the icehouse, but there was a stubborn tradition that ice water was "bad" for men working in hayfields under the hot sun.

So every hour I carried down a brown jug containing the innocent mixture of "molasses 'n' water" to the hands, each one of whom would pause in his work, throw the jug over his upper arm, drink deeply thereof, wipe the sweat off his forehead, say "Thanks, Bub," and go on making hay. I was only ten years old, but it was no hardship to carry the jug, and it was fun to see their Adam's apples working as they drank.

This was routine practice on our Connecticut farm. Mostly the farm hands — "hired men," we called them — came back to the house at noon and ate in the kitchen, after washing up at the pump outside. But in haymaking season each man sought a patch of shade, and his meal was carried to him there, to be eaten in the fields. I suppose the men's overheated bodies cooled off in the wisps of breeze drifting across the scorching "mowings" more effectively and comfortably than would have been possible in a hot summer kitchen. I am sure that my father did everything he could to make their lot as comfortable and healthy as possible. He worked with them, under the same conditions, setting them an example of careful, efficient labor. He differed from his men only in the fact that he was always cleanly shaved, that he gave orders and directions, and that he wore a silk shirt even in the hayfields. Nobody objected in the least to this token, for he was "the owner," and he had been to college, and everyone admitted that he was fair and square.

On such occasions, when the men were given their "dinners" out of doors, I always carried his victuals to Mr. Hardy, because I liked to sit with him while he ate and listen to his stories. I think he enjoyed talking, in his racy Connecticut vernacular, to such a fascinated audience of one. He was a Civil War veteran, like my father, who, however, had been too young to enlist until the last year of the war and had seen almost no active service. But Mr. Hardy was a soldier. Congress had given him a medal — of honor — and all men regarded him with respect.

As I look back and remember his stories, I think he must have been the most modest man I have ever known. Certainly he never thought of himself as a hero. He would accept no pension. "I'm able-bodied. I can work, can't I?" But, alas, he was not really able-bodied. He had been grievously wounded several times, and in 1895, when I fetched and carried for him and sat at his feet, it was pitiful to see his valiant efforts to fork hay on the wagon or do the other farming tasks which require muscular strength. He was thin and bent, but his face was brown and clean and his blue eyes bright and indomitable.

My father employed Mr. Hardy whenever there was work to give him, and treated him — I did not, at that time, know why — differently from the other hired men. He was poor, he lived alone, he was unsuccessful, and in New England then we rated people by their comparative "success." But he worked stoutly and asked no favors of anyone. It was generally conceded that Mr. Hardy, if a failure, was nevertheless a good man.

I remember the last day I served him. I brought him his dinner in a basket — cold meat 'n' potatoes, 'n' bread 'n' butter, 'n' cold coffee, 'n' pie. He was seated in the shade of an oak tree, leaning against a stack of hay. I put the food down beside him and sat down, hugging my knees. It was pleasant there, with the smell of the hay and the drone of the bees, and the good, warm feeling of the earth.

Mr. Hardy lay back against the haymow. "Thanks, Jackie," he said. "I don't seem to be hungry today. It's hot and this tree don't give much shade. Why, dammit, it's like that mean little oak tree down to Chancellorsville."

I said, "Oh, Mr. Hardy, you've told me about Antietam and the Wilderness, but you've never told me about Chancellorsville. What was it like?"

He said slowly, "I ain't never told nobody about Chancellorsville, and I don't aim to tell nobody — grown-up, that is. But I'd kind of like to tell somebody that don't know nothing — like you — about it, for the first and last time. You'll forget it, and it would kind of ease my mind."

Mr. Hardy hoisted himself a little higher on the haymow and made a pretense of eating some bread and meat. "Chancellorsville," he said, "was a bad battle, an awful bad battle. We didn't fight good and they was too many of them and I lost my captain."

"Who was he?" I asked.

"Why," he said, incredulously, "you oughta know that! He was Captain William Armstrong, commandin' Company B, 39th Connecticut. 'N' his twin brother, Ezra, was lootenant. He was younger by an hour or so, and they was identical twins. They never was two men as much alike — in looks, that is, for they was quite unlike inside. The lootenant was always stompin' around an' shoutin' an' wavin' his arms, an' the captain, he was always quiet an' soft-spoken an' brave an' gentle. He was a good man. I guess he was the best man I ever knowed."

He paused and took a sip of his cold coffee. Then he said, "Why, when we come to leave town to go in the cars to Hartford and then to Washington, their father — he was old Judge Armstrong, who lived in that big place up on Armstrong Hill — the Judge come up to me and says, 'Nathan, you look after my boys,' he said. 'They're younger than you be. You kind of keep an eye on them, for my sake,' he says. 'They is good boys,' he says. 'I will, Judge,' I says. 'I'll do my best.' An' he says to me, 'I know you will, Nathan Hardy.' "

"But tell me, Mr. Hardy," I broke in, for I was not interested in the Armstrong twins, "what happened at Chancellorsville?"

"It was a bad battle, as I said. Them Rebs come charging out of the woods, hollerin' and yellin' and helligolarrupin', and they was too many of them. The lootenant, he kept stomping up and down, shouting, 'Never give ground, boys! Stay where you are! Take careful aim! Never retreat!' Those was his words. I will never forget them, because he meant them. But my captain — I was next to him — says, 'They're too many; we can't stop 'em. Tell the men to retreat slowly, firing as often as they can reload.' Just then it hit him right in the chest. *Thunk!* was the noise it made; just like thet — *thunk!* I caught him as he fell, and the blood began to come out of his mouth. He tried to speak, but he was vomiting blood dreadful, so all he could do was to make faces, and his lips said, 'Tell Elizabeth . . .' and then he died. I put him down and noticed we was under a mean little oak tree on the edge of our trenches.

"Then they was around us, hairy men with bayonets, stabbin' and shootin' and yellin', and we soldiers had kind of drifted together in groups and the lootenant was shouting, 'Don't retreat, men!' and he got hit right in the knee and fell down; and so I picked him up and put him across my shoulder and started for the rear. He kep' hittin' me in the face and swearing, 'You damn coward! You left my brother there and you're making me retreat!' I says to him, 'Ezra, be reasonable; I'm takin' you to an ambulance. You ain't fit to fight, and as soon as I can I'm going back to bury William. They ain't goin' to shovel him into no trench,' I said. So he stopped hitting at me.

"I was strong then, and I musta carried him a mile or a mile and a few rods when we come to some stretcher men near a house, and I said, 'You take this officer to the nearest surgeon. They got to saw his leg off.' And they said, 'We ain't carryin' no wounded. We're a burial detail.' I said, pulling my pistol out, 'You will be if you don't carry this man. I'm kind of tuckered, but I ain't too tuckered to shoot.' So two of them carried him, and I went along with my pistol till we come to a place where surgeons was carving men up and I handed over the lootenant. He come to as I did so, and said, 'You scoundrel, you made me retreat. I'll never forgive you!' I said, 'Ezra, they're going to saw your leg off and you'll never fight again, but I'll bury William if it's the last thing I do.' He says, 'Is that a promise?' And I says, 'That's a promise. But it ain't a promise to you — it's one I made to your pa.'

"So I stayed with him and helped hold him while they sawed his leg off. They havin' run out of chloroform, it took four of us to hold him.

And when it was over he was unconscious, and they put him in a car with some others and took him away. So I went back to the house where the burial men were loafing. It was pretty ruined, but I found a shingle that was almos' clean and I wrote on it, in the light of a fire, 'cause it was dark then:

CAPT. WILLIAM ARMSTRONG
COMMANDING CO. B., 39 CONNECTICUT
He was an awful good man

"Then I borrowed a spade from this burial party. We had an argument about it, but I persuaded them with my pistol and I started off toward the Rebel lines. I hadn't gone very far when I come to a place which was thick with men moanin' and screamin' and lots that wasn't sayin' nothing at all. I didn't want to walk on them an' I couldn't help them, having nothing on me but a shingle and a spade and a pistol, an' I decided I couldn't find the captain in the dark anyhow, so I set down and tried to sleep, for I was tuckered. But they was one man bothered me. He kep' callin' out, 'Won't someone for Jesus Christ's sake kill me? Won't someone kill me?' And he kep' it up so long I knew he couldn't die and was in pain. So I crept around till I located him and I says, 'Is it bad, brother?' And he says, 'For Christ's sake kill me. I can't die.' So I felt around in my pockets and found a sulphur match and looked at him and he was all torn to pieces. And I said, 'I don't blame you. I'll do it.' And he says, 'God bless you.' So I took out my pistol and put it right between his eyes and shot him. Then I threw away my pistol. I set there waitin' for the dawn. It was a long time comin'.

"When it come gray, I started out with my shingle and my spade and I went along till I was challenged by the Rebel pickets and sentries. I answered, 'Union burial detail. I'm comin' for to bury my captain.' They begun shootin' at me and I don't know as I blame them. I was comin' out of the mist and they couldn't see that I was alone an' wasn't armed. So they shot real hard, and one bullet struck me in the left thigh and I fell down. Fortunately I had a belt, and I sat up and took it off and strapped it real tight over my wound, and my britches was tight at the waist so they didn't come down, and I got up and went on.

"They stopped shootin' and a man with a bayonet got up and said, 'Yank, you're my pris'ner.' And I said, 'I know I be, but I ain't your pris'ner till I bury my captain.' And I held up my shingle and spade. He said, 'Where's he lie?' And I said, 'About quarter mile from here and maybe a few rods, under a mean little oak tree; and,' I says, 'you take me there and I'll bury him and then I'm your pris'ner. They ain't goin' to stuff my captain into no ditch,' I says. He says, 'You may be crazy, Yank, or you may be a spy. You come with me an' I'll turn you over to the captain.'

" 'Your captain alive?' I asks.

" 'I reckon so,' he says.

" 'Mine's dead,' I says, 'and I aim for to bury him.'

"So he tuk me away with his bayonet in my back and the blood was squilchin' in my boot, but I got along to where his captain was and the captain asked questions, and the Rebel soldier, he tol' all he knew, an' the captain says, 'Where's he lie?' An' I says, 'By a mean little oak, where our lines was yesterday mornin'.'

"An' the captain says, 'That ain't far away. I'll send a detail to bury him.' I says, 'Ain't nobody goin' to bury the captain but me,' I says. 'After that, I'll be your pris'ner.'

"They was a young man dressed up all pretty with gold braid on his uniform, and he laughed kind of loud and he says, 'Saves us the trouble of buryin' him!' an' the captain turns to him, real stern, and says, 'Lootenant, this is a brave soldier,' he says, 'who come back under fire and was wounded to bury his company commander and give himself up as pris'ner. I will not have him insulted or laughed at,' he says. Then he turns to me an' says, 'What is your name an' rank?'

" 'Corporal Nathan Hardy, Co. B, 39th Connecticut,' I says.

"An' he says, 'Corporal, you and I an' these men,' turnin' around to the five or six Rebs who was listenin', 'will go together to find your captain.'

"So we went and I found him, underneath that mean little oak tree, and he looked dreadful. His eyes was open and they was an awful lot of blood on his shirt where his coat was open, and he was lyin' all sprangled out an' undignified. An' the first thing I done was to straighten him out. I spit on my sleeve and wiped the blood off his mouth the best I could. An' I closed his eyes an' buttoned his coat an' crossed his arms. They was kind of stiff, but I done it, an' I brushed him off and layed him out.

"Then I started diggin', an' it would have been easy if it hadn't been for my leg and all the blood in my boot. Six foot four or thereabouts it was, and three foot deep — not as deep as I wanted, but I couldn't dig no deeper, I was so tuckered. But it was an honest grave, for I was real handy with a spade in them days. Then I stood up and said, 'Will two o' you Rebs hand the captain to me?' Which they done, and I laid him

in the grave. An' as I stood lookin' down at him lyin' there, I says to myself, 'Ain't nobody goin' to shovel no dirt on the captain's face — nobody, nobody at all, not even me!' So I took my coat off and laid it over
him, coverin' up his face best I could. I didn't want to go to no Rebel
prison in my shirt, but I wouldn't have no one shovel dirt on the captain.

"Then the two Rebs pulled me out of the grave, real gentle and considerate. An' then I noticed they was a Rebel general there settin' on a
blood horse. How long he bin there I don't know. He looked at me and
see I was wounded and peaked, and he says, stern an' hard, 'Captain,
what's the meanin' of this? This man's wounded and weak,' he says. 'Do
you force wounded men to bury the dead?'

"The captain went over to him and began talkin' to him low and
earnest, seemed like, all the time I was fillin' in the grave. An' when I
had patted the mound even, so it looked good, and had stuck the shingle
in the new earth at the head of the grave, I come over to where the general was, limpin' and leanin' on my spade, an' I saluted — couldn't
help it; I kind of forgot he was a Rebel — an' I says, 'General, I'm
your pris'ner. I buried my captain. I ain't a great hand at askin' favors,
an' your captain and these Rebs has been real good to me. But I wanta
ask one more. I was raised Episcopal, and so was the captain. I'd kind
of like to say a prayer before I surrender.' "

Here Mr. Hardy seemed to doze for a little. "Where was I?" he asked,
rousing after a few minutes.

"You had just gone up to the general and asked if you could say a
prayer before you surrendered."

"Yes, yes, so it was. The general said, 'Corporal Hardy, I am an Episcopalian too, and you shall say your prayer.'

"So he dismounted and took off his hat, and he and I kneeled down
by the grave, and it was awful hard for me to kneel. And when we was
there kneelin' I looked up for a minute and all them Rebs was standin'
with their caps off and their heads bowed, nice and decent, just like
Northern people. An' then I had a dreadful time, for to save my life I
couldn't remember a prayer, not a line, not a word. I had heard the
burial service often enough and too often, what with Pa and Ma an' all
kinds of relatives, but my brains was all watery an' thin, seemed like, an'
I couldn't remember nothin' at all. I don't know how long 'twas till something come driftin' into my mind. It wa'n't from the burial service; 'twas
somethin' we used to chant in Evenin' Prayer. So I says it, loud as I
could, for I was gettin' awful feeble.

" 'Lord,' I says, 'now lettest Thou Thy servant depart in peace, according to Thy Word . . .' An' I couldn't remember or say any more. The general he helped me to my feet, spade an' all, an' I looked him in the face and, by creepers, they was tears in his beard. Soon as I could speak I says, 'General, you've been real good to me and I thank you. An' now I'm your pris'ner, wherever you want to send me.'

"An' he says, 'Corporal Hardy, you will never be a pris'ner of our people as long as I live and command this corps.'

"An' I broke in, awful scared he had misunderstood, and I says, 'General, you don't think I was prayin' for *me* to go in peace! I'm your pris'ner; I'm not askin' for no favors. I was thinkin' of the captain — and me too, perhaps, but not that way. I can go anywhere now. I — '

"He cut me short. 'Corporal Hardy,' he says, 'I know to Whom you was prayin' and why, an' I haven't misunderstood you at all. Captain,' he says, 'I want a detail of six men an' a stretcher and a flag of truce to take this brave soldier an' — an' Christian gentleman back to the Union lines; an' I want this message, which I have dictated and signed, delivered to the commanding officer to be forwarded through channels to the Secretary of War or the President. Those people can hardly decline this courtesy, under the circumstances. Wait, Carter, I wish to add a few lines.' So he put the paper against his saddle and he wrote for some time.

"Then, kind of in a dream, I heard the Rebel captain say, 'Sir, if the general permits, I would like to lead this detail to the Union lines and ask to be blindfolded and deliver your message to the Division commander.'

"An' the general says, 'Captain, I am very glad you made that request, and I commend your behavior. It is only fittin' that the officer escortin' Corporal Hardy with my message should be of field rank, and I shall put in my order for your promotion. You are a pretty good soldier, yourself,' he says — only he didn't say it that way.

"All this time I was kind of waverin' around, but I heard most all they said; and because I was feeble from losing blood an' the battle an' buryin' the captain an' a kind of feverish feelin', things begun to spin around, and I started walkin' this way and that way with my spade, tryin' to stand up, knowin' I couldn't much longer. I heard someone yell, 'Catch him!' An' the next thing I knowed I was in a bed of straw and they was probin' for the bullet in my leg. Then I don't remember nothin' till I woke up in a bed, a clean bed, with a nice-lookin' woman leanin' over me, wipin' my head with a cold, wet towel. I says, 'Where am I?'

"An' she says, 'You're in the hospital of the Sanitary Commission in

Washington. An' oh, Corporal Hardy,' she says, 'I'm so glad you're conscious, for today the President is comin' to give you the Medal of Honor.' An' I says, 'Listen, sister, I gotta get out of here. I don't care for no President or no medal — I gotta bury the captain. He's lyin' down there under a mean little oak. Gimme my clothes,' I says; 'I want a spade and a shingle.' An' she says, 'Corporal, you buried your captain an' buried him fine. That's why the President is comin' to see you. Now you just drink this and go to sleep for a while, and I'll wake you when the President comes.'

"So I drank it and kind of slept, and when I woke up there was Old Abe, the ugliest man I ever see, leanin' over and pinnin' something to my nightshirt, an' he says, 'Corporal Hardy, even the enemy call you a brave soldier and a good man. Congress has voted you this medal. God bless you,' he says."

Mr. Hardy yawned and closed his eyes, and leaned against the haymow. He had told the tale he had to tell — once, to one person.

"But, Mr. Hardy," I said, "what happened to the lieutenant, and who was Elizabeth?" I wanted the story all tied up in ribbons.

"Who?" he said. "The lootenant? Oh, Ezra come back and married Elizabeth and they went to live in Massachusetts. Seems he went aroun' sayin' he couldn't live in no town where people pointed at him and thought he had run away leavin' his dead brother. Naturally no one done so or thought so. But, for all his stompin' and shoutin', he was sensitive, an' he bore me a grudge for takin' him away. I don't see as how I could a done different. I'd promised the old Judge I'd look after his boys an' I've allus aimed to keep my promises."

Just then my father came up to us. It was unlike Mr. Hardy to sit in the shade while other men had started to work again, and Father looked worried. "How are you feeling, Nathan?" he asked.

"Why, John, I'm plumb tuckered out, and that's a fact. I don't know as I can do much more work today. Seems like I never did fare good under these mean little oak trees," and he glanced sharply at me with an expression that was almost a wink. We shared a secret.

Father looked startled, as if he thought Mr. Hardy's wits were wandering. "I tell you what, Nathan," he said, "you've had all the sun you need. I'll send the wagon and they'll take you up to the house, where you can be cool and rest for a while." And, for once in his life, Mr. Hardy made no protest over having "favors" done for him. Father took me aside. "Jackie," he said, "you run up to the house and tell your mother to make the bed in the spare room ready, and then you go to the village and tell Dr. Fordyce he's wanted. I don't like Nathan's looks."

Before I started running I glanced at Mr. Hardy, and I saw what Father meant. He was pale and flushed in the wrong places, though I hadn't noticed it at all when he was telling me about Chancellorsville.

So Mr. Hardy was put to bed in the spare room, and given such care and aid as we knew how to give. For several days he lay quietly enough, and, as I look back on it after all these years, I think that the weight and burden of his long, valiant struggle must suddenly have proved too great. He couldn't go on forever. Mr. Hardy was tuckered out.

Then for some time he alternated between unconsciousness and a mild delirium. He kept mumbling phrases: "Take that quid out o' your mouth. 'Tain't soldierly!" . . . "Ain't nobody goin' to bury the captain but me." I knew what lots of his bewildered sayings meant, but there were many which were obscure. I sat with him every day for an hour or so when the rest of the household were busy, and I had instructions to call my elders if Mr. Hardy needed help or became conscious.

One day he opened his eyes and said, "Here I am and I'm real easy in my mind — but I can't just remember what I said." I went out and called my parents, who told me to stay outside. But I listened and I heard Mr. Hardy say, "Call the boy in. He knows what I want said and I can't remember. He's young and 'twon't hurt him and he'll forget." So Mother beckoned me to come in and I said, "What can I do, Mr. Hardy?"

"You can say what I said for the captain when I knelt down with the general."

So I knelt down, and, having the parrotlike memory of childhood, I said, "You knelt down and so did the general, and then you couldn't remember any of the words of the burial service, but you did remember something that was sung in the evening, and you said, 'Lord, now lettest Thou Thy servant depart in peace, according to Thy Word . . .'" And I began to cry.

"That's right," he said very faintly, "that's right; that's it. Yes, Captain . . ."

My mother gathered me up and took me out and held me very close, rocking back and forth with me while I wept out how I loved Mr. Hardy and what a good man he was.

And that was why I was sent to my aunt and cousins at New London, where I could swim and fish and forget about battles and wounds and Mr. Hardy. But I didn't forget.

A True Story

Repeated Word for Word as I Heard It

by MARK TWAIN

*To understand Mark Twain, his friend Howells once said,
you must understand that he was both a Southerner and a
Westerner. This was Mark Twain's first contribution to the
Atlantic, and for it, after considerable discussion in the editorial offices, he was paid $60.*

NOVEMBER 1874

It was summertime, and twilight. We were sitting on the porch of the
farmhouse, on the summit of the hill, and "Aunt Rachel" was sitting
respectfully below our level, on the steps — for she was our servant,
and colored. She was of mighty frame and stature; she was sixty years
old, but her eye was undimmed and her strength unabated. She was a
cheerful, hearty soul, and it was no more trouble for her to laugh than
it is for a bird to sing. She was under fire, now, as usual when the day
was done. That is to say, she was being chaffed without mercy, and was
enjoying it. She would let off peal after peal of laughter, and then sit
with her face in her hands and shake with throes of enjoyment which
she could no longer get breath enough to express. At such a moment as
this a thought occurred to me, and I said, "Aunt Rachel, how is it that
you've lived sixty years and never had any trouble?"

She stopped quaking. She paused, and there was a moment of silence.
She turned her face over her shoulder toward me, and said, without
even a smile in her voice, "Misto C——, is you in 'arnest?"

It surprised me a good deal, and it sobered my manner and my
speech, too. I said, "Why, I thought — that is, I meant — why, you
can't have had any trouble. I've never heard you sigh, and never seen
your eye when there wasn't a laugh in it."

She faced fairly around, now, and was full of earnestness. "Has I had any trouble? Misto C——, I's gwyne to tell you, den I leave it to you. I was bawn down 'mongst de slaves; I knows all 'bout slavery, 'ca'se I ben one of 'em my own se'f. Well, say, my ole man — dat's my husban' — he was lovin' an' kind to me, jist as kind as you is to yo' own wife. An' we had chil'en — seven chil'en — an' we loved dem chil'en jist de same as you loves yo' chil'en. Dey was black, but de Lord can't make no chil'en so black but what they mother loves 'em an' wouldn't give 'em up, no, not for anything dat's in dis whole world.

"Well, sah, I was raised in ole Fo'ginny, but my mother she was raised in Maryland; an' my *souls* she was turrible when she'd git started! My *lan'* but she'd make de fur fly! When she'd git into dem tantrums, she always had one word dat she said. She'd straighten herse'f up an' put her fists in her hips an' say, 'I want you to understan' dat I wa'n't bawn in de mash to be fool' by trash! I's one o' de ole Blue Hen's Chickens, I is!' 'Ca'se, you see, dat's what folks dat's bawn in Maryland calls deyselves, an' dey's proud of it. Well, dat was her word. I don't ever forgit it, beca'se she said it so much, an' beca'se she said it one day when my little Henry tore his wris' awful, an' most busted his head, right up at de top of his forehead, an' de niggers didn't fly aroun' fas' enough to 'tend to him. An' when dey talk' back at her, she up an' she says, 'Look-a-heah!' she says, 'I want you niggers to understan' dat I wa'n't bawn in de mash to be fool' by trash! I's one o' de ole Blue Hen's Chickens, *I* is!' an' den she clar' dat kitchen an' bandage' up de chile herse'f. So I says dat word, too, when I's riled.

"Well, bymeby my ole mistis say she's broke, an' she got to sell all de niggers on de place. An' when I heah day dey gwyne to sell us all off at oction in Richmon', oh de good gracious! I know what dat mean!"

Aunt Rachel had gradually risen, while she warmed to her subject, and now she towered above us, black against the stars.

"Dey put chains on us, an' put us on a stan' as high as dis po'ch — twenty foot high — an' all de people stood aroun', crowds an' crowds. An' dey'd come up dah an' look at us all roun', an' squeeze our arm, an' make us git up an' walk, an' den say, 'Dis one too ole,' or 'Dis one lame,' or 'Dis one don't 'mount to much.' An' dey sole my ole man, an' took him away, an' dey begin to sell my chil'en an' take *dem* away, an' I begin to cry; an' de man say, 'Shet up yo' dam blubberin',' an' hit me on de mouf wid his han'. An' when de las' one was gone but my little Henry, I grab' *him* clost up to my breas' so, an' I ris up an' says, 'You shan't take him away,' I says, 'I'll kill de man dat tetches him!' I says. But my little Henry whisper an' say, 'I gwyne to run away, an' den I work an' buy yo' freedom.' Oh, bless de chile, he always so good! But dey got him — dey got him, de men did; but I took and tear de clo'es mos' off of 'em, an' beat 'em over de head wid my chain; an' *dey* give it to *me*, too, but I didn't mine dat.

"Well, dah was my ole man gone, an' all my chil'en, all my seven chil'en — an' six of 'em I hain't set eyes on ag'in to dis day, an' dat's twenty-two year ago las' Easter. De man dat bought me b'long' in Newbern, an' he took me dah. Well, bymeby de years roll on an' de waw come. My marster he was a Confedrit colonel, an' I was his family's cook. So when de Unions took dat town, dey all run away an' lef' me all by myse'f wid de other niggers in dat mons'us big house. So de big Union officers move in dah, an' dey ask me would I cook for *dem.* 'Lord bless you,' says I, 'dat's what I's *for.*'

"Dey wa'n't no small-fry officers, mine you, dey was de biggest dey *is;* an' de way dey made dem sojers mosey roun'! De Gen'l he tole me to boss dat kitchen; an' he say, 'If anybody come meddlin' wid you, you jist make 'em walk chalk; don't you be afeard,' he say; 'you's 'mong frens, now.'

"Well, I thinks to myse'f, if my little Henry ever got a chance to run away, he'd make to de Norf, o' course. So one day I comes in dah whah de big officers was, in de parlor, an' I drops a kurtchy, so, an' I up an' tole 'em 'bout my Henry, dey a-listenin' to my troubles jist de same as if I was white folks; an' I says, 'What I come for is beca'se if he got away and got up Norf whah you gemmen comes from, you might 'a' seen him, maybe, an' could tell me so as I could fine him ag'in; he was very little, an' he had a sk-yar on his lef' wris', an' at de top of his forehead.' Den dey look mournful, an' de Gen'l say, 'How long sence you los' him?' an' I say, 'Thirteen year.' Den de Gen'l say, 'He wouldn't be little no mo', now — he's a man!'

"I never thought o' dat befo'! He was only dat little feller to *me,* yit. I never thought 'bout him growin' up an' bein' big. But I see it den. None o' de gemmen had run acrost him, so dey couldn't do nothin' for me. But all dat time, do' I didn't know it, my Henry *was* run off to de Norf, years an' years, an' he was a barber, too, an' worked for hisse'f. An' bymeby, when de waw come, he ups an' he says, 'I'se done barberin',' he says; 'I's gwyne to fine my ole mammy, less'n she's dead.' So he sole out an' went to whah dey was recruitin', an' hired hisse'f out to de colonel for his servant; an' den he went all froo de battles everywhah, huntin' for his ole mammy; yes indeedy, he'd hire to fust one officer an' den another, tell he'd ransacked de whole Souf; but you see *I* didn't know nuffin 'bout dis. How was *I* gwyne to know it?

"Well, one night we had a big sojer ball; de sojers dah at Newbern was always havin' balls an' carryin' on. Dey had 'em in my kitchen, heaps o' times, 'ca'se it was so big. Mine you, I was *down* on sich doin's; be-c'ase my place was wid de officers, an' it rasp' me to have dem common sojers cavortin' roun' my kitchen like dat. But I alway' stood aroun' an' kep' things straight, I did; an' sometimes dey'd git my dander up, an' den I'd make 'em clar dat kitchen, mine I *tell* you!

"Well, one night — it was a Friday night — dey comes a whole plattoon f'm a *nigger* ridgment dat was on guard at de house — de house was headquarters, you know — an' den I was jist *a-bilin'*! Mad? I was jist *a-boomin'*! I swelled aroun', an' swelled aroun'; I jist was a-itchin' for 'em to do somefin for to start me. An' dey was a-waltzin' an' a-dancin'! *my*! but dey was havin' a time! an' I jist a-swellin' an' a-swellin' up! Pooty soon, 'long comes *sich* a spruce young nigger a-sailin' down de room wid a yaller wench round' de wais'; an' roun' an' roun' an' roun' dey went, enough to make a body drunk to look at 'em; an' when dey got abreas' o' me, dey went to kin' o' balancin' aroun', fust on one leg an' den on t'other, an' smilin' at my big red turban, an' makin' fun, an' I ups an' says, 'Git along wid you! rubbage!' De young man's face kin' o' changed, all of a sudden, for 'bout a second, but den he went to smilin' ag'in, same as he was befo'. Well, 'bout dis time, in comes some niggers dat played music an' b'long' to de ban', an' dey *never* could git along widout puttin' on airs. An' de very fust air dey put on dat night, I lit into 'em! Dey laughed, an' dat made me wuss. De res' o' de niggers got to laughin', an' den my soul *alive* but I was hot! My eye was jist a-blazin'! I jist straightened myself up, so — jist as I is now, plum to de ceilin', mos' — an' I digs my fists into my hips, an' I says, 'Look-a-heah!' I says, 'I want you niggers to understan' dat I wa'n't bawn in de mash to be fool' by trash! I's one o' de ole Blue Hen's Chickens, I is!' an' den I see dat young man stan' a-starin' an' stiff, lookin' kin' o' up at de ceilin' like he fo'got somefin, an couldn't 'member it no mo'. Well, I jist march' on dem niggers — so, lookin' like a gen'l — an' dey jist cave' away befo' me an' out at de do'. An' as dis young man was a-goin' out, I heah him say to an-other nigger, 'Jim,' he says, 'you go 'long an' tell de cap'n I be on han' 'bout eight o'clock in de mawnin'; dey's somefin on my mine,' he says; 'I don't sleep no mo' dis night. You go 'long,' he says, 'an' leave me by my own se'f.'

"Dis was 'bout one o'clock in de mawnin'. Well, 'bout seven, I was up an' on han', gittin' de officers' breakfast. I was a-stoopin' down by de stove — jist so, same as if yo' foot was de stove — an' I'd opened de stove do' wid my right han' — so, pushin' it back, jist as I pushes yo' foot — an' I'd jist got de pan o' hot biscuits in my han' an' was 'bout to raise up, when I see a black face come aroun' under mine, an' de eyes a-looking' up into mine, jist as I's a-lookin' up clost under yo' face now; an' I jist stopped *right dah,* an' never budged! Jist gazed, an' gazed, so; an' de pan begin to tremble, an' all of a sudden I *knowed!* De pan drop' on de flo' an' I grab his lef' han' an' shove back his sleeve — jist so, as I's doin' to you — an' den I goes for his forehead an' push de hair back, so, an' 'Boy!' I says, 'if you an't my Henry, what is you doin' wid dis welt on yo' wris' an' dat sk-yar on yo' forehead? De Lord God ob heaven be praise', I got my own ag'in!'

"Oh, no, Misto C——, *I* hain't had no trouble. An' no *joy!*"

Lee in Battle

by GAMALIEL BRADFORD, JR.

A native of Massachusetts and a man of frail physique, Gamaliel Bradford, Jr., husbanded his strength for the research and writing of biographical portraits.

AUGUST 1911

We like to imagine the master mind in a great conflict controlling everything, down to the minutest detail. But with vast modern armies this is far from being the case, even with the elaborate electrical facilities of today; and in Lee's time those facilities were much less complete. Lee himself indicated the difficulty humorously when he was remonstrated with for taking risks, and answered, "I wish someone would tell me my proper place in battle. I am always told I should not be where I am." And he expressed it with entire seriousness when he said, "During the battle my direction is of more harm than use; I must then rely on my division and brigade commanders. I think and I act with all my might to bring up my troops to the right place at the right moment; after that I have done my duty."

Some critics hold that Lee was inclined to carry the principle much too far. What impresses me in this, as in other things, is the nice balance of his gifts. Persons by nature predisposed to direct others almost always seek to direct them in everything. How wise and constant Lee's direction was, where he thought it needed, is shown by his son's remark: "We were always fully instructed as to the best way to get to Lexington, and, indeed, all the roads of life were carefully marked out for us by him." Yet the instant he reached the limit of what he felt to be his province, he drew back and left decision to others whom he knew to be, by nature or position, better qualified.

The amount of Lee's direction and influence seems to have varied greatly in different battles. At Fredericksburg he adopted a central position whence he could survey the whole field. Colonel Long's remarks in describing this must have given Longstreet exquisite pleasure. "In the battle Longstreet had his headquarters at the same place, so that Lee was able to keep his hand on the rein of his 'old war horse' and to direct him where to apply his strength." At Antietam critics are agreed that Lee's management of things was perfect. "He utilized every available soldier; throughout the day he controlled the Confederate operations over the whole field." On the other hand, in the Peninsular battles, owing perhaps to imperfect organization and staff arrangements, his hold on the machine was much less complete; and at Gettysburg the vast extension of his lines made immediate personal direction almost impossible, with results that were disastrous.

It is at Gettysburg that we get one of the most vivid of the few pictures left us of Lee in the very midst of the crash and tumult of conflict. It is from the excellent pen of General Alexander, who says that the commander-in-chief rode up entirely alone, just after Pickett's charge, "and remained with me for a long time. He then probably first appreciated the extent of the disaster, as the disorganized stragglers made their way back past us. . . . It was certainly a momentous thing to him to see that superb attack end in such a bloody repulse. But, whatever his emotions, there was no trace of them in his calm and self-possessed bearing. I thought at that time his coming there very imprudent, and the absence of all his staff officers and couriers strange. It could only have happened by his express intention. I have since thought it possible that he came, thinking the enemy might follow in pursuit of Pickett, personally to rally stragglers about our guns and make a desperate defense. He had the instincts of a soldier within him as strongly as any man. . . . No soldier could have looked on at Pickett's charge and not burned to be in it. To have a personal part in a close and desperate fight at that moment would, I believe, have been at heart a great pleasure to General Lee, and possibly he was looking for one."

And I ask myself how much of that born soldier's lust for battle, keen enjoyment of danger and struggle and combat, Lee really had. Certainly there is little record of his speaking of any such feeling. At various times he expressed a keen sense of all the horrors of war. "You have no idea of what a horrible sight a battlefield is." And again, "What a cruel thing is war; to separate and destroy families and friends, and mar the purest joys and happiness God has granted us in this world; to fill our hearts with hatred instead of love for our neighbors, and to devastate the fair face of this beautiful world." One vivid sentence, spoken in the midst of the slaughter of Fredericksburg, lights the man's true instincts like a flash: "It is well that war is so terrible, or else we might grow too fond of it."

As to Lee's personal courage, of course the only point to be discussed is the peculiar quality of it. Judging from his character generally and from all that is recorded of him, I should not take his courage to consist in a temperamental indifference to danger, a stolid disregard of its very existence, such as we find perhaps in Grant or Wellington. Though far from being a highly nervous organization, Lee was sensitive, imaginative; and I take it that he had to accustom himself to being under fire and was always aware of any elements of peril there might be about him.

Testimony to his entire coolness in battle is of course abundant. I do not know that there is any more striking general statement than that of Cooke in reference to the second battle of Bull Run: "The writer of these pages chanced to be near the commander at this moment and was vividly impressed by the air of unmoved calmness which marked his countenance and demeanor. Nothing in the expression of his face, and no hurried movement, indicated excitement or anxiety. Here, as on many other occasions, Lee impressed the writer as an individual gifted with the most surprising faculty of remaining cool and unaffected in the midst of circumstances calculated to arouse the most phlegmatic." A concrete instance of his self-possession in the midst of turmoil is narrated by a Union soldier: "A prisoner walked up to him and told him a Rebel had stolen his hat. In the midst of his orders he stopped and told the Rebel to give back the hat and saw that he done it, too."

I am not aware that Lee was wounded at any time during the war, or indeed in his life, except slightly at Chapultepec. His hands were severely injured just before Antietam, but this was by the falling of his horse. He was, however, again and again under fire. At Antietam, A. P. Hill, who was close to the general, had his horse's forelegs shot off. On another occasion, when Lee was sitting with Stuart and his staff, "a shell fell plump in their midst, burying in the earth with itself one of General Lee's gauntlets, which lay on the ground only a few feet from the general himself." In 1864 Lee was inspecting the lines below Richmond, and the number of soldiers gathered about him drew the enemy's fire rather heavily. The general ordered the men back out of range and he himself followed at his leisure; but it was observed that he stopped to pick up something. A fledgling sparrow had fallen from its nest, and he took it from the ground and tenderly replaced it, with the bullets whistling about him.

As the following incident shows, Lee was extremely solicitous about the unnecessary exposure of his men. Once, when he was watching the effect of the fire on an advanced battery, a staff officer rode up to him by the approach which was least protected. The general reprimanded him for his carelessness, and when the young man urged that he could not seek cover himself while his chief was in the open, Lee answered sharply, "It is my duty to be here. Go back the way I told you, sir." At another time Lee had placed himself in a very exposed position, to the horror of all his officers. They could not prevail upon him to come down, so finally General Gracie stepped forward and interposed himself between his commander and the enemy. "Why, Gracie," protested Lee, "you will certainly be killed." "It is better, General, that I should be killed than you. When you get down, I will." Lee smiled and got down.

When things became really critical, Lee completely threw aside all caution. In the terrific battles of the Wilderness, where at times it seemed as if Grant would succeed in breaking through, the Confederate general repeatedly (on three separate occasions, as it appears) rushed to the front to rally his men and charge, like Ney or Murat, at the head of them. "Go back, General Lee, go back!" shouted the soldiers. But he would not go back till they had promised to do as much for him as they could have done with him. And they did as much. No men could have done more.

It was this occasional fury of combativeness which made Longstreet assert that the general was sometimes unbalanced, not by any personal exposure or excitement, but by critical situations affecting the army as a whole. Longstreet, defending his own conduct at Gettysburg, urges that Lee was particularly overwrought at the time of that battle. In what is, to say the least, peculiar phraseology, he writes of his commander: "That he was excited and off his balance was evident on the afternoon of the first, and that he labored under that oppression till blood enough was shed to appease him." The suggestion that Lee required blood to appease him is grotesque, and his loyal admirers ridicule the idea that at Gettysburg he was unbalanced. But there is evidence besides Longstreet's that, once in a fight, he hated to give it up and perhaps occasionally allowed his ardor to overcome his discretion. The Prussian officer Scheibert remarks that while at Chancellorsville Lee was admirably calm, at Gettysburg he was restless and uneasy. General Anderson bears witness that at Gettysburg his chief was "very much disturbed and depressed."

The most heroic picture that is left us of Lee high-wrought by the excitement of battle and determined to fight to the end is the account, received by Henderson from a reliable eyewitness, of the chief's decision to remain north of the Potomac after Antietam. General after general rode up to the commander's headquarters, all with the same tale of discouragement and counsel of retreat. Hood was quite unmanned. "My God!" cried Lee to him, with unwonted vehemence, "where is the splendid division you had this morning?" "They are lying on the field where you sent them," answered Hood. Even Jackson did not venture to suggest anything but withdrawal. There were a few moments of oppressive silence. Then Lee rose erect in his stirrups and said, "Gentlemen, we will not cross the Potomac tonight. You will go to your respective commands, strengthen your lines, send two officers from each brigade towards the ford to collect your stragglers and bring them up. Many have come in. I have had the proper steps taken to collect all the men who are in the rear. If McClellan wants to fight in the morning, I will give him battle. *Go!*" They went, and in this case, at least, Lee's glorious audacity was justified; for he proved to all the world that McClellan did not dare attack him again.

However Lee's judgment may have been affected by the excitement of battle, it made little alteration in his bearing or manner. Fremantle tells us that the general's dress was always neat and clean, and adds, "I observed this during the three days fight at Gettysburg, when every one else looked and was extremely dirty." Stress of conflict sometimes seems to alter men's natures. Odd stories are told in the war books of officers quite saintly in common converse who in battle would swear like reprobates. Lee's politeness was always exquisite. It was only very, very rarely that some untoward incident stirred either his temper or his speech. "Probably no man ever commanded an army and, at the same time, so entirely commanded himself as Lee," says the cool-blooded Alexander. "This morning [after Chancellorsville] was almost the only occasion on which I ever saw him out of humor."

Nor was it only a question of mere politeness. Lee was as tender and sympathetic to man and beast in the fury of combat, in the chaos of defeat, as he could have been in his own domain at Arlington. After the great charge on the third day at Gettysburg, an officer rode up to him lashing an unwilling horse. "Don't whip him, Captain, don't whip him," protested the general. "I have just such another foolish beast myself, and whipping doesn't do any good." And as the tumult of disaster increased, the sympathy took larger forms of magnanimity than mere prevention of cruelty to animals. There was no faultfinding, no shifting of perhaps deserved blame to others, nothing but calmness, comfort, cheerfulness, confidence. "All will come right in the end; we'll talk of it afterwards, but in the meantime all good men must rally." "Never mind, General. All this has been my fault. It is I that have lost this fight, and you must help me out of it the best way you can."

So, with incomparable patience, tact, and energy, the great soldier held his army together after defeat and kept it in a temper and condition which went far to justify Meade's reluctance to follow up his success. Only, to complete the picture, one should turn to General Imboden's brief sketch, taken after the work was done and natural human exhaustion and despair claimed some little right over even a hero's nerve and brain. It must be remembered that this was a man fifty-six years old. Toward midnight Lee rode up to Imboden's command. "When he approached and saw us, he spoke, reined up his horse and endeavored to dismount. The effort to do so betrayed so much physical exhaustion that I stepped forward to assist him, but before I reached him, he had alighted. He threw his arm across his saddle to rest himself and fixing his eyes upon the ground, leaned in silence upon his equally weary horse; the two formed a striking group, as motionless as a statue. After some expressions as to Pickett's charge, etc., he added in a tone almost of agony, 'Too bad! Too bad! Oh, too bad!' "

With the portrait of Lee himself in the shock of battle we should put a background of his soldiers and their feeling as he came among them. We have already heard their passionate cry when he rushed to put himself at their head and charge into the thickest of the fight. "Go back, General Lee! Go back!" General Gordon, who loved to throw a high light of eloquence on all such scenes, describes this one with peculiar vividness, giving his own remonstrance, "These men are Georgians, Virginians, and Carolinians. They have never failed you on any field. They will not fail you now. Will you, boys?" and the enthusiastic answer, "No, no, no!" Those who like the quiet truth of history, even when it chills, will be interested in an eyewitness's simple comment on this picturesque narrative. "Gordon says, 'We need no such encouragement.' At this some of our soldiers called out, 'No, no!' Gordon continuing, said, 'There is not a soldier in the Confederate army who would not gladly lay down his life to save you from harm'; but the men did not respond to this last proposition."

It cannot be doubted, however, that Lee's personal influence in critical moments was immense. On one occasion, just before battle, there was heard to pass from mouth to mouth as a sort of watchword the simple comment, "Remember, General Lee is looking at us." Stuart's aide, Von Borcke, describes a scene which is immensely effective as showing how little the general relied on words, and how little he needed to. Lee was riding through the ranks before a charge. "He uttered no word. He simply removed his hat and passed bare-headed along the line. I had it from one who witnessed the act. 'It was,' said he, 'the most eloquent address ever delivered.' And a few minutes later he heard a youth, crying and reloading his musket, shout through his tears that 'any man who would not fight after what General Lee said was a damned coward.' "

Perhaps the most splendid battlepiece of Lee in the midst of his fighting soldiers is Colonel Marshall's account of the triumphant advance on the third day at Chancellorsville. The enemy were retiring and the troops swept forward through the tumult of battle and the smoke of woods and dwellings burning about them. Everywhere the field was strewn with the wounded and dying of both armies. "In the midst of this scene General Lee, mounted upon that horse which we all remember so well, rode to the front of his advancing battalions. His presence was the signal for one of those uncontrollable outbursts of enthusiasm which none can appreciate who have not witnessed them. The fierce soldiers, with their faces blackened with the smoke of battle, the wounded, crawling with feeble limbs from the fury of the devouring flames, all seemed possessed with a common impulse. One long unbroken cheer, in which the feeble cry of those who lay helpless on the earth blended with the strong voices of those who still fought, rose high above the roar of battle, and hailed the presence of the victorious chief. He sat in the full realization of all that soldiers dream of — triumph."

This was victory. But there came a day of defeat, when the Army of Northern Virginia, after four years of fighting and triumphing and suffering, shrunk almost to nothing, saw their great commander ride away to make his submission to a generous conqueror. Their love, their loyalty, their confidence, were no less than they had ever been. If he said further fighting was useless and inhuman, it must be so.

But this very absolute confidence increased the weight of the terrible decision. All these thousands trusted him to decide for them. He must decide rightly. What the burden was we can only imagine, never know. But under the noble serenity maintained by habitual effort, good observers detected signs of the struggle that must be taking place. "His face was still calm, but his carriage was no longer erect, as his soldiers had been used to see it. The trouble of those last days had already ploughed great furrows in his forehead. His eyes were red as if with weeping; his cheeks sunken and haggard; his face colorless. No one who looked upon him then, as he stood there in full view of the disastrous end, can ever forget the intense agony written upon his features. And yet he was calm, self-possessed, and deliberate." So great was his anguish that it wrung a wish to end it all, even from a natural self-control complete as his. "How easily I could get rid of this and be at rest. I have only to ride along the lines and all will be over. But," he quickly added, "it is our duty to live, for what will become of the women and children of the South if we are not here to support and protect them?"

So the decision had to be made. And he made it. "Then there is nothing left me but to go and see General Grant, and I would rather die a thousand deaths." His officers protested passionately, "Oh, General, what will history say of the surrender of the army in the field?" "Yes, I know, they will say hard things of us; they will not understand how we were overwhelmed by numbers; but that is not the question, Colonel; the question is, is it right to surrender this army? If it is right, then I will take all the responsibility."

The scene that ensued has been described often: the plain farmhouse room; the officers curious, yet respectful; the formal conversation, as always painfully unequal to the huge event it covered; the short, ungainly, ill-dressed man, as dignified in his awkwardness almost as the royal, perfectly appointed figure that conferred with him. Lee bore himself nobly, say his admirers; nobly, but a little coldly, say his opponents. And who shall blame him? Then it was over. One moment he paused at the door, as he went out, waiting for his horse, and as he paused, looking far into the tragic future or the tragic past, he struck his gauntleted hands together in a gesture of immense despair, profoundly significant for so self-contained a man. Then he rode away, back to his children, back to the Army of Northern Virginia, who had seen him daily for three years and now would never see him any more.

A Rebel's Recollections

by GEORGE CARY EGGLESTON

At the age of seventeen, George Cary Eggleston inherited his family's plantation in Amelia County, Virginia, and at twenty-one he saw service in the First Virginia Cavalry under Colonel Jeb Stuart. Thence he transferred to the field artillery, and in the final stage of the war he was in charge of a mortar fort at Petersburg. His series of articles entitled "A Rebel's Recollections," marked as they were by honor and fair-mindedness, showed that by 1874 the Atlantic had at last made its peace with the South.

DECEMBER 1874

I think we must have known from the begining of the campaign of 1864 that the end was approaching, and that it could not be other than a disastrous one. We knew very well that General Lee's army was smaller than it ever had been before. We knew, too, that there were no reinforcements to be had from any source. The conscription had put every man worth counting into the field already, and the little army that met General Grant in the Wilderness represented all that remained of the Confederate strength in Virginia. In the South matters were at their worst, and we knew that not a man could come thence to our assistance. Lee mustered a total strength of about sixty-six thousand men, when we marched out of winter quarters and began in the Wilderness that long struggle which ended nearly a year later at Appomattox. With that army alone the war was to be fought out, and we had to shut our eyes to facts very resolutely, that we might not see how certainly we were to be crushed. And we did shut our eyes so successfully as to hope in a vague, irrational way for the impossible, to the very end.

In the Wilderness we held our own against every assault, and the visible punishment we inflicted upon the foe was so great that hardly any man in our army expected to see a Federal force on our side of the river at daybreak next morning. We thought that General Grant was as badly hurt as Hooker had been on the same field, and confidently expected him to retreat during the night. When we moved by his left flank to Spottsylvania instead, we understood what manner of man he was, and knew that the persistent pounding, which of all things we were least able to endure, had begun. When at last we settled down in the trenches around Petersburg, we ought to have known that the end was rapidly drawing near. We congratulated ourselves instead upon the fact that we had inflicted a heavier loss than we had suffered, and buckled on our armor anew.

If General Grant had failed to break our power of resistance by his sledge-hammer blows, it speedily became evident that he would be more successful in wearing it away by the constant friction of a siege. Without fighting a battle he was literally destroying our army. The sharpshooting was incessant, and the bombardment hardly less so, and under it all our numbers visibly decreased day by day. During the first two months of the siege my own company, which numbered about a hundred and fifty men, lost sixty in killed and wounded, an average of a man a day; and while our list of casualties was greater than that of many other commands, there were undoubtedly some companies and regiments which suffered more than we.

There was no longer any room for hope except in a superstitious belief that Providence would in some way interfere in our behalf, and to that very many betook themselves for comfort. This shifting upon a supernatural power the task we had failed to accomplish by human means rapidly bred many less worthy superstitions among the troops. The general despondency, which amounted almost to despair, doubtless helped to bring about this result, and the great religious "revival" contributed to it in no small degree. I think hardly any man in that army entertained a thought of coming out of the struggle alive. The only question with each was when his time was to come, and a sort of gloomy fatalism took possession of many minds. Believing that they must be killed sooner or later, and that the hour and the manner of their deaths were unalterably fixed, many became singularly reckless and exposed themselves with the utmost carelessness to all sorts of unnecessary dangers.

"I'm going to be killed pretty soon," said as brave a man as I ever knew, to one day. "I never flinched from a bullet until today, and now I dodge every time one whistles within twenty feet of me."

I tried to persuade him out of the belief, and even got for him a dose of valerian with which to quiet his nerves. He took the medicine, but assured me that he was not nervous in the least.

"My time is coming, that's all," he said, "and I don't care. A few days more or less don't signify much." An hour afterward the poor fellow's head was blown off as he stood by my side.

One such incident — and there were many of them — served to confirm a superstitious belief in presentiments which a hundred failures of fulfillment were unable to shake. Meantime the revival went on. Prayer meetings were held in every tent. Testaments were in every hand, and a sort of religious ecstasy took possession of the army. The men had ceased to rely upon the skill of our leaders or the strength of our army for success, and not a few of them hoped now for a miraculous interposition of supernatural power in our behalf.

Men in this mood make the best of soldiers, and at no time were the fighting qualities of the Southern army better than during the siege. Under such circumstances men do not regard death, and even the failure of any effort they were called upon to make wrought no demoralization among troops who had persuaded themselves that the Almighty held victory in store for them and would give it them in due time. Disaster seemed only to strengthen the faith of many. They did their soldierly duties perfectly. They held danger and fatigue alike in contempt. It was their duty as Christian men to obey orders without question, and they did so in the thought that to do otherwise was to sin.

That the confidence bred of these things should be of a gloomy kind was natural enough, and the gloom was not dispelled, certainly, by the conviction of every man that he was assisting at his own funeral. Failure, too, which was worse than death, was plainly inevitable in spite of it all.

When at last the beginning of the end came, in the evacuation of Richmond and the effort to retreat, everything seemed to go to pieces at once. The best disciplinarians in the army relaxed instead of tightening their reins. The best troops became disorganized, and hardly any command marched in a body. Companies were mixed together, parts of each being separated by detachments of others. Flying citizens in vehicles of every conceivable sort accompanied and embarrassed the columns. Many commands marched heedlessly on without orders, and still others had instructions which it was impossible to obey in any case.

At Amelia Court House we should have found a supply of provisions. General Lee had ordered a train load to meet him there, but the interests of the starving army had been sacrificed to the convenience or the cowardice of the President and his personal following. The train had been hurried on to Richmond and its precious cargo of food thrown out there, in order that Mr. Davis and his people might retreat rapidly and comfortably from the abandoned capital. Then began the desertion of which we have heard so much. Up to that time, as far as I can learn, if desertions had occurred at all they had not become general; but now that the government, in flying from the foe, had cut off our only supply of provisions, what were the men to do? Many of them wandered off in search of food, with no thought of deserting at all. Many others followed the example of the government, and fled; but a singularly large proportion of the little whole stayed and starved to the last.

And it was no technical or metaphorical starvation which we had to endure, either, as a brief statement of my own experience will show. The battery to which I was attached was captured near Amelia Court House, and within a mile or two of my home. Seven men only escaped, and as I knew intimately everybody in the neighborhood, I had no trouble in getting horses for these to ride. Applying to General Lee in person for instructions, I was ordered to march on, using my own judgment, and rendering what service I could in the event of a battle. In this independent fashion I marched, with much better chances than most had to get food, and yet during three days and nights our total supply consisted of one ear of corn to the man, and we divided that with our horses.

The end came, technically, at Appomattox, but of the real difficulties of the war the end was not yet. The trials and the perils of utter disorganization were still to be endured, and as the condition in which many parts of the South were left by the fall of the Confederate government was an anomalous one, some account of it seems necessary to the completeness of this series of papers.

Our principal danger was from the lawless bands of marauders who infested the country, and our greatest difficulty in dealing with them lay in the utter absence of constituted authority of any sort. Our country was full of highwaymen of the most brutal description possible, and destitute even of the merit of presenting a respectable appearance. They were simply the deserters from fighting regiments on both sides and Negro desperadoes, who found common ground upon which to fraternize in their common depravity. They moved about in bands, from two to ten strong, cutting horses out of plows, plundering helpless people, and wantonly destroying valuables which they could not carry away. At the house of one of my friends where only ladies lived, a body of these men demanded dinner, which was given them. They then required the mistress of the mansion to fill their canteens with sorghum molasses, which they immediately proceeded to pour over the carpets and furniture of the parlor.

Outrages of this kind and worse were of everyday enactment, and there was no remedy. There was no state, county, or municipal government in existence among us. We had no courts, no justices of the peace, no sheriffs, no officers of any kind invested with a shadow of authority, and there were not men enough in the community, at first, to resist the marauders, comparatively few of the surrendered soldiers having found their way home as yet. Those districts in which the Federal armies were stationed were peculiarly fortunate. The troops gave protection to the people, and the commandants of posts constituted a government able to enforce order, to which outraged or threatened people could appeal. But these favored sections were only a small part of the whole. The troops were not distributed in detached bodies over the country, but were kept in considerable masses at strategic points, lest a guerrilla war should succeed regular hostilities; and so the greater part of the country was left wholly without law at a time when law was most imperatively needed.

I mention this not to the discredit of the victorious army or of its officers. They could not wisely have done otherwise. If the disbanded Confederates had seen fit to inaugurate a partisan warfare, as many of the Federal commanders believed they would, they could have annoyed the army of occupation no little; and so long as the temper of the country in this matter was unknown, it would have been in the last degree improper to station small bodies of troops in exposed situations. Common military prudence dictated the massing of the troops, and as soon as it became evident that we had no disposition to resist further, but were disposed rather to render such assistance as we could in restoring and maintaining order, everything was done which could be done to protect us. It is with a good deal of pleasure that I bear witness to the uniform disposition shown by such Federal officers as I came in contact with at this time, to protect all quiet citizens, to restore order, and to forward the interests of the community they were called upon to govern.

In one case I went with a fellow Confederate to the headquarters nearest me, eighteen miles away, and reported the doings of some marauders in my neighborhood, which had been more than usually outrageous. The general in command at once made a detail of cavalry and instructed its chief to go in pursuit of the highwaymen, and to bring them to him, dead or alive. They were captured, marched at a double-quick to the camp, and shot forthwith by sentence of a drumhead court-martial, a proceeding which did more than almost anything else could have done to intimidate other bands of a like kind. At another time I took to the same officer's camp a number of stolen horses which a party of us had managed to recapture from a sleeping band of desperadoes. Some of the horses we recognized as the property of our neighbors, some we did not know at all, and one or two were branded "C.S." and "U.S." The general promptly returned all the identified horses and lent all the others to farmers in need of them. These things gave us confidence and promoted good feeling.

It is difficult to comprehend, and impossible to describe, the state of uncertainty in which we lived at this time. We had surrendered at discretion, and had no way of discovering or even of guessing what terms were to be given us. We were cut off almost wholly from trustworthy news, and in the absence of papers were unable even to rest conjecture upon the expression of sentiment at the North. Rumors we had in plenty, but so many of them were clearly false that we were forced to reject them all as probably untrue. When we heard it confidently asserted that General Alexander had made a journey to Brazil and brought back a tempting offer to emigrants, knowing all the time that if he had gone he must have made the trip within the extraordinarily brief period of a few weeks, it was difficult to believe other news which reached us through like channels, though much of it ultimately proved true.

I think nobody in my neighborhood believed the rumor of Mr. Lincoln's assassination until it was confirmed by a Federal soldier whom I questioned upon the subject one day, a week or two after the event. When we knew that the rumor was true, we deemed it the worst news we had heard since the surrender. We distrusted President Johnson more than anyone else. Regarding him as a renegade Southerner, we thought it probable that he would endeavor to prove his loyalty to the Union by extra severity to the South, and we confidently believed he would revoke the terms offered us in Mr. Lincoln's amnesty proclamation; wherefore there was a general haste to take the oath and so to secure the benefit of the dead president's clemency before his successor should establish harsher conditions. We should have regarded Mr. Lincoln's death as a calamity, even if it had come about by natural means, and coming as it did through a crime committed in our name, it seemed doubly a disaster.

With the history of the South during the period of reconstruction, all readers are familiar, and it is only the state of affairs between the time of the surrender and the beginning of the rebuilding that I have tried to describe in this paper. But the picture would be inexcusably incomplete without some mention of the Negroes. Their behavior both during and after the war may well surprise anybody not acquainted with the character of the race. When the men of the South were nearly all in the army, the Negroes were left in large bodies on the plantations with nobody to control them except the women and a few old or infirm men. They might have been insolent, insubordinate, and idle, if they had chosen. They might have gained their freedom by asserting it. They might have overturned the social and political fabric at any time, *and they knew all this too.* They were intelligent enough to know that there was no power on the plantations capable of resisting any movement they might choose to make. They did know, too, that the success of the Federal arms would give them freedom. The fact was talked about everywhere, and no effort was made to keep the knowledge of it from them. They knew that to assert their freedom was to give immediate success to the Union cause. Most of them coveted freedom, too, as the heartiness with which they afterwards accepted it abundantly proves. And yet they remained quiet, faithful, and diligent throughout, very few of them giving trouble of any sort, even on plantations where only a few women remained to control them.

The reason for all this must be sought in the Negro character, and we of the South, knowing that character thoroughly, trusted it implicitly. We left our homes and our helpless ones in the keeping of the Africans of our households without any hesitation whatever. We knew these faithful and affectionate people too well to fear that they would abuse such a trust. We concealed nothing from them, and they knew quite as well as we did the issues at stake in the war.

The Negro is constitutionally loyal to his obligations as he understands them, and his attachments, both local and personal, are uncommonly strong. He speedily forgets an injury, but never a kindness, and so he was not likely to rise in arms against the helpless women and children whom he had known intimately and loved almost reverentially from childhood, however strongly he desired the freedom which such a rising would secure to him.

The Negroes remained quietly at work, many of them hoping, doubtless, that freedom for themselves and their fellows might somehow be wrought out, but they were wholly unwilling to make the necessary war upon the whites, to whom they were attached by the strongest possible bonds of affection. And so throughout the war they acted after their kind, waiting for the issue with the great, calm patience which is their most universal characteristic.

V

The Inward Life

The desire to draw close to nature, to be alone and self-sufficient, to escape from the attrition of daily commerce, and to live with the quiet fulfillment the city denies — this urgency presses upon many Americans, sometimes on the young but more often on those approaching forty, as they rebel against routine. It is a life force which has been variously celebrated in the Atlantic: *very early by the romantic, hardy Clarence King, who was so admired by his contemporaries, young Oliver Wendell Holmes, Jr., and young Henry Adams, for his feats of mountaineering in the high Sierra; it is the theme, stated or implicit, in the essays by John Muir and John Burroughs; it recurs again and again in papers by Charles D. Stewart and James Norman Hall and Thomas Barbour and Donald Culross Peattie, to mention a few.*

The inward life is inevitably attended by periods of deep misgiving and loneliness. We know that during his months at Walden, Thoreau was fortified by the pies Mrs. Emerson baked for him and still more by his sustaining friendship with Emerson; the reason for Thoreau's isolation and what it cost him we see in Thornton Wilder's illuminating, brilliant talk at Harvard. We see John Muir's search for the giant sequoias and how he struggled to impart the secret of that forest world to the aging Emerson, and in Thomas Wentworth Higginson's account of his thirty-year friendship with Emily Dickinson we are touchingly admitted to the confidence and loneliness of the village recluse.

It is clear that Miss Dickinson showed her poems to Higginson hoping for reassurance. In his replies he sent her his encouragement and his advice as to how to be more "orderly" in her versification. As his interest warmed, he came to recommend the poems to the proprietors of the Atlantic. *In her book* Ancestors' Brocades, *Millicent Todd Bingham reports the result:*

"My father," she writes, "told me that Colonel Higginson first recommended the poems to Houghton Mifflin Company for publi-

cation, as he was one of their readers at the time. They decided
against it. The poems, they said, were much too queer — the
rhymes were all wrong. They thought that Higginson must be losing his mind to recommend such stuff." Editors are not always infallible.

Helen Keller had to depend upon her inner resources to a
greater extent than any other person who ever wrote for the Atlantic. Hers was the inward life perforce, for she was struck blind,
deaf, and dumb, and when her inspired teacher, Mrs. Anne Sulli-
van Macy, tamed her as a child and then taught her to understand
with finger tips and lip reading, Helen had to imagine for herself a
universe whose dimmest outlines she could never hope to see again.
In January of 1933 Miss Keller wrote, at Ellery Sedgwick's suggestion, a touching paper entitled "Three Days to See." On the first
day, she tells us, she would want to see the people "whose kindness
and gentleness and companionship have made my life worth living," beginning of course with Mrs. Macy; the second day would
be devoted to the museums, particularly those holding the painting
and sculpture of the ages; and her third day would give her the
sights of Manhattan, from the dawn as she left her home in Forest
Hills, then the East River, then the view from the Empire State
Building, then Fifth Avenue, and so on to midnight when her Cin-
derella sight would close. Her paper is a remarkable feat of the imagination, and we must not sound ungrateful if we add that the
writing of it is of necessity less vivid than those we have selected
for this group.

The American Loneliness

by THORNTON WILDER

Playwright, novelist, and teacher, Thornton Wilder has done much to bridge the gap between the generations, and he was at his illuminating best in the Charles Eliot Norton Lectures which he delivered at Harvard in 1950.

AUGUST 1952

Walking to the auditorium where I am to lecture on Thoreau I pass Hollis Hall in which he lived as an undergraduate.

I think we can understand why on graduation he changed his name — David Henry became Henry David, peremptorily. Like Emerson before him he was a scholarship student. During his first year he had one coat — his mother and aunt had made it for him out of green homespun. That year the right students were wearing black. All his life he railed with particular passion against any discrimination that is based on dress. A classmate tells us that, as a student, Thoreau in conversation did not raise his eyes from the ground and that his hands were continually moist. That chapter over, he changed his name.

As I pass Hollis I become uncomfortable; I feel those extraordinary blue eyes not on me, but directed over me, in taciturn reproach. He set down a portrait of himself and he took pains with its details. He wished it to be known that he was direct, simple, forthright, candid, and uncomplicated. Many have taken him at his word; but no, his life and personality have more important things to tell us.

How hard it is to discuss Thoreau in the presence of the young. Many aspects of his life and thought lie in that sole territory which is inaccessible to young men and women. I never feel an incomprehension on their part when I treat of death or loss or passion; their imaginations can extend themselves — by that principle which Goethe called "anticipation" — to such matters. What is difficult is to treat of the slow attrition of the soul by the conduct of life, of our revolt against the workaday — the background of such works as Le Misanthrope *and* Don Quixote.

I must tell these young people, who are hurrying by me, that Thoreau met defeat in his impassioned demands upon Love, Friendship, and Nature; and yet I must tell them that at the same time he was an American who fought some of our battles for us, whose experience we are to follow with a sort of anxious suspense. The rewards we obtain from the contemplation of Thoreau, however, begin their consolatory and inspiriting effect upon us as we move through our forties.

I wish I were somewhere else.

Ladies and gentlemen:

We were talking last time about how difficult it is to be an American. We spoke of the support which a European receives from all those elements we call environment — place, tradition, customs: "I am I because my neighbors know me." Their environment is so thickly woven, so solid, that the growing boy and girl have something to kick against. The American, on the other hand, is at sea — disconnected from place, distrustful of authority, thrown back upon himself.

Here I am again.

And suddenly, as my eyes rest on the upturned faces before me, I am encouraged. It is in many ways a sad story I have to tell. Whenever I think of Thoreau I feel a weight about my heart, a greater weight than descends in thoughts of Poe or Emily Dickinson. Yet all of us here are Americans. My subject is the loneliness that accompanies independence and the uneasiness that accompanies freedom. These experiences are not foreign to anyone here. So forward.

Perceptive visitors to America from Europe are uniformly struck by what they call an "American loneliness" which they find no less present in that fretful and often hollow gregariousness we talked about last time.

Now there are several forms of this loneliness, and the one that occurs to us first is the sentimental form. In America the very word is sentimental and it makes us uncomfortable even to employ it. Yet we see this kind of loneliness about us everywhere; like the loneliness which springs from pride it is a consequence, a deformation, and a malady of that deeper form which we are about to discuss. Both proceed from the fact that the religious ideas current in America are still inadequate to explain the American to himself. The sentimental loneliness arises from the sense that he is a victim, that he was slighted when fortune distributed her gifts (though it is notably prevalent among those who seem to "have everything"); the proud loneliness arises from the sense of boundlessness which we described as related to the American geography and is found among those who make boundless moral demands on themselves and others.

Thoreau illustrates certain American traits connected with loneliness in an extreme and exaggerated form. He finally lost his battle — the typical American battle of trying to convert a loneliness into an enriched and fruitful solitude — but before he died (at forty-four, murmuring: "It is better some things should end") he furnished us many a bulletin of the struggle, many an insight, and many an aid.

Another of the most famous pages in American literature is that wherein Thoreau gives his reasons for going to live in solitude at Walden Pond. "I went to the woods because I wished to live deliberately, to front only the essential facts of life, and see if I could not learn what it had to teach, and not, when I came to die, discover that I had not lived. . . . Nor did I wish to practise resignation, unless it were quite necessary. . . . If [life] proved to be mean, why then to get the whole and genuine meanness of it, and publish its meanness to the world; or if it were sublime, to know it by experience, and be able to give a true account of it in my next excursion."

Thoreau's books are a sort of cento of transcriptions and amplifications of entries in his Journal. Here is what he wrote on the third day of his residence at the pond (July 6, 1845): "I wish to meet the facts of life — the vital facts, which are the phenomena or actuality which the Gods meant to show us — face to face, and so I came here. Life! who knows what it is, what it does?"

There are several things to notice about these passages: among them, first, that he will put his question as though no one had ever said anything valuable before; and, second, that in order to ask what life is, it is necessary to remove oneself from the human community.

Americans constantly feel that the whole world's thinking has to be done over again. They did not only leave the Old World, they repudiated it. Americans start from scratch. This is revolt indeed. All authority is suspect. And this is boundless presumption. I quoted Whitman's words in our last session ("It almost seems as if a poetry . . . suitable to the human soul were never possible before"). Poe, clutching some mathematics and physics he had acquired during a brief stay at West Point, launched into a description of how the universe came into being, and deduced the nature of God from his theory of the galaxies. He called his work *Eureka* and did not leave us in doubt that he felt that he had succeeded where the greatest minds had failed. Professional astronomers dismiss it with a smile, but we notice that the great French poet Paul Valéry, who occupied himself with mathematics for thirty years, tells us how great a role this book played in the growth of his thought.

Thoreau did some reading at Walden Pond, but it is astonishing how small a part it plays in this central inquiry of his life. He invokes neither the great philosophers nor the founders of religions. Every American is an autodidact; every American feels himself capable of being the founder of his own religion. At the end of the passage I have quoted from the Journal there is an allusion to his reading of the Sanskrit scriptures. It is an ironic jest: "to give a true account of it in my next excursion." He does not believe that our souls return to inhabit other bodies, though billions have reposed in that idea all that they know of hope and courage. He makes a jest of it — fit example, to him, of the uselessness of *other people's* thinking. There is something of this religious and metaphysical pioneer in us all. How often I have heard people say: "No, Mr. Wilder, we don't go to church. My husband and I each have our own religion — here — inside!" What student at the height of a lofty argument has not been heard to cry: "Listen, everybody! My theory is *this* . . ."?

To others this must all seem very deplorable. To Americans it is wearing and costing and often desolating; but such is the situation. The die is cast; and our interest in Thoreau is precisely that we see one of ourselves fighting, struggling, and finally fainting in this inescapable American situation. Thoreau asks, What is life? and he asks it in a world from which any considerable reliance on previous answers is denied him, and through his long inquiry he heard the closing of three doors — doors to great areas of experience on which he counted for aid and illumination, the doors to Love, Friendship, and Nature.

Here are the reverberations of these closing doors:

LOVE (October 27, 1851, aged 34): "The obstacles which the heart meets with are like granite blocks which one alone cannot remove. She who was the morning light is now neither the morning star nor the evening star. We meet but to find each other further asunder. . . ."

FRIENDSHIP (March 4, 1856, aged 38): "I had two friends. The one offered me friendship on such terms that I could not accept it, without a sense of degradation. He would not meet me on equal terms, but only to be to some extent my patron. . . . Our relation was one long tragedy. . . ."

NATURE: As early as July 16, 1851, Thoreau was saying, "Methinks my present experience is nothing; my past experience is all in all. I think that no experience which I have today comes up to, or is comparable with, the experiences of my boyhood. . . . Formerly, methought, nature developed as I developed, and grew up with me. My life was ecstasy. . . ."

The story of Thoreau's love is only beginning to be pieced together. The obstacles that separated him from this woman were indeed granite blocks. The expressions he gives to his love in his Journal are often strange "whirling words": "My sister, it is glorious to me that you live! . . . It is morning when I meet thee in a still cool dewy white sun light in the hushed dawn — my young mother — I thy eldest son" (lightly crossed through: "thy young father") ". . . whether art thou my mother or my sister — whether am I thy son or thy brother. . . . Others are of my kindred by blood or of my acquaintance but you are part of me. I cannot tell where you leave off and I begin." In another passage, Journal 1850, he says: "I am as much thy sister as thy brother. Thou art as much my brother as my sister."

We have reason to be surprised that the erotic emotion expresses itself in images borrowed from the family relationships. Yet such a coloring is present elsewhere in our writers of this period, in Whitman, in Melville (*Pierre*), and in Poe. In America the family is the nexus of an unusually powerful ambivalence. On the one hand, the child strains to break away and lead his own life. The young seldom settle down near their parents' home; less and less frequently do the parents end their days in the homes of their children; I have remarked that young people are increasingly eager for the moment when they are no longer financially dependent on their parents. On the other hand, the American — as we were saying — is exceptionally aware of the multitude of the human race; his loneliness is enhanced by his consciousness of those numbers. The family is at once an encroachment on his individualism and a seductive invitation to rejoin the human community at a level where he does not feel himself to be strange. Moreover, individualism has its arrogance. It has long been a tag that every American is king. Royalty marries only royalty. Other people aren't good enough. Thoreau elevates the woman he loves to his kinship. Poe's mother died when he was three; he lived the latter part of his life with his aunt and married his cousin. The blocks of granite which separated Thoreau from this "sister" were not all outside of him. The door of love closed and he never returned to it.

It was the friendship with Ralph Waldo Emerson that Thoreau described as "one long tragedy." The second friend who proved unworthy was William Ellery Channing, who seems to have enjoyed shocking Thoreau with an occasional ribaldry. Tragedy we too can call it, for few men could more have needed friendship, and few have been less ready to accommodate themselves to it. He wrote (June 11, 1855): "What if we feel a yearning to which no breast answers? I walk alone, my heart is full. Feelings impede the current of my thoughts. I knock on the earth for my friend. I expect to meet him at every turn; but no friend appears, and perhaps none is dreaming of me." Emerson knew that he was incapable of friendship, and the knowledge caused him some pain — brief pain, for Emerson had a short way with moral discomfiture; he mounted up into pink clouds and began to give voice to abstractions. This woeful triangle skirts the comic. A letter has recently come to light which gives Channing's view of a friendship with Emerson. Channing wrote to Elizabeth Hoar from New Bedford on December 23, 1856: ". . . how strange it seemed to hear W. [Waldo] lecturing on friendship. If he knew all the hearts he has frozen, he might better read something on the fall of human hopes. . . . I have never parted from him without the bitterest regret, not for having parted, but for having come. . . ."

Individualism! It is the point of honor of men and nations in this century. Every nation boasts that it is a nation of individualists and implies that the other nations are composed of sheep. ("You Americans — you all eat the same things; you repeat the same slogans; you read the same book of the month; the very streets in which you live have not even names, but merely numbers and letters!") Yet no man (and no nation) is as individualistic as he thinks he is; each is so in one area of his existence, and the extent to which he is — fortunately! — conformist in others is not apparent to him. Friendship is not incompatible with individualism, as the great pages of Montaigne have shown us, but it was incompatible in the lives of our Concord philosophers. Thousands of school children were formerly required to read Emerson's chaotic essay on the subject. For generations Emerson's style had the power to put the judgment to sleep, but one wonders what the teachers made of that farewell address to "our dearest friends": "Who are you? Unhand me: I will be dependent no more."

Thoreau's inability to come to terms with friendship was aggravated by the vastness of his expectations. To this day many an American is breaking his life on an excessive demand for the perfect, the absolute, and the boundless in realms where it is accorded to few — in love and friendship, for example. The doctrines of moderation and the golden mean may have flourished in Rome and in China (overcrowded and overgoverned countries), but they do not flourish here, save as counsels of despair. The injunction to be content with your lot and in the situation where God has placed you is not an expression of New World thinking. We do not feel ourselves to be subject to lot and we do not cast God in the role of a civil administrator or of a feudal baron.

Thoreau goes to the pond, then, to find an answer to the question, What is life? He will not admit other thinkers to his deliberations, and his answer will not reflect any *close* relation with his fellow men. With what frustrated passion, then, he turned to nature. Nature meant primarily the flora and fauna of the Concord River valley, though he made some trips elsewhere. Now that region has no tigers, avalanches, coral vipers, Black Forests, deserts, or volcanoes. Margaret Fuller warned her Concord friends of the dangers of accustoming themselves to a view of nature which omitted both cruelty and grandeur. On his walks Thoreau came upon some malodorous plants (June 26, 1852): "For what purpose has nature made a flower to fill the lowlands with the odor of carrion?" The question seems, to us, both biologically and philosophically a little *simpliste*.

Enough has already been written about the absence of a sense of evil in the work of the Concord essayists. It is only one of the elements that resulted in the gradually progressive grayness of the last volumes of Thoreau's Journal. Far more important is the fact that Thoreau asked of nature a gift which nature cannot, without coöperation, accord. He asked a continual renewal of moments of youthful ecstasy. Unhappy, indeed, is the boy or girl who has not known those moments of inexplicable rapture in the open air. There is a corresponding experience accorded to those in later years — awe. In ecstasy the *self* is infused with happiness; in awe the self recedes before a realization of the vastness and mystery of the non-self. Many never cross the bridge from one to the other. Thoreau despised and dreaded science; to inquire too narrowly into the laws of nature seemed to him to threaten those increasingly infrequent visitations of irrational joy. "If you would obtain insight, avoid anatomy," he wrote. With what a sad smile Goethe would have shaken his head over these words — for it was precisely from his studies of the skeleton of the vertebrates and the structure of plants that Goethe's life was flooded, even in the eighties, with an awe which retained much of the character of a juvenile ecstasy. Indeed, Goethe at eighty would not have written the words which Thoreau wrote at thirty-three: "In youth, before I lost any of my senses, I can remember that I was all alive, and inhabited my body with inexpressible satisfaction . . . !" As the years passed, Thoreau increasingly mourned his lost youth and the intoxication which nature had afforded him then. For a time the humming of the telegraph wires aroused transports; it was his "redeemer"; then they too lost their peculiar powers. Finally, in his last years he turns from the almost passive notation of the phenomena about him and introduces into his observations an element of progression and exploration into the unknown. He counts the rings in stumps and makes notes on the succession of trees. Those who are conversant with these things tell us that he is discovering the science of ecology. He seems, however, to be deriving no warming satisfaction from this innovation; his notes lie buried in his Journal and the work is repeated independently by others.

I am eager to arrive at all the things that call forth our admiration for Thoreau, but I must delay a moment to point out that we have brushed against two traits in him which are not characteristic of the American: the fixed orientation toward childhood, and the view of nature as engaged in close personal conversation with man. These are characteristic, however, of the region from which he came.

A portion of Massachusetts and several states of our South are enclaves or residual areas of European feeling. They were cut off, or resolutely cut themselves off, from the advancing tide of the country's modes of consciousness. Place, environment, relations, repetitions are the breath of their being. One evidence of it is a constant preoccupation with how old one is and a striking obsession with early youth (how many of the brilliant novels which have lately come to us from the South turn upon childhood). In New York and Chicago and the West, one's age is of relatively little importance; those who are *active* between twenty-five and sixty are contemporaries. They dine and dance and work and enjoy themselves together. This is bound up with the American sense of time. Time is something we create, we call into being, not something we submit to — an order outside us.

Similarly, there are aspects of Thoreau's relation to nature that are not those we feel to be prevalent elsewhere among us. The gods of glade and brook and pond are not the gods of plain, seacoast, forest, desert, and mountain. The former are almost in reach; one can imagine oneself in dialogue with them; they can enter into an almost personal relation with those who have turned from the company of men. But the gods of great space are enigmatic; we are never sure that we have read aright the message of their beauty and terror; we do not hastily put words into their mouths. Yet the more we feel an "otherness" in nature, the more we recognize that we ourselves are natural. "It appears to be a law," wrote Thoreau, in April 1852, "that you cannot have a deep sympathy with both man and nature." "I loved nature because she is not man, but a retreat from him." There is no such law, nor have any other American voices expressed any sentiment like it, unless we take note of a moment in Emily Dickinson's life when she wrote: "I thought that nature was enough / Till human nature came." Nature failed Thoreau, as it will ultimately fail anyone who wishes to divide it up, to pick and choose only limited congenial aspects of it, for ecstasy or for retreat, or who wishes to employ one aspect of it to confound another.

And the question: "Life! who knows what it is, what it does?" It would seem that Thoreau had considerably compromised his inquiry by divesting himself of the testimony and the companionship of others and by repeating his question to a wooded vale.

Yet millions have testified and are testifying to the powerful clarifications that he brought back from Walden Pond. And all his triumphs came from his embattled individualism, from pushing it to the limits that border on absurdity, and from facing — "face to face" — the loneliness consequent upon it. He came back with the answer that life, thought, culture, religion, government — everything — arises from subjectivity, from inwardness. Our sole self is the first and last judge of values, including the values of communal life.

Here I traced briefly the long, gradual millenniary convergence of emphasis on the individual — religion's, government's, art's; and showed how through an historical accident the settling of America, by that "selection of a selection" of European individualists, constituted an acceleration, perhaps a "leap" in the forward movement of this centering of emphasis.

Thoreau does not urge us to live in shacks merely to save money and time; to eschew railroad trains, newspapers, and the postal service; to lay in two sets of washable clothing and a bar of soap; to refuse these jobs which deform our souls between nine and five. These are not ends in themselves. "Simplify, simplify, simplify!" All these are injunctions in order that we may refine our ear to the promptings of our subjective, inward self. The evil of community is that it renders us stupid — and cowardly. Walden is a manual of self-reliance so much more profound than Emerson's famous essay that the latter seems to be merely on the level of that advice to melancholics which directs them to take walks and drink a lot of milk.

Thoreau did not merely meditate about the problem of living: he costingly, searchingly exemplified it, and his work rings with the validity of that single-minded commitment. One of the rewards of independence, apparently, is that you are certain that you are the master of your choices, you are not left to doubt whether or not you are free.

Yet there is no air of triumph about the latter end of Thoreau's life. It is difficult to be an American. In some aspects of his life and thought Thoreau is one of our most conspicuous, most outrageous Americans. But the spiritual situation in which these citizens of the New World find themselves is so new, so demanding, and so uncharted, that only by keeping in contact with its total demands can one maintain one's head above the surface. A partial American will drown. Thoreau did not grasp the New World sense of the innumerability of the human race — nor did Emerson, for all his employment of the word "universal." Thoreau had a parochial, a wood-lot view of nature and her mighty laws. Is there a Thoreau who can tell us that once one has grasped and accepted a basic solitude, all the other gifts come pouring back — love, friendship, and nature? One reads the life story of Thoreau with anxious suspense.
    And Abraham Lincoln?
    And Melville — and Poe?

Hunting Big Redwoods

by JOHN MUIR

John Muir, the Scottish-American naturalist who was instrumental in preserving the Yosemite National Park, contributed many papers to the Atlantic. *In 1875 he guided Emerson to the sequoias in the Mariposa Grove, but the sage was too old to spend the night in the open; thirty-two years later Muir took Theodore Roosevelt to the same spot, and this time they did camp out beneath the great trees.*

SEPTEMBER 1901

The Big Tree (*Sequoia gigantea*) is nature's forest masterpiece, and, as far as I know, the greatest of living things. It belongs to an ancient stock, as its remains in old rocks show, and has a strange air of other days about it, a thoroughbred look inherited from the long ago, the auld lang syne of trees. Once the genus was common, and with many species flourished in the now desolate Arctic regions, the interior of North America, and in Europe; but in long eventful wanderings from climate to climate only two species have survived the hardships they had to encounter, the *gigantea* and *sempervirens*: the former now restricted to the western slopes of the Sierra, the other to the Coast Mountains, and both to California, excepting a few groves of redwood which extend into Oregon.

The Pacific coast in general is the paradise of conifers. Here nearly all of them are giants, and display a beauty and magnificence unknown elsewhere. The climate is mild, the ground never freezes, and moisture and sunshine abound all the year. Nevertheless, it is not easy to account for the colossal size of the sequoias. The largest are about three hundred feet high and thirty feet in diameter. Who of all the dwellers of the plains and prairies and fertile home forests of round-headed oak and maple, hickory and elm, ever dreamed that earth could bear such growths? Sequoias are trees that the familiar pines and firs seem to know nothing about, lonely, silent, serene, with a physiognomy almost godlike, and so old that thousands of them still living had already counted their years by tens of centuries when Columbus set sail from Spain, and were in the vigor of youth or middle age when the star led the Chaldean sages to the infant Saviour's cradle. As far as man is concerned, they are the same yesterday, today, and forever, emblems of permanence.

Excepting the sugar pine, most of its neighbors with pointed tops seem to be forever shouting "Excelsior!" while the Big Tree, though soaring above them all, seems satisfied, its rounded head poised lightly as a cloud, giving no impression of trying to go higher. Only in youth does it show, like other conifers, a heavenward yearning, keenly aspiring with a long quick-growing top. Indeed, the whole tree, for the first century or two, or until a hundred to a hundred and fifty feet high, is arrowhead in form, and compared with the solemn rigidity of age, is as sensitive to the wind as a squirrel tail. The lower branches are gradually dropped as it grows older, and the upper ones thinned out, until comparatively few are left. These, however, are developed to great size, divide again and again, and terminate in bossy rounded masses of leafy branchlets, while the head becomes dome-shaped. Then, poised in fullness of strength and beauty, stern and solemn in mien, it glows with eager, enthusiastic life, quivering to the tip of every leaf and branch and far-reaching root, calm as a granite dome — the first to feel the touch of the rosy beams of the morning, the last to bid the sun good night.

Perfect specimens, unhurt by running fires or lightning, are singularly regular and symmetrical in general form, though not at all conventional, showing infinite variety in sure unity and harmony of plan. The immensely strong, stately shafts, with rich purplish-brown bark, are free of limbs for a hundred and fifty feet or so, though dense tufts of sprays occur here and there producing an ornamental effect, while long parallel furrows give a fluted, columnar appearance. The limbs shoot forth with equal boldness in every direction, showing no weather side. On the old trees the main branches are crooked and rugged, and strike rigidly outward, mostly at right angles from the trunk, but there is always a certain measured restraint in their reach which keeps them within bounds. No other Sierra tree has foliage so densely massed or outlines so finely, firmly drawn and so obediently subordinate to an ideal type. A particularly knotty, angular, ungovernable-looking branch, five to eight feet in diameter and perhaps a thousand years old, may occasionally be seen pushing out from the trunk, as if determined to break across the bounds of the regular curve; but, like all the others, as soon as the general outline is approached, the huge limb dissolves into massy bosses of branchlets and sprays, as if the tree were growing beneath an invisible bell glass against the sides of which the branches were molded, while many small varied departures from the ideal form give the impression of freedom to grow as they like.

Except in picturesque old age, after being struck by lightning and broken by a thousand snowstorms, this regularity of form is one of the Big Tree's most distinguishing characteristics. Another is the simple sculptural beauty of the trunk and its great thickness as compared with its height and the width of the branches; many of them being from eight to ten feet in diameter at a height of two hundred feet from the ground and seeming more like finely modeled and sculptured architectural columns than the stems of trees, while the great strong limbs are like rafters supporting the magnificent dome head.

The root system corresponds in magnitude with the other dimensions of the tree, forming a flat, far-reaching, spongy network, two hundred feet or more in width, without any taproot; and the instep is so grand and fine, so suggestive of endless strength, it is long ere the eye is released to look above it. The natural swell of the roots, though at first sight excessive, gives rise to buttresses no greater than are required for beauty as well as strength, as at once appears when you stand back far enough to see the whole tree in its true proportions.

The bark of full-grown trees is from one to two feet thick, rich cinnamon brown, purplish on young trees and shady parts of the old, forming magnificent masses of color with the underbrush and beds of flowers. Toward the end of winter the trees themselves bloom, while the snow is still eight or ten feet deep. The pistillate flowers are about three eighths of an inch long, pale green, and grow in countless thousands on the ends of the sprays. The staminate are still more abundant, pale yellow, a fourth of an inch long, and when the golden pollen is ripe they color the whole tree and dust the air and the ground far and near.

The cones are bright grass green in color, about two and a half inches long, one and a half wide, and are made up of thirty or forty strong closely packed rhomboidal scales, with four to eight seeds at the base of each. The seeds are extremely small and light, being only from an eighth to a fourth of an inch long and wide, including a filmy surrounding wing, which causes them to glint and waver in falling and enables the wind to carry them considerable distances from the tree.

The faint lisp of snowflakes, as they alight, is one of the smallest sounds mortal can hear. The sound of falling sequoia seeds, even when they happen to strike on flat leaves or flakes of bark, is about as faint. Very different are the bumping and thudding of the falling cones.

Most of them are cut off by the Douglas squirrel and stored for the sake of the seeds, small as they are. In the calm Indian summer these busy harvesters with ivory sickles go to work early in the morning, as soon as breakfast is over, and nearly all day the ripe cones fall in a steady pattering, bumping shower. Unless harvested in this way, they discharge their seeds and remain on the tree for many years. In fruitful seasons the trees are fairly laden. On two small specimen branches, one and a half and two inches in diameter, I counted four hundred and eighty cones. No other California conifer produces nearly so many seeds, excepting perhaps its relative, the redwood of the Coast Mountains. Millions are ripened annually by a single tree, and the product of one of the main groves in a fruitful year would suffice to plant all the mountain ranges of the world.

The dense tufted sprays make snug nesting places for birds, and in some of the loftiest, leafiest towers of verdure thousands of generations have been reared, the great solemn trees shedding off flocks of merry singers every year from nests like the flocks of winged seeds from the cones.

The Big Tree keeps its youth far longer than any of its neighbors. Most silver firs are old in their second or third century, pines in their fourth or fifth, while the Big Tree, growing beside them, is still in the bloom of its youth, juvenile in every feature, at the age of old pines, and cannot be said to attain anything like prime size and beauty before its fifteen hundredth year, or, under favorable circumstances, become old before its three thousandth. Many, no doubt, are much older than this. On one of the Kings River giants, thirty-five feet and eight inches in diameter, exclusive of bark, I counted upwards of four thousand annual wood rings, in which there was no trace of decay after all these centuries of mountain weather.

There is no absolute limit to the existence of any tree. Their death is due to accidents, not, as of animals, to the wearing out of organs. Only the leaves die of old age — their fall is foretold in their structure — but the leaves are renewed every year, and so also are the other essential organs, wood, roots, bark, buds. Most of the Sierra trees die of disease. Thus the magnificent silver firs are devoured by fungi, and comparatively few of them live to see their three hundredth birth year. But nothing hurts the Big Tree. I never saw one that was sick or showed the slightest sign of decay. It lives on through indefinite thousands of years, until burned, blown down, undermined, or shattered by some tremendous lightning stroke. No ordinary bolt ever seriously hurts sequoia. In all my walks I have seen only one that was thus killed outright.

I have seen silver firs, two hundred feet high, split into long peeled rails and slivers down to the roots, leaving not even a stump; the rails radiating like the spokes of a wheel from a hole in the ground where the tree stood. But the sequoia, instead of being split and slivered, usually has forty or fifty feet of its brash knotty top smashed off in short chunks about the size of cordwood, the beautiful rosy-red ruins covering the ground in a circle a hundred feet wide or more. I never saw any that had been cut down to the ground, or even to below the branches, except one in the Stanislaus Grove, about twelve feet in diameter, the greater part of which was smashed to fragments, leaving only a leafless stump about seventy-five feet high. It is a curious fact that all the very old sequoias have lost their heads by lightning.

The great age of these noble trees is even more wonderful than their huge size, standing bravely up, millennium in, millennium out, to all that fortune may bring them; triumphant over tempest and fire and time, fruitful and beautiful, giving food and shelter to multitudes of small fleeting creatures dependent upon their bounty.

One of my own best excursions among the sequoias was made in the autumn of 1875, when I explored the then unknown or little-known sequoia region south of the Mariposa Grove for comprehensive views of the belt and to learn what I could of the peculiar distribution of the species and its history in general. In particular, I was anxious to try to find out whether it had ever been more widely distributed since the glacial period; what conditions, favorable or otherwise, were affecting it; what were its relations to climate, topography, soil, and the other trees growing with it, and so forth; and whether, as was generally supposed, the species was nearing extinction.

I have done nearly all my mountaineering on foot, carrying as little as possible, depending on campfires for warmth, so that I might be light and free to go wherever my studies might lead. But on this sequoia trip, which promised to be long, I was persuaded to take a small wild mule with me to carry provisions and a pair of blankets. The friendly owner of the animal, having noticed that I sometimes looked tired when I came down from the peaks to replenish my bread sack, assured me that his "little Brownie mule" was just what I wanted — tough as a knot, perfectly untirable, low and narrow, just right for squeezing through brush, able to climb like a chipmunk, jump from boulder to boulder like a wild sheep, and go anywhere a man could go. But tough as he was, and accomplished as a climber, many a time in the course of our journey, when he was jaded and hungry, wedged fast in rocks or struggling in chaparral like a fly in a spider web, his troubles were sad to see, and I wished he would leave me and find his way home alone.

We set out from Yosemite about the end of August, and our first camp was made in the well-known Mariposa Grove. Here and in the adjacent pine woods I spent nearly a week, carefully examining the boundaries of the grove for traces of its greater extension without finding any. Then I struck out into the majestic trackless forest to the southeastward, hoping to find new groves or traces of old ones in the dense silver fir and pine woods about the head of Big Creek, where soil and climate seemed most favorable to their growth; but not a single tree or old monument of any sort came to light until I climbed the high rock called Wamellow by the Indians. Here I obtained telling views of the fertile forest-filled basin of the upper Fresno. Innumerable spires of the noble yellow pine were displayed rising one above another on the braided slopes, and yet nobler sugar pines with superb arms outstretched in the rich autumn light, while away toward the southwest, on the verge of the glowing horizon, I discovered the majestic domelike crowns of Big Trees towering high over all, singly and in close grove congregations. There is something wonderfully attractive in this king tree, even when beheld from afar, that draws us to it with indescribable enthusiasm, its superior height and massive smoothly rounded outlines proclaiming its character in any company; and when one of the oldest of them attains full stature on some commanding ridge, it seems the very god of the woods.

I ran back to camp, packed Brownie, and steered over the divide and down into the heart of the Fresno Grove. Then, choosing a camp on the side of a brook where the grass was good, I made a cup of tea and set off free among the brown giants, glorying in the abundance of new work about me. One of the first special things that caught my attention was an extensive landslip. The ground on the side of a stream had given way to a depth of about fifty feet, and with all its trees had been launched into the bottom of the stream ravine. Most of the trees — pines, firs, incense cedar, and sequoia — were still standing erect and uninjured, as if unconscious that anything out of the common had happened. Tracing the ravine alongside the avalanche, I saw many trees whose roots had been laid bare, and in one instance discovered a sequoia, about fifteen feet in diameter, growing above an old prostrate trunk that seemed to belong to a former generation. This slip had occurred seven or eight years ago, and I was glad to find not only that most of the Big Trees were uninjured, but that many companies of hopeful seedlings and saplings were growing confidently on the fresh soil along the broken front of the avalanche. These young trees were already eight or ten feet high, and were shooting up vigorously, as if sure of eternal life, though young pines, firs, and libocedrus were running a race with them for the sunshine, with an even start. Farther down the ravine I counted five hundred and thirty-six young sequoias on a bed of rough bouldery soil not exceeding two acres in extent.

The Forests of the Yosemite Park

APRIL 1900

During my first years in the Sierra I was ever calling on everybody within reach to admire the vast, billowy forests of conifers, but I found no one half warm enough until Emerson came. I had read his essays and felt sure that of all men he would best interpret the sayings of these noble mountains and trees. Nor was my faith weakened when I met him in Yosemite. He seemed as serene as a sequoia, his head in the empyrean; and forgetting his age, plans, duties, ties of every sort, I proposed a camping trip back in the heart of the mountains.

He seemed anxious to go, but considerately mentioned his party. I said: "Never mind. The mountains are calling; run away, and let plans and parties and dragging lowland duties all 'gang tap-sal-teerie.' We'll go up a cañon singing your own song, 'Good-by, proud world! I'm going home,' in divine earnest. Up there lies a new heaven and a new earth; let us go to the show." But alas, it was too late, too near the sundown of his life. The shadows were growing long, and he leaned on his friends. His party, full of indoor philosophy, failed to see the natural beauty and fullness of promise of my wild plan and laughed at it in good-natured ignorance, as if it were necessarily amusing to imagine that Boston people might be led to accept Sierra manifestations of God at the price of rough camping. Anyhow, they would have none of it and held Mr. Emerson to the hotels and trails.

After spending only five tourist days in Yosemite he was led away, but I saw him two days more; for I was kindly invited to go with the party as far as the Mariposa Big Trees. I told Mr. Emerson that I would gladly go to the sequoias with him, if he would camp in the grove. He consented heartily, and I felt sure that we would have at least one good wild memorable night round a sequoia campfire. Next day we rode through the magnificent forests of the Merced basin, and I kept calling his attention to the sugar pines, quoting his wood notes, "Come listen what the pine tree saith," and so forth, pointing out the noblest as kings and high priests, the most eloquent and commanding preachers of all the mountain forests, stretching forth their century-old arms in benediction over the congregations crowded about them. He gazed in devout admiration, saying but little, while his fine smile faded away.

Early in the afternoon, when we reached Clark's Station, I was surprised to see the party dismount. And when I asked if we were not going up into the grove to camp, they said: "No, it would never do to lie out in the night air. Mr. Emerson might take cold; and you know, Mr. Muir, that would be a dreadful thing." In vain I urged that only in homes and hotels were colds caught, that nobody ever was known to take cold camping in these woods, that there was not a single cough or sneeze in all the Sierra. Then I pictured the big climate-changing, inspiring fire I would make, praised the beauty and fragrance of sequoia flame, told how the great trees would stand about us transfigured in the purple light while the stars looked down between the great domes, ending by urging them to come on and make an immortal Emerson night of it. But the house habit was not to be overcome, nor the strange dread of pure night air, though it is only cooled day air with a little pure dew in it. So the carpet dust and unknowable reeks were preferred. And to think of this being a Boston choice! Sad commentary on culture and the glorious transcendentalism.

Accustomed to reach whatever place I started for, I was going up the mountain alone to camp and wait the coming of the party next day. But since Emerson was so soon to vanish, I concluded to stop with him. He hardly spoke a word all the evening, yet it was a great pleasure simply to be near him, warming in the light of his face as at a fire. In the morning we rode up the trail through a noble forest of pine and fir into the Mariposa Grove and stayed an hour or two, mostly in ordinary tourist fashion — looking at the biggest giants, measuring them with a tape line, riding through prostrate fire-bored trunks, and so forth, though Mr. Emerson was alone occasionally, sauntering about as if under a spell. As we walked through a fine group, he quoted, "There were giants in those days," recognizing the antiquity of the race. To commemorate his visit, Galen Clark, the guardian of the grove, selected the finest of the unnamed trees and requested him to give it a name. He named it Samoset, after the New England sachem, as the best that occurred to him.

The poor bit of measured time was soon spent, and while the saddles were being adjusted I again urged Emerson to stay. "You are yourself a sequoia," I said. "Stop and get acquainted with your big brethren." But he was past his prime and was now as a child in the hands of his affectionate but sadly civilized friends, who seemed as full of old-fashioned conformity as of bold intellectual independence. It was the afternoon of the day and the afternoon of his life, and his course was now westward down all the mountains into the sunset. The party mounted and rode away in wondrous contentment, apparently. I followed to the edge of the grove. Emerson lingered in the rear of the train, and when he reached the top of the ridge, after all the rest of the party were over and out of sight, he turned his horse, took off his hat, and waved me a last good-by.

I felt lonely, so sure had I been that Emerson of all men would be the quickest to see the mountains and sing them. Gazing awhile on the spot where he vanished, I sauntered back into the heart of the grove, made a bed of sequoia plumes and ferns by the side of a stream, gathered a store of firewood, and then walked about until sundown. The birds, robins, thrushes, and warblers that had kept out of sight came about me, now that all was quiet, and made cheer. After sundown I built a great fire, and as usual had it all to myself. And though lonesome for the first time in these forests, I quickly took heart again — the trees had not gone to Boston, nor the birds; and as I sat by the fire, Emerson was still with me in spirit, though I never again saw him in the flesh. He sent books and wrote, cheering me on; advised me not to stay too long in solitude. Soon he hoped my guardian angel would intimate that my probation was at a close. Then I was to roll up my herbariums, sketches, and poems (though I never knew I had any poems), and come to his house; and when I tired of him and his humble surroundings, he would show me to better people.

But there remained many a forest to wander through, many a mountain and glacier to cross, before I was to see his Wachusett and Monadnock, Boston and Concord. It was seventeen years after our parting on the Wawona Ridge that I stood beside his grave under a pine tree on the hill above Sleepy Hollow. He had gone to higher Sierras, and, as I fancied, was again waving his hand in friendly recognition.

Emily Dickinson's Letters

by THOMAS WENTWORTH HIGGINSON

Thomas Wentworth Higginson contributed a number of literary sketches to the early issues, and it was doubtless his reputation for befriending authors which prompted a recluse in Amherst to turn to him for encouragement and advice. Her name was Emily Dickinson, and in the letters she wrote him over a period of nearly thirty years she enclosed many of the best and earliest of her poems. The year after her death her poems were published, at the insistence of her sister, and on their release Higginson revealed to the public this extraordinary correspondence.

OCTOBER 1891

Few events in American literary history have been more curious than the sudden rise of Emily Dickinson into a posthumous fame only more accentuated by the utterly recluse character of her life and by her aversion to even a literary publicity. But for her only sister, it is very doubtful if her poems would ever have been printed at all; and when published, they were launched quietly and without any expectation of a wide audience; yet the outcome of it is that six editions of the volume have been sold within six months, a suddenness of success almost without a parallel in American literature.

One result of this glare of publicity has been a constant and earnest demand by her readers for further information in regard to her; and I have decided with much reluctance to give some extracts from her early correspondence with one whom she persisted in regarding — with very little ground for it — as a literary counselor and confidant. On April 16, 1862, I took from the post office in Worcester, Mass., where I was then living, the following letter:

MR. HIGGINSON, Are you too deeply occupied to say if my verse is alive?

The mind is so near itself it cannot see distinctly, and I have none to ask.

Should you think it breathed, and had you the leisure to tell me, I should feel quick gratitude.

If I make the mistake, that you dared to tell me would give me sincerer honor toward you.

I inclose my name, asking you, if you please, sir, to tell me what is true?

That you will not betray me it is needless to ask, since honor is its own pawn.

The letter was postmarked "Amherst," and it was in a handwriting so peculiar that it seemed as if the writer might have taken her first lessons by studying the famous fossil bird tracks in the museum of that college town. Yet it was not in the slightest degree illiterate, but cultivated, quaint, and wholly unique. Of punctuation there was little; she used chiefly dashes, and it has been thought better, in printing these letters, as with her poems, to give them the benefit in this respect of the ordinary usages. But the most curious thing about the letter was the total absence of a signature. It proved, however, that she had written her name on a card and put it under the shelter of a smaller envelope inclosed in the larger; and even this name was written — as if the shy writer wished to recede as far as possible from view — in pencil, not in ink. The name was Emily Dickinson. Inclosed with the letter were four poems, two of which have been already printed: "Safe in their alabaster chambers" and "I'll tell you how the sun rose"; together with the two that here follow. The first comprises in its eight lines a truth so searching that it seems a condensed summary of the whole experience of a long life:

> We play at paste
> Till qualified for pearl;
> Then drop the paste
> And deem ourself a fool.
>
> The shapes, though, were similar
> And our new hands
> Learned gem-tactics,
> Practicing sands.

Then came one which I have always classed among the most exquisite of her productions, with a singular felicity of phrase and an aerial lift that bears the ear upward with the bee it traces:

> The nearest dream recedes unrealized.
> 　　The heaven we chase,
> 　　Like the June bee
> 　　Before the schoolboy,
> 　　Invites the race,
> 　　Stoops to an easy clover,
> Dips — evades — teases — deploys —
> Then to the royal clouds
> 　　Lifts his light pinnace,
> 　　Heedless of the boy
> Staring, bewildered, at the mocking sky.
> 　　Homesick for steadfast honey,
> 　　Ah! the bee flies not
> Which brews that rare variety.

The impression of a wholly new and original poetic genius was as distinct on my mind at the first reading of these four poems as it is now, after thirty years of further knowledge; and with it came the problem never yet solved, what place ought to be assigned in literature to what is so remarkable, yet so elusive of criticism. The bee himself did not evade the schoolboy more than she evaded me; and even at this day I still stand somewhat bewildered, like the boy.

I remember to have ventured on some criticism which she afterwards called "surgery," and on some questions, part of which she evaded, as will be seen, with a naïve skill such as the most experienced and worldly coquette might envy. Her second letter, received April 26, 1862, was as follows:

Mr. Higginson, Your kindness claimed earlier gratitude, but I was ill, and write today from my pillow.

Thank you for the surgery; it was not so painful as I supposed. I bring you others, as you ask, though they might not differ. While my thought is undressed, I can make the distinction; but when I put them in the gown, they look alike and numb.

You asked how old I was? I made no verse, but one or two, until this winter, sir.

I had a terror since September, I could tell to none; and so I sing, as the boy does of the burying ground, because I am afraid.

You inquire my books. For poets, I have Keats, and Mr. and Mrs. Browning. For prose, Mr. Ruskin, Sir Thomas Browne, and the Revelations. I went to school, but in your manner of the phrase had no education. When a little girl, I had a friend who taught me Immortality; but venturing too near, himself, he never returned. Soon after my tutor died, and for several years my lexicon was my only companion. Then I found one more, but he was not contented I be his scholar, so he left the land.

You ask of my companions. Hills, sir, and the sundown, and a dog large as myself, that my father bought me. They are better than beings because they know, but do not tell; and the noise in the pool at noon excels my piano.

I have a brother and sister; my mother does not care for thought, and father, too busy with his briefs to notice what we do. He buys me many books, but begs me not to read them, because he fears they joggle the mind. They are religious, except me, and address an eclipse, every morning, whom they call their "Father."

But I fear my story fatigues you. I would like to learn. Could you tell me how to grow, or is it unconveyed, like melody or witchcraft?

You speak of Mr. Whitman. I never read his book, but was told that it was disgraceful.

I read Miss Prescott's Circumstance, but it followed me in the dark, so I avoided her.

Two editors of journals came to my father's house this winter, and asked me for my mind, and when I asked them "why" they said I was penurious, and they would use it for the world.

I could not weigh myself, myself. My size felt small to me. I read your chapters in the Atlantic, and experienced honor for you. I was sure you would not reject a confiding question.

Is this, sir, what you asked me to tell you? Your friend,

E. Dickinson

It will be seen that she had now drawn a step nearer, signing her name, and as my "friend." It will also be noticed that I had sounded her about certain American authors then much read, and that she knew how to put her own criticisms in a very trenchant way. With this letter came some more verses, still in the same birdlike script, as for instance the following:

> Your riches taught me poverty,
> Myself a millionaire
> In little wealths, as girls could boast,
> Till, broad as Buenos Ayre,
> You drifted your dominions
> A different Peru,
> And I esteemed all poverty
> For life's estate, with you.

Of mines, I little know, myself,
    But just the names of gems,
The colors of the commonest,
    And scarce of diadems
So much that, did I meet the queen
    Her glory I should know;
But this must be a different wealth,
    To miss it, beggars so.

I'm sure 'tis India, all day,
    To those who look on you
Without a stint, without a blame,
    Might I but be the Jew!
I'm sure it is Golconda
    Beyond my power to deem,
To have a smile for mine, each day,
    How better than a gem!

At least, it solaces to know
    That there exists a gold
Although I prove it just in time
    Its distance to behold;
Its far, far treasure to surmise
    And estimate the pearl
That slipped my simple fingers through
    While just a girl at school!

Here was already manifest that defiance of form, never through carelessness, and never precisely from whim, which so marked her. The slightest change in the order of words — thus, "While yet at school, a girl" — would have given her a rhyme for this last line; but no, she was intent upon her thought, and it would not have satisfied her to make the change. The other poem further showed, what had already been visible, a rare and delicate sympathy with the life of nature:

A bird came down the walk;
He did not know I saw;
He bit an angle-worm in halves
And ate the fellow raw.

And then he drank a dew
From a convenient grass,
And then hopped sidewise to a wall,
To let a beetle pass.

He glanced with rapid eyes
That hurried all around;
They looked like frightened beads, I thought;
He stirred his velvet head

Like one in danger, cautious.
I offered him a crumb,
And he unrolled his feathers
And rowed him softer home

Than oars divide the ocean,
Too silver for a seam —
Or butterflies, off banks of noon,
Leap, plashless as they swim.

It is possible that in a second letter I gave more of distinct praise or encouragement, for her third is in a different mood. This was received June 8, 1862.

DEAR FRIEND, Your letter gave no drunkenness, because I tasted rum before. Domingo comes but once; yet I have had few pleasures so deep as your opinion, and if I tried to thank you, my tears would block my tongue.

My dying tutor told me that he would like to live till I had been a poet, but Death was much of mob as I could master, then. And when, far afterward, a sudden light on orchards, or a new fashion in the wind troubled my attention, I felt a palsy, here, the verses just relieve.

Your second letter surprised me, and for a moment, swung. I had not supposed it. Your first gave no dishonor, because the true are not ashamed. I thanked you for your justice, but could not drop the bells whose jingling cooled my tramp. Perhaps the balm seemed better, because you bled me first. I smile when you suggest that I delay "to publish," that being foreign to my thought as firmament to fin.

If fame belonged to me, I could not escape her; if she did not, the longest day would pass me on the chase, and the approbation of my dog would forsake me then. My barefoot rank is better.

You think my gait "spasmodic." I am in danger, sir. You think me "uncontrolled." I have no tribunal.

Would you have time to be the "friend" you should think I need? I have a little shape: it would not crowd your desk, nor make much racket as the mouse that dents your galleries.

If I might bring you what I do — not so frequent to trouble you — and ask you if I told it clear, 'twould be control to me. The sailor cannot see the North, but knows the needle can. The "hand you stretch me in the dark" I put mine in, and turn away. I have no Saxon now:

> As if I asked a common alms,
> And in my wondering hand
> A stranger pressed a kingdom,
> And I, bewildered, stand;
> As if I asked the Orient
> Had it for me a morn,
> And it should lift its purple dikes
> And shatter me with dawn!

But, will you be my preceptor, Mr. Higginson?

With this came the poem already published in her volume and entitled "Renunciation"; and also that beginning "Of all the sounds dispatched abroad," thus fixing approximately the date of those two. I must soon have written to ask her for her picture, that I might form some impression of my enigmatical correspondent. To this came the following reply, in July 1862:

Could you believe me without? I had no portrait, now, but am small, like the wren; and my hair is bold, like the chestnut burr; and my eyes, like the sherry in the glass, that the guest leaves. Would this do just as well?

It often alarms father. He says death might occur, and he has moulds of all the rest, but has no mould of me; but I noticed the quick wore off those things, in a few days, and forestall the dishonor. You will think no caprice of me.

You said "Dark." I know the butterfly, and the lizard, and the orchis. Are not those *your* countrymen?

I am happy to be your scholar, and will deserve the kindness I cannot repay. . . .

Because you have much business, beside the growth of me, you will appoint, yourself, how often I shall come, without your inconvenience.

And if at any time you regret you received me, or I prove a different fabric to that you supposed, you must banish me.

When I state myself, as the representative of the verse, it does not mean me, but a supposed person.

You are true about the "perfection." Today makes Yesterday mean.

You spoke of Pippa Passes. I never heard anybody speak of Pippa Passes before. You see my posture is benighted.

To thank you baffles me. Are you perfectly powerful? Had I a pleasure you had not, I could delight to bring it.

YOUR SCHOLAR

This was accompanied by this strong poem, with its breathless conclusion.

Of tribulation, these are they,
    Denoted by the white;
The spangled gowns, a lesser rank
    Of victors designate.

All these did conquer; but the ones
    Who overcame most times,
Wear nothing commoner than snow,
    No ornaments but palms.

"Surrender" is a sort unknown
    On this superior soil;
"Defeat" an outgrown anguish,
    Remembered as the mile

Our panting ancle barely passed
    When night devoured the road;
But we stood whispering in the house,
    And all we said was "Saved!"
[Note by the writer of the verses.] I spelled ankle wrong.

It would seem that at first I tried a little — a very little — to lead her in the direction of rules and traditions; but I fear it was only perfunctory, and that she interested me more in her, so to speak, unregenerate condition. Still, she recognizes the endeavor. In this case, as will be seen, I called her attention to the fact that while she took pains to correct the spelling of a word, she was utterly careless of greater irregularities. It will be seen by her answer that with her usual naïve adroitness she turns my point:

DEAR FRIEND, Are these more orderly? I thank you for the truth.

I had no monarch in my life, and cannot rule myself; and when I try to organize, my little force explodes and leaves me bare and charred.

I think you called me "wayward." Will you help me improve?

I suppose the pride that stops the breath, in the core of woods, is not of ourself.

You say I confess the little mistake, and omit the large. Because I can see orthography; but the ignorance out of sight is my preceptor's charge.

Of "shunning men and women," they talk of hallowed things, aloud, and embarrass my dog. He and I don't object to them, if they'll exist their side. I think Carl would please you. He is dumb, and brave. I think you would like the chestnut tree I met in my walk. It hit my notice suddenly, and I thought the skies were in blossom.

Then there's a noiseless noise in the orchard that I let persons hear.

You told me in one letter you could not come to see me "now," and I made no answer; not because I had none, but did not think myself the price that you should come so far.

I do not ask so large a pleasure, lest you might deny me.

You say, "Beyond your knowledge." You would not jest with me, because I believe you; but, preceptor, you cannot mean it?

All men say "What" to me, but I thought it a fashion.

When much in the woods, as a little girl, I was told that the snake would bite me, that I might pick a poisonous flower, or goblins kidnap me; but I went along and met no one but angels, who were far shyer of me than I could be of them, so I haven't that confidence in fraud which many exercise.

I shall observe your precept, though I don't understand it, always.

I marked a line in one verse, because I met it after I made it, and never consciously touch a paint mixed by another person.

I do not let go it, because it is mine. Have you the portrait of Mrs. Browning?

Persons sent me three. If you had none, will you have mine?

YOUR SCHOLAR

A month or two after this I entered the volunteer army of the Civil War. In the summer of 1863 I was wounded, and in hospital for a time, during which came this letter in pencil, written from what was practically a hospital for her, though only for weak eyes:

DEAR FRIEND, Are you in danger? I did not know that you were hurt. Will you tell me more? Mr. Hawthorne died.

I was ill since September, and since April in Boston for a physician's care. He does not let me go, yet I work in my prison, and make guests for myself.

Carlo did not come, because that he would die in jail; and the mountains I could not hold now, so I brought but the Gods.

I wish to see you more than before I failed. Will you tell me your health? I am surprised and anxious since receiving your note.

Knowledge of your recovery would excel my own.

E. DICKINSON

From this time and up to her death (May 15, 1886) we corresponded at varying intervals, she always persistently keeping up this attitude of "scholar," and assuming on my part a preceptorship which it is almost needless to say did not exist. Always glad to hear her "recite," as she called it, I soon abandoned all attempt to guide in the slightest degree this extraordinary nature, and simply accepted her confidences, giving as much as I could of what might interest her in return.

Sometimes there would be a long pause, on my part, after which would come a plaintive letter, always terse, like this:

"Did I displease you? But won't you tell me how?"

Or perhaps the announcement of some event, vast to her small sphere, as this:

Carlo died.
Would you instruct me now?

E. DICKINSON

Or sometimes there would arrive an exquisite little detached strain, every word a picture, like this:

THE HUMMING-BIRD

A route of evanescence
With a revolving wheel;
A resonance of emerald;
A rush of cochineal.
And every blossom on the bush
Adjusts its tumbled head;
The mail from Tunis, probably,
An easy morning's ride.

In all this time — nearly eight years — we had never met, but she had sent invitations like the following:

DEAR FRIEND, Whom my dog understood could not elude others.

I should be so glad to see you, but think it an apparitional pleasure, not to be fulfilled. I am uncertain of Boston.

I had promised to visit my physician for a few days in May, but father objects because he is in the habit of me.

Is it more far to Amherst?

You will find a minute host, but a spacious welcome. . . .

If I still entreat you to teach me, are you much displeased? I will
be patient, constant, never reject your knife, and should my slowness
goad you, you knew before myself that

> Except the smaller size
> No lives are round.
> These hurry to a sphere
> And show and end.
> The larger slower grow
> And later hang;
> The summers of Hesperides
> Are long.

Afterwards, came this:

DEAR FRIEND, A letter always feels to me like immortality because
it is the mind alone without corporeal friend. Indebted in our talk to
attitude and accent, there seems a spectral power in thought that walks
alone. I would like to thank you for your great kindness, but never try
to lift the words which I cannot hold.

Should you come to Amherst, I might then succeed, though gratitude
is the timid wealth of those who have nothing. I am sure that you speak
the truth, because the noble do, but your letters always surprise me.

My life has been too simple and stern to embarrass any. "Seen of Angels," scarcely my responsibility.

It is difficult not to be fictitious in so fair a place, but tests' severe repairs are permitted all.

When a little girl I remember hearing that remarkable passage and
preferring the "Power," not knowing at the time that "Kingdom" and
"Glory" were included.

You noticed my dwelling alone. To an emigrant, country is idle except
it be his own. You speak kindly of seeing me; could it please your convenience to come so far as Amherst, I should be very glad, but I do not
cross my father's ground to any house or town.

Of our greatest acts we are ignorant. You were not aware that you
saved my life. To thank you in person has been since then one of my few
requests. You will excuse each that I say, because no one taught me.

At last, after many postponements, on August 16, 1870, I found myself face to face with my hitherto unseen correspondent. It was at her

father's house, one of those large, square, brick mansions so familiar in our older New England towns, surrounded by trees and blossoming shrubs without, and within exquisitely neat, cool, spacious, and fragrant with flowers. After a little delay, I heard an extremely faint and pattering footstep like that of a child in the hall, and in glided, almost noiselessly, a plain, shy little person, the face without a single good feature, but with eyes, as she herself said, "like the sherry the guest leaves in the glass," and with smooth bands of reddish chestnut hair. She had a quaint and nunlike look, as if she might be a German canoness of some religious order, whose prescribed garb was white piqué, with a blue net worsted shawl. She came toward me with two day lilies, which she put in a childlike way into my hand, saying softly, under her breath, "These are my introduction," and adding, also, under her breath, in childlike fashion, "Forgive me if I am frightened; I never see strangers, and hardly know what I say."

But soon she began to talk, and thenceforward continued almost constantly; pausing sometimes to beg that I would talk instead, but readily recommencing when I evaded. There was not a trace of affectation in all this; she seemed to speak absolutely for her own relief, and wholly without watching its effect on her hearer. Led on by me, she told much about her early life, in which her father was always the chief figure — evidently a man of the old type, *la vieille roche* of Puritanism — a man who, as she said, read on Sunday "lonely and rigorous books"; and who had from childhood inspired her with such awe that she never learned to tell time by the clock till she was fifteen, simply because he had tried to explain it to her when she was a little child, and she had been afraid to tell him that she did not understand and also afraid to ask anyone else lest he should hear of it. Yet she had never heard him speak a harsh word, and it needed only a glance at his photograph to see how truly the Puritan tradition was preserved in him.

He did not wish his children, when little, to read anything but the Bible; and when, one day, her brother brought her home Longfellow's *Kavanagh,* he put it secretly under the pianoforte cover, made signs to her, and they both afterwards read it. It may have been before this, however, that a student of her father's was amazed to find that she and her brother had never heard of Lydia Maria Child, then much read, and he brought *Letters from New York,* and hid it in the great bush of old-fashioned tree box beside the front door. After the first book she thought in ecstasy, "This, then, is a book, and there are more of them." But she did not find so many as she expected, for she afterwards said to me, "When I lost the use of my eyes, it was a comfort to think that there were so few real books that I could easily find one to read me all of them." Afterwards, when she regained her eyes, she read Shakespeare and thought to herself, "Why is any other book needed?"

She went on talking constantly and saying, in the midst of narrative, things quaint and aphoristic. "Is it oblivion or absorption when things pass from our minds?" "Truth is such a rare thing, it is delightful to tell it." "I find ecstasy in living; the mere sense of living is joy enough." She told me of her household occupations, that she made all their bread, because her father liked only hers; then saying shyly, "And people must have puddings," this very timidly and suggestively, as if they were meteors or comets. Interspersed with these confidences came phrases so emphasized as to seem the very wantonness of overstatement, as if she pleased herelf with putting into words what the most extravagant might possibly think without saying, as thus: "How do most people live without any thoughts? There are many people in the world — you must have noticed them in the street — how do they live? How do they get strength to put on their clothes in the morning?" Or this crowning extravaganza: "If I read a book and it makes my whole body so cold no fire can ever warm me, I know that is poetry. If I feel physically as if the top of my head were taken off, I know that is poetry. These are the only ways I know it. Is there any other way?"

She was much too enigmatical a being for me to solve in an hour's interview, and an instinct told me that the slightest attempt at direct cross-examination would make her withdraw into her shell; I could only sit still and watch, as one does in the woods; I must name my bird without a gun, as recommended by Emerson. Under this necessity I had no opportunity to see that human and humorous side of her which is strongly emphasized by her nearer friends, and which shows itself in her quaint description of a rural burglary contained in the volume of her poems. Hence, even her letters to me show her mainly on her exaltée side.

After my visit came this letter:

Enough is so vast a sweetness, I suppose it never occurs, only pathetic counterfeits.

Fabulous to me as the men of the Revelations who "shall not hunger any more." Even the possible has its insoluble particle.

After you went, I took Macbeth and turned to "Birnam Wood." Came twice "To Dunsinane." I thought and went about my work. . . .

The vein cannot thank the artery, but her solemn indebtedness to him, even the stolidest admit, and so of me who try, whose effort leaves no sound.

You ask great questions accidentally. To answer them would be events. I trust that you are safe.

I ask you to forgive me for all the ignorance I had. I find no nomination sweet as your low opinion.

Speak, if but to blame your obedient child.

You told me of Mrs. Lowell's poems. Would you tell me where I could find them, or are they not for sight? An article of yours, too, perhaps the only one you wrote that I never knew. It was about a "Latch." Are you willing to tell me? (Perhaps "A Sketch.")

If I ask too much, you could please refuse. Shortness to live has made me bold.

Abroad is close tonight and I have but to lift my hands to touch the "Heights of Abraham."

When I said, at parting, that I would come again some time, she replied, "Say, in a long time; that will be nearer. Some time is no time." We met only once again, and I have no express record of the visit. We corresponded for years, at long intervals, her side of the intercourse being, I fear, better sustained; and she sometimes wrote also to my wife, inclosing flowers or fragrant leaves with a verse or two. Once she sent her one of George Eliot's books, I think *Middlemarch,* and wrote, "I am bringing you a little granite book for you to lean upon." At other times she would send single poems, such as this:

THE BLUE JAY

No brigadier throughout the year
So civic as the jay.
A neighbor and a warrior too,
With shrill felicity
Pursuing winds that censure us
A February day,
The brother of the universe
Was never blown away.
The snow and he are intimate;
I've often seen them play
When heaven looked upon us all
With such severity
I felt apology were due
To an insulted sky
Whose pompous frown was **nutriment**

To their temerity.
The pillow of this daring head
Is pungent evergreens;
His larder — terse and militant —
Unknown, refreshing things;
His character — a tonic;
His future — a dispute;
Unfair an immortality
That leaves this neighbor out.

Then came the death of her father, that strong Puritan father who had communicated to her so much of the vigor of his own nature, and who bought her many books but begged her not to read them. Edward Dickinson, after service in the national House of Representatives and other public positions, had become a member of the lower house of the Massachusetts legislature. The session was unusually prolonged, and he was making a speech upon some railway question at noon, one very hot day (July 16, 1874), when he became suddenly faint and sat down. The house adjourned, and a friend walked with him to his lodgings at the Tremont House; where he began to pack his bag for home, after sending for a physician, but died within three hours. Soon afterwards, I received the following letter:

The last afternoon that my father lived, though with no premonition, I preferred to be with him, and invented an absence for mother, Vinnie [her sister] being asleep. He seemed peculiarly pleased, as I oftenest stayed with myself; and remarked, as the afternoon withdrew, he "would like it to not end."

His pleasure almost embarrassed me, and my brother coming, I suggested they walk. Next morning I woke him for the train, and saw him no more.

His heart was pure and terrible, and I think no other like it exists.

I am glad there is immortality, but would have tested it myself, before entrusting him. Mr. Bowles was with us. With that exception, I saw none. I have wished for you, since my father died, and had you an hour unengrossed, it would be almost priceless. Thank you for each kindness. . . .

Later she wrote:

When I think of my father's lonely life and lonelier death, there is this redress —

Take all away;
The only thing worth larceny
Is left — the immortality.

My earliest friend wrote me the week before he died, "If I live, I will
go to Amherst; if I die, I certainly will."
Is your house deeper off?

A year afterwards came this:

DEAR FRIEND, Mother was paralyzed Tuesday, a year from the evening father died. I thought perhaps you would care.

YOUR SCHOLAR

With this came the following verse, having a curious seventeenth-
century flavor:

A death-blow is a life-blow to some,
Who, till they died, did not alive become;
Who, had they lived, had died, but when
They died, vitality begun.

And these few fragmentary memorials — closing, like every human
biography, with funerals, yet with such as were to Emily Dickinson only
the stately introduction to a higher life — may well end with her description of the death of the very summer she so loved.

As imperceptibly as grief
The summer lapsed away,
Too imperceptible at last
To feel like perfidy.

A quietness distilled,
As twilight long begun,
Or Nature spending with herself
Sequestered afternoon.

The dusk drew earlier in,
The morning foreign shone,
A courteous yet harrowing grace
As guest that would be gone.

And thus without a wing
Or service of a keel
Our summer made her light escape
Into the Beautiful.

James Norman Hall

1887-1951

by ELLERY SEDGWICK

Ellery Sedgwick, who was editor of the Atlantic *from 1909 to 1938, first began to receive the manuscripts of James Norman Hall in 1912. Hall, a young graduate from Grinnell College, had come to Boston to work as an investigator for the Society for the Prevention of Cruelty to Children, and in the evening hours devoted himself to the writing of poems and of essays not many of which found their mark. Hall was cycling in England in the summer of 1914, and when the war broke out, he volunteered as a "Canadian" in Kitchener's Mob; later he was transferred and trained as a pilot in the Lafayette Escadrille. It was in these war years that his first major contributions began to appear in the* Atlantic. *From that time on, no contributor was more beloved.*

SEPTEMBER 1951

When James Norman Hall was born, the mold of Iowa clay was broken, never to be used again. Romance goes pulsing through the veins of many a farmer's son, but in Hall it had to break through gates and locks tight closed. Diffidence checked it; fastidiousness choked it; inertia, which so often paralyzes good in a bad world, might well have been the death of it. That he lived the life he did proves that all is possible. Providence may seem made of brass, but sometimes there is a streak of sympathy within, some latent trace of conscience, which cannot bear to lose an opportunity that may not come again.

Every quality of Hall's pulled hard against every other. Yet he won through, and luck, so indifferent to young men whose ambition does not lie on the surface, turned up trumps. Just because a dozen opposing traits so warred within him that forward motion seemed impossible, she produced Charles Nordhoff, quite obviously for the purpose of transferring the drawn battle within to a manlier contest with the outer world. Civil wars are forgotten when invasion comes, and just so Nordhoff's militant spirit denied Hall the privilege of wrestling peaceably with his own angel and forced him to put up his hands and fight. Nordhoff prodded and Hall accepted the challenge.

How well I remember the two boys — for still boys they were — when, the First World War over, they came to the *Atlantic* to take counsel concerning their lifework. One passionate desire they held in common, binding them together tighter than all the rest. Their intensest, freest life, each had lived alone, flying thousands of feet above the filth and beastliness of the trenches. When they fought their final battles, the Age of Chivalry was curiously reincarnate in another element, and now that peace had come they revolted against what seemed to them the sluttishness of modern life, where men fought not for a cause but selfishly, haggling for their dollars and their bread. To live they must find new heavens and new earth. So it was they went together to the South Seas.

What a contrast, those two young men! Nordhoff slightly scornful, very ambitious, Hall modest to a fault; Nordhoff skeptical and distrusting, Hall with no formulated belief but trusting absolutely in good. Both had a compelling sense of beauty; but for Nordhoff it was the beauty of strength and the outward world, for Hall the fairness of the inner, poetry and dream. Nordhoff was strikingly handsome in those days, a young David straight as a javelin, with aristocratic features and a manner that showed friendliness was not to be imposed upon. Hall wore a homely pleasantness about him reminding one, in spite of his soldiering abroad, of the good earth of his father's farm. Nordhoff had his inhibitions, too, but he was full of confidence and too eager to let doubts raise their interrogating heads. As he sat smiling in his chair, you knew that Hall's ambition was some lonely, lovely haven where he could dream out his dreams.

The isles of the South Seas turned out to have their less idyllic aspects. Sunshine and perfume are no aids to composition; spicy breezes and opaline wavelets play hob with work. There were times when the manna of the breadfruit tree offered their only supper, and fish their single source of vitamins; times when Nordhoff's leg, injured on barnacles, would not heal, when Hall feared his subtropical ailment might be the precursor of elephantiasis. Then Providence, long asleep, woke up.

Living within a mile or two of the young men, in a heavenly Tahitian garden, was their friend and guardian, Skipper Smith, of whom legend tells this story. Now legend has a great advantage over history through telling what ought to have happened, as history seldom takes pains to do. Long and arduously Professor Smith had toiled at his roll-top desk in Massachusetts Institute of Technology. One morning he was surveying in disgust this symbol of weary years. Suddenly he looked down and noted lying upon it an envelope with a lawyer's name printed in the corner. The letter ran somewhat as follows: "This will notify you that your aunt, Mrs. S., has named you as her exclusive heir. Her property valued at $500,000 can be converted into cash at your discretion." This pleasing missive Smith read three times. His unremembered affection for the dear old lady came vividly to mind. Instinctively his arms shot up, and down rolled the old top, closing with an everlasting click.

That very afternoon ex-Professor Smith called on his friend, Professor Barbour of the Peabody Museum. "Tom," he asked, "what is the most interesting thing a man like me can do?" The answer came back: "Cultivate dendrology in Borneo."

So dendrology it was, and Borneo too; but in after years Skipper Smith — for a layman's title had replaced the academic — had transported his garden to a still more enchanting spot in Tahiti, where he soon assumed paternal relations with our heroes. More than that, he wrote to me invaluable letters concerning their health and the more delicate matter of how much lotus-eating was good for them. I acted warily. Instead of direct subsidies, I sent money to the Skipper, instructing him to dole it out as if every dollar were the last — he to bear all reproaches, I to reap the reward. Meantime I saw to it that the war insurance policies should not lapse.

Of this confidential arrangement I think neither Hall nor Nordhoff ever knew the details. Certainly it was successful. While the hibiscus exhaled its delicate scent, the young noses were held fast to the grindstone.

Original causes are hard to seek, but it chanced that in my nursery at Stockbridge, Massachusetts, was a volume bound in red, bearing the title *Pitcairn's Island*. At eight I pored over this book and often served as one of the *Bounty's* crew mutinying under the old hemlock on the lawn. On one of his American holidays, Hall and I were sitting on my piazza. My vague memories coalesced. Conviction seized me that by opportunity, taste, and skill, Hall was the natural inheritor of the *Bounty* story.

Hall knew the tale well, and felt its power, but said he: "Nordy and I can't do the story without going to London, and that's expensive."

"No need of that," said I, "for I am going to London myself."

So it was that the following winter a huge packet of books went from

London to Tahiti, and besides the records a complete set of Smollett's novels to teach an eighteenth-century lingo. Also word reached me of a *Bounty* fan, a retired captain of the Royal Navy, who had spent untold hours shaping a model of the ship, carved according to exact specifications. Often Hall told me he came to know this so perfectly that, had he been given the chance of crawling over the deck of the original brig, he could have spotted every nail hole.

One providential service I was able to render at this time. There existed half a score of stories of the *Bounty,* but I noticed that they all covered the climacteric trial of the mutineers in very general terms. Inferring that all researches had been made in London, whereas the actual trial had been held in Plymouth, it seemed that a great advance could be made in enumerating details if the actual testimony could be secured. In the British Museum, I discovered one of those wonderfully learned ladies whose unrecorded burrowings make the reputations of the celebrated writers of history. At my direction, she went to Plymouth and copied the minutes of the trial. Now public records are not subject to copyright, but as the ensuing movie contract was important, the form of copyright was gone through with. The claim was carefully staked and the *Mutiny on the Bounty* by Nordhoff and Hall became attractive to producers, even at a price, beyond all alternatives at their free disposal.

To a huge public the mystifying trick of the *Bounty* was how two disparate figures, in full sight of the audience, could completely coalesce. Here were two totally different examples of God's creation suddenly become one, to all appearances indissoluble. The twain had visibly become one flesh. Neither could say like the happy bridegroom: "We two are one and I am *that one.*" There was neither first nor last; no clashes of style, no individual protuberances, no quirks of personal manner. David and Jonathan, Damon and Pythias, were like as one but not one. Nordhoff and Hall were no identical twins, no twin Dromios. They were the single author of a single book.

With Nordhoff and Hall complete success was due not to the similarity but to the diversity of the component halves. Neither half lost anything of his personality, but the sum of both was ampler and richer than either alone. Nordhoff gave energy and passion, Hall meditation and understanding. Nordhoff gave action, Hall beauty. Nordhoff's humor was in a higher key. Hall gave a quieter satisfaction. I defy the liveliest critic to pick up the volume and say "This is Hall, this Nordhoff."

Hall was a Christian in the least literal and most veracious sense. The Church meant nothing to him, though he doubtless approved it.

Missionaries stirred him to wrath. He judged them with a perverse judgment because the sense of sin which they imported had borne unhealthy fruit in the idyllic islands he loved so well. But his whole soul was enlisted in his detestation of America's darling sin, vulgarity.

The chiefest symbol of Yankee success is advertising, and advertising he loathed. In his simplicity he believed that merit would out, that the violet would not be hidden by the mossy stone. Here was a perpetual difficulty for his publisher. The most innocent intrusion of the first personal pronoun was an affront to him. When "I" unobtrusively appeared in a script of his, he looked at it as the basilisk looks at whatever it is the basilisk likes to pounce upon. He could as readily boast of his prowess in the air as allow the telephone poles of "I's" to run through a narrative passage. It was useless to tell him that the universal practice was not only harmless, but that the circuit made to avoid it was a literary offense. He would simply remark: "I did not set out to advertise myself."

As religion shapes the souls of men, so poetry shaped Hall's. He seldom quoted it aloud, but to himself he was forever repeating stanzas and poems and cantos of it. The poets of his youth were the poets of his maturity. He had no truck with the dissonance of today or with that obscurity which on a third reading deepens to opacity. Reverence for the masters cumbered, I think, his own efforts at verse. Overtones from choirs of the past hindered more than they helped him when he sought to rhyme on paper. But if his monument is not poetry, poetry made him what he was. It was the inner poetry of his being which gave him chivalry and kindness and love.

Men's works live after them. These are what we admire, but it is a man we love. I doubt if there was anyone with whom Jimmie Hall spent a chance hour who did not feel there was a difference between him and others, or that that difference was a precious thing. He was a wanderer in the world and was happiest alone or with a very, very few. Perhaps today he walks with Joseph Conrad, the adoration of his youth, whom, when an easy and natural opportunity came, he was too shy to approach; or with that strange and harassed genius, Lafcadio Hearn; for it was after these two he named his only son. Hall yearned for lonely places. Now he is in the loneliest of all. The world seemed to him crowded almost to suffocation. He felt fettered and cramped, and longed for endless reaches of space and time.

In immensity, he is at home.

V I

Love in America

Any record of love in America since 1857 must begin with the premise that decorum in speech, in print, and behavior has steadily given way before an ever-encroaching tolerance. Miss Gail Hamilton, a preserver of Boston morals in 1863, was sent by the Atlantic *to do an article on the Harvard Class Day festivities. She was not amused. One of her strictures was this:*

> Waltzing is a profane and vicious dance. Always. When it is prosecuted in the center of a great crowd, in a dusty hall, on a warm midsummer day, it is also a disgusting dance. Night is its only appropriate time. . . . The present mode of dress renders waltzing almost as objectionable in a large room as the boldest feats of a French ballet-dancer. I saw scores and scores of public waltzing-girls and among them all I saw but one who understood the art, or, at any rate, who practised the art, of avoiding an indecent exposure. Do I shock ears polite? I trust so.

Miss Hamilton could never have believed that the day would come when Harvard undergraduates would entertain their girl friends in their rooms unchaperoned, the only question being how late at night they could remain.

In those days the fastidious element in the Atlantic *audience reacted quickly. Upon the publication of the Countess Guiccioli's autobiography in 1869, Harriet Beecher Stowe sprang to the defense of Lady Byron. Lady Byron had been her friend, and in this battle of mistress versus wife, Mrs. Stowe told all — or at least all she knew — in an article which few could suffer through today entitled "The True Story of Lady Byron's Life." This was published in the* Atlantic *for September 1869, while the editor, James Fields, was abroad; in his absence the magazine was being run by young William Dean Howells, who had his misgivings but who yielded to the pressure of Dr. Holmes and the author. Mrs. Stowe's article proved to be a boomerang: whatever the readers may have felt for Lady Byron, they angrily resented Mrs. Stowe's hardly con-*

*cealed charges of incest, and within a short time 15,000 of them
canceled their subscriptions.*

*Decorum continued to rule as the century wore on, and the nov-
els which were serialized in the magazine abīded by the closed-door
rule: when the lovers were brought to the point of incandescence,
whether in a boudoir, barn, or tower (as in Thomas Hardy's Two
on a Tower, serialized in 1882), the novelist closed the door leaving the reader to imagine what went on. Confirmation came later,
for in Victorian fiction the wages of sin were usually a baby. Sex
plagued us in 1899 with our serialization of The Helpmate by
May Sinclair. Again the editor, Bliss Perry, was in Europe, and
again his assistant, Ferris Greenslet, took the risk, although in this
case with no hesitation. Perry got back in time to receive a sputter
of wrathful denunciations and some cancellations, but it is noticeable that they were only a fraction of what had come in response
to Mrs. Stowe.*

*The trouble was, the younger generation seemed to enjoy the
new freedom and to want more of it. For this they were reproved
by their elders, from time to time, in the* Atlantic. *But with the advent of the realists and the publication of Freud, love in America
became much more outspoken; fiction had entered upon its open-
door phase, and with each passing decade the door was opened
wider. The First World War had much to do with this, and neither the expostulations of Katharine Fullerton Gerould nor "Mrs.
Grundy" could slow things down. Even as Stuart P. Sherman conducted his genteel and oh so protracted* Conversations with Cor-
nelia *(1924) the vestiges of decorum were slipping.* Jurgen, Lady
Chatterley's Lover, A Farewell to Arms, Ulysses, Sanctuary, From
Here to Eternity, *and* The Kinsey Report — *these are a few of the
milestones we have passed on the way to a tolerance Miss Gail Hamilton could not have imagined.*

*It is part of the American paradox that we can stomach so much
that is literal and believe so much that is romantic. Through all of
this and despite the ever-increasing incidence of divorce, we still
believe in the happy ending; we still revere the words, "And they
married and lived happily ever after." Sometimes they do.*

Love in America

by RAOUL DE ROUSSY DE SALES

A Frenchman whose mother was American, Raoul de Roussy de Sales was one of the most acute and appreciative corre-spondents ever to write about America. His observations were in the great tradition of de Tocqueville; he represented Havas *and* Paris-Midi *in the fateful years leading up to 1940. He had published one book,* The Making of Tomorrow, *and was at work on a second, comparing the democracies of France and the United States, when his untimely death occurred.*

MAY 1938

America appears to be the only country in the world where love is a national problem.

Nowhere else can one find a people devoting so much time and so much study to the question of the relationship between men and women. Nowhere else is there such concern about the fact that this relationship does not always make for perfect happiness. The great majority of the Americans of both sexes seem to be in a state of chronic bewilderment in the face of a problem which they are certainly not the first to confront, but which — unlike other people — they still refuse to accept as one of those gifts of the gods which one might just as well take as it is: a mixed blessing at times, and at other times a curse or merely a nuisance.

The prevailing conception of love, in America, is similar to the idea of democracy. It is fine in theory. It is the grandest system ever evolved by man to differentiate him from his ancestors, the poor brutes who lived in caverns, or from the apes. Love is perfect, in fact, and there is nothing better. But, like democracy, it does not work, and the Americans feel that something should be done about it. Their statesmen are intent on making democracy work. Everybody is trying to make love work, too.

In either case the result is not very satisfactory. The probable reason is that democracy and love are products of a long and complicated series of compromises between the desires of the heart and the exactions of reason. They have a peculiar way of crumbling into ashes as soon as one tries too hard to organize them too well.

The secret of making a success out of democracy and love in their practical applications is to allow for a fairly wide margin of errors, and not to forget that human beings are absolutely unable to submit to a uniform rule for any length of time. But this does not satisfy a nation that, in spite of its devotion to pragmatism, also believes in perfection.

For a foreigner to speak of the difficulties that the Americans encounter in such an intimate aspect of their mutual relationship may appear as an impertinence. But the truth is that no foreigner would ever think of bringing up such a subject of his own accord. In fact, foreigners who come to these shores are quite unsuspecting of the existence of such a national problem. It is their initial observation that the percentage of good-looking women and handsome men is high on this continent, that they are youthful and healthy in mind and body, and that their outlook on life is rather optimistic.

If the newcomers have seen enough American moving pictures before landing here — and they usually have — they must have gathered the impression that love in America is normally triumphant, and that, in spite of many unfortunate accidents, a love story cannot but end very well indeed. They will have noticed that these love stories which are acted in Hollywood may portray quite regrettable situations at times and that blissful unions get wrecked by all sorts of misfortunes. But they never remain wrecked: even when the happy couple is compelled to divorce, this is not the end of everything. In most cases it is only the beginning. Very soon they will remarry, sometimes with one another, and always — without ever an exception — for love.

The observant foreigner knows, of course, that he cannot trust the movies to give him a really reliable picture of the American attitude toward love, marriage, divorce, and remarriage. But they nevertheless indicate that in such matters the popular mind likes to be entertained by the idea 1) that love is the only reason why a man and a woman should get married; 2) that love is always wholesome, genuine, uplifting, and fresh, like a glass of Grade A milk; 3) that when, for some reason or other, it fails to keep you uplifted, wholesome, and fresh, the only thing to do is to begin all over again with another partner.

Thus forewarned, the foreigner who lands on these shores would be very tactless indeed if he started questioning the validity of these premises. Besides, it is much more likely that he himself will feel thoroughly transformed the moment he takes his first stroll in the streets of New York. His European skepticism will evaporate a little more at each step, and if he considers himself not very young any more he will be immensely gratified to find that maturity and even old age are merely European habits of thought, and that he might just as well adopt the American method, which is to be young and act young for the rest of his life — or at least until the expiration of his visa.

If his hotel room is equipped with a radio, his impression that he has at last reached the land of eternal youth and perfect love will be confirmed at any hour of the day and on any point of the dial. No country in the world consumes such a fabulous amount of love songs.

Whenever I have gone back to France and listened to the radio, I have always been surprised to find that so many songs can be written on other subjects. I have no statistics on hand, but I think that a good 75 per cent of the songs one hears on the French radio programs deal with politics. There are love songs, of course, but most of them are far from romantic, and this is quite in keeping with the French point of view that love is very often an exceedingly comical affair.

In America the idea seems to be that love, like so much else, should be sold to the public, because it is a good thing. The very word, when heard indefinitely, becomes an obsession. It penetrates one's subconsciousness like the name of some unguent to cure heartaches or athlete's foot. It fits in with the other advertisements, and one feels tempted to write to the broadcasting station for a free sample of this thing called Love.

Thus the visitor from Europe is rapidly permeated with a delightful atmosphere of romanticism and sweetness. He wonders why Italy and Spain ever acquired their reputation of being the lands of romance. This, he says to himself, is the home of poetry and passion. The Americans are the real heirs of the troubadours, and station WXZQ is their love court.

To discover that all this ballyhoo about love (which is not confined to the radio or the movies) is nothing but an aspect of the national optimistic outlook on life does not take very long. It usually becomes evident when the foreign visitor receives the confidences of one or more of the charming American women he will chance to meet. This normally happens after the first or second cocktail party to which he has been invited.

The American woman entertains the delightful illusion that there *must* be some man on this earth who can understand her. It seems incredible to her that love, within legal bonds or outside of them, should not work out as advertised. From her earliest years she has been told that success is the ultimate aim of life. Her father and mother made an obvious success of their lives by creating her. Her husband is, or wants to be, a successful businessman. Success — the constant effort to make things work perfectly and the conviction that they can be made to — is the great national preoccupation.

And what does one do to make a success? Well, the answer is very simple: one learns how, or one consults an expert.

That is what her husband does when he wants to invest his money or improve the efficiency of his business. That is what she did herself when she decided to "decorate" her house. In the American way of life there are no insoluble problems. You may not know the answer yourself, but nobody doubts that the answer exists — that there is some method or some trick by which all riddles can be solved and success achieved.

And so the European visitor is put to the task on the presumption that the accumulation of experience which he brings with him may qualify him as an expert in questions of sentiment.

The American woman does not want to be understood for the mere fun of it. What she actually wishes is to be helped to solve certain difficulties which, in her judgment, impede the successful development of her inner self. She seldom accepts the idea that maladjustments and misunderstandings are not only normal but bearable once you have made up your mind that, whatever may be the ultimate aim of our earthly existence, perfect happiness through love or any other form of expression is not part of the program.

One of the greatest moral revolutions that ever happened in America was the popularization of Freud's works.

Up to the time that occurred, as far as I am able to judge, America lived in a blissful state of puritanical repression. Love, as a sentiment, was glorified and sanctified by marriage. There was a general impression that some sort of connection existed between the sexual impulses and the vagaries of the heart, but this connection was not emphasized, and the consensus of opinion was that the less said about it the better. The way certain nations, and particularly the French, correlated the physical manifestations of love and its more spiritual aspects was considered particularly objectionable. Love, in other words — and that was not very long ago — had not changed since the contrary efforts of the puritanically-minded and the romantic had finally stabilized it midway between the sublime and the parlor game.

The important point is that up to then (and ever since the first Pilgrims set foot on this continent) love had been set aside in the general scheme of American life as the one thing which could not be made to work better than it did. Each one had to cope with his own difficulties in his own way and solve them as privately as he could. It was not a national problem.

Whether or not people were happier under that system is beside the point. It probably does not matter very much whether we live and die with or without a full set of childish complexes and repressions. My own view is that most people are neither complex nor repressed enough as a rule; I wish sometimes for the coming of the anti-Freud who will complicate and obscure everything again.

But the fact is that the revelations of psychoanalysis were greeted in America as the one missing link in the general program of universal improvement.

Here was a system, at last, that explained fully why love remained so imperfect. It reduced the whole dilemma of happiness to sexual maladjustments, which in turn were only the result of the mistakes made by one's father, mother, or nurse, at an age when one could certainly not be expected to foresee the consequences. Psychoanalysis integrated human emotions into a set of mechanistic formulas. One learned with great relief that the failure to find happiness was not irreparable. Love, as a sublime communion of souls and bodies, was not a legend, nor the mere fancy of the poets. It was real, and — more important — practically attainable. Anybody could have it, merely by removing a few obstructions which had been growing within him since childhood like mushrooms in a dark cellar. Love could be made to work like anything else.

The profound effect of the Freudian revelation has lasted. From its materialistic interpretation of sexual impulses, coupled with the American longing for moral perfection, a new science has been born: the dialectics of love; and also a new urge for the American people — they want to turn out, eventually, a perfect product. They want to get out of love as much enjoyment, comfort, safety, and general sense of satisfaction, as one gets out of a well-balanced diet or good plumbing.

Curiously enough, this fairly new point of view which implies that human relationships are governed by scientific laws has not destroyed the romantic ideal of love. Quite the contrary. Maladjustments, now that they are supposed to be scientifically determined, have become much more unbearable than in the horse-and-buggy age of love. Husbands and wives and lovers have no patience with their troubles. They want to be cured, and when they think they are incurable they become very intolerant. Reformers always are.

Usually, however, various attempts at readjustment are made with devastating candor. Married couples seem to spend many precious hours of the day and night discussing what is wrong with their relationship. The general idea is that — according to the teachings of most modern psychologists and pedagogues — one should face the truth fearlessly.

This is a fine theory, but it has seldom been practiced without disastrous results. There are several reasons why this should be so. First of all, truth is an explosive, and it should be handled with care, especially in marital life. It is not necessary to lie, but there is little profit in juggling with hand grenades just to show how brave one is. Secondly, the theory of absolute sincerity presupposes that, if love cannot withstand continuous blasting, then it is not worth saving anyway. Some people want their love life to be a permanent battle of Verdun. When the system of defense is destroyed beyond repair, then the clause of hopeless maladjustment is invoked by one side, or by both. The next thing to do is to divorce and find someone else to be recklessly frank with for a season.

Another reason why the method of adjustment through truthtelling is not always wise is that it develops fiendish traits of character which might otherwise remain dormant.

I know a woman whose eyes glitter with virtuous self-satisfaction every time she has had a "real heart-to-heart talk" with her husband, which means that she has spent several hours torturing him, or at best boring him to distraction, with a ruthless exposure of the deplorable status of their mutual relationship to date. She is usually so pleased with herself after these periodical inquests that she tells most of her friends, and also her *coiffeur,* about it. "Dick and I had such a wonderful time last evening. We made a real effort to find out the real truth about each other — or, at least, I certainly did. I honestly believe we have found a new basis of adjustment for ourselves. What a marvelous feeling that is — don't you think so?"

Dick, of course, if he happens to be present, looks rather nervous or glum, but that is not the point. The point is that Dick's wife feels all aglow because she has done her bit in the campaign for the improvement of marital happiness through truth. She has been a good girl scout.

A man of my acquaintance, who believes in experimenting outside of wedlock, is unable to understand why his wife would rather ignore his experiments. "If I did not love her and if she did not love me," he argues, "I could accept her point of view. But why can't she see that the very fact that I want her to know everything I do is a proof that I love her? If I have to deceive her or conceal things from her, what is the use of being married to her?"

Be it said, in passing, that this unfortunate husband believes that these extramarital "experiments" are absolutely necessary to prevent him from developing a sense of inferiority, which, if allowed to grow, would destroy not only the love he has for his wife, but also his general ability in his dealings with the outside world.

Thus the problem of love in America seems to be resultant of conflicting and rather unrealistic ways of approaching it. Too many songs, too many stories, too many pictures, and too much romance on the one hand, and too much practical advice on the other. It is as if the experience of being in love could only be one of two things: a superhuman ecstasy, the way of reaching heaven on earth and in pairs; or a psychopathic condition to be treated by specialists.

Between these two extremes there is little room for compromise. That the relationship between men and women offers a wide scale of variations seldom occurs to the experts. It is not necessarily true that there is but one form of love worth bothering about, and that if you cannot get the de luxe model, with a life guarantee of perfect functioning, nothing else is worth while. It is not true either that you can indefinitely pursue the same quest for perfection, or that if a man and a woman have not found ideal happiness together they will certainly find it with somebody else. Life unfortunately does not begin at forty, and when you reach that age, in America or anywhere else, to go on complaining about your sentimental or physiological maladjustments becomes slightly farcical.

It is not easy, nor perhaps of any use, to draw any conclusion from all this, especially for a European who has lost the fresh point of view of the visitor because he lives here, and who is not quite sure of what it means to be a European any more. I sometimes wonder if there is any real difference between the way men and women get along — or do not get along — together on this side of the Atlantic and on the other. There are probably no more real troubles here than anywhere else. Human nature being quite remarkably stable, why should there be? But there is no doubt that the revolt against this type of human inadequacy is very strong indeed here, especially among the women who imagine that the Europeans have found better ways of managing their hearts and their senses than the Americans.

If this is at all true, I believe the reason is to be found in a more philosophical attitude on the part of the Europeans toward such matters.

There are no theories about marital bliss, no recipes to teach you how to solve difficulties which, in the Old World, are accepted as part of the common inheritance.

Men and women naturally want to be happy over there, and, if possible, with the help of one another; but they learn very young that compromise is not synonymous with defeat. Even in school (I am speaking more particularly of France now) they are taught, through the literature of centuries, that love is a phenomenon susceptible of innumerable variations, but that — even under the best circumstances — it is so intertwined with the other experiences of each individual life that to be over-romantic or too dogmatic about it is of little practical use. "*La vérité est dans les nuances*," wrote Benjamin Constant, who knew a good deal about such matters.

And, speaking of the truly practical and realistic nature of love, it is a very strange thing that American literature contains no work of any note, not even essays, on love as a psychological phenomenon. I know of no good study of the process of falling in and out of love, no analytical description of jealousy, coquettishness, or the development of tediousness. No classification of the various brands of love such as La Rochefoucauld, Pascal, Stendhal, Proust, and many others have elaborated has been attempted from the American angle. The interesting combinations of such passions as ambition, jealousy, religious fervor, and so forth, with love are only dimly perceived by most people and even by the novelists, who, with very few exceptions, seem to ignore or scorn these complicated patterns. These fine studies have been left to the psychiatrists, the charlatans, or the manufacturers of naïve recipes.

The reason for this neglect on the part of real thinkers and essayists may be that for a long time the standards imposed by the puritanical point of view made the whole study more or less taboo with respectable authors. And then the Freudian wave came along and carried the whole problem out of reach of the amateur observer and the artist.

Of course, nothing is lost. The field remains open, and there is no reason to suppose that love in America will not cease to be a national problem, a hunting ground for the reformer, and that it will not become, as everywhere else, a personal affair very much worth the effort it takes to examine it as such. All that is necessary is for someone to forget for a while love as Hollywood — or the professor — sees it, and sit down and think about it as an eternally fascinating subject for purely human observation.

The Love Letters of Mark Twain

Edited by DIXON WECTER

*In his courtship of Livy Langdon, Mark Twain, to win her
hand, took many pledges which were no easier to keep then
than now, especially for one of an explosive nature.*

NOVEMBER 1947

Except for Lincoln, no nineteenth-century American is more familiar
to the world than Mark Twain. His physical traits — the shock of rus-
set hair frosted by time to pure white, the hawk nose and piercing eye,
the white clothes and the Missouri drawl which dominated lecture platforms and after-dinner tables — were as unforgettable as the savor of
his personality, its drollery and corrosive wit.

Mark Twain the suitor and lover is an unknown by the light of his
literary works, since he has curiously little to say about the relation of
the sexes, beyond the calf love of Tom Sawyer and Becky, the oblique
study of miscegenation in *Pudd'nhead Wilson,* and a few Rabelaisian trifles never intended for the public. How, explicitly, did Samuel Clemens
woo for a year and a half and wed — when he was thirty-five and she
twenty-five — the only girl with whom he was ever deeply and incura-
bly in love? Recalling forty years later, after her death, how he had first
seen her face in a miniature carried by her brother on the *Quaker City*
cruise, he told a friend, "From that day to this she has never been out of
my mind."

The soul side that a man "shows a woman when he loves her" — to
quote from the Browning whose poetry Mark and Livy so often read together — is best disclosed by the letters which follow.

"The wild humorist from the Pacific slope" had been sent by a Sacramento newspaper in 1867 on what was in effect the first modern pleasure cruise, to Europe and the Holy Land. Among his company he found
a boon companion in Charles Langdon, a boy of eighteen, whose father,
Jervis Langdon, was a self-made coal magnate of Elmira, New York.

Another shipboard friend was Mary Mason Fairbanks, posting travel letters to her husband's Cleveland *Herald:* although only seven years Sam Clemens' senior, she became "Mother" Fairbanks to him, who "sewed my buttons on, kept my clothing in presentable trim, fed me on Egyptian jam (when I behaved) . . . and cured me of several bad habits," as he wrote his family. She undertook the "civilizing" process which Sam Clemens, son of frontier and mining camp, felt to be the predestined role of good and refined women — respecting matters like slang, profanity, tobacco, and liquor — which his future wife was soon solicited to continue. Mrs. Fairbanks also became the confidante of his impending courtship, together with Charlie Langdon, the girl's brother.

Olivia Langdon was a charming, sweet-faced, conventionally reared and overserious girl whose delicate health — after a fall on the ice, at the age of sixteen, resulted in two bedridden years which were ended by the ministrations of an osteopath with a streak of faith-healing — increased the protectiveness which her father and all the family had built around her. The whirlwind suit which the fiery-haired humorist began to pay her, following the return of the *Quaker City,* astonished and at first disconcerted the Langdons. They found his company diverting, but knowing nothing of his antecedents beyond his tales of pilothouse and mining camp, and his repute as a "phunny phellow," wondered whether he was a suitable mate for their only daughter. Nevertheless, Clemens was nothing if not persistent. On December 27, 1867, he first saw the original of the romantic face in the miniature; they met at the St. Nicholas Hotel in New York, where the Langdons were stopping; their first date was an expedition to Steinway Hall to hear Dickens read from *David Copperfield.* On New Year's Day, 1868, Clemens called upon her in the custom proper to that day, at the home of her friends, the Berrys, and (less conventionally) prolonged the call from noon till midnight.

A business trip to California delayed Mark Twain's suit of Livy Langdon, but upon his return in the late summer of 1868 he managed to coax an invitation to Elmira from her brother.

There was another visit in September. The most reliable account, with all its comic exaggeration, appears in an unpublished letter, now in the Huntington Library, which he wrote Mrs. Fairbanks shortly after the event: "After I had been a night and a day at Mr. Langdon's, Charlie and I got the wagon at 8 P.M. to leave for New York, and just as we sat down on the aftermost seat the horse suddenly started, the seat broke loose, and we went over backwards, Charlie falling in all sorts of ways and I lighting exactly on my head in the gutter and breaking my neck in eleven different places. . . . The seat followed Charlie out and split his head wide open, so that you could look through it just as if you were looking through a gorge in a mountain. There wasn't anything to intercept the view — which was curious, because his brains hadn't been knocked out. . . . But seriously, it came very near being a fatal mishap to both of us. . . ."

Livy's nursing was his heaven-sent opportunity, but his proposal just before leaving met with a rather frightened refusal. In all, she rejected him three times within as many months, meanwhile giving him permission to write to her as his "sister," and promising to remember him in her prayers. Never a conventional Christian believer, he invited her, probably with full sincerity, to convert him. With this gambit he drew from her a steady stream of answers to his soul-searching letters.

In late November 1868, in the midst of a lecture tour whose glowing press notices went not without effect upon the Langdons, the humorist suddenly reappeared at Elmira one morning with the words, "The calf has returned; may the prodigal have some breakfast?" At this time he won her shy acceptance, and her parents' consent, to a secret trial engagement. The first letter here was written as the jubilant suitor followed his lecture itinerary along the Great Lakes towns, a month after his acceptance.

> *Tecumseh* [*Mich.*]
> *Dec.* 27 [1868]

I got your letter at Charlotte, my dear, dear Livy, and I rather hoped to get one here, but it did not come. However, if one *should* come, it will be mailed to me at Cleveland. I find I shall be there at noon tomorrow, which is much sooner than I expected.

Yes, Livy, I *do* like to have you give me synopses of Mr. Beecher's sermons — and you need not suppose that I read them over once and then lay them aside for good, for I do not. I read them over and over again and try to profit by them. I got the printed sermon also, and have read that several times. Everything convicts me — so does this sermon. "A Christian is a fruit-bearer — a moral man is a vine that does not bear fruit." That is me, exactly. *I* do not swear, I do not steal, I do not murder, I do not drink. My "whole life is *not.*" I am "*not* all over." "Piety is the right performance of a common duty, *as well as the experience of a special moral emotion.*" I now perform all my duties as well as I can, but see what I lack! — I lack the *chief* ingredient of piety — for I lack (almost always) the "special moral emotion" — that inner sense which tells me that what I do I am doing *for love* of the Savior. I *can* be a Christian — I *shall* be a Christian — but when I feel as I feel today, it seems a far journey away. . . . I am glad you marked the sermon, Livy — why didn't you put in the margin what you and your father and mother *said* about the prominent passages? Yes, my little dear, I *shall* be glad to receive the *Plymouth Pulpit* as often as you will send it — and I *shan't* care to have an opinion of my own in the matter, notwithstanding your quiet sarcasm upon yourself, but I shall certainly like what you like — in jest or earnest you are right about *that*. Mark them, Livy.

As to the social drinking, give yourself no more uneasiness about it. O, my loved, my honored, my darling little Mentor! — for it had bothered my conscience so much ever since it seemed to me that day in the drawing room that you gave your consent to it *with a little reluctance,* that I have hardly taken a glass of ale or wine since but it seemed to me your kind eyes were upon me with a sort of gentle reproach in them — and so — well, I don't drink *anything,* now, dear, and so your darling noble old heart has been troubling itself all for nothing! But please don't let my *motive* distress you, Livy. You know the child must crawl before it walks — and I must do right for love of you while I am in the infancy of Christianity; and then I can do right for love of the Savior when I shall have gotten my growth. And especially don't give *this* instance any importance, for it is *no sacrifice,* because I have not now, and *never had,* any love for any kind of liquors, and not even a passable *liking* for any but champagne and ale, and only for these *at intervals.* I ought to be ever so grateful to you, Livy, for your brave confidence in me, and for the consideration you show for me in simply *suggesting* reforms when you could be such an absolute little tyrant if you chose. I do not know of anything I could refuse to do if you wanted it done. I am reasonably afraid that you'll stop me from smoking, some day, but if ever you do, you will do it with such a happy grace that I shall be swindled into the notion that I didn't *want* to smoke any more, anyhow! . . .

Livy, I do wish you were here, for it is very lonely in this solemn room on this solemn cloudy Sabbath. If I could only take you to my heart, now, and talk to you and hear your voice, I could want no other company, no other music. *This* letter of yours isn't cold, Livy — it couldn't be, when you say that the better you know me the better you love me. That is pleasant to hear from your lips. I do hope you may not cease to be able to speak those words until you shall have given me *all* your love and so shall have no more to give. I do *love* you, Livy! And don't you worry because you do not love me as well as I love you, Livy.

It isn't strange at all, that you can't do it — because I am not as lovable as you are — I lack a great deal of being as lovable as you, Livy. . . .

Of *course* I now think of many things that ought to have been said when I was with you, dear, but couldn't think of them then. I think I shall have to make out a *list,* against my next visit. Some of them I *did* think of — they were confessions — but they seemed of such trifling import that it appeared not worth while to waste priceless time upon them — and I think so yet. Still, I shall always be ready and willing to confess *anything* and *everything* to you, Livy, that you could possibly wish to know.

The supper bell has rung. . . .

Good-by darling — over these leagues of weary distance I cast a loving kiss.

SAML. L. C.

Jervis Langdon, a cautious father, asked Sam Clemens for character references before the engagement could be announced. As the latter remembered it years later in his *Autobiography,* he offered six names from the Pacific Coast, including two clergymen but omitting his very best friends out of scruple that they might lie loyally on his behalf. On his own hook Langdon wrote also to a former Elmira Sunday-school superintendent now clerking in a bank out West. All, it seems, leaned over backwards in their pious criticism, one clergyman and the former Sunday-school teacher adding "to their black testimony the conviction that I would fill a drunkard's grave," Mark recalled. Those sessions with newspaper cronies and *bon vivants* like Artemus Ward at the midnight bars of Virginia City and San Francisco arose from the buried years to threaten Mark's courtship with blight. In a mood of alarm mingled with unsparing honesty and a characteristic glint of grim humor, Clemens replied for the defense.

Cleveland
Dec. 29 [*1868*]

DEAR MR. LANGDON:

I wrote to the Metropolitan Hotel for your letter (of Dec. 8), and it overtook me two or three days ago at Charlotte, Mich. I will not deny that the first paragraph hurt me a little — hurt me a good deal — for when you speak of what I said of the drawing room, I see that you mistook the harmless overflow of a happy frame of mind for criminal frivolity. This is a little unjust — for although what I said may have been unbecoming, it surely was no worse. The subject of the drawing room cannot be more serious to you than it is to me. But I accept the rebuke, freely and without offer of defense, and am as sorry I offended as if I had *intended* offense.

All the rest of your letter is just as it should be. The language is as plain as ever language was in the world, but I like it all the better for that. I don't like to mince matters myself or have them minced for me. I think I am safely past that tender age when one cannot take his food save that it be masticated for him beforehand — and I would much prefer to suffer from the clean incision of an honest lancet than from a sweetened poison. Therefore it is even as you say: I have "too much good sense" to blame you for that part of the letter. Plain speaking does not hurt one.

I am not hurrying my love — it is my love that is hurrying *me* — and surely no one is better able to comprehend that than you. I fancy that Mrs. Langdon was the counterpart of her daughter at the age of twenty-three — and so I refer you to the past for explanation and for pardon of my conduct.

It is my desire as truly as yours, that sufficient time shall elapse to show you, beyond all possible question, what I *have been, what I am,* and what I am *likely to be.* Otherwise you could not be satisfied with me, nor I with myself. I think that much of my conduct on the Pacific Coast was not of a character to recommend me to the respectful regard of a high eastern civilization, but it was not considered blameworthy there, perhaps. We go according to our lights. I was just what Charlie would have been, similarly circumstanced, and deprived of home influences. I think all my references can say I never did anything mean, false, or criminal. They can say that the same doors that were open to me seven years ago are open to me yet; that *all* the friends I made in seven years are still my friends; that wherever I have been I can go again — and enter in the light of day and hold my head up; that I never deceived or defrauded anybody, and don't owe a cent. And they can say that I attended to my business with due diligence, and made my own living, and never asked anybody to help me do it, either. All the rest they can say about me will be *bad.* I can tell the whole story myself, without mincing it, and will if they refuse. . . .

As to what I am *going to be,* henceforth, it is a thing which must be *proven* and established. I am upon the right path — I shall succeed, I hope. Men as lost as I, have found a Savior, and why not I? I have hope — an earnest hope — a long-lived hope.

I wrote you and Mrs. Langdon a letter from Lansing, which will offend again, I fear — and yet, no harm was meant, no undue levity, no disrespect, no lack of reverence. The intent was blameless — and it is the *intent,* and not the *act* that should be judged, after all. Even men who take life are judged by this rule only.

They say the desire is so general, here, to have this public distressed again by a repetition of my lecture, that Mr. Fairbanks offers me $150 to repeat it the third week in January, and Mrs. Fairbanks offers to let me repeat it for the benefit of the Orphans' Home at a dollar a head and pay me nothing for it. I have accepted the latter proposition. I have received a second invitation from the Association I lectured for in Pittsburgh to come there and talk again. They have gotten up some little feeling there because of an unjust and angry criticism upon the lecture (it appeared in the *Dispatch*), and I think maybe that is the cause of these calls. I shall try to go, though really I am not disposed to quarrel with the *Dispatch's* opinion or make myself sad about it, either. I always liked to express my opinions freely in print, and I suppose the *Dispatch* people have a taste that runs in a similar direction. . . .

I believe I have nothing further to say, except to ask pardon for past offenses against yourself, they having been heedless, and not deliberate; and that you will —

(Mrs. Fairbanks has just come in and she says: "For shame! cut that letter short — do you want to wear out what endurance the poor man has left after his siege of illness?" This is a woman, Sir, whose commands are not to be trifled with — and so I desist.)

With reverent love and respect, I am

Sincerely
SAML. L. CLEMENS

According to Clemens's recollections, the upshot came later when they stood face to face. After reviewing these letters, his prospective father-in-law gravely asked, "Haven't you a friend in the world?" Clemens replied, "Apparently not." And then the shrewd old coal operator said, "I'll be your friend, myself. Take the girl. I know you better than they do."

Jan. 6, 1869

MY DEAREST LIVY:

. . . Make some more pictures of our own wedded happiness, Livy — with the bay window (which you shall have) and the grate in the living room — (which you shall have, likewise) and flowers, and pictures and books (which we will read together) — pictures of our future home — a home whose patron saint shall be love — a home with a tranquil "home atmosphere" about it — such a home as "our hearts and our God shall approve." And Livy, *don't* say at the bottom of it, "How absurd, perhaps wrong, I am to write of these things which are so uncertain." Don't, Livy, it spoils everything — and sounds so chilly. . . .

When I get starved and find that I have a little wife that knows nothing about cooking, and — Oh, my prophetic soul! *you* know anything about cookery! I would as soon think of your knowing the science of sawing wood! We shall have some peculiarly and particularly awful dinners, I make no manner of doubt, but I guess *we* can eat them, and other people who don't like them need not favor us with their company. That is a fair and proper way to look at it, I think.

You are such a darling faithful little correspondent, Livy. I can depend on you all the time, and I do enjoy your letters so much. And every time I come to the last page and find a blank area on it I want to take you in my arms and kiss you and wheedle you into sitting down and filling it up — and right away my conscience pricks me for wanting to make you go to work again when you have already patiently and faithfully wrought more than I deserve, and until your hand is cramped and tired, no doubt, and your body weary of its one position. . . .

I am all impatience to see the picture — and I do hope it will be a good one, this time. I want it to be *more* than a painted iron plate — I want it to be yourself, Livy — I want the eyes to tell me what is passing in the heart, and the hair and the vesture and the attitude to bring to me the vivid presentment of the grace that now is only vaguely glimpsed to me in dreams of you at night when I and the world sleep.

I shudder to think what time it may be! All the sounds are such *late* sounds! But though you were *here* to scold me, darling, I would *not* put this pen down till I had written *I love you, Livy!*

Good-by — Lovingly now and forever and forever.

SAML. L. C.

P.S. Can't stop to correct the letter, Livy.

Romance

by R. S.

MAY 1936

Replete with food, now satiate, somnolent,
He settles in the armchair with his port,
Lights a cigar and, like a runner spent,
Puffs as he turns from stock reports to sport.

With love-refracted reminiscent eyes
Wistful and timidly she watches him;
Her heart peers through the cruel years' disguise
And sees a youth, eager, erect and slim.

Out of the lamplight on the windowpane
He comes to meet her as she once adored him,
Leading his charger by the bridle rein,
His other hand outstretched to draw her toward him.

And thus she stands a moment, while her heart
Beats with the ticking clock. She turns her head.
He nods while reading, hardly hears her part.
"Good night, my dear, I think I'll go to bed."

Wedding Presents

by CHARLES W. MORTON

The author of light prose, Charles W. Morton has been the associate editor of the Atlantic *since 1941. Two collections of his* Atlantic *essays have been published in book form.*

MAY 1948

While American industry is trying for more regular year-round employment, marriages continue to bunch up in June. This puts an unnatural strain on the national economy, leading to hard feelings and even bad language in otherwise amiable households. The private citizen has just paid up his cold-weather obligations and convinced himself that there will never be another winter with quite so much unforeseen expense, when the cascade of engraved phraseology rolls over him.

"What are we going to do about Mary?" his wife asks him.

"Mary who?"

"Mary Jones, of course. I told you about her last week."

"What's the matter with her?"

"Nothing is the matter with her. She is getting married."

The householder tries to toss this aside with a quip: he doesn't intend to obstruct Mary's wedding plans or to "do anything" about the marriage. He babbles on, rather taken with his witticisms, but his wife hews to the line.

"Don't act like that," she says wearily. "You know we have to send them something."

The stereotype is familiar. Who is Mary's man? Never heard of him. Where is he from? Spokane? Mary is going to live in Spokane? Well, why on earth.

This conversation recurs for each of the horde of other imminent brides and grooms. The result never varies. Mary must have a suitable gift, because the invitation was not only to the wedding but also -- to the reception! The householder has been tapped, elected. He is an Old

Friend — that is, a donor. Not to respond, he is made to feel, would throw the bride into hysterics, delay the rites, blight the romance, and even lend a tinge of scandal to the whole project.

The rules demand that wedding gifts must have a permanent quality — no canned goods, potables, pots of cheese-in-wine, or sweet-grass baskets. Divorce statistics are showy, but the assumption holds that the wedding present is necessarily for the ages.

The donor-to-be never does learn who invented the rules, but his gift must be silver — sterling silver. Just as the Amsterdam diamond buyer can spot the imitation at forty paces, so can the wedding party identify plated ware even before the wrappings are off the package.

The smallest piece of silver which can qualify is a marmalade spoon. (A pickle fork is just a little too scrawny.) A seasoned donor could very well buy a gross or two of marmalade spoons and dispose of shopping risks once and for all. The less experienced Old Friends will flounder among candle snuffers and sugar tongs and even become trapped in bulky items like bowls (although you can sometimes find an extremely small bowl), candlesticks, and such.

Silversmiths realized long ago where all this was heading. Rather than lose their position to the tooled-leather crowd or Bohemian glass, they developed sterling silver objects of a truly remarkable thinness. An ounce of gold, flattened to a 150,000th part of an inch in thickness, can be made to cover hundreds of square feet, but the goldbeaters have nothing to compare, in thinness, with the "solid silver" used in wedding gifts. A careless flick from a polishing cloth will dent a wedding gift bowl. Wedding candlesticks, at those points not reinforced internally by concrete, sag and buckle under nothing more than the impact of tallow drippings. Another kind of "hollow ware" is found in the decoy carving knives and forks — very handsome, only don't ever squeeze the handles too firmly.

Some revision in the rules is plainly overdue. The theory of permanence is backfiring. A year later, the bride's friends can't tell whether that is a onetime picture frame or a coffeepot on her buffet. The donor, instead of being fondly recalled as the Old Friend who rallied round in the clutch, is denounced as a skinflint. He may even figure in the divorce proceedings. The more one analyzes the matter, the more inescapable becomes the case for the marmalade spoon. (About $3.75.)

While he is still learning the ropes, the donor will try to balance his books by means of the wedding reception. After all, he reasons, some champagne and sandwiches could be laid off against the marmalade spoon; with any luck, he might nearly break even. But wiser heads than his have schemed the reception. Champagne and sandwiches there will be, in seeming abundance; but no one, donors included, will deplete them by so much as a crust or cup.

The protective technique consists merely of inviting six times as many guests as there is room for. They are immobilized hub to hub in rooms that are too small and too hot. At short intervals, a waiter squirms his way through the crowd, holding aloft — well out of reach — a tray of delicacies, glasses, and a display bottle or two of French champagne. His air is purposive, he manages to keep right on moving, and the guests can only conclude that one of the bridal party has been taken faint, and yonder go her restoratives. From time to time, usually behind a screen, corks are popped and the donor's hopes revive, but he comes to realize that these are intended only as sound-effects. More waiters, taller men and holding the trays even higher, pass to and fro. More guests arrive, more sound-effects.

The donor struggles to an exit and goes home. The reception was ill-planned, he complains: how could they expect guests to get anything to eat or drink in such a paralyzing crush? It takes several receptions before the donor finally understands that the bride's mother always knows a thing or two about marmalade spoons and balancing books, herself.

Why American Marriages Fail

by ANNA A. ROGERS

A controversialist who believed a woman's place is in the home, Anna A. Rogers wrote a critical article, "Why American Mothers Fail"; a second article, entitled "Some Faults of American Men"; and a third, from which we have drawn the following passages.

SEPTEMBER 1907

That a large percentage of marriages achieve very little beyond a bare working compromise with happiness is not to be seriously denied. Nor is it to be doubted that there are more matrimonial catastrophes today than there were a generation ago. In fact, every recent decade has shown a marked increase in the evil of divorce in the United States out of all proportion to the growth of population. It is also a matter of statistics that the evil is growing more rapidly in our country than in Europe. Of course, this preponderance may be partly accounted for by the greater number of divorce courts on this side of the Atlantic. We have 2921 courts which have the power to grant divorces, as against England's one, Germany's twenty-eight, and France's seventy-nine.

Since during the last fifty years more radical changes by far have come in the social status of women than in that of men, there is a chance that at her door may lie the cause of at least some of this fast-growing social disease.

Three instances come uppermost: 1) Woman's failure to realize that marriage is her work in the world. 2) Her growing individualism. 3) Her lost art of giving, replaced by a highly developed receptive faculty.

First: Marriage is woman's work in the world, not man's. From whatever point it is viewed, physical or spiritual, as a question of civic polity or a question of individual ethics, it is her specific share of the world's work — first, last, and always; allotted to her by laws far stronger than she is. And the woman who fails to recognize this and acknowledge it has the germ of divorce in her veins at the outset.

Moonlit and springtime moods all to the contrary, the fact remains that marriage is not a man's work, but one of his dearest delusions, from which he parts begrudgingly. Moreover, it is not even necessary to him in the accomplishment of those things which *are* his work. It is generally no more than his dream of prolonging through years a humanly improbable condition. Happiness as a husband and father has always been his scarcely whispered prayer, his dearest secret hope, toward which all his idealism yearns. That numerous other and very potent motives enter into men's hearts is not in the least overlooked; it is only claimed that to the average man his future marriage is little more than a very beautiful dream.

But the wife who insists childishly upon treating marriage, either in theory or practice, as a beautiful dream, is forgetful of how very little is left of earnest lifework for a woman if she repudiates the dignified *duty* of wedlock placed upon her shoulders. Why should she not be taught the plain fact that no other work really important to the world has ever been done by a woman since "the morning of the world"? Only as a woman, with all that that entails upon her, is she alone, pre-

eminent, unapproachable. And yet apparently her whole energy is today bent upon dethroning herself!

The really small percentage of unmarried women who have the
blessing of paid work of any sort in their lives (as an absolute necessity
against starvation) are of the elect, and of course know it not! The rest
must wait for matrimony, if modest; struggle for it, if not. And then all
this unexpended feminine egoism, joined with unexpended physical energy, demands from the normally expended masculine egoism far more
of everything than he is at all prepared to give, far more than she has
any just claim to demand. More of his love, more admiration, more
time, more money — she wants more of them all to satisfy her recently
discovered Self. Ask the first girl of twenty who presents herself — let
her be the average badly educated, restless, pampered, passionate, but
shallow-natured maiden of the day, superb in physique, meager in sentiment — and note her answer as to what she demands (not hopes for!)
of her probable husband, quite irrespective of what he may get in
return.

He must be a god physically (that seems to be the modern American
girl's *sine qua non*); he must have wealth, brains, education, position, a
perfect temper, and a limitless capacity to adore her, kneeling. And he,
poor soul, after the first exigent mood, which soon passes, wants very
little more than peace and a place to smoke unmolested, combined
preferably with a guaranteed blindness to his general faults and particular fads. A recent public vote on this subject actually resulted in a
stronger poll for "sweet temper" than for any other masculine prerequisite in a wife.

In a broader aspect American women are as a whole pampered and
worshiped out of all reason, a condition which is sometimes found in
young civilizations.

Are Americans Polygamous?

by DAVID L. COHN

A Southern liberal with a number of highly readable books to his credit, David L. Cohn looks into the reasons for our ever-accelerating divorce rate with the calm objectivity of a bachelor.

AUGUST 1947

Our divorce rate has increased 600 per cent since the Civil War. Its trend is still upward. Two new marriages in five now end in divorce. (No one knows how many persons, unable to afford the luxury of divorce, simply "take up" with another mate.) Ten years hence, it is estimated, one marriage in two will conclude in the courts. Who says Americans are monogamous?

Business certainly could not endure as a stable system if two out of five business contracts reached the courts. What must be the effect upon marriage as the contracting parties enter upon it in a nation where so large a part of the contracts are broken? To what degree does the instability of American marriage breed instability?

The casualties of American marriage are higher than those of our wars, and more damaging to the country. You see the scars in the truncated spirit, the embittered heart, and the cynical mind. You see the wounds in the bewildered children of the divorced — displaced persons from the American home. Who shall calculate their pain and ingrowing misery?

Broken marriages indicate America's most unhappy national failure. For if a man fails in the central relationship of his life, if his family is shattered and the security of his children is destroyed, his home is obviously worthless.

This is not to decry the uses of divorce. It is to say that however "right" divorce may be in a given case, it nonetheless marks a grave breakdown in man's most important relationship. And since divorce is an omnipresent fact in our national life, with its rate constantly increasing, American marriage, on the evidence, is a monumental failure. How did this come to be?

Forty years ago, a woman who indulged in extramarital relations not only gravely endangered her marriage, but the penalty of discovery was often banishment from the society of so-called "nice" people. Forty years ago, a girl who indulged in premarital relations gravely endangered her chances of marriage. Today, as we know, effective prohibitions are no longer in force. The married woman who has a love affair may be the subject of gossip but, unless she uses a gun, is not an outcast within her own group. The premarital relations of girls, which have been stimulated by the war, are so common that young men, by their own testimony, no longer expect to marry a virgin. Thousands of girls' letters ask the same question of columnists for the lovelorn: "How can I be 'popular' and virginal?" There is no doubt that the change in our sexual morals over these forty years has had a direct effect upon our divorce rate.

I am not arguing that we are necessarily "worse" than our ancestors; I am simply looking certain facts in the face. Consider the car which enables couples to escape the eyes of the community; consider also the widespread knowledge of contraception which enables them to escape the biological consequences of their sexual acts. Who shall say how our elders might have behaved in the 1890s if these factors had then been present?

With our departure from the old sexual standards and with promiscuity made inviting by both world wars, one can mark the growing irresponsibility toward marriage. Marriage has been made almost meaningless by many who marry with the reservation that if they do not like the marriage, they will quickly get out of it. Whenever the parties enter into the marriage contract with an escape clause in their minds, it is a marriage of the market place, as when one buys a stove upon thirty days' trial. Yet such marriages, which in many cases are merely the expression of an unconscious desire to have the law bless a fleeting experimental mood, are performed every day, and this with the general approbation of the community, for they could neither exist without that approbation nor be conceived in an atmosphere hostile to them.

No people can take marriage seriously who take divorce lightly, even jocularly. Picture magazines display pages of photographs of divorce court scenes as casually as though they were fashion shows. Gossip columns, read by the millions, gleefully speculate upon prospective divorces among the well-known. Metropolitan newspapers carry announcements of the multiple marriages and divorces of the fashionable, for Names Make News. These facts are significant in any appraisal of our manners, since in our allegedly classless society the masses tend to ape the classes.

This is the land where we mouth noble words about marriage, and set up profitable red-light districts of divorce. These districts are Nevada, Arkansas, Florida, California, Wyoming — and others are eager to enter the trade. This is the country, and these are the states, where the marriage contract, alone among contracts, may be broken at will — even though, nine times out of ten, the breaking is a travesty of the law because it is an act of collusion between the parties.

In these districts no questions are asked. The test is simply that of a house of prostitution: ability and willingness to pay for the services demanded. Residence is established by hanging up your hat, and a hat for the hanging may be rented. Divorce is granted for good reason or no reason. The complainant's whim is the state's will. Divorce is big business. Competition is keen, and while the state, in its organized harlotry, does not send its girls to meet the train, the traveler is sure of a hearty welcome by the madam masquerading as a judge in what — God help us — is known as a court of justice. Competitive pressure has reduced the required period of legal residence in Nevada from six months to six weeks.

Business magazines report divorce business as they report sales of sewer pipe. Business Week (July 14, 1945) says:

> Estimates of what the divorce business means to Reno run from $3,000,000 to $4,000,000 a year. It costs . . . $500 to $600 to get a divorce in Reno. . . . Counsel fees vary widely. The basic fee is said to be $100 in Las Vegas, $150 in Reno. From there it ranges up to about $5000 for the average wealthy client, a great deal more for the fabulously rich (Gloria Vanderbilt is said to have paid $25,000 for her freedom; Barbara Hutton $50,000).

Nevada, with 0.1 per cent of our population, grants more than 2 per cent of our divorces. But the greatest increase in the divorce traffic was recorded in 1945 in Los Angeles County, California, where 17,083 decrees were entered. This is almost double the Nevada trade, and three times the divorce sales of a rising competitor — Miami, Florida.

We have, then, the revolting spectacle of several states scrambling for divorce business as they do for the tourist trade. Man's most significant personal relationship is sundered in an atmosphere of chicanery and buffoonery.

Why do our marriages fail so widely? The reasons are many and complex, but only a few can be touched upon here.

It may be that in this era of revaluation of values, we are slowly abandoning our ancient concepts of marriage and the family as we move toward new forms whose shapes are still inchoate. Man's relation to God, the state, the family, and marriage have all come under increasingly sharp scrutiny and have been subjected to various degrees of change since the French Revolution. Two hundred years ago there began the gradual dechristianization of the West, in the sense that man, not God, was enthroned at the center of the universe. The consequences are necessarily profound and all-pervasive. But mankind does not trust itself. The period since 1914 has been marked by wars, revolutions, crashings of empires, risings of dictators, and destruction unparalleled in history. Men yearn for a security which does not exist. They seek a faith which they do not find in their religions. Their moorings have been swept away. They scarcely know what to believe or where to turn.

Monogamous marriage, as we have known it, is challenged. For if repetitive divorces are permitted for capricious reasons — as in the notorious Tommy Manville case — we are tacitly establishing a legal halfway house between monogamy and polygamy. It is a polygamous relation accessible now only to the well-to-do. The ordinary man can no more afford the luxury of repetitive divorces than the ordinary Moslem, to whom polygamy is permitted by his faith, can afford four wives. But this is unimportant. What is important is that the law permits men to skip into and out of marriage at will, and the law is the expression of the will of the people. If we abandon monogamous marriage, it follows that we must also abandon our old concepts of the family and the relationship of parents to children.

It is too early to say precisely in what direction we are heading, but it is evident from the statistics of divorce that we are not heading in the direction of re-establishing monogamous marriage and the family in their once almost impregnable position. Marriage, as we know it, is an institution of relatively recent origin. Monogamous marriage is largely a product of the Western world. Cultures as great as ours, or greater, have long endured under other forms of marriage. And it may be that Americans, subconsciously believing that marriage and the family, as they have anciently existed, no longer suit their needs, are slowly changing them for other forms.

If we seek, however, specific reasons for our high divorce rate, we shall find them expressed in our attitudes and aspirations, in our character, in the manner in which we think and act. It is apparent, for example, that divorce lightly asked and lightly granted is individualism gone mad. It is an orgy of the ego. An anarchy within the law. It is an indulgence of the gratification of the immediate desires of man or wife without regard to family, children, or state. It is the case of *my* welfare and the rest be damned.

Although the landscape of America is cluttered with the wreckage of marriage, it is characteristic that we continue to foster a falsely romantic point of view toward it. Marriage is a difficult, if deeply rewarding, exercise in human relations. Perhaps it is even, as William Graham Sumner put it, "a state of antagonistic coöperation." Yet it is represented to the young by their elders, the movies, and slick magazine fiction, as a perpetual Christmas Eve with Tiny Tim passing double Martinis and saying "God bless you, every one." The deception is cruel and stupid. It is cruel because it is bound to bring about a mood of revulsion and disappointment in the mind of the deceived. It is stupid because it is no more a preparation for marriage than tree-sitting is a preparation for the ballet. And it is the expression of the dangerous mawkish romanticism of a people who refuse to subscribe to the first principle of becoming adult: to recognize that every blessing has its price.

We teach our young that to be married is automatically to be happy. We believe that everybody is, ought to be, or can be made happy; that all are entitled to happiness as to fresh air. One must be happy all the time; slap-happy if possible. But simultaneously, in our anarchy of impermanence, we believe that if we are not happy in one marriage we shall surely be happy in another. This is the miracle wrought by a change of address and laundry marks. Few people pursue happiness with such demoniac energy as we, briefly pausing at one roadside stand of illusion before rushing to another.

Happiness in marriage eludes those who make a dogma of it, and so they become foes to compromise. Marriage is, among other things, the art of the possible. Love is not "pure," but exists in combination with other things. It is interwoven with heredity, family or class tradition, religion, prejudices, predilections, and an infinite number of other qualities in an infinite number of variations.

The attitudes among us that destroy marriage are the result of our emotional and intellectual adolescence as a people. This, in my opinion, is the chief factor in our appalling divorce rate. The United States is the only country where the husband often is not — and does not want to be — a man, but a Boy. He wants, poor thing, not to be wived but to be mothered. Perhaps that is why he so often calls Maizie Mama, while Iwilla, his daughter, becomes Sister, and Joe, his son, becomes Brother. But Maizie dreamed of marrying a Man. Nobody told her that our men like to be giants in their offices and midgets in their homes. Yet all goes along well enough in the first years of marriage because Maizie finds it pleasant to mother her young boyish husband. But when the children come, she can far more satisfactorily discharge her maternal impulses through them. Then she begins to find it tiresome to baby her husband. She yearns to live with a Man, and since neither entered the marriage with mature attitudes toward it, while its contents made maturing impossible, Maizie soon is on her way to Reno. There she gets a divorce, and this time marries a man who wears knitted ties unlike the foulards affected by her first husband.

So, too, out of our immaturity, we have come to look upon marriage either as a relationship at will, or as a finality. In the first case we do not take it seriously. In the second case we see it murkily. Marriage is obviously not a finality but a beginning, since if it is to thrive, it must be constantly renewed. Marrying is a different thing from marriage, for the one implies something completed, while implicit in the other is the concept of becoming rather than being. Girls are brought up to look forward to marrying; then they may relax. Men marry to "settle down." But both may discover too late that a spiritual ferment, a search for a perfection never to be found, is the condition precedent to spiritual repose. We find such a concept tedious and emotionally tiring. It suggests the task never completed, the problem never solved. We want to do something and be done with it. Yet the fact that there are no finalities in marriage, nor even in divorce, makes little difference to us in our search for marital happiness. We continue to get divorced, change wives, breed various sets of children, and applaud when the speaker of the day comes to his thundering peroration — "And this, ladies and gentlemen, we must do not only for our own sake but for the sake of our children's children."

The City

The city and its influence for good and ill on the character of our country was a matter of conscience to the Atlantic *editors, and their concern increased as the incoming hordes of immigrants were jammed into tenement districts along the Atlantic seaboard. Fiction writers could take the romantic view, as did F. J. O'Brien, who remarked in his short story "The Wondersmith," which we published in October 1859, "I like a dirty slum; not because I am naturally unclean — I have not a drop of Neapolitan blood in my veins — but because I generally find a certain sediment of philosophy precipitated in its gutters. A clean street is terribly prosaic." But a more penetrating comment came from Charles Eliot Norton, the fastidious, more likely to be heard on art than the slums, who in his article on "Model Lodging-Houses in Boston," which appeared in June 1860, observed that "Life is not now to be reckoned by its 'threescore years and ten.' Its average duration in Boston is little above twenty years; in New York it is less than twenty years. Is the diminution of the length of life to go on from year to year?"*

The editors sought for the testimony of the newcomers and in Jacob A. Riis and Mary Antin the Atlantic *discovered two spokesmen whose articles, which were later to be published in book form, had an arousing impact on the country. Riis had come from Denmark; as a boy he had been scarred by the Danish slums, but the experiences which he encountered and uncovered in New York City were not tender by comparison. With the full power of his prose he blasted the corruption in City Hall which blocked the way to reform; his book,* The Making of an American, *was a challenge which had to be answered, and it is interesting that he sets the year 1879 as the time when the civic conscience awoke. Mary Antin was twelve, her father thirty-two, when the family landed in Boston. They were Russian Jews, formerly affluent, now stripped and driven into exile by the pogrom. They knew no English and had few resources to capitalize. In the public schools Mary found her liberation, and her articles on* The Promised Land *were a paean to the freedom and friendliness of the new world.*

But still the new bloodstreams flowed in and still there was congestion and misery and corruption. The beacon which Hull House became in Chicago was kindled by a small dedicated band led by Jane Addams and included such stalwarts as Julia Lathrop, Alice and Nora Hamilton, Mary Rozet Smith, and Harold Ickes. Their record was a shining one, and none tells it better than Miss Addams herself and Dr. Hamilton.

The fight still goes on, and to the age-old struggle against corruption in the City Hall must now be added the strenuous effort to revitalize the blighted areas of the old metropolis — to build new cities for old, as Robert Moses and William Zeckendorf have been doing in New York and as the Allegheny Conference under the lead of Richard Mellon, Wallace Richards, and Park H. Martin has done in Pittsburgh.

The Battle with the Slum

by JACOB A. RIIS

Jacob A. Riis, a native of Denmark, was twenty-one when he landed as an immigrant in New York on Whitsunday, 1870. He had known the tenements in Denmark and now he lived through the horror of the slums, which awaited every immigrant of that day. The experience fired him, when he became established as a journalist, to do some of his best writing for the Atlantic.

MAY 1899

The battle with the slum began the day civilization recognized in it her enemy. It was a losing fight until conscience joined forces with fear and self-interest against it. When common sense and the golden rule obtain among men as a rule of practice, it will be over. The two have not always been classed together, but here they are plainly seen to be allies. Justice to the individual is accepted in theory as the only safe groundwork of the commonwealth. When it is practiced in dealing with the slum, there will shortly be no slum. We need not wait for the millennium to get rid of it. We can do it now. All that is required is that it shall not be left to itself. When a man is drowning, the thing to do is to pull him out of the water; later there will be time for talking it over.

The slum complaint had been chronic in all ages, but the great changes which the nineteenth century saw, the new industry, political freedom, brought on an acute attack which threatened to become fatal. Too many of us had supposed that, built as our commonwealth was on universal suffrage, it would be proof against the complaints that harassed older states; but in fact it turned out that there was extra hazard in that. Having solemnly resolved that all men are created equal and have certain inalienable rights, among them life, liberty, and the pursuit of happiness, we shut our eyes and waited for the formula to work. It was as if a man with a cold should take the doctor's prescription to bed with him, expecting it to cure him. The formula was all right, but merely repeating it worked no cure. When after a hundred years we opened our eyes, it was upon sixty cents a day as the living wage of the workingwoman in our cities; upon knee pants at forty cents a dozen for the making; upon the Potter's Field taking tithe of our city life, ten per cent each year for the trench, truly the Lost Tenth of the slum. Our country had grown great and rich; through our ports was poured food for the millions of Europe. But in the back streets multitudes huddled in ignorance and want. The foreign oppressor had been vanquished, the fetters stricken from the black man at home; but his white brother, in his bitter plight, sent up a cry of distress that had in it a distinct note of menace. Political freedom we had won; but the problem of helpless poverty, grown vast with the added offscourings of the Old World, mocked us, unsolved. Liberty at sixty cents a day set presently its stamp upon the government of our cities, and it became the scandal and the peril of our political system.

So the battle began. Three times since the Civil War the slum confronted us in New York with its challenge. In the darkest days of the great struggle it was the treacherous mob; later on, the threat of the cholera, which found swine foraging in the streets as the only scavengers and a swarming host — but little above the hog in its appetites and in the quality of the shelter afforded it — peopling the back alleys. Still later the mob, caught looting the city's treasury with its idol, the thief Tweed, at its head, had, drunk with power and plunder, insolently defied the outraged community to do its worst. There were meetings and protests. The rascals were turned out for a season; the archthief died in jail. There are other fights to be fought in that war, other victories to be won, and it is slow work. It was nearly ten years after the great robbery before decency got the upper grip in good earnest. That was when the civic conscience awoke in 1879.

In that year the slum was arraigned in the churches. The sad and shameful story was told of how it grew and was fostered by avarice that saw in the homeless crowds from over the sea only a chance for business and exploited them to the uttermost, making sometimes a hundred per cent on the capital invested — always most out of the worst houses, from the tenants of which "nothing was expected" save that they pay the usurious rents — how Christianity, citizenship, human fellowship, shook their skirts clear of the rabble that was only good enough to fill the greedy purse, and how the rabble, left to itself, improved such opportunities as it found after such fashion as it knew; how it ran elections merely to count its thugs in, and fattened at the public crib; and how the whole evil thing had its root in the tenements, where the home had ceased to be sacred — those dark and deadly dens in which the family ideal was tortured to death and character was smothered, in which children were "damned rather than born" into the world, thus realizing a slum kind of foreordination to torment, happily brief in many cases. The Tenement House Committee long afterward called the worst of the barracks "infant slaughterhouses," and showed, by reference to the mortality lists, that they killed one in every five babies born in them.

The story shocked the town into action. Plans for a better kind of tenement were called for, and a premium was put on every ray of light and breath of air that could be let into it. Money was raised to build model houses, and a bill to give the health authorities summary powers in dealing with tenements was sent to the legislature. The landlords held it up until the last day of the session, when it was forced through by an angered public opinion. The power of the cabal was broken. The landlords had found their Waterloo. Many of them got rid of their property, which in a large number of cases they had never seen, and tried to forget the source of their ill-gotten wealth. Light and air did find their way into the tenements in a halfhearted fashion, and we began to count the tenants as "souls." That is one of our milestones in the history of New York. They were never reckoned so before; no one ever thought of them as "souls." So, restored to human fellowship, in the twilight of the air shaft that had penetrated to their dens, the first Tenement House Committee was able to make them out "better than the houses" they lived in, and a long step forward was taken. The Mulberry Bend, the wicked core of the "bloody Sixth Ward," was marked for destruction, and all slumdom held its breath to see it go. With that gone, it seemed as if the old days must be gone too, never to return. There would not be another Mulberry Bend. As long as it stood, there was yet a chance. The slum had backing, as it were.

The civic conscience was not very robust yet, and required many and protracted naps. It slumbered fitfully, waking up now and then with a start, while the politicians did their best to lull it back to its slumbers. I wondered often, in those years of delay, if it was just plain stupidity that kept the politicians from spending the money which the law had put within their grasp; for with every year that passed a million dollars that could have been used for small park purposes was lost.

Today we can count the months to the time when every child who knocks shall find a seat in our schools. We have a school census to tell us of the need. In that most crowded neighborhood in all the world, where the superintendent lately pleaded in vain for three new schools, five have been built, the finest in this or any other land — great, light, and airy structures, with playgrounds on the roof — and all over the city the like are going up. The briefest of our laws, every word of which is like the blow of a hammer driving the nails home in the coffin of the bad old days, says that never one shall be built without its playground. So the boy is coming to his rights.

The streets are cleaned; the slum has been washed. Even while I am writing, a bill is urged in the legislature to build in every senatorial district in the city a gymnasium and a public bath. It matters little whether it passes at this session or not. The important thing is that it is there. The rest will follow. A people's club is being organized to crowd out the saloon that has had a monopoly of the brightness and the cheer in the tenement streets too long. The labor unions are bestirring themselves to deal with the sweating curse, and the gospel of less law and more enforcement sits enthroned at Albany. Theodore Roosevelt will teach us again Jefferson's forgotten lesson, that "the whole art of government consists in being honest."

Of free soup there is an end. It was never food for free men. Our experience has taught us a new reading of the old word that charity covers a multitude of sins. It does. Uncovering some of them has kept us busy since our conscience awoke, and there are more left. The worst of them all, that awful parody on municipal charity, the police station lodging room, is gone after twenty years of persistent attack upon the foul dens — years during which they were arraigned, condemned, indicted by every authority having jurisdiction. The stale beer dives went with them, and the grip of the tramp on our throat has been loosened.

One after another, the outworks of the slum have been taken. The higher standards now set up on every hand, in the cleaner streets, in the better schools, in the parks and the clubs, in the settlements, and in the thousand and one agencies for good that touch and help the lives of the poor at as many points, will tell at no distant day and react upon the homes and upon their builders. Philanthropy is not sitting idle and waiting. It is building tenements on the humane plan that lets in sunshine and air and hope. It is putting up hotels deserving of the name for the army that just now had no other home than the cheap lodging houses which Inspector Byrnes fitly called "nurseries of crime." These are standards from which there is no backing down, and they are here to stay, for they pay. That is the test. Not charity, but justice — that is the gospel which they preach.

The Devil Baby at Hull House

by JANE ADDAMS

In 1899 Jane Addams, with her friend Ellen Gates Starr, rented the old Hull mansion in one of the worst of Chicago's slums. There her tact in handling people, her affection for children, her revulsion from cruelty and injustice soon made Hull House the most famous haven in the country. She was its director for forty-six years.

OCTOBER 1916

The knowledge of the existence of the Devil Baby burst upon the residents of Hull House one day when three Italian women, with an excited rush through the door, demanded that he be shown to them. No amount of denial convinced them that he was not there, for they knew exactly what he was like, with his cloven hoofs, his pointed ears, and diminutive tail; moreover, the Devil Baby had been able to speak as soon as he was born and was most shockingly profane.

The three women were but the forerunners of a veritable multitude; for six weeks the streams of visitors from every part of the city and suburbs to this mythical baby poured in all day long, and so far into the night that the regular activities of the settlement were almost swamped.

The Italian version, with a hundred variations, dealt with a pious Italian girl married to an atheist. Her husband vehemently tore a holy picture from the bedroom wall, saying that he would quite as soon have a devil in the house as that; whereupon the devil incarnated himself in her coming child. As soon as the Devil Baby was born, he ran about the table shaking his finger in deep reproach at his father, who finally caught him and in fear and trembling brought him to Hull House. When the residents there, in spite of the baby's shocking appearance, wishing to save his soul, took him to church for baptism, they found that the shawl was empty and the Devil Baby, fleeing from the holy water, ran lightly over the backs of the pews.

The Jewish version, again with variations, was to the effect that the

father of six daughters had said before the birth of a seventh child that
he would rather have a devil in the house than another girl, whereupon
the Devil Baby promptly appeared.

Save for a red automobile which occasionally figured in the story, and
a cigar which, in some versions, the newborn child snatched from his
father's lips, the tale might have been fashioned a thousand years ago.

Although the visitors to the Devil Baby included people of every degree of prosperity and education, even physicians and trained nurses
who assured us of their scientific interest, the story constantly demonstrated the power of an old wives' tale among thousands of people in
modern society who are living in a corner of their own, their vision fixed,
their intelligence held by some iron chain of silent habit. To such primitive people the metaphor apparently is still the very stuff of life; or,
rather, no other form of statement reaches them, and the tremendous
tonnage of current writing for them has no existence. It was in keeping
with their simple habits that the reputed presence of the Devil Baby at
Hull House did not reach the newspapers until the fifth week of his so-
journ — after thousands of people had already been informed of his
whereabouts by the old method of passing news from mouth to mouth.

During the weeks of excitement it was the old women who really
seemed to have come into their own, and perhaps the most significant
result of the incident was the reaction of the story upon them. It stirred
their minds and memories as with a magic touch; it loosened their
tongues and revealed the inner life and thoughts of those who are so often inarticulate. These old women enjoyed a moment of triumph, as if
they had made good at last and had come into a region of sanctions and
punishments which they understood.

Throughout six weeks, as I went about Hull House, I would hear a
voice at the telephone repeating for the hundredth time that day, "No,
there is no such baby"; "No, we never had it here"; "No, he couldn't have
seen it for fifty cents"; "We didn't send it anywhere because we never
had it"; "I don't mean to say that your sister-in-law lied, but there must
be some mistake"; "There is no use getting up an excursion from Mil-
waukee, for there isn't any Devil Baby at Hull House"; "We can't give
reduced rates because we are not exhibiting anything"; and so on and on.
As I came near the front door, I would catch snatches of arguments that
were often acrimonious: "Why do you let so many people believe it, if it
isn't here?" "We have taken three lines of cars to come, and we have as
much right to see it as anybody else"; "This is a pretty big place, of
course you could hide it easy enough." We had doubtless struck a

case of what the psychologists call the contagion of emotion, added to that aesthetic sociability which impels any one of us to drag the entire household to the window when a procession comes into the street or a rainbow appears in the sky.

But the Devil Baby was of course worth many processions and rainbows, and I will confess that, as the empty show went on day after day, I quite revolted against such a vapid manifestation of an admirable human trait. There was always one exception, however: whenever I heard the high, eager voices of old women, I was irresistibly interested and left anything I might be doing in order to listen to them.

Perhaps my many talks with these aged visitors crystallized thoughts and impressions that I had been receiving through years; or the tale itself may have ignited a fire, as it were, whose light illumined some of my darkest memories of neglected and uncomfortable old age, of old peasant women who had ruthlessly probed into the ugly depths of human nature in themselves and others. Many of them who came to see the Devil Baby had been forced to face tragic human experiences; the powers of brutality and horror had had full scope in their lives, and for years they had been acquainted with disaster and death. Such old women do not shirk life's misery by feeble idealism, for they are long past the stage of make-believe. They relate without flinching the most hideous experiences. "My face has had this queer twist for now nearly sixty years; I was ten when it got that way, the night after I saw my father do my mother to death with his knife." "Yes, I had fourteen children; only two grew to be men and both of them were killed in the same explosion. I was never sure they brought home the right bodies." But even the most hideous sorrows which the old women related had apparently subsided into the paler emotion of ineffectual regret, after memory had long done her work upon them; the old people seemed, in some unaccountable way, to lose all bitterness and resentment against life.

Perhaps those women, because they had come to expect nothing more from life and had perforce ceased from grasping and striving, had obtained, if not renunciation, at least that quiet endurance which allows the wounds of the spirit to heal. Through their stored-up habit of acquiescence, they vouchsafed a fleeting glimpse of that translucent wisdom so often embodied in old women but so difficult to portray.

Among the visitors were pitiful old women who, although they had already reconciled themselves to much misery, were still enduring more. "You might say it's a disgrace to have your son beat you up for the sake of a bit of money you've earned by scrubbing — your own man is different — but I haven't the heart to blame the boy for doing what he's seen all his life; his father forever went wild when the drink was in him and struck me to the very day of his death. The ugliness was born in the boy as the marks of the devil was born in the poor child upstairs."

This more primitive type embodies the eternal patience of those humble toiling women who through the generations have been held of little value, save as their drudgery ministered to their men. One of them related her habit of going through the pockets of her drunken son every payday, and complained that she had never got so little as the night before, only twenty-five cents out of fifteen dollars he had promised for the rent long overdue. "I had to get that as he lay in the alley before the door; I couldn't pull him in, and the copper who helped him home left as soon as he heard me coming and pretended he didn't see me. I have no food in the house nor coffee to sober him up with. I know perfectly well that you will ask me to eat something here, but if I can't carry it home, I won't take a bite nor a sup. I have never told you so much before. Since one of the nurses said he could be arrested for my nonsupport, I have been awfully close-mouthed. It's the foolish way all the women in our street are talking about the Devil Baby that's loosened my tongue — more shame to me."

There are those, if possible more piteous still, who have become absolutely helpless and can therefore no longer perform the household services exacted from them. One last wish has been denied them. "I hoped to go before I became a burden, but it was not to be"; and the long days of unwonted idleness are darkened by the haunting fear that "they" will come to think the burden too heavy and decide that the poorhouse is "the best." Even then there is no word of blame for undutiful children or heedless grandchildren, for apparently all that is petty and transitory falls away from austere old age; the fires are burnt out; resentments, hatreds, and even cherished sorrows have become actually unintelligible. It is as if the horrors through which these old people had passed had never existed for them, and, facing death as they are, they seem anxious to speak only such words of groping wisdom as they are able.

The vivid interest of so many old women in the story of the Devil Baby may have been an unconscious, although powerful, testimony that tragic experiences gradually become dressed in such trappings in order that their spent agony may prove of some use to a world which learns at the hardest; and that the strivings and sufferings of men and women long since dead, their emotions no longer connected with flesh and blood, are thus transmuted into legendary wisdom. The young are forced to heed the warning in such a tale, although for the most part it is so easy for them to disregard the words of the aged. That the old women who came to visit the Devil Baby believed that the story would secure them a hearing at home was evident, and as they prepared themselves with every detail of it, their old faces shone with a timid satisfaction. Their features, worn and scarred by harsh living, even as effigies built into the floor of an old church become dim and defaced by rough-shod feet, grew poignant and solemn. In the midst of their double bewilderment, both that the younger generation were walking in such strange paths and that no one would listen to them, for one moment there flickered up that last hope of a disappointed life, that it may at least serve as a warning while affording material for exciting narrations.

Sometimes in talking to one of them, who was "but a hair's breadth this side of the darkness," one realized that old age has its own expression for the mystic renunciation of the world. The impatience with all nonessentials, the craving to be free from hampering bonds and soft conditions, was perhaps typified in our own generation by Tolstoi's last impetuous journey, the light of his genius for a moment making comprehensible to us that unintelligible impulse of the aged.

Often, in the midst of a conversation, one of these touching old women would quietly express a longing for death, as if it were a natural fulfillment of an inmost desire. Her sincerity and anticipation were so genuine that I would feel abashed in her presence.

Such impressions were in their essence transitory, but one result from the hypothetical visit of the Devil Baby to Hull House will, I think, remain: a realization of the sifting and reconciling power inherent in memory itself. The old women, with much to aggravate and little to soften the habitual bodily discomforts of old age, exhibited an emotional serenity so vast and reassuring that I found myself perpetually speculating as to how soon the fleeting and petty emotions which seem so unduly important to us now might be thus transmuted; at what moment we might expect the perplexities of life to be brought under this appeasing memory, with its ultimate power to increase the elements of beauty and significance and to reduce, if not to eliminate, stupidity and resentment.

As our visitors to the Devil Baby came day by day, it was gradually evident that the simpler women were moved not wholly by curiosity, but that many of them prized the story as a valuable instrument in the business of living.

The legend exhibited all the persistence of one of those tales which have doubtless been preserved through the centuries because of their taming effects upon recalcitrant husbands and fathers. Shamefaced men brought by their womenfolk to see the baby but ill concealed their triumph when there proved to be no such visible sign of retribution for domestic derelictions. On the other hand, numbers of men came by themselves. One group from a neighboring factory, on their "own time," offered to pay twenty-five cents, a half dollar, two dollars apiece to see the child, insisting that it must be at Hull House because "the womenfolks had seen it." To my query as to whether they supposed we would exhibit for money a poor little deformed baby, if one had been born in the neighborhood, they replied, "Sure, why not?" "It teaches a good lesson, too," they added as an afterthought, or perhaps as a concession to the strange moral standards of a place like Hull House. All the members in this group of hard-working men, in spite of a certain swagger toward one another and a tendency to bully the derelict showman, wore that hangdog look betraying the sense of unfair treatment which a man is so apt to feel when his womankind makes an appeal to the supernatural. In their determination to see the child, the men recklessly divulged much more concerning their motives than they had meant to do, and their talk confirmed my impression that such a story may still act as a restraining influence in that sphere of marital conduct which, next to primitive religion itself, we are told, has always afforded the most fertile field for irrational taboos and savage punishments.

What story more than this could be calculated to secure sympathy for the mother of too many daughters, and contumely for the irritated father? The touch of mysticism, the supernatural sphere in which it was placed, would render a man perfectly helpless.

The story of the Devil Baby, evolved today as it might have been centuries before in response to the imperative needs of anxious wives and mothers, recalled the theory that woman first fashioned the fairy story, that combination of wisdom and romance, in an effort to tame her mate and to make him a better father to her children, until such stories finally became a rude creed for domestic conduct, softening the treatment that men accorded to women.

These first pitiful efforts of women, so widespread and powerful that we have not yet escaped their influence, still cast vague shadows upon the vast spaces of life, shadows that are dim and distorted because of their distant origin. They remind us that for thousands of years women had nothing to oppose against unthinkable brutality save "the charm of words," no other implement with which to subdue the fiercenesses of the world about them.

The American Miracle

by MARY ANTIN

Mary Antin, a Russian Jew, was twelve and her father thirty-two when the family landed in Boston. They had been people of affluence in Russia before the pogroms drove them out; now, stripped of possessions and with no English and no negotiable resources, they took refuge in the West End. It was in the public school that Mary first found her liberation, and this she went on to describe in a series of Atlantic *articles which became, in her famous book* The Promised Land, *a paean to the freedom of the New World.*

JANUARY 1912

Anybody who knows Boston knows that West and North ends are the wrong ends of that city. They form the tenement district, or, in the newer phrase, the slums of Boston. Anybody who is acquainted with the slums of any American metropolis knows that that is the quarter where poor immigrants foregather, to live, for the most part, as unkempt, half-washed, toiling, unaspiring foreigners; picturesque in the eyes of social missionaries, the despair of boards of health, the hope of ward politicians, the touchstone of American democracy.

But I saw a very different picture on my introduction to Union Place, off Wall Street in the West End. I saw two imposing rows of brick buildings, loftier than any dwelling I had ever lived in. Brick was even on the ground for me to tread on, instead of common earth or boards. Many friendly windows stood open, filled with uncovered heads of women and children. I thought the people were interested in us, which was very neighborly. I looked up to the topmost row of windows, and my eyes were filled with the May blue of an American sky!

Our initiation into American ways began with the first step on the new soil. My father found occasion to instruct or correct us even on the way from the pier to Wall Street, which journey we made crowded together in a rickety cab. He told us not to lean out of the windows, not to point, and explained the word "greenhorn." We did not want to be greenhorns, and gave the strictest attention to my father's instructions.

The first meal was an object lesson of much variety. My father produced several kinds of food, ready to eat, without any cooking, from little tin cans that had printing all over them. He attempted to introduce us to a queer, slippery kind of fruit, which he called "banana," but had to give it up for the time being. After the meal, he had better luck with a curious piece of furniture on runners, which he called "rocking chair." There were five of us newcomers, and we found five different ways of getting into the American vehicle of perpetual motion, and as many ways of getting out of it.

In our flat we did not think of such a thing as storing the coal in the bathtub. There was no bathtub. So in the evening of the first day my father conducted us to the public baths. As we moved along in a little procession, I was delighted with the illumination of the streets. So many lamps, and they burned until morning, my father said, and so people did not need to carry lanterns. In America, then, everything was free, as we had heard in Russia. Light was free; the streets were as bright as a synagogue on a holy day. Music was free; we had been serenaded, to our gaping delight, by a brass band of many pieces, soon after our installation on Union Place.

Education was free. That subject my father had written about repeatedly, as comprising his chief hope for us children, the essence of American opportunity, the treasure that no thief could touch, not even misfortune or poverty. It was the one thing that he was able to promise us when he sent for us, surer, safer than bread or shelter.

With our despised immigrant clothing we shed also our impossible Hebrew names. A committee of our friends, several years ahead of us in American experience, put their heads together and concocted American names for us all. Those of our real names that had no pleasing American equivalents they ruthlessly discarded, content if they retained the initials. My mother, possessing a name that was untranslatable, was punished with the undignified nickname of Annie. Fetchke, Joseph, and Edle Dvereh issued as Frieda, Joseph, and Dora, respectively. As for poor me, I was simply cheated. My Hebrew name being Maryashe in full — Mashke for short — Russianized into Marya (Mar-ya), my friends said it would hold good in English as *Mary;* which was very disappointing, as I longed to possess a really strange-sounding American name like the others.

I am forgetting the consolation I had, in this matter of names, from the use of my surname, which I have had no occasion to mention until now. My father, I found on my arrival, was *Mr. Antin* on the slightest provocation, and not, as in Polotzk, on state occasions alone. And so I was *Mary Antin,* and I felt very important to answer to such a dignified title. It was just like America that even plain people should wear their surnames on weekdays.

Father himself conducted me to school, with my brother and little sister. He would not have delegated that mission to the President of the United States. At last the four of us stood around the teacher's desk; and my father, in his impossible English, gave us over in her charge, with some broken word of his hopes for us that his swelling heart could no longer contain. I think Miss Nixon guessed what my father's best English could not convey. I think she divined that by the simple act of delivering our school certificates to her he took possession of America.

There were about half a dozen of us beginners in English, in age from six to fifteen. Miss Nixon made a special class of us, and aided us so skillfully and earnestly in our endeavors to "see-a-cat," and "hear-a-dog," and "look-at-the-hen," that we turned over page after page of the ravishing history, eager to find out how the common world looked, smelled, and tasted in the strange speech. The teacher knew just when to let us help each other out with a word in our own tongue — it happened that we were all Jews — and so, working all together, we actually covered more ground in a lesson than the native classes, composed entirely of the little tots.

If I was eager and diligent, my teachers did not sleep. As fast as my knowledge of English allowed, they advanced me from grade to grade, without reference to the usual schedule of promotions. She whom I found in the next grade became so dear a friend that I can hardly name her with the rest, though I mention none of them lightly. Her approval was always dear to me, first because she was Teacher, and afterwards, as long as she lived, because she was my Miss Dillingham. My father was right when he often said, in discussing my prospects, that ability would be promptly recognized in the public schools. Rapid as was my progress, on account of the advantages with which I started, some of the other "green" pupils were not far behind me: within a grade or two, by the end of the year. My brother, whose whole childhood had been one hideous nightmare, what with the stupid rebbe, the cruel whip, and the general repression of life in the Pale, surprised my father by the progress he made under intelligent, sympathetic guidance. Indeed, he soon had a reputation in the school that the American boys envied; and all through the school course he more than held his own with pupils of his age. So much for the right and wrong way of doing things.

There is a record of my early progress in English much better than my recollections, however accurate and definite these may be. I have several reasons for introducing it here. First, it shows what the Russian Jew can do with an adopted language; next, it proves that vigilance of our public-school teachers of which I spoke; and last, I am proud of it! That is an unnecessary confession, but I could not be satisfied to insert the record here, with my vanity unavowed.

This is the document, copied from an educational journal, a tattered copy of which lies in my lap as I write — treasured for fifteen years.

EDITOR *Primary Education:*

This is the uncorrected paper of a Russian child twelve years old, who had studied English only four months. She had never, until September, been to school even in her own country and has heard English spoken *only* at school. I shall be glad if the paper of my pupil and the above explanation may appear in your paper.

M. S. DILLINGHAM

Chelsea, Mass.

SNOW

Snow is frozen moisture which comes from the clouds.

Now the snow is coming down in feather-flakes, which makes nice snow-balls. But there is still one kind of snow more. This kind of snow is called snow-crystals, for its comes down in little curly balls. These snow crystals aren't quite as good for snow-balls as feather-flakes, for they (the snow-crystals) are dry: so they can't keep together as feather-flakes do.

The snow is dear to some children for they like sleighing.

As I said at the top — the snow comes from the clouds.

Now the trees are bare, no flowers are to see in the fields and gardens, (we all know why) and the whole world seems like asleep without the happy birds songs which left us till spring. But the snow which drove away all these pretty and happy things, try (as I think) not to make us at all unhappy; they covered up the branches of the trees, the fields, the gardens and houses, and the whole world looks like dressed in a beautiful white — instead of green — dress, with the sky looking down on it with a pale face.

And so the people can find some joy in it, too, without the happy summer.

MARY ANTIN

And now that it stands there, with *her* name over it, I am ashamed of my flippant talk about vanity. More to me than all the praise I could hope to win by the conquest of fifty languages, is the association of this dear friend with my earliest efforts at writing; and it pleases me to remember that to her I owe my very first appearance in print. Vanity is the least part of it, when I remember how she called me to her desk, one day after school was out, and showed me my composition — my own words, that I had written out of my own head — printed out, clear black and white, with my name at the end! Nothing so wonderful had ever happened to me before. My whole consciousness was suddenly transformed.

About the middle of the year I was promoted to the grammar school. Then it was that I walked on air. For I said to myself that I was a *student* now, in earnest, not merely a school girl learning to spell and cipher. I was going to learn out-of-the-way things, things that had nothing to do with ordinary life — things to *know*. When I walked home afternoons, with the great big geography book under my arm, it seemed to me that the earth was conscious of my step. Sometimes I carried home half the books in my desk, not because I should need them, but because I loved to hold them; and also because I loved to be seen carrying books. It was a badge of scholarship, and I was proud of it. I remembered the days in Vitebsk when I used to watch my cousin Hirshel start for school in the morning, every thread of his student's uniform, every worn copybook in his satchel, glorified in my envious eyes. And now I was myself even greater than he: for I knew English, and I could write poetry.

The public school has done its best for us foreigners, and for the country, when it has made us into good Americans. I am glad it is mine to tell how the miracle was wrought in one case. You should be glad to hear of it, you born Americans, for it is the story of the growth of your country; of the flocking of your brothers and sisters from the far ends of the earth to the flag you love; of the recruiting of your armies of workers, thinkers, and leaders. And you will be glad to hear of it, my comrades in adoption, for it is a rehearsal of your own experience, the thrill and wonder of which your own hearts have felt.

How long would you say, wise reader, it takes to make an American? By the middle of my second year in school I had reached the sixth grade.

When, after the Christmas holidays, we began to study the life of Washington, running through a summary of the Revolution, and the early days of the Republic, it seemed to me that all my reading and study had been idle until then. As I read how the patriots planned the Revolution, and the women gave their sons to die in battle, and the heroes led to victory, and the rejoicing people set up the Republic, it dawned on me gradually what was meant by *my country*. The people all desiring noble things, and striving for them together, defying their oppressors, giving their lives for each other — all this it was that made *my country*. It was not a thing that I *understood;* I could not go home and tell Fetchke about it, as I told her other things I learned at school. But I knew one could say "my country" and *feel* it, as one felt "God" or "myself." My teacher, my schoolmates, Miss Dillingham, George Washington himself, could not mean more than I when they said *my country,* after I had once felt it. For the Country was for all the Citizens, and *I was a Citizen.* And when we stood up to sing "America," I shouted the words with all my might. I was in very earnest proclaiming to the world my love for my new-found country.

> I love thy rocks and rills,
> Thy woods and templed hills.

Boston Harbor, Crescent Beach, Chelsea Square — all was hallowed ground to me. As the day approached when the school was to hold exercises in honor of Washington's Birthday, the halls resounded at all hours with the strains of patriotic songs; and I, who was a model of the attentive pupil, more than once lost my place in the lesson, as I strained to hear, through closed doors, some neighboring class rehearsing "The Star-Spangled Banner." If the doors happened to open, and the chorus broke out unveiled —

> Oh say, does that Star-Spangled Banner yet wave
> O'er the land of the free, and the home of the brave?

delicious tremors ran up and down my spine, and I was faint with suppressed enthusiasm.

Where had been my country until now? What flag had I loved? What heroes had I worshiped? Even the very names of these things had been unknown to me. Well I knew that Polotzk was not my country. It was *Goluth* — exile. On many occasions in the year we prayed to God to lead us out of exile. The beautiful Passover service closed with the words, "Next year, may we be in Jerusalem." Still, on childish lips, those words were no conscious aspiration; we repeated the Hebrew syllables after our elders, but without their hope and longing.

In very truth we were a people without a country. And as we had no country, so we had no flag to love. It was by no farfetched symbolism that the banner of the House of Romanoff became the emblem of our latter-day bondage in our eyes. Even a child would know how to hate the flag that we were forced, on pain of severe penalties, to hoist above our housetops, in celebration of the advent of one of our oppressors. And as it was with country and flag, so it was with heroes of war. We hated the uniform of the soldier, to the last brass button. On the person of a Gentile, it was the symbol of tyranny; on the person of a Jew, it was the emblem of shame.

So a little Jewish girl in Polotzk was apt to grow up hungry-minded and empty-hearted; and if, still in her out-reaching youth, she was set down in a land of outspoken patriotism, she was likely to love her new country with a great love, and to embrace its heroes in a great worship. Naturalization, with us Russian Jews, may mean more than the adoption of the immigrant by America: it may mean the adoption of America by the immigrant.

All Around the Town

by STEPHEN VINCENT BENÉT

The Atlantic *published a number of Stephen Vincent Benét's stories and poems, but none more appealing than his "All Around the Town," with its warmhearted Irish picture of Manhattan.*

APRIL 1940

I like it, winter or summer. But I guess I like it the best when it gets really hot and they turn on the fire hydrants for a while and the little kids splash in the water. That's when the noise lasts till after twelve and, if you look out of the window, you can see a man in his shirt sleeves and his fat wife beside him, sitting out in front of the store in a couple of kitchen chairs. I know nobody's supposed to. But that's the way I like New York.

No, I was born in Brooklyn, but I don't remember much about that. We moved to the East Side afterwards, before I could remember. The old man was a watch repairer — I guess that's where I get my liking for tinkering at things. He worked at Logan's, up on Fourteenth, and I remember how disappointed I was when I found he didn't own the whole store. He was Swiss and Ma was Irish, so I've got the two sides to me. They get along well enough, usually, but sometimes they fight.

I know now he had disappointments, but I didn't know it as a kid. He was always talking about a nice place in the country, with chickens, but he never got there. Once or twice, before I was born — I came along kind of late — he tried to set up in a small town. But something always happened, and he had to come back to the city. He didn't really object to it, but he felt it wasn't right to raise his kids there. But Ma always said it was up to her to take care of that. She did a good job by us, too, and she kissed me on both sides of my face when I got the silver medal for penmanship at St. Aloysius's. I didn't tell her it was because I'd promised Jerry Toole I'd beat the mush off him if he came in ahead of me. He was always the one to get the prizes, and I thought it was time I had one of my own to take home and show. My old man made a little wooden box for it and carved my initials on top. It took him quite a while to do it — he was a slow worker, but very careful — but it pleased him a lot. And me, too.

I guess I don't know how to tell a story, because, when I think about it, it gets all mixed up. They ask you what was the city like, in those days, and what are you going to tell them? I remember the horsecars, to be sure, and the gaslights in the streets, and the tangle of overhead wires, like a crazy spiderweb, and the big white stages. But, when you begin thinking back, you don't know if you're right or not. My old man had big gray mustaches that went out like a pair of wings, and he always wore a derby hat to his work. It was rounder, somehow, than they make derbies now — I'd recognize it among a million, but they don't have them any more. And, when Ma was baking, you could smell the clean, fresh bread all over the house. The first policeman I ever saw was standing under a gaslight, twirling his stick in front of his belly. We called him Mister Ryan and I thought him the greatest and largest man in the world. Well, that's the thing you remember. That, and the sprinkling carts, and the brown afternoon in the street, and the old woman who sold hot chestnuts, with her cheeks as red as red apples, a winter evening, under the El, when the horses were slipping on the ice.

All the same, it wasn't so big, then. I remember when the Flatiron was the biggest one and the out-of-town people bought postcards, just the way they do, this moment, with the Empire State. It got built without our knowing it, almost — it went up into the sky. Nobody decided about it — it stretched like a boy growing up, and now, there it is. The city, I mean — yes, the city. I remember my tall, laughing Irish uncles stamping into the house and swinging Ma from one to another of them and kissing her till she'd slap their faces. She was always little Katy, the bird, to them, though she'd had a great hand in bringing most of them up. I remember when Uncle Ally got in the Fire Department and his coming around, proud as Punch, to show us his new uniform. A well-setup man he was, and his helmet very impressive. He was killed in a big loft fire in the garment district, the year that I was sixteen. The whole wall fell like a stone and they couldn't get the bodies for two days.

All the same, they gave the three of them a Department funeral and there were pieces in all the papers about it. I think it helped break Ma's heart — he was her favorite brother. But I rode in the carriage with her and she sat up straight as a ramrod, in her new black clothes. Afterwards she had me cut the pieces out of the papers, and it wasn't till night that I heard her crying. I can hear the cry in my ears, though it's many years gone.

My old man and my uncles were polite enough to each other, but they didn't really get along. He liked to sit out on the stoop, after dinner, smoking his big pipe with the silver lid on it and reading the evening paper. But he was a quiet man, and when my uncles came in, full of life and gaiety, he'd have less to say than ever, though he always sent to the corner for the beer. He'd never have a drop of whiskey in the house, except for medicinal purposes — but he liked the steam beer at Schaeffer's, though I never saw him take too much. The day he came home with the chill, Ma made him a toddy, but even then he wouldn't take it. It scared me to see him in bed in the daytime. When you're young, you never think your parents can get sick or die. I remember that. But he got over it; and it wasn't till after I was married that he died.

He liked Eileen and she was very good to him — I'll always remember that. She used to call him Father Weiss — she was dainty in her conversation — but he'd always say, "Joost Poppa, *mein liebliches Kind.*" Then he'd stroke her hand, very gently, with the tips of his big, clever fingers. That was after Ma had gone, and we had the responsibility. The girls did what they could, but of course they had their families by then, except Nellie, and she wouldn't come to see him if any of the others were coming.

It wouldn't be held a disgrace, now — certainly not. The kids pray to go into the movies — and isn't that the same? But we held it a disgrace to us. I guess Nellie was my favorite sister — she took more after the uncles than the rest of us. She wasn't pretty, exactly, but she had a black-haired imp in her, and she was the first to marry of all the girls. I can see her face under the bridal veil, looking frightened. That's funny for Nellie O'Mara, the Wild Irish Rose. O'Mara was my grandda's name — she took it when she ran off with her piano pounder and started showing her legs on the public stage. The old man, queer enough, didn't mind so much — he had European ideas about the theater. But Ma was horrified and so were the other girls.

I was horrified myself — I had to fight three boys on account of it. And Nellie's husband, Ed Meany, would come around and sit on the stoop, looking as if he'd just had a tooth pulled and telling all he'd done for Nellie, and how, even now, he'd been willing to take her back. He was a good man, no doubt, but he talked till you'd feel like shooting him. It wasn't till I had my own trouble that I knew how he felt.

The other girls married all right and respectable — Grace and Kathleen — though I never did think much of Carl Schuhmacher. He always looked too much like one of his own sirloin steaks, but that was Grace's affair, not mine, and the meat market's a good business. We thought she could have done better for herself, but I don't know, as things turned out. He had some trouble, during the war, till young Carl was killed at Cantigny. I guess he's forgotten the trouble — I don't mean forgotten young Carl. They've still got the picture in the parlor, and the uniform looks queer, now. But he and John Pollard — that's Kathy's husband — get on a lot better than they did. There was feeling between the two families for a long time, over the meat-carving set and the Irish lace doilies. Well, Grace was always a grabber, and she did her best to make John Pollard feel small. But he got to be principal of Van Twiller for six months before they retired him — and I've seen his office. He was the steady sort that works up, and they couldn't keep him out of the position, though they tried. Now he's got the testimonial framed and it means something to him. I know that by the way he looks at it, now and then. Their youngest's teaching at Hunter, and they make a lot of that.

I can't say I've had a bad life, though it hasn't been quite what I expected. If I'd gone in with Uncle Martin — he was always the clever one! And I was his favorite, in a manner of speaking. But I couldn't stand the bother of politics — not even when he got to be district leader. He might have gone far, I think, but he picked the wrong side, in the Hall. That's the unforgivable mistake. Then, later on, he had his trouble — well, the jury disagreed at both trials. But it was all over the papers, and that sticks to a man. My clever, low-spoken uncle! I remember him always, a little disdainful of the rest of them, and you felt he took a drink to be friendly, and yet not to be really friendly. And then, at the trial, he was an old man, with jowls and white hair, answering just as clever and low-spoken as he always had, and yet not making a good impression. Because times had changed — that was all — and yet, how would he have done different? It was in his blood to rise by any means he could lay hands on, and pull up his family, too. But I'm glad that it didn't interest me — though he helped me get my first position.

Well, now, I was young and strong, though you might not think it. I wanted to go on the Force — but then the job came along. My old man wanted me to follow in his own line of business. But I didn't feel like messing around all day with little wheels and springs and an eyeglass stuck in one eye. They were building the subways in those days — well, that's how I started. It was good pay, for the time, and I wanted to marry Eileen.

It's queer what a man's work in life will turn out to be. You go around the top of the city — well, I know that, too. But it's underneath where I've worked, the strong part of my life. You don't often get to thinking of it — a man's work is his work, wherever it lies. But if it wasn't for thousands of men whose names you've never heard of, all living their lives underground, it wouldn't be a city, or the same city. I'd think of it, now and again, on the night shift, when things got quiet above. They'd have gone to sleep by then — yes, even the rich and proud — but we'd be working. It's hard to put to you so you'll understand it. You see the place in the street where it's planked over, and the taxi has to slow up, and you start to swear. But underneath there's the work gangs, and the lights.

It gives you a pride, in a way, to be part of it — at least at times. You feel as if the people just walking the streets were different people and didn't know. It's hard for me to explain that — I don't know the way to say it. But I'm glad I did what I did — if it did mean ending up in a change booth, and then the pension. It does for Martha and me.

Eileen always expected more of me, and maybe she was right to do so. But a young man, in his strength, that's bossing a gang — well, that's all a young man might like. He could well be wrong about it, but he'd have to be shown where he was wrong. But when I found out what was happening, I broke every stick of furniture in the flat. I did so. She wasn't afraid of me, either — I'd have killed her if she had been. But she stood there, cold and proud, with the look she'd had when I first saw her, the look of a woman untouched. He'd come as a boarder because we had the extra room that wasn't needed for the baby after all — a whey-faced, shrewd little man. I wasn't as angry at him, for some queer reason — I think he did his best to be decent, through it all. But she was ambitious, always, and we had no children.

Well, he made the money — he made a great deal before he died. Mrs. Loring Masters and the big house on Long Island and the children sent to fine colleges, except for the one that killed himself. When the daughter was married, I saw the picture in the paper, and she had just the look of Eileen. I wished her no ill — I wished her great good fortune. I wished her mother no ill — yet I wondered if the man had really touched her, after all. There were times when we lay beside each other, in our youth, and asked no better. I know that, for that is not something a man forgets. And it was the same with her. But she wanted other than that.

I don't know how to tell it all — I wish I knew. How am I to tell what it's like to come home, to the quiet street, after the night shift, with nothing but the milkman's horse clopping his way along — and be tired to bone and marrow and yet satisfied? How am I to tell what it's like, day after day? The city stretches and you don't notice it, till one day you go to the Park, and the buildings have grown up like a fence around it. I remember talking to my Uncle Matthew. He'd had thirty-five years on the Force and retired as inspector, and he should know if anyone did. Well, he talked about many changes, in an old man's voice, and how there was still as much law in the end of a night stick as in many law books. But he didn't really touch it.

It reminds me of the one time I went to Proctor's when Nellie was on the bill. She did well, and I was shamed to the bone, but I couldn't help applauding. The audience liked her, too — they knew she came from Third Avenue and was one of their own. I've given her change at the window, since, and she didn't know me. Nobody ever looks at the man in the change booth — nobody knows if he has a face. Why should I be worried about that? Well, I'm not, to tell you the truth. But it's given me a chuckle, now and then, when somebody's come along and said, "Why, Ed!"

Have I given you any idea? Most likely not. I've seen Teddy Roosevelt, the young dude back from the war, and his teeth were just the way they are in the pictures. I've shook hands with John McGraw — and seen the sudden, white, Irish rage on his face when somebody yelled "Muggsy" at him out of the crowd. I've seen the Mayor, by the Zoo, showing his boy the polar bears — and him in his queer black hat and people leaving him alone. But where do you begin and end? I remember John Pollard, that's educated, telling me once about some city in Europe where you dug down and under the city was the ruins of another city and under that ruin another till you could not come to the end of them. Now that's something any New Yorker could understand. It's Jimmy Walker's town and Rabbi Wise's, it's La Guardia's and J. P. Morgan's and Cardinal Spellman's, and the new strong hitter on the Yankees' and Katharine Cornell's. It belongs to the telephone repairmen and the Park Avenue dolls, to the fellow that peddles the racing sheets and the choirboys in the Cathedral and all the hackers in their cabs. Now how would I say whose town it was, precisely? Yet I'd like to know.

Well, now, there was my friend Louis Jordan, went into domestic service. It didn't seem work for a man to me, at first, and yet I liked him well. I ran into him first at Joe's place, the summer that Eileen had left me — a very dignified creature, though drink was his weakness. But you could neither smell it nor see it on him — at least at that time. The rich man he worked for had closed his house for the summer and left Louis and his wife the caretaking of it. A dignified creature, I say, with soft, puffy hands and a face not far off a priest's. His wife was a little thin woman, most respectable, in black. But when he got to know me well, he'd ask me back for a nip, now and then, at the house. Man, dear, you never saw a kitchen stove to equal that one — it could have roasted an ox. Then we'd have our nip and his wife would run the cards for me, very considerate and respectable, for she knew I'd had troubles. And all around us and over us was the big, grand, stately house with its pictures and its fine furniture, and yet we the only things alive in it, like mice in a cheese.

He took me through the whole of it, one warm Sunday afternoon. There was a bathtub of marble, though it looked like dusty stone, and the man of the house had twenty suits left in his closet, and yet he had others, for he'd not appear naked where he was. It gave me a queer feeling to see all those suits, hanging up on their hangers. Then, when we got back to the kitchen, we found that Mrs. Jordan had got hold of the gin bottle and was stretched out, highly respectable but stiff as a corpse, on the floor. So after that I knew his sorrow, as he had known mine.

Yet, the next winter, I happened to pass by the house. There was a red carpet down and all the fine carriages drawing up at the door. And just as the door opened I saw Louis Jordan, like a sentinel on post in his dress suit, receiving them all, with the young men to help him. Very fine he looked, and not like the man with his collar off that I'd drunk with, in the kitchen. And she, no doubt, was helping equally, with the ladies. Well, that's a long time ago, and the house is gone.

I've seen some queer sights, I have. I've stuck my head up from a manhole and seen six elephants, marching down Eighth Avenue, holding on to each other's tails. It was only for the circus in Madison Square Garden, but it gave you a turn. Then there was the bar the midgets used to frequent. I don't remember the name of it, but I stumbled in there one night and thought I'd gone mad when all the little faces turned at me. I've seen other things as well. I've seen them shower the ticker tape and the torn paper from the high buildings and got a glimpse of the face of the man they were welcoming. It might be one face or another, but it looked white and dazzled. And next week you'd have forgotten his name.

I used to go to the ball games often, with Martha, and that's a sight, too, when the game goes into extra innings and the crowd sits tight and the shadow begins to grow on the infield. Her brother was with the Giants, for a year — Swede Nansen, they called him — a tall, blond, slow-spoken boy. He could pitch with the best, on his day, but he liked farming better, which is a queer thing in a man. I remember the time he struck out nine Cubs in five innings, and the yelling of the crowd. But the next year his arm went bad on him and nothing could be done for it. He played for Atlanta a while — the South being recommended for him — then he gave up the game and settled down to his farming, and now, every Christmas, he sends us a box of pecans. But his record's still in the books, and the game where he beat Alexander. I should like to see him again, for he was a man I respected, but I doubt now that I will.

She's been a good wife to me, Martha, and never ashamed of a man that worked with his hands — though I do not do so any more. At one time we had the money, and that was a contrary experience. She was left five hundred dollars, and that sharp little fellow, Abe Leavis, told us what to buy. At first I felt queer, going into the grand office, but soon I saw my money was as good as another's. Yet, though I will not criticize any other man's work, it does not seem to me a man's occupation to do nothing but watch the figures change on a blackboard. They thought, for a while, that I was lucky, for those days had no sense to them at all. And indeed, I thought so myself. I've had men in their handmade suits ask me for advice, and take it, too. They'd have taken advice, at that time, from a horse, if the horse was winning on the market. Well, it was forty thousand dollars before it was nothing — so you can say that I've had the experience of riches. It takes a man's mind off his work — that's all I can say. But we had the sealskin coat for Martha — and the washing machine.

If I told you about Abe Leavis, that would be part of it, too. That was a rubber ball of a man, a rubber ball bounced up and down the pavements. I have seen him so thin and pitiful it would break your heart; I have seen him round and plump, with his pockets full of cigars. You could kill that man, but you could not put him down. But how he loved the smell and taste of the city! I'll forgive a man much for that. No, it wasn't my city he loved — it was Fifth and Park and the riches — the big shining toystore where everything's for sale. It was like a tonic to him to pay maybe twenty dollars for a pair of theater tickets and get there late for the play. But that's part of it, too.

Now there's whole sections and locations I've never seen. It wasn't so long ago that I visited my grandnephew, Francis. He married a Jewish girl when he'd finished his internship — a pretty, bright young thing — and they've got an apartment on the Grand Concourse. I walked twenty blocks after I'd left them and it was like another city. And yet it couldn't have been any other city. It couldn't have been.

I don't know if it's the two rivers make it — though I knew the captain of the *Michael T. McQuillan,* and a good man he was and told me the work there is to get the big, proud liners into dock. I don't know if it's the climate that makes it — the fine fall and the dirty winter, the hot summer and the spring that comes with the flower carts and touches your heart. It's a healthy climate, I've always thought, though others may differ. Now when Martha and I were first married we'd go as far as Far Rockaway for a bite of the summer. And that was a change and healthy — but I noticed we were glad to get back where you knew the look of the street. I don't know — I couldn't say — it's hard for me to tell.

Well, now, there's the being old. But we got along very comfortable. There's a lot of them move away — to Florida, let's say — and then they send you the postcards, saying what a fine time they're having. No doubt they are, if they like it, but I never could see it made them look any younger. There was my friend, the Dutchman, that retired from his delicatessen and went to live with his granddaughter at White Plains. It was a nice house, to be sure, and he kept the lawn very well cut. I congratulated him on that. Then he looked at me and there was a grief in his eyes. "Vy, Ed," he said, "it's all right. But you can't cut the lawn all day. I tell you, some nights I vake up and listen for the noise of the El. And, ven it ain't there, I feel old. Ed, I'd give ten dollars if Mrs. Burke was to come in — the fussy one — just to tell me she wouldn't put up with this kind of service no more." Then his granddaughter came to tell him it was time for his nap, and, though she was very polite, I knew I should go away. Thank God, I've been spared that — though we've neither chick nor child.

It's cool enough in the flat, and if there's a breeze we get it. And there's always something to look at — the boys playing ball in the streets, shouting under the light, summer evenings, and the taxis drawing up to the apartment house opposite, and a young woman coming out, with bare arms. Phil Kelly, the doorman there, is a friend of mine, though he comes from Ulster. They'd be surprised, in that house, if they knew the things that I know about them. I don't mean any ugly things — just the odd little circumstances. It's my hope that the pretty dark girl will marry the young man with glasses. He's steadier than the one that's better dressed. I'd like to tell her that, only how would I tell her?

There isn't a trace or a place of my childhood's house. There isn't a trace or a place of the house where I lived with Eileen. Now last year, when I went to the cemetery, it took me an hour to find Uncle Martin's grave, though they'd kept it decent, and he was a well-known man.

You'd think such a thing might make you sad, but again, it does not. It's comfortable, in a way, to be like the dust in the air. It's hard for me to tell it, and yet, what I mean is this. Last summer I went to the Fair, and that's a great sight, no doubt of it. Oh, the crowds and the proud buildings of the nations of the earth and the horns tooting "All around the town"!

It was some State Day when we went there, and there was the governor of the state, with the sirens blowing in front of him to clear the way. Well, I wouldn't remember which state it was, but that makes little difference. There were all the top hats there to receive him, and that's only courtesy. And yet he was swallowed up in the Fair itself, and, except for the people from his own state, there was no one knew he was there, or cared at all. So it came upon me, that day — sitting on a bench, with my feet tired — it all came upon me. For they all seemed to pass by me, the rich and the great and the proud, with the sirens blowing in front of them. And yet, that wasn't the city, and when the Fair itself was finished, there'd be many still in the city that hadn't even seen it. It was a fine sight to see, but they hadn't missed it, in their lives.

And so it was with the most of us — and with the city itself. For it wasn't the mayors and the millionaires and the Presidents — though I've walked by the President's house and seen him go in. It was my Uncle Ally and my Uncle Matthew, my friend Louis Jordan and my sister Nellie O'Mara, the boys that were on the gang with me and the boys that died underground. It's the small, new honeymoon couples, buying a coffee ring at the corner bakery, and the guards who walk the museums, clean and pudgy; the thieves in the morning roundup and the good men, like my old man, who live and die without notice. It's all that, and the moon at the end of the street where you never expected a moon.

I said, "Martha, I'm tired, I think," and she took me home. So next day, when I was no better, she called my grandnephew, Francis. He's been very kind, and, where some might be afraid of the hospital, I am not. It's a good sunny room, the ward, and the nurses very attentive to an old man. From where I lie on my back, I can see the river.

So, since it's to be that way, I'm glad it's to be that way. Wouldn't I have been the fool to go to a place like White Plains and die there? A man could hardly die easy in those foreign places — a man who's seen what I've seen. I'm aware there are other cities. The day orderly comes from London, and we've talked about that one.

I was born in Brooklyn, but we moved to the East Side, afterwards. I remember my mother's baking bread, and the Empire State, when it was new. You won't remember Swede Nansen, though his record's in the book, but I remember him. You won't remember Martin O'Mara, but he was part of it. You won't remember Logan's on Fourteenth Street, but it was a fine, large store.

When they bomb the town to pieces, with their planes from the sky, there'll be a big ghost left. When it's gone, they'd better let the sea come in and cover it, for there never will be one like it in the ages of man again.

Making Americans

from *Exploring the Dangerous Trades*

by ALICE HAMILTON

A pioneer in industrial medicine, a graduate of Bryn Mawr, and the first woman ever to teach at the Harvard Medical School, Dr. Alice Hamilton is the author of Exploring the Dangerous Trades, *the salient portions of which first appeared in the* Atlantic.

JANUARY 1943

I cannot describe Jane Addams. When I try, I get only bits of her, pieces that should be fitted together in a pattern of great beauty, but it is a pattern that I am unable to produce. All I can do is to give something of the impressions made upon me.

She had intellectual integrity; there was nothing of what George Meredith has called "merciful muddle" about her. She never sentimentalized the poor, or labor, or the half-baked young radicals, or the conscientious objectors; and so she could never be disillusioned or disappointed, because she had no illusions to start with. She never shrank from painful facts; she never refused to listen to damaging evidence. I well remember how indignant I was when she told me that she had invited a grief-stricken young couple to come for a visit, and I knew that those very people had treated her with a contemptible injustice born of panic and fear. When I reminded her of it, she said vaguely, "Why yes, that's true, they did. Strange, wasn't it?" And then she dropped it. She did not excuse them, for there was no excuse, but her pity was just as tender as if she had shut her eyes to the facts.

She was a pragmatist in the best sense before that word was popular. She held that anything one had learned in college and from travel must be tried out in actual life. "Truth must be put to the ultimate test, the test of the conduct it dictates and inspires." Her young womanhood was passed largely in study, reading, travel, for she was a semi-invalid for years; and she had had more than her fill of theoretical knowledge — it made her rather impatient. She turned from it eagerly to practical application, to action. As was natural, John Dewey, then in the University of Chicago, became one of her closest friends and counselors.

This practical approach, together with her complete absence of personal pride, made her ready to try out a new scheme and equally ready to drop it if it proved a failure. Always she held that a settlement should be a place for experiment and when a new enterprise had proved its worth the settlement ought to try to make the city take it over and go on to other new fields. And this happened again and again. Our playground, our public baths, our kindergarten, our volunteer probation officers and truant officers — all were taken over by the city; and though sometimes it seemed to us that we had managed these services better and more disinterestedly than the city did, Miss Addams insisted that it was a step forward from private charity to public responsibility, even when it was poorly done.

She never took a stand for the sake of consistency; she was no slave of her own theories. When we were in Paris just after the war, she shocked the French women of the pacifist group by accepting an invitation to a reception given her by a group of American doughboys who were waiting to be demobilized. The women begged me to remonstrate with her, to make her see that this would be a public abandonment of her principles. I labored in vain to convince them that she had no principles against conscripted men, whatever she thought of conscription, and that to hold herself aloof from them would require a fanatic belief in her own rightness which she never possessed.

She had two conflicting traits which sometimes brought her great unhappiness. She was very dependent on a sense of warm comradeship and harmony with the mass of her fellow men; but at the same time her clearsighted integrity made it impossible for her to keep in step with the crowd in many a crisis. Most reformers I have known have enjoyed, more or less, the sense of being in advance of their times, of belonging to a persecuted minority. Nothing of that was ever true of Jane Addams. The Pullman strike, the rise of the I.W.W., the war fever of 1914–1918, the sudden, panicky persecution of the radicals after the war — to mention only a few incidents — were for her the most painful of experiences, because she was forced by conviction to work against the stream, to separate herself from the great mass of her fellow countrymen. Nor did she ever fall into the mire of self-pity or take refuge in a sense of self-righteousness; she simply suffered from the spiritual loneliness which her farsighted vision had imposed on her.

One supremely lovely figure rises to my mind whenever I think of Hull House in the years from its founding to 1934, and that is the figure of Mary Rozet Smith, Jane Addams's closest friend and the most universally beloved person I have ever known. She left no mark on history but she left a deep mark on all who knew her even slightly, for she had a genius for personal relations. I suppose that means quick insight, warmth, and a "heart at leisure from itself." She was one of those persons whose biographies are never written but who have a deep abiding influence on their time. Her large, gracious home on Walton Place was a refuge for Miss Addams — who could hardly have carried on had she not been able to slip away from the West Side to it now and then — and a place of refreshment for many of the rest of us. And to Hull House her coming was not only a joy but a sustaining help in time of trouble and perplexity for all the years up to her death in 1934. Miss Addams survived her by only one year.

Hull House was a very attractive place. It was built in 1846 and on much the same plan as my grandfather's Fort Wayne house, which was five years older. There were the same hall and stairway, long drawing room with carved white marble mantelpieces, French windows at both ends, and the same lofty ceilings with elaborate cornices.

Life at Hull House was very simple so far as luxuries went, but it was full of beauty. The two founders had brought with them many charming furnishings, and whatever they bought later had the two qualities of durability and beauty. Our food was inexpensive, but dinner was served to us in a long, paneled dining room, lighted with chandeliers of Spanish wrought iron; breakfast, in a charming little coffeehouse built in imitation of an English inn. To me, the life there satisfied every longing — for companionship, for the excitement of new experiences, for constant intellectual stimulation, and for the sense of being caught up in a big movement which enlisted my enthusiastic loyalty.

My part in it was humble enough. At that time there were few of the social services which now we take as a matter of course. Hull House had to run its own day nursery, kindergarten, public baths, playground, as well as all the other activities which settlements still carry on. There were no baby clinics, and though I did not feel at all competent to treat sick babies I did venture to open a well-baby clinic, which very soon was taking in all the older brothers and sisters up to eight years of age. Miss Addams let me use the shower-bath room in the basement of the gymnasium and provided a dozen little bathtubs, soap, bathing towels, for most of the work of the "clinic" was bathing the children.

Living among the foreign-born makes one aware of ancient wrongs and oppressions which have left deep scars and lasting hatreds; and we Americans are the innocent inheritors of these hatreds and loyalties, which often complicate our national life. Of all the foreigners we met at Hull House the Poles were most difficult to deal with, for they were suspicious and hostile toward all outsiders. They thought any approach, no matter how friendly, meant some kind of governmental interference, and this attitude was easy to understand in a people who for centuries had known only oppressive government. They hated their Austrian rulers least, their German masters most. The Russians, they said, were cruel but they came down on you only at intervals; in between they forgot you and let you go your own way, but the Germans never.

The Poles were naturally fanatic Catholics and nationalists and they sent their children to the Polish Sisters' schools, not the public schools. I remember a German expert on primary education expressing to Miss Addams his amazement that this should be allowed. "Surely you should do everything to detach them from Poland, to make them Americans," he said. Miss Addams answered that if we attempted to force Americanization we should get the contrary result, and that as it was, the children learned English as fast as they could, dropping the old ways and adopting the new with almost incredible speed.

There were many Jews, Russian and Polish, in our neighborhood and always they made up the majority of the adult education classes. The Jews more than any others loved learning for its own sake and were ready to plunge into the study of Shakespeare, Browning, Ibsen, after a long day of factory work. Some of the Bohemians and Irish studied also, but the immigrants from Southern Europe cared more for the other things Hull House had to offer — dramatics, art, music, and social clubs where they could dance.

Settlement life shows clearly how deep and fundamental are the inequalities in our democratic country. The belief, so dear to Americans, that opportunity is open to all, that the exceptional child can rise to the highest position in the community if he will, is true in certain fields only: in politics, in business, even in the learned professions, but certainly not in the arts. One of the saddest things in the lot of the poor is the crushing down of artistic talent. "Chill penury" still freezes "the genial current of the soul," in spite of public schools and art museums and free concerts. My sister Norah, who had art classes in Hull House for several years, used to suffer again and again the grief of seeing some promising young artist, Italian or Mexican or Bohemian, leave school for the barren monotony of factory work, too tired after hours of it to do anything creative, his gift wasted.

As I look back I can remember the indignation I used to feel over the unfair and even cruel treatment I so often saw meted out to these immigrants; it was a feeling so strong that it even perverted my attitude toward my own country. When a visitor from uptown would glow with enthusiasm over a group of Hull House neighbors singing "America," I would feel only impatience. What reason had they to feel devotion to a country that treated them with callousness and injustice? My excursions into the dangerous trades only strengthened this feeling. And when we entered the war in 1917, that impression was so strong at the back of my mind that I could not join in the outburst of patriotism sweeping over the country.

I stopped over in Fort Wayne that May to visit my cousins. As I listened to their talk, full of deep devotion and admiration for our country, I realized that there was another America than the one I had been seeing for so many years; that my picture was one-sided, narrow. I must take a larger view. And as I looked back over my years at Hull House I could see that, hard as life had been for those uprooted Europeans, their path almost always had gone up, not down. Nearly every family, sooner or later, moved to better quarters, made its way up.

The Greeks moved fastest. They were single-minded in their pursuit of business; they came to our classes long enough to get a working knowledge of English, but they wasted no time over unpractical subjects. The Jews came next, for though they too were good in business, even then they had a wide range of other interests and some of them were dreamy idealists. Bohemians soon took the upper jobs in industry; Italians and Poles were slower to reach prosperity, but they too climbed up.

The only exceptions I ever met were a few Irish families which were wrecked by drink and went steadily down from bad to worse. An Irish policeman once said to me, "There's nothing better than a good Irishman and there's nothing worse than a bad one." It is true. Among the Irish I met in the slums were poets and artists. They had the manners and the charm of an old aristocracy — and they could sink to lower depths than any other immigrants. I wonder if those two things go together — that to be capable of the highest carries with it a capacity to fall the lowest. Certainly among the Irish wrecks from drink were some of the warmest, most generous, and most lovable people I have known.

Slums and City Planning

by ROBERT L. MOSES

*Robert L. Moses has made the most distinguished record of
any American entrusted with city planning. Serving fearlessly
under both parties, he has been head of the state park system
of New York; member of the City Planning Commission; and
chairman of the Triborough Bridge Authority since 1934.*

JANUARY 1945

In many cities the process of central decay has been encouraged and
speeded up by the building of rapid transit, railroad, road, and other facilities to minutely subdivided farms and estates in outlying sections and
the suburbs. The effects of this siphoning of people out of town were either not understood or were tacitly ignored by influential citizens and
even the press, not to speak of the promoters immediately interested. If
in New York City we had refrained from building so many miles of subways at twenty million dollars a mile and had put some of this money
into rehabilitating and making livable and attractive the older and central parts of town, millions of people would not today be crowded like
cattle into hurtling trains during the rush hours.

New York's leading real-estate operators at the turn of the century
have now passed on to what is conventionally known as their reward. I
devoutly hope this reward will be adequate, because they were without
question the most malignant influence on the city and its surroundings
in my lifetime. Their disservice to the community should be noted from
time to time so that it will not be repeated. These men perpetuated slum
conditions in outlying parts of the city. They created our slums of today
by selling small lots for big buildings and by preventing zoning, proper
building, and multiple-family regulations.

Everywhere these men left a slimy trail behind them which eventually had to be mopped up by public officials with money out of the public treasury. Almost every city has seen them, but I claim without pride

that we had the topnotchers in New York. Even the highbinder boys of the last Florida boom were only pale reflexes and imitations of our developers, auctioneers, subdividers, title-searching guarantee companies, surveyors, architects, and other come-on men. The fact that they were often extravagantly admired and praised as pioneers by their own generation and regarded as leading citizens by the next is one of the saddest commentaries on our urban civilization. It is, thank God, an era that is over, but we still have a tremendous price to pay for it — a price we are paying every day in the form of high taxes, bad living, economic dry rot, humiliation, disease, and crime.

Real-estate operators are only just beginning to recognize their responsibilities. Back in 1927, as Secretary of State, I organized and was head of the Real Estate Bureau of New York. The licensing law was never intended to be enforced. Its aim was to give real-estate operators the status of a profession without the responsibility and standards which are supposed to accompany this recognition. More and more the reputable real-estate men throughout the country are concluding that the time has come for statesmanship in place of irresponsible promotion.

It is safe to say that almost no city needs to tolerate slums. There are plenty of ways of getting rid of them. The only exceptions are in cities so decayed, so associated with temporary booms or exhausted natural resources, so lacking in morale and pride, so badly located as to trade, or so controlled by dirty politics, that the situation is hopeless.

It is a curious fact that thus far, in most of the older cities, more slum clearance has been accomplished indirectly than directly — that is, through clearance not for public, semipublic, or private housing, but for parks, playgrounds, parkways, expressways, boulevards, and other public improvements. I have made the statement a number of times in New York, and it has never been refuted, that my particular little group of demolition and building demons have without fanfare and social-worker abracadabra pulled down more old rookeries than all the housing experts and authorities put together. And the best thing about it is that we have substituted nothing for the rookeries but broad highways lined with landscaping and recreation facilities, open to the sun and the elements, and affording the very best incentive to further slum clearance.

It took the greater part of twenty years to persuade reactionaries, mossbacks, rural-minded legislators, sharpshooters for taxpayers' organizations, and legalistic comma-chasers that an arterial improvement, whether it be a parkway for restricted travel or an express route open to mixed traffic, is not simply a strip of pavement in a gasoline gully, but a genuine shoestring or ribbon improvement of the entire area through which it passes. It benefits not only those who travel in cars, but thousands who live along it or do business or seek recreation there.

New housing to take the place of slums must be completely subsidized with public money for persons of the lowest income; partly subsidized for the next higher income group; aided in other ways for a still higher income group, through limited-dividend schemes, FHA guarantees, or other similar devices; or left to private capital substantially encouraged if not actually financially helped by public capital. Usually a constitutional amendment is required to permit states and municipalities to enter this field. Most of the recent state constitutional amendments to clear the way for public, semipublic, and publicly aided private housing have been vague and verbose; they reflect, no doubt, the complexity and novelty of the problem, the mental confusion of the authors, and the ingenuity of the opponents who slip in those little interpolations known to the bill-drafting fraternity as "sleepers." The sleepers are the gremlins who wake up at the right time to show that the intent of the law is not what it was popularly supposed to be.

Completely subsidized government public housing was going up all over the country on an accelerated scale before the war with the use of federal, state, and local loans and grants, the exercise of the power of condemnation, and complete tax exemption. A curious feature of this public housing was that it became the common practice of all public housing agencies to omit wholly or partly the recreation, street, school, police, fire, utility, and other incidental and related improvements which should have been taken care of. These were left to chance or to subsequent municipal appropriations out of other funds.

I am a strong believer in subsidized public housing within proper limits, and have worked hard to support it, but I intend to be honest about it. The object of such housing is to have the government give the family of small income, at a rental from three eighths to one third of what an ordinary owner would have to charge and at half what a limited-dividend or redevelopment company would need to pay its way, an apartment built according to the highest standards and wholly beyond the reach of the next higher income groups. A subsidized tenant merely pays for the janitor. Stripped of tricky bookkeeping the situation is that he contributes nothing toward amortization, interest, and taxes. The public pays these bills so that the poor in a dislocated economy may have decent housing.

Obviously there is a limit to completely subsidized public housing.

You cannot rebuild all the slums for the persons of lowest income. This class must be taken care of, but we should not encourage more prudent and capable families to join it. The definition of persons of low income must not be constantly expanded and more and more liberally interpreted. Favoritism, bad politics, and a dozen other evils will crop up if this remedy is not kept within bounds.

One of the great difficulties with public housing subsidized by the federal and state governments is the tendency of distant opinionated bureaucrats to insist that if they pay the piper, they must call the tunes. This hurdle is by no means insurmountable. The best evidence to the contrary is afforded by the federal highway system and the matching of federal and state highway moneys — a process which has been carried on without attempts at federal domination over a period of more than a quarter of a century.

Everything possible should be done to encourage semipublic housing and the investment of funds of fiduciaries such as insurance companies and savings banks, as well as private capital, in slum clearance. The difficulty here lies in the fact that the land is almost always too expensive and building costs too high to keep the rent down to a figure within the reach of the second and third income groups. Another difficulty lies in the impossibility of acquiring numerous parcels of land in private ownership at anything like reasonable prices. As a few lots are bought and the existence of the project becomes noised about, prices rise, speculators intervene, promoters get busy, and selfish individuals figure that they can make a killing if they only hold out.

In this situation the power of eminent domain is the only salvation. Condemnation must be exercised for the private limited-dividend or redevelopment company by the city, state, or federal government. As soon as this happens the tendency of politicians and pressure groups is to impose all manner of restrictions on the company, not only on rentals but on the selection of tenants and on freedom of operation. All sorts of extraneous issues are injected into the problem.

These maneuvers frighten timid investors — particularly ultraconservative trustees of fiduciaries, who are not keen on assuming ownership where it is safer to take a mortgage. Private capital is discouraged from entering a field which at best is unexplored and highly speculative. An insurance company, bank, or limited-dividend company which wants to own, and not merely to lend, can buy a big piece of undeveloped land in the suburbs from one owner or institution at a low price and build attractive garden apartments on comparatively small coverage rather than venture into an old slum, where it must pay enormous prices for land which is usually overassessed and for buildings which are worthless and have to be torn down.

There remains another method of improvement of substandard and unsanitary areas, and that is rehabilitation. Rehabilitation has its dangers. It can easily become a slogan to attract landlords whose only object is to break down tenement-house and multiple-dwelling laws and to bring back into use rookeries which have been condemned as unfit for human habitation. Here again the old conflict between the perfectionists and the practical men breaks out.

The perfectionist does not want old buildings made sanitary and fireproof without changing their essential character. He says this move perpetuates the slum and gives it a new lease of life when it is about to die a natural death. He favors rehabilitation only if every third house is torn down and if the two remaining ones are completely rebuilt; and he can show that this process is so expensive that it is hardly worth while. Yet it is a fact that in most cities plenty of old tenements and other houses can be made safe, sanitary, and fairly comfortable for a number of years at reasonable cost.

Many of these old tenements are going to be lived in anyway — because there just cannot be enough public and semipublic new housing to take their place. This situation can be measurably improved by cutting through new streets and pedestrian lanes and by establishing small neighborhood parks and playgrounds. The average brick tenement has a good deal of life left, and people can live decently in crowded quarters if they have heat, hot water, bathrooms, fire escapes, light, and gas.

Another reason why these old houses will have to be used is that they constitute the only practical temporary quarters for those who are tossed out into the streets to make way for new public and semipublic housing projects. Obviously, tenants of buildings which are about to be razed must go somewhere, and they often represent families which are either not eligible to go back into the new public housing or do not have sufficient income to move into semipublic projects when they are completed.

A serious obstacle in the way of financing slum clearance lies in the unwillingness of organized labor to coöperate in any program which does not preserve its inalienable rights to hourly wages, jurisdictional disputes and strikes, and resistance to inventions and improvements in the building field. The notion that every effort to reduce building costs, every advance in building technique, is an attack on unionism and a conspiracy against the laboring man is so deep-seated that there seems no possibility of dislodging it. This attitude makes no sense, but it will not change until we deal with another generation of union officials educated in a better school.

It is unfortunate that in New York and many other cities public housing has pre-empted not the worst but the best of the acknowledged slum areas — that is, those favorably located on parks and waterfront, where values were comparatively low because of stables, junk shops, garages, and other cheap low buildings. The public housing experts have picked up the best and cheapest land at the lowest price. They have built up or planned their new communities on these favorable properties, leaving just behind them slums which will often have even less light and air than they had before and which in many cases constituted the areas on which the public housing should have been built. In other cases the so-called public housing experts have established projects in outlying sections where there were no slums at all, and have attracted there tenants from slum buildings. These old buildings have been left not empty but in many cases half filled, not quite bankrupting the owner or tossing the property into the hands of the bank or other mortgage holder.

There is another thing to think of, and that is the prevention of more slums through the decay and degeneration of residential properties which are being shifted from single-family to multi-family dwellings. These potential slums are being overbuilt because of zoning standards purposely kept low and inadequate by real-estate promoters and their cronies in the architectural profession, in banks which have made imprudent loans, and among the ranks of the builders, Chamber of Commerce members, and other building strategists. They all want to cash in on every nickel's worth of land which can be traded, bought, or actually built on.

In New York City we adopted our first zoning ordinance twenty-eight years ago in the face of the most bitter opposition and at a time when the attitude of the courts as to its constitutionality was not known. I know of no zoning ordinance with adequate and proper standards in any large city in the United States. All of them represented enormous concessions to powerful interests like those made in New York in 1916. In many cases the execution of these ordinances was placed in the hands of officials so timid, uncertain, or even corrupt as to ensure that no speculative builder on expensive land in congested areas would have much to worry about. When new standards become the law, we shall have done something to prevent future slums.

VIII

Portraits and Self-Portraits

The portrait in prose becomes noticeable in the Atlantic *under the fourth editor, Thomas Bailey Aldrich; prior to that, biography had been a bright strand in the extended historical studies of John Fiske, J. L. Motley, and W. H. Prescott. The portraits began by being eulogistic and, like the carefully ornate tombstones in an old burying ground, they marked the passing of the founding fathers.*

By the 1920s biography had become a regular feature, but the tone of the writing is quite different. The memorial note is seldom heard, and now when the eminent Victorians, as Strachey ironically called them, come back to us they have been cut down to size and judged with the healthy skepticism and guarded admiration we would apply to a contemporary in our home town. The change, I believe, was induced by several writers — by Strachey, of course, with his brilliant powers of sarcasm, by Henry Adams with his self-depreciation, by Sir Max Beerbohm with his half-affectionate mockery; it was induced by the disillusion and debunking which followed the First World War, and perhaps most of all it was induced by Dr. Freud, who gave us new tools for probing motivation.

"Our appetite for biography," in the words of Norman Douglas, "has become cannibalistic. Men cannot live, it seems, save by feeding on their neighbors' lifeblood."

Thoreau

by RALPH WALDO EMERSON

*The eulogy which Emerson delivered at Thoreau's funeral
was enlarged for publication in the* Atlantic. *It is one of the
most beautiful portraits we ever printed.*

AUGUST 1862

Henry David Thoreau was the last male descendant of a French ancestor who came to this country from the Isle of Guernsey. His character exhibited occasional traits drawn from this blood in singular combination with a very strong Saxon genius.

He was born in Concord, Massachusetts, on the 12th of July, 1817.
He was graduated at Harvard College in 1837, but without any literary
distinction. An iconoclast in literature, he seldom thanked colleges for
their service to him, holding them in small esteem, while yet his debt
to them was important. After leaving the university, he joined his
brother in teaching a private school, which he soon renounced. His father was a manufacturer of lead pencils, and Henry applied himself for
a time to this craft, believing he could make a better pencil than was
then in use. After completing his experiments, he exhibited his work
to chemists and artists in Boston, and having obtained their certificates to its excellence and to its equality with the best London manufacture, he returned home contented. His friends congratulated him
that he had now opened his way to fortune. But he replied that he
should never make another pencil. "Why should I? I would not do
again what I have done once." He resumed his endless walks and miscellaneous studies, making every day some new acquaintance with nature, though as yet never speaking of zoology or botany, since, though
very studious of natural facts, he was incurious of technical and textual
science.

At this time a strong, healthy youth, fresh from college, while all his
companions were choosing their profession or eager to begin some lu-
crative employment, it was inevitable that his thoughts should be exer-

cised on the same question, and it required rare decision to refuse all the accustomed paths and keep his solitary freedom at the cost of disappointing the natural expectations of his family and friends: all the more difficult that he had a perfect probity, was exact in securing his own independence and in holding every man to the like duty. But Thoreau never faltered. He was born protestant. He declined to give up his large ambition of knowledge and action for any craft or profession, aiming at a much more comprehensive calling, the art of living well. If he slighted and defied the opinions of others, it was only that he was more intent to reconcile his practice with his own belief. Never idle or self-indulgent, he preferred, when he wanted money, earning it by some piece of manual labor agreeable to him — as building a boat or a fence, planting, grafting, surveying, or other short work — to any long engagements. With his hardy habits and few wants, his skill in woodcraft, and his powerful arithmetic, he was very competent to live in any part of the world. It would cost him less time to supply his wants than another. He was therefore secure of his leisure.

A natural skill for mensuration, growing out of his mathematical knowledge, and his habit of ascertaining the measures and distances of objects which interested him — the size of trees, the depth and extent of ponds and rivers, the height of mountains, and the air-line distance of his favorite summits — this, and his intimate knowledge of the territory about Concord made him drift into the position of land surveyor. It had the advantage for him that it led him continually into new and secluded grounds and helped his studies of nature. His accuracy and skill in this work were readily appreciated, and he found all the employment he wanted.

He could easily solve the problems of the surveyor, but he was daily beset with graver questions, which he manfully confronted. He interrogated every custom and wished to settle all his practice on an ideal foundation. He was a protestant *à l'outrance,* and few lives contain so many renunciations. He was bred to no profession; he never married; he lived alone; he never went to church; he never voted; he refused to pay a tax to the state; he ate no flesh, he drank no wine, he never knew the use of tobacco; and, though a naturalist, he used neither trap nor gun. He chose, wisely, no doubt, for himself, to be the bachelor of thought and nature. He had no talent for wealth, and knew how to be poor without the least hint of squalor or inelegance. Perhaps he fell into his way of living without forecasting it much, but approved it with later wisdom. "I am often reminded," he wrote in his journal, "that, if

I had bestowed on me the wealth of Croesus, my aims must be still the same, and my means essentially the same."

He had no temptations to fight against — no appetites, no passions, no taste for elegant trifles. A fine house, dress, the manners and talk of highly cultivated people were all thrown away on him. He much preferred a good Indian, and considered these refinements as impediments to conversation, wishing to meet his companion on the simplest terms. He declined invitations to dinner parties, because there each was in everyone's way, and he could not meet the individuals to any purpose. "They make their pride," he said, "in making their dinner cost much; I make my pride in making my dinner cost little." When asked at table what dish he preferred, he answered, "The nearest."

He chose to be rich by making his wants few, and supplying them himself. In his travels, he used the railroad only to get over so much country as was unimportant to the present purpose, walking hundreds of miles, avoiding taverns, buying a lodging in farmers' and fishermen's houses, as cheaper and more agreeable to him, and because there he could better find the men and the information he wanted.

There was something military in his nature not to be subdued, always manly and able, but rarely tender, as if he did not feel himself except in opposition. He wanted a fallacy to expose, a blunder to pillory — I may say required a little sense of victory, a roll of the drum, to call his powers into full exercise. It cost him nothing to say No; indeed, he found it much easier than to say Yes. It seemed as if his first instinct on hearing a proposition was to controvert it, so impatient was he of the limitations of our daily thought. This habit, of course, is a little chilling to the social affections; and though the companion would in the end acquit him of any malice or untruth, yet it mars conversation. Hence, no equal companion stood in affectionate relations with one so pure and guileless. "I love Henry," said one of his friends, "but I cannot like him; and as for taking his arm, I should as soon think of taking the arm of an elm tree."

Yet, hermit and stoic as he was, he was really fond of sympathy, and threw himself heartily and childlike into the company of young people whom he loved, and whom he delighted to entertain, as only he could, with the varied and endless anecdotes of his experiences by field and river. And he was always ready to lead a huckleberry party or a search for chestnuts or grapes. Talking, one day, of a public discourse, Henry remarked that whatever succeeded with the audience was bad. But at supper a young girl, understanding that he was to lecture at the Ly-

ceum, sharply asked him "whether his lecture would be a nice, interesting story, such as she wished to hear, or whether it was one of those
old philosophical things that she did not care about." Henry turned to
her, and bethought himself, and, I saw, was trying to believe that he
had matter that might fit her and her brother, who were to sit up and
go to the lecture, if it was a good one for them.

He was a speaker and actor of the truth — born such — and was
ever running into dramatic situations from this cause. In any circumstance, it interested all bystanders to know what part Henry would take
and what he would say; and he did not disappoint expectation but used
an original judgment on each emergency. In 1845 he built himself a
small framed house on the shores of Walden Pond, and lived there two
years alone, a life of labor and study. This action was quite native and
fit for him. No one who knew him would tax him with affectation. He
was more unlike his neighbors in his thought than in his action. As
soon as he had exhausted the advantages of that solitude, he abandoned it. In 1847, not approving some uses to which the public ex-
penditure was applied, he refused to pay his town tax and was put in
jail. A friend paid the tax for him, and he was released. The like annoyance was threatened the next year. But, as his friends paid the tax,
notwithstanding his protest, I believe he ceased to resist. No opposition or ridicule had any weight with him. He coldly and fully stated
his opinion without affecting to believe that it was the opinion of the
company. It was of no consequence if everyone present held the opposite opinion.

No truer American existed than Thoreau. His preference of his
country and condition was genuine, and his aversion from English
and European manners and tastes almost reached contempt. He listened
impatiently to news or bon mots gleaned from London circles; and
though he tried to be civil, these anecdotes fatigued him. The men
were all imitating each other, and on a small mold. Why can they not
live as far apart as possible, and each be a man by himself? What he
sought was the most energetic nature; and he wished to go to Oregon,
not to London. "In every part of Great Britain," he wrote in his diary,
"are discovered traces of the Romans, their funereal urns, their camps,
their roads, their dwellings. But New England, at least, is not based
on any Roman ruins. We have not to lay the foundations of our houses
on the ashes of a former civilization."

But, idealist as he was, standing for abolition of slavery, abolition
of tariffs, almost for abolition of government, it is needless to say he

found himself not only unrepresented in actual politics, but almost equally opposed to every class of reformers. Yet he paid the tribute of his uniform respect to the Anti-Slavery Party. One man, whose personal acquaintance he had formed, he honored with exceptional regard. Before the first friendly word had been spoken for Captain John Brown, he sent notices to most houses in Concord that he would speak in a public hall on the condition and character of John Brown, on Sunday evening, and invited all people to come. The Republican Committee, the Abolitionist Committee, sent him word that it was premature and not advisable. He replied, "I did not send to you for advice, but to announce that I am to speak." The hall was filled at an early hour by people of all parties, and his earnest eulogy of the hero was heard by all respectfully, by many with a sympathy that surprised themselves.

It was said of Plotinus that he was ashamed of his body, and 'tis very likely he had good reason for it — that his body was a bad servant, and he had not skill in dealing with the material world, as happens often to men of abstract intellect. But Thoreau was equipped with a most adapted and serviceable body. He was of short stature, firmly built, of light complexion, with strong, serious blue eyes, and a grave aspect, his face covered in the late years with a becoming beard. His senses were acute, his frame well-knit and hardy, his hands strong and skillful in the use of tools. And there was a wonderful fitness of body and mind. He could pace sixteen rods more accurately than another man could measure them with rod and chain. He could find his path in the woods at night, he said, better by his feet than his eyes. He could estimate the measure of a tree very well by his eye; he could estimate the weight of a calf or a pig, like a dealer. From a box containing a bushel or more of loose pencils, he could take up with his hands fast enough just a dozen pencils at every grasp. He was a good swimmer, runner, skater, boatman, and would probably outwalk most countrymen in a day's journey. And the relation of body to mind was still finer than we have indicated. He said he wanted every stride his legs made. The length of his walk uniformly made the length of his writing. If shut up in the house, he did not write at all.

When I was planting forest trees and had procured half a peck of acorns, he said that only a small portion of them would be sound, and proceeded to examine them and select the sound ones. But finding this took time, he said, "I think if you put them all into water, the good ones will sink"; which experiment we tried with success. He could plan a garden, or a house, or a barn; would have been competent to lead a

"Pacific Exploring Expedition"; could give judicious counsel in the gravest private or public affairs.

He lived for the day, not cumbered and mortified by his memory. If he brought you yesterday a new proposition, he would bring you today another not less revolutionary. A very industrious man, and setting, like all highly organized men, a high value on his time, he seemed the only man of leisure in town, always ready for any excursion that promised well or for conversation prolonged into late hours. His trenchant sense was never stopped by his rules of daily prudence, but was always up to the new occasion. He noted — what repeatedly befell him — that after receiving from a distance a rare plant he would presently find the same in his own haunts. And those pieces of luck which happen only to good players happened to him. One day, walking with a stranger who inquired where Indian arrowheads could be found, he replied, "Everywhere," and, stooping forward, picked one on the instant from the ground. At Mount Washington, in Tuckerman's Ravine, Thoreau had a bad fall and sprained his foot. As he was in the act of getting up from his fall, he saw for the first time the leaves of the *Arnica mollis*.

His robust common sense, armed with stout hands, keen perceptions, and strong will, cannot yet account for the superiority which shone in his simple and hidden life. I must add the cardinal fact that there was an excellent wisdom in him, proper to a rare class of men, which showed him the material world as a means and symbol. This discovery, which sometimes yields to poets a certain casual and interrupted light, serving for the ornament of their writing, was in him an unsleeping insight; and whatever faults or obstructions of temperament might cloud it, he was not disobedient to the heavenly vision.

He understood the matter in hand at a glance, and saw the limitations and poverty of those he talked with, so that nothing seemed concealed from such terrible eyes. I have repeatedly known young men of sensibility converted in a moment to the belief that this was the man they were in search of, the man of men, who could tell them all they should do. His own dealing with them was never affectionate, but superior, didactic — scorning their petty ways — very slowly conceding, or not conceding at all, the promise of his society at their houses or even at his own. "Would he not walk with them?" "He did not know. There was nothing so important to him as his walk; he had no walks to throw away on company." Visits were offered him from respectful parties, but he declined them. Admiring friends offered to carry him at their own cost to the Yellowstone River, to the West Indies, to South America. But though nothing could be more grave or considered than his refusals, they remind one in quite new relations of that fop Brummel's reply to the gentleman who offered him his carriage in a shower, "But where will *you* ride, then?" — and what accusing silences, and what searching and irresistible speeches, battering down all defenses, his companions can remember!

Thoreau dedicated his genius with such entire love to the fields, hills, and waters of his native town that he made them known and interesting to all reading Americans and to people over the sea. The river on whose banks he was born and died he knew from its springs to its confluence with the Merrimack. He had made summer and winter observation on it for many years, and at every hour of the day and the night. Every fact which occurs in the bed, on the banks, or in the air over it: the fishes, and their spawning and nests, their manners, their food; the shad flies which fill the air on a certain evening once a year, and which are snapped at by the fishes so ravenously that many of these die of repletion; the conical heaps of small stones on the river shallows, one of which heaps will sometimes overfill a cart — these heaps the huge nests of small fishes; the birds which frequent the stream, heron, duck, sheldrake, loon, osprey; the snake, muskrat, otter, woodchuck, and fox on the banks; the turtle, hyla, and cricket which make the banks vocal; all were known to him, and, as it were, townsmen and fellow creatures; so that he felt an absurdity or violence in any narrative of one of these by itself apart, and still more of its dimensions on an inch rule, or in the exhibition of its skeleton, or the specimen of a squirrel or a bird in brandy. He liked to speak of the manners of the river, as itself a lawful creature, yet with exactness, and always to an observed fact. As he knew the river, so the ponds in this region.

One of the weapons he used, more important than microscope or alcohol receiver to other investigators, was a whim which grew on him by indulgence, yet appeared in gravest statement, namely, of extolling his own town and neighborhood as the most favored center for natural observation. He remarked that the flora of Massachusetts embraced almost all the important plants of America — most of the oaks, most of the willows, the best pines, the ash, the maple, the beech, the nuts. I think his fancy for referring everything to the meridian of Concord did not grow out of any ignorance or depreciation of other longitudes or latitudes, but was rather a playful expression of his conviction of the indifference of all places, and that the best place for each is where he stands. He expressed it once in this wise: "I think nothing is to be hoped from you, if this bit of mold under your feet is not sweeter to you to eat than any other in the world, or in any world."

The other weapon with which he conquered all obstacles in science was patience. He knew how to sit immovable, a part of the rock he rested on, until the bird, the reptile, the fish, which had retired from him, should come back and resume its habits, nay, moved by curiosity should come to him and watch him.

It was a pleasure and a privilege to walk with him. He knew the country like a fox or a bird, and passed through it freely by paths of his own. He knew every track in the snow or on the ground, and what creature had taken this path before him. One must submit abjectly to such a guide, and the reward was great. Under his arm he carried an old music book to press plants; in his pocket, his diary and pencil, a spy glass for birds, microscope, jackknife, and twine. He wore straw hat, stout shoes, strong gray trousers, to brave shrub oaks and smilax and to climb a tree for a hawk's or a squirrel's nest. He waded into the pool for the water plants, and his strong legs were no insignificant part of his armor. On the day I speak of he looked for the Menyanthes, detected it across the wide pool, and, on examination of the florets, decided that it had been in flower five days. He drew out of his breast pocket his diary, and read the names of all the plants that should bloom on this day, whereof he kept account as a banker when his notes fall due. The Cypripedium not due till tomorrow. He thought that, if waked up from a trance in this swamp, he could tell by the plants what time of the year it was within two days. The redstart was flying about, and presently the fine grosbeaks, whose brilliant scarlet makes the rash gazer wipe his eye, and whose fine clear note Thoreau compared to that of a tanager which has got rid of its hoarseness. Presently he heard a note which he called that of the night warbler, a bird he had never identified, had been in search of twelve years, which always, when he saw it, was in the act of diving down into a tree or bush, and which it was vain to seek; the only bird that sings indifferently by night and by day. I told him he must beware of finding and booking it, lest life should have nothing more to show him. He said, "What you seek in vain for, half your life, one day you come full upon all the family at dinner. You seek it like a dream, and as soon as you find it you become its prey."

His interest in the flower or the bird lay very deep in his mind, was connected with nature — and the meaning of nature was never attempted to be defined by him. He would not offer a memoir of his observations to the Natural History Society. "Why should I? To detach the description from its connections in my mind would make it no longer true or valuable to me: and they do not wish what belongs to it." His power of observation seemed to indicate additional senses. He saw as with microscope, heard as with ear trumpet, and his memory was a photographic register of all he saw and heard. And yet none knew better than he that it is not the fact that imports, but the impression or effect of the fact on your mind. Every fact lay in glory in his mind, a type of the order and beauty of the whole.

No college ever offered him a diploma or a professor's chair; no academy made him its corresponding secretary, its discoverer, or even its member: perhaps these learned bodies feared the satire of his presence. Yet so much knowledge of nature's secret and genius few others possessed, none in a more large and religious synthesis. For not a particle of respect had he to the opinions of any man or body of men, but homage solely to the truth itself; and as he discovered everywhere among doctors some leaning of courtesy, it discredited them. He grew to be revered and admired by his townspeople, who had at first known him only as an oddity. The farmers who employed him as a surveyor soon discovered his rare accuracy and skill, his knowledge of their lands, of trees, of birds, of Indian remains, and the like, which enabled him to tell every farmer more than he knew before of his own farm, so that he began to feel a little as if Thoreau had better rights in his land than he. They felt, too, the superiority of character which addressed all men with a native authority.

His poetry might be good or bad; he no doubt wanted a lyric facility and technical skill; but he had the source of poetry in his spiritual perception. He was a good reader and critic, and his judgment of poetry was to the ground of it. He could not be deceived as to the presence or absence of the poetic element in any composition, and his thirst for this made him negligent and perhaps scornful of superficial graces. He would pass by many delicate rhythms, but he would have detected every live stanza or line in a volume, and knew very well where to find an equal poetic charm in prose.

His own verses are often rude and defective. The gold does not yet run pure, is drossy and crude. The thyme and marjoram are not yet honey. But if he wants lyric fineness and technical merits, if he has not the poetic temperament, he never lacks the casual thought, showing that his genius was better than his talent. He knew the worth of the imagination for the uplifting and consolation of human life, and liked to throw every thought into a symbol.

While he used in his writings a certain petulance of remark in reference to churches or churchmen, he was a person of a rare, tender, and absolute religion, a person incapable of any profanation by act or by thought. Of course, the same isolation which belonged to his original thinking and living detached him from the social religious forms. This is neither to be censured nor regretted. Aristotle long ago explained it when he said, "One who surpasses his fellow citizens in virtue is no longer a part of the city. Their law is not for him, since he is a law to himself."

Thoreau was sincerity itself, and might fortify the convictions of prophets in the ethical laws by his holy living. It was an affirmative experience which refused to be set aside. A truth-speaker he, capable of the most deep and strict conversation; a physician to the wounds of any soul; a friend knowing not only the secret of friendship, but almost worshiped by those few persons who resorted to him as their confessor and prophet, and knew the deep value of his mind and great heart. He thought that without religion or devotion of some kind nothing great was ever accomplished: and he thought that the bigoted sectarian had better bear this in mind.

Had his genius been only contemplative, he had been fitted to his life; but with his energy and practical ability he seemed born for great enterprise and for command; and I so much regret the loss of his rare powers of action that I cannot help counting it a fault in him that he had no ambition. Wanting this, instead of engineering for all America, he was the captain of a huckleberry party. Pounding beans is good to the end of pounding empires one of these days; but if, at the end of years, it is still only beans!

But these foibles, real or apparent, were fast vanishing in the incessant growth of a spirit so robust and wise, and which effaced its defeats with new triumphs. His study of nature was a perpetual ornament to him, and inspired his friends with curiosity to see the world through his eyes and to hear his adventures. They possessed every kind of interest.

He had many elegances of his own, while he scoffed at conventional elegance. Thus he could not bear to hear the sound of his own steps, the grit of gravel, and therefore never willingly walked in the road, but in the grass, on mountains and in woods. His senses were acute, and he remarked that by night every dwelling place gives out bad air, like a slaughterhouse. He liked the pure fragrance of melilot. He honored certain plants with special regard, and, over all, the pond lily, then the gentian, the *Mikania scandens,* the "life everlasting," and a bass tree which he visited every year when it bloomed in the middle of July. He thought the scent a more oracular inquisition than the sight — more oracular and trustworthy. The scent, of course, reveals what is concealed from the other senses. By it he detected earthiness. He delighted in echoes, and said they were almost the only kind of kindred voices that he heard. He loved nature so well, was so happy in her solitude, that he became very jealous of cities and the sad work which their refinements and artifices made with man and his dwelling. The ax was always destroying his forest. "Thank God," he said, "they cannot cut down the clouds!"

I subjoin a few sentences taken from his unpublished manuscripts, not only as records of his thought and feeling, but for their power of description and literary excellence.

"Some circumstantial evidence is very strong, as when you find a trout in the milk."

"The chub is a soft fish, and tastes like boiled brown paper salted."

"I put on some hemlock boughs, and the rich salt crackling of their leaves was like mustard to the ear, the crackling of uncountable regiments. Dead trees love the fire."

"The bluebird carries the sky on his back."

"The tanager flies through the green foliage as if it would ignite the leaves."

"Nature made ferns for pure leaves, to show what she could do in that line."

"How did these beautiful rainbow tints get into the shell of the fresh-water clam, buried in the mud at the bottom of our dark river?"

"How can we expect a harvest of thought who have not had a seedtime of character?"

"I ask to be melted. You can only ask of the metals that they be tender to the fire that melts them. To nought else can they be tender."

There is a flower known to botanists, one of the same genus with our summer plant called "life everlasting," a Gnaphalium like that, which grows on the most inaccessible cliffs of the Tyrolese mountains, where the chamois dare hardly venture, and which the hunter, tempted by its beauty and by his love (for it is immensely valued by Swiss maidens), climbs the cliffs to gather, and is sometimes found dead at the foot, with the flowers in his hand. It is called by botanists the

Gnaphalium leontopodium, but by the Swiss *Edelweiss,* which signifies *noble purity.* Thoreau seemed to me living in the hope to gather this plant, which belonged to him of right. The scale on which his studies proceeded was so large as to require longevity, and we were the less prepared for his sudden disappearance. The country knows not yet, or in the least part, how great a son it has lost. It seems an injury that he should leave in the midst his broken task, which none else can finish — a kind of indignity to so noble a soul, that it should depart out of nature before yet he has really been shown to his peers for what he is. But he, at least, is content. His soul was made for the noblest society; he had in a short life exhausted the capabilities of this world; wherever there is knowledge, wherever there is virtue, wherever there is beauty, he will find a home.

Charles Darwin

by JOHN FISKE

When Asa Gray first began to study Darwin's Origin of Species in the summer of 1860, he was very uncomfortable with what he found. "Several features of the theory have an uncanny look," he wrote. "They may prove to be innocent but their first aspect is suspicious, and high authorities pronounce the whole thing to be positively mischievous." How complete was the Atlantic's conversion in the next twenty-two years will be seen in this appraisal by John Fiske, the historian, written directly after Darwin's death.

JUNE 1882

Today, while all that was mortal of Charles Darwin is borne to its last resting place in Westminster Abbey, by the side of Sir Isaac Newton, it seems a fitting occasion to utter a few words of tribute to the memory of the beautiful and glorious life that has just passed away from us. Though Darwin had more than completed his threescore and ten years, and though his life had been rich in achievement and crowned with success such as is seldom vouchsafed to man, yet the news of his death has none the less impressed us with a sense of sudden and premature bereavement. For on the one hand the time would never have come when those of us who had learned the inestimable worth of such a teacher and friend could have felt ready to part with him; and on the other hand Darwin was one whom the gods, for love of him, had endowed with perpetual youth, so that his death could never seem otherwise than premature.

There is, now and then, a mind — perhaps one in four or five million — which in early youth thinks the thoughts of mature manhood, and which in old age retains the flexibility, the receptiveness, the keen appetite for new impressions, that are characteristic of the fresh season of youth. Such a mind as this was Darwin's. To the last he was eager for new facts and suggestions, to the last he held his judgments in readiness

for revision; and to this unfailing freshness of spirit was joined a sagacity which, naturally great, had been refined and strengthened by half
a century most fruitful in experiences, till it had come to be almost
superhuman. When we remember how Alexander von Humboldt began
at the age of seventy-five to write his *Kosmos,* and how he lived to turn
off in his ninetieth year the fifth bulky volume of that prodigiously
learned book — when we remember this, and consider the great scientific value of the monographs which Darwin has lately been publishing
almost every year, we must feel that it is in a measure right to speak of
his death as premature.

After all, however, no one can fail to recognize in the career of Darwin the interest that belongs to a complete and well-rounded tale. When
the extent of his work is properly estimated, it is not too much to say
that among all the great leaders of human thought that have ever lived
there are not half a dozen who have achieved so much as he. In an age
that has been richer than any preceding age in great scientific names, his
name is indisputably the foremost. He has already found his place in the
history of science by the side of Aristotle, Descartes, and Newton. And
among thinkers of the first order of originality, he has been peculiarly
fortunate in having lived to see all the fresh and powerful minds of a
new generation adopting his fundamental conceptions and pursuing
their inquiries along the path which he was the first to break.

When Darwin was born, in 1809, the name which he inherited was
already a famous name. Dr. Erasmus Darwin, the friend of Priestley
and Watt and author of the *Botanic Garden,* was deservedly ranked
among the most ingenious and original thinkers of the eighteenth century in England. His brother, Robert Waring Darwin, was the author of
a work on botany which for many years enjoyed high repute. Of the sons
of Erasmus, one, Sir Francis Darwin, was noted as a keen observer of
animals; another, Charles, who died at the age of twenty-one from a dissection wound, had already written a medical essay of such importance
as to give his name a place in biographical dictionaries. Nor can it be
irrelevant to add that one of Darwin's sons has already, through his
study of the tides, achieved some remarkable results, which seem likely
to give him a high place among the astronomers of the present day.

There is one thing which a man of original scientific or philosophical
genius in a rightly ordered world should never be called upon to do. He
should never be called upon to "earn a living"; for that is a wretched
waste of energy, in which the highest intellectual power is sure to suffer
serious detriment, and runs the risk of being frittered away into hope-

less ruin. Like his great predecessor and ally, **Sir Charles Lyell,** Darwin was so favored by fortune as to be free from this odious necessity. He was able to devote his whole life with a single mind to the pursuit of scientific truth and to ministering in the most exalted way to the welfare of his fellow creatures. After taking his master's degree at Cambridge in 1831, at the age of twenty-two, an opportunity was offered Darwin for studying natural history on a grand scale. The *Beagle,* a ten-gun brig under the command of Captain Fitzroy, was then about to start on a long voyage, "to complete the survey of Patagonia and Tierra del Fuego . . . to survey the shores of Chili, Peru, and of some islands in the Pacific, and to carry a chain of chronometrical measurements round the world." As Captain Fitzroy had expressed a wish to have a naturalist accompany the expedition, Darwin volunteered his services, which the Lords of the Admiralty readily accepted — a fact which in itself is sufficient evidence of the reputation for scientific attainments which Darwin had already gained at that youthful age.

This memorable voyage, which lasted five years, was very fruitful in results. Owen, Hooker, Waterhouse, Berkeley, Bell, and other eminent naturalists took part in the publication of these results, which formed a very important contribution to the zoology and botany, and to the paleontology, of the countries visited in the course of the voyage. To this great series of volumes, which appeared between 1840 and 1846, Darwin contributed three from his own hand — the work on volcanic islands, the geological observations on South America, and the famous essay on coral reefs. In 1851–1853 Darwin published a *Monograph of the Cirripedia,* in two volumes octavo, and accompanied this about the same time with monographs of the various fossil genera of cirripeds (or barnacle family) in Great Britain. In recognition of his achievements, Darwin in 1853 received the royal medal from the Royal Society, and in 1859 the Wollaston medal from the Geological Society.

By this time his name had come to be known in all parts of the civilized world, so that when, in the year 1859, the *Origin of Species* was published, it at once attracted universal attention by reason of the eminence of its author.

Like the great works which had preceded it, the *Origin of Species* must be regarded as one of the results of the ever memorable voyage of the *Beagle.* In the course of this voyage Darwin visited the Galapagos Islands and was struck by the peculiar relations which the floras and faunas of this archipelago sustained to one another, and to the flora and fauna of the nearest mainland of Ecuador, distant some five hundred miles. These islands are purely volcanic in formation and have never at any time been joined to the South American continent.

From the study of the inhabitants of a single well-defined area, Darwin was led into a series of most grand and startling considerations relating to the past history of life upon our globe. The conclusions thus succinctly stated were amply confirmed by a survey of the distribution of organisms all over the earth, and thus was inaugurated the study of zoological and botanical geography. It has now become well established that in very few cases, if any, have animals and plants originated exactly in the places where we now find them, but that they are almost always the offspring of immigrants; and the study of the ancient migrations of the progenitors of living plants and animals has begun to throw a flood of light upon the history of the changes that have taken place in the physical geography of the earth.

The conception of the origin of species through "descent with modifications" having been thus forcibly suggested to Darwin by the facts of geographical distribution, it was still further strengthened by a study of the geological succession of extinct organisms and their relations to living organisms in the same areas. Such broad facts as the successive appearance of various sloth-like and armadillo-like animals in South America, or of various marsupials and monotremes in Australia, forcibly suggest the descent of the later forms from the earlier ones that lived in the same countries. Of like import is the general fact that in the course of geological succession any given organism is sure to be intermediate in character between those that have preceded and those that have followed it. But still more powerfully suggestive even than this is the fact that, in proportion as we go back in geologic time, we find the characteristics of plants and animals to be less and less distinctly specialized: so that, for example, in the Eocene period, instead of horses and tapirs such as now exist we find an animal something like a tapir and something like a horse; and instead of leopards and wolves and bears we find carnivorous animals, not specialized as of feline or canine or ursine family, but with some points of resemblance to all three, and with some points like opossums and wombats into the bargain. In conformity with this general principle, the arrangement of organisms according to their succession in geologic time would be like the branches and branchlets of a tree, which is the typical form of arrangement where the link that connects the facts arranged is the link of parentage.

But just here the facts of geological succession are reinforced, with truly overwhelming conclusiveness, by the great facts of classification in the animal and vegetable kingdoms. This branching tree-like arrangement, which alone correctly represents the relationships of organisms in their geological succession, is at the same time the only possible arrangement by which the likenesses and affinities among existing organisms can be represented with anything like an approach to correctness. The facts of paleontology exactly dovetail in with those of taxonomy, and serve to elucidate and emphasize them. Many eminent naturalists before Cuvier attempted to classify all animals in a linear series, but Cuvier proved once for all that no such arrangement is possible. The only feasible arrangement is that of groups within groups, diverging like the branches and twigs of what we aptly term a "family tree"; and this fact not only strongly suggests the theory of "descent with modifications" but is indeed utterly incompatible with any other theory.

Had Darwin done nothing but this, it would have given him a peculiar right to associate his name with the development theory, it would have established that theory on a basis of "convincing probability," and it would have entitled him to a high place in the history of scientific thought in the nineteenth century. But Darwin did not stop here. Convinced by such considerations as those just presented that the specific characters of plants and animals are not constant, but variable, he sought for some grand all-pervading *cause of variation* in organisms, and his search was crowned with success. This was the achievement which in his hands raised the development theory from the rank of a brilliant philosophical speculation into the rank of an irrefragable scientific discovery. This was the achievement which gave to mankind a new implement of research and a new insight into the workings of nature, and it was this which justifies us in placing Darwin's name beside those of Newton and Descartes.

The effect of Darwin's work has been, however, to remodel the theological conceptions of the origin and destiny of man which were current in former times. In this respect it has wrought a revolution as great as that which Copernicus inaugurated and Newton completed, and of very much the same kind. Again has man been rudely unseated from his imaginary throne in the center of the universe, but only that he may learn to see in the universe and in human life a richer and deeper meaning than he had before suspected. Truly, he who unfolds to us the way in which God works through the world of phenomena may well be called the best of religious teachers. In the study of the organic world, no less than in the study of the starry heavens, is it true that "day unto day uttereth speech, and night unto night showeth knowledge."

Dr. Holmes

by HORACE SCUDDER

*A wheelhorse for Houghton Mifflin in the closing years of
the century, Horace Scudder was editor of the Riverside Poets
and of the* Atlantic *from 1890 to 1898. On Holmes's death
he realized that the monopoly of American literature which
had once resided in Concord, Cambridge, and Boston was at
an end.*

DECEMBER 1894

It was thirty-seven years ago that Dr. Holmes published in the first
number of this magazine the opening number of a series which gave
distinction at once to the *Atlantic Monthly*. Since that day scarcely a
volume has appeared without a word from him, and many of the volumes
contain a poem, paper, or chapter of a novel in every number. So identified had he become with the fortunes of the magazine, that, the day
after his death, I received a communication addressed to him as editor.
It was very fortunate for all of us that he never was its editor, for he
would have been so scrupulous that he would have expended his energies on other people's work, and we should have missed some of his own.

The constancy with which he held to this medium of communication
with the reading public hints at a notable characteristic of his nature
which finds abundant expression in his writings. Dr. Holmes had the
passion of local patriotism. No one need be told who has read his stirring lyrics, his "Bread and the Newspaper," his oration on "The Inevitable Trial," and his sketch of Motley's life, how generous was his affection for the nation: but a great crisis brought these expressions to pass;
his familiar habit of mind was cordially local. His affection fastened
upon his college, and in his college on his class; he had a worthy pride
in the race from which he had sprung, and the noble clannishness which
is one of the safeguards of social morality; he loved the city of his life,
not with the merely curious regard of the antiquary, but with the passion
of the man who can be at home only in one place; and he held to New

England as to a substantial entity, not a geographical section of some greater whole.

It would be a perversion of logic to say that all this was the result of conditions of life; that the hard-working medical professor must stay at home, especially when, for a large part of his academic career, his duties permitted no long vacation, so that after the preliminary scamper over Europe which every young professional man was expected to make if he could, fifty years would elapse before the man, crowned with honors, should make a royal progress through England; that the lectures before the medical school precluded those general lecturing tours which gave Emerson and others acquaintance with remoter parts of the country. Dr. Holmes had his little experience of the lyceum. A truer account would reverse cause and effect. He did not travel because Boston and Nahant and Berkshire contented him. His laboratory was at hand; human nature was under his observation from the vantage ground of home. With the instinct of a man of science, he took for analysis that which was most familiar to him, assured that in the bit of the world where he was born and out of which he had got his nourishment, he had all he needed for the exercise of his wit.

He lived to see many changes in the large home to which he remained constant, and some of these changes were due to him. It may be doubted if any city so young as Boston ever acquired in its short life so distinct and self-centered a character. It is true that its founders brought with them a furnishing of customs, traditions, and ideas which gave the place at once a visionary ancestry of its own, and started it in life with a stock of notions; but the after life of the town down to the time when Holmes was a young man was singularly adapted to the creation of a personality such as is rare in modern times. With a very homogeneous population, a diversity of occupations, a commerce which gave its citizens the sense of being in the center of the world, a lively interest in politics and speculative theology which forbade intellectual stagnation, Boston was the head of a province, and had its own standards. So late as 1841, Mrs. Child could publish "Letters from New York" without raising a smile.

But when Dr. Holmes began his "Breakfast Table" series in the *Atlantic,* the great migration from Ireland had been going on for ten years, clippers had given way before ocean steamships, New York was draining the Connecticut Valley and the lower tier of New England states, manufacturers were establishing new centers of industrial interest, and political discussions were changing the center of gravity from party to moral principle. The great westward movement, also, had drawn Boston capital and Boston men into new relations, and the old days of provincial security and self-content were coming to an end.

It was then that Dr. Holmes with one hand held up to view the society whose integrity was about to disappear, and with the other helped to construct the new order that was to take its place. There is no more pathetic yet kindly figure in our literature than Little Boston. With poetic instinct, Dr. Holmes made him deformed but not ugly. He put into him a fiery soul of local patriotism, and transfigured him thus. Under the guise of a bit of nature's mockery he was enabled to give vent to a flood of feeling without arousing laughter or contempt.

If Dr. Holmes concealed himself behind the mask of Little Boston, he was more frankly in evidence under the humorous conceit of the Autocrat, and the service which he rendered in this character was an important one. He knew a society in which theological discussion was still largely concerned with abstractions and warfare was carried on under a set of rules which both parties recognized. Dr. Holmes used his wit not on one side or the other of prevailing controversies, though the conservative party undoubtedly regarded him as an assailant, but with the design of bringing to bear on fundamental questions that scientific spirit which was bred in him by his profession and penetrated by his genius. It was not so much the logic as the ingenuity, the wit, of science which he used to test a good many problems in spiritual life. He angered many at the time, but now that the heat of that day of discussions has gone down, it should be evident that Dr. Holmes had much more of the constructive temper than was then accredited to him, and that he was a poet dealing with fundamental things of the spirit, not a theologian. His good-natured raillery undermined conventions rather than sapped faith, and his wit was an acid which had no mordant power on that which was genuine. There were a good many shocks from his battery, but those who received the shocks were stung into a new vitality; and, taking his work by and large, it may be said to have had a tonic effect upon the society closest to it; a fresher breeze blew through the minds of men, and intellectual life was freer, more animated, and more on the alert.

This concentration of his power and his affection has had its effect on Dr. Holmes's literary fame. He is another witness, if one were needed, to the truth that identification with a locality is a surer passport to immortality than cosmopolitanism. The local is a good starting point from which to essay the universal. Thoreau perhaps affected a scorn of the world outside of Concord, but he helped make the little village a temple, and his statue is in one of the niches. Holmes, staying in Boston, has brought the world to his door, and a society which is already historic will preserve him in its amber. It is the power to transmute the near and tangible into something of value the world over which is the mark of genius, and Holmes had this philosopher's stone.

The death of Holmes removes the last of those American writers who form the great group. This wit and poet lingered long enough to bid each in turn farewell. No doubt a longer perspective will enable us ultimately to adjust more perfectly their relations to one another and to the time, but it is not likely that there will be any serious revision of judgment by posterity as to their place in the canon. When Lowell went, Whittier and Holmes remained, and we kept on, in the spirit of Wordsworth's maiden, counting over the dead and the living in one inseparate company. Now they are all in the past tense, and all in the present; for death has a way of liberating personality, setting it free from accidents, and giving it permanent relations.

In a few years the great body of literature read in the public schools of the nation will be the writings of Longfellow, Whittier, Hawthorne, Lowell, Emerson, Holmes, Bryant, and Irving. A common literature is essential to any true community of ideals; and in the work of producing a homogeneous nation out of the varied material which different races, different political orders, and different religious faiths have contributed since the war for the Union — a work which is largely committed to the public schools — there is no force comparable to a great, harmonious literature. Therefore, for a generation to come, the spiritual host which Holmes has just joined will be the mightiest force that can be reckoned with for the nationalization of the American people.

George Moore

by SIR MAX BEERBOHM

"A man must be judged by what is fine in him, not by what is trivial." So wrote Sir Max Beerbohm in this essay which gives us a hearing, seeing likeness of his friend George Moore.

When, where, did I first see my friend George Moore? It is odd that I do not remember my first sight of him. For I am sure there never was in heaven or on earth any one at all like him. It is conceivable that in the waters that are under the earth there *may,* vaguely luminous, be similar forms, and — stay, it isn't odd, after all, this lapse of my memory. It is explained by that quality of luminous vagueness which Moore's presence always had. There always was an illusory look about him — the diaphanous, vaporous, wan look of an illusion conjured up for us, perhaps by means of mirrors and by a dishonorable spiritualist. There was something blurred about him; his outlines seemed to merge into the air around him. He never seemed to enter or leave a room. Rather did he appear there, and in due time fade thence. It was always difficult to say at what moment he appeared: one had but become aware of his presence, which was always delightful, and later one found oneself missing him: he had gone. Thus would it be a strange feat indeed if now I remembered more than this: that somewhere in the early nineties the apparition of Moore had already been vouchsafed me.

Mentally, as well as physically, he was unique. He was always the same, and yet always new. Perhaps his novelty was in part due to his sameness. The outer and inner demeanor of almost every man is variable, changing with the circumstances he is in and the sort of people who are about him. Except Oscar Wilde, I never knew a man whose tone of mind and mode of expression, everywhere and with everyone, were so invariable as Moore's. And whereas Oscar Wilde's personality was in great measure a conscious and elaborate piece of work, and outshone other personalities by reason of the finer skill that had gone to the making of it, as well as to the richer materials from which it was made, Moore's slighter but not less peculiar personality was an entirely natural product. That he was intensely self-conscious is proved in all his many autobiographies. On the other hand, it is clear in his writings, and was still more clear to me in personal acquaintance with him, that he never exercised any positive guidance of himself. He was content to look on at himself, sometimes rather admiringly, more often disparagingly, always with absolute detachment. While he swam he looked on from the bank, and never when he sank did he offer himself a helping hand. For well or ill, he just let himself be; and as the spectacle of himself was too interesting to be interfered with even for his own sake, of course he wouldn't interfere with it to please Brown, Jones, and Robinson. It was for this reason that he was so dear to Wilson Steer, Tonks, and Walter Sickert, and indeed to all people who had the wit to enjoy in the midst of an artificial civilization the spectacle of one absolutely natural man.

Whatever was in his mind, no matter where he was nor what his audience, he said. And when he had nothing to say, he said nothing. Which of these courses in an average drawing room needs the greater courage — to say simply anything, or to sit saying simply nothing? I think I used to rate Moore's silences as his finer triumph. They were so long, so unutterably blank. And yet, in some remote way, they so dominated the current chatter. It was impossible not to watch him during them. He sat rather on the edge of his chair, his knees together, his hands hanging limp on either side of him. Limply there hung over his brow a copious wisp of blond hair, which wavered as he turned the long white oval of his face from one speaker to another. He sat wide-eyed, gaping, listening — no, one would not have said "listening" but hearing: it did not seem that his ears were sending in any reports to his brain. It would be an understatement to say that his face was as a mask which revealed nothing. His face was as a mask of gauze through which Nothing was quite clearly visible. And then, all of a sudden, there would appear — Something. There came a gleam from within the pale-blue eyes, and a sort of ripple passed up over the modeling of the flaccid cheeks; the chin suddenly receded a little further, and — *Voilà Moore qui parle! Silence, la compagnie! Moore parle.*

What Moore spoke of would be always something quite alien to the general theme. It would be some i-de-a that had lately been simmering in his brain. He had come to the conclusion that the eighteenth century was a *stoopid* century; or he had been reading Milton, and saw now that

Shelley was not a poet after all; or he saw now that women had no e-motion, but only logic. Always an i-de-a, delivered hot and strong, in gulps, as from the spout of a kettle boiling over. He had (as I have typographically suggested here) a way of dividing the syllables of his words, and of giving to each syllable an equal stress. Such words as *the* and *a* and *of* and *to* he pronounced as emphatically as any other word; and the effect was that they seemed to have an emphasis beyond all others: it was as though his voice *bulged* when he came to them. I suppose this habit of equal stress was due to his having lived among Frenchmen and talked French during his most malleable years. His Parisianism, grafted upon an imperishable brogue, gave to his utterance a very curious charm. Aided by his face and his gesture, this charm was irresistible. I say his "gesture" advisedly; for he had but one. The finger tips of his vague, small, inert, white hand continually approached his mouth and, rising thence, described an arc in the air — a sort of invisible suspension bridge for the passage of his i-de-a to us. His face, too, while he talked, had but one expression — a faintly illumined blank. Usually, when even the most phlegmatic of men is talking, you shall detect changes of expression. In Moore you never could. Usually the features of the most vivacious man's face retain the form that Nature assigned to them. But in Moore's face, immutable though the expression was, by some physical miracle the features were perpetually remolding themselves. It was not merely that the chin receded and progressed, nor merely that the oval cheeks went rippling in capricious hollows and knolls; the contours of nose and brow, they too, had their vicissitudes. You think I exaggerate? Well, I myself, with Moore there before me, did sometimes doubt the evidence of my own eyes. It was possible that my eyes had been deceived. But the point then is that no face save Moore's ever deceived them in just this way.

Sometimes he talked, as sometimes he also wrote in books, about ladies who had loved him. On such occasions, either because I had never met any of these ladies, or because the conventional English education instills into us a prejudice against that kind of disquisition, I used not to listen very attentively — used to revel merely in the visual aspect of this man of genius. Genius, assuredly, he had; not, I think, in his specifically creative work; but in criticism, yes. His novels, always interesting though they were, never seemed to me to have the quality of life. I saw them rather as experiments, made with admirable skill and patience and, as the years passed, on an ever-increasing scale — experiments which, though all the proper materials had been collected, and all the latest scientific formulae mastered, somehow failed of that final result for which they were made: creation of authentic life. Moore's habit of rewriting his earlier novels was in itself the deadliest criticism they could have. When once a novel has left the writer's hand, and been published, the characters, if they really live, are beyond his power. What they were, what they did, what happened to them, are things as unalterable now as the character and career of the late Queen Victoria. If they do not unalterably live for the man who made them, for whom shall they live? And if they do not live, how shall belated life be breathed into the clay? Vital magic, which was just what his novels lacked, was just what his criticisms had. No one but Ruskin has written more vividly than he, more lovingly and seeingly, about the art of painting; and no one has ever written more inspiringly than he, with a more infectious enthusiasm, about those writers whom he understood and loved, or more amusingly against those whom he neither understood nor liked. Of learning he had no equipment at all; for him everything was a discovery; and it was natural that Oscar Wilde should complain, as he did once complain to me, "George Moore is always conducting his education in public." Also, he had no sense of proportion. But this defect was in truth a quality. Whenever he discovered some new old master, that master seemed to him greater than any other; he would hear of no other. And it was just this frantic exclusiveness that made his adorations so fruitful: it was by the completeness of his surrender to one thing at a time that he possessed himself of that thing's very essence. The finest criticism is always passive, not active. Mastery comes only by self-surrender. The critic who justly admires all kinds of things simultaneously cannot love any one of them, any more than a lady can be simultaneously in love with more than one gentleman. That kind of critic is often (if I, who am of that kind, may be allowed to say so) very admirable. But it is the Moores who matter.

When I say that Moore could revere only one master at a time, I do not mean that he was always faithless to old idols. When he had exhausted his ecstasy at some new shrine, he would rise from his knees and, if no other new shrine were visible, would wander back to some old one. Turgenev, especially, had power to recapture and reinflame him ever. Almost the last time I met him was in one of these recurrent intervals. We were both weekend guests of Hugh Hammersley and his brilliant and beautiful wife. On Saturday evening, and on Sunday, Moore was rather blank. We could not tempt him to talk. I saw that he had risen from before some shrine and was temporarily at a loss. At dinner on Sunday I mentioned Turgenev. It was as though I had taken him by the hand, poor waif, and led him to the place where he would be. It was as though he leapt across the familiar threshold of the temple and fell prostrate at the shrine. At bedtime he was still talking of Turgenev with unflagging charm and power. And when, next morning, rather late, I came down to breakfast, there, fresh as a lily that had bloomed in the night — there at the breakfast table, with a fork in his right hand while his left described innumerable arcs over a plate of haddock — was Moore, talking of Turgenev to our polite host.

It is a pity for mankind that Moore's eloquence was all chamber music. When I said just now that he was always the same "everywhere" I meant that he was always the same among his diverse friends and acquaintances. In public he simply evaporated. In his *Ave* he has called himself "the only Irishman who could not make a speech"; and to this testimony I can add that he could not passably read a speech. I was a guest at that public dinner of which in *Ave* he has given an immortal account — the dinner held at the Shelbourne Hotel, Dublin, to inaugurate the Irish Literary Theatre; and well do I remember the woebegone way he murmured into his MS., making in that convivial and pugnacious company of orators no effect whatsoever. Nor was this the first time I had seen him wilt in the publicity he abhorred. In '96 Joseph Pennell sued "*The Saturday Review* and Another" for libel. "Another" was Walter Sickert, who had written the offending criticism. The case hinged on the difference between lithographs drawn on paper and lithographs drawn directly on the stone. Whistler, who was no longer on speaking terms with Sickert, nor on speaking terms with very many people besides Mr. and Mrs. Pennell, threw his mantle over the plaintiff. The friends of Sickert combined to throw their own modest little mantles over "Another." Moore was always accounted a rather selfish man; but the fact that he, with his horror of public appearances, did volunteer for service in the witness box, is proof that he could on occasion barter self for Auld Lang Syne. I can see him now, penned there, more than ever wraithlike in the harsh, bleak light of the court. He kisses the book, he acknowledges that his name is George Moore, and that he is an art critic; and dimly he conveys an impression that he prefers lithographs drawn directly on the stone. Up rises the cross-examining counsel: "Now, Mr. Moore, I want you to explain what claim you have to be regarded as an expert in this matter." Silence reigned. Moore's gaze wandered to the Judge, and then suddenly his tongue was loosened. "I knew Degas," he began; whereas down sat the cross-examining counsel with an eloquent gesture to Judge and jury; the Judge made a little gesture to the witness; the ordeal was over. But brief though that ordeal was, I hope it will not go unrecorded in the Golden Book of Friendship and Self-Sacrifice.

Sickert, Steer, Tonks — these, I think, were the friends he valued most. They were more or less coeval with him, and they were painters. It was with painters that he was happiest. To them he could talk, with the certainty that they would sympathize, about painting and about literature without being interrupted. They, on their side, revered him as the one mere critic with whom they could talk as with one of themselves. His face, too — that face transferred to canvas by so many painters since Manet — always entranced them with those problems of "planes" and "values" in which it abounded. He was always a sort of special *treat* to them. They went to him as children to a pantomime. Even more than his felicities of thought did they love those sudden infelicities which he alone could have uttered — those *gaffes* hailed with roars of delight that grew in volume while Moore stared around in simple wonderment. "I have been told," he said suddenly, one evening, "that Mi-chael An-ge-lo carved the Da-vid from a block of marble that had been im-properly quarried. Now if any one gave me a block of marble that had been im-properly quarried, I could no more carve the Da-vid than — than I could fly!" And then "What is the joke? Tell me the joke. If there is a joke, let me share it with you. If it is a good joke."

We know that the Irishman in England is not always what he seems. Moore, deep down in his breast, may have consciously cultivated and developed that innate quaintness which so pleased his friends. If he did so, this was his one little deviation from stark nature, and shall be forgiven him. But I don't really think he did so. Among people who refused ever to take him seriously, and were bent merely on teasing him, he would have dropped the pretense. One of these people — their ringleader, I might say — was Edmund Gosse, who loved to entertain Moore at his table for sake of the lavish entertainment he found in Moore. He had, it is true, a great admiration for Moore's endless patience in the craft of literature; but in social intercourse Moore was but the dearest, the least spared of all his butts. He drew Moore out, he goaded him, he danced around him, he lightly flew at him as a banderillero flies lightly at a bull, dexterously planting ornamental darts adown either flank of him. Moore never charged. He gazed mildly at his tormentor and patiently chewed the cud. He thought "Gosse is very wit-ty. I wish I were so wit-ty as Gosse," and was not at all deflected from his usual manner. "I have been reading," he would say, "a most as-tounding book."

GOSSE [*with a little start and a cry*]. Ah, I always forget that you can read — always I think of you as just a *writer*. But you learned to read when you were a child: I remember you once told me so, yes. And so you've been reading a book? Now [*beaming a quick sidelong glance to the company*] tell us what that book was.

MOORE [*diverting an absolutely blank gaze from host to company*]. I have been reading *Don Quixote*.

GOSSE [*dartingly*]. In the original Spanish, no doubt?

MOORE [*blankly envisaging him*]. No, in a translation. For of Spanish I know not one word. But now that I have read *Don Quixote* I am very sorry that I do not know Spanish, and that it is too late for me to learn Spanish.

GOSSE. Too late? Shame on such phrases! We'll go to learn Spanish together, you and I, hand in hand, every evening, to one of those night schools.

MOORE [*to the company*]. Ah, now Gosse is laughing at me, because Gosse is wit-ty, and if a man is as wit-ty as Gosse then he must have always somebody to laugh at.

GOSSE. Eliminate me, Moore! Or rather, regard me as the gravest and most receptive of my sex. And so you have been reading *Don Quixote* in a translation? Dear, dear! Dr. Douglas Hyde's translation into Erse?

MOORE [*his jaw dropping, and a sudden dawn of intense amusement visible in his eyes*]. Hyde has translated *Don Quixote* into Erse?

GOSSE. I've not the slightest doubt that he has. Ah [*lyrically*], what has he *not* done? What vistas of enchantment has he *not* opened up to the peasants who sit weeping around the waters of Shoo-na-Groo, and the peasants who go dreaming on the hills of Brau-na-Thingumy? Ah, if only poor dear Cervantes could know what delight — but there! You were just going to tell us all about him. Now we want to know just how he struck you.

MOORE. The most a-mazing thing a-bout the book is —

GOSSE. That Sancho Panza is obviously mad from the outset?

MOORE. I had not thought of that. [*Thinks of it, with growing pleasure in the idea.*] That is a good i-de-a, Gosse. I do not say that it is a true i-de-a. But an i-de-a is an i-de-a whether it be . . . [*His voice drifts into silence, then suddenly bursts forth.*] Why did not Cervantes treat Dulcin-e-a sub-jec-tive-ly? What manner of woman was she? Don Quix-ote speaks of her as his mistress. That is not e-nough. One wants to know, and so forth.

The foregoing dialogue is of course apocryphal. But it suggests, with no tinge of exaggeration that I can see in reading it, Gosse's way with Moore, Moore's with Gosse. Only, I haven't yet in these pages about Moore exemplified the goodness of his talk. I have merely said how good it was, and given examples of its queernesses. Oh, he too was often wit-ty. His mind, slow though it was in opposition, could leap swift and far on clear ground. Once, when the painting of "still life" was being discussed, he thus routed the conversation: "I don't care twopence about still life. Of what interest to me is it to see a picture of a bunch of grapes, a — a postage stamp, and a pair of corduroy trousers?" How perfectly delicious a generalization! Of a certain very handsome and statuesque actress, whose performances were much admired in the seventies, he said "I never could bear her. She was like *most* of the policemen, and *all* the barmaids, in London."

It was odd that whenever he dropped such crystals as these, he seemed to be as surprised by his friends' laughter as he was after one of his *gaffes*. Wit-ty, he was yet no judge of wit; and he would sometimes appropriate and repeat without acknowledgment very inferior remarks made by other people. I had a personal experience of this foible. On the Sunday evening before he went to Dublin for the inauguration of Irish drama, he and I had met at the Gosses'. He had been inveighing against Kipling; and, as we walked away together along Delamere Terrace, I said that I thought Kipling fifty years hence would be remembered no more nor less than Martin Tupper was remembered now. Moore paused under a lamppost. "That is a-mazingly good," he exclaimed. "Fifty years hence Kipling will be re-membered only as Martin Tupper is re-membered today! Oh but you really must let me say that in my speech!" Next morning he went to Dublin. I went next night. On Tuesday I was present at a luncheon which he has described in *Ave* — a luncheon given by T. P. Gill. I sat exactly opposite to Moore. Either Yeats or Gill mentioned the name of Kipling. "Oh," said Moore, "Kipling! Fifty years hence Kipling will be re-membered only as Martin Tupper is re-membered today!" We all laughed our appreciation, and I especially murmured "Capital!" Dear Moore had entirely forgotten me as maker of his remark. He didn't make it in his actual speech on the following Thursday. I suppose he had made a rule never to repeat himself.

It was said that in his books, too, he sometimes incorporated as his own the sayings of other people. When *Evelyn Innes* appeared, my friend Clyde Fitch, the brilliant American dramatist, an annual visitor to London, was startled at finding that the description of Evelyn's acting of Marguerite in Gounod's *Faust* was already familiar to him. A year or so before, he had written in an English weekly paper, *The Musician,* a detailed appreciation of Madame Calvé's interpretation of the part at Covent Garden Opera House. The article was one of about a thousand words. Almost all of these, with a very slight emendation here and there, had been appropriated by Moore. I asked Clyde Fitch what he was going to do about it. But Clyde was a very good-humored fellow, and said he wasn't going to do anything at all about it.

Often, when I met some perfect type of average English gentleman, I used to wonder in what degree he would have been more exciting, more of an individual, had he not gone to a public school and a university. In presence of a true eccentric, conversely, I would wonder how much of him this curriculum, had he been cast into it, might have marred. For academic debate within my breast no question was more fascinating than this: How far would Moore have been less Moorish if, in those malleable years of his, he had gone (say) to Eton and Oxford, instead of to Ballyhooly and Paris? It wouldn't really (I like to think) have made much difference. Oxford might in her own way have tinged, as Paris in hers tinged, his brogue. And he might have gone through life thinking his soul rather Oxfordish, even as he did go on thinking it rather Parisian. In his nonage, perhaps, Moore's soul did have a veneer of Paris; but this, thin and friable, was all gone before I knew him. A few years ago, a friend of mine, who knew him only by sight and repute, saw him one day in Paris. By collocation of dates, I think this must have been at the time when Moore, as he told us in *Ave,* had crossed the Channel in order that he might write in French that Irish play which was to be translated into English by Lady Gregory, and thence into Erse by Mr. O'Donaghue, and thence back into English by Lady Gregory for final and magical treatment by Yeats. My friend, who would have supposed from repute that in Paris on a fine afternoon Moore would either be making love to Mme. la Comtesse de Quelquechose in the Faubourg St. Germain or be bandying heterodoxies in a conclave of poets outside some little café on the Rive Gauche, was surprised to see him in the reading room of the Grand Hôtel, poring over the *Illustrated London News* and presently hovering impatient near the armchair of an old gentleman who for too long a time had been monopolizing *The Graphic*. In Paris he might have seemed to belong more or less to London; but not so in London. Wherever a true individuality may be found, there recognizably is *not* its home. Sometimes I used to see Moore dining in the Café Royal, on the ground floor — a haunt of which you could say that it was neither French nor English; neutral territory (like that reading room overseas); no man's land. Here seemed to be, not indeed a home for him, but a fairly congruous background. He himself, I think, knew that the other scenes of London looked rather odd in relation to him. "If you did not know me — if you just saw me in the street," he said once to Sickert, "what should you guess me to be?" The question demanded thought. "Should you not," he pursued, with a touch of impatience, "guess me to be an English country gentleman, who had come up to London to see his lawyer?" And then "What is the joke? Tell me the joke. If there is a joke," and so forth. No, assuredly, no passer-by would have attributed Moore to our simple English countryside. He could ride a horse well, I was told, and was quite a good shot, "but hang it!" Sir William Eden once said to me, "he always comes down to breakfast in pumps." And this reminds me that it was in shooting over the coverts at Windlestone that he met with an accident of which the sequel (as related by him to Sickert and myself) illustrated most exquisitely his indifference to the codes of behavior that govern us timid creatures of convention. A young man who was staying in the house, and was one of the shooting party, fired off his gun at some wrong moment, and in some wrong direction; and the result was that a spent shot, glancing off a tree, badly grazed the surface of one of Moore's eyes. The sufferer was hurried back to the house and surgically treated, and had to lie for some days in his darkened bedroom. On the second day, the guilty youth came to the bedside to express his contrition. "And what," we asked Moore, as he described the scene to us in London, "what did you say?" "I said 'Oh, go a-way. I do not want ever to see you. You are an id-i-ot. For heaven's sake, go a-way,' and I turned on my pillow." How much better, after all, because how much more sincere, this was than the prescribed "My dear fellow, it's nothing! Don't say another word! Sort o' thing might happen to anyone!" Such phrases as these would not have implied any true forgiveness; whereas Moore, having uttered his mind, was free to bear no ill will. The tone in which he spoke to us of the young man was perfectly good-humored. It might, of course, have been less so if the accident had been more serious. Luckily, no lasting damage had been done. "In fact," said Moore, unconsciously taking for a moment the famous posture of the Widow Wadman, "the eye is rather a pret-ti-er color."

The thought that passed through the mind of Julia Hazeltine, when she found the Maestro Jimson hiding under the table in the deserted houseboat — "Surely this is very strange behavior. He cannot be a man of the world!" — was precisely the thought raised by Moore in the minds of all worldly persons who met him for the first, or indeed the hundred-and-first, time. Yet neither would the unworldly have dreamed of claiming him for themselves. He shocked them. He was as one dangling to them the lures of levity and life. Of Edward Martyn, sitting stout in his tower at Tillyra, alone, cultivating his soul among his tomes of theology, Moore gave us in *Ave* a wonderful study — a study whose ridicule could not have been one tithe so good had it not been based on sympathy and affection. And Martyn, I believe, reciprocated fully these feelings. He liked to learn from Moore about modern painting, in return for what he taught him about old music. But certain it is that he was also afraid of Moore; and once, I am told, he gave to his fear deathless expression in a phrase, pensively uttered while he knocked the ashes from his pipe: "Well, he's a bhit of a bhank-holiday fellow, ye know, Moore is."

A marvelous phrase, that; an absolutely perfect rendering of the emotion behind it; but as a full judgment, of course, it cannot be accepted, nor have been intended. A man must be judged by what is fine in him, not by what is trivial; for the fine qualities must have deep roots within him, whereas trivial ones may thrive from the very surface. The bank-holiday side of Moore, if there it was, can count for nothing as against the fine things inside him — his matchless honesty of mind; his very real modesty about his own work; his utter freedom from jealousy; his loving reverence of all that in all arts was nobly done; and, above all, that inexhaustible patience of his, and courage, whereby he made the very most of the gifts he had, and earned for himself a gift which Nature had not bestowed on him: the specific gift of *writing*. No young man — nay, no young woman — ever wrote worse than young Moore wrote. It must have seemed to everyone that here was a writer who, however interesting he in himself might be, never would learn to express himself tolerably. Half-a-crown, we know, may be the foundation of a vast fortune. But what can be done without a penny? Some of the good writers have begun with a scant gift for writing. But which of them with no gift at all? Moore is the one instance I ever heard of. Somehow, in the course of long years, he learned to express himself beautifully. I call that great.

Herman Melville

by CLIFTON FADIMAN

Writer, editor, master of ceremonies par excellence, Clifton Fadiman acquired a reputation for urbanity as a book reviewer for the Nation, Stage, Harper's Bazaar *and the* New Yorker. *His evaluations of Tolstoi, Dostoevski, Ambrose Bierce, Henry James, and Dickens served as introductions to new editions of their works. The essay which follows was the introduction to the Heritage Press edition of* Moby Dick.*

OCTOBER 1943

Some twenty-odd years ago, on May 18, 1921, Justice Oliver Wendell Holmes, then eighty, in a letter to his lifelong friend, Sir Frederick Pollock, wrote: "Did I mention *Moby Dick,* by Herman Melville? I remember him in my youth. It seemed to me a great book — as ten years later may some of George Borrow's things, possibly influenced by him — but I should think a much greater man. It shook me up a good deal. It is wonderful already that a book published in 1851 doesn't seem thin, now. Hawthorne did when last I read *The Scarlet Letter.* Not so *Moby Dick.*"

Holmes, a man given to wide and impartial decisions, made no judicial error here. By common consent — but, interestingly enough, a consent given only during the last two decades — *Moby Dick* is one of the great books of the world. It does not "seem thin, now" any more than in 1921 it seemed thin to the lucky Balboas and Columbuses who then rediscovered its Pacific rhythms and Atlantic rages.

A minor proof of its greatness lies in the circumstance (always true of masterpieces) that, while there seems nothing new to say about it, we are forever trying our hands at further commentary. In the case of a minor work, no matter how interesting, critics sooner or later, happily, have their say, the river of annotation dribbles off, and the position of the work is more or less firmly established. But men and women will always attempt the seemingly impossible task of writing something new about Shakespeare and Dante — and Melville. That is, of course, because the meaning of a good minor work is clear and single while the meaning of a great major work is multiplex.

The greatest books rise from a profound level of wonder and terror, a level common to all humanity in all times and climes, but a level so deep that we are only at times aware of it. Occasionally a man — Cervantes or Dostoevski or Melville — lets down into this deep well the glorious, pitiful bucket of his genius, and he brings up a book, and then we read it, and dimly we perceive its source, and know that source to be something profound and permanent in the human imagination.

The mysterious liquid drawn from this well is never crystalline. Rather does each man, looking into it, see mirrored a different set of images, reflections, points of light, and layers of shadow. All great books are symbolical myths, overlaid like palimpsests with the meanings that men at various times assign to them.

Moby Dick is a book about Evil. Melville, with his characteristic irony, said of it, "I have written a wicked book and feel as spotless as the lamb." At no time in his life was Melville ever notably happy, but at thirty-two, when he sat down to the composition of his masterpiece, he was notably miserable, a sick, worried, and unhappily married man. Some of the poison of his personal life was undoubtedly discharged, veiled in symbols, into the book. But if this were the only impulse behind *Moby Dick,* it would be but a subjective work of the second order, like *Childe Harold*. Melville's despair was metaphysical as well as personal; his awareness of evil goes beyond his own constricted circumstances. His book is not a lament but a vision.

A pessimism as profound as Melville's, if it is not pathological — and his is not — can exist only in a man who, whatever his gifts, does not possess that of humor. There is much pessimism in Shakespeare but with it goes a certain sweetness, a kind of radiance. His bad men — Macbeth, Iago — may be irretrievable, but the world itself is not irretrievable. This sense of balance comes from the fact that Shakespeare has humor, even in the plays of his later period. Melville had none. For proof, reread Chapter 100, a labored, shrill, and inept attempt at laughter. Perhaps I should qualify these strictures, for there is a kind of vast, grinning, unjolly, sardonic humor in him at times — Ishmael's first encounter with Queequeg is an example. But this humor is bilious, not sanguine, and has no power to uplift the heart.

I said that *Moby Dick* was a book about Evil; and so it is. It is the nearest thing we have to an unchristian (though not an antichristian) epic. It is the other face of the Divine Comedy — the product of unfaith, as Dante's epic was the product of faith. But to believe in evil's reality is not to espouse it. Melville is as far removed from a pure champion of evil, like Hitler, as he is from a pure champion of good, like St. Francis. Ahab knows that good exists in the world, he even has his own moments of softening of the heart, but basically he is mesmerized by what is negative and disastrous. He cannot turn his mind away from Moby Dick.

The relationship between Ahab and the White Whale forms the central line of the story. Superficially this relationship is the same as that which animates any number of bloody Elizabethan tragedies of revenge. Ahab's leg has been torn off by Moby Dick; therefore he hates the whale; he pursues it to the death and is dragged down, in the very middle of his vengeance, to his own destruction: a sufficiently familiar pattern. But any grown-up reader of *Moby Dick* understands at once that this pattern is a mere blind, a concession to the brute fact that at bottom we still have no better way of portraying the storms of the soul than by means of physical action.

The subsurface meaning of the Ahab-Moby Dick relationship is that the two are one. Moby Dick is a monster thrashing about in the Pacific of Ahab's brain. It is as much a part of him as is his leg of ivory. The struggle that takes place on the vast marine or at the ends of a hundred harpoons is but Melville's method of exteriorizing the combat in the arena of Ahab's own chiaroscuro spirit.

> The White Whale swam before him as the monomaniac incarnation of all those malicious agencies which some deep men feel eating in them, till they are left living on with half a heart and half a lung. That intangible malignity which has been from the beginning; to whose dominion even the modern Christians ascribe one-half of the worlds; which the ancient Ophites of the east reverenced in their statue devil; — Ahab did not fall down and worship it like them; but deliriously transferring its idea to the abhorred white whale, he pitted himself, all mutilated, against it. All that most maddens and torments; all that stirs up the lees of things; all truth with malice in it; all that cracks the sinews and cakes the brain; all the subtle demonisms of life and thought; all evil, to crazy Ahab, were visibly personified, and made practically assailable in Moby Dick. He piled upon the whale's white hump the sum of all the general rage and hate felt by his whole race from Adam down; and then, as if his chest had been a mortar, he burst his hot heart's shell upon it.

Like his cousins, Faust and Hamlet, Ahab is a divided man, at odds with his own mortality, at odds with all the grief in the world, at odds with his own incapacity to enjoy the world's fair show, and therewith be content. The whole complex narrative of *Moby Dick,* with all its cetology and its digressions, is but the cunningly disguised soliloquy of a man in direst pain — pain which can cease only with suicide. And suicide is the true end of *Moby Dick,* the whale and the man, being one, turning upon each other simultaneously. There are certain men who are artists in suicide, who carve out for themselves, over many years, careers which have as their goal self-destruction. Ahab is such a man, and all his adventures, rages, conversations, soliloquies are but the joists and floorings of an immense structure of self-ruin.

If there is one grand type of character Melville knows to the last fiber and droplet of blood, it is the type self-dedicated to disaster. This self-dedication is a convoluted thing, never direct, never simple. Hamlet needs five acts and hundreds of lines of anguished poetry to achieve it. Ahab, in whom masochism is a complex art, cannot kill himself save in a roundabout manner, through the instrumentality of the White Whale. If there were no Moby Dick, it would be necessary for Ahab to invent one. In a sense, he is an invention, a white floating cancer in Ahab's own mind.

In the same way, to make sure that he will never deviate from this road, however curving, to disaster, Ahab strips himself of all associations that might waylay him into joy. He throws away his pipe in fury because it might bring him pleasure. Gifted, as he bitterly reflects, "with the high perception," he lacks "the low, enjoying power; damned, most subtly and most malignantly! damned in the midst of Paradise."

Just why he lacks "the low, enjoying power" Melville never tells us. He presents us with a fixed type; the causes of its fixity do not concern him. To give a certain surface rondure of motivation to Ahab's pessimism, he offers us the amputated leg, but we are not taken in by it; we know that this lightning-seared soul was deep in hell even in the days when he stood upon two feet of living bone. Moby Dick is a pretext, or, as Melville would say, a symbol.

Why do his men fear Ahab? Compare their emotion with that felt by the sailors toward Wolf Larsen in *The Sea Wolf.* In Jack London's novel the men are afraid of Larsen, another man, another creature; and therefore their fear is overcomable. But not one on the *Pequod,* however brave he be, can overcome his fear of Ahab, because the fear is seated in himself. His Ahab-fear is a fear of *himself,* or rather of the pit of blackness, the central dark mother lode of despair which every man at times knows to be within him. But we are afraid to confess this primordial horror. When we come upon one who, like Ahab, *does* confess it, exulting in his confession, we shrink back, as if we had looked in the mirror and seen there the horrid head of the Gorgon. It is this self-fear that explains Ahab's unholy domination of his crew. It explains too the desperate joy with which the men pursue Moby Dick, as if they felt that, by killing the monster, they could exorcise the fear and dispel with their puny harpoons the gathered and oppressive malice of the world.

It is generally recognized that the canons of the ordinary novel do not apply to *Moby Dick*. If we applied them we should be forced to put it down as an inept, occasionally powerful, but on the whole puzzling affair. This was the conventional opinion up to two decades ago. During those decades we have discovered *Moby Dick* to be a masterpiece. What caused this shift in perspective? To put it simply, we discovered how *Moby Dick* should be read. We must read it not as if it were a novel but as if it were a myth. A novel is a tale. A myth is a disguised method of expressing mankind's deepest terrors and longings. The myth uses the narrative form, and is often mistaken for true narrative. Once we feel the truth of this distinction, the greatness of *Moby Dick* becomes manifest: we have learned how to read it.

Moby Dick is a myth of Evil and Tragedy, as the Christian epic is a myth of Good and Salvation. "Both the ancestry and posterity of Grief go further than the ancestry and posterity of Joy," thinks Ahab; and this central brooding conviction threads every page of the story, even when it seems most concerned with try-pots, harpoons, and sperm oil.

The note is struck in the very opening sentence — surely the most magical first sentence in literature. "Call me Ishmael." Who is Ishmael? He is the narrator, but he is also Ahab (as all the characters of the book are partially Ahab) and he is also you and I, considered as eternal outcasts, which we are, the experience of birth being in a sense the casting-off of the moorings that attach us quite literally to mankind.

The *Pequod* seems a crowded world. Indeed it is a microcosm, with its philosophers, its men of action, its lunatics, its African savages and Polynesian cannibals. Yet, for all the shapes that man its boats or raise its sails, the *Pequod* is a heaving hell of lonely and grief-touched souls, whose solitudes are gathered up and made manifest in the figure of Ahab. Melville underlines this perception in the very abode of community itself, in the whaleman's chapel, where "each silent worshipper seemed purposely sitting apart from the other, as if each silent grief were insular and incommunicable."

The symbolic values of the book are not allegorically plain, as in *Pilgrim's Progress*, for Melville does not have Bunyan's Protestant certitude. They waver, shadowlike, at times emerging into the world of reality, at times descending into the subterranea of myth. For instance, Fedallah and his Malays do not merely "represent" the evil spirits conjured up by Ahab's necromantic power. They are in truth these very spirits. Yet at the same time they fulfill a solid and specific function aboard the *Pequod*. They are at one and the same time part of a whaling cruise and of Hell. It is this extraordinary ambiguity that gives *Moby Dick* its special murky atmosphere and which may have been responsible for the lack of understanding that was its portion for so many years.

Yet there should have been no misunderstanding, for Melville in a dozen passages reiterates that his story is not to be taken literally. The symbolism is not simple, no mere system of correspondences. It is rather the subtle atmosphere the whole story breathes. It is not imposed (except occasionally, and then the effect is creaky). "All visible objects," says Ahab, "are but as pasteboard masks. But in each event — in the living act, the undoubted deed — there, some unknown but still reasoning thing puts forth the moulding of its features from behind the unreasoning mask."

The poet is one, it has been said, who sees resemblances. Then Melville is all poet, for he sees little else, the world being for him a shadow show, a whale line but the halter round all men's necks, the very earth itself but the "insular Tahiti" in the soul of man, encompassed by the "appalling ocean" of "the horrors of the half-known life."

This vivid sense of an extra, invisible dimension in all things makes it possible for Melville's alembicating mind to mix such incongruities as angels and spermaceti, and distill an essence of beauty.

Finally, *Moby Dick* is America's most unparochial great book, less delivered over to a time and place than the work of even our freest minds, Emerson and Whitman. It is conceived on a vast scale, it shakes hands with prairie seas and great distances, it invades with its conquistador prose "the remotest secret drawers and lockers of the world." It has towering faults of taste, it is often willful and obscure, but it will remain America's unarguable contribution to world literature, so many-leveled is it, so wide-ranging in that nether world which is the defiant but secretly terror-stricken soul of man, alone and appalled by his aloneness.

John Dewey

by MAX EASTMAN

Max Eastman, the writer, studied under John Dewey at Columbia and was for years one of his most intimate friends.

DECEMBER 1941

John Dewey is the man who saved our children from dying of boredom as we almost did in school. The *Encyclopædia Britannica* in its article on Education puts it less succinctly: "By 1900 the centre of gravity had shifted from the subject-matter of instruction to the child to be taught. The school, in consequence, had begun to change from a place where children prepare for life . . . to a place where children live. . . . These changes, largely due to the teachings of John Dewey, have become dominant purposes of the American elementary school of the twentieth century." That is half of who John Dewey is, and the other half is a philosopher in the technical sense — a man who makes his living arguing about such questions as "How We Think" and "What Does Thought Do to Being?" The University of Paris, in conferring a degree upon him in 1930, described him as "the most profound and complete expression of American genius."

Two things make this grade-A brand of fame surprising. One is Dewey's perverse and obdurate neglect of it. The other is the total lack of fireworks in his nature. He has published 36 books and 815 articles and pamphlets, but if he ever wrote one quotable sentence it has got permanently lost in the pile. Not only is his own style dull, but this dullness infects everybody who has anything to say about his theories of education. A reform which might be described as a grown-up formulation of the necessity, long known to all lively-minded children, of raising hell in school has been put over in the language of the prosiest of disciplinary pedagogues. No flash of wit or poetry illumines it.

Perhaps Dewey's origin has something to do with this. He was born, like Calvin Coolidge, in Vermont, and he was born with the same trick of concealing whatever is, or is not, going on in his head under a non-committal exterior. Vermonters have a dry humor of understatement — an understatement so remote that you can't quite guess whether they are joking or just failing to warm up. His father was famous in a small way as a joker. He "kept store" in Burlington, a town of ten or twelve thousand, and sold more goods than anybody else in town because of the whimsical way he went at it. A sign outside reading "Hams and Cigars — Smoked and Unsmoked" apprised his customers that they would not be taken too seriously. On a frequently borrowed wheelbarrow he painted in big red letters "Stolen from A. S. Dewey." Notwithstanding his popularity, A. S. Dewey never got along very well because it hurt his feelings to ask people to pay their bills.

John slid into Vermont University at the early age of fifteen — an unusual accomplishment, but one which caused no particular comment, least of all from him. He slid through his first three college years also without throwing off any sparks or giving grounds to predict anything about his future. He joined the church during his sophomore year, and did so with sincere religious feeling but no profound experience of conversion. He was a good boy, and wanted to be better, and thought God would help him — that was all. As a result, his senior year at college was an ardent effort and adventure. He plunged heart and soul into his studies. He read and labored far into the night. He led his class, and got the highest marks on record in philosophy. The question was, What are you going to do with a nineteen-year-old philosopher?

An imaginative merchant named Johns Hopkins had just founded a new kind of research university in Baltimore, and Dewey's annunciation angel, Professor Huxley, had delivered the inaugural address. The new university was offering twenty $500 fellowships to be competed for by college graduates. Dewey tried for one and failed. (Thorstein Veblen also tried for one and failed.) But Dewey had an aunt with $500, and he borrowed that and went to Johns Hopkins anyway. After studying a year, he tried for the fellowship again and got it. He also got a job teaching the history of philosophy to undergraduates. So who said there wasn't a career in philosophy in America? To be sure there was no pay attached to this job, but then, on the other hand, he did not have to pay for the privilege of doing it. He was happy. He had found a wonderful teacher, a Hegelian named George Sylvester Morris. Unless you understand how exciting it is to fall in love with Hegel — and what hard work — there is very little Dewey can tell you about those three years at Johns Hopkins.

When Dewey took his Ph.D at Johns Hopkins, President Gilman offered him a loan to continue his studies in Germany. Dewey was deeply gratified, but said that he would rather not borrow money and felt perfectly at home in America. President Gilman also offered him some advice: "Don't be so bookish; don't live such a secluded life; get out and see people." That offer Dewey was more inclined to accept, although he did not know exactly how to act upon it. What he needed first was a job, and he spent another rather wistful summer in Burlington before he got one. It was a $900 job as instructor in philosophy at the University of Michigan, where his friend Morris was teaching.

In Michigan, Dewey began to "see people," and among the first he saw was a coed named Alice Chipman who lived in the same boarding-house with him. She was a strong-minded girl, descended from a family of radicals and freethinkers, an ardent woman suffragist, deeply religious but of no church, and brilliantly intolerant of "bunk." She was shorter than Dewey and thicker, not beautiful and not well dressed. By a purely physiological accident her eyelids hung so low over her eyes that to a timid judgment she looked dangerous. But her features were handsome in a strong way, and her mouth was gentle. Her pioneer grandfather had joined the Chippewa tribe of Indians and fought for their rights; he had also opposed Lincoln and the Civil War. She inherited his crusading spirit and his moral courage. And she had a passionate interest in the life of ideas. It was good luck — or was it good sense? — that Dewey fell in love with such a woman. Alice was a pupil in his classes. There was, in short, a full-sized moral and intellectual admiration between them. "No two people," Dewey once remarked, "were ever more in love."

They were married at the home of the Chippewa Copperhead in 1886. In the same year Dewey was made assistant professor and his salary was raised to $1600. The next year their first child, Fred, was born, and Dewey published his first book — significantly not a philosophy book at all, but a textbook in psychology. Dewey was willing to see psychology break loose from philosophy and become a natural science, and this book places him among the pioneers of that process.

The University of Chicago had been founded with a plentiful endowment by John D. Rockefeller, and its president, William R. Harper, had conceived the novel idea of combining the departments of philosophy, psychology, and education into one. In 1894 Dewey was invited to come to Chicago at a salary of $5000 and be the head of the whole thing. It was a piece of rare good luck, for Dewey's philosophy was taking more and more the aspect of a psychology of the thought process, and his interest in education was running neck and neck with his interest in philosophy. Moreover the Dewey family was growing, and was destined to grow far beyond the limits set by the income of any ordinary lay philosopher. Mrs. Dewey did not believe in birth control. Notwithstanding her freethinking grandparents, she held some streak of prudish puritanism that made her think it wicked to decide when and under what conditions you are going to bear children. The second child, Evelyn, had been born in 1890, and the third, Morris — named after Dewey's revered teacher — early in 1893. The difference between three and five thousand dollars was beginning to look important, and the letter from Chicago was in all ways a joyful piece of news.

Mrs. Dewey, they decided, would spend the summer in Europe with the children, and Dewey would go ahead to Chicago and earn some extra money teaching in the summer school. Dewey hated to say good-by to his two-year-old baby, Morris, for he had already made up his mind, by what signs it would be hard to say, that the child was a kind of saintly genius. This was not all a parent's fondness, either. A stranger on the boat going over made the peculiar remark: "If that child lives long enough there will be a new religion." Morris died of diphtheria in Milan, and even now, fifty years after, Dewey cannot mention the event without a catch in his throat.

Three other children were born in Chicago — Lucy, Gordon, and Jane — and thus there were still five of them rioting around the house during the best years of this philosopher's life. They did not disturb his meditations in the least.

It is customary to regard Dewey's educational theories as an inference from his instrumental philosophy, but more accurately they are an inference from his children. Dewey was interested in reforming education, and wrote a book about it long before he became an instrumental philosopher. The book was called *Applied Psychology,* and that indicates what his doctrine about education is. Education is life itself, so long as the living thing continues to grow. Education is growth under favorable conditions; the school is a place where those conditions should be regulated scientifically. That is about all there is to it.

The household also needed a little renovation along this line, and Dewey's influence on the relations between parents and their children has been as great as his influence on the schools. It was a reform that in the nature of the case began at home.

In his house at Ann Arbor, Dewey's study was directly under the bathroom, and he was sitting there one day, absorbed in a new theory of arithmetic, when suddenly he felt a stream of water trickling down his back. He jumped out of his chair and rushed upstairs to find the bathtub occupied by a fleet of sailboats, the water brimming over, and his small boy Fred busy with both hands shutting it off. The child turned as he opened the door, and said severely, "Don't argue, John — get the mop!"

You might think that a family of five children, brought up along these lines, would be something of a riot, and they did have a rare good time. But they were, as children go, a remarkably well-mannered bunch of rioters. They were at times, indeed, a little too well mannered. Jane used at the age of twelve to discuss the causes of prostitution in a disturbingly judicious manner. And Evelyn developed so early the poised and sagely humorous good sense which surrounds her now with loving friends that you wished sometimes she *would* be foolish for a minute.

Each of the two John Deweys, the philosopher and the educator, reached his high point in Chicago. In a book called *Studies in Logical Theory*, published in 1903, he formulated that practical American philosophy which was left in his head after Hegel's German cosmos "dropped away." All thinking, it declares — even Hegel's about his cosmos — is instrumental, and its truth is nothing more than its success in bringing human beings to their ends. Dewey finds rest in this idea because it closes, in a way that does less violence to common-sense reality than Hegel did, that chasm which he had felt yawning between the material and moral sciences. The material world is real, but our very knowledge of it is moral in the largest sense. It is practical. It is a solving of problems in the posing of which, and thus inevitably in their solution, human needs and aspirations play a vital part.

When William James came to Chicago a short time after Dewey's *Studies* were published, he spoke of the book — with a little too much modesty — as "the foundation of the philosophy of pragmatism." Dewey, equally modest, did not know that he had been founding pragmatism, and was greatly surprised when James greeted him in this way.

The other half of John Dewey reached its high point in the founding of an elementary school, two years after he came to Chicago. This school was regarded by him literally as the laboratory of the department of philosophy, and was called the Experimental or Laboratory School. But it has survived in history as the Dewey School, a name which might well be written "Do-y School," for "to learn by doing" was one of its chief slogans. Its founder had the rather naïve notion that in its operation he was putting his instrumental philosophy to an experimental test.

In these days when Dewey's ideas on education have become a part of our national culture, it is hard to imagine the clamor raised in 1896 by the idea of a laboratory school. "A school where they experiment with the children — imagine!" He could hardly have shocked the parents of the nineties more if he had proposed vivisection in a kindergarten. Even when closely examined, his idea seemed to be to let children do just what they wanted to, which was then generally regarded as equivalent to letting them go to hell. Dewey is, perhaps — or was — slightly utopian in his rebellion against the old puritanical pumping-in system of education, but he does not believe, and never did, in consecrating children's whims, much less in forcing them to have more whims than are natural to them. He has more horse sense than some of those who now run "modern schools" in his name. His idea was that life in school ought to be enough like life outside so that an interest in knowledge will arise in the child's mind as it did in the mind of the race — spontaneously. If you provide a sufficient variety of activities, and there's enough knowledge lying around, and the teacher understands the natural relation between knowledge and interested action, children can have fun getting educated and will love to go to school. That is the kind of thing Dewey was saying. And the little book, *School and Society,* in which he first said it, was translated into dozens of languages, including those as far away from home as Chinese and Japanese.

Dewey would never have started a Dewey School, however, if it hadn't been for Alice Chipman. Dewey never does anything except think — at least it often looked that way to Alice — unless he gets kicked into it. Nothing seems important to him but thinking. He is as complete an extrovert as ever lived, but the extroversion all takes place inside his head. Ideas are real objects to him, and they are the only objects that engage his passionate interest. If he gets hold of a new idea, he will sneak around the house with it like a dog with a bone, glancing up with half an eye at the unavoidable human beings and their chatter, hoping they won't bother him, and that's all. Only a man of this temperament who nevertheless took human lives and problems for his subject matter could have made the contribution Dewey has.

Mrs. Dewey would grab Dewey's ideas — and grab him — and insist that something be done. She had herself a brilliant mind and a far better gift of expression than his. And she was a zealot. She was on fire to reform people as well as ideas. She had an adoring admiration of his genius, but she had also a female impatience of the cumbersome load of ideological considerations he had to carry along when arriving at a decision. Her own decisions were swift, direct, and harshly realistic — not always aware of their grounds. "You always come at things backhanded," she would say. Dewey's view of his wife's influence is that she put "guts and stuffing" into what had been with him mere intellectual conclusions. He also recalls that she taught him not to be such an easy mark. He does not use that phrase. "She liberated me," he says, "from certain sentimental moralisms of the 'Judge not' variety, and taught me to respect my adverse as well as my favorable intuitions." In short, she kept pulling him down into the real world. And, as his own philosophy insisted that that is where a man ought to be, he was, theoretically at least, always willing to be pulled.

Mrs. Dewey, then, as might be guessed, was the principal of the Dewey School. To her — and to Ella Flagg Young, Chicago's famous superintendent of schools — belongs most of the credit for its concrete operation. Dewey calls Ella Flagg Young "the wisest person about actual schools I ever saw." "I would come over to her with these abstract ideas of mine," he says, "and she would tell me what they meant." Another woman memorable in this connection is Mrs. Charles R. Crane, who put up a large part of the money for the school and helped the Deweys raise the rest. Still another is Mrs. Emmons Blaine, who, besides sharing the enthusiasms of this little group of glowing reformers, shared in the McCormick dollars. Those dollars aided very considerably in the birth of the Dewey School, and it was from being forced to swallow a million of them at one gulp that the school rather suddenly died.

That sad story, which altered the direction and to some extent the tone of Dewey's whole life, has never been told. Mrs. Dewey wanted him to make a public statement at the time, but Dewey decided to swallow his chagrin, and so everybody else, for thirty-five years now, has been sitting decorously on the lid. The story is this:

Mrs. Blaine gave that million-dollar endowment originally to another educational reformer, and something of a genius too, named Colonel Parker, who founded a school with it called the Chicago Institute. Parker had more genius for handling children than for handling dollars by the million; and moreover he soon began to lose his health. With his consent, Mrs. Blaine finally proposed to President Harper that his school and Dewey's school unite, and the endowment be turned over to the university. At that time the Dewey School was a flourishing institution with 23 teachers and 140 children; it had none of the defects of the Chicago Institute; its theoretical principles, while similar, were not the same; and it had no need of a million dollars. The change was therefore vigorously resisted, and for one year staved off, by the parents of the children in the Dewey School. But Harper wanted that million dollars for the university, and the following year, while Dewey was conveniently absent in the East, he reopened the negotiations with Mrs. Blaine. When Dewey returned, the merger was all but accomplished. The president called him to his office and spoke with unction about "their dream at last realized." As Dewey had never dreamed this dream, but quite the opposite, and as Harper had never put up any money for the Laboratory School, Dewey felt that he might have been consulted before the realizing got quite so far along.

The interview was a tense one, and when President Harper asked him to come in on the final negotiations Dewey abruptly refused. "Since you've chosen to start this in my absence, I suggest that you finish it," he said. "After you get the terms arranged, I will decide whether I can coöperate or not."

"I should hate to go to the trustees," Harper said, "and tell them that your obstinacy had cost the university a million dollars."

Dewey explained that he was interested in an experiment in education, not in providing an endowment for the University of Chicago. He also told President Harper — although not in these crisp terms, I am sure — that if he did find it possible to come in he would expect a raise in salary from five to seven thousand dollars. President Harper expressed a fear that a salary of that size might embarrass him with his colleagues, but Dewey thought he could survive the pain. "That demand for more pay," Dewey says, "did more to make a man of me than any other act of my life!"

Another stipulation Dewey made was that Mrs. Dewey would continue to serve as principal of the school in the new setup, but President Harper had other ideas. He was aware that Mrs. Dewey had, as an administrator, the faults of her virtues. But she was the sole channel through which Dewey's ideas could naturally get down into action. She was too deeply bound up with bringing them down to be eased out as incidental to a "Dewey School." Dewey knew, besides, that his other trained teachers would be eased out in the same sly fashion. Nominally he would be head of the school, but he would be one man against a million dollars. He ended his last interview with President Harper, which was a hot one, by presenting his resignation.

That was the end of the Dewey School, and it was the end of a wholly joyful and very affluent epoch in Dewey's life.

Dewey, of course, was not many days out of a job. Aside from his rising fame in philosophy and education, he had recently filled a term as president of the American Psychological Association. J. McKeen Cattell took the initiative in getting him invited to Columbia as professor of philosophy, and it was stipulated in his contract that he continue to expound his views on education at Teachers College.

Both he and Mrs. Dewey might have recovered with more buoyance from the blow to their lifework had not fate chosen this moment to repeat, so exactly as to suggest deliberate malice, the tragedy of their previous personal loss. On a trip to Europe in the interval between jobs, their most gifted son, Gordon, died — in Ireland, and of typhoid fever.

A deeper wound, although perhaps he did not realize it, was the change in Mrs. Dewey. Stricken thus as a mother at the same time that she was deprived of any outlet for her violent zeal and genuine gift of leadership, she fell gradually into a habit of resentment. She grew caustic where she had been keen, captious where she had been critical. Her health began to decline. She had already done more work and borne more children than her physique, unless sustained by joy, was equal to. Her husband's bland way of going around with nothing on his mind but thoughts, when she herself so longed for action, got on her nerves. Increasingly, until her death in 1927, these habits of perpetual objection became fixed in her, and at the end, with arteriosclerosis and a high blood pressure that drove her literally crazy, she became, although still full of witty charm, impossible except for saints to live with. She was persuaded once to go away to a sanitarium, but in a day or two the doctor telephoned to say that she had left "without permission." After some anxious hours had passed, she herself telephoned from a friend's house to say that she was coming home. The road from there to her death was more than a tragic one. Dewey has had his full measure of sorrow.

Notwithstanding the mood in which the change was made, Dewey's eastward migration at forty was a good thing for him intellectually. He found a new group of stimulating minds at Columbia. His philosophic friendship with George H. Mead, a teammate in developing the philosophic implications of biology, was replaced by a more argumentative friendship with Frederick J. E. Woodbridge, a philosopher of the classic mold. Dewey says that he "learned a lot from Professor Woodbridge, but not what he was teaching." He learned a lot also from James Harvey Robinson, who used to begin his course in the intellectual history of Western Europe by remarking, "Now when I mention God, I want the class to relax"; from Charles Beard, who was teaching American history with a similar irreverence toward the founding fathers; and from Wesley Mitchell, who was leading a like revolt against the "economic man."

In general, ideas were sprouting up through the bricks at Columbia in those days, and Dewey's mind was happy there. Also he found it easier, while living in New York, to play a part in civic movements of national scope, to be a factor in the nation's political life, as is appropriate to a philosopher who believes that the truth of an idea lies in its practical effect. By taking an apartment at the corner of Broadway and 56th Street, he managed to surround himself with enough noise so that he could get some thinking done.

Later he moved out on Long Island, and preserved his contact with reality by raising eggs and vegetables and selling them to the neighbors. With characteristic vigor he learned all about farming, and actually earned money enough during one year to "pay for his keep." His farm was but a short walk from Walt Whitman's birthplace — where still the lilacs in the dooryard bloomed — and, like Walt Whitman, he loved the companionship of the humble earth. He loved to identify himself with lowly people. He was pleased when one day a hurry call came from a wealthy neighbor for a dozen eggs, and, the children being in school, he himself took the eggs over in a basket. Going by force of habit to the front door, he was told brusquely that deliveries were made at the rear. He trotted obediently around to the back door, feeling both amused and happy. Some time later he was giving a talk to the women's club of the neighborhood, and his wealthy customer, when he got up to speak, exclaimed in a loud whisper, "Why, that looks exactly like our eggman!"

Dewey looked like a young man then, a man just starting his career. He looked like the portraits of Robert Louis Stevenson, having the same flat hair and dark mustache and the same luminous eyes. Dewey's eyes are wells of dark, almost black, tenderly intelligent light such as would shine more appropriately out of a Saint Francis than a professor of logic. The rest of him is pleasant, but not quite so impressive.

He used frequently to come into the class in logical theory with his necktie out of contact with his collar, a sock down around his ankle, or a pants leg caught up into his garter. His hair always looked as though he had combed it with a towel, and being parted, if at all, in the middle, gave his face a rather ewe-like contour which emphasized the gentleness more than the penetration in those wondrous eyes. He would come in through a side door very promptly and with a brisk step. The briskness would last until he reached his chair, and then he would sag. With an elbow on the desk he would rub his hand over his face, push back some strands of his hair, and begin to purse his mouth and look vaguely off over the heads of the class and above the windows, as though he thought he might find an idea up there along the crack between the wall and the ceiling. He always would find one. And then he would begin to talk, very slowly and with little emphasis and long pauses.

He was thinking rather than lecturing, evolving a system of philosophy extempore, and taking his time about it. The process was impersonal and rather unrelated to his pupils — until one of them would ask a question. Then those glowing eyes would come down from the ceiling and shine into that pupil, and draw out of him and his innocent question intellectual wonders such as he never imagined had their seeds in his brain. Education does not, according to the Dewey system, mean "drawing out." But drawing out was never better done than it was in Dewey's classrooms. His instinctive and active deference, the unqualified giving of attention to whatever anybody, no matter how dumb and humble, may have to say, is one of the rarest gifts or accomplishments of genius. He embodies in his social attitude the essence of democracy.

Another trait of John Dewey's, very impressive in the classroom and very little conveyed in the above paragraphs, is his personal dignity. Careless as his dress used to be, he never seemed, as so many eccentric professors do, inwardly sloppy. You felt his moral force. You felt the rigorous self-discipline beneath his sagging manners. You felt also, or soon found out, that with all his taste for heresies John Dewey knows his trade. He is an expert philosopher. He has a prodigious memory, and is a learned scholar as well as an unforgetful friend.

There is one act of learning, however, which Dewey never performed and whose neglect, I fear, will stand against him in history. He never studied, at least until too recent years, the philosophy of Karl Marx. While occupying for two generations of young people the position of a leader in radical democracy, and that in a period when Marxism was sweeping the militant majority of them into the antidemocratic, or supposedly superdemocratic, camp, he was content always to say when the subject came up, "I have never read Marx. . . . I cannot speak with authority on the subject." He ought to have read Marx, and he ought to have spoken on the subject not only with authority but with vim. Marx was his chief enemy, the only other man on the left who backed a political program with a system of philosophy.

Soon after Dewey came to Columbia as professor of philosophy, New York City was turned upside down by a scandal attending the visit of the great Russian writer, Maxim Gorky. Gorky had come to solicit help for the Russian Revolution, and had brought with him his life companion, or common-law wife, the actress Madame Andreeva. It required but a hint from the Czar's officials to rouse the town against him. He was denounced in screaming headlines as a free-lover; hotels and private homes were closed in his face; he was virtually thrown into the streets. Even Mark Twain, although appealed to in the name of the republic of letters, refused to stand against the public hysteria. He turned his back with the rest. John Dewey offered his home, and the shelter of his prestige, to the bewildered Russian. Dewey in turn was violently attacked for this act of magnanimity, so violently that he seemed for a time in danger of losing his job. Mrs. Dewey stood behind him like a rock. "I would rather starve and see my children starve," she said between clenched teeth, "than see John sacrifice his principles."

In his more recent championship of a fair trial for Leon Trotsky on the treason charges made against him in Moscow, Dewey found no such support at home. The son and daughter-in-law who made their home with him after the marriage of his daughter Evelyn did all they could to dissuade him from taking the chairmanship of the Commission of Inquiry. He was too old for the journey to Mexico: he could not stand the discomfort and the change of food; he would contract some fatal disease. Dewey smiled at these anxious warnings. "I'll enjoy the trip," he said.

When Trotsky was asked afterwards for his impressions of John Dewey, he said, "Wonderful! He was the only man on the commission who didn't get sick!"

Dewey was no figurehead on that commission. He was, apart from the secretary, the one who did the work, and he was the one who made the decisions. He made them after an intense study of the Russian political situation in its historic development. He even went into its theoretical background to the extent of being able to deliver — at last — an authoritative judgment on the philosophy of Marxism.

The *Daily Worker,* of course, described his behavior as senile. The *New Masses* regretted that a great philosopher had made such a fool of himself in the sunset of his life — a remark on which Dewey's comment was, "Twilight is the usual expression." In the opinion of his colleagues on the commission Dewey conducted himself with the dignity of a judge and the shrewdness of a Vermont horse trader. He had answered his adverse critics in an essay written forty years before: "Better it is for philosophy to err in active participation in the living struggles and issues of its own age and times, than to maintain an immune monastic impeccability."

My Father: Leslie Stephen

by VIRGINIA WOOLF

It was a fond and literary household in which Virginia Woolf grew up. Her father was famous as a mountaineer, scholar, and editor of the Dictionary of National Biography; *he and his magnificent library formed her education. She learned also from her father's intimates, James Russell Lowell, who was her godfather, and Dr. Holmes, Hardy, Meredith, Ruskin, and John Morley, who were frequent visitors to the London house.*

MARCH 1950

By the time that his children were growing up, the great days of my father's life were over. His feats on the river and on the mountains had been won before they were born. Relics of them were to be found lying about the house — the silver cup on the study mantelpiece; the rusty alpenstocks that leaned against the bookcase in the corner; and to the end of his days he would speak of great climbers and explorers with a peculiar mixture of admiration and envy. But his own years of activity were over, and my father had to content himself with pottering about the Swiss valleys or taking a stroll across the Cornish moors.

That to potter and to stroll meant more on his lips than on other people's is becoming obvious now that some of his friends have given their own version of those expeditions. He would start off after breakfast alone, or with one companion. Shortly before dinner he would return. If the walk had been successful, he would have out his great map and commemorate a new short cut in red ink. And he was quite capable, it appears, of striding all day across the moors without speaking more than a word or two to his companion. By that time, too, he had written the *History of English Thought in the Eighteenth Century,* which is said by some to be his masterpiece; and the *Science of Ethics* — the book which interested him most; and *The Playground of Europe,* in which is to be found "The Sunset on Mont Blanc" — in his opinion the best thing he ever wrote. He still wrote daily and methodically, though never for long at a time.

In London he wrote in the large room with three long windows at the top of the house. He wrote lying almost recumbent in a low rocking chair which he tipped to and fro as he wrote, like a cradle, and as he wrote he smoked a short clay pipe, and he scattered books round him in a circle. The thud of a book dropped on the floor could be heard in the room beneath. And often as he mounted the stairs to his study with his firm, regular tread he would burst, not into song, for he was entirely unmusical, but into a strange rhythmical chant, for verse of all kinds, both "utter trash," as he called it, and the most sublime words of Milton and Wordsworth, stuck in his memory, and the act of walking or climbing seemed to inspire him to recite whichever it was that came uppermost or suited his mood.

But it was his dexterity with his fingers that delighted his children before they could potter along the lanes at his heels or read his books. He would twist a sheet of paper beneath a pair of scissors and out would drop an elephant, a stag, or a monkey, with trunks, horns, and tails delicately and exactly formed. Or, taking a pencil, he would draw beast after beast — an art that he practiced almost unconsciously as he read, so that the flyleaves of his books swarm with owls and donkeys as if to illustrate the "Oh, you ass!" or "Conceited dunce" that he was wont to scribble impatiently in the margin. Such brief comments, in which one may find the germ of the more temperate statements of his essays, recall some of the characteristics of his talk. He could be very silent, as his friends have testified. But his remarks, made suddenly in a low voice between the puffs of his pipe, were extremely effective. Sometimes with one word — but his one word was accompanied by a gesture of the hand — he would dispose of the tissue of exaggerations which his own sobriety seemed to provoke. "There are 40,000,000 unmarried women in London alone!" Lady Ritchie once informed him. "Oh, Annie, Annie!" my father exclaimed in tones of horrified but affectionate rebuke. But Lady Ritchie, as if she enjoyed being rebuked, would pile it up even higher next time she came.

The stories he told to amuse his children of adventures in the Alps — but accidents only happened, he would explain, if you were so foolish as to disobey your guides — or of those long walks, after one of which, from Cambridge to London on a hot day, "I drank, I am sorry to say, rather more than was good for me," were told very briefly, but with a curious power to impress the scene. The things that he did not say were always there in the background. So, too, though he seldom told anecdotes, and his memory for facts was bad, when he described a person — and he had known many people, both famous and obscure — he would convey exactly what he thought of him in two or three words. And what he thought might be the opposite of what other people thought. He had a way of upsetting established reputations and disregarding conventional values that could be disconcerting, and sometimes perhaps wounding, though no one was more respectful of any feeling that seemed to him genuine. But when, suddenly opening his bright blue eyes and rousing himself from what had seemed complete abstraction, he gave his opinion, it was difficult to disregard it. It was a habit, especially when deafness made him unaware that this opinion could be heard, that had its inconveniences.

"I am the most easily bored of men," he wrote, truthfully as usual; and when, as was inevitable in a large family, some visitor threatened to stay not merely for tea but also for dinner, my father would express his anguish at first by twisting and untwisting a certain lock of hair. Then he would burst out, half to himself, half to the powers above, but quite audibly, "Why can't he go? Why can't he go?" Yet such is the charm of simplicity — and did he not say, also truthfully, that "bores are the salt of the earth"? — that the bores seldom went, or, if they did, forgave him and came again.

Too much, perhaps, has been said of his silence; too much stress has been laid upon his reserve. He loved clear thinking; he hated sentimentality and gush; but this by no means meant that he was cold and unemotional, perpetually critical and condemnatory in daily life. On the contrary, it was his power of feeling strongly and of expressing his feeling with vigor that made him sometimes so alarming as a companion. A lady, for instance, complained of the wet summer that was spoiling her tour in Cornwall. But to my father, though he never called himself a democrat, the rain meant that the corn was being laid; some poor man was being ruined; and the energy with which he expressed his sympathy — not with the lady — left her discomfited. He had something of the same respect for farmers and fishermen that he had for climbers and explorers. So, too, he talked little of patriotism, but during the South African War — and all wars were hateful to him — he lay awake thinking that he heard the guns on the battlefield. Again, neither his reason nor his cold common sense helped to convince him that a child could be late for dinner without having been maimed or killed in an accident. And not all his mathematics together with a bank balance which he insisted must be ample in the extreme could persuade him, when it came to signing a check, that the whole family was not "shooting Niagara to ruin," as he put it. The pictures that he would draw of old age and the bankruptcy court, of ruined men of letters who have to support large families in small houses at Wimbledon (he owned a very small house at Wimbledon), might have convinced those who complain of his understatements that hyperbole was well within his reach had he chosen.

Yet the unreasonable mood was superficial, as the rapidity with which it vanished would prove. The checkbook was shut; Wimbledon and the workhouse were forgotten. Some thought of a humorous kind made him chuckle. Taking his hat and his stick, calling for his dog and his daughter, he would stride off into Kensington Gardens, where he had walked as a little boy, where his brother Fitzjames and he had made beautiful bows to young Queen Victoria and she had swept them a curtsy; and so, round the Serpentine, to Hyde Park Corner, where he had once saluted the great Duke himself; and so home. He was not then in the least "alarming"; he was very simple, very confiding; and his silence, though one might last unbroken from the Round Pond to the Marble Arch, was curiously full of meaning, as if he were thinking half aloud, about poetry and philosophy and people he had known.

He himself was the most abstemious of men. He smoked a pipe perpetually, but never a cigar. He wore his clothes until they were too shabby to be tolerable; and he held old-fashioned and rather puritanical views as to the vice of luxury and the sin of idleness. The relations between parents and children today have a freedom that would have been impossible with my father. He expected a certain standard of behavior, even of ceremony, in family life. Yet if freedom means the right to think one's own thoughts and to follow one's own pursuits, then no one respected and indeed insisted upon freedom more completely than he did. His sons, with the exception of the Army and Navy, should follow whatever professions they chose; his daughters, though he cared little enough for the higher education of women, should have the same liberty. If at one moment he rebuked a daughter sharply for smoking a cigarette — smoking was not in his opinion a nice habit in the other sex — she had only to ask him if she might become a painter, and he assured her that so long as she took her work seriously he would give her all the help he could. He had no special love for painting; but he kept his word. Freedom of that sort was worth thousands of cigarettes.

It was the same with the perhaps more difficult problem of literature.

Even today there may be parents who would doubt the wisdom of allowing a girl of fifteen the free run of a large and quite unexpurgated library. But my father allowed it. There were certain facts — very briefly, very shyly he referred to them. Yet "Read what you like," he said, and all his books, "mangy and worthless," as he called them, but certainly they were many and various, were to be had without asking. To read what one liked because one liked it, never to pretend to admire what one did not — that was his only lesson in the art of reading. To write in the fewest possible words, as clearly as possible, exactly what one meant — that was his only lesson in the art of writing. All the rest must be learned for oneself. Yet a child must have been childish in the extreme not to feel that such was the teaching of a man of great learning and wide experience, though he would never impose his own views or parade his own knowledge. For, as his tailor remarked when he saw my father walk past his shop up Bond Street, "There goes a gentleman that wears good clothes without knowing it."

In those last years, grown solitary and very deaf, he would sometimes call himself a failure as a writer; he had been "jack of all trades, and master of none." But whether he failed or succeeded as a writer, it is permissible to believe that he left a distinct impression of himself on the minds of his friends. Meredith saw him as "Phoebus Apollo turned fasting friar" in his earlier days; Thomas Hardy, years later, looked at the "spare and desolate figure" of the Schreckhorn and thought of

> him,
> Who scaled its horn with ventured life and limb,
> Drawn on by vague imaginings, maybe,
> Of semblance to his personality
> In its quaint glooms, keen lights, and rugged trim.

But the praise he would have valued most, for though he was an agnostic nobody believed more profoundly in the worth of human relationships, was Meredith's tribute after his death: "He was the one man to my knowledge worthy to have married your mother." And Lowell, when he called him "L.S., the most lovable of men," has best described the quality that makes him, after all these years, unforgettable.

The Incorruptible Sinclair Lewis

by PERRY MILLER

Outward bound for a year of teaching at European universities, Perry Miller, professor of American literature at Harvard University, encountered on the boat a novelist whose work he had been discussing for many years — Sinclair Lewis. Their friendship sparked on sight, and they saw much of each other during the last year of Lewis's life.

APRIL 1951

The first night out of New York on the *Nieuw Amsterdam,* September 7, 1949, my wife said, "That man going out of the bar looks like Sinclair Lewis." I caught a side glimpse — which I shall forever behold — of that long figure, its head tilted back, its narrow shoulders heightened and compressed, an elastic-jointed puppet held two inches off the deck by invisible strings, so that the longest pair of legs ever attached to so short a body jerked their way across the room in a motion that had nothing to do with the ordinary act of walking.

I had the good fortune never to have met him before; hence we had never quarreled. When he had been working (if that is the word for what he did in preparation for the worst book he ever pieced together) upon *The God-Seeker,* he had wanted to consult an out-of-print work of mine on New England theology. I offered, through the bookseller, to send him my own copy; he found another somewhere, and never replied. Now I was to discover that this sort of thing Lewis did not forget. Of all the men I have ever known, his gratitude — for such a trifle — was the most profound and the most lasting. The point being that one thing really counted — his work. He and I were friends within five minutes, because we did not have to explain anything.

It took no astuteness to realize that Sinclair Lewis was dying. He had barely recovered from a siege of pneumonia (on this voyage he was not drinking): his hand shook, and the wavering of his legs meant that he

was unsteady on them. With him was his brother, Dr. Claude Lewis of Saint Cloud, Minnesota — of whom Red had not seen much in recent decades, who was six years older than he, and who addressed him as "Hal." Dr. Lewis looked a good ten years younger: Red's myth — to which he clung with inexhaustible solicitude — was that he was about to introduce Claude for the first time to the immemorial riches of Europe. He asked my advice morning and evening as to just how gradually and circumspectly he should spring the art galleries and cathedrals on brother Claude, so as not to heap too much into the initiation.

The whole business was infinitely comic: Dr. Lewis is a distinguished surgeon, of eminent common sense, who can and does find his way about the world by his own native shrewdness. And when it comes to the conventional "sightseeing," Red Lewis was about the most unperceptive and blundering of all the myriads of tourists this country annually exports.

For the sake of the record, let me say that during Lewis's last year, I saw much of him — simply because I was in Europe and able to reach him. We perfected a little fiction between us that my wife and I, his newest friends, were his oldest and only friends. This gambit often grew rather harrowing as his perpetual mulling over the past disclosed the number of former friends who were now estranged, or at any rate out of touch. He received staggering quantities of mail, most of which (when he was with us) he never opened. In October he came to Holland and delivered a lecture at the University of Leiden.

In December of 1949 he had found, in the Cook's Tourist Office at Florence, Alexander Manson, who became his secretary, chauffeur, nurse, and interpreter. I gather that Aleck and his lovely Tina were with him to the end. I knew that Lewis had tried this "secretary" arrangement before, and that it had ended in repeated disasters; but Aleck Manson is something special; he knows Europe completely, speaks the languages, can repair a car or order a dinner, tell a story or comprehend a picture, and both he and his wife devoted themselves to Lewis with a disregard of self that would take all the recent history of Europe to explain. The beauty and poignance of the story is that Aleck instantly knew, and never for a moment imagined anything else, what Lewis signified as an artist. I am a countryman of Sinclair Lewis, as Aleck is not; and I grew up with his novels a part — a very great part — of my experience; most of those who read this did likewise. It took me all these years, and then the illumination of his discourse, and after that Aleck's by no means blind consecration, to realize what a terrifying thing it is to be in at the death of a lion. I use the word lion not in the flip sense of a target for hostesses: I mean it in the primitive sense of a leonine beast who roars his last defiance from a cave in the rocks.

You may think that this is melodramatic overstatement as against some of the facts. Externally they are shabby enough. During the winter, while he worked on his novel, he managed — with Aleck's help — to keep away from the bottle. As soon as he finished the manuscript, he started drinking, until his Florentine physician forbade him spirits. When I reached him in April, he was guzzling quantities of red wine, and despite Aleck's strenuous efforts, he generally succeeded in knocking himself out by afternoon. At a Florence restaurant he commanded the orchestra to play the sentimental tunes of his earlier escapades; he peeled off and flung about five-thousand-lira notes — Babbitt on a spree — until Aleck could get him out and pour him into the car. By August he was drinking only beer, but he had already had two serious heart attacks and should not have touched even that.

I suppose hundreds of people in three decades have seen Sinclair Lewis drunk; no doubt he made a vast public spectacle of himself. I cannot say what kept him going through the years of creativity; I do know that at the end of it, his back to the wall, facing himself drunk or sober, he did not flinch. There was something positively reckless about it. He was not drinking because he was miserable and wanted solace; neither was he what you would call a drunkard. He was no disenchanted, alcoholic Scott Fitzgerald, drinking compulsively. There may not have been much joy in what Red was doing, but there was still plenty of defiance. Remember, this was not Walter Scott collecting his retainers about him in feudal glory; this was not Zola declining in the realization of an enshrined place in the Academy. This was just an American who had written himself out, to whom the Nobel Prize was no canonization but merely one of those things that happen, for whom the dignity of the artist had no external supports, and who yet somehow maintained it, as Poe and Whitman did, on the terms which this nation imposes upon its artists — terms that Lewis gladly, as a matter of fact, imposed upon himself for fear he might otherwise take himself too solemnly.

This was something that ran deep and strong in him — his hatred for pomposity. I don't mean his treasuring the hypocrisies of Main Street or the sanctimoniousness of Elmer Gantry: that was something else entirely. I mean his attitude toward himself as a writer and toward writing in general. It was too serious a business to be taken solemnly. In the last

months he had a game he would play with Aleck — it went on inter-
minably — in which he was the stuffy, grandiose German Professor and
Aleck was the trembling *Privatdocent;* the point of the game (aside from
letting Lewis show off his German, for he was vain about his smattering
of languages) was that the Herr Professor Dr. Geheimrat made a damn
fool of himself. It was a way of throwing bricks at high silk hats. It was
a Mark Twain gesture, it was deeply and embarrassingly American, but
it was also more: it was a myth-maker thumbing his nose at those who
would reduce myth to literalness.

Being a professor of literary history, I wanted to find out what he derived from. The answer was instructive: Dickens. He knew Dickens by
heart. There was little to be gained by asking him about what had come
in between, about realists and naturalists. He had read here and there,
but most of them meant little to him, except for Shaw and Wells, who
to him were primarily writers that showed what might be done with
Dickensian exaggeration in a modern situation. The most valuable and
most plausible thing in his account of his own beginnings was the perfect naturalness and inevitability with which, it had seemed to him, a
young writer of about 1910, with Dickens as a model, would proceed
to make social comedy out of America.

Yes, he recognized that by now the generation of the twenties, himself the foremost, were being defined in historical terms and treated as
radical departures, as collectively a great break with the past. He had
no such sense of the story at all; as for most of the "influences" which,
according to our historians, brought about the revolution, he was unaware of them or else heard about them only after their effect on his own
work had been detected by some ingenious critic. He would agree that
up to a point it had been a matter of the time and place; as he talked
about the coming of the deep-freeze, television, and the high-powered
automobile to Gopher Prairie, he saw that he had caught Main Street
just at the turning point, at a now vanished point, and that his book
was already a matter of history — and then he would take flight into
fantasy, showing that he had never been and could never be capable
of thinking in terms of history. He was in love with mythological and
typological creations like Micawber and Gradgrind, and all his effort
had been to evoke such genii out of the American bottle. It was a constricted and stoppered vessel he had — as he saw it — to work with,
which is one reason he vented so much rage upon it. His incantations
had to be more labored than those of Dickens, who was in a position to

summon up, with a wave of the hand so to speak, a Pecksniff or a Mr. Squeers. In America there had to be a vaster quantity of documented fact before Lewis could extract from it a Babbitt or a Gantry, just as there had to be all the knowledge of the River before Mark Twain could set Huck Finn afloat upon it.

Lewis listened to, and sometimes was impressed by, what the critics said of his books as providing a panorama of the civilization, but for him Babbitt and Gantry and Arrowsmith were creations; he was still trying the old art when he wrote such pathetically documented things as *The Prodigal Parents* or *Cass Timberlane*. He was still trying it his last winter, and told me with affected complacence, as though one should say that Winston Churchill had dropped in yesterday, that in the new book Mr. and Mrs. Dodsworth had reappeared.

In this view, the lecture he gave for my class at Leiden was immensely revealing: most of the students were bewildered, because it was not anything they expected or wanted Sinclair Lewis to say. He worked on it carefully, and his notes reside now in the University Library. It was his last effort at any such sustained discourse. His argument was that America is not new, it is actually very old. He proved this first by dwelling on the antiquity of the Indian culture; how that was linked to the present American civilization so as to furnish us with its venerability never became quite clear. Secondly, he insisted, Americans all brought with them the civilization of Europe, and consequently their culture is as old as any European. He then blamed the Europeans for the antics of the Americans: because they expect us to act like wild Indians, we are obliged to put on a show for them. If you listen to the second half of a sentence uttered by the visiting American, he said, it will be a logical, sensible statement, but the first half will contain some "Oh boy" or "Gee whiz" or "What the hell" to assist the European in keeping up his illusion.

This from the author of *Babbitt!* If I was amused, my students were puzzled, because the primary (and almost the only) assumption among literate Europeans is that the recent literature of America is a sociological report on the horrors of a materialistic order, that all our artists hate it and want, like Lewis, to escape to Europe. In part, Lewis's speech was sheer perversity: he got fun out of scandalizing the European stereotype. He, like all of us, was troubled over the charge that the American literature of protest, with himself as Exhibit A, was confirming Europeans in their anti-Americanism. But there was something else at work in him when he wrote this lecture, which I think is fundamental in his best work. I stumbled upon it early in our friendship by telling him that as a boy in Chicago I had wanted to devote myself to the ancient history of the Near East. Nothing I ever said to him made his eyes shine so much. He too had wanted, more than anything in the world, to be an Egyptologist.

Don't ask me if this is true (although Claude did remember that the boy Hal had spouted a lot about Babylonia): my point is only that he announced this to have been the great dream of his youth and swore that it was the adventure yet to come. While his strength was visibly failing, even after the heart attacks commenced, he descanted on how he and Aleck were to set out in the fall, work their way through Sicily, then go to Egypt and Damascus and Assyria, and at last penetrate to Persepolis. I do not know how much history he read, but he loved to pontificate about Rameses II and the queen of Palmyra.

Was it a trauma of escapism? Maybe. In ordinary terms, I think it was something simpler: it was a thin little boy in Sauk Center dreaming (over an unfinished book) about the gorgeous panoply of Ashur-bani-pal. Remember how many times the majestic syllables of ancient history are invoked in his ironic addresses to America, how "Ur of the Chaldees" had for him a magic sound, and how it seemed the supreme comment upon the tin Lizzie standing before the Bon Ton store that for this the pyramids were built and Hannibal crossed the Alps.

I said good-by to him one night in Zurich; Aleck was taking him the next day to Turin, and he and I knew that we would never meet again. The next morning, before breakfast, he telephoned: he wanted me to tell him whether Rangoon is a port for ocean-going vessels and the precise dates when Generals Lee and Grant died.

I suppose he knew that he would never get to Egypt. He probably would have been as restless before the pyramids as he was in the cathedral of Antwerp, and would have distracted his attention from the sublimity of the pile by finding some ridiculous detail off to one side, or by looking at his watch and worrying about whether he could get back to the hotel on time. But that is not what concerns us. One of the most perceptive of my friends in Leiden came from his lecture exhilarated; when I asked her what she liked about it, she replied with unhesitating emphasis, "His fanaticism." That, she said, is what Europe needs, and she went on to contrast him and Dodsworth with Henry James: where James made so exquisite an effort to comprehend the special essence of every European place, to stretch his sensibility into the fine web that would catch the slightest reverberations, Lewis (like Dodsworth) stood intransigent and incorruptible. For this listener, and several others, his lecture had not been what he may consciously have intended it, the rebuttal of a flimsy European stereotype about America; it was much more: it was a revelation of the sources of his energy as an artist, of the act of dedication he had performed so thoroughly that he could never, whether flamboyant or, as now, sick and battered, do anything but exemplify it. My friend said that she was reading *Babbitt* with new eyes.

The difficulty is that too few in America have read him with such eyes. Perhaps I might put my contention more bluntly (although it loses much if stated so flatly): it is all very well to call Lewis a realist because he heaped up the furnishings of the Kennicotts' parlor or because he could mimic to the last grammatical atrocity the jabberings of the man who knew Coolidge, but at the heart of him Lewis was what we must call, for lack of a better word, a romancer. He loved telling stories, and even in this last year, in the ebb of his powers, could start with almost anything and make the draft of a novel out of it. I have never heard anything so fascinating, and it made the Dickens clue trebly revelatory.

Lewis could have earned a comfortable living writing stories for magazines; in fact, before *Main Street* he was doing exactly that. What kept him from being just a spinner of yarns was not something more sophisticated in him — not any doctrinal adherence to, or even comprehension of, the tenets of realism or naturalism — but something more primitive. The scrupulous documentation was the working of a conscience. This organ does not operate so strenuously in easy living or in facile writing; it becomes tormenting only when there is some deep psychic dislocation, some wrong done — or some hurt felt.

I gather that few of Red's friends got along with him for any period without certain stormy scenes. I had mine the night before his lecture, when we were invited for dinner by the Rector Magnificus of Leiden University. Professor van Groningen is a civilized, gentle classicist; his wife is witty and, fortunately, comprehends the world. They both had behaved with quiet heroism in the war, and are what in Holland is known as "conservative" on the Indonesian question (which means that they regret the American policy), but I never had any difficulty discussing it with them.

This night, I started the dinner off by remarking that the Amsterdam paper had called Claude the younger brother. (There is no way I can tell this story that reflects the slightest credit on me.) At the table, the van Groningens intimated their attitude toward Indonesia, whereupon Red launched into a patriotic tirade, of the sort he had voluminously burlesqued, in which the embattled Indonesians became American patriots at Valley Forge and his Dutch hosts supercilious Tories in London of 1776. I completed the ruin of the evening by asking the Rector to have Dr. Lewis escorted through the Faculty of Medicine on the morrow, managing by an inspiration of stupidity to say that Claude had heard his brother before and did not need to hear him again. The resulting scene was Red Lewis at his most histrionic: we were all denounced and assured that the lecture would never be delivered. The situation was saved only by the wit of Mevrouw van Groningen, who told funny stories, mostly at her own expense, while Lewis sulked like a child, until he came out of it, put his hand on my arm, and said of his hostess, "Wouldn't Frans Hals have liked to paint her!"

Somehow, my wife and I got them back to the hotel. Claude pulled me aside and whispered as he went up to bed, "He's been like that since he was a boy."

Lewis was contrite, but of course wouldn't admit it; he took us into the bar, and then the confession came. It's been that way from the beginning, he said. I wanted to write, and I've worked like hell at it, and the whole of Sauk Center and my family and America have never understood that it is work, that I haven't just been playing around, that this is every bit as serious a proposition as Claude's hospital. When you said that Claude did not want to hear my lecture, Lewis told me, you set up all the resentments I have had ever since I can remember.

If much of this sounds petulant, it was. It was also the story of the artist in America. It was a revelation of the sources of what the perceptive Dutch woman found his redeeming fanaticism. It may have been bad manners but it was freedom, passionate and consuming. It was the *élan* that went into the writing of the great novels of the twenties, which makes them, in the guise of ferocious attacks upon America, celebrations of it. For at the end of the lecture on the next day, he said something which I believe he seldom brought himself to avow, which certainly he never put in print: "I wrote *Babbitt* not out of hatred for him but out of love." I am afraid that in the books of his later years Sinclair Lewis wrote much that allows only one interpretation. All this immense America had to be poured through him; there was too much of it, and finally he took merely to reporting it, as Whitman, when his vitality flagged, catalogued it. But Lewis never got altogether away from the ambiguity that informs his five triumphs of the 1920s.

Over and over again, after he had mailed the manuscript of this last book, when he would try to enjoy Italian scenery or the Swiss Alps, he would come back, with the reiteration of obsession, to asserting that he had written twenty-three novels about America, that nobody could ask more of him, that he had done his duty by his country. "I love America," he would shout into the unoffending European atmosphere; "I love it, but I don't like it." As a closing statement on the career of Sinclair Lewis, this assuredly does not, whatever else you say about it, allow of only a single, and certainly not of a literal, interpretation.

Mr. Churchill

by ISAIAH BERLIN

Attached to the British Embassy in Washington during World War II, Isaiah Berlin became an all but legendary figure in the capitals of both nations while still in his early thirties. After the war he served in the Embassy at Moscow. By profession a teacher, he is the Ritchie Professor of Philosophy at Oxford, and today, Sir Isaiah.

SEPTEMBER 1949

In the now remote year 1928, the eminent English poet and critic Herbert Read published a book dealing with the art of writing English prose. Writing at a time of bitter disillusion with the false splendors of the Edwardian era, and still more with the propaganda and phrasemaking occasioned by the First World War, Read praised the virtues of simplicity. If simple prose was often dry and flat, it was at least honest. If it was at times awkward, shapeless, and bleak, it did at least convey a feeling of truthfulness. Above all, it avoided the worst of all temptations — inflation, self-dramatization, the construction of flimsy stucco façades, either deceptively smooth or covered with elaborate baroque detail which concealed a dreadful inner emptiness.

The time and mood are familiar enough: it was not long after Lytton

Strachey had set a new fashion by his method of exposing the cant or muddleheadedness of eminent Victorians, after Bertrand Russell had unmasked the great nineteenth-century metaphysicians as authors of a monstrous hoax played upon generations eager to be deceived, after Keynes had successfully pilloried the follies and vices of the Allied statesmen at Versailles. This was the time when rhetoric and even eloquence were held up to obloquy as camouflage for literary and moral Pecksniffs, unscrupulous charlatans who corrupted artistic taste and discredited the cause of truth and reason, and at their worst incited to evil and led a credulous world to disaster. It was in this literary climate that Read, with much skill and discrimination, explained why he admired the last recorded words spoken to Judge Thayer by the poor fish peddler Vanzetti — moving, ungrammatical fragments uttered by a simple man about to die — more than he did the rolling periods of celebrated masters of fine writing widely read by the public at that time.

He selected as an example of the latter a man who in particular was regarded as the sworn enemy of all that Read prized most highly — humility, integrity, humanity, individual freedom, personal affection — the celebrated but distrusted paladin of imperialism and the romantic conception of life, the swashbuckling militarist, the vehement orator and journalist, the most public of public personalities in a world dedicated to the cultivation of private virtues, the Chancellor of the Exchequer of the Conservative Government then in power, Winston Churchill.

After observing that "these three conditions are necessary to Eloquence — firstly an adequate theme, then a sincere and impassioned mind, and lastly a power of sustainment, of pertinacity," Read drove his thesis home with a quotation from the first part of Churchill's *World Crisis,* which had appeared some four years previously, and added: "Such eloquence is false because it is artificial . . . the images are stale, the metaphors violent, the whole passage exhales a false dramatic atmosphere . . . a volley of rhetorical imperatives." He went on to describe Churchill's prose as being high-sounding, redundant, falsely eloquent, declamatory, which, in Read's words, derived from undue "aggrandization of the self" instead of "aggrandization of the theme"; and condemned it root and branch.

Read's view was well received by the young men who were painfully reacting against anything which appeared to go beyond the naked skeleton of the truth, at a time when not only rhetoric but noble eloquence seemed outrageous hypocrisy. Read spoke, and knew that he spoke, for a post-war generation; the sequel to so much magnificence was very bitter, and left behind it a heritage of hatred for the grand style as such. The victims and casualties of the disaster thought they had earned the right to be rid of the trappings of an age which had so heartlessly betrayed them.

Nevertheless Read and his audience were profoundly mistaken. What he and they denounced as so much tinsel and hollow pasteboard was in reality solid: it was this author's natural means for the expression of his heroic, highly colored, sometimes oversimple and even naïve, but always absolutely genuine, vision of life. Read saw only an unconvincing, sordidly transparent pastiche, but this was an illusion. The reality was something very different: an inspired, if unconscious, attempt at a revival. It went against the stream of contemporary thought and feeling only because it was a deliberate return to a formal mode of English utterance which extends from Gibbon and Dr. Johnson to Peacock and Macaulay, a weapon created by Churchill in order to convey his particular vision. In the bleak and deflationary twenties it was too bright, too big, too vivid, too unsubtle for the sensitive and sophisticated epigoni of the age of imperialism, who, living an inner life of absorbing complexity and delicacy, became unable and certainly unwilling to admire the light of a day which had destroyed so much of what they had trusted and loved. From this Read recoiled; but his analysis of his reasons is unconvincing.

Read had, of course, a right to his own scale of values, but it was a blunder to dismiss Churchill's prose as a false front, a hollow sham. Revivals are not false as such: the Gothic Revival, for example, represented a passionate and intense attitude toward life, and while some examples of it may appear bizarre, it sprang from a deeper sentiment and had a good deal more to say than some of the thin and "realistic" styles which followed; the fact that the creators of the Gothic Revival found their liberation in going back into a largely imaginary past in no way discredits them or their achievement. There are those who, inhibited by the furniture of the ordinary world, come to life only when they feel themselves actors upon a stage, and, thus emancipated, speak out for the first time, and are then found to have much to say. There are those who can function freely only in uniform or armor or court dress, see only through certain kinds of spectacles, act fearlessly only in situations which in some way are formalized for them, see life as a kind of play in which they and others are assigned certain lines which they must speak. So it happens — the last war afforded plenty of instances of this — that people of a shrinking disposition perform miracles of courage when life has been dramatized for them, when they are on the battlefield; and might continue to do so if they were constantly in uniform and life were always a battlefield.

This need for a framework is not "escapism," not artificial or abnormal or a sign of maladjustment. Often it is a vision of experience in terms of the strongest single psychological ingredient in one's nature: not infrequently in the form of a simple struggle between conflicting forces or principles, between truth and falsehood, good and evil, right and wrong, between personal integrity and various forms of temptation and corruption (as in the case of Read), or between what is conceived as permanent and what is ephemeral, or the material and the immaterial, or between the forces of life and the forces of death, or between the religion of art and its supposed enemies — politicians or priests or philistines. Life may be seen through many windows, none of them necessarily clear or opaque, less or more distorting than any of the others. And since we think largely in words, they necessarily take on the property of serving as an armor. The style of Dr. Johnson, which echoes so frequently in the prose of *Their Finest Hour,* particularly when the author indulges in a solemn facetiousness, was itself in its own day a weapon offensive and defensive; it requires no deep psychological subtlety to perceive why a man so vulnerable as Johnson — who belonged mentally to the previous century — had constant need of it.

Churchill's dominant category, the single, central, organizing principle of his moral and intellectual universe, is an historical imagination so strong, so comprehensive, as to encase the whole of the present and the whole of the future in a framework of a rich and multicolored past. Such an approach is dominated by a desire — and a capacity — to find fixed moral and intellectual bearings, to give shape and character, color and direction and coherence, to the stream of events.

This kind of systematic "historicism" is, of course, not confined to men of action or political thinkers: the great Roman Catholic thinkers see life in terms of a firm and lucid historical structure, and so, of course, do Marxists, and so did the Romantic historians and philosophers from whom the Marxists are directly descended. Nor do we complain of "escapism" or perversion of the facts until the categories adopted are thought to do too much violence to the "facts." To interpret, to relate, to classify, to symbolize are those natural and unavoidable human activities which we loosely and conveniently describe as thinking.

We complain, if we do, only when the result is too widely at variance with the common outlook of our own society and age and tradition.

Churchill sees history — and life — as a great Renaissance pageant: when he thinks of France or Italy, Germany or the Low Countries, Russia, India, Africa, the Arab lands, he sees vivid historical images — something between Victorian illustrations in a book of history and the great procession painted by Benozzo Gozzoli in the Riccardi Palace. His eye is never that of the neatly classifying sociologist, the careful psychological analyst, the plodding antiquary, the patient historical scholar. His poetry has not that anatomical vision which sees the naked bone beneath the flesh, skulls and skeletons and the omnipresence of decay and death beneath the flow of life. The units out of which his world is constructed are simpler and larger than life, the patterns vivid and repetitive like those of an epic poet, or at times like those of a dramatist who sees persons and situations as timeless symbols and embodiments of eternal, shining principles. The whole is a series of symmetrically formed and somewhat stylized compositions, either suffused with bright light or cast in darkest shadow, like a legend by Carpaccio, with scarcely any nuance, painted in primary colors with no half tones, nothing intangible, nothing impalpable, nothing half spoken or hinted or whispered: the voice does not alter in pitch or timbre.

The archaisms of style to which Churchill's wartime speeches have accustomed us are indispensable ingredients of the heightened tone, the formal chronicler's attire, for which the solemnity of the occasion calls. Churchill is fully conscious of this: the style should adequately respond to the demands which history makes upon the actors from moment to moment. "The ideas set forth," he wrote in 1940 about a Foreign Office draft, "appeared to me to err in trying to be too clever, to enter into refinements of policy unsuited to the tragic simplicity and grandeur of the times and the issues at stake."

His own narrative consciously mounts and swells until it reaches the great climax of the Battle of Britain. The texture and the tension are those of a tragic opera, where the very artificiality of the medium, both in the recitative and in the arias, serves to eliminate the irrelevant dead level of normal existence and to set off in high relief the deeds and sufferings of the principal characters. The moments of comedy in such a work must necessarily conform to the style of the whole and be parodies of it; and this is Churchill's practice. When he says that he viewed this or that "with stern and tranquil gaze," or informs his officials that any "chortling" by them over the failure of a chosen scheme "will be viewed with great disfavour by me," or describes the "celestial grins" of his collaborators over the development of a well-concealed conspiracy, he does precisely this; the mock heroic tone — reminiscent of *Stalky & Co.* — does not break the operatic conventions. But conventions though they be, they are not donned and doffed by the author at will: by now they are his second nature, and have completely fused with the first; art and nature are no longer distinguishable. The very formal pattern of his prose is the normal medium of his ideas, not merely when he sets himself to compose, but in the life of the imagination which permeates his daily existence.

Churchill's language is a medium which he invented because he needed it. It has a bold, ponderous, fairly uniform, easily recognizable rhythm which lends itself to parody (including his own) like all strongly individual styles. A language is individual when its user is endowed with sharply marked characteristics and succeeds in creating a medium for their expression. The origins, the constituents, the classical echoes which can be found in Churchill's prose are obvious enough; the product is, however, unique. Whatever the attitude that may be taken toward it, it must be recognized as a large-scale phenomenon of our time. To ignore or deny this would be blind or frivolous or dishonest. The utterance is always, and not merely on special occasions, formal (though it alters in intensity and color with the situation), always public, Ciceronian, addressed to the world, remote from the hesitancies and stresses of introspection and private life.

The quality of Churchill's historical writing is that of his whole life. His world is built upon the primacy of public over private relationships, upon the supreme value of action, of the battle between simple good and simple evil, between life and death; but above all, battle. He has always fought. "Whatever you may do," he declared to the demoralized French ministers in the bleakest hour of 1940, "we shall fight on for ever and ever and ever," and under this sign his own whole life has been lived.

What has he fought for? The answer is a good deal clearer than in the case of other equally passionate but less consistent men of action. Churchill's principles and beliefs on fundamental issues have never faltered. He has often been accused by his critics of inconstancy, of veering and even erratic judgment, as when he changed his allegiance from the Conservative to the Liberal Party, to and fro. But with the exception of the issue of protection, when he supported the tariff as

Chancellor of the Exchequer in Baldwin's cabinet in the twenties, this charge, which at first seems so plausible, is spectacularly false. Far from changing his opinions too often, Churchill has scarcely, during a long and stormy career, altered them at all. If anyone wishes to discover his views on the large and lasting issues of our time, he need only set himself to discover what Churchill has said or written on the subject at any period of his long and exceptionally articulate public life, in particular during the years before the First World War: the number of instances in which his views have in later years undergone any appreciable degree of change will be found astonishingly small.

The apparently solid and dependable Baldwin adjusted his attitudes with wonderful dexterity as and when circumstances required it. Chamberlain, long regarded as a grim and immovable rock of Tory opinion, altered his policies — more serious than Baldwin, he pursued policies, not being content with mere attitudes — when the party or the situation seemed to him to require it. Churchill remained inflexibly attached to first principles.

It is the strength and coherence of his central, lifelong beliefs that has provoked greater uneasiness, more disfavor and suspicion, in the central office of the Conservative Party than his vehemence or passion for power or what was considered his wayward, unreliable brilliance. No strongly centralized political organization feels altogether happy with individuals who combine independence, a free imagination, and a formidable strength of character with stubborn faith and a single-minded, unaltering view of the public and private good. Churchill, who believes that "ambition, not so much for vulgar ends but for fame, glints in every mind," knows with an unshakable certainty what he considers to be big, handsome, noble, and worthy of pursuit by someone in high station, and what, on the contrary, he abhors as being dim, gray, thin, likely to lower or destroy the play of color and movement in the universe. Tacking and bending and timid compromise may commend themselves to those sound men of sense whose hopes of preserving the world they defend are shot through with an often unconscious pessimism; but if the policy they pursue is likely to slow the tempo, to diminish the forces of life, to lower the "vital and vibrant energy" which he admires, say, in Lord Beaverbrook, Churchill is ready for attack.

Churchill is one of the diminishing number of those who genuinely believe in a specific world order: the desire to give it life and strength is the most powerful single influence upon everything which he thinks and imagines, does and is. When biographers and historians come to describe and analyze his views on Europe or America, on the British Empire or Russia, on India or Palestine, or even on social or economic policy, they will find that his opinions on all these topics are set in fixed patterns, set early in life and later only reinforced. Thus he has always believed in great states and civilizations in an almost hierarchical order, and has never, for instance, hated Germany as such: Germany is a great, historically hallowed state; the Germans are a great historic race and as such occupy a proportionate amount of space in Churchill's world picture. He denounced the Prussians in the First World War and the Nazis in the Second; the Germans, scarcely at all. He has always entertained a glowing vision of France and her culture, and has unalterably advocated the necessity of Anglo-French collaboration. He has always looked on the Russians as a formless, quasi-Asiatic mass beyond the walls of European civilization. His belief in and predilection for the American democracy are too well known to need comment — they are the foundation of his political outlook.

His vision in foreign affairs has always been consistently romantic. The struggle of the Jews for self-determination in Palestine engaged his imagination in precisely the way in which the Italian Risorgimento captured the sympathies of his Liberal forebears. Similarly his views on social policy conform to those Liberal principles which he received at the hands of the men he most admired in the great Liberal administration of the first decade of this century — Asquith, Haldane, Grey, above all Lloyd George before 1914 — and he has seen no reason to change them, whatever the world might do; and if these views, progressive in 1910, seem less convincing today, that flows from Churchill's unalterable faith in the firmly conceived scheme of things which he established within himself long ago, once and for all.

It is an error to regard the imagination as a mainly revolutionary force — if it destroys and alters, it also fuses hitherto isolated beliefs, insights, mental habits, into strongly unified systems. These, if they are filled with sufficient energy and force of will — and, it may be added, fantasy, which is less frightened by the facts and creates ideal models in terms of which the facts are ordered in the mind — sometimes transform the outlook of an entire people and generation.

The British statesman most richly endowed with these gifts was Disraeli, who in effect conceived that imperialist mystique, that splendid but most un-English vision which, romantic to the point of exoticism, full of metaphysical emotion, to all appearances utterly opposed to everything most soberly empirical, utilitarian, antisystematic in the British tradition, bound its spell on the mind of England for two generations.

Churchill's political imagination has something of the same magical power to transform. It is a magic which belongs equally to demagogues and great democratic leaders: Franklin Roosevelt, who as much as any man altered his country's inner image of itself, of its character and its history, possessed it in a high degree. But the differences between him and the Prime Minister of Britain are far greater than the similarities, and to some degree epitomize the differences of continents and civilizations. The contrast is brought out vividly by the respective parts which they played in the war which drew them so closely together.

The Second World War in some ways gave birth to less novelty and genius than the First World War. It was, of course, a greater cataclysm, fought over a wider area, and altered the social and political contours of the world at least as radically as its predecessor, perhaps more so. But the break in continuity in 1914 was far more violent. The years before 1914 look to us now, and looked even in the twenties, as the end of a long period of largely peaceful development broken suddenly and catastrophically. In Europe, at least, the years before 1914 were viewed with understandable nostalgia by those who after them knew no real peace.

The period between the wars marks a decline in the development of human culture if it is compared with that sustained and fruitful period which makes the nineteenth century seem a unique human achievement, so powerful that it continued, even during the war which broke it, to a degree which seems astonishing to us now. The quality of literature, for example, which is surely one of the most reliable criteria of intellectual and moral vitality, was incomparably higher during the war of 1914–1918 than it has been after 1939. In Western Europe alone these four years of slaughter and destruction were also years in which works of genius and talent continued to be produced by such established writers as Shaw and Wells and Kipling, Hauptmann and Gide, Chesterton and Arnold Bennett, Beerbohm and Yeats, as well as such younger writers as Proust and Joyce, Virginia Woolf and E. M. Forster, T. S. Eliot and Alexander Blok, Rilke, Stefan George, and Valéry. Nor did natural science, philosophy, and history cease to develop fruitfully. What has the recent war to offer by comparison?

Yet perhaps there is one respect in which the Second World War did outshine its predecessor: the leaders of the nations involved in it were, with the significant exception of France, men of greater stature, psychologically more interesting than their prototypes. It would hardly be disputed that Stalin is a more fascinating figure than the Czar Nicholas II; Hitler more arresting than the Kaiser; Mussolini than Victor Emmanuel; and, memorable as they were, President Wilson and Lloyd George yield in the attribute of sheer historical magnitude to Franklin Roosevelt and Winston Churchill.

"History," we are told by a celebrated authority, "is what Alexander did and suffered." This notion, despite all the efforts of the social sciences to overthrow it, remains a good deal more valid than rival hypotheses, provided that history is defined as that which historians actually do. At any rate Churchill accepts it wholeheartedly, and takes full advantage of his opportunities. And because his narrative deals largely in personalities and gives individual genius its full and sometimes more than its full due, the appearance of the great wartime protagonists in his pages gives his narrative some of the quality of an epic, whose heroes and villains acquire their stature not merely — or indeed at all — from the importance of the events in which they are involved, but from their own intrinsic human size upon the stage of human history; their characteristics, involved as they are in perpetual juxtaposition and occasional collision with one another, set each other off in vast relief.

Comparisons and contrasts are bound to arise in the mind of the reader which sometimes take him beyond Churchill's pages. Thus Roosevelt stands out principally by his astonishing appetite for life and by his apparently complete freedom from fear of the future; as a man who welcomed the future eagerly as such, and conveyed the feeling that whatever the times might bring, all would be grist to his mill, nothing would be too formidable or crushing to be subdued and used and molded into the pattern of the new and unpredictable forms of life, into the building of which he, Roosevelt, and his allies and devoted subordinates would throw themselves with unheard-of energy and gusto. This avid anticipation of the future, the lack of nervous fear that the wave might prove too big or violent to navigate, contrasts most sharply with the uneasy longing to insulate themselves so clear in Stalin or Chamberlain. Hitler too, in a sense, showed no fear, but his assurance sprang from a lunatic's cunning vision, which distorted the facts too easily in his favor.

So passionate a faith in the future, so untroubled a confidence in one's power to mold it, when it is allied to a capacity for realistic appraisal of its true contours, implies an exceptionally sensitive awareness, conscious or half-conscious, of the tendencies of one's milieu, of the desires, hopes, fears, loves, hatreds, of the human beings who compose it, of what are impersonally described as social and individual "trends." Roosevelt had this sensibility developed to the point of genius. He acquired the symbolic significance which he retained throughout his Presidency largely because he sensed the tendencies of his time and their projections into the future to a most uncommon degree. His sense, not only of the movement of American public opinion but of the general direction in which the larger human society of his time was moving, was what is called uncanny. The inner currents, the tremors and complicated convolutions of this movement, seemed to register themselves within his nervous system with a kind of seismographical accuracy. The majority of his fellow citizens recognized this — some with enthusiasm, others with gloom or bitter indignation. Peoples far beyond the frontiers of the United States rightly looked to him as the most genuine and unswerving spokesman of democracy known to them, the most contemporary, the most outward-looking, free from the obsessions of an inner life, with an unparalleled capacity for creating confidence in the power of his insight, his foresight, and his capacity to identify himself with the ideals of humble people.

This feeling of being at home not merely in the present but in the future, of knowing where he was going and by what means and why, made him, until his health was finally undermined, buoyant and gay; made him delight in the company of the most varied and opposed individuals, provided that they embodied some specific aspect of the turbulent stream of life, stood actively for the forward movement in their particular world, whatever it might be. And this inner *élan* made up, and more than made up, for faults of intellect or character which his enemies — and his victims — never ceased to point out. He seemed genuinely unaffected by their taunts: what he could not abide was, before all, passivity, stillness, melancholy, fear of life or preoccupation with eternity or death, however great the insight or delicate the sensibility by which they were accompanied.

Churchill stands at almost the opposite pole. He too does not fear the future, and no man has ever loved life more vehemently and infused so much of it into everyone and everything that he has touched. But whereas Roosevelt, like all great innovators, had a half-conscious premonitory awareness of the coming shape of society, not wholly unlike that of an artist, Churchill, for all his extrovert air, looks within, and his strongest sense is the sense of the past.

The clear, multicolored vision of history, in terms of which he conceives both the present and the future, is the inexhaustible source from which he draws the primary stuff out of which his universe is so solidly built, so richly and elaborately ornamented. So firm and so embracing an edifice could not be constructed by anyone liable to react and respond like a sensitive instrument to the perpetually changing moods and directions of other persons or institutions or peoples. And indeed Churchill's strength lies precisely in this: that, unlike Roosevelt, he is not equipped with numberless sensitive antennae which communicate the smallest oscillations of the outer world in all its unstable variety. Unlike Roosevelt, and unlike Gladstone and Lloyd George for that matter, he does not reflect a social or moral world in an intense and concentrated fashion; rather he creates one of such power and coherence that it becomes a reality and alters the external world by being imposed upon it with irresistible force. As this history of the war shows, he has an immense capacity for absorbing facts, but they emerge transformed by the categories which he powerfully imposes on the raw material into something which he can use to build his own massive, simple, impregnably fortified inner world.

Roosevelt, as a public personality, was a spontaneous, optimistic, pleasure-loving ruler who dismayed his assistants by the gay and apparently heedless abandon with which he seemed to delight in pursuing two or more totally incompatible policies, and astonished them even more by the swiftness and ease with which he managed to throw off the cares of office during the darkest and most dangerous moments. Churchill too loves pleasure, and he too lacks neither gaiety nor a capacity for exuberant self-expression, together with the habit of blithely cutting Gordian knots in a manner which often upset his experts; but he is not a frivolous man. His nature possesses a dimension of depth — and a corresponding sense of tragic possibilities, which Roosevelt's lighthearted genius instinctively passed by.

Roosevelt played the game of politics with virtuosity, and both his successes and his failures were carried off in splendid style; his performance seemed to flow with effortless skill. Churchill is acquainted with darkness as well as light. Like all inhabitants and even transient visitors of inner worlds, he gives evidence of seasons of agonized brooding and slow recovery. Roosevelt might have spoken of sweat and blood, but when Churchill offered his people tears, he spoke a word which might have been uttered by Lincoln or Mazzini or Cromwell but not Roosevelt, greathearted, generous, and perceptive as he was.

Not the herald of the bright and cloudless civilization of the future, Churchill is preoccupied by his own vivid world, and it is doubtful how far he has ever been aware of what actually goes on in the heads and hearts of others. He does not react, he acts; he does not mirror, he affects others and alters them to his own powerful measure. Writing of Dunkirk he says: "Had I at this juncture faltered at all in the leading of the nation, I should have been hurled out of office. I was sure that every Minister was ready to be killed quite soon, and have all his family and possessions destroyed, rather than give in. In this they represented the House of Commons and almost all the people. It fell to me in these coming days and months to express their sentiments on suitable occasions. This I was able to do because they were mine also. There was a white glow, overpowering, sublime, which ran through our island from end to end." And on the twenty-eighth of June of that year he told Lord Lothian, then ambassador in Washington, "Your mood should be bland and phlegmatic. No one is downhearted here."

These splendid sentences hardly do justice to his own part in creating the feeling which he describes. For Churchill is not a sensitive lens which absorbs and concentrates and reflects and amplifies the sentiments of others; unlike the European dictators, he does not play on public opinion like an instrument. In 1940 he assumed an indomitable stoutness, an unsurrendering quality on the part of his people, and carried on. If he did not represent the quintessence and epitome of what his fellow citizens feared and hoped in their hour of danger, this was because he idealized them with such intensity that in the end they approached his ideal and began to see themselves as he saw them: "the buoyant and imperturbable temper of Britain which I had the honour to express" — it was indeed, but he had a lion's share in creating it. So hypnotic was the force of his words, so strong his faith, that by the sheer intensity of his eloquence he bound his spell upon them until it seemed to them that he was indeed speaking what was in their hearts and minds. If it was there, it was largely dormant until he had awoken it within them.

After he had spoken to them in the summer of 1940 as no one has ever before or since, they conceived a new idea of themselves which their own prowess and the admiration of the world has since established as a heroic image in the history of mankind, like Thermopylae or the defeat of the Spanish Armada. They went forward into battle transformed by his words. The spirit which they found within them he had created within himself from his inner resources, and poured it into his nation, and took their vivid reaction for an original impulse on their part, which he merely had the honor to clothe in suitable words. He created a heroic mood and turned the fortunes of the Battle of Britain not by catching the mood of his surroundings (which was not indeed at any time one of craven panic or bewilderment or apathy, but was somewhat confused; stouthearted but unorganized) but by being impervious to it as he has been to so many of the passing shades and tones of which the life around him has been composed.

The peculiar quality of heroic pride and sense of the sublimity of the occasion arises in him not, as in Roosevelt, from delight in being alive and in control at a critical moment of history, in the very change and instability of things, in the infinite possibilities of the future whose very unpredictability offers endless possibilities of spontaneous moment-to-moment improvisation and large imaginative moves in harmony with the restless spirit of the time. On the contrary, it springs from a capacity for sustained introspective brooding, great depth and constancy of feeling — in particular, feeling for and fidelity to the great tradition for which he assumes a personal responsibility, a tradition which he bears upon his shoulders and must deliver, not only sound and undamaged but strengthened and embellished, to successors worthy of accepting the sacred burden.

Bismarck once said something to the effect that there was no such thing as political intuition: political genius consisted in the ability to hear the distant hoofbeat of the horse of History — and then by superhuman effort to leap and catch the horseman by the coattails. No man has ever listened for this fateful sound more eagerly than Winston Churchill, and in 1940 he made the heroic leap. "It is impossible," he writes of this time, "to quell the inward excitement which comes from a prolonged balancing of terrible things," and when the crisis finally bursts he is ready because after a lifetime of effort he has reached his goal.

The position of the Prime Minister is unique: "If he trips he must be sustained; if he makes mistakes they must be covered; if he sleeps he must not be wantonly disturbed; if he is no good he must be poleaxed," and this because he is at that moment the guardian of the "life of Britain, her message and her glory." He trusted Roosevelt utterly, "convinced that he would give up life itself, to say nothing about office, for the cause of world freedom now in such awful peril." His prose records the tension which rises and swells to the culminating moment, the Battle of Britain — "a time when it was equally good to live or die." This bright, heroic vision of the mortal danger and his will to conquer, born in the hour when defeat seemed not merely possible but probable, is the product of a burning historical imagination, feeding not upon the data of the outer but of the inner eye: the picture has a shape and simplicity which future historians will find it hard to reproduce when they seek to assess and interpret the facts soberly in the gray light of common day.

The Prime Minister was able to impose his imagination and his will upon his countrymen, and enjoy a Periclean reign, precisely because he appeared to them larger and nobler than life and lifted them to an abnormal height in a moment of crisis. It was a climate in which men do not usually like — nor ought to like — living; it demands a violent tension which, if it lasts, destroys all sense of normal perspective, over-dramatizes personal relationships, and falsifies normal values to an intolerable extent. But, in the event, it did turn a large number of inhabitants of the British Isles out of their normal selves and, by dramatizing their lives and making them seem to themselves and to each other clad in the fabulous garments appropriate to a great historic moment, transformed cowards into brave men, and so fulfilled the purpose of shining armor.

This is the kind of means by which dictators and demagogues transform peaceful populations into marching armies; it was Churchill's unique and unforgettable achievement that he created this necessary illusion within the framework of a free system without destroying or even twisting it; that he called forth spirits which did not stay to oppress and enslave the population after the hour of need had passed; that he saved the future by interpreting the present in terms of a vision of the past which did not distort or inhibit the historical development of the British people by attempting to make them realize some impossible and unattainable splendor in the name of an imaginary tradition or of an infallible, supernatural leader. Churchill was saved from this frightening nemesis of romanticism by a sufficiency of that libertarian feeling which, if it sometimes fell short of understanding the tragic aspects of modern despotisms, remained sharply perceptive — sometimes too tolerantly, but still perceptive — of what is false, grotesque, contemptible in the great frauds upon the people practiced by totalitarian regimes. Some of the sharpest and most characteristic epithets are reserved for the dictators: Hitler is "this evil man, this monstrous abortion of hatred and defeat." Franco is a "narrow-minded tyrant" of "evil qualities" holding down a "blood-drained people." No quarter is given to the Pétain regime, and its appeal to tradition and the eternal France is treated as a repellent travesty of national feeling. Stalin in 1940–1941 is "at once a callous, a crafty, and an ill-informed giant."

This very genuine hostility to usurpers, which is stronger in him than even his passion for authority and order, springs from a quality which Churchill conspicuously shares with the late President Roosevelt — uncommon love of life, aversion for the imposition of rigid disciplines upon the teeming variety of human relations, the instinctive sense of what promotes and what retards or distorts growth and vitality. But because the life which Churchill so loves presents itself to him in an historical guise as part of the pageant of tradition, his method of constructing historical narrative, the distribution of emphasis, the assignment of relative importance to persons and events, the theory of history, the architecture of the narrative, the structure of the sentences, the words themselves, are elements in an historical revival as fresh, as original, and as idiosyncratic as the neoclassicism of the Renaissance or the Regency. To complain that this is not contemporary, and therefore in some way less true, less responsive to modern needs, than the noncommital, neutral glass and plastic of those objective historians who regard facts and only facts as interesting and, worse still, all facts as equally interesting — what is this but craven pedantry and blindness?

The differences between the President and the Prime Minister were at least in one respect something more than the obvious differences of national character, education, and even temperament. For all his sense of history, his large, untroubled, easygoing style of life, his unshakable feeling of personal security, his natural assumption of being at home in the great world far beyond the confines of his own country, Roosevelt was a typical child of the twentieth century and of the New World; while Churchill, for all his love of the present hour, his unquenchable appetite for new knowledge, his sense of the technological possibilities of our time, and the restless roaming of his fancy in considering how they might be most imaginatively applied, despite his enthusiasm for Basic English, or the siren suit which so upset his hosts in Moscow — despite all this, Churchill remains a European of the nineteenth century.

The difference is deep, and accounts for a great deal in the incompatibility of outlook between him and the President of the United States, whom he admired so much and whose great office he held in awe. Something of the fundamental unlikeness between America and Europe, and perhaps between the twentieth century and the nineteenth, seemed to be crystallized in this remarkable interplay. It may perhaps be that the twentieth century is to the nineteenth as the nineteenth was to the eighteenth century. Talleyrand once made the well-known observation that those who had not lived under the *ancien régime* did not know what true *douceur de la vie* had been. And indeed, from our distant vantage point, this is clear: the earnest, romantic young men of the early part of the nineteenth century seemed systematically unable to understand or to like the attitude to life of the most civilized representatives of the prerevolutionary world, particularly in France, where the break was sharpest; the subtlety, the irony, the minute vision, the perception of and concentration upon fine differences in character, in style, the preoccupation with barely perceptible dissimilarities of hue, the extreme sensibility which makes the life of even so "progressive" and forward-looking a man as Diderot so unbridgeably different from the larger and simpler vision of the Romantics, is something which the nineteenth century lacked the historical perspective to understand.

Suppose that Shelley had met and talked with Voltaire, what would he have felt? He would most probably have been profoundly shocked — shocked by the seemingly limited vision, the smallness of the field of awareness, the apparent triviality and finickiness, the almost spinsterish elaboration of Voltaire's malice, the preoccupation with tiny units, the subatomic texture of experience; he would have felt horror or pity before such wanton blindness to the large moral and spiritual issues of his own day — causes whose universal scope and significance painfully agitated the best and most awakened minds; he might have thought him wicked, but even more he would have thought him contemptible, too sharp, too small, too mean, grotesquely and unworthily obscene, prone to titter on the most sacred occasions, in the holiest places.

And Voltaire, in his turn, would very probably have been dreadfully bored, unable to see good cause for so much ethical eloquence; he would have looked with a cold and hostile eye on all this moral excitement: the magnificent Saint-Simonian vision of one world (which so stirred the left-wing young men half a century later), altering in shape and becoming integrated into a neatly organized man-made whole by the application of powerfully concentrated, scientific, technical, and spiritual resources, would to him have seemed a dreary and monotonous desert, too homogeneous, too flavorless, too unreal, apparently unconscious of those small, half-concealed but crucial distinctions and incongruities which gave individuality and savor to experience, without which there could be no civilized vision, no wit, no conversation, certainly no art deriving from a refined and fastidious culture. The moral vision of the nineteenth century would have seemed to him a dull, blurred, coarse instrument unable to focus those pin points of concentrated light, those short-lived patterns of sound and color, whose infinite variety as they linger or flash past are comedy and tragedy — are the substance of personal relations and of worldly wisdom, of politics, of history, and of art.

The reason for this failure of communication was not a mere change in the point of view, but the kind of vision which divided the two centuries. The microscopic vision of the eighteenth century was succeeded by the macroscopic eye of the nineteenth. The latter saw much more widely, saw in universal or at least in European terms; it saw the contours of great mountain ranges where the eighteenth century discerned, however sharply and perceptively, only the veins and cracks and different shades of but a portion of the mountainside. The object of vision of the eighteenth century was smaller and its eye was closer to the object. The enormous moral issues of the nineteenth century were not within the field of its acutely discriminating gaze: that was the devastating difference which the Great French Revolution had made, and it led to something not necessarily better or worse, uglier or more beautiful, profounder or more shallow, but to a situation which above all was different in kind.

Something not unlike this same chasm divides America from Europe (and the twentieth century from the nineteenth). The American vision is larger and more generous; its thought transcends, despite the parochialism of its means of expression, the barriers of nationality and race and differences of outlook, in a big, sweeping, single view. It notices things rather than persons, and sees the world (those who saw it in this fashion in the nineteenth century were considered Utopian eccentrics) in terms of rich, infinitely moldable raw material, waiting to be constructed and planned in order to satisfy a world-wide human craving for happiness or goodness or wisdom. And therefore to it the differences and conflicts which divide Europeans in so violent a fashion must seem petty, irrational, and sordid, not worthy of self-respecting, morally conscious individuals and nations; ready, in fact, to be swept away in favor of a simpler and grander view of the powers and tasks of modern man.

To Europeans this American attitude, the large vista possible only for those who live on mountain heights or vast and level plains affording an unbroken view, seems curiously flat, without subtlety or color, at times appearing to lack the entire dimension of depth, certainly without that immediate reaction to fine distinctions with which perhaps only those who live in valleys are endowed, and so America, which knows so much, to them seems to understand too little, to miss the central point. This does not, of course, apply to every American or European — there are natural Americans among the natives of Europe and vice versa — but it seems to characterize the most typical representatives of these disparate cultures.

In some respects Roosevelt half-consciously understood and did not wholly condemn this attitude on the part of Europeans; and even more clearly Churchill is in many respects in instinctive sympathy with the American view of life. But by and large they do represent different outlooks, and the very high degree to which they were able to understand and admire each other's quality is a tribute to the extraordinary power of imagination and delight in the variety of life on the part of both. Each was to the other not merely an ally, the admired leader of a great people, but a symbol of a tradition and a civilization; from the unity of their differences they hoped for a regeneration of the Western world.

Roosevelt was intrigued by the Russian Sphinx; Churchill instinctively recoiled from its alien and to him unattractive attributes. Roosevelt on the whole, thought that he could cajole Russia and even induce her to be assimilated into the great society which would embrace mankind; Churchill, on the whole, remained skeptical.

Roosevelt was imaginative, optimistic, Episcopalian, self-confident, cheerful, empirically-minded, fearless, and steeped in the idea of social progress; he believed that with enough energy and spirit anything could be achieved by man; he shrank as much as any English schoolboy from probing underneath the surface, and saw vast affinities between the peoples in the world, out of which a new, freer, and richer order could somehow be built. Churchill was imaginative and steeped in history, more serious, more intent, more concentrated, more preoccupied, and felt very deeply the eternal differences which would make such a structure difficult of attainment. He believed in institutions and permanent characters of races and classes and types of individuals. His government was organized on clear principles; his personal private office was run in a sharply disciplined manner. His habits, though unusual, were regular. He believed in a natural, a social, almost a metaphysical order which it was neither possible nor desirable to upset.

Roosevelt believed in flexibility, improvisation, the fruitfulness of using persons and resources in an infinite variety of new and unexpected ways; his bureaucracy was somewhat chaotic, perhaps deliberately so. His own office was not tidily organized, he practiced a highly personal form of government. He maddened the advocates of institutional authority, but it is doubtful whether he could have achieved his ends in any other way.

These dissimilarities of outlook went deep, but both were large enough in scope and both were genuine visions, not narrowed and distorted by personal idiosyncrasies and those disparities of moral standard which so fatally divided Wilson, Lloyd George, and Clemenceau. The President and the Prime Minister often disagreed; their ideals and their methods were widely different; in some of the memoirs and gossip of Roosevelt's entourage much has been made of this; but the point was that the discussion was conducted on a level of which both heads of government were conscious. They may have opposed but they never wished to wound each other; they may have issued contrary instructions but they never bickered; when they compromised, as they so often did, they did so without a sense of bitterness or defeat, but in response to the demands of history or one another's traditions and personality.

Each appeared to the other in a romantic light high above the battles of allies or subordinates; their meetings and correspondence were occasions to which both consciously rose; they were royal cousins and felt pride in this relationship, tempered by a sharp and sometimes amused, but never ironical, perception of the other's peculiar qualities. The relationship born during the great historical upheaval, somewhat aggrandized by its solemnity, never flagged or degenerated, but retained a combination of formal dignity and exuberant high spirits which can scarcely ever before have bound the heads of states. Each was personally fascinated not so much by the other, as by the idea of the other, and infected him by his own peculiar brand of high spirits.

The relationship was made genuine by something more than even the solid community of interest or personal and official respect or admiration — namely, by the peculiar degree to which they liked each other's delight in the oddities and humors of life and their own active part in it. This was a unique personal bond, which Harry Hopkins understood and encouraged to the fullest degree. Roosevelt's sense of fun was perhaps the lighter, Churchill's a trifle grimmer. But it was some-

thing which they shared with each other and with few, if any, statesmen outside the Anglo-American orbit; their staffs sometimes ignored
or misunderstood it, and it gave a most singular quality to their association.

Roosevelt's public utterances differ by a whole world from the dramatic masterpieces of Churchill, but they are not incompatible with
them in spirit or in substance. Roosevelt has not left us his own account
of his world as he saw it; and perhaps he lived too much from day to
day to be temperamentally attracted to the performance of such a task.
But both were thoroughly aware of their commanding position in the
history of the modern world, and Churchill's account of his stewardship is written in full consciousness of this responsibility.

It is a great occasion, and he treats it with corresponding solemnity.
Like a great actor — perhaps the last of his kind — upon the stage of
history, he speaks his memorable lines with a large, unhurried and
stately utterance in a blaze of light, as is appropriate to a man who
knows that his work and his person will remain the object of scrutiny
and judgment to many generations. His narrative is a great public performance and has the attribute of formal magnificence. The words, the
splendid phrases, the sustained quality of feeling, are a unique medium
which convey his vision of himself and of his world, and will inevitably,
like all that he has said and done, reinforce the famous public image,
which is no longer distinguishable from the inner essence and the true
nature of the author: of a man larger than life, composed of bigger and
simpler elements than ordinary men, a gigantic historical figure during
his own lifetime, superhumanly bold, strong, and imaginative, one of
the two greatest men of action his nation has produced, an orator of
prodigious powers, the savior of his country, a legendary hero who
belongs to myth as much as to reality, the largest human being of our
time.

I X

Questions of Faith

Science and religion have had two shocking collisions in the At-
lantic's *century, and the first occurred in* 1859 *with the publica-*
tion of The Origin of Species by Charles Darwin. *The book*
dealt a staggering blow to those of orthodox belief. Asa Gray, who
reviewed the volume in July 1860, would clearly have been happier, as a critic puts it, if one could take up the Darwinian theory
at the point where existing species were introduced, relying on the
doctrine of special creation to get the show going. Louis Agassiz,
the most distinguished of American scientists, opposed Darwin
with all the brilliance he could muster, and because of his influence other contributors were at first standoffish. But the elder
Henry James and his son William (who reviewed Darwin's sequel,
The Variation of Animals and Plants under Domestication) *played*
the devil's advocate, and the Atlantic *had openly become a convert*
to Darwinism before Darwin's death.

We cannot now rekindle the intensity and animosity of the con-
flict; what we can testify to is the deep and troubled seriousness
with which it was taken by writers and readers alike.

It is important to remember that in questions of faith the Atlan-
tic *has never feared to be unorthodox. The Autocrat was not ortho-*
dox, neither was Emerson, and if we praised the popular Henry
Ward Beecher it was certainly not because his views were conventional. Unitarians were admittedly strong in our councils, but they,
too, could be put to the test, for the magazine was fundamentally
nonsectarian.

Our Puritan heritage must account in part for the magazine's
distrust of Roman Catholicism; the suspicions shipped over from
England and from time to time expressed in our columns were not
only those of the parochial Yankee but of Protestants generally who
have grown alarmed as the power of the Church has waxed in the
land. As the incoming tides of Irish and Italian immigrants flooded

into New England, it was only natural that resentment would be felt by the natives who in a matter of decades were rivaled and dispossessed of political control. This resentment has undoubtedly animated the distaste for Catholicism.

Under the editorship of Ellery Sedgwick (1908–1938) the magazine seemed almost to enjoy needling the Church, and articles by renegade priests, usually anonymous, were a recurring feature. Yet in fairness it must be added that this same editor, a profound admirer of Governor Alfred E. Smith, drew out of him in the heat of the presidential campaign the most lucid and loyal statement that has yet been written by an American Catholic in high office.

Our questions of faith today are not as single-minded as they were in 1860 when Goldwin Smith was so troubled by the decline in influence of organized religion; for us such questions have been broadened and intensified by the release of atomic energy and by the awful wonder: Does man have the moral strength to prevent atomic destruction? This is the second great collision.

The Mystic's Experience of God

by RUFUS M. JONES

A Quaker of light and leading, during his four decades as a professor of philosophy at Haverford College, Rufus M. Jones was the best loved and most quoted Friend in America.

NOVEMBER 1921

According to those who have been there, the experience that we call mystical is charged with the conviction of real, direct contact and commerce with God. It is the almost universal testimony of those who are mystics that they find God through their experience. John Tauler says that in his best moments of "devout prayer and the uplifting of the mind to God," he experiences "the pure presence of God" in his own soul; but he adds that all he can tell others about the experience is "as poor and unlike it as the point of a needle is to the heavens above us."

There are many different degrees of intensity, concentration, and conviction in the experiences of different individual mystics, and also in the various experiences of the same individual from time to time. There has been a tendency in most studies of mysticism to regard the state of ecstasy as *par excellence* mystical experience. That is, however, a grave mistake. The calmer, more meditative, less emotional, less ecstatic experiences of God possess greater constructive value for life and character than do ecstatic experiences which presuppose a peculiar psychical frame and disposition. The seasoned Quaker, in the corporate hush and stillness of a silent meeting, is far removed from ecstasy, but he is not the less convinced that he is meeting with God.

The more normal, expansive mystical experiences come apparently when the personal self is at its best. Its powers and capacities are raised to an unusual unity and fused together. The whole being, with its accumulated submerged life, *finds itself*. The process of preparing for any high achievement is a severe and laborious one; but nothing seems easier in the moment of success than is the accomplishment for which the life has been prepared. There comes to be formed within the person what Aristotle called "a dexterity of soul," so that the person does with ease what he has become skilled to do. A mystic of the fourteenth century stated the principle in these words: "It is my aim to be to the Eternal God what a man's hand is to a man."

There are many human experiences which carry a man up to levels where he has not usually been before, and where he finds himself possessed of insight and energies that he had hardly suspected were his until that moment. One leaps to his full height when the right inner spring is reached. We are quite familiar with the way in which instinctive tendencies in us, and emotions both egoistic and social, become organized under a group of ideas and ideals into a single system, which we call a sentiment, such as love, or patriotism, or devotion to truth. It forms slowly, and one hardly realizes that it has formed until some occasion unexpectedly brings it into full operation and we find ourselves able with perfect ease to overcome the most powerful inhibitory and opposing instincts and habits, which until then had usually controlled us. Literary and artistic geniuses supply us with many instances in which, in a sudden flash, the crude material at hand is shot through with vision, and the complicated plot of a drama, the full significance of a character, or the complete glory of a statue stands revealed, as if, to use R. L. Stevenson's illustration, a jinni had brought it on a golden tray as a gift from another world. Abraham Lincoln, striking off in a few intense minutes his Gettysburg address, as beautiful in style and perfect in form as anything in human literature, is as good an illustration as we need of the way in which a highly organized person, by a kindling flash, has at his hand all the moral and spiritual gains of a lifetime.

We come now to the central question of our consideration: Do mystical experiences settle anything? Are they purely subjective and one-sided, or do they prove to have objective reference and so to be two-sided? Do they take the experiment across the chasm that separates "self" from "other"?

The most striking effect of such experience is not new fact-knowledge, not new items of empirical information, but new moral energy, heightened conviction, increased caloric quality, enlarged spiritual vision, an unusual radiant power of life. In short, the whole personality, in the case of the constructive mystics, appears to be raised to a new level of life and to have gained from somewhere many calories of life-feeding, spiritual substance. We are quite familiar with the way in which adrenalin suddenly flushes into the physical system and adds a new and incalculable power to brain and muscle. Under its stimulus a man can carry out a piano when the house is on fire. May not, perhaps, some energy, from some Source with which our spirits are allied, flush our inner being with forces and powers by which we can be fortified to stand the universe and more than stand it?

I believe that mystical experiences do, in the long run, expand our knowledge of God, and do succeed in verifying themselves. Mysticism is a sort of spiritual protoplasm, which underlies, as a basic substance, much that is best in religion, in ethics, and in life itself. It has generally been the mystic, the prophet, the seer, who have spotted out new ways forward in the jungle of our world or lifted our race to new spiritual levels. Their experiences have in some way equipped them for unusual tasks, have given supplies of energy to them which their neighbors did not have, and have apparently brought them into vital correspondence with dimensions and regions of reality that others miss. The proof that they have found God, or at least a domain of spiritual reality, is to be seen rather in the moral and spiritual fruits which test out and verify the experience.

Consciousness of beauty or of truth or of goodness baffles analysis as much as consciousness of God does. These values have no objective standing ground in current psychology. They are not things in the world of space. They submit to no adequate causal explanation. They have their ground of being in some other kind of world than that of the mechanical order, a world composed of quantitative masses of matter in motion. These experiences of value, which are as real for experience as stone walls are, make very clear the fact that there are depths and capacities in the nature of the normal human mind which we do not usually recognize, and of which we have scant and imperfect accounts in our textbooks. Our minds taken in their full range, in other words, have some sort of contact and relationship with an eternal nature of things far deeper than atoms and molecules.

Only very slowly and gradually has the race learned, through finite symbols and temporal forms, to interpret beauty and truth and goodness, which, in their essence, are as ineffable and indescribable as is the mystic's experience of God. Plato often speaks as if he had high moments of experience when he rose to the naked vision of beauty — beauty "alone, separate, and eternal," as he says. But, as a matter of fact, however exalted heavenly and enduring beauty may be in its essence, we know *what it is* only as it appears in fair forms of objects, of body, of soul, of actions; in harmonious blending of sounds or colors; in well-ordered or happily combined groupings of many aspects in one unity, which is as it ought to be. Truth and moral goodness always transcend our attainments, and we sometimes feel that the very end and goal of life is the pursuit of that truth or that goodness which eye hath not seen nor ear heard. But whatever truth we do attain, or whatever goodness we do achieve, is always concrete. Truth is just this one more added fact that resists all attempt to doubt it. Goodness is just this simple everyday deed that reveals a heroic spirit and a brave venture of faith in the midst of difficulties.

So, too, the mystic knowledge of God is not some esoteric communication, supplied through trance or ecstasy; it is an intuitive personal touch with God, felt to be the essentially real, the bursting forth of an intense love for Him, which heightens all the capacities and activities of life, followed by the slow laboratory effects which verify it. "All I could never be" now *is*. It seems possible to stand the universe — even to do something toward the transformation of it. And if the experience does not prove that the soul has found God, it at least does this: it makes the soul feel that proofs of God are wholly unnecessary.

The Nun and the Dramatist

Letters of GEORGE BERNARD SHAW

At the time of her death in 1953 it was said of Dame Laurentia McLachlan, the Abbess of Stanbrook, that "she gave herself to everyone who needed her help; she was a person without frontiers." The letters which passed between herself and George Bernard Shaw are the revelation of a friendship in which the faith of each was put to the test.

JULY 1956

On October 1, 1924, Shaw made Dame Laurentia a gift of a copy of *St. Joan* complete with the Preface which as yet she had not seen, since it formed an independent essay written only in May 1924, some time after the play itself had been produced. "I am in possession of my own *St. Joan*," she wrote to Sydney Cockerell, "adorned with the inscription

'To Sister Laurentia from Brother Bernard'! Mr. Shaw is becoming quite monastic. I have thanked him and said that if I thought I had anything to say after reading the Preface, I should ask leave to say it."

Much of the Preface could not but win Dame Laurentia's whole-hearted approval. She was not likely to quarrel with Shaw's assertion that "there is no Rationalism so rationalistic as Catholic Rationalism." As a Catholic she was as free as he was to believe or disbelieve in private revelations, to which only a purely human or probable authority is attached; and no Catholic should ever be deceived into thinking that the saints and angels of St. Joan's or any other saint's visions, clothed in rich garments and visible to the eye in bodies which they do not in reality possess, are anything but symbols whose appearance accords with the ideas of the person who sees them, or those of the painters of his day. One of the greatest visions — that of the four living creatures round about the throne in the Apocalypse — has largely been borrowed by St. John from the prophet Ezekiel, who himself adapted the image from the gigantic bas-reliefs of the Assyrian palaces familiar to the eyes of every Jew during the Captivity. God transmits His light through the mists of familiar surroundings and individual outlook, and revelations have to be understood in a spiritual sense. It was precisely because St. Joan herself took her visions too literally that she misinterpreted their real significance. With so much Dame Laurentia was in agreement. But when Shaw went on to urge that Catholicism was not Catholic enough, since the Church's blunders deter Freethinkers from joining it and a Church which has no place for Freethinkers has neither future in modern culture nor belief in the validity of its own doctrines, Dame Laurentia immediately challenged him to define what he meant by Freethought. She suspected that his Freethought was synonymous with false thought — truth alone makes a man free.

Unfortunately her letters to Bernard Shaw cannot now be recovered, and in only two instances did she keep rough drafts. The gist of her letter of thanks for the gift of *St. Joan* may, however, be gathered from one she wrote on January 2, 1925, to Sydney Cockerell. Although in point of time it was written after G.B.S.'s letter, it will be necessary to transcribe it first in order to appreciate his references:

The enclosed came on Christmas Day from Brother Bernard — a remarkable letter which pleases me greatly in spite of its heresies. . . . The first paragraph of the second sheet [the paragraph beginning "I am quite aware . . ."] refers to my remark about the Church's objection to

Freethinking. I said that to my mind no thinker was so free as a Catholic — the limitations being in the direction of good sense and ensuring *right* thinking, that it is not freedom to be able to think contrary to objective truth. . . . Then I could not resist quoting a remark made to me a few days before by Dom Bouré, the French monk who lives here. Speaking of these things and Protestantism, he said: "Ma Mère, le protestantisme démolit la cervelle"! I thought I could not deprive Brother Bernard of that fine thought. The reference to the Book of Wisdom means that I had referred him to that Book, viii, 9–15, for the passage chosen as a lesson on St. Joan's feast. I think you will agree that the choice could scarcely be bettered. I shall not bother Br. B. again, but when he next shakes my bars I shall make some further remarks.

Her letter to Shaw had been accompanied with a copy of a small book entitled *The Godly Instructions and Prayers of Blessed Thomas More Written in the Tower of London 1535* recently printed at Stanbrook in preparation for the tercentenary of the monastery's foundation. His reply, the first letter of a series extending over a period of twenty-six years until his death in 1950, is here given in its entirety.

My dear Sister Laurentia

In reading heathen literature like mine you must always allow for the special meaning given by the Church to the word supernatural. Also you must remember that I am addressing an audience not exclusively Catholic, including not only Protestants and Modernists of all sorts, but also Indians and Orientals whose religion has an iconography entirely different to the Christian one. Whether God makes different iconographies for different peoples, or whether he lets us all make our own iconography, it is clear that to a pious Hindoo or Moslem St. Michael and St. Catherine mean nothing, just as to a Worcester dairymaid Allah and Brahma mean nothing. Christ in His metaphor of the tares and the wheat, has given us a very plain warning to let Allah and Brahma and Vishnu alone, as if our rash missionaries pluck them out of the Arab and Hindu soul, they will pluck all the religion out of that soul as well. This explains why missionary converts are usually undesirables.

It was therefore necessary for me to present Joan's visions in such a way as to make them completely independent of the iconography attached to her religion. But I did not therefore deprive the visions of their miraculous character. If she had been born at the other side of the Ural mountains she would have seen, not St. Michael, but Mahomet or

Buddha or Vishnu or Lao-tse. She would perhaps have spat at the blessed Michael just as, being what she was, a Western Christian, she would have spat at "the accurst Mahound." God adapts his method of revelation to the powers and faculties and knowledge of his creatures. We cannot, for instance, believe that God would have mocked Joan with a written revelation which she could not read; yet that would not be a more inconsiderate proceeding than sending a messenger in whose existence she did not believe. The divine inspiration takes the path of least resistance; and whether you believe that the messengers are real persons or illusions — and I have to leave this an open question to retain the interest of the modernists, who would otherwise reject the inspiration with the objectivity of the vision in the same violent regurgitation — the inspiration loses none of its divinity either way.

This does not please the many Catholics who are not really catholic at all, as they cling consciously or unconsciously to the doctrine of exclusive salvation, which carries with it the doctrine of exclusive revelation; but if I wrote in terms of this doctrine I should, from their point of view, be calling, not sinners, but the righteous to salvation; and my book would reach no further than the penny lives of the saints which they sell in the Churches in Ireland. I want my sound to go out into all lands.

I am quite aware that Catholicism has produced much more audacious philosophic speculation than Protestantism. What is more, there is no Rationalism so rationalistic as Catholic Rationalism. When the monk said that Protestantism destroys the brain I think he meant that Protestantism leads men to break through the limits of reason, just as the mathematicians did when, finding they could get no further with possible quantities, they assumed impossible ones like the square root of minus X. I exhausted rationalism when I got to the end of my second novel at the age of twenty-four, and should have come to a dead stop if I had not proceeded to purely mystical assumptions. I thus perhaps destroyed my brain; but inspiration filled up the void; and I got on better than ever. I suspect that monk's orthodoxy. *"Cucullus non facit monachum."*

I am delighted to learn that my St. Joan is yours also. It sets my mind completely at ease: I know now that I have done the trick. The passage from the Book of Wisdom amazed me. For having chosen it may all the sins of the Church be forgiven!

Thanks for the St. Thomas More book, which is excellently printed. Some bits of it are very good; but the Psalm part of it is a mere literary exercise, quite out of character with his personal attitude toward his enemies. To make a clean breast of it to you, I do not like the Psalms: they seem to me to be the classic examples of fool's comfort. Comforting people by telling them what they would like to believe when both parties know that it is not true is sometimes humane, and always to be let off with a light penance as between two frail mortals; but it should not be admitted to the canon. I like Wisdom ever so much better.

I must stop, or I shall begin by kicking my cloven hoof too obviously for your dignity and peace; but I mean well, and find great solace in writing to you instead of to all the worldly people whose letters are howling to be answered.

On the 26th we sail to Madeira for six weeks or thereabouts. When we are next touring your neighborhood I shall again shake your bars and look longingly at the freedom at the other side of them.

Faithfully
G. Bernard Shaw

But if Bernard Shaw was deaf to the appeal of the Psalms, he showed himself surprisingly alive to the implications of the contemplative life and to the freedom paradoxically symbolized by the double iron grille. Chesterton said of him: "There is always something about him which suggests that in a sweeter and more solid civilization he would have been a great saint. He would have been a saint of a sternly ascetic, perhaps of a sternly negative type. But he has this strange note of the saint in him: that he is literally unworldly." Indeed, one is led to wonder how far the man who discarded the George of his Christian name and became the Brother Bernard of Dame Laurentia's letters was secretly influenced by admiration for his namesake, the Abbot of Clairvaux, in his choice of a vegetarian regime Cistercian in its austerity, his love of our Lady, and the government of his thought by what he termed "mystical assumptions." The coolness and effrontery originating from his extreme shyness, the love of shocking lion-hunters with outrageous remarks, and — most Irish of all his traits — the levity with which he disguised his deepest feelings found no place before Dame Laurentia. Brilliant, disconcerting, and dynamic he could not help being; yet his fundamental humility, tact, and quick understanding became more and more apparent in his relations with her as the years passed.

In 1931 Shaw set out on his journey to the Holy Land, Egypt, and Italy. To a letter from Dame Laurentia wishing him Godspeed and asking for a little stone from Jerusalem, he sent a note on March 15, 1931, to assure her he had not forgotten her petition: "Just a hurried line in the middle of my packing as I leave Jerusalem for Nazareth. Later on I will write fully about my pilgrimage and the extraordinary difficulty in finding a real relic for you in this City of Destruction where relics are thrust on you for sale (by Jews) at every corner."

Two days later the promise to write a real letter was splendidly fulfilled. Accompanied by two snapshots of Jerusalem and Bethlehem not too happily focused, and by a portrait of the writer on board ship with his fellow traveler, Dean Inge, entitled "The Temptation: The Devil and the Dean of St. Paul's. Marseilles. March 4, 1931," the letter, written on green paper selected presumably in honor of St. Patrick, occupies thirteen sheets roughly nine inches by six in measurement. The chief, if not the only, record of Bernard Shaw's impressions of his tour throughout the Holy Land, this very personal document is a masterpiece of exact observation from start to finish.

St. Patrick's Day in Damascus, 1931

DEAR SISTER LAURENTIA

This Holy Land is in a queer situation from the Crusader's point of view, which is officially your point of view. The British representative in Jerusalem is also the representative, precisely, of Pontius Pilate; and when Communist Messiahs turn up, as they actually do from time to time under Russian influences, he is bound to handle the case on Pilatical lines. What would any medieval Christian saint — or say Richard Coeur de Lion — say if miraculously resuscitated in Jerusalem today? Saladin and the followers of the accurst Mahound vanquished at last by the Christian British Empire. The circumcised crucifiers of Christ scattered through the ghettos of Europe. The Cross triumphant over all the Promised Land, over Christ's birthplace, over his sepulchre, over the Mount of the Beatitudes and over the bloodstained plain (which Christ overlooked from that Mount) on which Saladin smashed the last effort of the Crusaders to resist him, over Galilee and Samaria, Bethlehem, Nazareth, Capernaum, over the waters on which he walked and the hillsides from which he preached, over Nain and Cana and Bethany, over Jordan in which he was baptized, and the unknown Golgotha on which he was duly executed according to the official routine by the predecessor of Mr. Keith Roach.

So far, praised be God, Richard would say, probably adding a stentorian Hep, hep, hep!

But when Richard was further informed that the use England had made of its victory was to hand over all that sacred territory to the descendants and co-religionists of Saladin and to those of Annas and Caiphas, having promised it to both for their help in the war, and that Pontius now had his hands full with the job of keeping the peace between them, he would surely either start a new crusade or return to his tomb in disgust with a world gone entirely mad.

I ask myself whether I shall persuade Sister Laurentia to get a hundred days indulgence, a tailor-made short skirt, gaiter boots, a Fair Isle pull-over, a smart waterproof, a field glass and camera, a brown sun umbrella lined with red, and a Revelation suitcase, and hasten hither to see for herself what she has imagined at Stanbrook. I leave the question unanswered; but I will tell you what might happen to you because it has happened to me.

You would enter the Holy Land at night under a strong impression made on you in Egypt, not by the Tutankhamen trash which the tourists are now mobbing, but by something seen under the pyramids. A pyramid is just as big as its royal builder is old; and it is always finished. If he dies a baby, there is his monument ready for him, like this: △. If he grows

up, his tomb grows with him △ △ △ and so on, if he lives

as long as Cheops, to △.

There was a redhaired queen who made a tomb for herself and her daughters, deep under tons of pyramid and rock, and set two great artists, Rahay a painter and Yentaf a sculptor, to work in it. Whether the redhaired one and her brood were very fine ladies, or whether the two fine artists made fine ladies of them I do not know; but when you see that row of sculptured women come alive in a hundred candle power electric sunlight without a shadow of death or fear on their shining faces and pleasantly courteous eyes or a line or contour in their whole bodies that is not exquisite, and when you turn to their magnificently designed portraits on the wall, the impression you receive is beyond description in our lower language, as of an order of beings completely redeemed from sin and vulgarity and all the plagues of our degradation, and yet not in the least geniuses, as Michael Angelo would have made them, but girls whom you might enlist for Stanbrook without expecting them to excel in doing as well as in being. You might question their vocation on the ground that they seem to have no religion nor to need any, having achieved excellence and being content to leave it at that; but the impression would be all the more astonishing. And that to those who served them fifty tons of solid stone seemed as easy to move and handle as a little water in a spoon, gets far beyond our miracles which are wondered at as miracles and taken as divine testimonies, and lifts us into a region in which the miraculous is no longer miraculous but gigantically normal, and immortality a thing to be achieved in a turn of the hand.

Under such impressions you find yourself in the Holy Land by night, with strange new constellations all over the sky and the old ones all topsy turvy, but with the stars soft and large and down quite close overhead in a sky which you feel to be of a deep and lovely blue. When the light comes you have left the land of Egypt with its endlessly flat Delta utterly behind, and are in a hilly country, with patches of cultivation wrested from the omnipresent stones, which you instantly recognize with a strange emotion which intensifies when you see a small boy coming down one of the patches, and presently, when he has passed away, a bigger boy of about thirteen, beginning to think, and at last, when he too has vanished, a young man, very grave and somewhat troubled, all three being dressed just as Christ dressed. (Here I break off, to resume on the night of the 20th, between Cyprus and Rhodes, at sea.) The appearance of a woman with an infant in her arms takes on the quality of a vision. On this first hour you do not improve. It gives you the feeling that here Christ lived and grew up, and that here Mary bore him and reared him, and that there is no land on earth quite like it.

Later on the guides try to be more exact. This, they tell you, is the stable in the inn. This is the carpenter shop. This is the upper chamber where the Last Supper was served. You know that they are romancing — that there is not a scrap of evidence for the possible identifications and that no inn or stable ever existed in a natural cavern in the limestone rock without light or fresh air. In Nazareth you know that Mary used the well in the street because there was (and is) no other well in the town to use; but the water she drew is gone, and the new water, with taps affixed by the British mandatory Government, is anybody's and everybody's water. Everything else in Nazareth except its natural beauty as a hill town is a fraud, meanly commemorated by an unattractive and unimpressive church. But for these frauds every stone in Nazareth would be sacred with possibilities. Because one muddy bend of the Jordan is labeled as the spot on which the dove descended, the whole river is desecrated to make trade for the stall that sells the mud in bottles. I swam in the lake of Tiberias with a pleasant sense that this, at least, was Christ's lake on which nobody could stake out the track on which he walked or the site from which the miraculous draught of fishes was hauled. It is better to have Christ everywhere than somewhere, especially where he probably wasnt.

The hills rise almost into mountains over the train to Jerusalem, which winds between them so sinuously that you can see its tail from the window. When you arrive you are surprised: the place has a flourishing modern suburban air, and the new fashionable villa-land is mentioned as The New Jerusalem. When your very modern hotel has completed your disenchantment you make for the old Jerusalem and the church of the Holy Sepulchre. And the only possible comment on it is that of Dean Inge (he is with us on this trip) "Why seek ye the living among the dead? He is not here." (When Dean Inge says the right thing it is so very right that he is privileged to say a hundred wrong things that dont matter.) A sort of case can be made for the sepulchre: it is at least possible that what remains of the chamber in the rock after its smashing up by the Moslem persecutions may be the family vault of Joseph of Arimathea; but when on the same floor a few yards off they show you Calvary (not a hill) with the sockets of the three crosses, it is irresistibly revealed to you that Saint Helena was a humbug who, when the court was ordered to turn Christian, was quite determined to outshine the Queen of Heaven by a galaxy of visions and miracles that would show the world that Roman queens would enter the new temples as goddesses and not as Syrian peasants cradling their infants in mangers. I know that sort of woman almost as well as you must. I have seen her court in the mosaics of Ravenna, where the attempt of the imperial court ladies to look pious is ludicrously unsuccessful.

The church of the Holy Sepulchre, to eyes accustomed to western architecture of the same period, is a second rate affair; and the squabbles of the sects over their "rights" in it are not edifying. I duly squeezed myself into the sepulchre, and tipped the queerly robed priest who touched my hands with oil to the extent of five piastres, looking as credulous as I could so as not to hurt his feelings; but my thought was that you would be disappointed. For the rest of the day I damned Jerusalem up hill and down dale; and when they took me to the Mount of Olives (practically oliveless) and showed me the famous view of the city my only comment was "Just like Buxton." But one's appreciation is more complex than that. When you stand on the stone from which the Ascension took place you feel at the same moment everything that the legend means you to feel and a purely comic amusement at the notion of Jesus going up to the highest attainable point as a taking-off place for his celestial flight. Your faith and your tourist's observation jostle one another in the queerest fashion.

Next day I discovered Jerusalem. I went to the great plain of stone on which the Temple stood, and on which the Mosque of Omar (who didnt build it) stands. And there I found the charm and sanctity of Jerusalem. Christ has been worshiped in both the mosques; Omar was a man after God's own heart; and Mahomet's horse sprang to heaven with him from the great rock which the Mosque of Omar enshrines, and which is a nobly beautiful building in spite of the utterly anachronistic Corinthian capitals of the red pillars of granite which bother one all over the Holy Land, and which are so Roman and common. The Kaiser gilt the Corinthian heavily so that they might hit you harder in the eye. Mahomet respected Christ and taught his followers to do the same; and it is perhaps the failure of the Christians to respect Mahomet equally that makes Islam and Israel more impressive in the east than Christendom. Still, the history of the place is such a record of iconoclasms, massacres, persecutions, spoliations, demolitions, and delendings (in Cato's sense) by Turks, Romans, and any conqueror who happened to come along, that the only general verdict possible is that of the King of Brobdingnag. God must feel sick when he looks at Jerusalem. I fancy he consoles himself by turning to Stanbrook.

You asked me for a relic from Calvary. But St. Helena's Calvary is only a spot on a church pavement, jealously guarded, and with nothing removable about it. Where the real Calvary is nobody knows; for the hills outside the city are innumerable. The alleged Via Dolorosa I traversed in a motor car hooting furiously at the children to get out of the way. The praetorium can be reasonably identified as in the palace of Herod, which Titus kept as a fortress for his garrison when he as nearly as possible left not one stone on another of the rest of the city; but as you cannot tell where Calvary was you cannot tell the way from the praetorium to it.

So off I went to Bethlehem, a beautifully situated hill town; and from the threshold of the Church of the Nativity I picked up a little stone, a scrap of the limestone rock which certainly existed when the feet of Jesus pattered about on it and the feet of Mary pursued him to keep him in order; for he was a most inconsiderate boy when his family was concerned, as you would realize if you traveled over the distance (at least a day's journey without a Rolls Royce) his mother had to go back to look for him when he gave her the slip to stay and argue with the doctors of divinity. In fact I picked up two little stones; one to be thrown blindfold among the others in Stanbrook garden so that there may always be a stone from Bethlehem there, though nobody will know which it is and be tempted to steal it, and the other for your own self. You shall have them when I return, unless I perish on the way, in which case I shall present myself at the heavenly gate with a stone in each hand, and St. Peter will stand at attention and salute the stones (incidentally saluting ME) when he has unlocked the gate and flung it open before me. At least he would if it were ever locked, which I dont believe.

I have been writing all this in scraps; but there must be an end to everything, even to a letter to you; besides, I finished with the Holy Land at Patmos three days ago, the intervening two days having been spent among heathen idols in and around Athens. For climbing up that frightfully stony road to the top of the mountain where the Greek monastery stands I shall claim indulgence for every sin I ever committed and a few hundred which I still hope to commit. The man who wrote the Book of Revelations, who was *not* the John of the fourth gospel (the Dean assures me that his Greek was disgracefully ungrammatical) ought to have married St. Helena. I *know* he was a drug addict, as all the wickednesses of which he accuses God, all the imaginary horrors, all the passings of a thousand years in a second and the visions of universes breaking into three pieces, are the regular symptoms of drug action and delirium tremens. The book is a disgrace to the Bible and should never have been admitted to the canon.

I began this on the 17th March and it is now the 26th! You can spend a week of your scanty leisure in reading it, and then sell the manuscript to Cockerell for the Fitzwilliam and endow a chapel to St. Bernard at Stanbrook with the proceeds. The writing of it has been very restful to the soul of your brother

affectionately

G. BERNARD SHAW

"Brother Bernard's is a splendid document," was Dame Laurentia's brief comment, "the least merit being its brilliancy. I believe his criticisms are such as I should have made myself if I had been there, and his appreciations seem to me to be most just. The tenderness of some passages is beautiful and reveals, I imagine, the soul of the real G.B.S."

Man Against Darkness

by W. T. STACE

After twenty years in the British Civil Service in Ceylon, in the course of which he rose to be Mayor of Colombo and Controller of Revenue, W. T. Stace came to Princeton University, where he has been professor of philosophy since 1932.

SEPTEMBER 1948

The Catholic bishops of America recently issued a statement in which they said that the chaotic and bewildered state of the modern world is due to man's loss of faith, his abandonment of God and religion. For my part I believe in no religion at all. Yet I entirely agree with the bishops. It is an oversimplification to speak of *the* cause of so complex a state of affairs as the tortured condition of the world today. Its causes are doubtless multitudinous. Yet allowing for some element of oversimplification, I say that the bishops' assertion is substantially true.

Jean-Paul Sartre, the French existentialist philosopher, labels himself an atheist. Yet his views seem to me plainly to support the statement of the bishops. So long as there was believed to be a God in the sky, he says, men could regard him as the source of their moral ideals. The universe, created and governed by a fatherly God, was a friendly habitation for man. We could be sure that, however great the evil in the world, good in the end would triumph and the forces of evil would be routed. With the disappearance of God from the sky all this has changed. Since the world is not ruled by a spiritual being, but rather by blind forces, there cannot be any ideals, moral or otherwise, in the universe outside us. Our ideals, therefore, must proceed only from our own minds; they are our own inventions. Thus the world which surrounds us is nothing but an immense spiritual emptiness. It is a dead universe. We do not live in a universe which is on the side of our values. It is completely indifferent to them.

There is a popular belief that some particular scientific discoveries or theories, such as the Darwinian theory of evolution, or the views of geologists about the age of the earth, or a series of such discoveries, have done the damage. It would be foolish to deny that these discoveries have had a great effect in undermining religious dogmas. But this account does not at all go to the heart of the matter. Religion can probably outlive any scientific discoveries which could be made. It can accommodate itself to them. The root cause of the decay of faith has not been any particular discovery of science, but rather the general spirit of science and certain basic assumptions upon which modern science, from the seventeenth century onward, has proceeded.

It was Galileo and Newton — notwithstanding that Newton himself was a deeply religious man — who destroyed the old comfortable picture of a friendly universe governed by spiritual values. And this was effected, not by Newton's discovery of the law of gravitation nor by any of Galileo's brilliant investigations, but by the general picture of the world which these men and others of their time made the basis of the science, not only of their own day, but of all succeeding generations down to the present. That is why the century immediately following Newton, the eighteenth century, was notoriously an age of religious skepticism. Skepticism did not have to wait for the discoveries of Darwin and the geologists in the nineteenth century. It flooded the world immediately after the age of the rise of science.

Neither the Copernican hypothesis nor any of Newton's or Galileo's particular discoveries were the real causes. Religious faith might well have accommodated itself to the new astronomy. The real turning point between the medieval age of faith and the modern age of unfaith came when the scientists of the seventeenth century turned their backs upon what used to be called "final causes." The final cause of a thing or event meant the purpose which it was supposed to serve in the universe, its cosmic purpose. What lay back of this was the presupposition that there is a cosmic order or plan and that everything which exists could in the last analysis be explained in terms of its place in this cosmic plan, that is, in terms of its purpose.

Plato and Aristotle believed this, and so did the whole medieval Christian world. For instance, if it were true that the sun and the moon were created and exist for the purpose of giving light to man, then this fact would explain why the sun and the moon exist. We might not be able to discover the purpose of everything, but everything must have a purpose. Belief in final causes thus amounted to a belief that the world is governed by purposes, presumably the purposes of some overruling mind.

This belief was not the invention of Christianity. It was basic to the whole of Western civilization, whether in the ancient pagan world or in Christendom, from the time of Socrates to the rise of science in the seventeenth century.

The founders of modern science — for instance, Galileo, Kepler, and Newton — were mostly pious men who did not doubt God's purposes. Nevertheless they took the revolutionary step of consciously and deliberately expelling the idea of purpose as controlling nature from their new science of nature. They did this on the ground that inquiry into purposes is useless for what science aims at: namely, the prediction and control of events. To predict an eclipse, what you have to know is not its purpose but its causes. Hence science from the seventeenth century onward became exclusively an inquiry into causes. The conception of purpose in the world was ignored and frowned on. This, though silent and almost unnoticed, was the greatest revolution in human history, far outweighing in importance any of the political revolutions whose thunder has reverberated through the world.

For it came about in this way that for the past three hundred years there has been growing up in men's minds, dominated as they are by science, a new imaginative picture of the world. The world, according to this new picture, is purposeless, senseless, meaningless. Nature is nothing but matter in motion. The motions of matter are governed, not by any purpose, but by blind forces and laws. Nature on this view, says Whitehead — to whose writings I am indebted in this part of my paper — is "merely the hurrying of material, endlessly, meaninglessly." You can draw a sharp line across the history of Europe dividing it into two epochs of very unequal length. The line passes through the lifetime of Galileo. European man before Galileo — whether ancient pagan or more recent Christian — thought of the world as controlled by plan and purpose. After Galileo, European man thinks of it as utterly purposeless.

It is this which has killed religion. Religion could survive the discoveries that the sun, not the earth, is the center; that men are descended from simian ancestors; that the earth is hundreds of millions of years old. These discoveries may render out of date some of the details of older theological dogmas, may force their restatement in new intellectual frameworks. But they do not touch the essence of the religious vision itself, which is the faith that there is plan and purpose in the world, that the world is a moral order, that in the end all things are for the best. This faith may express itself through many different intellectual dogmas, those of Christianity, of Hinduism, of Islam. All and any of these intellectual dogmas may be destroyed without destroying the essential religious spirit. But that spirit cannot survive destruction of belief in a plan and purpose of the world, for that is the very heart of it. Religion can get on with any sort of astronomy, geology, biology, physics. But it cannot get on with a purposeless and meaningless universe.

If the scheme of things is purposeless and meaningless, then the life of man is purposeless and meaningless too. Everything is futile, all effort is in the end worthless. A man may, of course, still pursue disconnected ends, money, fame, art, science, and may gain pleasure from them. But his life is hollow at the center. Hence the dissatisfied, disillusioned, restless spirit of modern man.

The picture of a meaningless world, and a meaningless human life, is, I think, the basic theme of much modern art and literature. Certainly it is the basic theme of modern philosophy. According to the most characteristic philosophies of the modern period from Hume in the eighteenth century to the so-called positivists of today, the world is just what it is, and that is the end of all inquiry. There is no reason for its being what it is. Everything might just as well have been quite different, and there would have been no reason for that either. When you have stated what things are, what things the world contains, there is nothing more which could be said, even by an omniscient being. To ask any question about *why* things are thus, or what purpose their being so serves, is to ask a senseless question, because they serve no purpose at all. For instance, there is for modern philosophy no such thing as the ancient problem of evil. For this once famous question presupposes that pain and misery, though they seem so inexplicable and irrational to us, must ultimately subserve some rational purpose, must have their places in the cosmic plan. But this is nonsense. There is no such overruling rationality in the universe. Belief in the ultimate irrationality of everything is the quintessence of what is called the modern mind.

It is true that, parallel with these philosophies which are typical of the modern mind, preaching the meaninglessness of the world, there has run a line of idealistic philosophies whose contention is that the world is after all spiritual in nature and that moral ideals and values are inherent in its structure. But most of these idealisms were simply philosophical expressions of romanticism, which was itself no more than an unsuccessful counterattack of the religious against the scientific view of things. They perished, along with romanticism in literature and art, about the beginning of the present century, though of course they still have a few adherents.

At the bottom these idealistic systems of thought were rationalizations of man's wishful thinking. They were born of the refusal of men to admit the cosmic darkness. They were comforting illusions within the warm glow of which the more tender-minded intellectuals sought to shelter themselves from the icy winds of the universe. They lasted a little while. But they are shattered now, and we return once more to the vision of a purposeless world.

Along with the ruin of the religious vision there went the ruin of moral principles and indeed of all values. If there is a cosmic purpose, if there is in the nature of things a drive toward goodness, then our moral systems will derive their validity from this. But if our moral rules do not proceed from something outside us in the nature of the universe — whether we say it is God or simply the universe itself — then they must be our own inventions. Thus it came to be believed that moral rules must be merely an expression of our own likes and dislikes. But likes and dislikes are notoriously variable. What pleases one man, people, or culture displeases another. Therefore morals are wholly relative.

This obvious conclusion from the idea of a purposeless world made its appearance in Europe immediately after the rise of science, for instance in the philosophy of Hobbes. Hobbes saw at once that if there is no purpose in the world there are no values either. "Good and evil," he wrote, "are names that signify our appetites and aversions; which in different tempers, customs, and doctrines of men are different. . . . Every man calleth that which pleaseth him, good; and that which displeaseth him, evil."

This doctrine of the relativity of morals, though it has recently received an impetus from the studies of anthropologists, was thus really implicit in the whole scientific mentality. It is disastrous for morals because it destroys their entire traditional foundation. That is why philosophers who see the danger signals, from the time at least of Kant, have been trying to give to morals a new foundation, that is, a secular or nonreligious foundation. This attempt may very well be intellectually successful. Such a foundation, independent of the religious view of the world, might well be found. But the question is whether it can ever be a *practical* success, that is, whether apart from its logical validity and its influence with intellectuals, it can ever replace among the masses of men the lost religious foundation. On that question hangs perhaps the future of civilization. But meanwhile disaster is overtaking us.

The widespread belief in "ethical relativity" among philosophers, psychologists, ethnologists, and sociologists is the theoretical counterpart of the repudiation of principle which we see all around us, especially in international affairs, the field in which morals have always had the weakest foothold. No one any longer effectively believes in moral principles except as the private prejudices either of individual men or of nations or cultures. This is the inevitable consequence of the doctrine of ethical relativity, which in turn is the inevitable consequence of believing in a purposeless world.

Another characteristic of our spiritual state is loss of belief in the freedom of the will. This also is a fruit of the scientific spirit, though not of any particular scientific discovery. Science has been built up on the basis of determinism, which is the belief that every event is completely determined by a chain of causes and is therefore theoretically predictable beforehand. It is true that recent physics seems to challenge this. But so far as its practical consequences are concerned, the damage has long ago been done. A man's actions, it was argued, are as much events in the natural world as is an eclipse of the sun. It follows that men's actions are as theoretically predictable as an eclipse. But if it is certain now that John Smith will murder Joseph Jones at 2:15 P.M. on January 1, 1963, what possible meaning can it have to say that when that time comes John Smith will be *free* to choose whether he will commit the murder or not? And if he is not free, how can he be held responsible?

It is true that the whole of this argument can be shown by a competent philosopher to be a tissue of fallacies — or at least I claim that it can. But the point is that the analysis required to show this is much too subtle to be understood by the average entirely unphilosophical man. Because of this, the argument against free will is generally swallowed whole by the unphilosophical. Hence the thought that man is not free, that he is the helpless plaything of forces over which he has no control, has deeply penetrated the modern mind. We hear of economic determinism, cultural determinism, historical determinism. We are not responsible for what we do because our glands control us or because we are the products of environment or heredity. Not moral self-control, but the doctor, the psychiatrist, the educationist, must save us from doing evil. Pills and injections in the future are to do what Christ and the prophets have failed to do. Of course I do not mean to deny that doctors and educationists can help. And I do not in any way mean to belittle their efforts. But I do wish to draw attention to the weakening of moral controls, the repudiation of personal responsibility which, in the popular thinking of the day, result from these tendencies of thought.

No civilization can live without ideals, or to put it in another way, without a firm faith in moral ideas. Our ideals and moral ideas have in the past been rooted in religion. But the religious basis of our ideals has been undermined, and the superstructure of ideals is plainly tottering. None of the commonly suggested remedies on examination seems likely to succeed. It would therefore look as if the early death of our civilization were inevitable.

Of course we know that it is perfectly possible for individual men, very highly educated men, philosophers, scientists, intellectuals in general, to live moral lives without any religious convictions. But the question is whether a whole civilization, a whole family of peoples, composed almost entirely of relatively uneducated men and women, can do this. Of course, if we could make the vast majority of men as highly educated as the very few are now, we might save the situation. And we are already moving slowly in that direction through the techniques of mass education. But the critical question seems to concern the time lag. Perhaps in a few hundred years most of the population will, at the present rate, be sufficiently highly educated and civilized to combine high ideals with an absence of religion. But long before we reach any such stage, the collapse of our civilization may have come about. How are we to live through the intervening period?

I am sure that the first thing we have to do is to face the truth, however bleak it may be, and then next we have to learn to live with it. Let me say a word about each of these two points. What I am urging as regards the first is complete honesty. Those who wish to resurrect Christian dogmas are not, of course, consciously dishonest. But they have that kind of unconscious dishonesty which consists in lulling oneself with opiates and dreams. Those who talk of a new religion are merely hoping for a new opiate. Both alike refuse to face the truth that there is, in the universe outside man, no spirituality, no regard for values, no friend in the sky, no help or comfort for man of any sort. To be perfectly honest in the admission of this fact, not to seek shelter in new or old illusions, not to indulge in wishful dreams about this matter, this is the first thing we shall have to do.

I do not urge this course out of any special regard for the sanctity of truth in the abstract. It is not self-evident to me that truth is the supreme value to which all else must be sacrificed. Might not the discoverer of a truth which would be fatal to mankind be justified in suppressing it, even in teaching men a falsehood? Is truth more valuable than goodness and beauty and happiness? To think so is to invent yet another absolute, another religious delusion in which Truth with a capital T is substituted for God. The reason why we must now boldly and honestly face the truth that the universe is nonspiritual and indifferent to goodness, beauty, happiness, or truth is not that it would be wicked to suppress it, but simply that it is too late to do so. In the end we cannot do anything else but face it. Yet we stand on the brink, dreading the icy plunge. We need courage. We need honesty.

Now about the other point, the necessity of learning to live with the truth. This means learning to live virtuously and happily, or at least contentedly, without illusions. And this is going to be extremely difficult because what we have now begun dimly to perceive is that human life in the past, or at least human happiness, has almost wholly depended upon illusions. It has been said that man lives by truth, and that the truth will make us free. Nearly the opposite seems to me to be the case. Mankind has managed to live only by means of lies, and the truth may very well destroy us. If one were a Bergsonian one might believe that nature deliberately puts illusions into our souls in order to induce us to go on living.

The illusions by which men have lived seem to be of two kinds. First, there is what one may perhaps call the Great Illusion — I mean the religious illusion that the universe is moral and good, that it follows a wise and noble plan, that it is gradually generating some supreme value, that goodness is bound to triumph in it. Secondly, there is a whole host of minor illusions on which human happiness nourishes itself. How much of human happiness notoriously comes from the illusions of the lover about his beloved? Then again we work and strive because of the illusions connected with fame, glory, power, or money. Banners of all kinds, flags, emblems, insignia, ceremonials, and rituals are invariably symbols of some illusion or other. The British Empire, the connection between mother country and dominions, is partly kept going by illusions surrounding the notion of kingship. Or think of the vast amount of human happiness which is derived from the illusion of supposing that if some nonsense syllable, such as "sir" or "count" or "lord" is pronounced in conjunction with our names, we belong to a superior order of people.

There is plenty of evidence that human happiness is almost wholly based upon illusions of one kind or another. But the scientific spirit, or the spirit of truth, is the enemy of illusions and therefore the enemy of human happiness. That is why it is going to be so difficult to live with the truth.

There is no reason why we should have to give up the host of minor illusions which render life supportable. There is no reason why the lover should be scientific about the loved one. Even the illusions of fame and glory may persist. But without the Great Illusion, the illusion of a good, kindly, and purposeful universe, we shall *have* to learn to live. And to ask this is really no more than to ask that we become genuinely civilized beings and not merely sham civilized beings.

I can best explain the difference by a reminiscence. I remember a fellow student in my college days, an ardent Christian, who told me that if he did not believe in a future life, in heaven and hell, he would rape, murder, steal, and be a drunkard. That is what I call being a sham civilized being. On the other hand, not only could a Huxley, a John Stuart Mill, a David Hume, live great and fine lives without any religion, but a great many others of us, quite obscure persons, can at least live decent lives without it.

To be genuinely civilized means to be able to walk straight and to live honorably without the props and crutches of one or another of the childish dreams which have so far supported men. That such a life is likely to be ecstatically happy I will not claim. But that it can be lived in quiet content, accepting resignedly what cannot be helped, not expecting the impossible, and thankful for small mercies, this I would maintain. That it will be difficult for men in general to learn this lesson I do not deny. But that it will be impossible I will not admit since so many have learned it already.

Man has not yet grown up. He is not adult. Like a child he cries for the moon and lives in a world of fantasies. And the race as a whole has perhaps reached the great crisis of its life. Can it grow up as a race in the same sense as individual men grow up? Can man put away childish things and adolescent dreams? Can he grasp the real world as it actually is, stark and bleak, without its religious or romantic halo, and still retain his ideals, striving for great ends and noble achievements? If he can, all may yet be well. If he cannot, he will probably sink back into the savagery and brutality from which he came, taking a humble place once more among the lower animals.

Second Coming

by JOHN MOFFITT

APRIL 1956

Were you there,
Were you there,
When they crucified
My Lord?
When they struck
His holihood,
When they nailed him
To the rood,
When they drew
His burning blood?
(I was there,
I was there,
And I saw him
Hanging there,
Felt the thunder
In my soul
Smite the thunder
In the air.)

Were you there,
Were you there,
When he stood
Beside the tomb,
In the garden
In the morn,
Risen from
Gehenna's womb?
(I was there,
I was there,
And I saw him

Standing there,
Saw his patient
Lonely smile,
Fairer far
Than all things fair,
And I heard
His plighted word
To return
Among us here.)

Were you there,
Were you there,
When he kept
His pledge to men,
When he came
To earth again?
When they cast him
In the dust,
When they broke
His fervid trust,
When they sealed
A nation's doom
In the name
Of kingdom come,
When they dropped
The cobalt bomb?
(I was there,
I was there,
And I saw him
Weeping there,

Saw the pitiless
Sharp crown
Pressing close
About his hair,
And I saw
The seraphim
As they swung
Their swords of flame,
And I saw
The victims' feet
All around
The Judgment Seat,
And I felt

The wrath of God
Like a vast
Devouring cloud,
And I watched
The world go down
In a cloud
Of dust and doom,
To the bottom
Of the pit.
And my Lord,
And my Lord,
Rose and followed
After it.)

Catholic and Patriot

by ALFRED E. SMITH

In the spring of 1927, before he had been nominated for President, while he was still Governor of New York State, Alfred E. Smith was subjected to a series of questions by Charles C. Marshall, a New York lawyer, as to whether he could give undivided allegiance to his country were he elected. The Governor's ringing affirmative, which he wrote after consultation with Father Duffy, Catholic Chaplain of the 165th Infantry, is the memorable creed of an American Catholic.

MAY 1927

CHARLES C. MARSHALL, ESQ.
DEAR SIR:

In your open letter to me in the April *Atlantic Monthly* you "impute" to American Catholics views which, if held by them, would leave open to question the loyalty and devotion to this country and its Constitution of more than twenty million American Catholic citizens. I am grateful to you for defining this issue in the open and for your courteous expression of the satisfaction it will bring to my fellow citizens for me to give "a disclaimer of the convictions" thus imputed. Without mental reservation I can and do make that disclaimer. These convictions are held neither by me nor by any other American Catholic, as far as I know.

Taking your letter as a whole and reducing it to commonplace English, you imply that there is conflict between religious loyalty to the Catholic faith and patriotic loyalty to the United States. Everything that has actually happened to me during my long public career leads me to know that no such thing as that is true. I have taken an oath of office in this state nineteen times. Each time I swore to defend and maintain the Constitution of the United States. All of this represents a period of public service in elective office almost continuous since 1903. I have never known any conflict between my official duties and my religious belief. No such conflict could exist. Certainly the people of this state recognize no such conflict. They have testified to my devotion to public duty by electing me to the highest office within their gift four times. You yourself do me the honor, in addressing me, to refer to "your fidelity to the morality you have advocated in public and private life and to the religion you have revered; your great record of public trusts successfully and honestly discharged." During the years I have discharged these trusts I have been a communicant of the Roman Catholic Church. If there were conflict, I, of all men, could not have escaped it, because I have not been a silent man but a battler for social and political reform. These battles would in their very nature disclose this conflict if there were any.

I regard public education as one of the foremost functions of government and I have supported to the last degree the State Department of Education in every effort to promote our public school system. The largest single item of increased appropriations under my administration appears in the educational group for the support of common schools. Since 1919, when I first became Governor, this item has grown from $9 million to $82.5 million. My aim — and I may say I have succeeded in achieving it — has been legislation for child welfare, the protection of working men, women, and children, the modernization of the state's institutions for the care of helpless or unfortunate wards, the preservation of freedom of speech and opinion against the attack of wartime hysteria, and the complete reorganization of the structure of the government of the state.

I did not struggle for these things for any single element, but in the interest of all of the eleven million people who make up the state. In this work I had the support of churches of all denominations. I probably know as many ecclesiastics of my Church as any other layman. During

my long and active public career I never received from any of them anything except coöperation and encouragement in the full and complete
discharge of my duty to the state. Moreover, I am unable to understand
how anything that I was taught to believe as a Catholic could possibly
be in conflict with what is good citizenship. The essence of my faith is
built upon the Commandments of God. The law of the land is built
upon the Commandments of God. There can be no conflict between
them.

Instead of quarreling among ourselves over dogmatic principles, it
would be infinitely better if we joined together in inculcating obedience
to these Commandments in the hearts and minds of the youth of the
country as the surest and best road to happiness on this earth and to
peace in the world to come. This is the common ideal of all religions.
What we need is more religion for our young people, not less; and the
way to get more religion is to stop the bickering among our sects which
can only have for its effect the creation of doubt in the minds of our
youth as to whether or not it is necessary to pay attention to religion
at all.

I know your imputations are false when I recall the long list of
other public servants of my faith who have loyally served the state. You
as a lawyer will probably agree that the office of Chief Justice of the
United States is second not even to that of the President in its influence
on the national development and policy. That court by its interpretation
of the federal Constitution is a check not only upon the President himself but upon Congress as well. During one fourth of its history it has
been presided over by two Catholics, Roger Brooke Taney and Edward
Douglass White. No one has suggested that the official conduct of either
of these men was affected by any unwarranted religious influence or that
religion played with them any part other than it should play in the like
of every God-fearing man.

And I know your imputations are false when I recall the tens of
thousands of young Catholics who have risked and sacrificed their lives
in defense of our country. These fundamentals of life could not be true
unless your imputations were false.

I come now to the speculation with which theorists have played for
generations as to the respective functions of Church and State. You
claim that the Roman Catholic Church holds that, if conflict arises, the
Church must prevail over the State. What is this conflict about which
you talk? It may exist in some lands which do not guarantee religious
freedom. But in the wildest dreams of your imagination you cannot con-

jure up a possible conflict between religious principle and political duty in the United States, except on the unthinkable hypothesis that some law were to be passed which violated the common morality of all God-fearing men. And if you can conjure up such a conflict, how would a Protestant resolve it? Obviously by the dictates of his conscience. That is exactly what a Catholic would do. There is no ecclesiastical tribunal which would have the slightest claim upon the obedience of Catholic communicants in the resolution of such a conflict. As Cardinal Gibbons said of the supposition that "the Pope were to issue commands in purely civil matters":

> He would be offending not only against civil society, but against God, and violating an authority as truly from God as his own. Any Catholic who clearly recognized this would not be bound to obey the Pope; or rather his conscience would bind him absolutely to disobey, because with Catholics conscience is the supreme law which under no circumstances can we ever lawfully disobey.

Under our system of government the electorate entrusts to its officers of every faith the solemn duty of action according to the dictates of conscience. I may fairly refer once more to my own record to support these truths. No man, cleric or lay, has ever directly or indirectly attempted to exercise Church influence on my administration of any office I have ever held, nor asked me to show special favor to Catholics or exercise discrimination against non-Catholics.

It is a well-known fact that I have made all of my appointments to public office on the basis of merit and have never asked any man about his religious belief. In the first month of this year there gathered in the Capitol at Albany the first Governor's cabinet that ever sat in this state. It was composed, under my appointment, of two Catholics, thirteen Protestants, and one Jew. The man closest to me in the administration of the government of the state of New York is he who bears the title of Assistant to the Governor. He had been connected with the Governor's office for thirty years, in subordinate capacities, until I promoted him to the position which makes him the sharer with me of my every thought and hope and ambition in the administration of the state. He is a Protestant, a Republican, and a thirty-second-degree Mason. In my public life I have exemplified that complete separation of Church from State which is the faith of American Catholics today.

I next come to education. You admit that the Supreme Court guaranteed to Catholics the right to maintain their parochial schools; and you ask me whether they would have so ruled if it had been shown that children in parochial schools were taught that the state should show discrimination between religions, that Protestants should be recognized only as a matter of favor, that they should be intolerant to non-Catholics, and that the laws of the state could be flouted on the ground of the imaginary conflict. My summary answer is: I and all my children went to a parochial school. I never heard of any such stuff being taught or of anybody who claimed that it was. That any group of Catholics would teach it is unthinkable.

I summarize my creed as an American Catholic. I believe in the worship of God according to the faith and practice of the Roman Catholic Church. I recognize no power in the institutions of my Church to interfere with the operations of the Constitution of the United States or the enforcement of the law of the land. I believe in absolute freedom of conscience for all men and in equality of all churches, all sects, and all beliefs before the law as a matter of right and not as a matter of favor. I believe in the absolute separation of Church and State and in the strict enforcement of the provisions of the Constitution that Congress shall make no law respecting an establishment of religion or prohibiting the free exercise thereof. I believe that no tribunal of any church has any power to make any decree of any force in the law of the land, other than to establish the status of its own communicants within its own church. I believe in the support of the public school as one of the cornerstones of American liberty. I believe in the right of every parent to choose whether his child shall be educated in the public school or in a religious school supported by those of his own faith. I believe in the principle of noninterference by this country in the internal affairs of other nations and that we should stand steadfastly against any such interference by whomsoever it may be urged. And I believe in the common brotherhood of man under the common fatherhood of God.

In this spirit I join with fellow Americans of all creeds in a fervent prayer that never again in this land will any public servant be challenged because of the faith in which he has tried to walk humbly with his God.

ALFRED E. SMITH

Christianity and Human Rights

by BARBARA WARD

An English Catholic who served with distinction as the foreign editor of the London Economist, *Barbara Ward is the author of* Policy for the West *and* Faith and Freedom.

DECEMBER 1947

If religion is accepted as a factor determining society *in its own right,* then one statement can be made with certainty about the relationship between Western democracy and religion. It is that Western democracy emerged from a profoundly religious civilization, and whether or not it could have grown from irreligious roots, we know from history that in fact it did not do so. If for a moment I may take the example of British society, which, with the United States, is the most typical example of Western democracy, the extent to which our political and social tradition is steeped in Christianity can hardly be exaggerated. Some of the most formative institutions in our country — Parliament, the boroughs, the universities, the law courts, and the older public schools — go back in unbroken tradition to the Catholic Middle Ages, and a vestigial religious atmosphere clings to them to this day. When, in the seventeenth century, the British revolution was fought, the men who opposed the centralizing and autocratic tendencies of the Stuart kings fought for the "ancient liberties" of the law courts and of Parliament. They felt they were preserving a medieval tradition, and the conservative character of their revolution was one reason why English society, in spite of regicide, suffered no violent break with the past such as ruined the cohesion of French society at the French Revolution.

Nor was the influence of religion simply traditional. At two turning points in English history, Christianity played a decisive part. In the eighteenth century John Wesley broke away from the narrow Anglicanism of his day and took the Gospel to the poor. His reforms led to the tremendous expansion of the Nonconformist or free churches, which in their turn decisively influenced the beginning of the trade-union and labor movements in Britain. The first British organizers of labor were lay preachers, and to this day there is nothing incongruous when the Archbishop of Canterbury opens the Labor Party's National Conference, or when the socialist Minister of Education preaches from the Methodist pulpit.

The other decisive religious trend in British democracy lay in the astonishing grip of religion on all classes of British society in the nineteenth century. The men and women who first took reform into the prisons, the galleys, the mines, the factories, and the workhouses were Christians. The greatest and most typical politician of the day — Gladstone — was a churchman almost before he was a parliamentarian. A deep sense of personal obligation and religious responsibility dominated that intensely dynamic and creative period in whose aftermath the British people to some extent live even today. Whether or not British democracy could have developed without Christianity, it has not in fact done so and the onus of proof lies with those who would seek to prove that the connection between them is inessential and that the one can continue without the other.

I cannot speak with the same certainty of American society, yet even a superficial knowledge of America's history suggests how powerful were the religious forces which molded its democratic form of society. The first colonists founded societies so thoroughly religious that some of them were almost theocracies. The drafters of the American Declaration of Independence and of the Constitution may not all have been Christian, yet both documents breathe the spirit of a natural law and of a divine order which were bedrocks of European political and religious thought. The women who took "law and order" with them in the covered wagons based both on Christianity, and it was their faith that was in part, at least, responsible for the astonishingly rapid pacification and settlement of the frontier. And at the greatest crisis of the young republic, surely its religious genius found expression in Abraham Lincoln, who to many people — not only Americans — is one of the most Christian statesmen the world has seen.

No one will deny the strength of the other forces that have molded America, but the strength of the Christian strand is so formidable that once again those who wish to prove it immaterial to the development of democracy will not be able to bring in history to give evidence on their side. The answer of history is irrefutable. Democracy and religion have so far been inseparable.

I do not wish to make too great a claim for the lessons of history. History does not prove that Christianity inevitably produces Western democracy. The experience of the Orthodox Church in Russia or of the Catholic Church in Spain is an example of the coexistence of religion and autocracy. The lesson of history is more limited. It is only that Western democracy has not in fact developed except in constant interrelation with Christianity, and that, particularly in the formative phases, the influence of Christian faith has been overwhelmingly strong.

When I go on to discuss the further problem — whether democracy can develop or survive without Christianity — the argument becomes in part an expression of faith. Personally I believe that democracy, the highest and most civilized form of society yet evolved by man, cannot realize its full potentialities without Christianity. Moreover, I do not believe that it can preserve its achievements without religious faith.

It seems to me that there are certain attitudes toward life, certain basic beliefs that come to us from the Christian faith, which are more essential to democracy than, say, the maintenance of reasonable economic standards, or freedom from invasion, or a situation in a temperate climate, or any of the other material factors which are often held to be indispensable to the maintenance of free society. One such belief is a belief in a moral order superior to the convenience of men or of man-made society. Every great civilization has felt, more or less strongly, that human laws have their validity not because of social convenience but because they mirror a divine order which is above all human appetites and ambitions. Acceptance of such an order is important in that it gives greater sanction to personal responsibility and good behavior — and no democracy can survive without a high measure of unforced personal responsibility among its citizens.

Even more important, belief in a morality which transcends the temporal order and its needs and conveniences is a vital factor in securing one of the essential characteristics of democratic society — the limitation of the state's authority. When the medieval priest and lawyer, Bracton, wrote that "the king is under God and the law," he was expressing a principle of cardinal importance for democratic society. He was striking at the foundations of royal and therefore of state absolutism. This belief — that the power of the state was limited by law — was, as I have indicated, one of the chief factors in the struggle in Britain against the claim of the Stuart kings to govern by Divine Right; and in the United States it took the form of limiting the power of the state by a written constitution. Today, modern theories — of racialism, of class interest, of "mass democracy" — have undermined the belief in the essentially limited authority of the state, and to my mind it is no coincidence that these theories have also abandoned all conception of a natural law in which is mirrored a divine order.

And this pre-Christian relationship of government and governed should remind us of another factor introduced into the world by Christianity and without which democracy is inconceivable — the belief in the infinite value of human personality and the essential equality of human souls. That these beliefs are profound acts of faith can be realized by glancing round any large assembly of people. To the eye of reason or the eye of science, men clearly are neither essentially equal nor equally valuable. And we have seen in our own time how easily this faith can be thrown aside, how easily Jews can be massacred by the million in the name of racial purity, and Balts and Poles and Trotskyites and political opponents murdered in the name of "people's democracy." The act of faith essential to democracy — belief in human equality and human personality — springs traditionally from the Christian faith in the Fatherhood of God. It may be possible to maintain it without that faith, but one can at least say that in the twentieth century the fading of belief in God has coincided with a growing ferocity and inhumanity of the relation of man to man.

It is a curious paradox that the most revolting forms of cruelty, the most appalling exhibitions of the lust for power, and the most frenzied search for material gratification have, in our own time, coincided with an almost complete rejection of the idea of sin. I do not want to go into the reasons for this — the growing belief in economic determinism, the growing influence of Freudian psychology — but I do wish to stress my own belief that acceptance of the fact and possibility of sin is essential to the preservation of democracy. It is not simply that to admit the possibility of sin is to accept personal responsibility. This fact is certainly important, but the decisive influence of the sense of sin seems to me to operate at the level of government. The great tragedy of today is the number of men and groups and classes who are ready to massacre and torture their neighbors in order to achieve the rigid Utopia of their dreams — the Aryan paradise, the Marxist classless society. The more convinced they are of the utter infallibility of their political creed, the more ready they are to kill their opponents for daring to stand in the way of the realization of absolute perfection.

It is perhaps by the violence and brutality of our economic struggle that we, in Western society, have most gravely endangered the future of our democracy. The sense of pity, the sympathetic understanding of the weak, the acceptance of failure as part of life and possibly as a redeeming and constructive part of life, came from a religious faith unique in history, whose God shared human suffering, even to a shameful death on the Cross. I do not know that we can preserve a profoundly human society — for that, in the last analysis, is what democracy is — if we lose that faith.

Again and again I have spoken of faith — the religious faith that underlies democracy, my own faith in the vital link between them. But some will dismiss faith and say that the ideal democracy of the future will not need superstition and must be based on the clear light of reason and enlightened self-interest. I do not believe it. I do not believe that men, save in brief moments of anarchy and despair, live without faith. Our age, which has seen the weakening and undermining of democracy, is an age of tremendous faiths — faith in National Socialism, in Communism, in Caesar worship, in the Divine Emperor. If faith in God drains out of society, faith in lesser gods flows in. If the supreme Godhead of the prophets and the philosophers and the mystics is banished, in His place rush in the idols of the tribe. Perhaps democracy can survive without a faith, but history gives no proof of it. And our new faiths have been without exception fatal to democracy.

One last point: the quality of a free society depends essentially upon the quality of its citizens. When Montesquieu wrote that virtue must be the distinguishing quality of republics, he was only underlining the necessity of democracies to depend upon the integrity, the responsibility, and the good will of their people. But is this essential quality of goodness so easy to produce? Let me give an analogy.

Three things above all others have been recognized by the philosophers as ends in themselves, as things which exist on their own merit, fit objects of human effort and search. The first is beauty, the second truth, the third goodness. Up to a certain point the claims of beauty and truth are recognized in most societies today. The artist, the scientist, and the scholar hold an honored place. Moreover, many people recognize, however dimly, that the quality of beauty and the appreciation of truth in society as a whole depend upon the number of men and women of genius who are prepared to devote themselves wholeheartedly and without stint to the realization of beauty and the search for truth. A great artistic age is an age of great artists. An age of supreme scientific achievement is an age of great scientists. It is the work and dedication of great men and women that raise the whole tone and level of society.

But when it comes to the third of the three absolutes — goodness — the absolute upon which the temper of a free society most obviously depends, do we find anything comparable to the work of great scientists and great artists? Only in religious faith, only — in our own society — in Christianity, do we find anything like the same effort to produce souls as heroic in their goodness as great artists and scientists are wholehearted in their pursuit of beauty and truth. It is these saints and mystics, these geniuses of goodness, who in the last analysis seem to me to be the only founts from which the spiritual vitality, the force of goodness in free society will flow. Some of the first founders of democracy in America called themselves a society of saints. Their ambition vaulted too high perhaps, but I doubt whether democracy will survive if it is to become at any time a society without saints.

More Truth than Poetry

from As I Remember Him

by HANS ZINSSER

Scientist and poet, Dr. Zinsser began the writing of As I Remember Him *on his return from China, where he had been fighting the outbreak of typhus. He was suffering, he knew, from incurable leukemia, and he was writing against a deadline. The knowledge intensified his perception. Under this pressure he projected the life story of a fellow scientist, whom he identified simply with the initials "R.S." Was it his alter ego? We shall never know, but the resulting book, of which this is the final section, takes rank with* The Education of Henry Adams.

MAY 1940

We are living in an age in which the sciences not only are transforming the structure of society and the habits of men, but are equally confirming an orderliness of natural forces vaguely suspected, hitherto, by philosophers and great artists. Goethe recognized this orderliness and put his finger on the eternal quandary of the philosophers — that the creative force, whatever it might be, was powerless to modify the course of its own creation — when he said: *"Die Natur wirkt nach ewigen, notwendigen, dergestalt göttlichen Gesetzen, dass die Gottheit selbst daran nichts ändern könnte."* The criticism of the future, therefore, to have any value, will demand a fundamental comprehension at least of the effects of the new understanding of nature upon human thoughts and affairs. For, after all, it is awareness of the scene as a whole which must form the equipment of the critic.

In response to such a need, there has arisen a literature, largely contributed by distinguished physicists — Eddington, Jeans, Dingle, and Millikan among them — who began to contemplate the modern world in its broader relations from a base line of deep scientific wisdom. But, as has ever been the case with physicists, they soon gave the poor earth little thought in their preoccupations with the universe. Yet some of them, notably Dingle, have tried to apply the logical processes of scientific method to the criticism of art; and a more than usually well-informed literary critic, I. A. Richards, made an attempt to meet these efforts halfway by approaching the scientific point of view from literature as a base.

From none of these did R.S. gain much comfort. He became, however, a profound admirer of Whitehead, who, it seemed to him, combined — in the wide horizon of his mature wisdom — deep erudition of the sciences with sensitiveness to aesthetic values, appearing in this regard to possess some of the qualities, less creative but perhaps more contemporaneously sound, of a Goethe. It was in Whitehead's diagnosis of the sick world that R.S. recognized his own, less learnedly arrived at, to the effect that with the rapid development of industrialism and urbanization (both consequences of the scientific control of natural forces) there was a neglect of the "aesthetic qualities of the new material environment"; there was a limitation of the "moral outlook" at a time when it was most needed. The "moral pace of progress," says Whitehead, "requires a greater force of direction," but a grooved professionalism (also a consequence of the headlong rush of science) has brought it about that "the leading intellects lack balance" and "the task of coördination is left to those who lack either the force or the character to succeed in some definite career." The corrective, therefore, it seemed to R.S., should lie not in the checking of science, but rather in catching up with it.

It is one thing to make a diagnosis, quite another to devise an operation or a remedy. Whitehead was by no means the only diagnostician who put his finger on the modern world's McBurney's point. But he was the particular one who — standing, in the tranquillity of his wisdom, *"au-dessus de la mêlée"* — seemed to make the situation objectively clear to R.S. There was in many other critics, especially those like Babbitt and other lesser humanists, in writers, poets, and artists generally, a feebly masked resentment against the scientists, who seemed to them to usurp too much of the modern world's attention. They appeared to feel toward science somewhat as the Church did in the sixteenth century.

To R.S. this was confusing, since, with his own profound distrust of mere fact accumulated without philosophical and aesthetic coördination, the philosopher and the great artist were to him the architects who must build the cultural edifice of the future, using science — among other things — as an indispensable part of their equipment. But he found among most of his friends little or no appreciation of the fact that the last forty years had witnessed an era of enlightenment in man's understanding both of nature and of himself which was not incomparable to the epoch beginning with Galileo.

And yet the specific developments of the modern period, in their correlation of matter and energy and in the application of the exact sciences to biology, appeared to R.S. to bring scientific thought and its effects much closer than ever before to the everyday lives of men. Some of the landmarks of this era he pointed out to me.

New understanding was coming from all directions, often from the least-expected sources of supposedly "pure academic" investigation. The beauty of the situation was this growing integration of all the sciences in biological research.

But at the same time similar things were happening in biology itself. Up to 1900, the Darwinian conceptions of evolution by continuous natural selection and Weismann's ideas of heredity had remained virtually unchanged. Almost simultaneously, in 1900, Bateson and De Vries rediscovered the work of Mendel. The laws deduced by Mendel in his experiments with sweet peas, the conception of the dominance or recessive nature of certain qualities and a numerical relationship between the appearance of the dominant and the recessive in hybrids, became the basis of the modern knowledge of heredity. When the effects of the Mendelian theory of unit characteristics were correlated with microscopic studies of cell cleavage, the carriers of hereditary qualities were sought in the chromosomes of the nuclei of the germ cells, and work such as that of Edmund B. Wilson, on the manner in which chromosomes divide before cell cleavage and are united in pairs in the new cells, strengthened the growing belief that there was some connection between the two. The idea was formulated by Sutton, and in 1910 Thomas H. Morgan brought the matter to a definite conception by his work on the fruit fly.

From these studies originated the idea of genes within the chromosomes — the linkage of numerous hereditary factors in one chromosome. Modern genetics became a logical, if not entirely a precise, science. And soon these principles found application in medicine. A large number of human qualities, ailments, and deformities could now be traced to genetic origin, and for some of them it has already been possible to determine which are dominant and which recessive. Such knowledge made it possible to differentiate many physical and physiological defects into those which are hereditary and those which are due to extraneous causes. It may establish certain principles of human breeding in extreme cases where physical defects are known to be dominant.

Yet there is no rational basis for immediately embarking on a totalitarian regulation of marriage on a eugenic basis. That is an old story, tried out — as Castle has indicated — in Sparta and advocated in the Darwinian period by Galton. But social instincts, cultural struggle, and emotional factors are too complex and strong to be even temporarily overcome by a farseeing plan of man-husbandry which cannot be expected to take hold effectively in less than many generations of a control abhorrent to the strongest physiological urge. Moreover, there may be much justifiable difference of opinion concerning the desirable traits toward which such breeding might aim. A six-toed or hunchbacked critic might be judged a more desirable citizen than a morally defective Adonis; or a tuberculous Chopin or a neurotic Shelley than a normal delicatessen merchant. And as far as the socially valuable characteristics are concerned, J. B. S. Haldane holds out the hopeful suggestion that since the virtuous are often rewarded by poverty, and since the poor breed quicker than the rich, we may possibly expect some slight, though slow, improvement. His mathematical treatment of the subject does not, at any rate, support the kind of eventual system which, one imagines, some eugenists might approve — that is, limiting procreation to those holding a "fornication license" from the State House, with number plates appropriately attached. Even science must leave some things to what Ehrlich called *Die Uralte Protoplasma-Weisheit*.

Thus, thought R.S., science, instead of helping to release mankind from toil, poverty, and war, actually seemed to be accelerating materialism, hatred, and the forces of destruction. And in its fundamental aspects science was demonstrating that, however deeply it might penetrate into the mechanisms of nature and the universe, it would never — alone — solve the ultimate problems or appease that hunger of the spirit, that yearning toward an ethical ideal, which, in one form or another, he believed to be an inherent, biological attribute of human beings, as strong as the hungers of the body. For its existence, what more convincing scientific proof could be desired than the irresistible force with which the teachings of Buddha and of the New Testament had swept across the world and had conquered the imaginations of men, often to the disadvantage of their material interests and racial supremacies? R.S. had seen many of his most admired and distinguished scientific contemporaries, despairing of the powers of reason alone, seek spiritual sanctuary either — acknowledgedly *faute de mieux* — in the arms of the established Church, or, more deplorably, in some form of mysticism.

Both the desire for and the guidance toward such "aesthetic apprehension," as Whitehead calls it, were apparent. Yet less and less were they effective in arresting the downward course of our civilization. Some regulating force was needed, something of the heart. Was recourse to supernatural authority the only alternative for this apprehension of the higher values of existence, he asked himself. If so, it appeared to him, the outlook was dark. For the masses of the people, once lured away from a weakening religious control, would be more and more delivered, spiritually hog-tied, to the mercy of pure material forces. It seemed to him that the sole hope lay in a powerful development of the arts.

It was too much to expect, of course, that in times as complex as our own, with huge populations of widely diverse interests and educational backgrounds, the best in art could find its way, unaided, into the hearts and minds of the people. The output of artistic endeavor good, bad, and terrible, sincere and insincere, was too overwhelming, and too strong the temptation for commercial exploitation of the spurious and the corruption of taste. Here, thought R.S., was a situation which called desperately for the development of sound criticism in its broadest sense; in which the art of criticism might become one of the most important factors in civilization. Critics were needed to interpret, to segregate, to create judgment, to come out of their ivory towers and carry the battle for aesthetic standards into the world of everyday life.

Never before was there such an important function for great critics, thought R.S., critics who — like Goethe, Coleridge, Sainte-Beuve, or Taine — could lead the intelligent and sensitive up hills whence they could see many things to gladden their hearts and enrich their spirits, which, unguided, they might never have beheld. Then, filtering down-ward from the few to the many, standards and taste might eventually emerge. At any rate, art might regain the dignity to which it is entitled by man's need of it.

But a great critic, said Voltaire, is "an artist who possesses great knowledge and taste without prejudice and without envy," and he adds: "*Cela est difficile à trouver.*"

In spite of Voltaire's definition of a critic, R.S. wanted to air his own views on modern art, and incidentally on the critics who, he thought, were more and more devoting their talents to an almost scientific de-fense of the obscure, incomprehensible, and psychologically aberrant performances of modernistic experimenters.

I was a little nervous about letting R.S. — who was, in my opinion, artistically quite naïve — stick out his neck in his self-imposed role as a critic. Since his own preoccupation, outside of science, had been chiefly with poetry, I asked him, instead of criticizing the work of contempo-raries, to tell me what it was that gave him satisfaction in the poetry he read and which he tried to write himself. I add his reply more from the desire to give a complete picture of the man than from any idea that his views were either original or profound.

"Poetry," he said, "has been to me much like horses. Though I was often cheated in consequence, I never enjoyed critically appraising a horse, walking around it, feeling its hocks, looking at its teeth, and then seeing other people ride it. A horse meant little to me until I could feel it under me, swing with the rhythm of its gaits, rise over fences with it, and lean over its neck in the exhilaration of its galloping vigor.

"And so a poem means nothing to me unless it can carry me away with the gentle or passionate pace of its emotion, over obstacles of reality into meadows and covers of illusion. Nor is it the material that mat-ters — whether it be the old stirrings of nature and love, or war, or whether it deals with the tragedies and complexities of human fate. The sole criterion for me is whether it can sweep me with it into emotion or illusion of beauty, terror, tranquillity, or even (Herder to the con-trary) disgust — as in Baudelaire — so long as it arouses fundamental feelings or reflections which, encountered without the poet, might have passed half realized, like a tongue of flame or a flying leaf. For the poet arrests emotions at their points of greatest supportable heat — just short of the melting point, as it were — and can hold in that perfect state, permanent in his words and meters, those feelings and comprehensions which pass too quickly to be held through the minds of ordinary men.

The poet imprisons them in words or color or marble, so that we lesser men can contemplate them and recognize in them our own hearts and minds."

This was the last serious conversation I had with R.S.

R.S. returned from his last professional journey badly damaged. On the steamer he was humiliated by the fact that not only occasional youngsters but even a British general of approximately his own age could outlast him at deck tennis. Also the sun, instead of tinging his skin a healthy brown, turned him the lemon yellow of the sunburned anemic. He made a tentative diagnosis on himself before arrival in port.

So when he got home he went to see an old friend, a doctor, who had pulled him through a nasty infection a few years before. This friend was one of those precious individuals whom nature had meant to be physicians. He was fond of R.S. and showed it most helpfully by his affectionate abstinence from any expression of sympathy. And R.S. told me that together this good friend and he stood for a long time at the office window, looking out at the Charles River Basin. It was one of Lowell's June days, in the early afternoon. Bright sunshine was reflected from the water and from dozens of little white sails on the dinghies that were racing along the Cambridge shore. The Esplanade was alive with contented men and women, strolling and sitting on the benches; and the sounds of playing children came up through the open window like the voices of many birds. The world looked a bright and attractive place.

But in those few minutes, R.S. told me, something took place in his mind that he regarded as a sort of compensatory adjustment to the thought that he would soon be dead. In the prospect of death, life seemed to be given new meaning and fresh poignancy. It seemed, he said, from that moment as though all that his heart felt and his senses perceived was taking on a "deep autumnal tone" and an increased vividness. From now on, instead of being saddened, he found — to his own delighted astonishment — that his sensitiveness to the simplest experiences, even for things that in other years he might hardly have noticed, was infinitely enhanced.

When he awoke in the mornings, the early sun striking across the bed, the light on the branches of the trees outside his window, the noise of "his" sparrows, and the sounds of the awakening street aroused in him all kinds of gentle and pleasing memories of days long past which had left their imprints — indelible but, until now, not consciously realized — of contentment and happiness. It was quite the opposite of the "woe of the remembering of happy times" in Canto V of the *Inferno*. R.S. felt a deeper tenderness for the people whom he loved, and a warmer sympathy and understanding for many whose friendship he had lost in one way or another.

Each moment of the day, every prospect on meadow or hill or sea, every change of light from dawn to dusk, excited him emotionally with an unexpected clarity of perception and a new suggestiveness of association. Thinking of the shortness of the time still left him, he reread the books that had meant much to him at the various stages of his life and found them more moving, more deeply wise, or more hilariously robust, according to their natures. Everything that went on about him or within him struck upon his heart and mind with a new and powerful resonance. So, on the whole, he was far from either meriting or desiring sympathy. The only thing that depressed him at all in those days was the thought of horses. He couldn't stand the sight of his saddles, his bridles, and the various bits that hung about his bedroom — and which he now packed out of sight in the cellar.

As his malady progressed, he had another variety of experience which, to some others more conditioned to religious belief than he was, might have signified an intimation of the separateness of body and soul. He said to me: "Here I am, *me* as always. My mind more alive and vivid than ever before; my sensitiveness keener; my affections stronger. I seem for the first time to see the world in clear perspective; I love people more deeply and more comprehensively; I seem to be just beginning to learn my business and see my work in its proper relationship to science as a whole; I seem to myself to have entered into a period of stronger feelings and saner understanding. And yet here am I — essentially unchanged except for a sort of distillation into a more concentrated *me* — held in a damaged body which will extinguish me with it when it dies. If it were a horse I was riding that went lame or broke its neck, or a ship on which I was traveling that sprang a leak, I could transfer to another one and leave the old vehicle behind. As it is, my mind and my spirit, my thoughts and my love, all that I really am is inseparably tied up with the failing capacities of these outworn organs.

"Yet," he continued, apostrophizing in a serio-comic mood, "poor viscera, I can hardly blame you! You have done your best, and have served me better than could be expected of organs so abused. When I think of the things that have flowed over and through you! Innumerable varieties of fermented hops and malt and of the grapes of all coun-

tries and climates; to say nothing of the distillates, flavored and un-
flavored: cognac, whiskeys, and gin. No, no, my organs! I cannot feel
that you have let me down. It is quite the other way round. Only now
it seems so silly that you must take me with you when I am just beginning to get dry behind the ears."

Though he had these spells of half-humorous revolt against the idea
that his personality and his increasing joy of living should be so helplessly at the mercy of his deteriorating body, he was still grateful that, in
his case, it was this and not the mind that was going to pieces first. He
was not at any time tempted to seek strength in wishful surrender to a
religious faith in which far greater men than he had taken refuge just
before death. When this had, astonishingly, happened in the cases of
several of his intimate friends, he regarded it as a capitulation of the
mind to the fatigue of suffering. Indeed, he became more firm in his
determination to see things out consistently along his own lines of
resignation to agnostic uncertainty — as his father had done before
him. Moving further away, therefore, from faith in any comprehensible
conception of God, he yet grew closer in conviction of the wisdom and
guiding integrity of the compassionate philosophy of Christ.

As his disease caught up with him, R.S. felt increasingly grateful for
the fact that death was coming to him with due warning, and gradually.
So many times in his active life he had been near sudden death by accident, violence, or acute disease; and always he had thought that rapid
and unexpected extinction would be most merciful. But now he was
thankful that he had time to compose his spirit, and to spend a last
year in affectionate and actually merry association with those dear to
him. He set down this feeling in his last sonnet:

> Now is death merciful. He calls me hence
> Gently, with friendly soothing of my fears
> Of ugly age and feeble impotence
> And cruel disintegration of slow years.
> Nor does he leap upon me unaware
> Like some wild beast that hungers for its prey,
> But gives me kindly warning to prepare:
> Before I go, to kiss your tears away.
>
> How sweet the summer! And the autumn shone
> Late warmth within our hearts as in the sky,
> Ripening rich harvests that our love had sown.
> How good that ere the winter comes, I die!
> Then, ageless, in your heart I'll come to rest
> Serene and proud, as when you loved me best.

It is apparent, therefore, that in his last months R.S. achieved a certain degree of philosophical tranquillity and resignation. It would be a mistake, however, to suppose that, apart from his purely personal reactions to his own fate and his immediate environment, he was less confused at the time of his death than in his youth. When he gazed beyond the circle of his own work, his family and friends, into the rushing world about him, he was completely bewildered. He had a little the same resentful feeling that he remembered having when, as a boy, he had walked through Normandy and had to jump into the ditch to let one of the recently invented automobiles rattle by — knowing that its passengers would have dinner at the town where he expected to arrive two days later. It was all moving too fast for him. Indeed, he was not sure whether the world that was rushing by was going forward or backward. He wondered whether he had not, perhaps, been born a little too late and remained unable to catch up with his time.

The world to which he had been born had not alone speeded up with that acceleration of which Henry Adams complained, but had actually seemed to change direction. Scientific progress had brought as much sorrow as happiness. With immensely enhanced powers of production, millions were out of work and starving. Not only were ideas of democracy and individual freedom which he had accepted as the gradually evolved goals of centuries of struggle being denied, but entire nations were frantically intent on destroying them. Great racial masses seemed willing to fight and perish, if necessary, for their own enslavement. New so-called "ideologies" were tearing up the foundations of all that men had thought firm and permanently established. Something had cracked in the old Western civilization, and its walls and lofty towers — cemented with the sweat and blood of their forefathers — were tumbling about men's ears. And the intellectual calamity seemed to be that no one could say whether the turmoil was the result of avoidable stupidity or of the operation of laws of economic and social evolution that were acting on mankind as other laws had acted on the dinosaur and the saber-toothed tiger.

But in all these things he could never tell, before he died, whether the fault was in him or in the trends he disliked. He didn't admit this, of course, and remained to the last argumentatively arrogant. But I knew that at the time of his death he was as thoroughly bewildered as any thoughtful individual of our time is bound to be.

All of which goes to prove that R.S. was really a quite ordinary person about whom it was hardly worth while to write a book.

X

The Shape of Things to Come

The feeling of expansion and of expectation was in the air. An American naval officer, Captain A. T. Mahan, was prompted to look ahead when he heard the plans for cutting a canal through the Isthmus of Panama, and what he wrote about the urgent need of our defenses in the Pacific was read and marked by Theodore Roosevelt. In the spring of 1898, before our sudden and smashing victory over Spain, Richard Olney, who had been Secretary of State under Cleveland, foretold the necessity of the Anglo-American alliance; he was quoted in full on the front page of the New York Times and, the day following, on the front page of The Times of London. We turned into the twentieth century with these new concepts and this new apprehension of destiny, and under the successive editorships of Walter Hines Page and Bliss Perry, a new note of prophecy was heard in the magazine.

This was not just local talk. Brooks Adams on monopoly, F. M. Taussig on free trade, Arthur Pound on the iron man in industry, were three who translated the current event into terms of national consequence. In three articles which Pound published in the autumn of 1921 he anticipated by more than a decade the findings of the Lynds in Middletown. Pound based his study on close observation of actual conditions in a single typical Michigan city in the automotive belt. He had been born in Flint when it was a little agricultural community; in the two decades leading up to the publication of his book the population of his home town had increased tenfold, due mostly to the influx of non-natives who came either to tend automatic machines or to supply the wants of those who did. His was the Atlantic's first view of "the new automation," and the prediction that came with it was both true and startling.

In the fall of 1925, spurred on by Ellery Sedgwick, William Z. Ripley, Professor of Political Science at Harvard, began a survey of the new legal devices by which the common stockholder was being dispossessed of his traditional rights of control. His first article, "From Main Street to Wall Street," burst in the January issue of 1926, and Sedgwick employed sandwich men to advertise the attack by parading up and down Wall Street. That issue sold out, and copies in New York were going at a dollar apiece before the supply was exhausted. Ripley's probing and unsparing criticism continued in subsequent issues, anticipating by eight years the regulations which were finally made law by the creation of the Securities and Exchange Commission in 1934 and the passage of the Public Utilities Act. Ripley blazed that trail.

Just as Nathaniel Hawthorne on the deck of the Monitor knew that the days of the sailing ship were at an end, so Dr. David Bradley, as he worked with his Geiger counter on the atoll and the dead ships of Bikini to protect the Navy personnel from the effects of radiation, received the full premonition of atomic warfare. His small book, No Place to Hide, *was a sensation in 1948, when it first appeared in the* Atlantic; *it told Americans that their citadel of defense was gone for good.*

It is the gleam in the eye of such prophets which we see here; we show the prophecy at the point of contact, and the dates are important in emphasizing how far these writers were ahead of their time.

1867 ———— Westward Growth

The development of American commercial power as against the world is secondary to the internal development of our own resources, and to the indissoluble bond of national union afforded by this inland route from the Atlantic to the Pacific, and by its future connections with every portion of our territory. In thirty years, California will have a population equal to that of New York today, and yet not be half full, and the city of St. Louis will number a million souls. New York City and San Francisco, as the two great entrepôts of trade, Chicago and St. Louis as its two vital centers, and New Orleans at the mouth of our great national canal, the Mississippi, will become nations rather than cities, outstripping all the great cities of ancient and modern history. As far as the resources of the West are concerned, one Pacific railroad with two or three branches will not suffice; we may need a road along every parallel.

The West is still in a large degree terra incognita. We know it only in parts. We are indeed aware that California is already competing with Russia and the cis-Mississippi states in the production of cereals, and that the mineral region of the West now annually yields gold and silver worth one hundred million dollars. But California's agricultural resources are almost untouched, while the best "leads" of the vast mineral region are not worked, from the fear of a savage race. Missouri extends over thirty-five million acres of arable land, two million of which are the alluvial margins of rivers and twenty thousand are high rolling prairie; but five sevenths of the soil is yet fallow. We see Denver and other cities of the Far West spring up in a day; but their growth, marvelous as it is, arises from the circumstance that they are great mineral centers, and is cramped and partial, depending upon an insecure overland route extending over hundreds of miles, via Salt Lake, to Atchison.

The Pacific railroad will quicken this development to its full possibilities; it will populate the West in a few years; and along its lines will spring up a hundred cities, which will advance in the swift march of national progress just in proportion to their opportunities for rapid communication with the older centers of opulence and culture. The corollary of the Pacific railroads is the transfer of the world's commerce to

America, and the substitution of New York for Paris and London as the world's exchange. In the train of these immeasurable events must come the wealth and the culture which have hitherto been limited to Europe.

From "Our Pacific Railroads" by James Knowles Medbery, December 1867

1877———The Caliber of Congress

Now, more than ever before, the people are responsible for the character of their Congress. If that body be ignorant, reckless, and corrupt, it is because the people tolerate ignorance, recklessness, and corruption. If it be intelligent, brave, and pure, it is because the people demand those high qualities to represent them in the national legislature. Congress lives in the blaze of "that fierce light which beats against the throne." Now, as always, Congress represents the prevailing opinions and political aspirations of the people.

Our national safety demands that the fountains of political power shall be made pure by intelligence, and kept pure by vigilance; that the best citizens shall take heed to the selection and election of the worthiest and most intelligent among them to hold seats in the national legislature; and that when the choice has been made, the continuance of their representative shall depend upon his faithfulness, his ability, and his willingness to work.

Congress must always be the exponent of the political character and culture of the people; and if the next centennial does not find us a great nation, with a great and worthy Congress, it will be because those who represent the enterprise, the culture, and the morality of the nation do not aid in controlling the political forces which are employed to select the men who shall occupy the great places of trust and power.

From "A Century of Congress" by James A. Garfield, July 1877

1890———The Panama Canal

Our self-imposed isolation in the matter of markets and the decline of our shipping interest in the last thirty years have coincided singularly with an actual remoteness of this continent from the life of the rest of the world. The writer has before him a map of the North and South Atlantic oceans, showing the direction of the principal trade routes and the proportion of tonnage passing over each; and it is curious to note what deserted regions, comparatively, are the Gulf of Mexico, the Caribbean Sea, and the adjoining countries and islands.

When the Isthmus is pierced this isolation will pass away, and with it the indifference of foreign nations. From wheresoever they come and whithersoever they afterward go, all ships that use the Canal will pass through the Caribbean. Whatever the effect produced upon the prosperity of the adjacent continent and islands by the thousand wants attendant upon maritime activity, around such a focus of trade will center large commercial and political interests. To protect and develop its own, each nation will seek points of support and means of influence in a quarter where the United States has always been jealously sensitive to the intrusion of European powers.

Whether they will or no, Americans must now begin to look outward. The growing production of the country demands it. An increasing volume of public sentiment demands it. The position of the United States, between the two Old Worlds and the two great oceans, makes the same claim, which will soon be strengthened by the creation of the new link joining the Atlantic and Pacific. The tendency will be maintained and increased by the growth of the European colonies in the Pacific, by the advancing civilization of Japan, and by the rapid peopling of our Pacific states with men who have all the aggressive spirit of the advanced line of national progress. Nowhere does a vigorous foreign policy find more favor than among the people west of the Rocky Mountains.

The military needs of the Pacific states, as well as their supreme importance to the whole country, are yet a matter of the future, but of a future so near that provision should immediately begin. Three things are needful: First, protection of the chief harbors by fortifications and coast-defense ships, which gives defensive strength, provides security to the community within, and supplies the bases necessary to all military operations. Secondly, naval force, the arm of offensive power, which alone enables a country to extend its influence outward. Thirdly, it should be an inviolable resolution of our national policy that no European state should henceforth acquire a coaling position within three thousand miles of San Francisco — a distance which includes the Sandwich and Galapagos islands and the coast of Central America.

From "The United States Looking Outward" by A. T. Mahan,
December 1890

1898——The Advertiser and the Daily Press

We have not yet hit on the best plan of getting at "public opinion." Elections at best tell us only what half the people are thinking; for no party nowadays wins an electoral victory by much over half the voters. So that we are driven back, for purposes of observation, on the newspaper press.

Our confidence in this is based on the theory, not so much that the newspapers make public opinion, as that the opinions they utter are those of which their readers approve. But this ground is being made less tenable every year by the fact that more and more newspapers rely on advertising rather than on subscriptions for their support and profits, and agreement with their readers is thus less and less important to them. The old threat of "stopping my paper" if a subscriber came across unpalatable views in the editorial columns is therefore not so formidable as it used to be, and is less resorted to. The advertiser, rather than the subscriber, is now the newspaper bogie. He is the person before whom the publisher cowers and whom he tries to please, and the advertiser is very indifferent about the opinions of a newspaper. What interests him is the amount or quality of its circulation. What he wants to know is how many persons see it, not how many persons agree with it. The consequence is that the newspapers of largest circulation, published in the great centers of population where most votes are cast, are less and less organs of opinion, especially in America. In fact, in some cases the advertisers use their influence — which is great, and which the increasing competition between newspapers makes all the greater — to prevent the expression in newspapers of what is probably the prevailing local view of men or events. There are not many newspapers which can afford to defy a large advertiser.

From "The Growth and Expression of Public Opinion" by E. L. Godkin,
January 1898

1898——Anglo-American Alliance

The mission of this country is not merely to pose but to act. There is such a thing for a nation as a "splendid isolation" — as when for a worthy cause, for its own independence or vital interests, it unshrinkingly opposes itself to a hostile world. But isolation that is nothing but a shirking of the responsibilities of high place and great power is simply ignominious. If we shall sooner or later — and we certainly shall — shake off the spell of the Washington legend and cease to act the role of a sort of international recluse, it will not follow that formal alliances with other nations for permanent or even temporary purposes will soon or often be found expedient. On the other hand, with which of them we shall as a rule practically coöperate cannot be doubtful. From the point of view of our material interests alone, our best friend as well as most formidable foe is that world-wide empire whose navies rule the seas and which on our northern frontier controls a dominion itself imperial in extent and capabilities.

There is a patriotism of race as well as of country — and the Anglo-American is as little likely to be indifferent to the one as to the other. Family quarrels there have been heretofore and doubtless will be again, and the two peoples, at the safe distance which the broad Atlantic interposes, take with each other liberties of speech which only the fondest and dearest relatives indulge in. Nevertheless, that they would be found standing together against any alien foe by whom either was menaced with destruction or irreparable calamity, it is not permissible to doubt. Nothing less could be expected of the close community between them in origin, speech, thought, literature, institutions, ideals — in the kind and degree of the civilization enjoyed by both. In that same community, and in that coöperation in good works which should result from it, lies, it is not too much to say, the best hope for the future not only of the two kindred peoples but of the human race itself.

From "International Isolation of the United States" by Richard Olney,
May 1898

1910——Monopoly

In our universe, so far as we know, there is no such thing as a stable equilibrium. There is only change; and competition, by the process of elimination of the weak, led inexorably to monopoly. Taking human history altogether, I apprehend that monopoly is rather the natural condition of mankind than competition, for, to go no further than the beginning, an organized social system can exist on no other foundation than monopoly. Justice must be a monopoly. There can be no competition in justice. That the state, and not the citizen, shall punish wrong, is the first principle of civilization.

Yet although, as we can now see, the evolution of monopoly from competition was inevitable, it had not been foreseen, much less provided for, and it paralyzed the nineteenth-century intelligence; for in less than a single generation, the whole vital movement of the age passed beyond the domain of law.

Modern society, as reorganized after the French Revolution, posited as its fundamental principle that if buyer and seller were left free, they would come together, substantially on what Adam Smith called the "natural price"; if one man asked more than a normal profit for his goods, another would be content with less for the same article, the supposition being that there would always be more than one seller, or, as we say, an open market.

Since 1870 these conditions have vanished as utterly as have the conditions of the Stone Age. Competition has exterminated the weak until monopoly is left as the survivor; and with the advent of monopoly, buying and selling passes out of the region of contract into the domain of grant, which involves legal conceptions foreign to our notions. Grant precludes choice, except the choice of abstinence, which is often impossible. For example, if a person wishes to buy a ton of coal he may ask a price, but if he does not like the price named by the dealer he has no redress, for the price of coal is fixed by monopoly. He must pay what is asked, or go without.

But the monopoly is a natural phenomenon, as inexorable as the steam, the electricity, and the explosives which have created it under the guidance of the scientific mind. To attack monopoly is to attack the vital principle of our civilization. We may destroy monopoly, but with it we shall destroy civilization itself. The alternatives are to bring monopoly under the jurisdiction of the courts or else for the monopolist to enroll an armed police which shall enforce his will upon the majority without their consent. Impartial tribunals are a prerequisite to consent by the governed. Without impartial tribunals there can only be force or chaos.

From "A Problem in Civilization" by Brooks Adams, July 1910

1910——Free Trade

The dependence of our manufacturing industries on tariff duties is enormously exaggerated. The constant shouting about foreign pauper labor has brought about a state of pusillanimity among the manufacturers themselves. Most of them know virtually nothing about foreign conditions. They are familiar only with their own business and with that which touches their daily routine. Foreign competition has been nonexistent for years. What its real possibilities are, they do not know. But the politicians and those few shrewder manufacturers who have cleverly formed plans for aid to special industries have incessantly predicted wholesale ruin unless the tariff system were maintained without the change of a dot.

A searching inquiry would show, I am convinced, that our present system of extremely high duties could be greatly pruned without any disturbance of vested interests. One great gain from such an overhauling of the tariff would be to lessen its importance in the public mind. To the economist nothing is more nauseating than the cry about prosperity and the tariff. From much of the current campaign talk, one would suppose that the country would go to certain ruin if a single duty were reduced by a fraction of a per cent. Manufacturing industries in general are in the main not dependent on protection. This country of ours is certain to be a great manufacturing one under any tariff system. Still less is our general prosperity dependent on the tariff. Our natural resources, our vigor, industry, and intelligence, our training in school and college and shop, the enterprise and judgment of our business leaders — these are the things on which material welfare depends.

I would not have the reader infer that I am an unqualified free trader, or that this view of the tariff problem leads immediately, or even ultimately, to complete abolition of all except revenue duties. But few economists would say a good word for such an exaggerated protectionist policy, one so intolerant of foreign competition and foreign supply, as the United States has been following in the McKinley tariff of 1890, in the Dingley tariff of 1897, and now, with but slight change of essentials, in the Payne-Aldrich tariff of 1909. When duties of 50, 80, and 100 per cent come to be looked upon as normal protectionist rates; when ingenious devices and "jokers" are resorted to in order to bring about such high rates without its being made plain that this is the thing really aimed at and accomplished; when, by the logrolling process, the policy comes to be applied indiscriminately to any and every article without scrutiny of the possibility of ultimate cheapening or the promise of social or political gain — then it is time to call a halt.

I would not undertake to foretell whether free trade will be abandoned in Great Britain, or protection in the United States. But the outlook is certainly for a moderation of extreme protectionist policies. The various nations which have stirred each other to measures of commercial warfare — and the United States has been most aggressively guilty in this regard — seem to be wearying of a game which each can play with effect against the other. The indications are for some sort of compromise all around; an illogical proceeding, perhaps, but a very human one. In this moderated course of action the United States is likely to join; and all sorts of persons, whatever their opinions (or lack of opinions) as to the goal ultimately to be reached, will think and vote in favor of pruning a protectionist system which has become so rigidly and intolerantly restrictive as ours.

From "The Tariff and the Tariff Commission" by F. W. Taussig,
December 1910

1921 ——— Automation

THE RISE OF JUVENILE DELINQUENCY

The majority of youths, male and female, no longer need to be told how to earn their living. Days after the law that sets limits on child labor leaves them free to work at the machines, they will be earning big money — practically as much as they ever will earn. There is little to learn; the mills can teach that better and cheaper than the schools. The pockets of these children are full of money at an age when their fathers earned less than a living wage as apprentices. They are economically independent of home and of social control. They have the eternal belief of youth that the preceding generation is fossilized, and the buying power to act upon their belief. They buy pleasures, buy companions, buy glad raiment; they try — desperately — to buy happiness. And fail. Yet they are splendid raw material for citizens. They met every war need more than half way; fought and fell; sacrificed and saved — during the emergency. Their faults are those of youth plus affluence.

Herein lies the explanation of our youthful delinquency. Our "bad men" of this winter are mostly minors. In a town dominated by automatic machines, the educational program is to train youths for the right use of leisure. Precisely here is the point of my argument. Education for leisure, under the conditions of automatic production, is education for life. What was once a privilege for an arrogant aristocracy has become a necessity for an arrogant democracy. Unless American gentlemen and gentlewomen appear in due time and in sufficient numbers our civilization will be wrecked by machine-made barbarians, unable — though their machines compass the globe — to replace what they have destroyed.

THE DEGRADATION OF THE MACHINE TENDER

There develops among the workers in highly automatized plants a chronic dissatisfaction which cannot be explained away. It seems to be proof against high wages and good conditions. Welfare work, bonuses, shop councils, even profit sharing do not drive it out. Clatter and haste are contributing factors; so, also, are indoor confinement, monotony of task, distance from the mill boss, repression of personality, strict regimentation of effort, and the scant opportunity afforded for the play of the craftsman instinct, the joy in production.

But the basic cause lies deeper. Even the simple annals of the medieval poor must have been crowded with adventure as compared with the systematic, colorless, bare-of-drama tasks of the modern factory. The worker is there in the factory not because he wants to be, but because he needs the money and can discover no other means of getting it. Yet there is that stirring within him which informs him, even before the voice of the agitator reinforces the conviction, that this is no life for a real man. He gets, literally, no fun out of his labors. Our tenders of ma-

chines are being starved in their souls; and while there may be seda-
tives for that malady, there is no specific. Soon or late all peoples will be
brought to the ordeal by the Iron Man.

From "The Iron Man in Industry" by Arthur Pound, October to
December 1921

1925——Atomic Energy

If we could utilize the forces which we know now to exist inside the
atom, we should have such capacities for destruction that I do not know
of any agency, other than divine intervention, which would save humanity from complete and peremptory nullification. But the remoteness
of the day when we shall use these forces may best be judged by an
analogy.

We cannot make apparatus small enough to disintegrate or fuse
atomic nuclei, any more than we can make it large enough to reach to
the moon. We can only bombard them with particles of which perhaps
one in a million hit, which is like firing keys at a safe door from a machine gun a mile away in an attempt to open it. We do occasionally open
it, but the process is very uneconomical. It may be asked why we cannot
bring our machine gun nearer or improve our aim. To do this would require the construction of apparatus on the same infinitesimal scale as
the structure of the chemical atom.

Now we can arrange atoms into various patterns. For example, we
can arrange carbon, hydrogen, and oxygen atoms in patterns which constitute the molecules of sugar, glycerine, or alcohol at will. This is called
chemical synthesis. We have been doing it by rule-of-thumb methods for
thousands of years and are just beginning to know a little about it. But
even chemical molecules are much too large for our purposes. We can
no more ask a chemist to build our apparatus than expect a theatrical
scene painter or a landscape gardener to do us a miniature. We know
very little about the structure of the atom and almost nothing about how
to modify it, and the prospect of constructing such an apparatus seems
to me to be so remote that when some successor of mine is lecturing to
a party spending a holiday on the moon, it will still be an unsolved —
though not, I think, an ultimately insoluble — problem.

From "Chemistry and Peace" by J. B. S. Haldane, January 1925

1926———Stock Market Regulation

Several millions of our fellow citizens are part owners in the $70 billion capitalization of American corporations, according to the federal tax returns, in the year 1923. Individual and partnership forms of business organization disappeared in favor of the corporation even before the war. But since the war, and particularly in this heyday of prosperity, the facile initiating and legal minds have hit upon something which puts once and for all at rest the last vestige of the owner's power to participate in prudent and efficient management of property. These last two years, 1924–25, promise to go down in history — like the Year of the Plague — as the Years of the Split Common Stock and the Vanishing Stockholder.

Even before the World War the practice was not uncommon, outside of railroads, of setting off preferred shares as nonvoting. The amount of these issues was in those days adjusted to the tangible assets, leaving the common shares to represent the equity, which depended upon successful management to be secured by the exercise of the voting rights. The late invention now splits up these common shares. To be in the mode one has, let us call it, a "Class A participating" common stock, with a first lien on earnings after satisfaction of all prior claims of preferred stocks and bonds. This leaves a "Class B" common stock representing, according to circumstances, the cream, the scum, the froth, or the sediment of the business; for the full voting rights attach exclusively to these Class B common shares, none, or only a minority, of which are offered to the public at all. The appetite for the preferred shares may sometimes be whetted by a flavoring of the Class A common shares, but not of those which carry votes. The recent "Dodge Brothers, Inc.," is typical. A banking house buys up a private business for, it has been said, $146 million or thereabouts. This sum, and more too, they recover — if the plan works out — by the sale to the public, for $160 million, of bonds and preferred stock at par and 1.5 million *nonvoting* shares of Class A common stock. But not a single one of the 500,000 Class B voting (no par) common shares are thus sold. The promoters have virtually paid themselves a handsome profit for the assumption of the entire directorial power, having mortgaged the property to the full amount of its original cost through outstanding bonds and preferred stock, including both assets and capitalized earning power. And the amazing thing is that this final deathblow to the exercise of voting rights by the general public has brought no voice of protest. Yet the plan bears every appearance of a bald and outrageous theft of the last tittle of responsibility for management of the actual owners by those who are setting up these financial erections. Isn't it the prettiest case ever known of having a cake and eating it too?

There is of late another financial practice, also, which greatly accentuates this nullification of the ordinary shareholder. This is the wide distribution of stock to employees and the consumers of the corporation's product, whether electric service, steel, or what not. The effect in any event is bound to be cumulative with that of the insinuation of professional management power between ownership and operation.

Corporations have always been susceptible to control by concentration of voting power. Far less than half of the capital stock may be as effective for such control as possession of an actual majority. But it is elemental that the larger the number of shareholders, the more easily may a small concentrated block of minority shares exercise sway over all the rest. With a dozen owners, probably 51 per cent will be necessary for dominance. With 300,000 scattered holdings, a possible 15 to 20 per cent of the votes can never be overmatched at an election.

This present tendency to strip the public shareholders of their voting rights may be checked either through revision of our corporation laws or by a vigorous attitude on the part of the courts. Direct action by the investing class, by boycotting all such offerings of securities, may give even more immediate results. But, in either or any event, no other safeguard against misuse of power by insiders is so likely to be effective as publicity.

Whatever is to be done about the affairs, either of private corporations dealing in the necessaries of life in more than any one state in the union, or with, let us say, the Associated Gas and Electric Company, must evidently be done on a larger basis than a single commonwealth affords. It is inconceivable that joint giant power commissions should be set up by different groups of states, each group corresponding to the especial scope and extent of the particular corporation which it is intended to supervise. The answer, alas, seems to be always the same. If anything needs doing, there is but one agency to which to turn — exercise of the federal power.

From "From Main Street to Wall Street" by William Z. Ripley,
January 1926

1933———Fascism Versus Democracy

The current experience of the United States will show, I suspect, that Fascism is not the inevitable form which a non-Bolshevist society must take, but rather that it is abnormal and pathological. Philosophically, Fascism is a movement whose leaders are civilians in riding boots. Politically, it is an entirely new type of tyranny, both personal and demagogic — a tyranny which for the first time in history exploits the mob spirit in an era of universal suffrage and gives to the supreme leaders irresponsible power as limitless as that of the modern state. In contrast to this picture, we now see in America a leader who has never played the role of hero or savior and whose greatest ambition appears to be to look like a common human being, a member of the middle class by voluntary affiliation. Without frowning or putting on a mask of ferocity, he has taken on his shoulders the heaviest burden that any President ever assumed; he does not shirk the responsibility, and he stands ready to give an account of his stewardship when the time comes.

In spite of the novelty of Roosevelt's experiments, perhaps the most appropriate term for this new American way of grappling with social and economic unrest is still the good old word "democracy."

From "Fascism in the Making" by Max Ascoli, November 1933

1948———The Bomb

Friday, August 9 — This afternoon I was assigned to make a survey of the *New York*. This venerable old battlewagon, constructed about 1914, was pretty badly hit by the Bikini test bombs. Her superstructures aft are a jungle of steel, and she has been taking in water enough in the stern to require almost continuous pumping. Radioactive material has leaked into her after compartments and has come in through every portal and companionway above. Stores of food, hundreds of pounds of coffee, and even the drinking water have had to be condemned.

All previous attempts at decontamination have been notably unsuccessful. The decks have been sluiced down with water. When this caused no reduction in radioactivity, buckets of soap were broken out. Still the same result.

Today a trial was being made of alkali. The main deck forward had not been touched as yet, and here we proposed to run the experiment. I made a careful survey of the deck, finding the intensity to vary a great deal in a matter of feet. One gets the impression that fission products have become most fixed in the tarry calking of the planking and in rusty spots in the metal plates.

When the survey was complete the Chief turned his booted, sweating, profane, and laughing crew loose with brushes, water, and a barrel of lye. Yet when the hydraulics were done and the deck was rinsed clean again, another survey showed the invisible emanations to be doing business as usual. The portly Chief stood watching the dial of my Geiger counter, completely bewildered. The deck was clean — anybody could see that — clean enough for the Admiral himself to eat his breakfast off of. So what was all this goddam radioactivity?

Finally he could stand it no longer: "Here, Doc, let me listen to that gadget, will you?"

I fitted the headphones over his ears. He stood moving the gadget over the deck as I had done, and listening intently. He shook his head: "Must be fouled up. I only get static now."

"That's all you ever get, Chief. What did you expect — Dorothy Lamour?"

He looked dubious: "Well, what are they, them clicks? Do they mean anything?"

"They sure do, Chief. Each of those clicks is a little bullet shooting through your body. You get enough of them and they will kill you. You don't know it, but this deck is a booby trap."

Still unconvinced, but taken with the gadget, he went off for a cruise around his deck. He'd seen two wars fought out from that deck. He wasn't particularly concerned about a stray bullet or two. Finally he hove to, beside a stanchion, where several of his men were resting. They grinned at him as he surveyed the area. Then suddenly he straightened up.

"Here, you guys," he said with gruff authority, "get the hell off that stanchion. Can't you see you're sittin' on a goddam booby trap?"

The sailors took off of that stanchion as though 440 volts had hit them, dusting off their jeans and feeling behind as if they expected to find something sticking there. Feeling nothing, they laughed.

Saturday, August 10 — Operation Crossroads as an experiment is being abandoned. A skelcton Task Force will remain out here to keep the target vessels afloat, and a skeleton Radiological Safety Section will stay to carry on the public health work. Volunteers are being rounded up for the job. Most of the trained scientific personnel, being civilian and pressed with teaching and research engagements stateside, will have to leave, and so of course will the higher echelon of Navy personnel.

Things have not gone according to plan. The target fleet, which was to have steamed triumphantly back to Pearl and the Golden Gate, invincible as ever, will remain here at anchor, blackened with flame and streaked with foamite and rust, until the ships can be safely disposed of. Some may eventually be towed to the West Coast; many will certainly be sunk in deep water.

A few ships, notably the submarines, have been given clearance to go to Pearl Harbor for repairs and further decontamination, but the rest remain. Some inkling of the danger which persists aboard these ships can be gleaned from the conditions imposed by the Admiral on all future operations. All work henceforth will be confined to that necessary for closing up the ships. This is a momentous decision, a momentous admission, and there are many reasons behind it. Among those which are no secret are:

1. That these ships are fouled up with radioactivity to a degree far greater than was anticipated.

2. That this coat of radioactive paint cannot be scrubbed off or removed by any of the ordinary measures, short of chipping off all the paint and rust and uprooting all the planking from the outsides of the ships.

3. That there is a real hazard from elements present which cannot be detected by the ordinary methods.

One of these is plutonium. We have to assume the presence of plutonium on these ships because it is impossible for a bomb to be 100 per cent efficient. In the instant of explosion not all atoms of plutonium can undergo fission. Some do. The rest are blown apart to a subcritical concentration and the chain reaction dies out.

The degree of efficiency of the bomb is top secret, but recent studies with the alpha counter have established the presence of alpha emitters, among them plutonium. These studies include samples of paint from ships' decks, samples of rust, and even air samples taken from within ships by means of a vacuum cleaner device and filter paper.

Sunday, October 6 — It would seem that our work out here is about at an end. The derelict fleet may go on indefinitely, being pumped out or towed away to sink. All thought of decontaminating the ships and getting them under way again is, of course, out of the question, and save for the effects of weathering and rusting, one could study these ships as well ten years from now as today. The recent announcement by the President, canceling Test Charlie (the deep-water shot), would seem to be the final *coup de grâce* for Operation Crossroads.

The Crossroads Tests at first glance might seem to have been a failure. From a military point of view the two shots confirmed what was already known of the effectiveness of a chain reaction as an explosive, and certainly proved beyond all expectations what was feared concerning the poisoning of land, sea, and air with radioactivity. Scientifically what was learned in the crude laboratory of Bikini remains to be evaluated and declassified from the archives of military secrecy.

But *the greatest failure of all in these tests has been in apprehending their sociological implications.* Evidently the bomb has failed to impress more than a few congenital pessimists with the full scope of its lethal potential. This error in publicity — an error of omission — might be justifiable on the basis of strict military secrecy. In the long run, however, the one thing more dangerous than informed governments abroad will be an uninformed American opinion making our policies. The question is not political so much as biological. It is not just the security of a political system but the survival of the race that is at stake in the indiscriminate use of atomic energy for political coercion. Its unique problems are self-evident; there is nothing about them so profound as to require translation by a scientist. Among them are:

1. That there is no real defense against atomic weapons.

2. That there are no satisfactory countermeasures and methods of decontamination.

3. That there are no satisfactory medical or sanitary safeguards for the people of atomized areas.

4. That the devastating influence of the bomb and its unborn relatives may affect the land and its wealth — and therefore its people — for centuries through the persistence of radioactivity.

These facts are substantiated in theory by experiments upon thousands of animals, and in practice by Hiroshima, Nagasaki, and Bikini. It is in this sense that the Crossroads Tests have been anything but failures. Hastily planned and hastily carried out, they may have only sketched in the gross outlines of the real problem; nevertheless, those outlines show pretty clearly the shadow of the colossus which looms behind tomorrow.

Thursday, October 10 — What was learned at Bikini of a scientific or military nature may have been of value. Unfortunately, much of it is disguised in the esoteric idiom of the scientist. The really great lessons of that experiment, however, belong to no special group but to all mankind. The atomic era, fortunately or otherwise, is now man's environment, to control or to adapt himself to as he can.

Atomic research daily gathers momentum with its full train of military and social implications. For good or for ill we have embarked on this blind program.

There is no way back.

From "No Place to Hide" by David Bradley, M.D., December 1948

1950——The One-paper Town

The final going down of the New York *Sun* is said to have thrown twelve hundred newspaper workers out of employment. The individual tragedies involved in this catastrophe are justly regarded as of more than local concern; they have a large social significance as evidence of the constricting limits of one field of human endeavor, that of daily journalism. Daily newspaper work, if not a dying profession, is certainly a shrinking one.

News is rapidly assuming the status of water, communication, and electricity. Supplying it calls for an immense, and increasing, capital investment and very large daily expenditures. Whether it comes through newspapers, by radio-television, or through the movies, it involves the employment of millions of dollars and thousands of men; and only great capitalists, usually in the form of great corporations, can undertake it. This means that supplying news assumes every day more of the nature of a natural monopoly.

It is already collectivized to a high degree. The Associated Press, the United Press, and the International News Service are all essentially coöperatives, even when, as in the case of INS, they preserve the form of private ownership. The local newspaper is simply an outlet, as is the individual member of a coöperative chain-store group.

What the country needs is not the abolition of editorial writers, but more, many more, and better ones. But as daily newspapers decrease in numbers there are fewer positions open to such men; and as the corporate form grows vaster and more complex, their independence is more and more restricted. My suggestion is that the editorial writer is badly placed on a daily newspaper, and that his position grows worse with every newspaper that collapses. The number of contending opinions has been reduced by 40 per cent since 1929, by the disappearance of daily newspapers in that proportion.

Added to economic giantism, this plainly points to the day when most cities will rely for news of record on one huge journal, issued twice — and in large cities possibly three times — a day.

But no one will look to it for opinion any more than people now look to the telephone or the electric-light company for opinion. That will be supplied by a multitude of four-page sheets sold for a cent but written by exceptionally alert and well-informed men. Not being burdened with responsibility for millions of other people's money, as a conscientious executive of a large newspaper is, they will say what they think, and they will usually think accurately. Opinion must find some other channel. What the channel will be, only the seventh son of a seventh son is competent to guess. But it will be found. To doubt it would be to doubt the final perseverance of intelligence.

From "The Monopoly of News" by Gerald W. Johnson, September 1950

X I

Dogs

You either love dogs or you don't, and only those who do can write about them. We have published some memorable dog stories in the Atlantic. *Two of the best, too long for inclusion here, were* Flush, A Biography, *by Virginia Woolf, and* The Voice of Bugle Ann, *by MacKinlay Kantor. There is one aspect of dog literature not always perceived by the reader: the dog's nose is of utmost importance and the story will often depend on scents and smells. This is the most atrophied of the human senses, and as a result the writer may run short of sufficient adjectives and adverbs.*

Moses

by WALTER D. EDMONDS

For Walter D. Edmonds, author of Drums Along the Mohawk
and Long Haul, *the Mohawk Valley was the favorite setting
for his stories, and for many an autumn at his farm in Boonville, Moses was his hunting companion.*

AUGUST 1938

It was a long climb. The scent was cold, too; so faint that when he found it behind the barn he could hardly trust himself. He had just come back from Filmer's with a piece of meat, and he had sat down behind the barn and cracked it down; and a minute later he found that scent reaching off, faint as it was, right from the end of his nose as he lay.

He had had the devil of a time working it out at first, but up here it was simple enough except for the faintness of it. There didn't appear to be any way to stray off this path; there wasn't any brush, there wasn't any water. Only he had to make sure of it, when even for him it nearly faded out, with so many other stronger tracks overlaying it. His tail drooped, and he stumbled a couple of times, driving his nose into the dust. He looked gaunt when he reached the spot where the man had lain down to sleep.

The scent lay heavier there. He shuffled round over it, sifting the dust with an audible clapping of his nostrils to work out the pattern the man had made. It was hard to do, for the dust didn't take scent decently. It wasn't like any dust he had ever come across, either, being glittery, like mica, and slivery in his nose. But he could tell after a minute how the man had lain, on his back, with his hands under his head, and probably his hat over his eyes to shield them from the glare which was pretty dazzling bright up this high, with no trees handy.

His tail began to cut air. He felt better, and all of a sudden he lifted up his freckled nose and let out a couple of short yowps and then a good chest-swelled belling. Then he struck out up the steep going once more. His front legs may have elbowed a little, but his hind legs were full of spring, and his tail kept swinging.

That was how the old man by the town entrance saw him, way down below.

The old man had his chair in the shadow of the wall with a black and yellow parasol tied to the back of it as an extra insurance against the sun. He was reading the Arrivals in the newspaper, the only column that ever interested him; but he looked up sharply when he heard the two yowps and the deep chest notes that, from where he sat, had a mysterious floating quality. It was a little disturbing; but when he saw a dog was the cause he reached out with his foot and shoved the gate hard, so that it swung shut and latched with a sound like a gong. Only one dog had ever come here, and that sound had been enough to discourage him; he had hung round for a while, though, just on the edge, and made the old man nervous. He said to himself that he wasn't going to watch this one, anyway, and folded the paper in halves the way the subway commuter had showed him and went on with the Arrivals.

After a while, though, he heard the dog's panting coming close and the muffled padding of his feet on the marble gate stone. He shook the paper a little, licked his thumb, and turned over half a sheet and read on through the Arrivals into the report of the Committee on Admissions. But then, because he was a curious old man, and kindhearted, noticing that the panting had stopped — and because he had never been quite up to keeping his resolves, except once — he looked out of the gate again.

The dog was sitting on the edge of the gate stone, upright, with his front feet close under him. He was a rusty-muzzled, blue-tick foxhound, with brown ears, and eyes outlined in black like an Egyptian's. He had his nose inside the bars and was working it at the old man.

"Go away," said the old man. "Go home."

At the sound of his voice the hound wrinkled his nose soberly and his tail whipped a couple of times on the gate stone, raising a little star dust.

"Go home," repeated the old man, remembering the dog that had hung around before.

He rattled the paper at him, but it didn't do any good. The dog just looked solemnly pleased at the attention, and a little hopeful, and allowed himself to pant a bit.

"This one's going to be worse than the other," the old man thought, groaning to himself as he got up. He didn't know much about dogs anyway. Back in Galilee there hadn't been dogs that looked like this one — just pariahs and shepherds and the occasional Persian greyhound of a rich man's son.

He slapped his paper along the bars; it made the dog suck in his tongue and move back obligingly. Peter unhooked his shepherd's staff from the middle crossbar, to use in case the dog tried to slip in past him, and let himself out. He could tell by the feeling of his bare ankles that there was a wind making up in the outer heavens and he wanted to get rid of the poor creature before it began really blowing round the walls. The dog backed off from him and sat down almost on the edge, still friendly, but wary of the shepherd's staff.

"Why can't the poor dumb animal read?" thought Peter, turning to look at the sign he had hung on the gatepost, which read:

TAKE NOTICE

NO

DOGS

SORCERERS

WHOREMONGERS

MURDERERS

IDOLATERS

LIARS

WILL BE

ADMITTED

When he put it up, he had thought it might save him a lot of trouble; but it certainly wasn't going to help in the case of this dog. He expected he would have to ask the Committee on Admissions to take the matter up, and he started to feel annoyed with them for not having got this animal on the list themselves. It was going to mean a lot of correspondence and probably the Committee would send a memorandum to the Central Office suggesting his retirement again, and Peter liked his place at the gate. It was quiet there, and it was pleasant for an old man to look through the bars and down the path, to reassure the frightened people, and, when there was nothing else to do, to hear the winds of outer heaven blowing by.

"Go away. Go home. Depart," he said, waving his staff; but the dog only backed down on to the path and lay on his wishbone with his nose between his paws.

Peter went inside and sat down and tried to figure the business out. There were two things he could do. He could notify the Committee of the dog's arrival, or he could give the information to the editor. The Committee would sit up and take notice for once if they found the editor had got ahead of them. It would please the editor, for there were few scoops in Heaven. And then, as luck would have it, the editor himself came down to the gate.

The editor wasn't Horace Greeley or anybody like that, with a reputation in the newspaper world. He had been editor of a little country weekly that nobody in New York or London or Paris had ever heard of. But he was good and bursting with ideas all the time. He was now.

"Say, Saint Peter," he said, "I've just had a swell idea about the Arrivals column. Instead of printing all the 'arrivals' on one side and then the 'expected guests' on the other, why not just have one column and put the names of the successful candidates in upper-case type? See?" He shoved a wet impression under Peter's nose and rubbed the back of his head nervously with his ink-stained hand. "Simple, neat, dignified."

Peter looked at the galley and saw how simple it would be for him, too. He wouldn't have to read the names in lower case at all. It would make him feel a lot better not to know. Just check the upper-case names as they came to the gate.

He looked up at the flushed face of the editor, and his white beard parted over his smile. He liked young, enthusiastic men, remembering how hard, once, they had been to find.

"It looks fine to me, Don," he said. "But the Committee won't like losing all that space in the paper, will they?"

"Probably not," the editor said ruefully. "But I thought you could pull a few wires with the Central Office for me."

Peter sighed. "I'll try," he said. "But people don't pay attention to an old man, much, Don. Especially one who's been in service."

The editor flushed and muttered something about bums.

Peter said gently, "It doesn't bother me, Don. I'm not ashamed of the service I was in." He looked down to his sandals. He wondered whether there was any of the dust of that Roman road left on them after so long a time. Every man has his one great moment. He'd had two. He was glad he hadn't let the second one go. "I'll see what I can do, Don."

It was a still corner, by the gate; and, with both of them silently staring off up the Avenue under the green trees to where the butterflies were fluttering in the shrubbery of the public gardens, the dog decided to take a chance and sneak up again.

He moved one foot at a time, the way he had learned to do behind the counter in the Hawkinsville store, when he went prospecting towards the candy counter. These men didn't hear him any more than the checker players in the store did, and he had time to sniff over the gatepost thoroughly. It puzzled him; and as the men didn't take any notice, he gumshoed over to the other post and went over that, too.

It was queer. He couldn't smell dog on either of them and they were the best-looking posts he had ever come across. It worried him some. His tail drooped and he came back to the gate stone and the very faint scent on it, leading beyond the gate, that he had been following so long. He sat down again and put his nose through the bars, and after a minute he whined.

It was a small sound, but Peter heard it.

"That dog," he said.

The editor whirled round, saying "What dog?" and saw him.

"I was going to let you know about him, only I forgot," said Peter. "He came up a while ago, and I can't get rid of him. I don't know how he got here. The Committee didn't give me any warning and there's nothing about him in the paper."

"He wasn't on the bulletin," said the editor. "Must have been a slip-up somewhere."

"I don't think so," said Peter. "Dogs don't often come here. Only one other since I've been here, as a matter of fact. What kind of a dog is he anyway? I never saw anything like him." He sounded troubled and put out, and the editor grinned, knowing he didn't mean it.

"I never was much of a dog man," he said. "But that's a likely-looking foxhound. He must have followed somebody's scent up here. Hi, boy!" he said. "What's your name? Bob? Spot? Duke?"

The hound lowered his head a little, wrinkled his nose, and wagged his tail across the stone.

"Say," said the editor. "Why don't I put an ad in the Lost and Found? I've never had anything to put there before. But you better bring him in and keep him here till the owner claims him."

"I can't do that," said Peter. "It's against the Law."

"No dogs. Say, I always thought it was funny there were no dogs here. What happens to them?"

"They get removed," said Peter. "They just go."

"That don't seem right," the young editor said. He ruffled his back hair with his hand. "Say, Saint," he asked, "who made this law anyway?"

"It's in Revelations. John wasn't a dog man, as you call it. Back in Galilee we didn't think much of dogs, you see. They were mostly pariahs."

"I see," said the editor. His blue eyes sparkled. "But say! Why can't I put it in the news? And write an editorial? By golly, I haven't had anything to raise a cause on since I got here."

Peter shook his head dubiously.

"It's risky," he said.

"It's a free country," exclaimed the editor. "At least nobody's told me different. Now probably there's nothing would mean so much to the owner of that dog as finding him up here. You get a genuine dog man and this business of passing the love of women is just hooey to him."

"Hooey?" Peter asked quietly.

"It just means he likes dogs better than anything. And this is a good dog, I tell you. He's cold-tracked this fellow, whoever he is, Lord knows how. Besides, he's only one dog, and look at the way the rabbits have been getting into the manna in the public garden. I'm not a dog man, as I said before, but believe me, Saint, it's a pretty thing on a frosty morning to hear a good hound high-tailing a fox across the hills."

"We don't have frost here, Don."

"Well," said the editor, "frost or no frost, I'm going to do it. I'll have to work quick to get it in before the forms close. See you later."

"Wait," said Peter. "What's the weather report say?"

The editor gave a short laugh.

"What do you think? Fair, moderate winds, little change in temperature. Those twerps up in the bureau don't even bother to read the barometer any more. They just play pinochle all day, and the boy runs that report off on the mimeograph machine."

"I think there's a wind making up in the outer heavens," Peter said. "When we get a real one, it just about blows the gate stone away. That poor animal wouldn't last a minute."

The editor whistled. "We'll have to work fast." Then, suddenly his eyes blazed. "All my life I wanted to get out an extra. I never had a chance, running a weekly. Now, by holy, I will."

He went off up the Avenue on the dead run. Even Peter, watching him go, felt excited.

"Nice dog," he said to the hound; and the hound, at the deep gentle voice, gulped in his tongue and twitched his haunches. The whipping of his tail on the gate stone made a companionable sound for the old man. His beard folded on his chest and he nodded a little.

He was dozing quietly when the hound barked.

It was a deep, vibrant note that anyone who knew dogs would have expected the minute he saw the spring of those ribs; it was mellow, like honey in the throat. Peter woke up tingling with the sound of it and turned to see the hound swaying the whole hind half of himself with his tail.

Then a high loud voice shouted, "Mose, by Jeepers! What the hell you doing here, you poor dumb fool?"

Peter turned to see a stocky, short-legged man who stuck out more than was ordinary, both in front and behind. He had on a gray flannel shirt and blue denim pants, and a pair of lumberman's rubber packs on his feet, with the tops laced only to the ankle. There was a hole in the front of his felt hat where the block had worn through. He wasn't, on the whole, what you might expect to see walking on that Avenue. But Peter had seen queer people come to Heaven and he said mildly, "Do you know this dog?"

"Sure," said the stout man. "I hunted with him round Hawkinsville for the last seven years. It's old Mose. Real smart dog. He'd hunt for anybody."

"Mose?" said Peter. "For Moses, I suppose."

"Maybe. He could track anything through hell and high water."

"Moses went through some pretty high water," said Peter. "What's your name?"

"Freem Brock. What's yours?"

Peter did not trouble to answer, for he was looking at the hound; and he was thinking he had seen some people come to Heaven's gate and look pleased, and some come and look shy, and some frightened, and some a little shamefaced, and some satisfied, and some sad (maybe with memories they couldn't leave on earth), and some jubilant, and a whole quartette still singing "Adeline" just the way they were when the hotel fell on their necks in the earthquake. But in all his career at the gate he had never seen anyone express such pure, unstifled joy as this raw-boned hound.

"Was he your dog?" he asked Freeman Brock.

"Naw," said Freem. "He belonged to Pat Haskell." He leaned his shoulder against the gatepost and crossed one foot over the other. "Stop that yawping," he said to Mose, and Mose lay down, wagging. "Maybe you ain't never been in Hawkinsville," he said to Peter. "It's a real pretty village right over the Black River. Pat kept store there and he let anybody take Mose that wanted to. Pretty often I did. He liked coming with me because I let him run foxes. I'm kind of a fox hunter," he said, blowing out his breath. "Oh, I like rabbit hunting all right, but there's no money in it. Say," he broke off, "you didn't tell me what your name was."

"Peter," said the old man.

"Well, Pete, two years ago was Mose's best season. Seventy-seven fox was shot ahead of him. I shot thirty-seven of them myself. Five crosses and two blacks in the lot. Yes sir. I heard those black foxes had got away from the fur farm and I took Mose right over there. I made three hundred and fifty dollars out of them hides."

"He was a good dog, then?" asked Peter.

"Best foxhound in seven counties," said Freem Brock. He kicked the gate with his heel in front of Mose's nose and Mose let his ears droop. "He was a fool to hunt. I don't see no fox signs up here. Plenty of rabbits in the Park. But there ain't nobody with a gun. I wish I'd brought my old Ithaca along."

"You can't kill things here," said Peter.

"That's funny. Why not?"

"They're already dead."

"Well, I know that. But it beats me how I got here. I never did nothing to get sent to this sort of place. Hell, I killed them farm foxes and I poached up the railroad in the *pre*-serve. But I never done anything bad."

"No," said Saint Peter. "We know that."

"I got drunk, maybe. But there's other people done the same before me."

"Yes, Freem."

"Well, what the devil did I get sent here for, Pete?"

"Do you remember when the little girl was sick and the town doctor wouldn't come out at night on a town case, and you went over to town and made him come?"

"Said I'd knock his teeth out," said Freem, brightening.

"Yes. He came. And the girl was taken care of," said Peter.

"Aw," Freem said, "I didn't know what I was doing. I was just mad. Well, maybe I'd had a drink, but it was a cold night, see? I didn't knock his teeth out. He left them in the glass." He looked at the old man. "Jeepers," he said. "And they sent me here for that?"

Peter looked puzzled.

"Wasn't it a good reason?" he asked. "It's not such a bad place."

"Not so bad as I thought it was going to be. But people don't want to talk to me. I tried to talk to an old timber-beast named Boone down the road. But he asked me if I ever shot an Indian, and when I said no he went along. You're the only feller I've seen that was willing to talk to me," he said, turning to the old man. "I don't seem to miss likker up here, but there's nowhere I can get to buy some tobacco."

Peter said, "You don't have to buy things in Heaven."

"Heaven?" said Freeman Brock. "Say, is that what this is?" He looked frightened all at once. "That's what the matter is. I don't belong here. I ain't the kind to come here. There must have been a mistake somewhere." He took hold of Peter's arm. "Listen," he said urgently. "Do you know how to work that gate?"

"I do," said Peter. "But I can't let you out."

"I got to get out."

Peter's voice grew gentler.

"You'll like it here after a while, Freem."

"You let me out."

"You couldn't go anywhere outside," Peter said.

Freem looked through the bars at the outer heavens and watched a couple of stars like water lilies floating by below. He said slowly, "We'd go some place."

Peter said, "You mean you'd go out there with that dog?"

Freem flushed.

"I and Mose have had some good times," he said.

At the sound of his name, Mose's nose lifted.

Peter looked down at the ground. With the end of his shepherd's staff he thoughtfully made a cross and then another overlapping it and put an X in the upper left-hand corner. Freem looked down to see what he was doing.

"You couldn't let Mose in, could you, Pete?"

Peter sighed and rubbed out the pattern with his sandal.

"I'm sorry," he said. "The Committee don't allow dogs."

"What'll happen to the poor brute, Pete?"

Peter shook his head.

"If you ask me," Freem said loudly, "I think this is a hell of a place."

"What's that you said?"

Peter glanced up.

"Hello, Don," he said. "Meet Freem Brock. This is the editor of the paper," he said to Freem. "His name's Don."

"Hello," said Freem.

"What was that you said about Heaven being a hell of a place?" asked the editor.

Freem drew a long breath. He took a look at old Mose lying outside
the gate with his big nose resting squashed up and sideways against the
bottom crossbar; he looked at the outer heavens, and he looked at the
editor.

"Listen," he said. "That hound followed me up here. Pete says he
can't let him in. He says I can't go out to where Mose is. I only been in
jail twice," he said, "but I liked it better than this."

The editor said, "You'd go out there?"

"Give me the chance."

"What a story!" said the editor. "I've got my extra on the Avenue
now. The cherubs will be coming this way soon. It's all about the
hound, but this stuff is the genuine goods. Guest prefers to leave
Heaven. Affection for old hunting dog prime factor in his decision. It's
human interest. I tell you it'll shake the Committee. By holy, I'll have
an editorial in my next edition calling for a celestial referendum."

"Wait," said Peter. "What's the weather report?"

"What do you think? Fair, moderate winds, little change in temperature. But the Central Office is making up a hurricane for the South
Pacific and it's due to go by pretty soon. We got to hurry, Saint."

He pounded away up the Avenue, leaving a little trail of star dust in
his wake.

Freem Brock turned on Saint Peter.

"He called you something," he said.

Peter nodded.

"Saint."

"I remember about you now. Say, you're a big shot here. Why can't
you let Mose in?"

Peter shook his head.

"I'm no big shot, Freem. If I was, maybe — "

His voice was drowned out by a shrieking up the Avenue.

"Extry! Extry! Special edition. Read all about it. Dog outside Heaven's
gate. Dog outside . . ."

A couple of cherubs were coming down the thoroughfare, using their
wings to make time. When he saw them, Freem Brock started. His
shoulders began to itch self-consciously and he put a hand inside his
shirt.

"My gracious," he said.

Peter, watching him, nodded.

"Everybody gets them. You'll get used to them after a while. They're
handy, too, on a hot day."

"For the love of Pete," said Freem.

"Read all about it! Dog outside Heaven's gate. Lost dog waiting outside . . ."

"He ain't lost!" cried Freem. "He never got lost in his life."

" 'Committee at fault,' " read Peter. "Thomas Aquinas isn't going to like that," he said.

"It don't prove nothing," said Freem.

"Mister, please," said a feminine voice. "The editor sent me down. Would you answer some questions?"

"Naw," said Freem, turning to look at a young woman with red hair and a gold pencil in her hand. "Well, what is it you want to know, lady?"

The young woman had melting brown eyes. She looked at the hound. "Isn't he cute?" she asked. "What's his name?"

"Mose," said Freem. "He's a cute hound all right."

"Best in seven counties," said Peter.

"May I quote you on that, Saint?"

"Yes," said Peter. "You can say I think the dog ought to be let in." His face was pink over his white beard. "You can say a hurricane is going to pass, and that before I see that animal blown off by it I'll go out there myself — I and my friend Freem. Some say I'm a has-been, but I've got some standing with the public yet."

The girl with red hair was writing furiously with a little gold glitter of her pencil. "Oh," she said.

"Say I'm going out too," said Freem. "I and Pete."

"Oh," she said. "What's your name?"

"Freeman Brock, Route 5, Boonville, New York, U.S.A."

"Thanks," she said breathlessly.

"How much longer before we got that hurricane coming?" asked Freem.

"I don't know," said the old man, anxiously. "I hope Don can work fast."

"Extry! Owner found. Saint Peter goes outside with hound, Moses. Committee bluff called. Read all about it."

"How does Don manage it so fast?" said Peter. "It's like a miracle."

"It's science," said Freem. "Hey!" he yelled at a cherub.

They took the wet sheet, unheeding of the gold ink that stuck to their fingers.

"They've got your picture here, Pete."

"Have they?" Peter asked. He sounded pleased. "Let's see."

It showed Peter standing at the gate.

"It ain't bad," said Freem. He was impressed. "You really mean it?" he asked. Peter nodded.

"By cripus," Freem said slowly, "you're a pal."

Saint Peter was silent for a moment. In all the time he had minded Heaven's gate, no man had ever called him a pal before.

Outside the gate, old Mose got up on his haunches. He was a weather-wise dog, and now he turned his nose outward. The first puff of wind came like a slap in the face, pulling his ears back, and then it passed. He glanced over his shoulder and saw Freem and the old man staring at each other. Neither of them had noticed him at all. He pressed himself against the bars and lifted his nose and howled.

At his howl both men turned.

There was a clear gray point way off along the reach of the wall, and the whine in the sky took up where Mose's howl had ended.

Peter drew in his breath.

"Come on, Freem," he said, and opened the gate.

Freeman Brock hesitated. He was scared now. He could see that a real wind was coming, and the landing outside looked almighty small to him. But he was still mad, and he couldn't let an old man like Peter call his bluff.

"All right," he said. "Here goes."

He stepped out, and Mose jumped up on him and licked his face.

"Get down, darn you," he said. "I never could break him of that trick," he explained shamefacedly to Peter. Peter smiled, closing the gate behind him with a firm hand. Its gong-like note echoed through Heaven just as the third edition burst upon the Avenue.

Freeman Brock was frightened. He glanced back through the bars, and Heaven looked good to him. Up the Avenue a crowd was gathering. A couple of lanky, brown-faced men were in front. They started toward the gate.

Then the wind took hold of him, and he grasped the bars and looked outward. He could see the hurricane coming like an express train running through infinity. It had a noise like an express train. He understood suddenly just how the victim of a crossing accident must feel.

He glanced at Peter.

The old Saint was standing composedly, leaning on his staff with one hand, while with the other he drew Mose close between his legs. His white robe fluttered tight against his shanks and his beard bent sidewise like the hound's ears. He had faced lack of faith in others; what was worse, he had faced it in himself; and a hurricane, after all, was not so much. He turned to smile at Freem. "Don't be afraid," he said.

"O.K.," said Freem, but he couldn't let go the gate.

Old Mose, shivering almost hard enough to rattle, reached up and licked Peter's hand.

One of the brown-faced men said, "That's a likely-looking hound. He the one I read about in the paper?"

"Yep," said Freem. He had to holler now.

Daniel Boone said, "Let us timber-beasts come out with you, Saint, will you?"

Peter smiled. He opened the gate with a wave of his hand, and ten or a dozen timber-beasts — Carson, Bridger, Nat Foster — all crowded through and started shaking hands with him and Freeman Brock. With them was a thin, mild-eyed man.

"My name's Francis," he said to Freem when his turn came. "From Assisi."

"He's all right," Daniel Boone explained. "He wasn't much of a shot, but he knows critters. We better get holt of each other, boys."

It seemed queer to Freem. Here he was going to get blown to eternity and he didn't even know where it was, but all of a sudden he felt better than he ever had in his life. Then he felt a squirming round his legs and there was Mose, sitting on his feet, the way he would on his snowshoes in cold weather when they stopped for a sandwich on earth. He reached down and took hold of Mose's ears.

"Let her blow to blazes," he thought.

She blew.

The hurricane was on them. The nose of it went by, sweeping the wall silver. There was no more time for talk. No voices could live outside Heaven's gate. If a man had said a word, the next man to hear it would have been some poor heathen aborigine on an island in the Pacific Ocean, and he wouldn't have known what it meant.

The men on the gate stone were crammed against the bars. The wind dragged them bodily to the left, and for a minute it looked as if Jim Bridger were going, but they caught him back. There were a lot of the stoutest hands that ever swung an axe in that bunch holding on to Heaven's gate, and they weren't letting go for any hurricane — not yet, at any rate.

But Freem Brock could see it couldn't last that way. He didn't care, though. He was in good company, and that was what counted the most.

He wasn't a praying man, but he felt his heart swell with gratitude, and he took hold hard of the collar of Mose and felt the license riveted on. A queer thing to think of, a New York State dog license up there. He managed to look down at it, and he saw that it had turned to gold, with the collar gold under it. The wind tore at him as he saw it. The heart of the hurricane was on him now like a million devils' fingers.

"Well, Mose," he thought.

And then in the blur of his thoughts a dazzling bright light came down and he felt the gate at his back opening and he and Peter and Francis and Daniel and the boys were all drawn back into the peace of Heaven, and a quiet voice belonging to a quiet man said, "Let the dog come in."

"Jesus," said Freem Brock, fighting for breath, and the quiet man smiled, shook hands with him, and then went over and placed his arm around Peter's shoulders.

They were sitting together, Freem and Peter, by the gate, reading the paper in the morning warmth, and Peter was having an easy time with the editor's new type arrangement. "Gridley," he was reading the uppercase names, "Griscome, Godolphin, Habblestick, Hafey, Hanlon, Hartwell, Haskell . . ."

"Haskell," said Freem. "Not Pat?"

"Yes," said Peter. "Late of Hawkinsville."

"Not in big type?"

"Yes."

"Well, I'll be . . . Well, that twerp. Think of that. Old Pat."

Peter smiled.

"By holy," said Freem. "Ain't he going to be amazed when he finds Mose up here?"

"How's Mose doing?"

"He's all right now," said Freem. "He's been chasing the rabbits. I guess he's up there now. The dew's good."

"He didn't look so well, I thought," Peter said.

"Well, that was at first," said Freem. "You see, the rabbits just kept going up in the trees and he couldn't get a real run on any of them. There, he's got one started now."

Peter glanced up from the paper.

Old Mose was doing a slow bark, kind of low, working out the scent from the start. He picked up pace for a while, and then he seemed to strike a regular knot. His barks were deep and patient.

And then, all of a sudden, his voice broke out — that deep, ringing, honey-throated baying that Freem used to listen to in the late afternoon on the sand hills over the Black River. It went away through the public gardens and out beyond the city, the notes running together and fading and swelling and fading out.

"He's pushing him pretty fast," said Freem. "He's going to get pretty good on these rabbits."

The baying swelled again; it came back, ringing like bells. People in the gardens stopped to look up and smile. The sound of it gave Peter a warm tingling feeling.

Freem yawned.

"Might as well wait here till Pat Haskell comes in," he said.

It was pleasant by the gate, under the black and yellow parasol. It made a shade like a flower on the hot star dust. They didn't have to talk, beyond just, now and then, dropping a word between them as they sat.

After a while they heard a dog panting and saw old Mose tracking down the street. He came over to their corner and lay down at their feet, lolling a long tongue. He looked good, a little fat, but lazy and contented. After a minute, though, he got up to shift himself around, and paused as he sat down, and raised a hind leg, and scratched himself behind his wings.

Dog in a Car

by DAVID McCORD

JULY 1936

He grins a little as they drive him by.
Of what his nose needs there's a fresh supply
Round every corner, up the rainy field:
He has no daily walk of equal yield.
His head hangs out, his tongue out farther still;
His bark is bolder from that window sill.
His nose is longer on the modern breeze —
His father being Scotch, not Pekingese.

Dogs

A lesser breed on leash or running loose
Would find his comradeship of little use;
A dog transported by the family Ford
Rides far beyond the days he loved or warred.
His ancestors on purely urban smells
Leaned hard enough, but they had nothing else.
They hadn't won to his synthetic taste:
Investigation kept them out of haste.

You drive a dog from state to other state;
His senses meet with scents he can't relate.
He hasn't time. His little nostrils twitch.
Was that a rabbit, mole, or brindle bitch?
His eye grows bright. He reaches out in space.
The local brothers hardly see his face.
He's whirling through a night of strange impact —
Of atavistic cats he once attacked.

Mickey

by EDWARD WEEKS

The ninth and present editor of the Atlantic, *Edward Weeks
has a special spot in his heart for spaniels and Kerry blues.*

AUGUST 1947

Overhead the oak leaves stir against the cloudless blue, and the
shadow in which I am reading ripples like running water. At my feet on
the borderline between the sunny and the cool grass lies Mickey dozing,
gray muzzle pointed toward the driveway up which the family will return from their expedition. Periodically he rouses himself, shakes the
catkins from his black curls, and moves closer to the sun. His movement
renews the scolding of the mother robin in the bittersweet and interrupts
my intake of print. I watch him, and through the forming impressions
of the book in my lap, memory thrusts its feeling.

This is probably our last summer together. Mickey is sixteen and that is a great age for a cocker spaniel given to eating any old thing; indeed a great age for any dog. Implicit in every friendship is the trust that it will never break. Mick has no reason to doubt us, but we who note his fading hearing and his inability to spot us at any distance on the beach live with the warning to make these months good.

I remember William Morton Wheeler's remarking on the silent communication between dogs, and how, when he had taken one of his for a walk through the Arboretum, the others would gather about the traveler instantly on his return and by scent and emanation have all the news in a matter of seconds. On the Common with other dogs Mick is eager, quivering, and gregarious when I am along, and hair-on-end belligerent when accompanying his mistress. In canine years he is now well past the century mark, so it is small wonder that dogs in their prime have only a passing curiosity in what he has to say. They pause, there is the usual tail-wagging introduction. Then, while he is still standing on his dignity, they suddenly lope off. Mick will start after and then resign himself to his own grass, which he scratches up with a "What the hell." For ladies he has, I gather, the charm of an aging colonel. There is a honey-colored spaniel who, after the nosing, will describe mad circles about him as he stands immovable on the moonlit Common. But if she pushes him too roughly he loses his balance and shows his lip, and so they part.

At home his expressions are stressed for our benefit. His humor, as when with jaws open and tongue half a yard out he stands there grinning; his sneeze of expectation; his mutter — a kind of controlled yip — of annoyance; his jumping recognition of those most important words in a city dog's vocabulary, "Going out" and "Down country" (is it the special note that colors our voices as we say them?); his sharp demanding bark when his water dish is empty or when brownies, his passion, are cooking — these are a language no one could miss. So too his boredom when, after a decent interval in our friend's house, he fetches his leash and stands obdurate with it in his jaws.

And in his play, he loves to tease. Mickey came to us when he was three weeks old, and in the pecking order he established himself as a contemporary of my daughter Sara and as a senior in every respect to young Ted. In his youth we spent the winters in an apartment on the Fenway, and here Mickey devised a series of games for his own and our amusement. There was one he liked to play with a Malaga grape. A grape would be given him and he would go through the motions of chewing it. Then he would lie down facing us, his head cocked on one side. With a sudden twist he would fling the grape, perfectly intact, over his shoulder and pounce upon it as it rolled along the rug or under the table. Again the mock seriousness of swallowing it, the fixed stare in our direction, and again, the quick projection. The wonder was that he could keep this up for such a long time without puncturing the thin-skinned grape.

He loved to tease Sara about her dollhouse. The open rooms were just right for his inspection, and the inmates — known as Mr. and Mrs. Brewster — were much to his taste. He would stand gazing into the living room until he was sure Sara was watching him; then with a quick dart he would seize one of the little dolls and be off, up the hall, through the kitchen, through the dining room, across the living room, and into the hall again. It was a lovely circle, and Sara could seldom catch him without the help of May, the cook. Sara's revenge was unpremeditated. One evening she set Mr. and Mrs. Brewster at the dinner table and served each of them a chocolate-covered Ex-lax for their supper, and after she had gone to sleep Mickey ate both. On rising the next morning, I found that he had used the bathroom in a hurry, and Sara, all un-knowing, supplied the perfect caption at breakfast: "Now, Mother, I told you the dolls were alive. They ate their candy."

I remember those times when he seemed to speak my language, once for instance when in his puppyhood he was sick from a distemper injec-tion. He began vomiting at midnight and at four I got the car and drove him to the vet's. He was so weak that he leaned limply against the corner of seat and door, but in answer to my hand his eyes said, "I'm sorry to be such a mess. But I *am* sick." And again, years later, when he had to apologize for his hunting. It was summer and our little cottage adjoined the orchard and vegetable garden of our big neighbor. At sundown rab-bits would make free with the tender lettuce and carrots, and their scent — when Mickey got it — drove him wild. One evening from our screened porch I spotted a cottontail in the green. Mick was asleep, but quietly opening the door I pointed him at the quarry and he got the idea. Rabbit and spaniel disappeared over the horizon with yips marking every second bound. Two hours went by, and then in darkness there was Mick scratching at the screen. "No luck," he said, and in his mouth was the half-eaten carrot the rabbit had dropped in his haste. "No luck."

Mickey is by his nature a hunter and a retriever. But now, with his teeth gone, his retrieving is limited to fishermen's corks as they curve ahead of him on the beach, and to apples in the orchard. As a hunter he fancied himself, and for years he nourished a grudge against squirrels.

I used to tease him about this. Walking close to one of our oaks, I would peer up into the leaves and touch the bark significantly; whereupon Mick would leave the ground jumping and scrabbling as high as my arm.

The squirrels, for their part, enjoyed the feud: they knew he could never catch them. I remember one summer day when Mickey was lying on the open porch soaking up the sun which radiated from the warm boards. Close to the house stood an old apple tree, one of whose branches reached over the porch. Along this bridge, as Mickey slept, stole one of his bushy-tailed enemies. With mathematical precision the squirrel nipped clean a hard green apple, which hit the porch with a thump an inch from Mickey's nose. It was as nice a piece of natural comedy as I have ever witnessed, and the aftermath was noisy.

That dogs remember, we know from their habits and from their twitching dreams when they are so palpably reliving some activity. But how far back does their memory reach, and do those little half-uttered cries indicate that, like man, they are long haunted by old fears? If so, then Mick may still feel the most painful terror of domesticated animals — the fear of desertion. The autumn of his second year, my wife and I had to answer a sudden call to New York. We closed the cottage, packed up the daughter, and to save time left the pup with the maid. She took him to her home in Watertown, and from it he escaped in search of us. That was on Friday afternoon. They saw him for an instant at the garbage pail Saturday morning, and then he was gone for good.

By our return on Monday there wasn't a clue. We drove the unfamiliar streets and we put our appeal in the newspapers and on the air. In twenty-four hours we had heard from seventeen spaniel owners, fifteen of whom had lost their own dogs. But one of them gave us a tip. In their search they had seen a small black dog in the vast reaches of the Watertown Arsenal. So, with the Governor's permission, we drove through the gates — this was long before the war — to explore the cement strips which led between the huge closed buildings. A sergeant's son gave us hope. "Sure," he said, "a little black dog. He's here all right, only you can't get close to him." "Don't scare him," I said. "Find him if you can."

Whistling and calling, we went to point after point, and once on the knoll above a huge oil tank I thought I heard the short familiar bark, but nothing moved. Three hours later we came back to the same spot, and there was the boy lying full-length on the cement wall aiming an imaginary gun. "The buffalo is down here," he called. Ten yards farther, and I saw Mick's nest and his unmistakable head. "Mickey," I shouted. Then up the slope he came on the dead run, his ears brown pancakes of burr.

Is it the fear of our leaving him that so troubles him when he can now no longer hear us as we move about the house? The sight of an open suitcase makes him more doleful than does a thunderstorm. When we pack for the country there is no way to tell him that he will surely come too. In his heart of hearts Mick knows that he is dependent upon four people, and no comfort of maid or sitter can distract his vigil when we are gone for the evening. Our woods are his woods. The squirrels who used to scold him he no longer hears. He begins not to hear us. But we shall hear him long after he is gone.

The World Wars

To those of us who were in it but not old enough to have seen it coming, the outbreak of the First World War was an adventure that called forth an unsuspected patriotism. In training at Plattsburg young men fretted lest they not get to France before it was over, and an old war horse like T.R. groaned aloud because President Wilson would not let him go. The tension mounted all during the slow-moving months while the United States stood on the sidelines. Then anxiety began to sway our sympathies. As the British casualties and the atrocity stories from Belgium were received, as we read The First Hundred Thousand *by Ian Hay and* Mr. Britling Sees It Through *by H. G. Wells, the voice in our common heritage cried out. To the* Atlantic's *wartime editor, Ellery Sedgwick, it was clear that the country must support the Allies, and the English writers who pled this cause in our columns, Henry Massingham and H. W. Nevinson, were joined by Americans as respected as Frank H. Simonds.*

It is almost impossible to recapture today the feeling of dedication and self-sacrifice with which the first volunteers were imbued, but you hear the true note of it in the sonnets of Rupert Brooke. This valiance came home to readers of the Atlantic *in letters from the American ambulance drivers and in the exploits of American pilots in the Lafayette Escadrille. It was the prompting spirit in the most popular of our war stories, "England to America," by Margaret Prescott Montague. Miss Montague, a Virginian, wrote of the leave which young Lieutenant Skipworth Cary of Virginia had spent in Devonshire. A pilot in the R.F.C., the lieutenant had been invited to stay with the parents of his English flight commander. He is gently though somewhat distantly entertained; not till the last day of his leave do the parents break their reserve to tell him that their son had been shot down in action even before he, the American, arrived.*

As one looks back, it is amazing to see how much writing of a nonbelligerent nature went forward despite the war: Galsworthy was at work on The Forsyte Saga *and Max Beerbohm on* Seven Men; *Somerset Maugham published* Of Human Bondage *in* 1915; *Lord Dunsany* The Last Book of Wonder *in* 1916; *Bernard Shaw finished* Heartbreak House *in* 1917, *and that same year saw the appearance of* Prufrock and Other Observations *by T. S. Eliot. On the Continent Joyce was at work on* Ulysses, *Norman Douglas on* South Wind, *D. H. Lawrence on his poems* Amores.

By 1917 *the fervor of self-sacrifice was burning itself out, and to poets who were soldiers — Siegfried Sassoon, Osbert Sitwell, Robert Graves, and Wilfred Owen, the bloody carnage in the mud of Flanders became appalling, too great to be borne in silence, and they rebelled.*

When the World War was renewed in 1939, *it had a good deal less of what James Norman Hall had called "high adventure" left in it. Its coming had been foreseen; it had been rehearsed with bloody casualties in Spain. The temperament of the German people and their reasons for following Hitler were analyzed with piercing candor by the German exile Emil Ludwig. But nothing could stay our fate. We were as if walking in our sleep and could not turn away. The fighting, when it came, with tanks, flame throwers, and napa bombs, was grimmer than ever before. Men went in with determination but no exhilaration: the only song was heard in the desert and the favorite, sung by both sides in the cool of the evening, was "Lili Marlene." This time it was total war, which absorbed the young and which paralyzed and suspended the writing of those at home. From London, in intervals between the bombing, we heard a man speaking: we heard Churchill's prose, we heard* The Burning of the Leaves, *those poems in which Laurence Binyon made indelible the burning of the city; we heard the Elizabethan prose of H. M. Tomlinson, Eliot's* Four Quartets, *and the evocative recollection of an England lost forever, Sir Osbert Sitwell's* Autobiography.

Here in America, which never felt the devastation of the bombs, one lived on the dispatches of the war correspondents and found a soporific in fiction written by women for other women whose men were away.

The German Mind

by EMIL LUDWIG

A German biographer driven into exile by Hitler, Emil Ludwig was living in Switzerland in February 1938. With war once more impending, he wrote his masterly analysis of the German temperament.

FEBRUARY 1938

The man who regards raw materials as more important than a people's philosophy, or believes that figures decide history and not feelings, is liable to be surprised by a sudden outburst of national character. Philosophers, and only philosophers, have accurately forecast developments: that has held good from Plato and Cicero to Nietzsche, and we have a modern example in Norman Angell, who in 1912 foretold all that happened later, or Bernard Shaw, who did it in 1931 for this country in New York. Statesmen who have no philosophers to advise them are lost. If, before the war, the international secret services had busied themselves with other people's character instead of their guns, the Germans would have known what the Anglo-Saxon character means, and would never have ventured on the war. Today, if the Americans and the English would study the German character, they might yet ward off the war which threatens. That is my reason for writing on this subject, which I studied for twenty years.

The decisive difference between the spiritual history of Germany and that of other peoples lies in the opposition between the state and mind. While the great epochs of English and French culture coincide with the epochs of power of the two nations, Germany was always powerless without and torn within when German culture was flourishing. But whenever she was powerful and united as regards the outside world, spiritual values declined. You can trace this process from Erasmus to Planck, over five centuries. Goethe, the greatest event in German history, was doomed to develop in a Germany torn within and defeated without, and the seven-starred constellation of German music, from

Bach to Schubert, rose above the prostration of the nation as an airplane rises above a bank of mist.

This separation of state and mind, which is the same at all epochs, in all classes, and in the various provinces, has created the image of a double Germany which is a source of great confusion outside. How is it, other countries ask repeatedly, that the land of Goethe and Beethoven is perpetually relapsing into barbarism? The reason is simply that the ordinary man, in the long run, admires and imitates the men who represent power. As the greatest banker or the most celebrated professor entered society behind the riding boots and decorations of colonels and counts, even the astronomer tried to appear in uniform, as long as he had to tread this earth. The students tried to look as soldierly as possible and hacked each other's faces in duels, and he was most admired whose face most resembled a beefsteak. Those very uniforms and duels are once more the greatest fashion in Germany today. The lieutenant has again become the flapper's ideal.

The consequence of this German military organization was a regular anarchy of the spirit. The conception of the state, adapted to the mind of the *Junker,* unspiritual and overweening, was separated from the ideals of the mind. Obedience and organization were raised from their position as third-rate necessities to first-rate virtues and approved by those who needed them in their own interests. The Germans are the only nation on earth who obey with passion, and not out of necessity. And so the will to freedom departed into the provinces of the mind and created German individualism.

Here we have one of the profoundest differences between the German and the French national character. For in Germany profound obedience prevails in political and social life, but an equally profound resistance to rules in the intellectual life; in France it is exactly the other way round. If a French writer uses a subjunctive which is not in the *Encyclopédie,* he is accused of having broken a law; but if a notice is put up telling people to walk to the right, the Parisian will certainly walk to the left.

The eternal war between these neighbors only becomes clear in the light of their radically different characters. What the one has the other lacks. What weakens the one strengthens the other.

Here we have, side by side, an overorganized and an underorganized people, a mystical beside a logical, and an aggressive beside a defensive one. The Germans distrust French grace, the French distrust Germany's gravity. In France a man wants to be left alone, hating even to have his name at his own door; in Germany there is a man to organize everything, even amusement. In France the authorities are polite, but letters often go astray; in Germany the authorities snarl at you, but your letters get there. In France even the head of the state is plain Monsieur; in Germany every butcher and baker and candlestick maker must have a title. The Frenchman loves his cat, because it keeps to itself and takes orders from nobody, just like its master. The German loves the police dog, which stands obedient, asking with its eyes which enemy it shall fall upon, just like its master. Obedience is despised in France, worshiped in Germany.

In Berlin, after the war, when the Republic had given orders to the police to get rid of their harsh ways in traffic regulation, I was shouted at in good Prussian manner by a policeman for being on the wrong side of the street. After he had done, he said quietly, "Well, I could not be more polite than that!"

Some years later, in Paris, when crossing the road outside the "nails," an *agent de ville* rather gruffly called me to attention. Then, as if regretting his military tone, he came up close to me and said, "I do it myself if I'm not in uniform."

And now these two men are condemned by God to live side by side for a thousand years!

To the lack of freedom, to the passion for obedience, we must add a third radical trait of the German character — their musicality, without which it is quite impossible to understand them. This is their refuge from overorganization. Yet a people cannot be the most musical on earth with impunity; and it is no accident that the English and the Germans — cousins, as they say — have developed their strength in exactly opposite directions: the most musical nation is the least political, while the politically strongest one has produced the fewest musicians. The music of the German rises from the mystic elements in his nature and has helped to strengthen them.

After the war was lost, the entire people sought their refuge in Beethoven. More Beethoven was played in Germany than ever before. During the Republic, for instance, the biggest popular theater in Berlin performed the Ninth Symphony every New Year's Eve, beginning at eleven fifteen, so that with the stroke of midnight the great Hymn to Joy rang out to the world.

This mystic bent in the German character is most dangerous in politics. Present rulers have made use of it to give a mystical meaning even to power, so that the German's wonted worship of the uniform is now bathed in religious light.

For three centuries a warlike people had learned that the state is upheld by might and that might is more important than mind. For a century this theory had led them to victory and expansion. A nation which slavishly worships its rulers will hold *itself* guilty rather than them. When Hindenburg, therefore, invented the legend of the dagger which had struck the German army in the back, he was sure of being believed. Today every German believes it: every boy and every girl is taught that the Germans neither began nor lost the war. This double lie has been used to convince the Germans that, on the eve of victory, they were cheated of it by a diabolical conspiracy of Jews and Socialists.

Today the world is faced with a Germany just as ready to fight and to die, just as obedient, disciplined, and armed, as she was in 1914; but then she was a flourishing and rich nation, hard-working and inventive, arrogant, it may be, but sociable, and so she could only be driven to war by being told she had been attacked. Today, on the other hand, she feels strong but misjudged, born to rule, yet cheated of victory. Today she stands in clattering armor before the world demanding vengeance. The Germans are the more dangerous today because they are fighting not for the preservation but for the restoration of what they call their honor.

For the Germans do not want raw materials or colonies or Russian cornfields. They want something much more ideal. They do not want war in order to sink their own oil wells or to plant their own cotton. They want victory. They want war in order to revenge the crime the world committed when it fell upon them in the midst of peace and then, although they offered conciliation and negotiation while standing deep in an enemy country, cheated them in a malicious peace and crowned their dishonor by prohibiting their arms.

They are not satisfied with the admiration of the world for their four years' resistance in the war, nor with the world's acclamation, after the defeat, of German science, shipping and aircraft, authors and musicians, chemists and biologists. That is not honor as a soldier people understands it. Honor means victory by arms, and it is not by chance that Herr Hitler, at every popular festival, calls on the assembled thousands to shout with him "*Sieg-heil!*"

If the Germans want victory, that victory is to be won only in Paris. Who imposed the shame of Versailles upon them? The French. Nobody reflects that if it had not been for the intervention of Wilson the French would have won the left bank of the Rhine, the holy river with which

Germany's most ancient national memories are connected. Nobody reflects that the Germans, during the war, had determined to keep nearly all the country they had occupied. The monstrous conditions which the Germans imposed on the defeated Russians and Rumanians in their peace treaties of 1917–1918 do not justify the errors of Versailles.

What is branded into the soul of every school child is the scene in the mirror hall of Versailles. This scene has bred in the Germans a feeling of inferiority which they must get rid of at all costs. In that very Versailles, Bismarck had stood and founded the German Empire on French soil. A bold thought — the thought of a poet! It was a wonder that in 1871 the French accepted it, and, thirty years later, the overwhelming majority had lost even their ideas of revenge — a satisfied people that would on no account proceed to aggression. And now in 1919, forty-eight years later, in that very mirror hall, the Tiger sat, forcing the Germans to sign a peace which disarmed them. That is the scene that is provoking the new war.

We German pacifists, writing ten years for a European coalition and for the League, hoped once that an understanding between two equally gifted neighbors might replace the eternal idea of revenge. We forgot that one of these two peoples is more vital, younger, more cramped for room, more accustomed to privation than the other. If the French, mature, stable, and averse to change, bore their defeat for forty years without aggression, if it was the *victor himself* who invaded their country a second time in 1914, how much more likely it is that the defeated German will repeat the move. That is what we Europeans hoped to overcome. We were wrong: the German character disowned us.

It is a mistake to say that Hitler is not Germany. In his demagogism, he unites just those incentives which goad the German mind to frenzy. He resembles Wagner in his histrionic instinct. It is from Wagner that Hitler has adopted his endless melodies — that is, the wearisome repetition of the same few themes; the splendor of the processions and choruses, the burning thirst for success, the bluster, the brutality and blamelessness, which make Wagner's work so effective can all be observed in the way Hitler works on his audience.

He is altogether most effective in his speeches, and he is the first popular orator modern Germany has ever had. Up to 1900, no German minister had ever made a speech outside the Reichstag; Bismarck was eighty before he spoke to the people. Wilhelm II had already won his influence over the Germans by his oratory, without which there would have been no World War. Hitler is like him in so many ways that he might be called Wilhelm III. The history of modern Germany will one day record that the people let themselves be gulled twice by the poses of a neurasthenic.

For here we have a power of suggestion that has carried away the whole nation. Do not believe that it is merely a party government! Although millions are discontented today, no one has the courage to bring about a change. They complain of high prices, the scarcity of butter, low wages, the lack of free speech, but that does not mean revolution. A people that loves order more than freedom does not revolt.

Three years ago it was thought the generals would overthrow Hitler. But their history shows that they will take advantage of any form of power as long as it is to their profit. Hitler gave them back their power, position, and wealth; in fact, the uniformed Germans are the only ones who have gained by the regime. But no German officer in the hour of need — with the exception of three naval officers — died for the Emperor. The rest disappeared or went over to the Republic; none defended the twenty-two royal houses in November 1918. Will they stay with the leader to whom they have sworn loyalty, if it does not suit them any longer?

If he is overthrown, it will certainly be by his own men, and not by Communists and democrats. It was always so in the German Sagas — Hagen stabs Siegfried from behind. Hagen's descendant of today can hope to sell guns and gain honor in the coming war. But the lower middle classes, who will have to pay for it with their lives, have only the satisfaction of seeing themselves reflected in their *Führer*. For the secret of his success is that he is of them.

The dormant elements of revolution in Germany consist of a few million workmen — who are, however, very difficult to organize — of the clergy, and other religious-minded men of both creeds. The priests who go to prison rather than give up the Bible, and the workmen who set their paper in small print in cellars — these real heroes of the Germany of today are not strong enough for revolution *now*. But they are the precursors of those who, when the war comes, will represent the other Germany in much greater strength than in 1914. Then the other, the great side of the German character will come again to the top.

Leaves from a Surgeon's Journal

by HARVEY CUSHING

Dr. Harvey Cushing, celebrated brain surgeon, arrived in Paris in April 1915 and immediately began operating on head cases in the French hospitals. He served with the B.E.F. in 1917 and with the A.E.F. to the end of the war. He was at Passchendaele and again in the Argonne. He did as many as nine delicate head operations in twenty-four hours. And the strain left him as tense as a piano wire. For relief he jotted down on the backs of temperature charts and all kinds of paper a diary which eventually ran close to half a million words. From it the Atlantic *published, in a series of articles, his* Leaves from a Surgeon's Journal.

OCTOBER–DECEMBER 1934

Saturday, April 24, 1915 — This afternoon, in response to a call to the Ambulance for all of its many cars, Boothby and I went in one of them to La Chapelle, which is the present single distributing station for all the wounded forwarded to Paris.

Red Cross ambulances of every pattern and from a great many hospitals were being picked up from all sides as we neared our destination — a rather unusual sight here at midday, for the authorities do not like to have the recent wounded carted through the streets by day even though it be in closed cars; and as a matter of fact the larger number of our admissions occur in the late hours or at night.

A large, high building, once a freight shed, I presume, possibly 250 feet long, has been transformed for the present purpose. The train runs in on a single track behind a curtained-off side of the building — curtained off by a huge heavy black canvas which opens at one place through which the wounded successively come — first the *petits blessés* on foot, then the men in chairs, then the *grands blessés* on stretchers.

The impressive thing about it is that it is all so quiet. People talk in low voices; there is no hurry, no shouting, no gesticulating, no giving of direction — nothing Latin about it whatsoever. And the line of wounded — tired, grimy, muddy, stolid, uncomplaining, bloody. It would make you weep. Through the opening in the curtain, beyond which one of the cars of the train could be seen, they slowly emerged one by one, cast a dull look around, saw where they were to go, and then doggedly went, one after the other, each hanging on to his little bundle of possessions. Many of them were Moroccans, though for the most part they were downright French types. Those with legs to walk on had heads or bodies or arms in bandages or slings, in the hurried applying of which, day before yesterday, uniforms and sleeves had been ruthlessly slit open. Not a murmur, not a grunt — limping, shuffling, hobbling — in all kinds of bedraggled uniforms, the new gray-blue as well as the old dark blue with red trousers — home troops and African Zouaves and occasionally a marine, for they too have been in the trenches of late.

The procession wound directly by us, for the American Ambulance drivers are privileged to go into this part of the shed, owing to their known willingness to lend a hand. They were sitting in a quiet group, evidently moved, though many of them had been through the Marne days when cattle trains would come in with the wounded on straw, without food or water for two or more days, stinking and gangrenous. Things of course are very different now, and here at La Chapelle, Dr. Quenu, of Hôpital Cochin reputation, has finally got a perfect system arranged to replace the utter confusion of those early weeks.

It has been only two days since these fellows were hit, and many of them, regarded as sitting cases, have stuck it out, believing they could walk off the train. But not all could. One poor boy, who collapsed before us, they put on a stretcher and took to the emergency booth. Others had to be helped as they walked on between the two rows of booths to the farther end of the building, where were two large squares of benches arranged in a double row about an iron brazier in which a warm charcoal fire was glowing; for it was a cold, raw, and drizzly afternoon.

The wounded all have their tags dangling from a button somewhere — a tag from the *poste de secours,* another from the *ambulance de première ligne,* and possibly one or two more indicating where they had stopped for a dressing; and in addition, on the train, to save trouble, each has been chalked somewhere on his coat with a big B (*blessé*) or an M (*malade*), so that they can be sorted readily.

It was soon whispered about that this lot had come from Ypres and that they had all suffered greatly from some German *gaz asphyxiant;* but I hardly believed the talc, or thought I had misunderstood, until this evening's communiqué bears it out. Many of them were coughing; but then, most of the wounded still come in with a bronchitis. We have heard rumors for some days of a movement of German troops in the direction of Ypres, and this attack is apparently the result.

By the time the wounded were all congregated, many Red Cross nurses were serving them hot soup and other things, ending up with the inevitable cigarette. The men were quiet, immovable, sitting where and how they first slumped down on their benches. No conversation — just a stunned acceptance of the kindly efforts to comfort them.

Quenu, though busy, was very polite — they all are — pretended he knew me and asked if I should like to see the room where the *petits pansements* were being made. Among the several who had been singled out as needing immediate dressings because of pain, dislodged bandages, or recent bleedings, was the poor boy we had seen collapse as he walked out of the train. He had a high fever and a trifling first-aid dressing on his badly fractured left arm. This was surely enough, but when the young doctor cut off his circa six layers of clothing an undressed chest wound in his right pectoral region was disclosed. We then sat him up and found the wound of exit near the shoulder blade — at which the boy said, *"C'est bon, je guérirai."* He was in our lot and I saw him landed later at Neuilly spitting blood.

When we got back to the Ambulance, the air was full of tales of the asphyxiating gas which the Germans had turned loose on Thursday — but it is difficult to get a straight story. A huge, low-lying, greenish cloud of smoke with a yellowish top began to roll down from the German trenches, fanned by a steady easterly wind. At the same time there was a terrifically heavy bombardment. The smoke was suffocating and smelled to some like ether and sulphur, to another like a thousand sulphur matches, to still another like burning rosin. One man said that there were about a thousand Zouaves of the Bataillon d'Afrique in the lines and only sixty got back — either suffocated or shot as they clambered out of the trenches to escape. Another of the men was *au repos* five kilometers away and says he could smell the gas there. He, with his fellows, was among those of the reserves who were called on to support the line, but by the time they got up the Germans were across the canal, having effectively followed up their smudge. They seem to have been driven out later, or at least these men thought they had been. We'll have to await the official communiqués, and perhaps not know even then. In any event, there's devil's work going on around Ypres, and the heralded spring drive seems to have been initiated by the Germans.

Sunday, April 25 — It has apparently been a large affair at Ypres, with the Germans the aggressors. Several hundred more wounded at La Chapelle this morning — all the ambulance men out — all our beds full.

Wednesday, April 28 — We are still very busy and the hospital is crowded. I had a strange time operating for DuBouchet on one of his patients — Lafourcode in No. 77 — supposed to have a *gouttière* bullet wound of the skull, which I did not question, though murmuring something about the desirability of an X ray.

At all events, I was persuaded to take the case in hand and it proved to be not a gutter wound at all, the presumed wound of exit being merely where the man had fallen and cut his head on some sharp object. The track of the missile, along which an aluminum probe could be passed, led directly downward toward the base of the brain. This afternoon an X ray showed a fragment of *obus* just over the sella — not a bullet at all.

Thursday, April 29 — Several unsuccessful trials this morning to extract the shell fragment by the aid of the magnet from the brain of poor Lafourcode. I was afraid to use the huge probe which they have and so determined to make, or have made, another — of which later. We had tried every possible thing in our own cabinet and in those on the lower floors without success. Finally, while I was at lunch, Boothby hit upon precisely what was needed in the shape of a large wire nail about six inches long, the point of which he had carefully rounded off.

Well, there was the usual crowd in the X-ray room and approaching corridor, and much excitement when we let the nail slide by gravity into the central mechanism of smiling Lafourcode; for at no time did he have any pressure symptoms, and all of these procedures were of course without an anesthetic. While the X-ray plate was being developed to see whether the nail and missile were in contact, who should drop in but Albert Kocher with a friend from Berne; and then shortly a card was sent in by Tom Perry's friend, Salomon Reinach of the French Institute, author of the *History of Religions* and much else.

So all together we finally traipsed into the first-floor operating room, where Cutler mightily brings up the magnet and slowly we extract the nail — and — there was nothing on it! Suppressed sighs and groans. I tried again, very carefully — with the same result. More sighs, and people began to go out. A third time: nothing. By this time I began to grumble: "Never saw anything of this kind pulled off with such a crowd. Hoodooed ourselves from the start. Should have had an X ray made when the man first entered the hospital." The usual thing, as when one begins to scold his golf ball.

I had taken off my gloves and put the nail down; but then, let's try just once more. So I slipped the brutal thing again down the track, three and a half inches to the base of the brain, and once more Cutler gingerly swung the big magnet down and made contact. The current was switched on and as before we slowly drew out the nail — and there it was, the little fragment of rough steel hanging on to its tip.

Much emotion on all sides, especially on the part of A. Kocher and Salomon Reinach, both of whom could hardly bear it.

[On July 22, 1917, Dr. Cushing, with a surgical team, was detached from his unit and sent forward to work in a British Casualty Clearing Station at a place known as "Mendinghem," near Poperinghe. Here he remained during the long-drawn-out attack (July–October) on the Passchendaele ridges.]

Tuesday, July 31 — The third battle of Ypres opened today — zero hour at 3:50 A.M. After a week of good weather came the deluge.

Wednesday, 1:30 A.M. — One of the disadvantages of our picturesque camp came home to me as I felt my way to this soggy red tent. Pitch black, pouring rain, and has been, I believe, nearly all this fearful day — two ambulance trains of the new variety, about a mile long, vestibuled so you can't climb under or over the couplings, standing between the officers' quarters and the hospital encampment — your electric torch burned out — trying to stick to slippery duckboards about a foot wide. Depressing for a well man, but imagine what these poor wounded devils have had to go through today, and what those still lying out are enduring. The pre-operative hut is still packed with untouched cases, so caked in wet mud that it's often a task to strip them and find out what they've got.

Thursday, August 2, 2:30 A.M. — Pouring cats and dogs all day — also pouring cold and shivering wounded, covered with mud and blood. Some G.S.W.'s (gunshot wounds) of the head, when the mud is scraped off, prove to be trifles — others of unsuspected gravity. The pre-operation room is still crowded; one can't possibly keep up with them, and the unsystematic way things are run drives one frantic. The news, too, is very bad. The greatest battle of history is floundering up to its middle in a morass, and the guns have sunk even deeper than that. *Gott mit uns* was certainly true for the enemy this time.

Operating from 8:30 A.M. one day till 2 A.M. the next; standing in a pair of rubber boots, and periodically full of tea as a stimulant, is not healthy. It's an awful business, probably the worst possible training in surgery for a young man, and ruinous for the carefully acquired technique of an oldster. Something over 2000 wounded have passed, so far, through this one C.C.S. There are fifteen similar stations behind this battle front.

10:30 P.M. We're about through now with this particular episode. Around 30,000 casualties, I believe — a small advance here and there, and that's about all.

Operating again all day, and finished up at 9 P.M. with an extraction of a large piece of shell from a man's badly infected ventricle with the magnet; then dinner, and now to bed. It still rains. A lot of wounded must have drowned in the mud.

Saturday, August 4 (really 3:30 A.M. on the 5th) — Another night helping Johnnie and Blake as long as I could stand up. I think the teams do better work by night than by day, and it is noticeable that the night shifts are composed of the emergency teams. Urgent operations on more rotting men. One case I did had a gross gas infection of the brain. My particular grouse lies in the fact that no one protests against locking tight every door of a twenty-car ambulance train between the hospital and our camp. There are two alternatives — to feel your way around in a sea of mud or to crawl under. I crawled under tonight and nearly cracked my head. I'll feel less peevish later.

Sunday, August 5, 8:30 A.M. — I do. Except for the fact that my ragged batman, Ashford by name, says there are orders not to provide us with our customary inch of bath water — that we must henceforth go to the bathing tent. This structure lies in the hospital grounds on the other side of the barricaded track. "Zink," who is a joyful American attached here, said at breakfast that he had thought it out fully and told his particular batman to bring him some weak tea. He says it makes a fine lather.

Three years ago today England declared war against Germany. About four months ago we did.

Easter

by NORA CONNOLLY

The daughter of one of the Irish leaders of the Easter Upris-
ing of 1916, Nora Connolly tells of the iron reprisals which
left such bitterness in the hearts of the Irish and English
alike. Since the Atlantic *published her memorable article,*
Miss Connolly has become both a wife and a member of the
Irish Senate.

NOVEMBER 1916

On Easter Monday morning, 1916, Irish men and women declared
their belief in their country's right to national independence and their
willingness to die if need be to win that right.

They took possession of the capital and hoisted over it the green,
white, and orange flag of the Irish republic. Unfortunately, owing to the
demobilizing order issued by Sean MacNeill, the Republican forces were
small, not very much larger than a battalion of the English Army. On
Easter Monday morning there were only nine hundred men in arms, but
at the end of the week about fifteen hundred men surrendered.

The fight was short, but it was a good, clean, able one. Fifteen hundred men held the city for a week against a force of twenty-five thousand English soldiers, supplied with armored cars, field guns, rifles, and
all the necessary equipment of an army of war.

It was a week full of heroic incidents. At Mount Street Bridge a body
of two thousand English soldiers with full war equipment was held at
bay for over twelve hours by five rebels armed only with rifles. When,
near the end of the fight, the ammunition was giving out, two of the
men went for supplies; the remaining three gave no sign that their numbers were lessened. A little later one was killed and then one man held
the fort while the other buried his dead comrade. Two forts overlooking
O'Connell's Bridge were held by six men, three in each. They were not
killed, although shot and shell were poured into the forts. When they
could hold out no longer they made their way to the General Post Of-

fice. These six were what was known in Dublin as Kimmage men — men who had been born in England or Scotland and, in most cases, had never been in Ireland before; men who, knowing the day was near, came over to Ireland to make ready.

It seemed to me, in those days, that they were like the reserve men who are mobilized by a nation on the eve of going to war. Most of these men spoke with a Scotch or English accent, and an amusing story is told of one of them. A party of seven was evacuating one of the forts and making an attempt to gain the General Post Office. The street was swept with machine-gun bullets. They had to cross the street. They took a zig-zag course, one after another — the first, second, third, and fourth men crossed in safety, and the fifth was so struck by this that in the middle of the street he stopped to remark to the man behind him, "Blimy, this is gryte!" and then made his way across. Our men seemed to lead charmed lives. Their casualties were marvelously small — one hundred and fifty killed and wounded — the dead numbering about thirty.

I was first sent to the North of Ireland with a dispatch on Easter Monday morning. I was commandant of the Ambulance Corps going North, and had all my medical supplies with me. Unfortunately, the men had received the demobilizing order and believing there was to be no rebellion they had returned home, so there was no need for me.

When I was going back to Dublin, I went to stay the night in a house that had just been searched by the military, and a small amount of ammunition had been taken from there by them. I had to pass through the military on my way to the house, and as I was in a motorcar with all my bundles, they evidently came to the opinion that I was bringing more ammunition there, as they paid the house another visit at two o'clock in the morning. They searched the whole house again, questioned me closely, took my address, and went through my kit bag. They finally left, seizing all my medical supplies and not disdaining to take my haversack containing two days' rations. This frightened the lady of the house and she asked me to leave. She said she did not want an arrest from her house. I left early the next morning.

I had sent a young girl ahead with a dispatch some time before. Feeling myself responsible for her, I did not care to return to Dublin without her. I started for the town she was in. The lady of the house told me it was not five miles away. I decided to walk: to go by train I would have had to pass the inspection of a constabulary, and that was the last thing I desired. I set out at seven o'clock, and walked all day on a lonely mountain road — mountains on one side of me, bogs on the other, and never a tree for shade, and never a house to get a drink in. The sun was roasting that day, and I was heavily laden. I had my uniform on, under a skirt and mackintosh, and was carrying the kit bag of the other girl and my own. I walked until I was completely worn out, not able to go more than a few yards at a time. Near my journey's end I met the girl I was looking for. She took me to the house she was staying in. In that house, I learned that I had walked nearly twenty miles.

I rested that night and in the morning the little girl and I started for Dublin. We took a train which brought us to Dundalk. When we arrived there the station was full of military and constabulary. We asked if we could get to Dublin, and were told the only train going there was a military one, and that the lines were in the hands of the military. We decided to walk. We learned from the automobile signs that it was fifty-six miles to Dublin. We started on our road after lunch and we walked all that day. We had to pass a military barricade at a place called Dunleer, some eight miles from Drogheda.

We were rather nervous. We did not want to be stopped, for we did not know the name of the next village. If we were asked where we were going we could not say — it would be worse than folly to say "Dublin" — but we passed it, however, and walked until dark. We thought it possible that there might be military or police patrols, and as no hotel was near, we did not desire to arouse suspicion by asking for a night's shelter, so we decided to lie out in the field that night. We did so, and a most uncomfortable night it was. It was very cold. A heavy mist came down and soaked into our clothes. We watched for the dawn, then we resumed our walk and reached Drogheda in time for seven o'clock mass.

We had no adventures until we came to Balbriggan. There was another military barricade there, which we managed to pass while the soldiers were having a heated discussion with three men they desired to search. At 7:30 on Sunday night we arrived on the outskirts of Dublin. There we learned the dreadful news that our men were surrendering and that my father was wounded and a prisoner in Dublin Castle.

I saw my father the following Tuesday. He was in bed, his wounded leg resting in a cage. There was an officer of the R.A.M.C. in his room all the time I was with him. He was very weak and pale and his voice was very low. I asked if he was suffering much pain. He said no, but that he had been propped up in the bed and court-martialed and the strain was very great. I was very much depressed at hearing that. I had been thinking that there would be no attempt to shoot him till he was well; but I knew then that if he was court-martialed while he was unable to sit up, the authorities would not hesitate to shoot him while he was wounded.

He was very cheerful, as he lay in his bed making plans for our future. He gave my mother, who was with me, a message to Skeffington, asking him to get some of the songs published. It nearly broke my mother's heart to think she could not tell him that his good comrade and friend had already been murdered by English soldiers. (Before we were permitted to see my father, we were asked to give our word of honor that we would give him no news from the outside.) I tried to tell him some news, however. I told him that Captain Mellows was still out with his men in the Galway hills. He smiled and said, "They were always good boys." I told him that Lawrence Ginnell was fighting for the men in the House of Commons. "Good man, Larry!" he said. "He can always be depended upon."

He was very proud of his men. "It was a good clean fight," he declared. "The cause cannot die now. It will put an end to recruiting. Irishmen now realize the absurdity of fighting for the freedom of another country while their own is still enslaved." He praised the brave women and girls. "No one can ever say enough to honor them," he said.

He told me about one young boy who was carrying his stretcher when the rebels were trying to retreat from the burning Post Office. The street they were crossing was swept with bullets. If a bullet came near the stretcher, the boy would move his body to shield my father. He was so young-looking that my father asked his age. "I am fourteen, sir," he replied. My father's eyes lit up while he was telling this story. At the end, he said, "We cannot fail. Those young boys will never forget."

When next I saw my father, it was at midnight on Thursday, May the eleventh. A motor ambulance came to the house. The officer who accompanied it said my father was very weak and wanted to see his wife and eldest daughter. My mother believed this, as when she had last seen my father he was very weak and suffering much pain. He had told her that he never slept without morphine. Nevertheless, she was a trifle apprehensive, for she asked the officer to tell her if they were going to shoot my father. The officer said he could tell her nothing.

It seemed to take hours to get to the Castle, and when we were stopped by the sentries the minutes seemed hours. Finally we were passed in and were taken to my father's room at once. We were surprised to see on the small landing outside his room about a dozen soldiers encamped. They had their beds and full equipments with them. Six were on guard at the top of the stairs, and in the little alcove leading to his room were three more; all had their rifles with fixed bayonets.

We entered the room; my father had his head turned to the door. When he saw us he said, "Well, Lillie, I suppose you know what this means."

My mother cried out, "Oh James, it's not that, it's not that!"

"Yes, Lillie, I fell asleep tonight for the first time, and they wakened me at eleven to tell me I was to die at dawn."

My mother broke down, laid her head on his bed and sobbed heart-breakingly.

My father patted her head and said, "Don't cry, Lillie, you will un-man me."

My mother sobbed, "But your beautiful life, James, your beautiful young life!"

"Well, Lillie," he said, "hasn't it been a full life and isn't this a good end?"

I was crying, too. He turned to me at the other side of his bed, and said, "Don't cry, Nora, there is nothing to cry about."

"I won't cry," I said.

He patted my hand and said, "That's my brave girl." He then whispered to me, "Put your hand here," making a movement under the bed-clothes. I put my hand where he indicated. "Put it under the clothes." I did so and he slipped a paper into my hand. "Smuggle that out," he said, "it is my last statement."

Mother was sitting at the other side of the bed, her face growing grayer and older every minute. My father turned to her and said, "Re-member, Lillie, I want you and the girls to go to America; it will be the best place for them. Leave the boy at home in Ireland. He was a brick and I am proud of him."

My mother could only nod her head. My father tried to cheer her up by telling her about a man who had come to the Post Office during the revolution to buy a penny stamp, and how indignant he was when he was told he could not get one. He turned to me then and said, "I heard poor Skeffington was shot." I said, "Yes," and then told him that all his staff, the best men in Ireland, were gone. He was silent for a while. I think he thought that he was the first to be executed. I told him the pa-pers had said that it was promised in the House of Commons there would be no more shootings. "England's promises!" was all he said to that.

The officer then told us we had only five minutes more. Mother was nearly overcome. We had to give her water. My father tried to clasp her in his arms but he could barely lift his head and arms from the bed.

"Time is up," the officer said. My father turned to say good-by to me. I could not speak. He said, "Go to your mother."

I tried to bring her away. I could not move her. She stood as if turned to stone. The nurse came forward and helped her away. I ran back and kissed my father again; then the door was shut and we saw him no more.

We were brought back to the house. My mother went to the window, pulled back the curtain, and stood watching for the dawn, moaning all the while. I thought her heart would break and that she would die.

We went to the Castle in the morning to ask for my father's body. They would not give it to us. A kind nurse managed to get a lock of my father's hair which she gave to my mother.

That is all we have of him now.

Wilfred Owen
by SIR OSBERT SITWELL

It was while serving in the Grenadier Guards that Sir Osbert Sitwell, biographer and poet, first came to know Wilfred Owen, the English poet who was killed one week before the Armistice in 1918.

AUGUST 1950

Wilfred Owen! This is a name that has gathered a continual accretion of fire. It glows. It lives clothed in flame. On the day when at last the news came that the Second World War was over, under circumstances so terrible and portentous as to overshadow any feeling of happiness; in that strange desert of a holiday created for public rejoicing in which there yet could exist no feeling of joy, certain lines drifted into my mind:

> Red lips are not so red
>   As the stained stones kissed by the English dead.
> Kindness of wooed and wooer
> Seems shame to their love pure.
> O love, your eyes lose lure
>   When I behold eyes blinded in my stead!

For an instant, I could not remember who had written them, and then, with the shock that comes when one recognizes another of the distorted repetitions of history, I identified them, and in consequence today take up my pen to salute, across the intervening gap of over thirty years, the genius of a poet killed at the end of the First World War. So long ago; yet it was just such a summer day as this when I last saw him.

I did not know Wilfred Owen for long, hardly for more than a year, I suppose, but the friendships we possessed in common, notably with Siegfried Sassoon and Robert Ross, and the fact that we were deeply in sympathy in our views concerning the war and its conduct soon matured our relationship.

He manifested a tremendous capacity for admiration, for reverence; a quality which perhaps every poet, however much of a rebel he may be in other directions, must possess. It showed in his conduct toward contemporaries and elders no less than in his attitude toward the great who had gone before. It sounds from much of his early verse; in the last stanza, for example, of the poem he wrote in the summer of 1912, when he was nineteen, "On Seeing a Lock of Keats' Hair."

> It is a lock of Adonais' hair!
> I dare not look too long; nor try to tell
> What glories I see glistening, glistening there.
> The unanointed eye cannot perceive their spell.
> Turn ye to Adonais; his great spirit seek.
> O hear him; he will speak!

The quality of greatness that differentiates him from other war poets is in the truth both of his poetry and of his response to war. If he can be properly called a War Poet — since, greater than that, he was a Poet — he may be the only writer who answers truly to that description; the first, as he may be the last, for the very phrase *War Poet* indicates a strange twentieth-century phenomenon, the attempt to combine two incompatibles. There had been no War Poets in the Peninsular, Crimean, or Boer wars. But war had suddenly become transformed by the effort of scientist and mechanician into something so infernal, so inhuman, that it was recognized that only their natural enemy, the poet, could pierce through the armor of horror with which they were encased, to the pity at the human core; only the poet could steadily contemplate the struggle at the level of tragedy. The invention of the atomic bomb again changed these values: for war has once more altered its character, and an Atomic-Bomb Poet is one not to be thought of.

No, Owen was a *poet* — a War Poet only because the brief span of his maturity coincided with a war of hitherto unparalleled sweep, viciousness, and stupidity. Alone of contemporary poets he fused, without confusing, the thoughts and emotions of war; but his compassionate heart could have been moved by other matters to the same profound and poignant expression.

His feelings about the struggle in which he was involved are stated by implication in his finest poems; they are summarized more forthrightly still in the following passage from a letter he wrote while in hospital in the spring of 1917:

> Already I have comprehended a light which never will filter into the dogma of any national church: namely, that one of Christ's essential commands was: passivity at any price! Suffer dishonour and disgrace, but never resort to arms. Be bullied, be outraged, be killed; but do not kill. It may be a chimerical and an ignominious principle, but there it is. It can only be ignored, and I think pulpit professionals are ignoring it very skilfully and successfully indeed. . . . And am I not myself a conscientious objector with a very seared conscience? . . . Christ is literally in "no man's land." There men often hear His voice: Greater love hath no man than this, that a man lay down his life for a friend. Is it spoken in English only and French? I do not believe so. Thus you see how pure Christianity will not fit in with pure patriotism.

In a document found among his papers — a curious, fragmentary work of genius intended as a preface for his unpublished poems, and composed at the Front in the weeks immediately before he was killed — he writes:

> Above all I am not concerned with Poetry.
> My subject is War, and the pity of War.
> The Poetry is in the Pity.
> . . . All a poet can do to-day is warn. That is why
> the true poet to-day must be truthful.

"The Poetry is in the Pity." Yes, but it is also, in Owen's case, in the poetry. It is through the poetry of it that Pity makes her voice heard. All through his poems, even those he wrote when a boy, runs not only the same deeply flowing stream of feeling, but the same individual music, both like and unlike that of the great poets at the beginning of the previous century, of whom he was the heir. As a poet, he advanced, moreover, both in content and technique, by natural degrees from the conventional to the original, instead of beginning, as do so many writers, by being original when young and then lapsing later into the academic. His use of assonances was a profound modification of traditional English verse usage, and found its perfect expression in the most famous and the most moving of his poems, "Strange Meeting," as great a poem as exists in our tongue. Let us turn then,

> Turn ye to Adonais; his great spirit seek.
> O hear him; he will speak!

What do we hear; what are the young to hear from him?

> . . . Whatever hope is yours,
> Was my life also; I went hunting wild
> After the wildest beauty in the world,
> Which lies not calm in eyes, or braided hair,
> But mocks the steady running of the hour,
> And if it grieves, grieves richlier than here.
> For by my glee might many men have laughed,
> And of my weeping something had been left,
> Which must die now. I mean the truth untold,
> The pity of war, the pity war distilled.
> Now men will go content with what we spoiled.
> Or, discontent, boil bloody, and be spilled.
> They will be swift with swiftness of the tigress,
> None will break ranks, though nations trek from progress.

The material facts of Wilfred Owen's short life are soon told. He was born at Plas Wilmot, Oswestry, on March 18, 1893. Even in his earliest years, he loved, as we might have presumed, the sound of words: for his mother said, "He was always a very thoughtful, imaginative child — not very robust, and never cared for games. As a little child his greatest pleasure was for me to read to him, even after he could read himself." He was educated at the Birkenhead Institute across the river from Liverpool, to which city his family had moved. About the age of thirteen or fourteen, he showed a passionate desire for learning, and began to reveal the great power that poetry exercised over him.

Between his fourteenth and sixteenth years he spent two holidays in France, a country for which he developed a great affection. In 1910, he matriculated at the London University. His early verses, written with the greatest diffidence at this time, reflect his continual reading of Keats, and the adoration he cherished for him. In 1913, a serious illness led to his seeking a more equable winter climate in France, where he accepted an engagement as tutor at Bordeaux — a post he filled for some two years.

This period must have been most important in his development; he was keenly appreciative of the beauty of the mountains; and he was fortunate enough to become acquainted with Laurent Tailhade, the poet. Tailhade, it is clear from the work of both of them, exercised no direct influence upon the young man. Indeed, there is little sign in his work of any influences save those of Shakespeare, the Bible, and Keats — especially Keats: and this is unexpected, because of all the poets of the English Romantic age he was the most perfect, and therefore, you would have presumed, the least likely quarry for others to work; because it is generally the great but incomplete poet who is the father of those to come. No doubt Tailhade's conversation and his knowledge of the French literary world were of the greatest interest to Owen. It was plainly a happy interval, and his poems written at this time show a light and gaiety that events were soon to deny to them forever. During this score of months he grew to understand the French way of thinking and to learn to talk and write in French, though about this accomplishment he remained typically diffident.

Owen's professional contract prevented him from returning until 1915, and in that year he came home and joined the Artists' Rifles, being gazetted later to the Manchester Regiment. He was posted to the Second Battalion on the Somme front, where sharp fighting was already in progress, in January 1917. His letters of the time present with perfect veracity and consummate skill the life of the infantry officer of those years in France and Flanders. Each war produces its own particular harvest of horrors for the soldier, and those of the 1914–1918 struggle — in addition to such flimsy but none the less abiding troubles as that which the poet notes in the words "Since I set foot on Calais quays I have not had dry feet" — were boredom, mud, and, in especial, No Man's Land, the space between the enemy trenches and our own. Of this, since it is important to realize out of what suffering the fullness of his poetry was born, I give the following description from one of Owen's letters:

It is like the eternal place of gnashing of teeth; the Slough of Despond could be contained in one of its crater-holes; the fires of Sodom and Gomorrah could not light a candle to it — to find the way to Babylon the Fallen. It is pock-marked like a body of foulest disease, and its odour is the breath of cancer. I have not seen any dead. I have done worse. In the dank air I have *perceived* it, and in the darkness, *felt.* . . . No Man's Land under snow is like the face of the moon, chaotic, crater-ridden, uninhabitable, awful, the abode of madness.

After months of hard service and almost intolerable cold — for the winter of 1916–1917 was particularly severe — Owen was taken into

No. 1 General Hospital suffering from neurasthenia, and probably from concussion, the result of a fall into a cellar, of being blown up, and of exhaustion. Thence he was sent first to the Welsh Hospital at Netley, and finally to the Craiglockhart War Hospital for nervous cases, near Edinburgh — an establishment housed in a building which he compared to "a decayed hydro." Here he led an active life, lecturing and editing the hospital magazine, and took lessons in German — no doubt to prepare himself for future intercourse with the Germans, the majority of whom he held to be fellow victims of war — from Frank Nicholson, the then librarian of Edinburgh University, who gave to Edmund Blunden a most living account of him as he was at this time. In it he describes how Owen took him out to tea, after one of these lessons, in a café, the only occasion on which they were alone and able to speak freely. He had with him a collection of photographs of mutilated and wounded men which he had made in order to bring home to the unimaginative the horrors that others faced for them. Owen spoke of them to Nicholson, and started to raise his hand to his breast pocket to bring them out, but then, suddenly realizing perhaps that his companion was not one to whom it was necessary to emphasize the horrors of war, refrained.

Later on the same occasion he spoke to Nicholson — and this is important — on the problem of literary form, and how he believed that he had discovered a medium for himself through the substitution of a play of vowels for pure rhyme. (In this connection it must be remarked that quite apart from the mastery in the matter of assonances and dissonances which his work shows, and that can only be the result of long practice, many of his early poems manifest his preoccupation with this technical device.) In a letter to me, Nicholson says:

> What really drew me to him so strongly was the beauty of his personality. I bear a certain grudge against myself for not having, on the occasion to which you refer, pursued the subject of his "new" poetic technique more sympathetically and more intelligently than I did. I fancy he was then more or less feeling his way toward that vowel-music which he made so peculiarly his own and used with such tremendous effect in some of his later war poems. When he spoke to me of enlarging the older traditional rhyme-range of English verse in this fashion I could only think of such freedoms as poets like Tennyson had occasionally indulged in — for example in some of the Lady of Shalott stanzas — and I failed to grasp how immensely different in character Owen's experiments were.

During the first weeks at Craiglockhart, Owen was depressed. On August 8 he wrote:

> . . . I am a sick man in hospital, by night; a poet, for quarter of
> an hour after breakfast; I am whatever and whoever I see while going
> down to Edinburgh on the train: greengrocer, policeman, shopping
> lady, errand-boy, paper-boy, blind man, crippled Tommy, bank-clerk,
> carter, all of these in half an hour; next a German student in earnest.

At this very moment of his life's lowest ebb there arrived in the same
hospital a new patient, Siegfried Sassoon, whose celebrated book of
poems, *The Old Huntsman,* had recently made its appearance. Owen admired the newcomer, his work, and the moral courage of his pacifism —
which, indeed, was in part responsible for his being in the sanatorium —
equally.

The younger man summoned up his courage and called on Sassoon.
He showed him some poems, and persuaded him, too, to give some of his
work to the hospital magazine, which Owen was editing. *The Hydra,* as
it was called, was thus privileged to publish two famous poets of the war.
The friendship that started in this manner gave Owen hope, and a new
vision of life, so that from now onward, in the short year that opened up
before him, his full stature, which grew continually until the end, was
revealed. Within a year, everything was changed; he now both understood his own capacity and was sure of his strength. Two years before he
had written:

> *To be able* to write as I *know how to,* study is necessary: a period
> of study, then of intercourse with kindred spirits, then of isolation.
> My heart is ready, but my brain unprepared, and my hand untrained.

But now, in November 1917, in a letter to Siegfried Sassoon, he says:

> Know that . . . I held you as Keats + Christ + Elijah + my
> Colonel + my father-confessor + Amenophis IV in profile. What's
> that mathematically? . . . If you consider what the above names
> have severally done for me, you will know what you are doing. And
> you have *fixed* my Life — however short. You did not light me: I
> was always a mad comet; but you have fixed me. I spun round you a
> satellite for a month, but I shall swing out soon, a dark star in the
> orbit where you will blaze.

For all the modesty of demeanor and manner that showed so touchingly when one met him, he possessed, as every poet must possess, his
ambitions: in his own words "lesser than Macbeth's and greater, not so
happy but much happier." Now they were realized. On the last day of
the last year he was to complete — 1917 — he wrote to his mother:

And so I have come to the true measure of man. I am not dissatisfied [with] my years. Everything has been done in bouts: Bouts of awful labour at Shrewsbury and Bordeaux; bouts of amazing pleasure in the Pyrenees, and play at Craiglockhart; bouts of religion at Dunsden; bouts of horrible danger on the Somme; bouts of poetry always; of your affection always; of sympathy for the oppressed always. I go out of this year a poet, my dear mother, as which I did not enter it. I am held peer by the Georgians; I am a poet's poet. I am started. The tugs have left me; I feel the great swelling of the open sea taking my galleon.

Alas, he sailed the open sea for only a few more months — ten, to be precise — but in that time produced imperishable poems.

Though to Siegfried Sassoon belongs the glory of having discovered Wilfred Owen, and of having helped him and launched him, it was through Robert Ross that I first heard of the new poet. The younger men who would be found at Robbie's were usually writers and often poets, and he would often ask me to come and meet them. I was not surprised, therefore, when, in September 1917, he telephoned to me and invited me to come round to his rooms on Half-Moon Street the next evening after dinner. He said it was very important, and when I inquired why, he told me that a newly discovered poet called Wilfred Owen, a friend whom Siegfried had met at Craiglockhart, was dining with him at the Reform, and that he wanted me to meet him. He gave promise of being a remarkable poet, Robert Ross added, and he asked me especially "not to frighten him" for he was the most diffident and sensitive of men.

Accordingly, I went round at the hour named, and there, in the comfortable warmth of Robbie's sitting room, I saw a young officer of about my age — he was three months younger than myself — of sturdy, medium build and wearing a khaki uniform. His face was rather broad, and I think its most unusual characteristics were the width of eyes and forehead and the tawny, rather sanguine skin, which proclaimed, as against the message of his eyes — deep in color, and dark in their meaning — a love of life and a poet's enjoyment of air and light. His features were mobile but determined, and his hair short and of a soft brown. His whole appearance, in spite of what he had been through, gave the impression of being somewhat young for his age, and, though he seemed perfectly sure of himself, it was easy to perceive that by nature he was shy.

His voice — what does his voice sound like across the years? A soft modulation, even-toned, but with a warmth in it (I almost hear it now), a well-proportioned voice that signified a sense of justice and of compassion. With his contemporaries he talked with ease. Only in the presence of such literary nabobs of the period as Wells and Bennett could he scarcely bring himself to speak; and this silence, apart from being rooted in his natural modesty and good manners, was due, I think, to the immense esteem in which he held literature and those who practiced the profession of author. His residence in France may have deepened this attitude of respect, and almost awe, which had in it nothing of the Englishman's casual approach to books. To him they were all-important, while poetry was the very crown of life, and constituted its meaning.

The following year he sent me some of his poems, among them his magnificent "Mental Cases":

> Who are these? Why sit they here in twilight?
> Wherefore rock they, purgatorial shadows.

The others are "Disabled," "Parable of the Old Men and the Young," "The Last Laugh," "The Last Word," "Soldiers' Dreams," "Arms and the Boy," and an early poem, untitled, beginning

> Long ages past, in Egypt thou wert worshipped
> And thou wert wrought from ivory and beryl.

"The Last Laugh" and "The Last Word" are similar versions of the same unpublished poem, and are not among the first rank of his work. The early poem and "Soldiers' Dreams" also remain unpublished, and each of the rest presents variations from the published text. But this was not unusual with Owen, for many manuscript versions exist of nearly all his poems. The version I possess of "Mental Cases" offers an interesting alternative three lines for the four that appear at the end of the poem in the book *The Poems of Wilfred Owen*. The published version runs:

> — Thus their hands are plucking at each other;
> Picking at the rope-knouts of their scourging;
> Snatching after us who smote them, brother,
> Pawing us who dealt them war and madness.

whereas in my copy it is:

> Thus their fingers pick and pluck each other,
> Picking the hard scourge that scourged them, brother,
> Plucking us who dealt them war and madness.

The last time I saw Wilfred Owen was on an afternoon of full summer, a Saturday in July 1918. He had let me know that he was coming to London, and I had been able to arrange to take him and Siegfried Sassoon to hear Violet Gordon Woodhouse play the harpsichord and clavichord, and she made the afternoon stand out as an oasis in the desert of war. For over two hours she played Bach, Mozart, and the early English composers to us, as only she could play them. Wilfred Owen felt deeply the appeal of music, and he was dazed with happiness at the fire and audacity of the player.

After hearing Mrs. Gordon Woodhouse, Owen, Siegfried Sassoon, and I went back to my house on Swan Walk — or rather we first sat in the Physic Garden opposite, under the mulberry trees. We walked across to the house for tea and then returned to sit in the Garden. It was the ideal of a summer afternoon: various shrubs, late-flowering magnolias and the like, were in blossom, there was a shimmer and flutter in the upper leaves, and a perfection of contentment and peacefulness, unusual in the tense atmosphere of a hot day in London, especially during a war, breathed over the scene. So listlessly happy was Owen that he could not bring himself to leave the Garden to go to the station and catch the train he had arranged to take.

That afternoon, so untouched by premonition, was yet full of lamentable fate. Those persons who, thinking he was not yet fit for foreign service, were seeking to find him a post at home, suddenly desisted. Had they continued, Wilfred Owen might well be alive today; but within a week he was ordered to attend for medical inspection, and knew that he was going out to France again. "I am glad," he wrote. "That is I am much gladder to be going out again than afraid. I shall be better able to cry my outcry, playing my part." A little more than a month later, he embarked once more for France. He rejoined his old battalion, and after winning the Military Cross in October, he was killed in an attempt to cross the Sambre Canal, on November 4, a week before the Armistice.

It was some weeks before his friends heard of his death: he had disappeared into the gray mists of those autumnal regions which had swallowed so many young lives — but never one that could be a greater loss to England than this. His death occurred many years ago now, but it is only a short period since one of his friends wrote to me: "I have found many letters lately of Wilfred Owen's, and looking back over the time since the last war, I see how much easier all our lives would have been if he had lived." These words bear true witness, both to his influence on his friends and to their feeling for him.

Flesh and Blood

by LAURENCE CRITCHELL

This story by Laurence Critchell, lieutenant in the 101st Airborne Division, was our first to touch without dodging the theme of men and women cut off from their mates, decent people so emotionally starved they hardly knew where to turn. "Flesh and Blood" was an Atlantic First which received the O. Henry Award for 1945.

JANUARY 1945

It was still raining outside. It was so wet that even the crows had ceased their arguments from tree to tree. The only sounds in the whole local English world were the dripping of water on the tent walls and a lonesome fragment of music now and then from the direction of the area where the enlisted men lived. Lieutenant Stack wholeheartedly missed his wife. He had been in England for so long now that sometimes the memory of her grew a little dim, like the memory of so many things at home. Missing her, she seemed very close. She was standing at the door of the tent in the dim wet gloom, wearing a white dress. He got up and shook himself. He'd do something. He'd have to do something. Walk to town, maybe. Any change at all, even town, was better than this somberness, those dripping trees, that far-off music.

He felt a little sorry for himself. An hour ago the other officers — all of them except the O.D. — had gone to a dance at the club, seven miles away. He had stayed behind because of classes for Monday. *On the retraction of the bolt, the driving spring is compressed on the driving spring rod, cushioning the force of the recoil. The remainder of this force is absorbed in the buffer plates, which, when adjusted in tension, vary the cyclic rate of fire.* He was heartily sick of that gun.

The latrine was cold. There was no hot water; the enlisted men who were detailed as firemen had gone to a Red Cross dance in town several hours before. He cursed a little under his breath. It was nine days since the rain had started; now everything was damp — the boards, the floor, the walls, even the two mirrors. He studied his face critically in the glass. Thinner and older. There were small crow's-feet around his eyes. He wondered what his wife would think of him when he got back. He remembered what she had looked like that afternoon when he had come home and told her he had to go overseas. She had sat and looked at him and smiled, as she had promised to do, but slow tears came in her eyes and ran down her cheeks. Even after all these months, his memory of that moment was vivid. It warmed him inwardly as he shaved.

To be married and in love and overseas was, he reflected, a mixed blessing. At home he scarcely ever looked at other women. But over here it was different. He envied the single officers' freedom of mind. At the party tonight some Army nurses were coming down from the near-by evacuation hospital; everybody would have Scotch, brought from London, and when they returned they would have had enough excitement to keep them quiet for the week to follow — or reasonably quiet. War did funny things to men and women. If you were married and in love with your wife you could go for quite a while with just the memory of the things you did together for company. But there were other times when that solace failed, home grew very far away, the remembered intimacies dim.

Rain and work did it sometimes. He felt it strongly tonight. As he changed his parachute wings from the shirt to the blouse he wondered if when he got to town he would stay by himself. It was fairly easy to find a girl in town. The English civilian girls were friendly and the WAFS and the ATS were just as lonely as all soldiers. When he swung on his raincoat a stray passage from Charlotte Brontë came back to him out of the English gloom and the rain — something from *Jane Eyre:* that principles were only for the times when the senses ruled. Then he laughed at himself and swung out into the rain.

It was a long walk to town. He was lucky. A jeep on its way out of the area had been stopped at the gate by the sentry.

"Going to town?" he asked the driver.

The man nodded. Lieutenant Stack climbed into the front seat. They went very fast once they were clear of the gate. The driver said he was going to the railroad station to pick up an officer. Stack lit a cigarette. He leaned in out of the wind to smoke it.

The countryside looked sodden after so much rain. The haystacks, piled only the week before, had settled down to half their former size and now were dull yellow. Save for a single woman on a bicycle, who pulled her skirts over her knees as they passed, no one was abroad. The jeep swept up onto an overpass above some railroad tracks and then for a little space ran parallel with a train, which clicked along quietly not far from them. Its smoke was whiter than the sober clouds. Hedgerows flickered by. A few houses, cobblestones, a pub. And then suddenly they were in town.

"Where are you going, sir?"

Stack named the better of the two movie houses. "You can let me off at the station," he said. "I'll walk the rest of the way."

But the driver drove all the way to the theater. "Damn!" Stack said as they came up. "I've seen it."

The people waiting to get inside looked at them curiously as they went away. On another bridge along the road a small blonde girl was talking to a soldier. She caught Stack's eye as he went past. He smiled at her. That was harmless, at any rate. But he went on thinking about her — and he was still thinking about her when the driver let him off at the Regal. *Lifeboat* was playing. He did not tell the man that he had seen this one too. He returned the salute and walked down the street.

Beddingford on busy weekdays looked a little like a French fisher-town. It had the same bustle, the same smallness, the same kind of smells. The meat shops had the old familiar odors of raw meat and marble, the breadshops smelled like French breadshops, and one sometimes looked to see people carrying long rolls. But the queues of women lined up to get their rations of food on weekdays were not the sort of thing Stack remembered of pre-war France.

Nor were the powdered eggs in the store windows, the pitiful emptiness of the restaurants, which were almost too cold, the ration stamp notations on the suits in the clothing stores. In the stationery places you could buy writing paper with the insignia of the ATS or the WRENS on it, but the plain writing pads were only scratch paper and the books were almost all old ones.

The people who shopped looked shabby. The women wore no stockings. Only the younger girls had any lipstick — American soldiers had given it to them. They were cheery people but they were hard pressed for the necessities of life, and sometimes you got the impression that they looked a little weathered, like their old brown houses, the worn-down cobblestones, the eternal gray sky.

This night was Saturday. Everyone was out. As Stack walked toward the Quarter Arms Hotel, where there was a bar, he looked at the girls who passed him. His flesh was hungry. He had lost the vivid awareness of his wife. The war seemed utterly meaningless. One girl, passing, brushed against him. He jumped. Well, he thought, it served him right. He should have gone to the party, got high, forgotten everything — retractions of bolts, absorption of recoil, Monday's commitments, his wife — everything.

The bar of the Quarter Arms Hotel was paneled in wood, like the smoking room of an English club. Despite this luxury, it was still considered a pub by the men of the town, who came into it in their working clothes and stood about smoking and talking. For some reason, few women came into the place. On this evening an American WAC, a second lieutenant, blonde, plump, and rather pretty, was standing at the doorway talking to some glider pilots. She was the only woman. The room was thick with tobacco smoke. Stack pushed his way through the knots of men to the bar, saying "Thank you," as was the English custom.

A captain of his acquaintance was standing there. "Going to the dance?" asked the man.

Stack paused. "Too late, isn't it?"

"There's another bus supposed to come by in ten minutes. It's the last one."

Stack shook his head slowly. "I'll think it over," he said. Then, to the girl: "Bitters, please." She was thin and tall and not pretty.

"One, three and a half," she said, bringing him the glass. He gave her a half crown and waited for the change, swallowing the bitters in large mouthfuls. It was served in a smaller glass than the ales and had a sharper flavor; it was the only English drink he cared for. When the girl gave him the change, he moved into the center of the room. This was his last chance, he reflected. He could catch the bus and go out to the dance and that would be the end of that. He stood by a table and drank the bitters, wondering what to do. A staff sergeant beside him lifted his glass to someone across the room. Fragments of conversation came to him: ". . . doing all right, you know . . ." and "Birdy was the jockey for the Duke of Westminster. . . ."

He wondered what his wife would want him to do. She was unselfish — she'd tell him to go. She told him that when he left. She trusted him. And that was the whole trouble: he wished he trusted himself. He knew what happened to him over here when there were women around. The war had made it that way. Friends killed, death something to be checked off on a roster, youngsters with the fuzz scarcely off their cheeks machine-gunning other men. *On the retraction of the bolt . . .* It put you off your balance. You wanted to go out and drink and raise hell and kiss all the girls in the world and make it up somehow — you were not quite sure how. Principles were for the times — But what were principles in a world where youngsters out of high school, who should have been making love and growing up and learning a job, were busy machine-gunning other men?

He took the unfinished bitters and joined the captain. But the bus never came.

In the next half hour he visited the other three pubs in town. They were dark little places full of smoke and conversation, where drinks were served through a little window like a cashier's cage and where American soldiers stood around and joked with the villagers. Well-behaved, quiet soldiers, looking neatly dressed. But he could not find anyone to talk to. He wandered for a while through the back streets of town where the poor people lived and he crossed the bridge by the railroad where he had seen the girl with blonde hair. But she was gone. In desperation at last he took a place in the queue of people waiting to see the second showing of *Lifeboat*. He would go home after that.

As he joined the line, someone came up and stood beside him. It was a girl. She wore a neat tweed suit. The collar of her blouse under her raincoat was clean and starched. Her hair was clean, too, and it had been recently waved. She wore no stockings, but that was common enough in England; her shoes were neat. He looked at her face. She was not unattractive, he thought. She looked intelligent. She had her profile to him, but he could see that her eyes were blue. She was frowning a little. He looked away. The queue of people moved up and as he followed she moved with him.

He wondered about her. She didn't seem to be the kind of person you spoke to easily. But he liked her looks and he could tell that she was conscious of him. His wife was vague in his mind. If he had wanted someone to talk to in the early part of the evening, now, after walking through the rainy streets of town alone, he was desperate for it. He was too far gone for argument. The right or wrong of it could come later. As he moved toward the booth he thought of how he would do it. It was simple enough. He would buy two tickets and look at her as he stepped aside, and if she followed him that would be that.

There were only two more couples to go. It was now or not at all. He fumbled in his wallet for a ten-shilling note and glanced once again at the girl. He was ashamed to realize that his heart was pounding. The last couple had gone. The girl stepped aside for him and he understood then that she would go with him if he wished. He did not think of his wife.

"Two, please," he said, looking at the girl. This time their eyes met. He looked back at the cashier. "Two and nine." Then he stepped aside with the tickets, and the girl, after a moment of hesitation, followed him into the theater.

By American standards it was dark inside the theater. There were no half-lights and the exit lamps were only small bulbs. He and the girl waited in the darkness for the usher to come back. They could see nothing. He was wondering what to say to her, when she broke the silence first. "I've seen this before," she said. "In London."

"So have I," he answered. "In New York." She laughed. He was pleased by her voice. It was low and rather toneless but it sounded sensible. They stumbled down the aisle in the wake of the bobbing flashlight.

Of the two cinemas in Beddingford, the Regal was the more modest. Upstairs, where there was a restaurant, you could sit in comparative grandeur, helped to your seat by a girl with a very bright flashlight. Tickets for the balcony cost as much as four and six, where downstairs they cost only two and nine. But the downstairs seats were better. The air was cooler there and — since people could smoke anywhere in the theater — clearer.

Little by little as his eyes grew accustomed to the darkness he could make out the audience sitting around them — two English officers of the Royal Engineers directly in front, one wearing horn-rimmed spectacles; two girls at his side and, beyond them, a very fat woman who was alone. The fat woman looked over once and smiled at them. He was pleasantly conscious of being a couple.

"Do you like her?" asked the girl, leaning close to him to whisper.

"Who?"

"Tallulah Bankhead."

"Sometimes."

"I do," said the girl, straightening up. He looked at her once and met her eyes. He could feel his blood mount a little. He was surprised how hungry he had been for the touch of a woman. Even the sight of her sitting beside him in the dimness was pleasing. Her whispered comments were critical and sensible, he decided. And he liked the fragrance of her hair when she leaned close. He tried to think of things to whisper back to her. It made him feel a little like a schoolboy. He realized that the war had done this; he was accustomed to living in the field. With the girl he felt young, inexperienced. It made him smile. When the picture ended he was so lost in thoughts that he forgot to stand still at the first bars of "God Save the King."

"It was better the second time," she said when they were outside. She refused the cigarette he offered her.

"Where would you like to go?" he asked, lighting one himself.

"There really isn't any place, you know. The pubs are closed by now" — she looked at her watch — "and they don't have any clubs here as they do in London."

"Let's just walk, then."

"All right," cheerfully. "We can walk to where I live, if you like. There's an RAF field out there, you know."

He could think of few things he cared less about, that moment, than the Royal Air Force. But he nodded and took her arm and they started out. It was ten o'clock, yet the sky was still bright. She was a good walker. She had the firm, independent stride of the young English girl. For the first time that evening the cold rainy wind in his face was pleasurable.

"I never know whether I like England or hate it," he said aloud, smiling.

"Why should you hate it?"

"It's the first foreign country I've ever been in that I can't leave when I want to."

"That sounds rather spoiled."

"Don't the English think all Americans are spoiled?"

"Yes," she said candidly. "Don't you?"

He nodded. They both laughed at that. He told her his name. Hers was Leslie Bean. She was married. Her husband was a maritime lawyer in London. They had been separated for half a year. She worked for the Food Administration Bureau in Beddingford and lived with her sister and was trying to save enough money for a divorce. "It'll be a bit of a pull, I'm afraid," she said ruefully. "I make five pounds a week and that has to do for everything."

Ashamed of his own income of a hundred pounds a month, after what they had just said about Americans, he said nothing. They crossed a canal bridge and came into that part of town where the houses thinned out and gave way to trees and hedgerows. Shortly they passed the RAF airdrome, where it was noisy with motors and gusts of wind. He thought of where the pilots would be in a little while and grimaced. A few WAFS on bicycles, their stockings black, went by them with a ting-a-ling. This made the girl smile.

"You know," she said amusedly, "it's going to be hard for a lot of English girls when the war is over."

"How do you mean?"

"I mean that a lot of them have got used to the American soldiers. You people — I don't know — you all seem so well built, physically." She looked at him appreciatively and laughed. "Then you're more direct and you talk more. Our men are so quiet. It takes ages and ages to get to know them; and even when you do get to know them, they don't say very much."

"They're talkative enough when they're together," he said, thinking of the pubs.

"They're at home among themselves."

"One thing I've found out about you," he said. "I thought the English were shy. That's not true."

"It's because of the war. The war has done a lot of things for us."

For a while after that their footsteps on the wet road were the only sounds. The rain had turned to a light drizzle. In the prolonged twilight of that time of year in England the small hills, the small fields, the great trees, looked oddly precise. It was lonesome once they were past the airdrome. He began to be conscious of her physically again. He wondered what had happened between her and her husband.

"My husband is living with another woman," she said unexpectedly.

"Oh." He was silent again. The tone of her voice made him feel a little sorry for her.

"Tell me about your wife," she urged.

"How can a man tell anybody else about his wife?"

"Try."

"She's the sort of woman who looks at home in a field in summer, in a white dress, waiting for the children to catch up with her."

"I do envy her."

"You needn't."

"D'you suppose she'd mind your being with me?"

"I guess she would," he said. "But I think she'd understand."

"You're happily married."

"Yes."

"Marriage is funny." She was quiet for a moment, thinking. "When you get married you think it's the end of everything — everything you did before and the kind of person you were, everything. And you're glad. And for a while it's that way. But when you get used to it — " She sighed. "Well, you start becoming the person you were beforehand.

Which you don't want. And presently, if things don't work out too well, you wonder if you were ever married at all. It feels like a dream."

He was struck by the wretchedness in her voice. He put his arm around her waist. She seemed not to have noticed. They walked along quietly, saying nothing. The forest ended in a row of fields, ambushed behind hedges. "This way," she said, turning into a narrow country lane. Once under the trees the tardy night closed around them. There was a smell of wet flowers. The trees arched overhead, making a shelter, and in the gloom he could just barely see her moving beside him. But he was conscious of her body moving as they walked.

"How much farther?" he asked.

"To the next bend."

When they came to a rotted log set back off the road near the hedge he stopped. "Let's sit here for a few minutes," he said.

They found a flat space on the log where the rot had weathered down into a natural seat. He offered her a cigarette and for a little while they smoked and said nothing. The world of town had withdrawn. Somewhere out of sight in the fields beyond the hedgerow a cowbell clanked now and then. There was no other sound. A few gnats found them; then a breeze that sent a shower of drops down from the leaves overhead blew the gnats away. She shivered a little. He put his arm around her. They talked for a space and were silent again, musing, and finally she turned up her head.

"Funny, isn't it?" she said a moment later. She had a stick in her hand and was turning over the leaves underfoot, one by one. "I mean this sort of thing," she said. "Does it seem wrong?"

"No."

"It doesn't to me, either. And yet it should be. It should be all wrong. Then sometimes you do the right thing and get married properly, just as everything should be, and everything goes all wrong." She poked a hole through a sodden leaf. "I don't understand."

"Perhaps you think too much," he ventured.

"You do, too," indignantly. He grinned and was silent. The rain had stopped. The last light of the day had not yet died outside the trees, but in the forest it was wholly dark. They smoked another cigarette and after a while she put her head on his shoulder, wearily and simply. The smell of her hair was clean and rich. "Perhaps it's the war," she said dreamily. "If the war hurts you, you get to needing someone. If marriage hurts you, you get to needing someone, too."

"I guess you've hit it," he said.

"You're an odd sort of person to be a paratrooper."

"It was a case of getting out of an ivory tower by jumping."

"Have you done it?"

"Let's not talk," he said.

They had come to the deep center of the night. In the sheltered lane under the heavy trees there was no light, no sound, no movement. Even the lonely clank of the cowbell had ceased. He had stopped wondering about anything. At other times in his life there had been things like this. It was wrong and yet it was right. He bent down to her again.

"Do you think I'm cheap?" she asked at length.

"No."

"I'm not, you know. It's just that — " She waited and shook her head. "I don't know. I don't understand."

"None of us do, these days," he said.

She buried her head on his shoulder. Somewhere out of sight a crow made a funny wailing sound, like a lost dog. Off toward London, very far away, there was a faint whisper of an explosion. He turned and took her into his arms.

If you hated the war enough, he thought as he tramped back along the wet road to camp, it made you love people. If you saw enough death, the love — or the desire — was just as ready and sudden as the death was. You loved the women and the men equally — those who were involved in it. You loved those you were responsible for, even if they rejected it. You read their mail because you had to, and it broke you sometimes, the pitiful letters they wrote. You put them in the guardhouse when they got wild and did crazy things, and they looked bewildered and wretched because the whole thing from start to finish was beyond their comprehension — beyond anybody's comprehension. They were just kids, kids from home, and you didn't understand them but you loved them. And presently you had to take them across that stretch of water, and then some of them were scratched off the roll by a clerk at Personnel and afterwards you had to send their effects home. Some people got hardened to war, he reflected. He didn't.

A solitary cyclist honked at him from behind. When the whickering of the tires had died out on the road the only sound was the wind in the telephone wires. So that was how it was — you loved the people who were in it with you, men and women equally. And if you needed a woman sometimes, that was because there was a deficiency in war that got into your bones, and the deficiency was simply life itself. War was just as far removed from the ordinary things of home as violence was. He remembered a young man of his platoon who had been wounded in the stomach on the morning of D plus three and who was still conscious when he undid the boy's clothing and looked at the horror of what had happened to him. The other men had torn a door off a wrecked house to use as a stretcher; and all the boy had asked for while he waited was a cigarette. He died on the way to the aid station, and when they set him down on the ground the cigarette in his hand was still smoking.

"Got any goom, mister?" It was a group of children, up late. He shook his head, smiling at them. "Got any coppers then?" they demanded. Fishing up the coppers the girl had given him in change at the hotel, he presented one to each of the smallest.

"You're a sergeant, you are," said the smallest girl with decision.

"He is not," said one of the others indignantly. "He's a lootenant."

"You're a *loo*tenant," reclassified the smallest girl gravely. She fingered her penny. "You got a long ways to go to get home."

"How do you know?" he asked, grinning.

"We was in *your* tent," the small girl announced defiantly. "Wasn't we, Joy? In *his* tent?"

"It's time you youngsters were in bed," he said, looking at his watch.

"We've been in an air raid," announced one of them. "In London."

"What time is it?" asked the oldest girl.

"Ten minutes after twelve," he said.

"Lum!" She was startled. "Come along, you." She shepherded the youngsters before her. "Here comes a jeep!" screamed the small one. "You can get a ride!"

But the jeep was full of soldiers who passed him with a laughing shout, "Got any gum, chum?" He turned on his way alone.

The O.D. was in the enlisted men's kitchen, cooking himself a pot of coffee. To save himself the trouble of blacking-out the windows, he had left the lights off. Stack saw the flashlight. "Help yourself," said the man as he went in. "You'll find sugar and cream over there on the shelf."

Stumbling through the room, Stack helped himself. He felt suddenly cheerful. The coffee was strong and hot and it tasted better than the coffee they cooked for the daily meals. He stood by the open door and drank it gratefully.

"Where've you been?" asked the O.D.

"To town."

"Anything new?"

"Not a thing."

He lit a cigarette and inhaled it deeply. He felt more at peace than he had felt in months. He did not understand it, but it was so. He had done what he had promised himself never to do again, as long as he lived, and yet he felt at peace. The balance had been restored. What was stranger still, he had found his wife again. Already the incident of the evening was going back into that part of his mind where he kept the memory of the flesh and the blood, the quick and the dead — those things that would never be wholly understood by him and never understood at all by the people back home. In their place had come his wife. He had her back.

Outside, a dark wind stirred through the branches. But beyond the trees, where the shower of drops set the crows to a sleepy murmuring of protest among themselves, the sky had begun to clear. A few stars were out.

Death of a Bomber

by JOHN CIARDI

Machine Gunner on a B-29, Saipan

MAY 1945

We saw the smoke. The blue skull of the sky
Scarred on the black trail of the running fire.
The world came out of doors and every eye
Turned on the afternoon, while higher and higher
The sirens mounted and the watchers' breath
Drew in and waited to be first with death.

It was a choice: to parachute or ride.
It was a race: fire against altitude.
He chose to land. Which way would fire decide
Lapping the tanks, racing to be renewed
Into the thundering of exploded gas
While the charred midgets cometed to grass?

We stood and watched and each man watched his own
Possible future flaming to arrive.
By never ending inches she came down
Bringing the living back to stay alive.
Still with a sky unclosed, we saw her shed
The first burned metal, flaking down and dead.

We counted distances by fractional
Unending seconds till her wheels might touch;
While fire grew wider till it lavished all
The warping wing, and something came to clutch
The circling silence of the afternoon,
And the long smoke rode her like a black dragoon.

First feet, then inches. Still a roof above
The blurring ground, the burning engine spat
Clear from the melted wing and dove
Spilling its flame into the landing mat.
And still the wing held and the sky thinned out
Between her and the ground, and with a shout

We heard the brakes squeal, saw the midgets dive
Like dervishes toward grass and rise and run
Across the sweet returning of their lives.
We counted out the crew and one by one
We saw death leave us, and from roof and wall
The held breath broke, as sudden as a squall.

We stood in circles when they brought them in,
And offered cigarettes and held the match,
Not certain where to let their lives begin,
Or held our breaths after the silent watch.
And then it thawed, and inches past a doom
Were all the spaces of the afternoon.

We turned and waited till the fire reached home
And saw the tanks blow and the monstrous cloud —
Orange and black upon the air's blue room —
Slant up through miles of air, the emptied shroud
Still holding us. And crackling down below
We heard the roasted ammunition go.

It took an hour to burn down and be done.
We watched and memorized it flame by flame,
Our faces mirrored in the afternoon
With death gone by and fire become a game.
And when we left the last fire and last smoke
Someone began a drawn-out bedroom joke.

To the Finish

A Letter from Iwo Jima

by EDGAR L. JONES

A graduate of Dartmouth, Edgar L. Jones served as an ambulance driver with the British Eighth Army in Africa and was eventually invalided home with dysentery. He recovered in time to be sent as the Atlantic *correspondent covering the last bitter fighting in the Pacific.*

JUNE 1945

DEAR MR. WEEKS:

Our empty transport vessel with its deck-load of beaten-up landing craft is rolling heavily on the long voyage home from Iwo Jima. To provide quarters for casualties, the sick bay has been expanded until half the bunks, built in tiers of four, are now occupied by the wounded remnants of the Fourth Marines who rode the ship into battle.

The doctors aboard this particular ship are specialists in eye surgery and mental cases, so that in bed after bed one passes men who have lost their eyesight or their sanity. The same small boats which headed valiantly for the beach on D Day returned again and again on succeeding days with litter-loads of pain-crazed bodies; not really men, just bodies, which were salted down as the heavy seas broke over the bows of the lurching landing craft, jarred into sickening consciousness as the waves hurled the boats against the high walls of the transport, and finally lifted, two stretchers to a crane-load, onto the flat, steady decks of the ship which was to take them home.

Some of the more fortunate ones died during the night, and in the morning the bodies, so tightly wrapped in gray blankets that they seemed pygmy size, were lined up on deck, waiting for the same small boats to take them ashore for burial. Among the less fortunate are one man who is faceless from the end of his nose to his hairline, and another whose right side is paralyzed, whose left arm is gone, and whose one remaining eye stares out of a pulpy mass of flesh. The doctors, who with such skill and untiring attention have kept these bodies alive, come into the wardroom, remove their rubber gloves and face masks, and sit over their coffee in brooding silence.

The brig contains the only Japanese prisoners, nine of them, to be captured prior to our departure on D plus ten. There were two others, but they died aboard ship, and two of the remaining are unconscious most of the time. The same small boats which took the first waves of Marines ashore and brought the endless waves of wounded back again also transported to the safety of the ship's brig those of the enemy who still had a breath of life.

In many ways the crews of those small boats were the heroes of the battle of Iwo Jima, because, tough as the Japanese were, the heavy seas were tougher. The prevailing winds reversed themselves during the first ten days, so that instead of being on the leeward side of the island, the beachhead was exposed to the sullen fury of the Pacific Ocean. Because Iwo Jima is a volcano rising straight out of the sea, there is no shallow water. The box-shaped landing craft were tossed about like egg crates caught on the crest of a spring flood. Unprotected by breakwaters or coral reefs, the boats were swamped by six-foot breakers as soon as their bows rammed into the volcanic sand. The boats floundered, sank, and were spewn along the shore to form twisted barricades of debris.

Despite their losses, the boat crews continued to shuttle men and materials. The men rarely slept, and depended for food upon having some-one aboard a transport pass down K rations and an occasional sandwich. The crew of one small boat from this ship, manned like so many others by Coast Guard personnel, went four days and nights without relief. The men could barely walk when they finally came aboard to sleep.

The waves hit the beach at an angle, swinging the boats sidewise and overturning them before the ramps could be let down. The Marine beach parties and Seabees had to resort to bulldozers and stern lines to keep the craft at right angles to the shore long enough to roll the matériel onto the sand. While a bulldozer with a tow chain kept the ramp anchored in the sand, a small tug with a stout line on the stern strained against the current to prevent the landing craft from being swept broadside against the shoreline. As the men rushed to unload vehicles, ammunition, and food, the breakers swarmed over the sterns of the landing craft, swamping some and leaving the rest half filled with water. The crews were never dry.

As if the seas were not enough to contend with, the Japanese had the entire beach under mortar and shell fire, so that the men never knew when a shell would explode in their midst. Our transport was lying close offshore, enabling the correspondents to go onto the beach each morning and return at night to such luxuries as a hot shower, warm meals, and a dry bed. Even when we reached the beach on the morning of the seventh day, a flurry of mortar shells hit the landing craft to our left and right. We were free to scramble through the deep sand to the nearest hole, but the crew of the boat was left to manhandle the cargo with no more protection than a steel helmet.

Each of the half-dozen beaches had a beachmaster who stood on high ground with a microphone and directed unloading operations. A powerful battery of loudspeakers carried his commands to landing craft waiting to come in, to bulldozer crews, and to Marine working parties. Though shells burst around him, the beachmaster stood his ground and with a caustic voice of assurance kept the traffic moving with invectives interlarded with: "You there in boat number 457, whatja got 'board? All right, ride in on the next breaker. Hey, you cat drivers, get the hell down here with your tails in the water. Clear that truck out of there. You Marines start moving or we'll bury you under. Drop the hawser! *Drop the hawser!* Swing her starboard." And so on.

Working with the beachmasters were the floating traffic cops, the men in control boats who remained a few hundred yards offshore and regulated the successive waves of landing craft. Beyond them were the destroyers, blasting away with their five-inch guns whenever the Marines struck an enemy strong point; and still farther out, riding at anchor, were the transports, tankers, LCT's, cargo vessels, and floating drydocks. On the horizon one could see the small, fast ships in the antisubmarine patrol, and somewhere out of sight were the aircraft carriers which sent forth fighters and fighter bombers whenever enemy tanks or pillboxes were discovered. The larger units of the fleet, the battleships and cruisers, stood by, after having finished their three-day bombardment prior to the invasion, and fired their heavy guns only when a specific target required a salvo of eight- or sixteen-inch shells for permanent liquidation.

Two years ago, and possibly even one year ago, American forces would have lost the battle of Iwo Jima. The island was more heavily fortified than any previous one captured. The knee-deep volcanic sand stopped all vehicles in their tracks, and the heavy seas littered the two-mile beach with the shredded remains of boats, tanks, half-tracks, amphibious trucks, and jeeps. Yet the bulldozers were brought ashore to open lanes through the deep sand. Steel tracks were laid to enable tanks and trucks to reach more solid terrain; cranes were set up along the beach; heavy artillery was hauled ashore, along with steam rollers, road graders, and prime movers. The entire operation followed a tested pattern which neither the Japs nor the weather could stop.

American tacticians had learned much between Tarawa and Iwo Jima about island-to-island fighting, but so had the Japanese. The landing followed a pattern which in three years has become a tradition: a long period of bombing from the air, a shorter flurry of concentrated naval gunfire, a final assault at close range which utilized every type of weapon that floats or flies, and then the Marines landed. The Japanese knew what to expect, and had planned accordingly. The bombings they could not stop, so they went underground where the bombs could not reach them. The rocky cliffs of Iwo were so soft that a man with a pick and shovel could dig himself a comfortable cave in a day.

For sixty-eight consecutive days the Army bombed Iwo. The Japanese lost all their planes and most of their surface installations, but they and their guns survived. On the sixty-ninth day, at dawn, the American Navy began its bombardment; the Japanese remained in hiding during the three days that the Navy poured a record tonnage of explosives on the island. They could not stop the Fleet any more than they could the Army bombers, so they did not try.

Their defense was based on not giving away their positions or revealing their strength until an actual landing was attempted. They had only a handful of coastal batteries; and the only time I saw one of them in action, it hit a ship. The Japanese policy was not to fire unless they were sure they could not miss. They allowed endless waves of carrier planes to make their bombing runs unmolested, but they practically threw the island at observation planes which served as the eyes of the Fleet.

Their defense plan was a simple one; they dug their guns into the high ground in such a way that they had the beaches in a cross fire. Because they did not intend to fire back at the Fleet, it was unnecessary to have their guns facing the sea. The advantages of such a plan are obvious. They could mount their guns in reinforced caves which had only small openings facing inland. The Fleet could have circled the island for weeks and still not have been able to bring direct fire to bear on the entrances of the caves. The guns dug into Mount Suribachi pointed to the north, while those in the cliffs overlooking the northern end of the beach faced to the south. The Fleet was firing from the east and west.

Had the Navy known the exact location of the caves, they might have had some success in firing over Suribachi into the cliffs on the northern part of the island, and vice versa; the Japanese, however, shrewdly avoided revealing their positions. They had the beach completely covered, and the beach was all they were interested in.

I go into this at length to counteract any notion that the Fleet did not give adequate support to the landing parties. For three days prior to D Day I was on a light cruiser. No fleet ever moved in closer and unloaded so many high explosives on so small a stretch of land. For two of those three days a heavy mist obscured the island, so that even the observation planes hovering overhead could not tell with certainty where the shells were landing or how much damage they were doing. The Japanese camouflaged the entrances of their caves. Once the camouflage was torn away, succeeding salvos found their mark. In other places, however, the caves had armor-plated doors as protection, and luck was as essential as accuracy in knocking them out. The entire faces of hills tumbled down, but it was still anyone's guess whether the right caves had been sealed off in the process.

In walking around Iwo later, I saw cement blockhouses which the Navy had pulverized into pieces so small that I could have picked up and carried away what was left as a souvenir. The face of Suribachi had been pushed back fifteen feet. Remains of some Japanese showed the effect of eight- and sixteen-inch shells exploding at close range, and there were others dead without a scratch on them. The heads were grotesquely misshapen by concussion, however, just as though someone had taken a ball of putty and squeezed it. When the Navy had a definite target to aim at, it left no doubt of its firepower.

Whether Iwo will have any lasting military significance is something which men out here argue about. In the midst of mobile warfare, Iwo nearly proved that a stationary defense was invulnerable, but there were too many flukes working against the invaders to make any generalization possible. Probably the most significant thing about the battle for Iwo was its inevitableness. No American operation was less secret. Everyone in the Pacific, including the Japanese, knew that the island had to be taken, knew approximately when it would be taken, and how it would be taken. This does not imply faulty security. It simply means that Iwo was next on the list of steppingstones to Tokyo, and there was only one way to capture it.

The island could not be knocked out from the air or sea. It had to be stormed when the typhoon season had passed, and when the prevailing winds were such that the eastern beaches were on the leeward side of the island. The master stroke of American strategy was having a task force at large between Iwo and Japan. This left the Japanese on Iwo without air or naval support.

The Japanese, under the command of an artillery officer, fought a smarter battle with better weapons than in any previous engagement. With an abrupt change of tactics, they fought with the skill of the German Army. Yet 20,000 Japanese did not stop 40,000 Marines from landing in small boats from the open sea. Any evaluation of opposing tactics must, I suppose, be based on which side won, unless future historians prove that the Japanese made the United States pay more for Iwo than the island was worth.

The first time I went onto the beach was D Day plus four. I went in with a large group of Fourth Division Marines. The beach was another Anzio. The Japanese were lobbing shells into supply dumps, ammunition depots, communication centers, and every other place where they saw men or machinery concentrated. No man on the beach felt secure. The Americans held about one square mile of low ground at that point, most of which I toured. Everywhere men were struggling: to keep landing craft from submerging, to dig roads in the deep sand, to push mired trucks onto solid ground, to haul equipment to sheltered locations, and to fight nature for the chance to get on with the battle. And all the time the Japanese shells whined down and tore into sand and flesh with indiscriminate fury.

Trying as the volcanic sand of Iwo proved to be, it was also a blessing. The Japanese shells buried themselves, and the sand absorbed most of the shrapnel. Usually a man was killed instantly by having a shell land beside him in the foxhole, or he escaped without injury. This did not hold true when a shell landed in a boat, or when one dropped in the midst of a beach party. What impressed me most, however, was the absence of dead Japanese. Some had been buried, of course, and others had died underground, but it was unnatural to find so few bodies after so much fighting. There were American bodies — more than 3000 of them buried or not yet buried — but where were the Japanese? Everyone I questioned simply pointed to the hills on the left and right and swore fervently.

Iwo was unlike any war I had ever seen. It was a fight to the finish, with no man asking for quarter until he was dead. Of the nearly 20,000 American casualties, approximately two thirds were wounded, but all except a few score of the 20,000 Japanese died where they fell. There is such a thing as dying decently, but not on Iwo. I do not believe anything practical can be achieved by describing men blown apart. Veterans of two and three years of war in the Pacific were sickened. An estimated 26,000 men died in eight square miles of fighting.

I returned to Iwo on D Day plus six, seven, and eight. By that time the Marines had captured territory where Japanese had lain dead in the hot sun for more than a week. I crawled into pillboxes burned out by flame throwers, and into deep caves where the Japanese had been burning their own dead to conceal the extent of their losses. I was torturing myself to look at the results of war, because I think it is essential for civilians occasionally to hold their noses and see what is going on.

The sight on Iwo which I could not force myself to see again was the section of the beach allotted for an American cemetery. The chaplains were endeavoring to identify each body and hold a brief, individual service for each man to be buried in the black sands of the barren island. Naturally the chaplains and the burial parties were far behind in their work. The dead were brought in faster than they could be buried.

On the afternoon I walked by, there was half an acre of dead Marines stretched out so close together that they blanketed the beach for two hundred yards. The stench was overpowering. There, in mangled lots, not laid in neat rows, was part of the price paid for Iwo. All I could think of as I hurried by was the old priest who died in Dostoevski's *The Brothers Karamazov* and shocked his followers by decomposing before the burial service. The smell of one's countrymen rotting in the sun is a lasting impression.

Perhaps one becomes accustomed to it. To me it was an experience which made it impossible for me to return to Iwo. Undoubtedly I shirked my duty, but I never could have been an impartial observer after that. I cannot evaluate the battle for Iwo objectively. The Marines fought with courage and determination seemingly beyond human capabilities. They died the hard way.

As ever,
EDGAR JONES

Pacific Lament

In memory of William Hickey, a member of the crew
of the U.S.S. *Growler,* lost at sea in February 1944.

by CHARLES OLSON

MARCH 1946

Black at that depth
turn, golden boy no more
white bone to bone, turn
hear who bore you weep
hear him who made you
deep there on ocean's floor
turn
as waters stir;
turn, bone of man.

Cold as a planet is
cold, beat of blood no more
the salt sea's course
along the bone jaw white
stir, boy, stir
motion without motion
stir, and hear
love come down.

Down as you fell
sidewise, stair to green stair
without breath, down
the tumble of ocean
to find you, bone
cold and new among the ships
and men and fish askew.

You alone o golden boy no more
turn now and sleep
washed white by water
sleep in your black deep
by water out of which man came
to find his legs, arms, love, pain.
Sleep, boy, sleep
in older arms than hers,
rocked by an older father;
toss no more,
love;
sleep.

Herald Angels Miss the Boat

by AGNES NEWTON KEITH

An American married to a British civil servant, Agnes New-
ton Keith spent twenty years of her maturity in the islands of
the South Pacific. From 1934 *until* 1942 *she and her hus-*
band made their headquarters in Sandakan, North Borneo,
and from those years came her prize-winning Atlantic *book,*
Land Below the Wind. *Her great war book,* Three Came
Home, *was the painful, compassionate account of her three*
years in a Japanese prison camp.

DECEMBER 1946

If it was possible to hate one time more than another in camp, I hated
Christmas. Then was the time material and spiritual paupery hurt.
Christmas, 1944, was the worst. The Christian religion taught us that
the promise of the Saviour was peace on the earth, good will to men.
He showed us the way by love. The irony of celebrating His birth and
teaching, while we were following their antithesis, overcame me.

Then we had another rice cut; four-year-old George had a toothache
again; I heard that my husband, Harry, was ill; and Christmas was
coming.

I wanted to cut it all out; I felt that I could not pretend. I suggested to the other mothers that, as both energy and materials were nonexistent now, we should keep Christmas as the Sisters did, as a religious festival only, and agree not to give any presents to our children. If no child had anything, they could not compare, they would not be sad. But the majority of mothers felt that the children would be disappointed if they did not receive gifts, as we had made things for them the two previous Christmas seasons in camp. And if some children had gifts, then they all must have.

So the Christmas rush started. We cut off sleeves, shortened dresses, cut off collars, sacrificed anything, in the excitement of creating, to get bits of material out of which to make presents. Many of us had slept in evening dresses for a year or so, our nightgowns being worn out; now the good parts of these were sacrificed. We unraveled stockings and socks to get thread to sew with. I had one pair of kid gloves which I cut up to make dolls' shoes. Out of bits and pieces of every sort of material, we made small dolls and fancy animals, and never have I seen their like for originality. Nothing was what it seemed to be.

Their bodies were made of flesh-colored underpants or nighties or beige stockings, and stuffed with kapok, tea, or shredded rags. Hair was made of hemp, unraveled from the ends of rope, or else of wool. Faces were embroidered on, or rubbed on with pastel, or painted. I had a few pastels which the Japanese Domei news reporter had given me when he had posed me for a propaganda picture of "artist at play" the year before; these I used, combined with my own lipstick and rouge, to paint faces. I put the pastels on with a wet match stick to make them more lasting, and finished each face with a coat of my face powder.

The Christmas before, I had done fifty dolls' faces for people this way, and nearly exhausted my make-up and patience. Now I said that I would trade each doll's face for a scrap of extra food, or smokes. The barter did not discourage trade as much as I had hoped.

We cut blocks of soft rubberwood and carved small toys; we used liquid rubber tapped from the rubber tree in camp to glue things together. And anything with any claim of edibility was bartered for and hoarded until The Day. If I hadn't been exhausted anyway, if I hadn't grudged the energy and time, if my heart had been in it, it might have been fun.

The day came. The children went wild. The barrack was bedlam, the holiday bustle was there, the excitement and comparing and quarreling. Each Sister came along with a food titbit for some child, and contributions arrived all morning. Gifts came from their fathers, permitted by the Japs: scooters, swords, guns, carts, and blocks, made of soft rubberwood, put together with nails made from the twisted-off barbs of barbed wire.

The Japanese office sent word that we were to meet our husbands for half an hour, in the field outside the barbed wire. We put on our make-up and went.

Lieutenant Nekata, who had charge of our camp, was there, looking benevolent or malevolent, according to your interpretation of him. Miss Takata, the interpreter, was there, announcing and pronouncing the rules and regulations and taboos of the occasion with her own natural vocal arrangements, which surpassed any ordinary loudspeaker. The armed guards were there, sweating and prodding their way among us. Colonel Suga, the Commandant, was there, sweeping by in his motorcar, he bowing, we bowing. Sweet biscuits arrived to be distributed to the children.

We sat with our husbands quietly under the trees. They held their children lovingly to them, and yearned over them. But the children would not have much of that. They were outside the barbed wire today, in the fields with the trees and the stream, running wild, climbing trees, picking flowers, burrs, buds, any living wild thing, running free. Fathers were secondary to freedom.

Harry looked ill, always more ill, always more thin. At the end of half an hour the parting came. As always, I felt that I had forgotten the most important things, that I had not made it clear enough that the only thing that mattered now was to be with him again; that I had talked about food, and hunger, and anxiety, when all that I should have said was, I love you.

We parted. The men were mustered and marched off down the road. Some looked back, striving to hold the moment longer. Always there was the feeling that danger, destruction, death, would strike before we met again. Always each meeting seemed the last. I looked after them as far as I could see. Was it better, or was it worse, to meet like this, I wondered.

In the afternoon we had the Christmas tree. It had been sent from the men's camp with all the decorations on it, made by the civilians and the British soldiers, and arranged for by George Colley, the American from Manila. George had no children, but there was no child in camp whom he did not father, send presents to, feed sugar to, whenever he had it.

The tree was pleasant, a small Dacrydium with bending boughs. Flowers and tiny scraps of colored cloth or string or paper were used to make it bright. The smaller gifts were hung on the tree, and the heavy ones placed under. It was like every Christmas tree, the shrine of great promise. A Christmas angel in spangles, with limbs of seduction and face of enticing dissipation, teetered drunkenly on top, created by Fifi, the British Tommy, in the likeness of a prisoner's dream.

Long before the presents were distributed the boys had spotted the best ones. These were two wooden motor trucks, a train, and a large and splendid ship carved of rubberwood. These were outstanding and stupendous, they were manly and pretentious. All over the tree were hung various-colored stuffed animals and dolls: giraffes, tigers, elephants, zebras, spotted ponies, dogs, cats, bunnies, and golliwoggs — whimsical, fanciful, phony. We thought they were wonderful, considering — considering — but who wants to consider.

At the foot of the tree the boys all crowded and handled and grabbed and dribbled on and panted over the trucks, the boat, and the train.

George said happily, "That's mine, isn't it, Mum? That big big big boat?"

"I don't think so, darling. That is so very big it must be for the biggest boy. But there is *something* lovely for you on the tree; I know there is."

"I want the boat, Mum."

"But all the boys want the boat, and they can't all have it. You must wait and see."

"But I want it, Mum."

"Wait and see."

The distribution started. George waited breathless and confident, to receive his boat. I was praying; if only one child could have that boat, it might as well be George!

One by one the gifts were distributed. Still George didn't have his, and the boat was still there. And then George was handed a white pony with red spots and an orange mane and a beautiful Christmas card: *To George.*

"Say thank you, George."

"Thank you. But when do I get the boat?"

"That is for someone else, dear. You have your present now."

"I don't want this pony. I want that boat."

"I think we'd better go home now, George." Something was about to start!

Just then the boat was presented to Vicki. It was actually taken and held by Vicki, and it was removed by Vicki.

George watched it go. His world broke into bits. This was worse than the war, or being hungry, or toothache. This was the end of everything. So he acted accordingly.

Oh, George, my darling, I know just how you feel. I would have got it for you if I could. I didn't know in time. But it was too late then for me to make one, or smuggle one, or steal one.

It wasn't nice of you to throw that pony on the ground and stamp on it. It wasn't nice to scream and shout, "I hate that bad-smell pony!" It wasn't nice, but I know how you feel.

Dusk comes, quiet comes, children sleep. Christmas is over again. I say my prayers: "O God, before next Christmas comes, give me a boat to give my son."

Return Trip to the Stone Age

by JOHN P. MARQUAND

In 1945, John P. Marquand, the novelist, was in the West Pacific as a correspondent attached to the Navy. And in 1947, he accompanied Admiral Louis Denfeld, at that time Commander of the Pacific Fleet, on an inspection trip that eventually took them to Truk.

APRIL 1949

A Pacific atoll is the loneliest sight in the world, but from the air it is one of the most beautiful. From a height, one can perceive all the opalescent color gradations created by the sun, the sand, the coral, and the startlingly clear Pacific water as it touches the first bench of the outer atoll reef and merges into purples and violets and whites around the coral heads and then into the more delicate greens and blues in the shallower lagoon. The ringlike atoll itself with its dazzling white sand, its dots of coconut palm, and its untidy shrubbery of pandanus is thus always surrounded by a mass of changing color. From the air it becomes a punctuation mark in an interminable waste of ocean.

There were several of these punctuation marks between the main Marshalls and the Carolines, but they were only a preview to the Truk formation. Truk, as we approached it in the late forenoon, was completely in the clear, without a wisp of vapor to hide it, rising from the midst of a cobalt and silver sea. Unlike the atolls of the Marshalls, which seldom could have stood more than eight feet above high-tide mark, Truk seemed like a part of a submerged continent.

As our plane began letting down, the lagoon became a large round lake, protected by a circle of barrier reef as perfect almost as if it had been drawn by a geometric compass. There was room for ten navies to anchor in the Truk lagoon, and three good channels through the reef. Rising nearly in the center of this clear and beautifully sheltered body of water were five ancient volcanic peaks, now islands, covered with a deeper, richer, emerald verdure than is common with Pacific islands further north; and, like freckles, there were tinier islands scarcely to be noticed from a circling plane, both inside and outside the coral barrier. The Truk islands, which shelter about 11,000 natives, have names that sound as remote from civilization as they really are — Moen, Dublon, Fefan, Udot, Fala, Tol, Polie, and Onamue.

As the plane headed toward the island of Moen, which was Truk's administrative center, as it lost altitude and as the flaps came down, it was possible to see a concrete pier, a crane, and a few abandoned buildings. These were left by the Japanese, and except for some rusted hulls of shipping, were the most impressive signs I saw of the earlier occupation. The airstrip on which we landed was also Japanese, but the control tower and the Quonset huts and the Quonset roofs of the administration buildings a little way up the hill gave it the customary American look.

Ours was the last plane to come into Truk before the strip was closed, but there was no sign of abandonment that morning. The Naval Island Commander and his staff and the native constabulary and even some Boy Scouts were out to meet the plane. The constabulary were dressed in shorts and wore bluish helmets and were armed with what appeared to be salvaged Japanese weapons. They were well turned out and stood at stiff attention, but they looked no more military than the Marshallese. Their features were irregular but agreeable, their eyes dark and intelligent, their height only medium. None had the Grecian, athletic build of the Polynesian, and none possessed his coördination or physical beauty. It was warm on the airstrip, too warm for clothing, and yet I was just as pleased that the Trukese constabulary were not turned out in G-strings. Not one of them would have looked like a beach boy on Waikiki.

As we drove in jeeps from the airstrip to the administration building and the hospital higher up the hill, over a dusty, glary coral road, we were to encounter an experience almost unique in post-war history. Moses Arkana, the chief of the Truk atoll, emerged from his office building — another Quonset hut set up by Naval Government — to greet us. The chief wore khaki trousers, a khaki shirt, and sneakers. He was a short, stoutish man in his late fifties and he had a quiet and moderate command of English because in his youth he had shipped before the mast aboard a tramp steamer that had anchored off the atoll.

When we asked if there was anything that he and his people wanted, he made the surprising statement that his people were comfortable and doing very well and that they wanted nothing. When he was asked again if he was sure about this, he said that they would like a few fishhooks. His people had nearly forgotten the art of fishing.

The chief, whose life had been spent under Spanish, German, and Japanese domination, explained that the Trukese had been discouraged from fishing by the Japanese, possibly for reasons of security. Their canoes had been taken from them, and Japanese fishermen had been imported from Okinawa, who had carried on a commercial industry until the outbreak of the war.

It must not be assumed, however, that the Truk islanders follow the hardy seafaring tradition of other Caroline natives. Captain Walter Karig, U.S.N.R., who has recently traveled extensively in these regions, has pointed out to me that the Trukese have always been exporters rather than sailors, using boatmen from Puluwat to carry their processed goods through the Carolines — a fragrant cosmetic oil composed of coconut and frangipani blossoms, and a yellow vegetable dye called turmeric, still used on the atoll, not to mention tortoise shell and pearl shell. They had only done lagoon fishing and had purchased outriggers for the purpose from such canoe-building islands as Mokil.

Now that the natives wanted to fish again in the lagoon, they no longer had boats. They had almost forgotten the fishing grounds and besides, the Japanese, in the months of starvation that had faced them immediately before they surrendered, had dynamited portions of the lagoon and had thinned out the fish considerably. However, Chief Moses was sure they could get some if they could get fishhooks.

We then walked to the small hospital that cared for all the natives on the Truk islands. The Naval doctor in charge was a young man with great enthusiasms. His wife, who had come with him, was a trained nurse. Together with a very few enlisted personnel, they had trained a group of Trukese girls for nursing and Trukese men for orderlies. They were also conducting a general school for health and sanitation, which was designed to send intelligent natives to teach hygiene on the outer islands.

These efforts, the doctor said, were already beginning to bear fruit. Tuberculosis was common in the atoll, but their main problem was the familiar tropical yaws, a filth disease, which was now being controlled largely by the graduates of his school. Infant mortality and death from childbirth were also a Trukese problem. An effort was now being made to bring expectant mothers from the outer islands to the maternity ward, where they would have proper care, but sometimes this was difficult because the outer islanders still had taboos and prejudices and still lived without clothes and other benefits of civilization.

The prize patient in the hospital was suffering from elephantiasis, that lymphatic, glandular disease caused by the bite of the Culex mosquito. He had been picked up by a health team from an outer island and he seemed pleased to exhibit his monstrous deformity, which was going to be treated in a few days by an operation.

The doctor said that the natives' diet was like that of any other Pacific islanders; fish, plantain, breadfruit, coconut, taro root, and yam. Since the departure of the Japanese, the food situation had been bad because the starving troops had cut the hearts from thousands of coconut palms. There was also a second agricultural menace in the form of a land snail imported by the Japanese for food from the island of Madagascar. This giant African snail, apparently freed from the natural enemies which controlled it in Madagascar, was multiplying in huge numbers and devouring the new leaves of breadfruit trees and attacking the yam patches.

Nevertheless, life was not hard for the Trukese. In their genial climate, no great efforts at agriculture were necessary. Food in the main still dropped from trees, if one waited long enough beneath them.

Invasions from the outer world may have threatened the balance of life on Truk, but even from the front seat of the jeep it was possible to lapse into one of those daydreams so apt to overtake visitors to Pacific islands, and to think of the Truk atoll as it must have looked before the first European ships discovered it, bringing such gadgets as iron nails, Christianity, and disease. The lagoon, the steep mountain slopes, and their luxurious verdure must have looked very much as they still do. The influence of the West was superficial, yet curiously blighting.

There were no outrigger canoes, no villages of thatch on Moen. On a causeway running through a mangrove swamp some Trukese were making minor repairs on the road surface, and all were sedately dressed in shirts and trousers in spite of the steamy heat of midday. The doctor explained that missionaries had indoctrinated all natives on the main islands with such a sense of modesty that bodily exposure was most uncommon, and workmen seldom removed their shirts.

The missionaries, it seemed, had done an exceptional job on Truk. There was a story that in 1934, when the Japanese were staging some sort of celebration, they asked if the Moen natives would oblige with their songs and dances, only to discover that these had been forgotten long ago. It was wrong to dance, and the only songs the Trukese knew were some moldy European hymns.

On the far side of the mangrove swamp stood a Trukese settlement. The buildings of this tiny village looked worse than any in an American hobo jungle. They seemed to have been constructed principally from tin cans and packing cases, but after all there was no lumber industry in Truk, and boards and nails were at a premium. Rickety as the buildings were, the natives evidently preferred them to pandanus thatch. The main building was a Catholic church, recently constructed, framed with the wood of the breadfruit tree and roofed with gasoline tins. Two black-gowned Portuguese priests conducted us through it, but barriers of language forbade communication.

Then we climbed halfway up the mountain on a rocky, washed-out road to the Island Commander's bungalow, where we had lunch. Sitting on his veranda, looking out to sea, we all seemed like transients. The head of the Island Government told of other islands on the atoll and showed us handcrafts — baskets and mats woven from pandanus leaves, a fine cloth woven from vegetable fiber, and wooden masks and models of outrigger canoes. In spite of the closeness of the islands in the atoll to each other, many, he said, were seldom visited and in many there was still a Stone Age civilization. The truth was that Truk had no great natural resources, nothing much a predatory white man would want, except the harbor facilities of its beautiful lagoon, and it might well be that even this would not be wanted either, now that the strategical areas were shifting north.

It was too bad, an officer was saying, that this magnificent anchorage, large enough for adequate dispersal in case of air bombing, could not be towed six hundred miles north, for then it would make a better base than Guam, but there seemed to be no use for Truk in its present situation.

Since the American occupation there is only one Trukese product that has achieved any wide sort of popularity. This is the native love stick, which may still be used on the outer islands but surely not on Moen. The love stick is an intricately carved piece of wood whittled by a native suitor and shown to the girl of his choice, who becomes so familiar with its individual carvings that if the stick is pushed through the thatch of her hut on a dark night, she knows that it belongs to the man of her choice and is glad to join him outside in the starlight. The Naval personnel landing on Truk had carried the story of the love stick over most of the Pacific, so that when we were there, even the sedate natives of Moen were manufacturing them in quantities and they could be bought for twenty-five cents apiece.

As we were due in Manila in time for dinner, it was necessary to leave Truk shortly after luncheon. I can remember the languid heat, the acute sense of loneliness, and my feeling of disappointment at the sight of that jerry-built village. I can remember wondering too what could be more practical than that village and what could possibly be done by an enlightened civilization to make the life of the Trukese happier and more fruitful. Aside from some medical attention, I was not able to think of much.

I could even imagine that the kindest thing the outer world could do for Truk would be to leave it alone. If this idea has any value, perhaps happier days are coming to the atoll, because as one reads the news from China and listens to the rumblings of revolt in the East Indies, it may be that a silence will settle over the Central Pacific, that a curtain of neglect will fall again over Micronesia, and that the natives there will be driven back to their old skills for survival. The rest of the world may be dissecting atoms and cosmic rays, but in Truk they want fishhooks and to learn again how to build and handle a boat in the lagoon.

Atlantic Fiction

Reading habits change, and in no field have the changes been so drastic as in fiction. Readers have no such leisure for their books as they enjoyed a hundred years ago, and they have almost no pa tience left for those endless passages of description in which Sir Walter Scott excelled. They read today with a nervous expectancy; they have been trained to expect a dialogue which will be swift and revelatory; they have great tolerance in matters of sex and violence. They are not disturbed by the intricacies of the subconscious mind, but they are disturbed by purple passages. They read their books in snatched-at time, in intervals of seldom longer than an hour or two, and their magazines are given even shorter shrift.

At the outset the Atlantic *had a novel — usually an American novel — running serially in every issue, and not infrequently there were two. It was the practice to begin them in January, publish them in installments of fifteen or twenty pages, and stretch them out for a year if possible. The longer they lasted the more the novelist was paid, and Henry James, who had a good business head on his shoulders, made the record when he managed to extend one of his novels* (The Tragic Muse) *for seventeen consecutive months.*

William Dean Howells made the most of this feature. During his decade as the editor he serialized no less than seven of his own books, including Their Wedding Journey *and* The Lady of the Aroostook — *indeed, as he tells us, he needed every morning for the writing of his fiction, as he became more and more of a novelist and less and less of an editor. He also printed five by his friend Henry James, including* The American *and* The Portrait of a Lady.

Thomas Bailey Aldrich gave first place to F. Marion Crawford. Scudder scored with Sarah Orne Jewett, especially The Country of the Pointed Firs, *and Walter Hines Page is said to have doubled the magazine circulation — from seven thousand to fourteen thousand — with Mary Johnston's* To Have and to Hold.

But interest in the prolonged serial began to dry up in the twentieth century, and when in 1909 Ellery Sedgwick took over the magazine it is noticeable that although he picked an occasional good novel — the work of Anne Douglas Sedgwick, the first two Whiteoak books by Mazo de la Roche, and Rogue Male *by Geoffrey Household, to name a few — he was beginning to place much more reliance upon the short story. Since we could not outbid the wealthier fiction magazines, the* Atlantic *has had to play the part of discoverer. For years we have put a premium on the discovery of young American writers, and we have to our credit an extraordinary list of* Atlantic Firsts *— those who made their national debut in our columns — Ernest Hemingway, Wilbur Daniel Steele, James Norman Hall, Jessamyn West, Eudora Welty, Thomas Heggen, Louis Auchincloss, and Richard Bissell being a fair sample. The vitality of such young talent has kept the magazine fresh.*

To build this list we had to take chances, and quite often to publish the rejects of other magazines. Ray Long, for twenty years the editor of Cosmopolitan, *received from the Hearst representative in Paris a short story about a prize fighter written by an unknown. "I read the story. It left me cold. Absolutely cold. For the life of me I couldn't see why my associate had got so excited about it. I rejected the story. Next it went to* Scribner's. *Maxwell Perkins, one of the most astute editors in the land, liked the story fairly well, but thought it should be cut down. Hemingway (the author) refused to do the cutting. . . . Next it went to the* Saturday Evening Post. *And bounded back like a rubber ball. Next* Collier's. *Same result. And then one night I picked up the* Atlantic Monthly *and started to read 'Fifty Grand,' just to see what they had done with it. They hadn't done a thing. But Ellery Sedgwick, editor of the* Atlantic, *had seen in the story what Bill Lengel had seen in it, and what the others, myself heading the list, had overlooked." This was Ernest Hemingway's first story to appear in a magazine of general circulation.*

The stories we have selected are all by American authors, and several of them were Atlantic Firsts. *The lack of space has compelled us to omit the work of many who are dear to us, including our most loyal English contributors. We had John Galsworthy in his richest period, and a little, though not the best, of Rudyard Kipling. We have had E. M. Forster and H. E. Bates and Geoffrey Household, Mary Lavin and Lord Dunsany; had we not confined ourselves to a native choice we could have filled half this book with the best of their work.*

Fifty Grand

by ERNEST HEMINGWAY

The present editor was the first reader for the Atlantic *when this story of Ernest Hemingway's came to us in manuscript. It was certainly different from anything we had seen before; it hit with a wallop, but it was irresistibly good, and the verdict was unanimous.*

JULY 1927

"How are you going yourself, Jack?" I asked him.

"You seen this Walcott?" he says.

"Just in the gym."

"Well," Jack says, "I'm going to need a lot of luck with that boy."

"He can't hit you, Jack," Soldier said.

"I wish to hell he couldn't."

"He couldn't hit you with a handful of birdshot."

"Birdshot'd be all right," Jack says. "I wouldn't mind birdshot any."

"He looks easy to hit," I said.

"Sure," Jack says, "he ain't going to last long. He ain't going to last like you and me, Jerry. But right now he's got everything."

"You'll left-hand him to death."

"Maybe," Jack says. "Sure. I got a chance to."

"Handle him like you handled Kid Lewis."

"Kid Lewis," Jack said. "That kike!"

The three of us, Jack Brennan, Soldier Bartlett, and I, were in Handley's. There were a couple of broads sitting at the next table to us. They had been drinking.

"What do you mean, kike?" one of the broads says. "What do you mean, kike, you big Irish bum!"

"Sure," Jack says. "That's it."

"Kikes," this broad goes on. "They're always talking about kikes, these big Irishmen. What do you mean, kikes?"

"Come on. Let's get out of here."

"Kikes," this broad goes on. "Whoever saw you ever buy a drink? Your wife sews your pockets up every morning. These Irishmen and their kikes. Ted Lewis could lick you, too."

"Sure," Jack says. "And you give away a lot of things free, too, don't you?"

We went out. That was Jack. He could say what he wanted to when he wanted to say it.

Jack started training out at Danny Hogan's health farm over in Jersey. It was nice out there, but Jack didn't like it much. He didn't like being away from his wife and the kids, and he was sore and grouchy most of the time. He liked me and we got along fine together; and he liked Hogan, but after a while Soldier Bartlett commenced to get on his nerves. A kidder gets to be an awful thing around a camp if his stuff goes sort of sour. Soldier was always kidding Jack, just sort of kidding him all the time. It wasn't very funny and it wasn't very good and it began to get to Jack.

It was sort of stuff like this. Jack would finish up with the weights and the bag and pull on the gloves. "You want to work?" he'd say to Soldier.

"Sure. How you want me to work?" Soldier would ask. "Want me to treat you rough like Walcott? Want me to knock you down a few times?"

"That's it," Jack would say. He didn't like it any, though.

One morning we were all out on the road. We'd been out quite a way and now we were coming back. We'd go along fast for three minutes and then walk a minute, and then go fast for three minutes again. Jack wasn't ever what you would call a sprinter. He'd move around fast enough in the ring if he had to, but he wasn't any too fast on the road. All the time we were walking Soldier Bartlett was kidding him. We came up the hill to the farmhouse.

"Well," says Jack, "you better go back to town, Soldier."

"What do you mean?"

"You better go back to town and stay there."

"What's the matter?"

"I'm sick of hearing you talk."

"Yes?" says Soldier.

"Yes," says Jack.

"You'll be a damn sight sicker when Walcott gets through with you."

"Sure," says Jack, "maybe I will. But I know I'm sick of you."

So Soldier went off on the train to town that same morning. I went down with him to the train. He was good and sore.

"I was just kidding him," he said. We were waiting on the platform. "He can't pull that stuff with me, Jerry."

"He's nervous and crabby," I said. "He's a good fellow, Soldier."

"The hell he is. The hell he's ever been a good fellow."

"Well," I said, "so long, Soldier."

The train had come in. He climbed up with his bag.

"So long, Jerry," he says. "You be in town before the fight?"

"I don't think so."

"See you then."

He went in and the conductor swung up and the train went out. I rode back to the farm in the cart. Jack was on the porch writing a letter to his wife. The mail had come and I got the papers and went over on the other side of the porch and sat down to read. Hogan came out the door and came over to me.

"Did he have a jam with Soldier?"

"Not a jam," I said. "He just told him to go back to town."

"I could see it coming," Hogan said. "He never liked Soldier much."

"No. He don't like many people."

"He's a pretty cold one," Hogan said.

"Well, he's always been fine to me."

"Me too," Hogan said. "I got no kick on him. He's a cold one, though."

Hogan went in through the screen door and I sat there on the porch and read the papers. It was just starting to get fall weather and it's nice country there in Jersey up in the hills, and after I read the paper through I sat there and looked out at the country and the road down below against the woods, with a car going along it, lifting the dust up. It was fine weather and pretty nice-looking country. Hogan came to the door and I said, "Say, Hogan, haven't you got anything to shoot out here?"

"No," Hogan said. "Only sparrows."

"Seen the paper?" I said to Hogan.

"What's in it?"

"Sande booted three of them in yesterday."

"I got that on the telephone last night."

"You follow them pretty close, Hogan?" I asked.

"Oh, I keep in touch with them."

"How about Jack?" I says. "Does he still play them?"

"Him?" said Hogan. "Can you see him doing it?"

Just then Jack came around the corner with the letter in his hand. He's wearing a sweater and an old pair of pants and boxing shoes.

"Got a stamp, Hogan?" he asks.

"Give me the letter," Hogan said. "I'll mail it for you."

"Say, Jack," I said. "Didn't you used to play the ponies?"

"Sure."

"I knew you did. I knew I used to see you out at Sheepshead."

"What did you lay off them for?" Hogan asked.

"Lost money."

Jack sat down on the porch by me. He leaned back against a post. He shut his eyes in the sun.

"Want a chair?" Hogan asked.

"No," said Jack. "This is fine."

"It's a nice day," I said. "It's pretty nice out in the country."

"I'd a damn sight rather be in town with the wife."

"Well, you only got another week."

"Yes," Jack says. "That's so."

We sat there on the porch. Hogan was inside at the office.

"What do you think about the shape I'm in?" Jack asked me.

"Well, you can't tell," I said. "You got a week to get around into form."

"Don't stall me."

"Well," I said, "you're not right."

"I'm not sleeping," Jack said.

"You'll be all right in a couple of days."

"No," says Jack, "I got the insomnia."

"What's on your mind?"

"I miss the wife."

"Have her come out."

"No. I'm too old for that."

"We'll take a long walk before you turn in, and get you good and tired."

"Tired!" Jack says. "I'm tired all the time."

He was that way all week. He wouldn't sleep at night and he'd get up in the morning feeling that way — you know, when you can't shut your hands.

"He's stale as poorhouse cake," Hogan said. "He's nothing."

"I never seen Walcott," I said.

"He'll kill him," said Hogan. "He'll tear him in two."

"Well," I said, "everybody's got to get it sometime."

"Not like this, though," Hogan said. "They'll think he never trained. It gives the farm a black eye."

"You hear what the reporters said about him?"

"Didn't I! They said he was awful. They said they oughtn't to let him fight."

"Well," I said, "they're always wrong, ain't they?"

"Yes," said Hogan. "But this time they're right."

"What the hell do they know about whether a man's right or not?"

"Well," said Hogan, "they're not such fools."

"All they did was pick Willard at Toledo. This Lardner, he's so wise now, ask him about when he picked Willard at Toledo."

"Aw, he wasn't out," Hogan said. "He only writes the big fights."

"I don't care who they are," I said. "What the hell do they know? They can write, maybe, but what the hell do they know?"

"You don't think Jack's in any shape, do you?" Hogan asked.

"No. He's through. All he needs is to have Corbett pick him to win for it to be all over."

"Well, Corbett'll pick him," Hogan says.

"Sure. He'll pick him."

That night Jack didn't sleep any either. The next morning was the last day before the fight. After breakfast we were out on the porch again.

"What do you think about, Jack, when you can't sleep?" I said.

"Oh, I worry," Jack says. "I worry about property I got up in the Bronx. I worry about property I got in Florida. I worry about the kids. I worry about the wife. Sometimes I think about fights. I think about that kike Ted Lewis and I get sore. I got some stocks and I worry about them. What the hell don't I think about?"

"Well," I said, "tomorrow night it'll be all over."

"Sure," said Jack. "That always helps a lot, don't it? That just fixes everything all up, I suppose. Sure."

He was sore all day. We didn't do any work. Jack just moved around a little to loosen up. He shadowboxed a few rounds. He didn't even look good doing that. He skipped the rope a little while. He couldn't sweat.

"He'd be better not to do any work at all," Hogan said. We were standing watching him skip rope. "Don't he ever sweat at all any more?"

"He can't sweat."

"Do you suppose he's got the con? He never had any trouble making weight, did he?"

"No, he hasn't got any con. He just hasn't got anything inside any more."

"He ought to sweat," said Hogan.

Jack came over skipping the rope. He was skipping up and down in front of us, forward and back, crossing his arms every third time.

"Well," he says, "what are you buzzards talking about?"

"I don't think you ought to work any more," Hogan says. "You'll be stale."

"Wouldn't that be awful?" Jack says and skips away down the floor, slapping the rope hard.

That afternoon John Collins showed up out at the farm. Jack was up in his room. John came out in a car from town. He had a couple of friends with him. The car stopped and they all got out.

"Where's Jack?" John asked me.

"Up in his room, lying down."

"How is he?"

I looked at the two fellows that were with John.

"They're friends of his," John said.

"He's pretty bad," I said.

"What's the matter with him?"

"He don't sleep."

"Hell," said John. "That Irishman could never sleep."

"He isn't right," I said.

"Hell," John said. "He's never right. I've had him for ten years and he's never been right yet."

The fellows with him laughed.

"I want you to shake hands with Mr. Morgan and Mr. Steinfelt," John said. "This is Mr. Doyle. He's been training Jack."

"Glad to meet you," I said.

"Let's go up and see the boy," the fellow called Morgan said.

"Let's have a look at him," Steinfelt said.

We all went upstairs.

"Where's Hogan?" John asked.

"He's out in the barn with a couple of his customers," I said.

"He got many people out here now?"

"Just two."

"Pretty quiet, ain't it?" Morgan said.

"Yes," I said. "It's pretty quiet."

We were outside Jack's room. John knocked on the door. There wasn't any answer.

"Maybe he's asleep," I said.

"What the hell's he sleeping in the daytime for?"

John turned the handle and we all went in.

Jack was lying asleep on the bed. He was face down and his face was in the pillow. Both his arms were around the pillow.

"Hey, Jack!" John said to him.

Jack's head moved a little on the pillow. "Jack!" John says, leaning over him. Jack just dug a little deeper in the pillow. John touched him on the shoulder. Jack sat up and looked at us. He hadn't shaved and he was wearing an old sweater.

"Hell! Why can't you let me sleep?" he says to John.

"Don't be sore," John says. "I didn't mean to wake you up."

"Oh no," Jack says. "Of course not."

"You know Morgan and Steinfelt," John said.

"Glad to see you," Jack says.

"How do you feel, Jack?" Morgan asks him.

"Fine," Jack says. "How the hell would I feel?"

"You look fine," Steinfelt says.

"Yes, don't I?" says Jack. "Say," he says to John. "You're my manager. You get a big enough cut. Why the hell didn't you come out here when the reporters was out? You want Jerry and me to talk to them?"

"I had Lew fighting in Philadelphia."

"What the hell's that to me?" Jack says. "You're my manager. You get a big enough cut, don't you? You aren't making me any money in Philadelphia, are you? Why the hell aren't you out here when I ought to have you?"

"Hogan was here."

"Hogan," Jack says. "Hogan's as dumb as I am."

"Soldier Bahtlett was out here wukking with you for a while, wasn't he?" Steinfelt says, to change the subject.

"Yes, he was out here," Jack says. "He was out here, all right."

"Say, Jerry," John said to me. "Would you go and find Hogan and tell him we want to see him in about half an hour?"

"Sure," I said.

"Why the hell can't he stick around?" Jack says. "Stick around, Jerry."

Morgan and Steinfelt looked at each other.

"Quiet down, Jack," John said to him.

"I better go find Hogan," I said.

"All right, if you want to go," Jack says. "None of these guys are going to send you away, though."

Hogan was out in the gym in the barn. He had a couple of his health-farm patients with the gloves on. They neither one wanted to hit the other for fear the other would come back and hit him.

"That'll do," Hogan said when he saw me come in. "You can stop the slaughter. You gentlemen take a shower and Bruce will rub you down." They climbed through the ropes and Hogan came over to me.

"John Collins is out with a couple of friends to see Jack," I said.

"I saw them come up in the car."

"Who are the two fellows with John?"

"They're what you call wise boys," Hogan said. "Don't you know them two?"

"No," I said.

"That's Happy Steinfelt and Lew Morgan. They got a poolroom."

"I been away a long time," I said.

"Sure," said Hogan. "That Happy Steinfelt's a big operator."

"I've heard his name," I said.

"He's a pretty smooth boy," Hogan said. "They're a couple of sharp-shooters."

"Well," I said, "they want to see us in half an hour."

"You mean they don't want to see us until a half an hour?"

"That's it."

"Come on in the office," Hogan said. "To hell with those sharp-shooters."

After about thirty minutes or so Hogan and I went upstairs. We knocked on Jack's door. They were talking inside the room.

"Wait a minute," somebody said.

"To hell with that stuff," Hogan said. "When you want to see me I'm down in the office."

We heard the door unlock. Steinfelt opened it.

"Come on in, Hogan," he says. "We're all going to have a drink."

"Well," says Hogan, "that's something."

We went in. Jack was sitting on the bed. John and Morgan were sitting on a couple of chairs. Steinfelt was standing up.

"You're a pretty mysterious lot of boys," Hogan said.

"Hello, Danny," John says.

"Hello, Danny," Morgan says and shakes hands.

Jack doesn't say anything. He just sits there on the bed. He ain't with the others. He's all by himself. He was wearing an old blue jersey and an old pair of pants and had on boxing shoes. He needed a shave. Steinfelt and Morgan were dressers. John was quite a dresser, too. Jack sat there looking Irish and tough.

Steinfelt brought out a bottle and Hogan brought in some glasses and everybody had a drink. Jack and I took one and the rest of them went on and had two or three each.

"Better save some for your ride back," Hogan said.

"Don't you worry. We got plenty," Morgan said.

Jack hadn't drunk anything since the one drink. He was standing up and looking at them. Morgan was sitting on the bed where Jack had sat.

"Have a drink, Jack," John said and handed him the glass and the bottle.

"No," Jack said, "I never like to go to these wakes."

They all laughed. Jack didn't laugh.

They were all feeling pretty good when they left. Jack stood on the porch when they got into the car. They waved to him.

"So long," Jack said.

We had supper. Jack didn't say anything all during the meal except "Will you pass me this?" or "Will you pass me that?" The two health-farm patients ate at the same table with us. They were pretty nice fellas. After we finished eating we went out on the porch. It was dark early.

"Like to take a walk, Jerry?" Jack asked.

"Sure," I said.

We put on our coats and started out. It was quite a way down to the main road, and then we walked along the main road about a mile and a half. Cars kept going by and we would pull out to the side until they were past. Jack didn't say anything. After we had stepped out into the bushes to let a big car go by, Jack said, "To hell with this walking. Come on back to Hogan's."

We went along a side road that cut up over the hill and cut across the fields back to Hogan's. We could see the lights of the house up on the hill. We came around to the front of the house and there, standing in the doorway, was Hogan.

"Have a good walk?" Hogan asked.

"Oh, fine," Jack said. "Listen, Hogan. Have you got any liquor?"

"Sure," says Hogan. "What's the idea?"

"Send it up to the room," Jack says. "I'm going to sleep tonight."

"You're the doctor," Hogan says.

"Come on up to the room, Jerry," Jack says.

Upstairs Jack sat on the bed with his head in his hands.

"Ain't it a life?" Jack says.

Hogan brought in a quart of liquor and two glasses.

"Want some ginger ale?"

"What do you think I want to do — get sick?"

"I just asked you," said Hogan.

"Have a drink?" said Jack.

"No, thanks," said Hogan. He went out.

"How about you, Jerry?"

"I'll have one with you," I said.

Jack poured out a couple of drinks. "Now," he said, "I want to take it slow and easy."

"Put some water in it," I said.

"Yes," Jack said. "I guess that's better."

We had a couple of drinks without saying anything. Jack started to pour me another.

"No," I said, "that's all I want."

"All right," Jack said. He poured himself out another big shot and put water in it. He was lighting up a little.

"That was a fine bunch out here this afternoon," he said. "They don't take any chances, those two."

Then a little later, "Well," he says, "they're right. What the hell's the good in taking chances?

"Don't you want another, Jerry?" he said. "Come on, drink along with me."

"I don't need it, Jack," I said. "I feel all right."

"Just have one more," Jack said. It was softening him up.

"All right," I said.

Jack poured one for me and another big one for himself.

"You know," he said, "I like liquor pretty well. If I hadn't been boxing I would have drunk quite a lot."

"Sure," I said.

"You know," he said, "I missed a lot, boxing."

"You made plenty of money."

"Sure, that's what I'm after. You know I miss a lot, Jerry."

"How do you mean?"

"Well," he says, "like about the wife. And being away from home so much. It don't do my girls any good. 'Who's your old man?' some of those society kids'll say to them. 'My old man's Jack Brennan.' That don't do them any good."

"Hell," I said. "All that makes a difference is if they got dough."

"Well," says Jack, "I got the dough for them all right."

He poured out another drink. The bottle was about empty.

"Put some water in it," I said. Jack poured in some water.

"You know," he says, "you ain't got any idea how I miss the wife."

"Sure."

"You ain't got any idea. You can't have an idea what it's like."

"It ought to be better out in the country than in town."

"With me now," Jack said, "it don't make any difference where I am. You can't have an idea what it's like."

"Have another drink."

"Am I getting soused? Do I talk funny?"

"You're coming on all right."

"You can't have an idea what it's like. They ain't anybody can have an idea what it's like."

"Except the wife," I said.

"She knows," Jack said. "She knows, all right. You bet she knows."

"Put some water in that," I said.

"Jerry," says Jack, "you can't have an idea what it gets to be like."

He was good and drunk. He was looking at me steady. His eyes were sort of too steady.

"You'll sleep, all right," I said.

"Listen, Jerry," Jack says. "You want to make some money? Get some dough down on Walcott."

"Yes?"

"Listen, Jerry." Jack put down the glass. "I'm not drunk now, see? You know what I'm betting on him? Fifty grand."

"That's a lot of dough."

"Fifty grand," Jack says, "at two to one. I'll get twenty-five thousand bucks. Get some money on him, Jerry."

"It sounds good," I said.

"How can I beat him?" Jack says. "It ain't crooked. How can I beat him? Why not make money on it?"

"Put some water in that," I said.

"I'm through after this fight," Jack says. "I'm through with it. I got to take a beating. Why shouldn't I make money on it?"

"Sure."

"I ain't slept for a week," Jack says. "All night I lay awake and worry my can off. I can't sleep, Jerry. You ain't got an idea what it's like when you can't sleep."

"Sure."

"I can't sleep. That's all. I just can't sleep. What's the use of taking care of yourself all these years when you can't sleep?"

"It's bad."

"You ain't got an idea what it's like, Jerry, when you can't sleep."

"Put some water in that," I said.

Well, about eleven o'clock Jack passes out and I put him to bed. Finally he's so he can't keep from sleeping. I helped him get his clothes off and got him into bed.

"You'll sleep, all right, Jack," I said.

"Sure," Jack says, "I'll sleep now."

"Good night, Jack," I said.

"Good night, Jerry," Jack says. "You're the only friend I got."

"Oh, hell," I said.

"You're the only friend I got," Jack says. "The only friend I got."

"Go to sleep," I said.

"I'll sleep," Jack says.

Downstairs Hogan was sitting at the desk in the office reading the papers. He looked up. "Well, you get your boy friend to sleep?" he asks.

"He's off."

"It's better for him than not sleeping," Hogan said.

"Sure."

"You'd have a hell of a time explaining that to these sport writers, though," Hogan said.

"Well, I'm going to bed myself," I said.

"Good night," said Hogan.

In the morning I came downstairs about eight o'clock and got some breakfast. Hogan had his two customers out in the barn doing exercises. I went out and watched them.

"One! Two! Three! Four!" Hogan was counting for them. "Hello, Jerry," he said. "Is Jack up yet?"

"No. He's still sleeping."

I went back to my room and packed up to go in to town. About nine thirty I heard Jack getting up in the next room. When I heard him go downstairs I went down after him. Jack was sitting at the breakfast table. Hogan had come in and was standing beside the table.

"How do you feel, Jack?" I asked him.

"Not so bad."

"Sleep well?" Hogan asked.

"I slept, all right," Jack said. "I got a thick tongue, but I ain't got a head."

"Good," said Hogan. "That was good liquor."

"Put it on the bill," Jack says.

"What time you want to go in to town?" Hogan asked.

"Before lunch," Jack says. "The eleven o'clock train."

Hogan went out.

"Sit down, Jerry," Jack said.

I sat down at the table. Jack was eating a grapefruit. When he'd find a seed he'd spit it out in the spoon and dump it on the plate.

"I guess I was pretty stewed last night," he started.

"You drank some liquor."

"I guess I said a lot of fool things."

"You weren't bad."

"Where's Hogan?" he asked. He was through with the grapefruit.

"He's out in front in the office."

"What did I say about betting on the fight?" Jack asked. He was holding the spoon and sort of poking at the grapefruit with it.

The girl came in with some ham and eggs and took away the grapefruit.

"Bring me another glass of milk," Jack said to her. She went out.

"You said you had fifty grand on Walcott," I said.

"That's right," Jack said.

"That's a lot of money."

"I don't feel too good about it," Jack said.

"Something might happen."

"No," Jack said. "He wants the title bad. They'll be shooting with him, all right."

"You can't ever tell."

"No. He wants the title. It's worth a lot of money to him."

"Fifty grand is a lot of money," I said.

"It's business," said Jack. "I can't win. You know I can't win anyway."

"As long as you're in there you got a chance."

"No," Jack says. "I'm all through. It's just business."

"How do you feel?"

"Pretty good," Jack said. "The sleep was what I needed."

"You might do good."

"I'll give them a good show," Jack said.

After breakfast Jack called up his wife on the long distance. He was inside the booth telephoning.

"That's the first time he's called her up since he's out here," Hogan said.

"He writes her every day."

"Sure," Hogan says. "A letter only costs two cents."

Hogan said good-by to us, and Bruce, the nigger rubber, drove us down to the train in the cart. "Good-by, Mr. Brennan," Bruce said at the train. "I sure hope you knock his can off."

"So long," Jack said. He gave Bruce two dollars. Bruce had worked on him a lot. He looked kind of disappointed. Jack saw me looking at Bruce holding the two dollars.

"It's all in the bill," he said. "Hogan charged me for the rubbing."

On the train going into town Jack didn't talk. He sat in the corner of the seat with his ticket in his hatband and looked out of the window. Once he turned and spoke to me. "I told the wife I'd take a room at the Shelby tonight," he said. "It's just around the corner from the Garden. I can go up to the house tomorrow morning."

"That's a good idea," I said. "Your wife ever see you fight, Jack?"

"No," Jack says. "She never seen me fight."

I thought, he must be figuring on taking an awful beating if he doesn't want to go home afterward. In town we took a taxi up to the Shelby. A boy came out and took our bags and we went in to the desk.

"How much are the rooms?" Jack asked.

"We only have double rooms," the clerk says. "I can give you a nice double room for ten dollars."

"That's too steep."

"I can give you a double room for seven dollars."

"With a bath?"

"Certainly."

"You might as well bunk with me, Jerry," Jack says.

"Oh," I said, "I'll sleep down at my brother-in-law's."

"I don't mean for you to pay it," Jack says. "I just want to get my money's worth."

"Will you register, please?" the clerk says.

He looked at the names. "Number 238, Mr. Brennan."

We went up in the elevator. It was a nice big room with two beds and a door opening into a bathroom. "This is pretty good," Jack says.

The boy who brought us up pulled up the curtains and brought in our bags. Jack didn't make any move, so I gave the boy a quarter. We washed up and Jack said we better go out and get something to eat.

We ate a lunch at Jimmy Handley's place. Quite a lot of the boys were there. When we were about half through eating, John came in and sat down with us. Jack didn't talk much.

"How are you on the weight, Jack?" John asked him. Jack was putting away a pretty good lunch.

"I could make it with my clothes on," Jack said. He never had to worry about taking off weight. He was a natural welterweight and he'd never gotten fat. He'd lost weight out at Hogan's.

"Well, that's one thing you never had to worry about," John said.

"That's one thing," Jack says.

We went around to the Garden to weigh in after lunch. The match was made at a hundred forty-seven pounds at three o'clock. Jack stepped on the scales with a towel around him. The bar didn't move. Walcott had just weighed and was standing with a lot of people around him.

"Let's see what you weigh, Jack," Freedman, Walcott's manager, said.

"All right, weigh *him* then," Jack jerked his head toward Walcott.

"Drop the towel," Freedman said.

"What do you make it?" Jack asked the fellows who were weighing.

"Hundred and forty-three pounds," the fat man who was weighing said.

"You're down fine, Jack," Freedman says.

"Weigh *him*," Jack says.

Walcott came over. He was a blond with wide shoulders and arms like a heavyweight. He didn't have much legs. Jack stood about half a head taller than he did.

"Hello, Jack," he said. His face was plenty marked up.

"Hello," said Jack. "How you feel?"

"Good," Walcott says. He dropped the towel from around his waist and stood on the scales. He had the widest shoulders and back you ever saw.

"One hundred and forty-six pounds and twelve ounces."

Walcott stepped off and grinned at Jack.

"Well," John says to him, "Jack's spotting you about four pounds."

"More than that when I come in, Kid," Walcott says. "I'm going to go and eat now."

We went back and Jack got dressed. "He's a pretty tough-looking boy," Jack says to me.

"He looks as though he'd been hit plenty of times."

"Oh yes," Jack says. "He ain't hard to hit."

"Where are you going?" John asked when Jack was dressed.

"Back to the hotel," Jack says. "You looked after everything?"

"Yes," John says. "It's all looked after."

"I'm going to lie down a while," Jack says.

"I'll come around for you about a quarter to seven and we'll go and eat."

"All right."

Up at the hotel Jack took off his shoes and his coat and lay down for a while. I wrote a letter. I looked over a couple of times and Jack wasn't sleeping. He was lying perfectly still, but every once in a while his eyes would open. Finally he sits up. "Want to play some cribbage, Jerry?"

"Sure," I said.

He went over to his suitcase and got out the cards and the cribbage board. We played cribbage and he won three dollars off me. John knocked at the door and came in.

"Want to play some cribbage, John?" Jack asked him.

John put his kelly down on the table. It was all wet. His coat was wet, too.

"Is it raining?" Jack asks.

"It's pouring," John says. "The taxi I had got tied up in the traffic and I got out and walked."

"Come on, play some cribbage," Jack says.

"You ought to go and eat."

"No," says Jack. "I don't want to eat yet."

So they played cribbage for about half an hour and Jack won a dollar and a half off him.

"Well, I suppose we got to go eat," Jack says. He went to the window and looked out.

"Is it still raining?"

"Yes."

"Let's eat in the hotel," John says.

"All right," Jack says. "I'll play you once more to see who pays for the meal."

After a little while Jack gets up and says, "You buy the meal, John," and we went downstairs and ate in the big dining room.

After we ate we went upstairs and Jack played cribbage with John again and won two dollars and a half off him. Jack was feeling pretty good. John had a bag with him with all his stuff in it. Jack took off his shirt and collar and put on a jersey and a sweater, so he wouldn't catch cold when he came out, and put his ring clothes and his bathrobe in a bag.

"You all ready?" John asks him. "I'll call up and have them get a taxi."

Pretty soon the telephone rang and they said the taxi was waiting.

We rode down in the elevator and went out through the lobby, and got in the taxi and rode around to the Garden. It was raining hard, but there was a lot of people outside on the streets. The Garden was sold out. As we came in on our way to the dressing room I saw how full it was. It looked like half a mile down to the ring. It was all dark. Just the lights over the ring. "It's a good thing, with this rain, they didn't try and pull this fight in the ball park," John said.

"They got a good crowd," Jack says.

"This is a fight that would draw a lot more than the Garden could hold."

"You can't tell about the weather," Jack says.

John came to the door of the dressing room and poked his head in. Jack was sitting there with his bathrobe on; he had his arms folded and was looking at the floor. John had a couple of handlers with him. They looked over his shoulder. Jack looked up. "Is he in?" he asked.

"He's just gone down," John said.

We started down. Walcott was just getting into the ring. The crowd gave him a big hand. He climbed through between the ropes and put his two fists together and smiled and shook them at the crowd, first at one side of the ring, then at the other, and then sat down. Jack got a good hand coming down through the crowd. Jack is Irish, and the Irish always get a pretty good hand. An Irishman don't draw in New York like a Jew or an Eyetalian, but they always get a good hand. Jack climbed up and bent down to go through the ropes, and Walcott came over from his corner and pushed the rope down for Jack to go through. The crowd thought that was wonderful. Walcott put his hand on Jack's shoulder and they stood there just for a second.

"So you're going to be one of these popular champions," Jack says to him. "Take your goddam hand off my shoulder."

"Be yourself," Walcott says.

This is all great for the crowd. How gentlemanly the boys are before the fight! How they wish each other luck!

Solly Freedman comes over to our corner while Jack is bandaging his hands and John is over in Walcott's corner. Jack put his thumb through the slit in the bandage and then wrapped his hand nice and smooth. I taped it around the wrist and twice across the knuckles.

"Hey," Freedman says. "Where do you get all that tape?"

"Feel of it," Jack said. "It's soft, ain't it? Don't be a hick."

Freedman stands there all the time while Jack bandages the other hand, and one of the boys that's going to handle him brings the gloves and I pull them on and work them around.

"Say, Freedman," Jack asks. "What nationality is this Walcott?"

"I don't know," Solly says. "He's some sort of a Dane."

"He's a Bohemian," the lad who brought the gloves said.

The referee called them out to the center of the ring and Jack walks

out. Walcott comes out smiling. They met and the referee put his arm
on each of their shoulders.

"Hello, Popularity," Jack says to Walcott.

"Be yourself."

"What do you call yourself Walcott for," Jack says. "Didn't you
know he was a nigger?"

"Listen — " says the referee, and he gives them the same old line.
Once Walcott interrupts him. He grabs Jack's arm and says, "Can I
hit when he's got me like this?"

"Keep your hands off me," Jack says. "There ain't no moving picture
of this."

They went back to their corners. I lifted the bathrobe off Jack and
he leaned on the ropes and flexed his knees a couple of times and scuffed
his shoes in the rosin. The gong rang and Jack turned quick and went
out. Walcott came toward him and they touched gloves, and as soon as
Walcott dropped his hands Jack jumped his left into his face twice.
There wasn't anybody ever boxed better than Jack. Walcott was after
him, going forward all the time with his chin on his chest. He's a hooker
and he carries his hands pretty low. All he knows is to get in there and
sock. But every time he gets in there close, Jack has the left hand in his
face. It's just as though it's automatic. Jack just raises the left hand up
and it's in Walcott's face. Three or four times Jack brings the right
over, but Walcott gets it on the shoulder or high up on the head. He's
just like all these hookers. The only thing he's afraid of is another one
of the same kind. He's covered everywhere you can hurt him. He don't
care about a left hand in his face.

After about four rounds Jack has him bleeding bad and his face all
cut up, but every time Walcott's got in close he's socked so hard he's
got two big red patches on both sides just below Jack's ribs. Every time
he gets in close, Jack ties him up, then gets one hand loose and upper-
cuts him, but when Walcott gets his hands loose he socks Jack in the
body so they can hear it outside in the street. He's a socker.

It goes along like that for three rounds more. They don't talk any.
They're working all the time. We worked over Jack plenty, too, in between the rounds. He don't look good at all, but he never does much
work in the ring. He don't move around much, and that left hand is just
automatic. It's just like it was connected with Walcott's face and Jack
just had to wish it in every time. Jack is always calm in close, and he
doesn't waste any juice. He knows everything about working in close,
too, and he's getting away with a lot of stuff. While they were in our

corner I watched him tie Walcott up, get his right hand loose, turn it, and come up with an uppercut that got Walcott's nose with the heel of the glove. Walcott was bleeding bad and leaned his nose on Jack's shoulder so as to give Jack some of it, too, and Jack sort of lifted his shoulder sharp and caught him against the nose, and then brought down the right hand and uppercut him again.

Walcott was sore as hell. By the time they'd gone five rounds he hated Jack's guts. Jack wasn't sore; that is, he wasn't any sorer than he always was. He certainly did use to make the fellows he fought hate boxing. That was why he hated Kid Lewis so. He never got the Kid's goat. Kid Lewis always had about three new dirty things Jack couldn't do. Jack was as safe as a church all the time he was in there as long as he was strong. He certainly was treating Walcott rough. The funny thing was, it looked as though Jack was an open classic boxer. That was because he had all that stuff, too.

After the seventh round Jack says, "My left's getting heavy."

From then he started to take a beating. It didn't show at first. But instead of him running the fight it was Walcott was running it. Instead of being safe all the time, now he was in trouble. He couldn't keep Walcott out with the left hand now. It looked as though it was the same as ever, only now, instead of Walcott's punches just missing him, they were just hitting him. He took an awful beating in the body.

"What's the round?" Jack asked.

"The eleventh."

"I can't stay," Jack says. "My legs are going bad."

Walcott had been just hitting him for a long time. It was like a baseball catcher pulls the ball and takes some of the shock off. From now on Walcott commenced to land solid. He certainly was a socking machine. Jack was just trying to block everything now. It didn't show what an awful beating he was taking. In between the rounds I worked on his legs. The muscles would flutter under my hands all the time I was rubbing them. He was sick as hell.

"How's it go?" he asked John, turning around, his face all swollen.

"It's his fight."

"I think I can last," Jack says. "I don't want this bohunk to stop me."

It was going just the way he thought it would. He knew he couldn't beat Walcott. He wasn't strong any more. He was all right, though. His money was all right and now he wanted to finish it off right to please himself. He didn't want to be knocked out.

The gong rang and we pushed him out. He went out slow. Walcott came right out after him. Jack put the left in his face and Walcott took it, came in under it, and started working on Jack's body. Jack tried to tie him up and it was just like trying to hold on to a buzz saw. Jack broke away from it and missed with the right. Walcott clipped him with a left hook and Jack went down. He went down on his hands and knees and looked at us. The referee started counting. Jack was watching us and shaking his head. At eight John motioned to him. You couldn't hear on account of the crowd. Jack got up. The referee had been holding Walcott back with one arm while he counted.

When Jack was on his feet Walcott started toward him.

"Watch yourself, Jimmy," I heard Solly Freedman yell to him.

Walcott came up to Jack looking at him. Jack stuck the left hand at him. Walcott just shook his head. He backed Jack up against the ropes, measured him, and then hooked the left very light to the side of Jack's head and socked the right into the body as hard as he could sock just as low as he could get it. He must have hit him five inches below the belt. I thought the eyes would come out of Jack's head. They stuck way out. His mouth come open.

The referee grabbed Walcott. Jack stepped forward. If he went down, there went fifty thousand bucks. He walked as though all his insides were going to fall out.

"It wasn't low," he said. "It was a accident."

The crowd were yelling so you couldn't hear anything.

"I'm all right," Jack says. They were right in front of us.

The referee looks at John and then he shakes his head.

"Come on, you dirty Polack," Jack says to Walcott.

John was hanging on to the ropes. He had the towel ready to chuck in. Jack was standing just a little way out from the ropes. He took a step forward. I saw the sweat come out on his face like somebody had squeezed it, and a big drop went down his nose.

"Come on and fight," Jack says to Walcott.

The referee looked at John and waved Walcott on.

"Go in there, you slob," he says.

Walcott went in. He didn't know what to do either. He never thought Jack could have stood it. Jack put the left in his face. There was all this yelling going on. They were right in front of us. Walcott hit him twice. Jack's face was the worst thing I ever saw — the look on it. He was holding himself and all his body together, and it all showed on his face. All the time he was thinking and holding his body in where it was busted.

Then he started to sock. His face looked awful all the time. He started to sock with his hands low down by his side, swinging at Walcott. Walcott covered up and Jack was swinging wild at Walcott's head. Then he swung the left and it hit Walcott in the groin and the right hit Walcott right bang where he'd hit Jack. Way low. Walcott went down and grabbed himself there and rolled and twisted around.

The referee grabbed Jack and pushed him toward his corner. John jumps into the ring. There was all this yelling going on. The referee was talking with the judges and then the announcer got into the ring with the megaphone and says, "Walcott on a foul."

The referee is talking to John and he says, "What could I do? Jack wouldn't take the foul. Then when he's groggy he fouls him."

"He'd lost it anyway," John says.

Jack's sitting on the chair. I've got his gloves off and he's holding himself in down there with both hands.

"Go over and say you're sorry," John says into his ear. "It'll look good."

Jack stands up and the sweat comes out all over his face. I put the bathrobe around him and he holds himself in with one hand under the bathrobe and goes across the ring. They've picked Walcott up and they're working on him. There's a lot of people in Walcott's corner. Nobody speaks to Jack. He leans over Walcott.

"I'm sorry," Jack says. "I didn't mean to foul you."

Walcott doesn't say anything. He looks too damned sick.

"Well, you're the champion now," Jack says to him. "I hope you get a hell of a lot of fun out of it."

"Leave the kid alone," Solly Freedman says.

"Hello, Solly," Jack says. "I'm sorry I fouled your boy."

Freedman just looks at him.

Jack went over to his corner walking that funny jerky way, and we got him down through the ropes and through the reporters' tables and out down the aisle. A lot of people want to slap Jack on the back. He goes out through all that mob in his bathrobe to the dressing room. It's a popular win for Walcott. That's the way the money was bet in the Garden.

Once we got inside the dressing room Jack lay down and shut his eyes.

"We want to get to the hotel and get a doctor," John says.

"I'm all busted inside," Jack says.

"I'm sorry as hell, Jack," John says.

"It's all right," Jack says.

He lies there with his eyes shut.

"They certainly tried a nice double cross," John said.

"Your friends Morgan and Steinfelt," Jack said. "You got nice friends."

He lies there; his eyes are open now. His face has still got that awful drawn look.

"It's funny how fast you can think when it means that much money," Jack says.

"You're some boy, Jack," John says.

"No," Jack says. "It was nothing."

A Worn Path

by EUDORA WELTY

Eudora Welty is a native of Jackson, Mississippi. "A Worn Path" was the first of a remarkable trilogy which Miss Welty contributed to the Atlantic *in 1941, the others being "Powerhouse" and "Why I Live at the P.O."*

FEBRUARY 1941

It was December — a bright frozen day in the early morning. Far out in the country there was an old Negro woman with her head tied in a red rag, coming along a path through the pine woods. Her name was Phoenix Jackson. She was very old, and small, and she walked slowly in the dark pine shadows, moving a little from side to side in her steps, with the balanced heaviness and lightness of a pendulum in a grandfather clock. She carried a thin small cane made from an umbrella, and with this she kept tapping the frozen earth in front of her. This made a grave and persistent noise in the still air that seemed meditative, like the chirping of a solitary little bird.

She wore a dark striped dress reaching down to her shoe tops, and an equally long apron of bleached sugar sacks, with a full pocket: all neat and tidy, but every time she took a step she might have fallen over her shoelaces, which dragged from her unlaced shoes. She looked straight ahead. Her eyes were blue with age. Her skin had a pattern all its own of numberless branching wrinkles, and as though a whole little tree stood in the middle of her forehead, but a golden color ran underneath, and the two knobs of her cheeks were illumined by a yellow burning under the dark. Under the red rag her hair came down on her neck in the frailest of ringlets, still black, and with an odor like copper.

Now and then there was a quivering in the thicket. Old Phoenix said, "Out of my way, all you foxes, owls, beetles, jack rabbits, coons, and wild animals! Keep out from under these feet, little bobwhites. Keep the big wild hogs out of my path. Don't let none of those come running my direction. I got a long way." Under her small black-freckled hand her cane, limber as a buggy whip, would switch at the brush as if to rouse up any hiding things.

On she went. The woods were deep and still. The sun made the pine needles almost too bright to look at, up where the wind rocked. The cones dropped as light as feathers. Down in the hollow was the mourning dove — it was not too late for him.

The path ran up a hill. "Seem like there is chains about my feet, time I get this far," she said, in the voice of argument old people keep to use with themselves. "Something always take a hold of me on this hill — pleads I should stay."

After she got to the top, she turned and gave a full, severe look behind her where she had come. "Up through pines," she said at length. "Now down through oaks."

Her eyes opened their widest and she started down gently. But before she got to the bottom of the hill a bush caught her dress.

Her fingers were busy and intent, but her skirts were full and long, so that before she could pull them free in one place they were caught in another. It was not possible to allow the dress to tear. "I in the thorny bush," she said. "Thorns, you doing your appointed work. Never want to let folks pass — no, sir. Old eyes thought you was a pretty little *green* bush."

Finally, trembling all over, she stood free, and after a moment dared to stoop for her cane.

"Sun so high!" she cried, leaning back and looking, while the thick tears went over her eyes. "The time getting all gone here."

At the foot of this hill was a place where a log was laid across the creek.

"Now comes the trial," said Phoenix. Putting her right foot out, she mounted the log and shut her eyes. Lifting her skirt, leveling her cane fiercely before her like a festival figure in some parade, she began to march across. Then she opened her eyes, and she was safe on the other side.

"I wasn't as old as I thought," she said.

But she sat down to rest. She spread her skirts on the bank around her and folded her hands over her knees. Up above her was a tree in a pearly cloud of mistletoe. She did not dare to close her eyes, and when a little boy brought her a plate with a slice of marble cake on it she spoke to him. "That would be acceptable," she said. But when she went to take it there was just her own hand in the air.

So she left that tree, and had to go through a barbed-wire fence. There she had to creep and crawl, spreading her knees and stretching her fingers like a baby trying to climb the steps. But she talked loudly to herself: she could not let her dress be torn now, so late in the day, and she could not pay for having her arm or her leg sawed off if she got caught fast where she was.

At last she was safe through the fence and risen up out in the clearing. Big dead trees, like black men with one arm, were standing in the purple stalks of the withered cotton field. There sat a buzzard.

* "Who you watching?"

In the furrow she made her way along.

"Glad this not the season for bulls," she said, looking sideways, "and the good Lord made his snakes to curl up and sleep in the winter. A pleasure I don't see no two-headed snake coming around that tree, where it come once. It took a while to get by him, back in the summer."

She passed through the old cotton, and went into a field of dead corn. It whispered and shook, and was taller than her head. "Through the maze now," she said, for there was no path.

Then there was something tall, black, and skinny there, moving before her.

At first she took it for a man. It could have been a man dancing in the field. But she stood still and listened, and it did not make a sound. It was as silent as a ghost.

"Ghost," she said sharply, "who be you the ghost of? For I have heard of nary death close by."

But there was no answer, only the ragged dancing in the wind.

She shut her eyes, reached out her hand, and touched a sleeve. She found a coat and inside that an emptiness, cold as ice.

"You scarecrow," she said. Her face lighted. "I ought to be shut up for good," she said with laughter. "My senses is gone. I too old. I the oldest people I ever know. Dance, old scarecrow," she said, "while I dancing with you."

She kicked her foot over the furrow, and with mouth drawn down shook her head once or twice in a little strutting way. Some husks blew down and whirled in streamers about her skirts.

Then she went on, parting her way from side to side with the cane, through the whispering field. At last she came to the end, to a wagon track, where the silver grass blew between the red ruts. The quail were walking around like pullets, seeming all dainty and unseen.

"Walk pretty," she said. "This the easy place. This the easy going." She followed the track, swaying through the quiet bare fields, through the little strings of trees silver in their dead leaves, past cabins silver from weather, with the doors and windows boarded shut, all like old women under a spell sitting there. "I walking in their sleep," she said, nodding her head vigorously.

In a ravine she went where a spring was, silently flowing through a hollowed log. Old Phoenix bent and drank. "Sweet gum makes the water sweet," she said, and drank more. "Nobody know who made this well, for it was here when I was born."

The track crossed a swampy part where the moss hung as white as lace from every limb. "Sleep on, alligators, and blow your bubbles." Then the cypress trees went into the road. Deep, deep it went down between the high, green-colored banks. Overhead the live oaks met, and it was as dark as a cave.

A big black dog with a lolling tongue came up out of the weeds by the ditch. She was meditating, and not ready, and when he came at her she only hit him a little with her cane. Over she went in the ditch, like a little puff of milkweed.

Down there, her senses drifted away. A dream visited her, and she reached her hand up, but nothing reached down and gave her a pull. So she lay there and presently went to talking. "Old woman," she said to herself, "that black dog came up out of the weeds to stall you off, and now there he sitting on his fine tail, smiling at you."

A white man finally came along and found her — a hunter, a young man, with his dog on a chain.

"Well, Granny!" he laughed. "What are you doing there?"

"Lying on my back like a June bug waiting to be turned over, mister," she said, reaching up her hand.

He lifted her up, gave her a swing in the air, and set her down. "Anything broken, Granny?"

"No, sir, them old dead weeds is springy enough," said Phoenix, when she had got her breath. "I thank you for your trouble."

"Where do you live, Granny?" he asked, while the two dogs were growling at each other.

"Away back younder, sir, behind the ridge. You can't even see it from here."

"On your way home?"

"No, sir, I going to town."

"Why, that's too far! That's as far as I walk when I come out myself, and I get something for my trouble." He patted the stuffed bag he carried, and there hung down a little closed claw. It was one of the bobwhites, with its beak hooked bitterly to show it was dead. "Now you go on home, Granny!"

"I bound to go to town, mister," said Phoenix. "The time come around."

He gave another laugh, filling the whole landscape. "I know you old colored people! Wouldn't miss going to town to see Santa Claus!"

But something held Old Phoenix very still. The deep lines in her face went into a fierce and different radiation. Without warning, she had seen with her own eyes a flashing nickel fall out of the man's pocket on to the ground.

"How old are you, Granny?" he was saying.

"There is no telling, mister," she said, "no telling."

Then she gave a little cry and clapped her hands, and said, "Git on away from here, dog! Look! Look at that dog!" She laughed as if in admiration. "He ain't scared of nobody. He a big black dog." She whispered, "Sic him!"

"Watch me get rid of that cur," said the man. "Sic him, Pete! Sic him!"

Phoenix heard the dogs fighting, and heard the man running and throwing sticks. She even heard a gunshot. But she was slowly bending forward by that time, further and further forward, the lids stretched down over her eyes, as if she were doing this in her sleep. Her chin was lowered almost to her knees. The yellow palm of her hand came out from the fold of her apron. Her fingers slid down and along the ground under the piece of money with the grace and care they would have in lifting an egg from under a setting hen. Then she slowly straightened up; she stood erect, and the nickel was in her apron pocket. A bird flew by. Her lips moved. "God watching me the whole time. I come to stealing."

The man came back, and his own dog panted about them. "Well, I scared him off that time," he said, and then he laughed and lifted his gun and pointed it at Phoenix.

She stood straight and faced him.

"Doesn't the gun scare you?" he said, still pointing it.

"No, sir, I seen plenty go off closer by, in my day, and for less than what I done," she said, holding utterly still.

He smiled, and shouldered the gun. "Well, Granny," he said, "you must be a hundred years old, and scared of nothing. I'd give you a dime if I had any money with me. But you take my advice and stay home, and nothing will happen to you."

"I bound to go on my way, mister," said Phoenix. She inclined her head in the red rag. Then they went in different directions, but she could hear the gun shooting again and again over the hill.

She walked on. The shadows hung from the oak trees to the road like curtains. Then she smelled wood smoke, and smelled the river, and she saw a steeple and the cabins on their steep steps. Dozens of little black children whirled around her. There ahead was Natchez shining. Bells were ringing. She walked on.

In the paved city it was Christmas time. There were red and green electric lights strung and crisscrossed everywhere, and all turned on in the daytime. Old Phoenix would have been lost if she had not distrusted her eyesight and depended on her feet to know where to take her.

She paused quietly on the sidewalk, where people were passing by. A lady came along in the crowd, carrying an armful of red, green, and silver-wrapped presents; she gave off perfume like the red roses in hot summer, and Phoenix stopped her.

"Please, missy, will you lace up my shoe?" She held up her foot.

"What do you want, Grandma?"

"See my shoe," said Phoenix. "Do all right for out in the country, but wouldn't look right to go in a big building."

"Stand still then, Grandma," said the lady. She put her packages down on the sidewalk beside her and laced and tied both shoes tightly.

"Can't lace 'em with a cane," said Phoenix. "Thank you, missy. I doesn't mind asking a nice lady to tie up my shoe when I gets out on the street."

Moving slowly and from side to side, she went into the stone building and into a tower of steps, where she walked up and around and around until her feet knew to stop.

She entered a door, and there she saw nailed up on the wall the document that had been stamped with the gold seal and framed in the gold frame, which matched the dream that was hung up in her head.

"Here I be," she said. There was a fixed and ceremonial stiffness over her body.

"A charity case, I suppose," said an attendant who sat at the desk before her.

But Phoenix only looked above her head. There was sweat on her face; the wrinkles shone like a bright net.

"Speak up, Grandma," the woman said. "What's your name? We must have your history, you know. Have you been here before? What seems to be the trouble with you?"

Phoenix only gave a twitch to her face as if a fly were bothering her.

"Are you deaf?" cried the attendant.

But then the nurse came in.

"Oh, that's just old Aunt Phoenix," she said. "She doesn't come for herself; she has a little grandson. She makes these trips just as regular as clockwork — she lives away back off the Old Natchez Trace." She bent down. "Well, Aunt Phoenix, why don't you just take a seat? We won't keep you standing, after your long trip." She pointed.

The old woman sat down, bolt upright in the chair.

"Now, how is the boy?" asked the nurse.

Old Phoenix did not speak.

"I said, how is the boy?"

But Phoenix only waited and stared straight ahead, her face very solemn and withdrawn into rigidity.

"Is his throat any better?" asked the nurse. "Aunt Phoenix, don't you hear me? Is your grandson's throat any better since the last time you came for the medicine?"

With her hands on her knees, the old woman waited, silent, erect, and motionless, just as if she were in armor.

"You mustn't take up our time this way, Aunt Phoenix," the nurse said. "Tell us quickly about your grandson, and get it over. He isn't dead, is he?"

At last there came a flicker and then a flame of comprehension across her face, and she spoke. "My grandson. It was my memory had left me. There I sat and forgot why I made my long trip."

"Forgot?" The nurse frowned. "After you came so far?"

Then Phoenix was like an old woman begging a dignified forgiveness for waking up frightened in the night. "I never did go to school — I was too old at the Surrender," she said in a soft voice. "I'm an old woman without an education. It was my memory fail me. My little grandson, he is just the same, and I forgot it in the coming."

"Throat never heals, does it?" said the nurse, speaking in a loud, sure voice to Old Phoenix. By now she had a card with something written on it, a little list. "Yes. Swallowed lye. When was it — January — two — three years ago — "

Phoenix spoke unasked now. "No, missy, he not dead, he just the same. Every little while his throat begin to close up again, and he not able to swallow. He not get his breath. He not able to help himself. So the time come around, and I go on another trip for the soothing-medicine."

"All right. The doctor said as long as you came to get it, you could have it," said the nurse. "But it's an obstinate case."

"My little grandson, he sit up there in the house all wrapped up, waiting by himself," Phoenix went on. "We is the only two left in the world. He suffer and it don't seem to put him back at all. He got a sweet look. He going to last. He wear a little patch-quilt and peep out, holding his mouth open like a little bird. I remembers so plain now. I not going to forget him again, no, the whole enduring time. I could tell him from all the others in creation."

"All right." The nurse was trying to hush her now. She brought her a bottle of medicine. "Charity," she said, making a check mark in a book.

Old Phoenix held the bottle close to her eyes, and then carefully put it into her pocket.

"I thank you," she said.

"It's Christmas time, Grandma," said the attendant. "Could I give you a few pennies out of my purse?"

"Five pennies is a nickel," said Phoenix stiffly.

"Here's a nickel," said the attendant.

Phoenix rose carefully and held out her hand. She received the nickel and then fished the other nickel out of her pocket and laid it beside the new one. She stared at her palm closely, with her head on one side.

Then she gave a tap with her cane on the floor. "This is what come to me to do," she said. "I going to the store and buy my child a little windmill they sells, made out of paper. He going to find it hard to believe there such a thing in the world. I'll march myself back where he waiting, holding it straight up in this hand."

She lifted her free hand, gave a little nod, turned around, and walked out of the doctor's office. Then her slow step began on the stairs, going down.

The Journey to Hanford

by WILLIAM SAROYAN

We published William Saroyan early and often; his manuscripts were — and are — a maze of inked-in insertions. So too were his galley proofs, for he never ceased struggling to improve the text, and gave up only when he knew that the narrative was actually being printed. This story was published after The Daring Young Man on the Flying Trapeze *and before* My Heart's in the Highlands.

APRIL 1938

The time came one year for my sad uncle Jorgi to fix his bicycle and ride twenty-seven miles to Hanford, where it seems there was a job. I went with him, although at first there was talk of sending my cousin Vask instead.

The family didn't want to complain about having among its members a fool like Jorgi, but at the same time it wanted a chance, in the summertime, to forget him for a while. If he went away and got himself the job in Hanford, in the watermelons, all would be well. Jorgi would earn a little money and be out of the way. That was the important thing — to get him out of the way.

"To hell with him and his zither both," my grandfather said. "When you read in a book that a man sits all day under a tree and plays a zither and sings, believe me, that writer is an impractical man. Money, that's the thing. Let him go and sweat under the sun for a while. Him and his zither both."

"You say that now," my grandmother said, "but wait a week. Wait till you begin to need music again."

"That is nonsense," my grandfather said. "When you read in a book that a man who sings is one who is truly a happy man, that writer is a dreamer, not a merchant in a thousand years. Let him go. It is twenty-seven miles to Hanford. That is a good intelligent distance."

"You speak that way now," my grandmother said, "but you'll be a melancholy man in three days. I shall see you walking around like a tiger. I am the one who shall see that. Seeing that, I am the one who shall laugh."

"You are a woman," my grandfather said. "When you read in a book with hundreds of pages of small print that a woman is truly a creature of wonder, that writer has turned his face away from his wife and is dreaming. Let him go away on his bicycle, him and his zither both."

"It is simply that you are not young any longer," my grandmother said. "That is the thing that is making you roar."

"Close your mouth," my grandfather said. "Close it, or here comes the back of my hand."

My grandfather looked about the room at his children and grand-children.

"I say he goes to Hanford on his bicycle," he said. "What do you say?"

Nobody spoke.

"Then that's settled," my grandfather said. "Now, who shall we send with him? Which of the uncouth of our children shall we punish, sending him with Jorgi to Hanford? When you read in a book that a journey to another city is a pleasant experience for a young man, that writer is probably a man of eighty or ninety who as a child once went in a wagon two miles from home. Who shall we punish? Vask? Shall Vask be the one? Step up here, boy."

My cousin Vask got up from the floor and stood in front of the old man, who looked down at him furiously, twisted his enormous mus-taches, cleared his throat, and put his hand over the boy's face. His hand practically covered the whole head. Vask didn't move.

"Shall you go with your uncle Jorgi to Hanford?" my grandfather said.

"If it pleases my grandfather, I shall," Vask said.

The old man began to make faces, thinking it over.

"Let me think a moment," he said. "Jorgi's spirit is the foolish one of our tribe. Yours is also. Is it wise to put two fools together?"

He turned to the others.

"Let me hear your spoken thoughts on this theme," he said. "Is it wise to put an old fool and a young one together, of the same tribe? Will it profit anyone? Speak aloud so I may consider."

"I think it would be the natural thing to do, under the circum-stances," my uncle Zorab said. "A fool and a fool. The man to work, the boy to keep house and cook."

"Perhaps," my grandfather said. "Let's consider. A fool and a fool, one to work, the other to keep house and cook. Can you cook, boy?"

"Of course he can cook," my grandmother said. "Rice, at least."

"Is that true, boy, about the rice?" my grandfather said. "Four cups of water, one cup of rice, one teaspoonful of salt. Do you know about the trick of making it come out like food instead of swill, or are we dreaming?"

"Of course he can cook rice," my grandmother said.

"The back of my hand is on its way to your mouth," my grandfather said. "Let the boy speak for himself. He has a tongue. Can you do it, boy? When you read in a book that a boy answers an old man wisely, that writer is probably a Jew, bent on exaggeration. Can you make it come out like food, not swill?"

"I have cooked rice," Vask said. "It came out like food."

"Was there enough salt to it?" my grandfather said. "If you lie, remember my hand."

Vask hesitated a moment.

"I understand," my grandfather said. "You are embarrassed about the rice. What was wrong with it? Truth is all that pleases me. Speak up fearlessly. If it is the truth fearlessly, no man can demand more. What embarrasses you about the rice?"

"It was too salty," Vask said. "We had to drink water all day and all night, it was so salty."

"No elaboration," my grandfather said. "Only what is true. The rice was too salty. Naturally you had to drink water all day and all night. We've all eaten that kind of rice. Don't think because you drank water all day and all night that you are the first Armenian who ever did that. Just tell me that it was too salty. I'm not here to learn. I *know*. Just say it was too salty and let me try to determine if you are the one to go."

My grandfather turned to the others. He began to make faces again.

"I think this is the boy to go," he said, "but speak up, any of you who have something to say. Salty is better than swill. Was it light in texture, boy?"

"It was light in texture," Vask said.

"I believe this is the one to send," my grandfather said. "The water is good for the gut. Shall it be this boy here, Vask Garoghlanian, or who?"

"On second thought," my uncle Zorab said, "two fools, out and out, perhaps not, though the rice is not swill. I nominate Aram. Perhaps he should go. He deserves to be punished."

Everybody looked at me.

"Aram?" my grandfather said. "You mean the boy who laughs, the loud-laughing boy? You mean light-footed, bright-eyed, loud-laughing Aram Garoghlanian?"

"Who else would he mean?" my grandmother said. "You know very well who he means."

My grandfather turned slowly and for half a minute looked at my grandmother.

"When you read in a book," he said, "about some man who falls in love with a girl and marries her, that writer is truly referring to a very young man who has no idea she is going to talk out of turn right up to the time she is ready to go into the ground, at the age of ninety-seven. That writer is thinking of a younger type of man.

"Do you mean Aram?" he said. "Aram Garoghlanian?"

"Yes," my uncle Zorab said.

"What has he done to deserve this awful punishment?" my grandfather said.

"*He knows,*" my uncle Zorab said.

"Aram Garoghlanian," my grandfather said.

I got up and stood in front of my grandfather. He put his big hand over my face and rubbed it. I knew he was not angry, though, because his hand was gentle.

"What have you done, boy?" my grandfather said.

I began to laugh, remembering the things I had done. My grandfather listened a moment and then began laughing with me.

Only he and I laughed. The others didn't dare laugh. My grandfather had instructed them not to laugh unless they could laugh like him. I was the only Garoghlanian in the world who could laugh like him.

"Aram Garoghlanian," my grandfather said, "tell me. What have you done?"

"Which one?" I said.

My grandfather turned to my uncle Zorab.

"Which one?" he said. "Tell the boy which mischief to acknowledge. There appear to be several."

"He knows which one," my uncle Zorab said.

"Do you mean," I said, "telling the neighbors you are crazy?"

My uncle Zorab refused to speak.

"Or do you mean," I said, "going around talking the way you talk?"

"This is the boy to send with Jorgi," my uncle Zorab said.

"Can you cook rice?" my grandfather said.

He didn't care to go into detail about my making fun of my uncle Zorab. If I could cook rice, I should go with Jorgi to Hanford. That was what it came to. Of course I wanted to go, no matter what the writer was who wrote that it was a fine experience for a boy to travel to a strange city. Fool or liar or anything else, I *wanted* to go.

"I can cook rice," I said.

"Salty or swill, or what?" my grandfather said.

"Sometimes salty," I said. "Sometimes swill. Sometimes perfect."

"Let's consider," my grandfather said.

He leaned against the wall, considering.

"Three large glasses of water," he said to my grandmother.

My grandmother went to the kitchen and after a moment returned with three large glasses of water on a tray. My grandfather drank one glass after another, then turned to the others, making many thoughtful faces.

"Sometimes salty," he said. "Sometimes swill. Sometimes perfect. Is this the boy to send to Hanford?"

"Yes," my uncle Zorab said. "The only one."

"So be it," my grandfather said. "That will be all. I wish to be alone."

I moved to go. My grandfather took me by the neck.

"Stay a moment," he said.

When we were alone he said, "Talk the way your uncle Zorab talks."

I did so and my grandfather roared with laughter.

"Go to Hanford," he said. "Go with the fool Jorgi and make it salty or make it swill or make it perfect."

In this manner I was assigned to be my uncle Jorgi's companion on his journey to Hanford.

We set out the following morning before daybreak. I sat on the crossbar of the bicycle and my uncle Jorgi on the seat, but when I got tired I got off and walked, and after a while my uncle Jorgi got off and walked, and I rode. We didn't reach Hanford till late that night.

We were supposed to stay in Hanford till the job ended, after the watermelon season. That was the idea. We went around town looking for a house to stay in, a house with a stove in it, gas connections, and water. We didn't care about electricity, but we wanted gas and water. We saw six or seven houses and then we saw one my uncle Jorgi liked, so we moved in that night. It was an eleven-room house, with a gas stove, a sink with running water, and a room with a bed and a couch. The other rooms were all empty. My uncle Jorgi lighted a candle, brought out his zither, sat on the floor, and began to play and sing. It was beautiful; it was melancholy sometimes and sometimes funny, but it was always beautiful. I don't know how long he played and sang before he realized he was hungry, but all of a sudden he got up off the floor and said, "Aram, I want rice."

I made a pot of rice that night that was both salty and swill, but my uncle Jorgi said, "Aram, this is wonderful."

The birds got us up at daybreak.

"The job," I said. "You begin today, you know."

"Today," my uncle Jorgi groaned.

He walked tragically out of the empty house and I looked around for a broom. There was no broom, so I went out and sat on the steps of the front porch. It seemed to be a nice region of the world in daylight. It was a street with only four houses. There was a church steeple in front of the house, two blocks away. I sat on the porch about an hour. My uncle Jorgi came up the street, on his bicycle, zigzagging joyously.

"Not this year, thank God," he said, leaping off the bicycle.

"What?" I said.

"There is no job," he said. "No job, thank God."

"No job?" I said.

"No job, thank our Heavenly Father," he said.

"Why not?" I said.

"The watermelons," he said.

"What about them?" I said.

"The season is over," he said.

"That isn't true," I said.

"The season is over," he said. "Praise God, the watermelons are all harvested."

"Who said so?"

"The farmer himself. The farmer himself said so."

"He just said that," I said, "because he didn't want to hurt your feelings. He just said that because he knew your heart wouldn't be in your work."

"Praise God," my uncle Jorgi said, "the whole season is over. All the fine, ripe watermelons have been harvested."

"What are we going to do?" I said. "The season is just beginning."

"It's ended," he said. "We shall dwell in this house a month and then go home. We have paid six dollars rent and we have money enough for rice. We shall dream here a month and then go home."

"With no money," I said.

"But in good health," he said. "Praise God, who ripened them so early this year."

My uncle Jorgi danced into the house to his zither, and before I could decide what to do about him he was playing and singing, and it was so beautiful I didn't even get up and try to chase him out of the house. I just sat on the porch and listened.

We stayed in the house a month and then went home. My grandmother was the first to see us.

"It's about time you two came home," she said. "He's been raging like a tiger. Give me the money."

"There is no money," I said.

"Did he work?" my grandmother said.

"No," I said. "He played and sang the whole month."

"How did your rice turn out?" she said.

"Sometimes salty," I said. "Sometimes swill. Sometimes perfect. But he didn't work."

"His father mustn't know," she said. "I have money."

She lifted her dress and got some currency out of a pocket in her pants and put it in my hands.

"When he comes home," she said, "give him this money."

She looked at me a moment, then added: *"Aram Garoghlanian."*

"I will do as you say," I said.

When my grandfather came home he began to roar.

"Home already?" he said. "Is the season ended so soon? Where is the money he earned?"

I gave him the money.

"I won't have him singing all day," my grandfather roared. "There is a limit to everything. When you read in a book that a father loves a foolish son more than his wise sons, that writer is a bachelor."

In the yard, under the almond tree, my uncle Jorgi began to play and sing. My grandfather came to a dead halt and began to listen. He sat down on the couch, took off his shoes, and began to make faces.

I went into the kitchen to get three or four glasses of water to quench the thirst from last night's rice. When I came back to the parlor the old man was stretched out on the couch, asleep and smiling, and his son Jorgi was singing hallelujah to the universe at the top of his beautiful, melancholy voice.

Gold Is Not Always

by WILLIAM FAULKNER

This is an unusual story to come from William Faulkner. He sent it to us in the grim days of 1940, and the laughter in it was a welcome relief from the strain. Ten years later he came into his own when in December 1950 he went to Stockholm to receive the Nobel Prize for Literature.

NOVEMBER 1940

When they drew near the commissary, Lucas said: "You wait here." "No, no," the salesman said. "I'll talk to him. If I can't sell it to him, there ain't a — " Then the salesman stopped. He did not know why. He was young, not yet thirty, with the slightly soiled snap and dash of his calling, and a white man. Yet he stopped and looked at the Negro in battered overalls, whose face showed only that he was at least sixty, who was looking at him not only with dignity but with command.

"You wait here," Lucas said. So the salesman leaned against the lot fence in the bright August morning while Lucas went on up the hill and mounted the gnawed steps beside which a bright-coated young mare with a blaze and three stockings stood under a heavy comfortable saddle, and entered the commissary, with its ranked shelves of tinned food and tobacco and patent medicines, its hooks from which hung trace chains and collars and hames, and where, at a roll-top desk beside the front window, his landlord was writing in a ledger. Lucas stood quietly looking at the back of the white man's neck until the other looked around. "He's done come," Lucas said.

Edmonds swiveled his chair about, back-tilted. He was already glaring at Lucas before the chair stopped moving; he said with astonishing violence: "No!"

"Yes," Lucas said.

"No!"

"He done fotch the machine with him," Lucas said. "I seed hit work."

I buried a dollar in my back yard this morning and it went right straight to whar it wuz and found it. He just wants three hundred dollars for it. We gonter find that money tonight and I can pay it back tomorrow morning."

"No!" Edmonds said. "I tell you and tell you and tell you there ain't any money buried around here. You've been here sixty years. Did you ever hear of anybody in this country with enough money to bury? Can you imagine anybody in this country burying anything worth as much as two bits that some of his kinfolks or friends or neighbors or acquaintances ain't dug up long ago?"

"You're wrong," Lucas said. "Folks finds it all the time. Ain't I told you about them two strange white men that come in here after dark one night three years ago and dug up twenty-two thousand dollars and got out again before anybody even seed um? I seed the hole whar they had done filled it up again. And the churn hit was buried in."

"Hah," Edmonds said. "Then how do you know it was twenty-two thousand dollars?" But Lucas only looked at him. It was not stubbornness. It was an infinite, an almost Jehovah-like patience, as if he, Lucas, were engaged in a contest, partially for the idiot's own benefit, with an idiot. "Your paw would a lent me three hundred dollars if he was here," he said.

"Well, I ain't," Edmonds said. "You've got damn near three thousand dollars in the bank. If I could keep you from wasting any of that on a damn machine to find buried money, I would. But then, you ain't going to use any of your money, are you? You've got more sense yourself than to risk that."

"It looks like I'm gonter have to," Lucas said. "I'm gonter ask you one more time — "

"No!" Edmonds said, again with that astonishing and explosive violence. Lucas looked at him for a time, almost contemplative. He did not sigh.

"All right," he said.

When he returned to the salesman, his son-in-law was there too — a lean-hipped, very black young man with a ready face full of white teeth and a ruined Panama hat raked above his right ear.

The salesman looked once at Lucas's face and hunched himself away from the fence. "I'll go talk to him," he said.

"No," Lucas said. "You stay away from there."

"Then what you going to do about it?" the salesman said. "Here I've come all the way from St. Louis — and how you ever persuaded them to send this machine out without any down payment in the first place, I still don't see. And I'll tell you right now, if I got to take it back and turn in an expense account for this trip and no sale, something is — "

"We ain't doing no good standing here, nohow," Lucas said. The other two followed him, back to the gate and the highroad, where the salesman's car stood. The divining machine rested on the rear seat and Lucas stood in the open door, looking at it — an oblong metal box with a handle for carrying at each end, compact and solid, efficient and businesslike and complex with its knobs and dials, and Lucas standing over it, sober and bemused. "And I seed hit work," he said. "I seed hit with my own eyes."

"Well?" the salesman said. "What you going to do? I've got to know, so I can know what to do, myself. Ain't you got three hundred dollars?" Lucas mused upon the machine. He did not look up yet.

"We gonter find that money tonight," he said. "You put in the machine and I'll show you whar to look, and we'll go halves on hit."

"Ha, ha, ha," the salesman said harshly. "Now I'll tell one."

"We bound to find hit, cap-tin," the son-in-law said. "Two white men slipped in here three years ago and dug up twenty-two thousand dollars one night and got clean away wid hit fo' daylight."

"You bet," the salesman said. "And you knew it was exactly twenty-two thousand because you found where they had throwed away the odd cents."

"Naw, sir," the son-in-law said. "Hit mought a been even more than twenty-two thousand dollars. Hit wuz a big churn."

"George Wilkins," Lucas said, still half inside the car and still without turning his head.

"Sir," the son-in-law said.

"Shut up." Now Lucas turned and looked at the salesman; again the salesman saw a face quite sober, even a little cold, quite impenetrable. "I'll swap you a mule for it."

"A mule?" the salesman said.

"When we find that money tonight, I'll buy the mule back for your three hundred dollars." The son-in-law had begun to bat his eyes rapidly. But nobody was looking at him. Lucas and the salesman looked at one another — the shrewd, suddenly attentive face of the young white man, the absolutely impenetrable face of the Negro.

"Do you own the mule?"

"How could I swap hit to you ef'n I didn't?"

"Let's go see it," the salesman said.

"George Wilkins," Lucas said.

"Sir," the son-in-law said. He was still batting his eyes constantly and rapidly.

"Go up to my barn and get my halter," Lucas said.

Edmonds found the mule was missing as soon as the stablemen brought the drove up from pasture that evening. She was a three-year-old, eleven-hundred-pound mare mule named Alice Ben Bolt, and he had refused three hundred dollars for her in the spring. But he didn't even curse. He merely dismounted and stood beside the lot fence while the rapid beat of his mare's feet died away in the darkling night and then returned, and the head stableman sprang down and handed him his flashlight and pistol. Then, himself on the mare and the two Negroes on saddleless mules, they went back across the pasture, fording the creek, to the gap in the fence through which the mule had been led. From there they followed the tracks of the mule and of the man who led her in the soft earth along the edge of a cotton field, to the road. And here too they could follow them, the head stableman walking and carrying the flashlight, where the man had led the unshod mule in the softer dirt which bordered the gravel. "That's Alice's foot," the head stableman said. "I'd know hit anywhar."

Later Edmonds would realize that both the Negroes had recognized the man's footprints too. But at the time his very fury and concern had short-circuited his normal sensitivity to Negro behavior. They would not have told him who had made the tracks even if he had demanded to know, but the realization that they knew would have enabled him to leap to the correct divination and so save himself the four or five hours of mental turmoil and physical effort which he was about to enter.

They lost the tracks. He expected to find the marks where the mule had been loaded into a waiting truck, whereupon he would return home and telephone to the sheriff in Jefferson and to the Memphis police to watch the horse-and-mule markets tomorrow. There were no such marks. It took them almost an hour to find where the tracks had vanished onto the gravel, crossing it, descending through the opposite roadside weeds, to reappear in another field a hundred yards away. Supperless, raging, the mare which had been under saddle all day unfed too, he followed the two shadowy mules at the backstretched arm of the second walking Negro, cursing the darkness and the puny light which the head stableman carried, on which they were forced to depend.

Two hours later they were in the creek bottom four miles away. He was walking too now, lest he knock his brains out against a limb, stumbling and thrashing among brier and undergrowth and rotting logs and branches where the tracks led, leading the mare with one hand and fending his face with the other arm and trying to watch his feet, so that he walked into one of the mules, instinctively leaping in the right direction as it lashed out at him with one hoof, before he discovered that the Negroes had stopped. 'Then, cursing out loud now and moving quickly again to avoid the invisible second mule which would be somewhere to his left, he discovered that the flashlight was now off and he too saw the faint, smoky glare of the lightwood torch among the trees ahead. It was moving. "That's right," he said rapidly. "Keep the light off." He called the second Negro's name. "Give the mules to Dan and come back here and take the mare." He waited, watching the light, until the Negro's hand fumbled at his. Then he released the reins and moved around the mules, drawing his pistol and still watching the moving flame. "Hand me the flashlight," he said. He took the light from that fumbling hand too. "You and Oscar wait here."

"I better come wid you," the Negro said.

"All right," Edmonds said. "Give Oscar the mules." He didn't wait, though from time to time he could hear the Negro behind him, both of them moving as quietly and rapidly as possible. The rage was not cold now. It was hot, and there was an eagerness upon him, a kind of vindictive exultation as he plunged on, heedless of brush or log, the flashlight in his left hand and the pistol in his right, gaining rapidly on the moving torch, bursting at last out of the undergrowth and into a sort of glade, in the center of which two men stood looking toward him, one of them carrying before him what Edmonds believed at first to be some kind of receptacle of feed, the other holding high over his head the smoking pine knot. Then Edmonds recognized George Wilkins's ruined Panama hat, and he realized not only that the two Negroes with him had known all the time who had made the footprints, but that the object which Lucas was carrying was not any feedbox and that he himself should have known all the time what had become of his mule.

"You, Lucas!" he shouted. George flung the torch, arching, but the flashlight already held them spitted; Edmonds saw the white man now, snap-brim hat, necktie, and all, risen from beside a tree, his trousers rolled to the knees and his feet invisible in caked mud. "That's right," Edmonds said. "Go on, George. Run. I believe I can hit that hat without even touching you." He approached, the flashlight's beam contracting onto the metal box which Lucas held before him, gleaming and glinting among the knobs and dials. "So that's it," he said. "Three hundred dollars. I wish somebody would come into this country with a seed that had to be worked every day, from New Year's right on through to Christmas. As soon as you niggers are laid by, trouble starts. I ain't going to worry with Alice tonight, and if you and George want to spend the rest of it walking back and forth with that damn thing, that's your business. But I want that mule to be in her stall by sunup. Do you hear?" Edmonds had forgotten about the white man until he appeared beside Lucas.

"What mule is that?" he said. Edmonds turned the light on him for a moment.

"My mule, sir," he said.

"I've got a bill of sale for that mule," the other said. "Signed by Lucas here."

"Have you now," Edmonds said. "You can make lamplighters out of it next winter."

"Is that so?" the other said. 'Look here, Mister What's-your-name — " But Edmonds had already turned the light back to Lucas, who still held the divining machine before him.

"On second thought, I ain't going to worry about that mule at all," he said. "I told you this morning what I thought about this business. But you're a grown man; if you want to fool with it, I can't stop you. But if that mule ain't in her stall by sunup tomorrow, I'm going to telephone the sheriff. Do you hear me?"

"I hears you," Lucas said.

"All right, big boy," the salesman said. "If that mule is moved from where she's at until I'm ready to move her, I'm going to telephone the sheriff. Do you hear that too?" This time Edmonds jumped, flung the light beam at the salesman, furious and restrained.

"Were you talking to me, sir?" he said.

"No," the salesman said. "I'm talking to him. And he heard me." For a while longer Edmonds held the light beam on the other. Then he dropped it, so that only their legs and feet showed, planted in the pool and its refraction as if they stood in a pool of dying water. He put the pistol back into his pocket.

"Well, you and Lucas have got till daylight to settle that. Because that mule is to be back in my barn at sunup." He turned and went back to where Dan waited, the light swinging and flickering before him; presently it had vanished.

"George Wilkins," Lucas said.

"Sir," George said.

"Find that pine knot and light it again." George did so; once more the red glare streamed away in thick smoke, upward against the August stars of more than midnight. "Now grab a holt of this thing," Lucas said. "I got to find that money now."

But when day broke they had not found it, the torch paling away in the wan, dew-heavy light, the white man asleep on the wet earth now, drawn into a ball against the dawn's wet chill, unshaven, with his dashing city hat, his necktie, his soiled shirt and muddy trousers rolled to his knees, and his mud-caked feet whose shoes gleamed with polish yesterday. They waked him. He sat up, cursing. But he knew at once where he was, because he said: "All right now. If that mule moves one foot out of that cotton house, I'm going to get the sheriff."

"I just wants one more night," Lucas said. "That money's here."

"What about that fellow that says the mule is his?"

"I'll tend to him in the morning. You don't need to worry about that. Besides, ef'n you try to move that mule yourself, the sheriff gonter take her away from you. You leave her whar she's at and lemme have one more night with this-here machine. Then I kin fix everything."

"All right," the other said. "But do you know what it's going to cost you? It's going to cost you just exactly twenty-five dollars more. Now I'm going to town and go to bed."

He put Lucas and George out at George's gate. They watched the car go on down the road, already going fast. George was batting his eyes rapidly. "Now whut we gonter do?" he said. Lucas roused.

"Eat your breakfast quick as you can and come on to my house. You got to go to town and get back here by noon."

"I needs to go to bed too," George said. "I'm bad off to sleep too."

"Ne'mine about that," Lucas said. "You eat your breakfast and get up to my house quick." When George reached his gate a half hour later, Lucas met him, the check already written out in his laborious, cramped, but quite legible hand. It was for fifty dollars. "Get it in silver dollars," Lucas said. "And be back here by noon."

It was just dusk when the salesman's car stopped again at Lucas's gate, where Lucas and George, carrying a long-handled shovel, waited. The salesman was freshly shaved and his face looked rested; the snap-brim hat had been brushed and his shirt was clean. But he now wore a pair of cotton khaki pants still bearing the manufacturer's stitched label and still showing the creases where they had been folded on the store's shelf. He gave Lucas a hard, jeering stare as Lucas and George approached. "I ain't going to ask if my mule's all right," he said. "Because I don't need to. Hah?"

"Hit's all right," Lucas said. He and George got into the rear seat beside the divining machine. The salesman put the car into gear, though he did not move it yet.

"Well?" he said. "Where do you want to walk tonight? Same place?"

"Not there," Lucas said. "I'll show you whar. We was looking in the wrong place. I misread the paper."

"You bet," the salesman said. "It's worth that extra twenty-five bucks to have found that out — " The car had begun to move. He stopped it so suddenly that Lucas and George, squatting gingerly on the front edge of the seat, lurched forward before they caught themselves. "You did what?" the salesman said.

"I misread the paper," Lucas said.

"What paper? Have you got a letter or something that tells where some money is buried?"

"That's right," Lucas said.

"Where is it?"

"Hit's put away in the house," Lucas said.

"Go and get it."

"Ne'mine," Lucas said. "I read hit right this time." For a moment longer the salesman sat, his head turned over his shoulder. Then he looked forward. He put the car in gear again.

"All right," he said. "Where's the place?"

"Drive on," Lucas said. "I'll show you."

It was not in the bottom, but on a hill overlooking the creek — a clump of ragged cedars, the ruins of old chimneys, a depression which was once a well or a cistern, the old worn-out fields stretching away and a few snaggled trees of what had been an orchard, shadowy and dim beneath the moonless sky where the fierce stars of late summer swam. "Hit's in the orchard," Lucas said. "Hit's divided, buried in two separate places. One of them's in the orchard."

"Provided the fellow that wrote you the letter ain't come back and joined it all up again," the salesman said. "What are we waiting on? Here, Jack," he said to George, "grab that thing out of there." George lifted the divining machine from the car. The salesman had a flashlight himself now, quite new, thrust into his hip pocket. He didn't put it on at once. "By God, you better find it first pop this time. We're on a hill now. There probably ain't a man in ten miles that can walk at all that won't be up here inside an hour, watching us."

"Don't tell me that," Lucas said. "Tell hit to this-here three hundred and twenty-five dollar buzz-box I done bought."

"You ain't bought this box yet, big boy," the salesman said. "You say one of the places is in the orchard. All right. Where?"

Lucas, carrying the shovel, went on into the old orchard, the others following. The salesman watched him pause, squinting at trees and sky to orient himself, then move on again, pause again. "We kin start here," he said. The salesman snapped on the light, handcupping the beam on to the metal box which George carried. "All right, Jack," he said. "Get going."

"I better tote it," Lucas said.

"No," the salesman said. "You're too old. I don't know yet that you can even keep up with us. Get on, Jack!" So Lucas walked on George's other side, carrying the shovel and watching the small bright dials in the flashlight's contracted beam as they went back and forth across the orchard. He was watching also, grave and completely attentive, when the needles began to spin and jerk and then quiver. Then he held the box and watched George digging into the light's concentrated pool and saw the rusted can come up at last and the bright cascade of silver dollars about the salesman's hands and heard the salesman's voice: "Well, by God! By God!" Lucas squatted also; they faced each other across the pit.

"I done found this much of hit, anyhow," he said. The salesman, one hand upon the scattered coins, made a slashing, almost instinctive blow with the other as if Lucas had reached for the coins. Squatting, he laughed harshly at Lucas across the pit.

"*You* found? This machine don't belong to you, old man."

"I bought hit," Lucas said.

"With what?"

"A mule," Lucas said. The other laughed at him, harsh and steady across the pit. "I give you a billy sale for hit."

"Which never was worth a damn. It's in my car yonder. Go and get it whenever you want to." He scrabbled the coins together, back into the can. He rose quickly out of the light, until only his legs showed in the new, still-creased cotton pants. He still wore the same low black shoes. He had not had them shined again — only washed. Lucas rose also, more slowly. "All right," the salesman said. "This ain't hardly any of it. Where's the other place?"

"Ask your finding machine," Lucas said. "Ain't it supposed to know?"

"You damn right it does," the salesman said.

"Then I reckon we can go home," Lucas said. "George Wilkins."

"Sir," George said.

"Wait," the salesman said. He and Lucas faced each other in the darkness, two shadows, faceless. "There wasn't over a hundred here. Most of it is in the other place. I'll give you ten per cent."

"Hit was my letter," Lucas said. "Hit ain't enough."

"Twenty. And that's all."

"I wants half," Lucas said. "And that mule paper, and another paper to say the finding machine belongs to me."

"Tomorrow," the salesman said.

"I wants hit now," Lucas said. The invisible face stared at his own invisible one. Both he and George seemed to feel the windless summer air moving to the trembling of the white man's body.

"How much did you say them other fellows found?"

"Twenty-two thousand dollars," Lucas said.

"Hit mought a been more," George said. "Hit wuz a big — "

"All right," the salesman said suddenly. "I'll give you a bill of sale for the machine as soon as we finish."

"I wants it now," Lucus said. They went back to the car. While Lucas held the flashlight, they watched the salesman rip open his patent brief case and jerk out of it and fling toward Lucas the bill of sale for the mule. Then they watched his jerking hand fill in the long printed form with its carbon duplicates and sign it and rip out one of the duplicates.

"You get possession tomorrow morning," he said. "It belongs to me until then. O.K.?"

"All right," Lucas said. "What about them fifty dollars we done already found? Does I get half of them?" This time the salesman just laughed, harsh and steady and without mirth. Then he was out of the car. He didn't even wait to close his brief case. They could see him half running back toward the orchard, carrying the divining machine and the flashlight both.

"Come on," he said. "Bring the spade." Lucas gathered up the two papers, the bill of sale which he had signed for the mule, and the one which the salesman had signed for the divining machine.

"George Wilkins," he said.

"Sir," George said.

"Take that mule back whar you got hit. Then go tell Roth Edmonds he can quit worrying folks about her."

Lucas mounted the gnawed steps beside which the bright mare stood beneath the heavy saddle, and entered the commissary, with its ranked shelves of tinned food, the hooks from which hung collars and trace chains and hames and ploughlines, its smell of molasses and cheese and leather and kerosene. Edmonds swiveled around from the roll-top desk. "Where've you been?" he said. "I sent word two days ago I wanted to see you."

"I was in bed, I reckon," Lucas said. "I been had to stay up all night for the last three nights. I can't stand hit no more like when I was a young man."

"So you've found that out at last, have you? What I wanted to see you about is that damn St. Louis fellow. Dan says he's still hanging around here. What's he doing?"

"Hunting buried money," Lucas said.

"What?" Edmonds said. "Doing what, did you say?"

"Hunting buried money," Lucas said. "Using my finding box. He rents it from me. That's why I been had to stay up all night. To go with him and make sho' I'd get the box back. But last night he never turnt up, so I reckon he's done gone back wherever it was he come from."

Edmonds sat in the swivel chair and stared at him. "Rents it from you? The same machine he sold you?"

"For twenty-five dollars a night," Lucas said. "That's what he chawged me to use hit one night. So I reckon that's the regular rent. Leastways, that's what I chawges." Edmonds stared at him as he leaned against the counter with only the slight shrinkage of the jaws to show that he was an old man, in his clean, faded overalls and shirt and the open vest looped across by a heavy gold watch chain, and the thirty-dollar handmade beaver hat which Edmonds's father had given him forty years ago above the face which was not sober and not grave but wore no expression whatever. It was absolutely impenetrable. "Because he was looking in the wrong place," Lucas said. "He was looking up there on that hill. That money is buried down there by the creek. Them two white men that slipped in here that night three years ago and got clean away with twenty-two thousand dollars — " At last Edmonds got himself out of the chair onto his feet. He was trembling. He drew a deep breath, walking steadily toward the old Negro leaning against the counter, his lower lip full of snuff. "And now that we done got shut of him," Lucas said, "me and George Wilkins — " Walking steadily toward him, Edmonds expelled his breath. He had believed it would be a shout, but it was not much more than a whisper.

"Get out of here," he said. "Go home. And don't come back. Don't ever come back. When you need supplies, send your wife after them."

Lead Her Like a Pigeon

by JESSAMYN WEST

A Californian whose antecedents go back to the Quaker settlements in Indiana, Jessamyn West made her debut in the Atlantic. *We were fortunate to publish most of her first book in the* Atlantic, *and helped her find the title for it,* The Friendly Persuasion.

DECEMBER 1944

It was deep in May. Fingers had lifted the green strawberry leaves and had found fruit beneath them. The bees had swarmed twice. Cherries, bright as Christmas candles, hung from the trees. Wheat was heading up. The wind was from the south and sent a drift of locust blossoms like summer snow, Mattie thought, through the air.

She left her churn on the back porch and stood for a minute by the springhouse with uplifted face to see how locust snow felt; but the wind died down and no more blossoms fell, so she went back to her churning.

She counted slowly as she moved the dasher up and down. She was keeping track of the least and most strokes it took to bring butter. This at any rate was not going to be a least-time. "Eighty-eight, eighty-nine — " Josh and Labe were putting horsehairs into the rain barrel to turn into worms. The hired man stuck his head out of the barn door, saw her, and directly pulled it in again.

"Mattie," called her mother, "get finished with thy churning and ride over to the Bents' with some rocks." Mattie could smell the rocks baking: raisins and hickory nuts all bedded down together in sweet dough.

"Lavony Bent's as queer as Dick's hatband," her mother called above the slap and gurgle of the dasher, "half Indian and a newcomer. She needs a token to show she's welcome."

Listening, Mattie slowed her churning. "Bring that butter humping," her mother said. "Thee'll have to get a soon start or it'll get dark on thee." She came to the kitchen door, rosy from the oven's heat, bringing Mattie a new-baked rock.

"Day fading so soon," she said. Mattie looked at her mother because of the sadness in her voice, and felt uncertainty and sorrow herself.

"There'll be another to match it tomorrow," her mother promised. "Its equal or better, Mattie. That red sky's a sure sign."

The butter was slow coming — only five strokes short of the most she had ever counted. "Thee'd best go as thee is, Mattie."

"In this?" said Mattie.

"Who's to see?" asked her mother. "None but Bents and hoot owls at this hour."

Mattie wouldn't have named them together — hoot owls and the black-haired brown-faced boys she had watched walking riverward with fishing poles over their shoulders.

"Once thee starts combing and changing, it'll be nightfall."

So Mattie rode as she was to the Bents', barefoot and in her blue anchor print which had faded until the anchors were almost as pale as the sea that lapped about them.

She carried the rocks in a little wooden box her mother intended to make into a footstool. So far, it was only painted white, with cranes and cattails on each side. The brown cattails were set onto the box with so much paint that they curved up plump as real ones beneath Mattie's exploring thumb.

Old Polly walked like a horse in a dream — slow — slow. Tonight, a short way on the pike and then across the wood lot. Mattie ate a rock, pulled down a limb to see it spring back in place, remembered what she had heard about the Bents.

"Never seen a more comfortable sight in my life," her father called one day, and there on a padded chair was Sile Bent riding down the pike in his manure wagon, sitting and reading like a man at ease in his parlor. "Wonderful emancipation," her father said. "Thee mark it, Mattie. The spirit of man's got no limitations."

Sile Bent read and farmed. His boys, all but Gardiner, fished and farmed. "Gardiner's a reader like his pa," said Mattie's father. "Off to Normal, studying to be a teacher. He figures on getting shut of the manure wagon and having just the book left."

But the day she rode through meant more to Mattie than her destination. In the woods it was warm and sheltered, and the sun, setting, lay like butter on the new green leaves.

At the far edge of the woods she stopped for a minute at the old Wright place. A little white tumbling-down house, empty for years, stood there — a forgotten house; but flowers still came up about it in the patterns in which Mrs. Wright had planted them. It was a sad, beautiful sight, Mattie thought, to see flowers hands had planted growing alone in the woods with not an eye to note whether they did well or not: the snowball bush where the front gate had been, spice pinks still keeping to their circle by the steps, and white flags, gold-powdered now at sunset, by the ruined upping block. A pair of doves, as she watched, slid down from the deep shadows of the woods and wheeled about in the sunlit clearing as if coming home. Mattie stretched a hand to them. "Thee don't act like wildings," she said.

She slipped down from fat Old Polly and, carrying her box of cookies, went to pick some flags. These flowers and buildings have known people for too long, she thought, to be happy alone. They have grown away from their own kind and forgotten the language of woods and doves and long to hear household words again. To hear at bedtime a woman coming to the door for a sight of stars and saying, "There'll be rain before morning. A circle round the moon — and the cock crowing. It's a sure sign." Or a man at morning, scanning the sky as he hitches up his suspenders, "A weather breeder. Have to hustle the hay in."

Mattie talked for the house and flowers to hear as she gathered the flags and laid them across the top of the cookie-filled footstool.

"If it's a dry summer I'll bring some water," she said. "I couldn't bear to lie abed a hot night, and you parching here. I'll carry buckets from the branch if the well's dry, and some night I'll come and light a candle in the house so it'll look like olden times. I'll sing a song in the house and it'll be like Mrs. Wright playing on her melodeon again."

"Sing now, why don't you?"

She was bending over the flags, but she wasn't frightened, the voice was so quiet. It was a young man's voice, though, and she dropped the flags in her hand onto her bare feet before she turned to face him.

"No human would enjoy my singing — only maybe an old house that can't be choosy."

"I'm not choosy, either."

"No, I'm on an errand to take some rocks to Lavony Bent. I only stopped to pick some flags."

"Well, I'm Gard Bent," the boy said, "and I'll walk along home with you. What's your name?"

"Martha Truth Birdwell. Only I'm mostly called Mattie."

"Martha Truth Birdwell. That's as pretty as any song. If he had known you" — and Gardiner Bent held up the book he was carrying — "he'd have written a poem called 'Martha Truth.'"

Mattie saw the name on the book. "He mostly writes of Jeans and Marys," she said. Now maybe this Bent boy wouldn't think she was a know-nothing, barefooted and talking to herself. "Thee take the rocks on to thy ma. I've dallied here so long it'll be dark going home through the wood lot."

"No, I'll walk back with you to the pike. Ma'd never forgive me if I let you go home with your box empty. The boys have been on the river this afternoon. They'll have a fine mess of catfish. Can I help you onto your horse?"

Mattie would dearly have liked being handed onto her horse had she been rightly dressed and Old Polly saddled, but that would have to wait for another time. She would not be hoisted like a sack of meal, plopped barefoot onto a saddleless horse. She stood stock-still, the flags covering her feet, and said nothing.

"I'll get the rest of my books," the boy said.

While he was gone Mattie led Old Polly to the upping block and settled herself as sedately as if she were riding sidesaddle, one bare foot curled daintily beneath her.

Old Polly stepped slowly along in the dusk down the back road that led to the Bents', and Gard walked beside her. There wasn't much Indian about him, Mattie thought, unless it was his black hair and his quiet, toed-in walk. But his hair wasn't Indian straight, and his eyes weren't black at all, but the color of the sandstone in a go-to-meeting watch fob. It was a pleasing face, a face she did not tire of regarding. Her eyes searched its tenderness and boldness in the May dusk.

"I thought thee was away at Vernon, studying at the Normal."

"I was, but it's out. Now I'm studying to take the teachers' examinations. I've got the promise of the school at Rush Branch when I pass. That's why I come to Wright's — to study where it's quiet. If it gets dark on you, you could see your way home by the fireflies, they're so thick," he finished, as if ashamed of telling so much of himself.

"Fireflies. Is that what thee calls lightning bugs?"

"Elsewhere they're known as fireflies."

It was full sunset before they reached the Bent place. Lavony Bent was cleaning fish on a stump at the edge of the yard. Sile Bent was on the back steps getting the last of the light onto the book he was reading. Two black-haired boys were rolling about on the ground wrestling; a third was trying to bring a tune from a homemade-looking horn. There weren't any flowers or grass about the Bents' house. The yard was trodden flat and swept clean.

Gard called out, "Ma, this is Martha Truth Birdwell come to bring you some cookies."

Mrs. Bent didn't stop her fish-cleaning, but looked up kindly enough. "Light down, Martha Truth, light down. I knowed your folks years ago when we's all younger than you are now."

Sile Bent closed his book on his finger and walked over to Mattie. He was a little, plump man with a big head of red hair and a silky red mustache. "If it isn't Spring!" he said. "Spring riding a white horse and with flowers in her hands."

Mattie was too taken aback to answer, but Gard laughed. "She's got a box of cookies under the flowers, Pa."

Mattie handed the box of cookies and the white flags to him. "Spring for looks and Summer for gifts," said Sile Bent, and took a rock in two bites, shaking the crumbs from his mustache like a water-drenched dog.

Mattie was afraid to talk to this strange man who carried a book as if it had been a pipe or a jackknife, and spoke of her as though she were absent, or a painted picture.

Mrs. Bent took the head from a still quivering catfish with a single clean stroke. The boy with the horn started a tune she knew, but he couldn't get far with it. "Lead her like a pigeon — Lead her like a pigeon — " he played over and over. Mattie's ears ached to hear the next notes, to have the piece played through to its ending, not left broken and unfinished. Her mind hummed the tune for him:

> Lead her like a pigeon,
> Bed her like a dove.
> Whisper when I'm near her,
> "You're my only love."

But the horn could not follow. "Lead her like a pigeon," it said once more, then gave up.

The wrestlers groaned and strained. They turned up the earth beneath them like a plow. A catfish leaped from the stump and swam again, most pitifully, in the dust.

"I'll have to be turning homewards," Mattie spoke suddenly. "Could I have my box? Ma's fixing to make a footstool of it."

Mrs. Bent sent Gard into the house to empty the cookies; then she lined the footstool with leaves and filled it with fish.

"There's a mess of fish for your breakfast," she said. "Tell your ma she's so clever at sharing I can't hope to keep pace with her."

As they went out of the yard, Mattie once more on Old Polly, and

Gard walking beside her, Sile Bent called after them, "Persephone and Pluto. Don't eat any pomegranate seeds, Martha Truth."

"What does he mean?" asked Mattie. What Mr. Bent had said didn't sound like English to her.

"Persephone was a girl," Gard said, "the goddess of spring, and Pluto, another god, stole her away to live underground with him. And while she was gone it was winter on earth."

"She's back on earth now, isn't she?" Mattie asked, watching the wink of lightning bugs among the dark leaves.

"Yes, she's back again," Gard said.

They parted at the edge of the woods, where Mattie could see the lights of home glimmering down the road. Supper was over when she brought her box of catfish into the kitchen, and the dishes half washed.

"Sit down, child," her mother said, "and have thy supper. What kept thee?"

"The Bents all talk a lot," said Mattie. "It didn't seem polite to go and leave them all talking."

"They'll not be hindered by thy leaving, never fear. Eat, eat. Thy food will lose its savor."

"I can't eat," Mattie said. "I don't seem to have any relish for victuals." She got the dish towel from the rack and started drying.

"Was thee fanciful," asked her mother, who never attributed fright to anything but fancy, "crossing the wood lot?"

"No. Gardiner Bent came with me."

"The Normal School boy?"

"Yes," said Mattie. "He's learned. Flowers. Fireflies. Poetry. Gods and goddesses. It's all one to him," she declared ardently. "He can lay his tongue to anything and give thee a fact about it. Oh, he's full of facts. He's primed for an examination and knows more than he can hold in."

Mattie made the plates she dried fly through her hands like thistledown — as if they were weightless as thistles and as imperishable. Her hands were deft but they had not her mother's flashing grace, and they were silent; they could not play the tune she envied, the tinkling bell-like song of her mother's wedding ring against the china; the constant light clatter of gold against glass and silver that said, "I'm a lady grown and mistress of dishes and cupboards."

Mattie hummed a little.

"What's thee humming?" her mother asked. "Seems like I've heard it."

" 'Lead Her Like a Pigeon,' " Mattie said, smiling.

"Play-party tune." Her mother held her hands above the soapy water and looked far away. "Weevily wheat. Once I was tempted to lift my foot to that."

Lift her foot! Mattie looked at her mother, the Quaker preacher, whose foot now never peeped from beneath her full and seemly skirts. Once tempted — The wedding-ring music began again, but Mattie was watching, not drying. A long time ago tempted; yes, there was something in the way her mother would bury her face in a cabbage rose, or run to the door when Father's spring wagon turned off the pike, that showed her the black-haired girl who once listened to that music.

"Who does the Bent boy favor, Mattie?"

"His mother, I reckon. But handsomer. He's got a face to remember," Mattie said earnestly. "A proud, learned face. He's got eyes the color of sandstones. When he walks there isn't any up and down. It's a pleasure to watch him walk."

Mattie's mother put a washed skillet on the still warm stove to dry. "After a good heart," she said, "the least a woman can do is pick a face she fancies. Men's so much alike and many so sorry, that's the very least. If a man's face pleasures thee, that doesn't change. That is something to bank on. Thy father," she said, "has always been a comely man."

She turned back to her dishpan. "Why, Mattie," she said, "what's thee crying about?"

Mattie would not say. Then she burst out: "Pushing me off. Pushing me out of my own home. Thee talking about men that way — as if I would marry one. Anxious to be shut of me." She cried into her already wet dish towel. "My own mother," she sobbed.

"Why, lovey," her mother said, and went to her, but Mattie buried her face more deeply in her dish towel and stumbled up the back stairs. "My own mother," she wailed.

"What's the trouble? What's Mattie taking on about?"

Eliza Birdwell looked up at her husband, filling the doorway from the sitting room like a staunch timber. "Well, Jess," she said, "I think Mattie got a sudden inkling of what leaving home'll be like."

"Leaving home?" asked Jess. "Getting married? Thee think that's a crying matter, Eliza?"

Eliza looked at the face that had always pleasured her. "Thee knows I don't, Jess," she said.

Jess smiled. "Seems like," he said, "I have a recollection of some few tears thee shed those first — " But Eliza would have none of that. "Tsk, tsk," she said, her wedding ring beating a lively tattoo against the last kettle, "tsk, tsk, Jess Birdwell."

"Thee happy, now?" Jess asked, smiling.

Eliza wouldn't say, but she hummed a little raveling of a song.

"Seems as if I know that," Jess said. "A long time ago."

"Like as not," Eliza agreed, and handed him the pan to empty.

Jess went out with it, trying the tune over. "Tum-te-tum-te-tum. I can't name it," he said when he came back, "but it runs in my mind I know it."

"Thee knows it, Jess, never fear," Eliza said. She took the empty pan from him, her wedding ring making one more musical note.

Creole Love Song

by NATHANIEL LaMAR

Nathaniel LaMar, who was educated at Phillips Exeter and at Harvard, is now in his early twenties; a very talented Negro writer, he has recently been awarded an Atlantic grant with which to bring to completion his first novel.

JUNE 1955

I used to work for the LaBotte family. That's how I know what I'm going to tell you about Jemmie LaBotte. They lived up on Bayou Street in one of those big pink stucco houses with a wide tile porch and tall windows with fancy, yellow frosty-looking windowpanes.

Old man LaBotte was a doctor. He was queer in a way. I used to hear some of the white people around town say he was nothing but a "ham-fat" doctor. I never could quite get the straight of it. I do know one thing, though. He didn't go around like the other white doctors in New Orleans did. I mean he never went around to highfalutin people like the kind of fine ladies his wife was always playing bridge with. As far as I know, he didn't treat anybody but the Creoles down in the Quarter. Some people said it was because Dr. LaBotte was a Creole himself. They said that about Mrs. LaBotte too; but I didn't believe it. He used to come down to the Quarter whenever somebody got hurt on their job or beat up in a fight. He had a smart way about him; he could always get money out of his patients. I know a lot of people that didn't pay their house rent or their electric bills, but Dr. LaBotte got money out of them. He had a shiny green car, and whenever he came driving through the Quarter everybody would get in their windows and doorways and start yelling and waving at him; even old people.

I'd shout just like the rest of them. "Hey! Hey! There go Doctor. Doctor! Doctor! Hey there, Dr. LaBotte!!!"

That's the way we'd go on. Sometimes he'd have his son Jemmie in the car with him. That was before Jemmie went off to medical school. Jemmie was almost grown, but he'd hang out of the car window and laugh when we'd shout.

Dr. LaBotte used to come to see my Aunt Albertine sometimes. My parents went to Chicago when I was little, and they didn't come back. So I lived with Aunt Albertine. She was young and pretty — had a lot of men always hanging around our house after her. She had yellow skin and long brown hair; and she had a fine shape. She used to drink a lot. But the thing about her was that she knew it was bad for her. So she'd make me go out to a pay-station phone and call up Dr. LaBotte to come see her. I don't know what he'd do for her because she wasn't really sick. He talked to her; that was about all. But he could get her out of her drinking moods and she'd be all right for a while.

One day in the springtime Dr. LaBotte came to see us when Aunt Albertine was coming out of one of her moods. I was surprised, because he came to talk about me. "Why don't you let Emory come see if he'd like to work for us up at our house, 'Tine? Light work — kind of helping around the house — you know. He could save, maybe — go back and finish high school in a little bit."

At first Aunt Albertine didn't say anything. Finally she sized me up and said, "He fifteen. Let him do what he want to. *I* don't care. It ain't like he was going far off." She could tell I wanted to go by the way I was looking at her.

So I began working up at the LaBottes'. I think it was March when I started, and Jemmie LaBotte came home from medical school that June. He was a lot like his daddy; he laughed like him and acted just about like him. He was glad to be back home. Some days he'd roam through the house just smiling, like he'd never seen it before. And every evening he'd go walking down in the Quarter. Maybe he was hunting for somebody to cure, people said. I guess Dr. LaBotte was glad Jemmie was home too. He laughed more than I'd heard him laugh when Jemmie wasn't there.

Jemmie LaBotte didn't pay me much attention. I'd pass by him in the

house and he always looked like he was thinking to himself, or sometimes he'd be talking to his mother and daddy. Sometimes he sat in the
living room and read all the morning. I knew they were medical books;
most of them were old and had pages as flimsy as tissue paper.

One day I asked him, "You remember all you read?"

"Yeah. I sure do." He laughed when he said it; he was a friendly
somebody after all. "They make you — in a medical school."

"But you're not going back, are you? Your mother says you're a doctor
now."

"I want to do what Daddy's doing — doctor up people down there
where you live." I could see he meant it.

I wondered why Jemmie LaBotte didn't have any friends. Once in a
while somebody would call him on the phone and he'd talk a little while
to whoever it was, but he never went anywhere much.

It got so Jemmie and his daddy argued. They'd sit out on the front
porch late in the afternoon. I could hear them through the screen door.
The old man's voice would be squeaky and high like he was afraid of
something. "You sure you want to stay in New Orleans and practice?"
he'd say. "You could always go back up there and study another year,
if you wanted. You could be a specialist!" They'd talk a long time, and
Jemmie would get worked up and keep telling Dr. LaBotte how much
he wanted to be just like him. Jemmie LaBotte was always so serious
about everything. "I don't want you to quit, Daddy," he'd say. "I'm not
trying to make you *quit*. I just want to go down there with you."

"You don't know how they live — it's hard to get to know. I understand every one of 'em down there." Dr. LaBotte's voice sounded so old.
I don't think I'd ever thought he was old before. It was almost pitiful
the way he kept trying so hard to get Jemmie's mind off staying in New
Orleans; like there was something in New Orleans he was ashamed of.

Mrs. LaBotte took Jemmie's side. She must have thought old man
LaBotte was jealous of Jemmie's being young and right out of school.
Most of the time Dr. LaBotte wouldn't say anything to her when she
started talking, because he knew what she was leading up to. "You
know good and well you ought to let Jemmie make some of your calls for
you — 'specially those late calls. It'd be better for *him* to go down there
in the Quarter at night when you're tired."

It got so when somebody from the Quarter called up old man LaBotte
he'd get his bag and leave the house before Mrs. LaBotte and Jemmie
had a chance to ask him where he was going. And when he was home he
stayed shut up in the little office room and acted crabbed.

Mrs. LaBotte was the one who finally did it. One morning Dr. LaBotte didn't come out of his bedroom early like he usually did. And Mrs. LaBotte tiptoed around, because she said he needed rest. That bedroom door stayed closed even when the phone started ringing. It was an old man called David calling up from a grocery store. He wanted to tell Dr. LaBotte he had the "choky-feeling" in his chest again and he couldn't lie down and sleep. So Mrs. LaBotte went in the bedroom. But there wasn't any fussing between them. All Dr. LaBotte said was "Tell Jemmie he can go down there — he wants to go." I think Mrs. LaBotte had worn him down to nothing.

I went down to the Quarter with Jemmie LaBotte because I knew where David's house was. It's hard to find a place you're looking for in the Quarter because the house numbers are all faded off. I'm telling you the truth, it felt good riding through the Quarter in old man LaBotte's shiny car, because everybody *really did* look when they saw it was me.

David's house was like the rest of the houses down there; the weatherboards were old and needed some paint. And it had fancy rusty iron banisters around the front porch, with iron flowers and curls. The room old David was in had the shades down and it was black-dark, except David had a little candle sitting in a piece of saucer on his chiffonier. Jemmie LaBotte didn't know what that little candle was for. He didn't pay it much attention at first; but I knew. You see old folks always burning a candle when they're afraid they're going to die, or afraid somebody in their family is going to die. Sometimes you're supposed to put pepper on the candle because everybody says it'll keep the worms from eating you after you're dead. David was propped up on a pillow. I sat down on a little stool by the door. Jemmie said, "You know good and well you ought to have some air in here, hot as it is." And then he went over to the window to let up the shade.

But old David screwed up his face at Jemmie LaBotte. "I wish you wouldn't be messin' wid that window shade, 'cause that air out there got things in it bad for my feeling right here." He hit his chest with his wrinkled-up little hand. I could see he didn't like Jemmie LaBotte.

"Air never did hurt anybody's heart trouble," Jemmie LaBotte said.

"Your daddy don't never make me keep no air in here if I don't want none." I think that was the first thing that got Jemmie. And then old David wouldn't let Jemmie touch him with the needle. He held out those skinny old arms like he was scared to death. "Naw! Naw! You ain't going to put that thing in me. I don't want to have that thing sticking in my arm. And your daddy don't never stick me with none, either!"

I felt sorry for Jemmie LaBotte. He stood there like he didn't know what to do. Old David kept on hollering, "Oh Jesus! Oh Jesus! You going to stick me with that *thing*. Your daddy don't never do nothing like that!" Finally Jemmie LaBotte just took a good hold on his arm and jabbed him very quick; and you'd have thought David was having a baby by the way he was taking on. But after that I started feeling good toward Jemmie LaBotte, because I liked the way he just went on and stuck the needle in anyhow. And he tried to be nice to old David after he gave him that shot: he told him to be quiet because he was through and ready to go, and he said he hoped he'd rest easier.

But old David wasn't ready for Jemmie to go away. "You ain't going to give me nothing like what your daddy give me when he come?"

"What'd my daddy give you?"

"Some kind of stuff — "

"What stuff does he give you?"

"That stuff what make me sleep a lot. *You know*, Mr. Jemmie La-Botte." He kept smiling a sly, hateful smile. "Your daddy always give me a piece of paper that I can get it with at the drug-store-man's. Your daddy say it's codeine."

"My daddy didn't give you any codeine. Where'd you get that, talking about codeine? Don't you know your heart's too bad for you to be taking anything like that?"

"Well, that's what your daddy say it was. Codeine. Make me sleep." He winked at Jemmie LaBotte like he expected him to understand something. "Your daddy give me that stuff instead of all that sticking me with that goddam old needle."

I don't know what made me think I had to say something; because it wasn't my business. But Jemmie LaBotte had such a funny look on his face all of a sudden I said, "Don't pay attention to old man big-head David. They say he don't never tell the truth about nothing." And we went out of the house with David still begging for the "sleepy stuff."

Jemmie LaBotte just asked me one thing while we were going back to Bayou Street. "Why'd old David have that little candle? How come he didn't have the electric light on?"

"That's the way a lot of folks do when they're scared of sickness. You smell how that candle was making that stink in there?"

"I'd have made him put it out if I'd known that was what it was."

"A lots of people keep a sick candle," I said. "I bet your daddy never did try to make anybody put out their sick candle. They wouldn't do it anyhow — for him or nobody else." He didn't say anything after that.

The day after we went down to old David's, Mrs. LaBotte called me out on the porch and she tried to make me think she just wanted me to sit out there and rock back and forth in the rocker and talk to keep her company. But she kept on trying to get it out of me about what happened when we went down to the Quarter. I didn't tell her a thing, though. It wasn't my business.

But I did tell Aunt Albertine how Mrs. LaBotte tried to pick me and Aunt Albertine said, "You better be careful — that's all *I* can say." She'd seen old man David that day at the grocery up on Ogechee Street and he was telling everybody Jemmie LaBotte was a good-for-nothing doctor; and then he'd roll up his sleeve and show the little place the needle made. Aunt Albertine said he was clowning and telling everybody Jemmie LaBotte was nothing but "ca-ca."

About a week went by and old man LaBotte didn't seem to be getting better of whatever was wrong with him; at least he didn't come out of his room. And Mrs. LaBotte kept saying all he needed was rest and for people to let him alone and not worry him. There was something wrong between him and Jemmie ever since the day Jemmie went down to David's. But as far as I know, Jemmie hadn't even seen him since then; so I didn't understand what it could be. Then one Sunday morning early a lady named Mrs. Clara called up the house to ask for Dr. LaBotte because her little girl was having a fit. It was so early Jemmie and Mrs. LaBotte didn't even bother to tell Dr. LaBotte.

Jemmie LaBotte took me with him again, and we went driving fast through those gray little snaky-looking streets in the Quarter. We saw a lot of people walking the sidewalks; some of them were still drunk from Saturday night. When we got to Mrs. Clara's house she was out in a funny kind of silk dress washing the steps to her front porch with a jar full of pepper-water. She was real fat and she had her behind turned up to us because she was down on her knees scrubbing the steps; and at first it looked funny. But she turned around and it was pitiful because her big fat face was screwed up and she was crying. The pepper-water had the front steps smelling loud like grease and vinegar. So Jemmie LaBotte asked her what that stuff was and why she wasn't in the house with her little girl. Mrs. Clara said, "I ain't in there 'cause I got to wash with this old pepper-water. Keeps off bad things from coming in the house — keep 'um way from my baby." Jemmie LaBotte told her she had no business believing in such things and he made her put down the jar with the pepper-water in it. But she kept on saying, "Your own daddy

— your flesh-and-blood daddy — your daddy — he say it's fine if I want to wash off them front steps with my pepper-water!"

I sat on the porch while Jemmie LaBotte was inside. I'd seen that little girl lots of times with Mrs. Clara when they'd be walking up Ogechee Street. Her name was Monica and she was about eight years old, and she was pretty because she had a round face with a funny kind of purple eyes and light, hay-colored hair. But you could tell something was wrong with her because she walked so slow and funny and held her head like her neck was made out of rubber.

When Mrs. Clara came to the screen door with Jemmie LaBotte she was saying, "Ain't you going to give her none of them pink pills what make her sleep? Your daddy say them be good for her — they make her lay real quiet so she don't have no more of them fits. She don't roll her eyes or nothing if she have them pink pills."

Jemmie LaBotte kept looking at the little thing around Mrs. Clara's neck. It was hanging on a greasy string. I don't think he knew what it was, but I did, because my Aunt Albertine always has one so she'll be sure to have good luck. It was a little ball of hair; only this was a ball of hay-colored hair. Mrs. Clara and Jemmie were both acting upset.

"I'm not going to give her anything to make her sleep, because it wouldn't be good for her. She had a *fit!* It's not good for her to go to sleep on medicine, I don't care *what* my daddy told you." So we left, and Mrs. Clara stood on her front porch; and she was crying and sprinkling pepper-water because she said Jemmie LaBotte must be evil and she didn't even want the smell of him around her house. "You ain't no good kind of a man like *Doctor*" was the last thing we heard her say.

Then Jemmie LaBotte told his mother. They sat in the living room on that big settee and he told her how old David asked him for codeine and said Dr. LaBotte always gave it to him. And he told her how he didn't want to believe a thing like that on his daddy; but he told her what happened with Mrs. Clara. "That little girl's name is Monica, and the whites of her eyes are all dulled over. Like she's been asleep a *long* time! She's had a lot of codeine — I can tell she has."

Once Mrs. LaBotte looked up and saw me standing in the doorway, but she turned her head away. Dr. LaBotte came in the living room; I don't know whether he heard them or what. But Jemmie didn't act like he was there. "I thought my daddy was something." He said it just like the old man wasn't there at all.

And Dr. LaBotte said, "They do magic down there, Juanita!" When he called her name Mrs. LaBotte put her little handkerchief up to her mouth. She made a choking noise. And you should've seen *Dr.* LaBotte — the way he blazed his eyes. "Real magic — *real!*" he said. "And they won't stop. They wouldn't stop it for me. What in the world makes you think *I* could make them stop?"

"You've got them so all they want is codeine. You think codeine can do an epileptic fit any good, Daddy?"

"I told you — you don't know how they are. You think they'll take medicine, don't you?"

"You're bad as they are. You put them all to sleep. You can put them to sleep all right!"

Dr. LaBotte said, "You get so you'll do anything for them if you can just get 'em to love you." And then he went out of the living room and left Mrs. LaBotte and Jemmie still sitting there on the settee. He walked away slow, like he was so old.

From then on strange things started going on. Jemmie LaBotte could hardly wait until some more of the old man's patients called up so he could go back down to the Quarter. It got so the main thing for Jemmie was his big idea about making them like him down there.

But Jemmie LaBotte didn't know the word had got around about him. It just takes one mouth to spread things in the Quarter, and David and Mrs. Clara ran their mouths a plenty. Everybody down there was whispering old man LaBotte was sick and going to die and his boy didn't know a thing to do for him or anybody. His boy wasn't nothing but "ca-ca" and a good-for-nothing. That's what they said about Jemmie LaBotte. David told everybody he could feel funny things crawling in his arm where Jemmie LaBotte stuck him with that needle. And Mrs. Clara said her Monica was bloody-eyed and always screaming with fits, because Jemmie LaBotte didn't give her the sleepy-stuff that would quiet her down.

Then one day Jemmie LaBotte got tired of waiting. He must've known what was wrong by that time. So he went down to the Quarter. That evening when I got home Aunt Albertine told me, "Jemmie LaBotte come driving down here today. Folks say he was trying to see old David and when David found out he locked up his door on him."

Aunt Albertine laughed about Jemmie LaBotte because she was just like the rest of them; she didn't think he was anything.

But I give him credit. He tried hard in the Quarter. He tried to get David and Mrs. Clara to believe he wanted to do them some good. But David would always lock his door, and Mrs. Clara wouldn't even let him come up on her front porch. It got so bad people would sit in their windows and laugh whenever they'd see him coming. But he kept on going down there.

Then one day he did get a phone call. It was August then, and that day was rainy. The house was quiet like somebody was dead or going to die. And it was so hot all the windows and doors were open and you could hear the rain hitting the gardenia bushes out in the front yard. Whoever it was calling sounded like they were crying. All they said was for somebody to come down to Mama Callie's house quick. So Jemmie went down there by himself. I could see he wasn't thinking about taking me down here with him that day. But I wouldn't have gone anyhow, because I didn't like that old Mama Callie.

When I was little I used to go over to her house with Aunt Albertine. Aunt Albertine never has stopped going to Mama Callie's because Mama Callie knew her when she was just knee-high. In the first place I didn't like Mama Callie because she was always coughing. Everybody knew she had t.b., and she was sleepy-looking and slow-talking because she stayed all doped up on codeine to ease her coughing spells. She must have been about seventy-five years old, and she had a sister named Alena who was somewhere around fifty. She and Alena spent all day making little charms and things; and they sold them to a lot of people. Like if Mrs. Clara wanted a hair ball out of little Monica's hair she'd cut off a snip of hair and take it to Mama Callie, and Mama Callie would do things like dip it in hot chicken fat and tie it on a string and wrap it up for a week in senna leaves. Then she'd give it back to Mrs. Clara when it was ready to do some good.

Sometimes on a hot day you'd walk past their house and you'd see Mama Callie and Alena sitting in the open window and Mama Callie would always be singing something in French. She said that song was a Creole song her father taught her when she was a little girl. They say she was real proud of that, because her and Alena's father was a Frenchman. Anyway, whenever she and Alena sat in the window Mama Callie would hold her old sleepy-looking face out the window to see who was walking up and down the street. Alena, who liked men, would be just sitting there beside Mama Callie brushing her hair. She had hair that came down to her shoulders and she always brushed it with a brush soaked in strong tea to keep it from getting gray.

When Jemmie LaBotte came back from Mama Callie's he looked discouraged, and he didn't say a thing. But that evening Alena was going around telling everybody in the Quarter about how when Jemmie La-Botte got to Mama Callie she'd had a hemorrhage and blood was coming out of her nose and mouth all over the bed sheets. Alena said, "He come bringing his fancy bag with them bottles in it. He thought he was going to give Callie one of them needles of his, but me and Callie wouldn't even let him get near the bed. I told him he wasn't going to touch my Callie!" Alena was bragging about how she told Jemmie La-Botte right to his face they'd just called him so he could give Mama Callie some codeine. But he wouldn't give her any, and he started telling Alena how much Mama Callie needed a hospital, or at least some medicine. Alena laughed. "That Jemmie LaBotte wanted to pay me money to let him stick Callie with one of them shiny needles — pay me *money!* Callie and me told him if he couldn't put her to sleep there wasn't nothing he could do. We fixed him. Callie, bad off as she was, she couldn't help but laugh at him. We fixed him all right!"

Alena said she warmed up some pig oil with mustard seeds and went to work on Mama Callie and started rubbing her all over with it right there in front of Jemmie LaBotte. "He was just standing there looking. And he looked like he couldn't take his eyes off. He couldn't even stop looking for nothing. Like a young'un watching his daddy in the bed with his ma." Everybody laughed at Alena's saying that. "I could see he didn't like it for nothing, but there wasn't a thing he could do about me rubbing up Callie with that hog grease. Callie was warm, and shiny as she could be when I got through with her. He just stood up there like he had that hog grease on his brain — stood there just looking 'cause that's all he could do — look."

Alena almost bragged herself to death talking about it. She said before he left their house Jemmie LaBotte cursed her and Mama Callie out and told them there wasn't anything he could do for anybody like them. "But you know what I say to that Jemmie LaBotte? I told him we can make him do anything we God-a-mighty please. I say to him we can low-more make him come right straight back down here anytime we want to. We going to show him better'n we can tell him."

About a week after all that happened Jemmie LaBotte asked me if I knew Mama Callie and Alena, and I told him yes. Then he started talking about how queer they were. He talked so fast; like he couldn't tell me quick enough. I didn't see why he was acting so worried. "That old Mama Callie — you know what she did? She wouldn't even let me put a stethoscope on her. You ever see all the little baskets in there — in her bedroom? They were all full of leaves!"

I knew the little baskets he was talking about. "Yeah. They're willow leaves."

"You know what she does with them?"

"Naw," I said, "I never did know."

I knew what those willow leaves were for, but I didn't tell him because I didn't see what difference it made to him.

One evening Mama Callie called up again; Jemmie LaBotte didn't seem to want to go down there. But his mother couldn't see why. "You ought to go on if they called you, Jemmie," she kept saying. She was so proud of him because she thought he was everything old man La-Botte never *had* been. "You have to go right on down there, even if that old lady won't let you attend to her — she *called* you."

Mama Callie and Alena must have known he'd come, because they told Aunt Albertine and a lot of other people to be on the lookout if they wanted to see the car when it drove up. Mama Callie was feeling weak and puny, but she was sitting in the window singing that little French song, and Alena was sitting beside her brushing her hair with that brush she kept wetting in a bowl of tea. Sure enough, Jemmie La-Botte did come. And Mama Callie told Aunt Albertine he tried to give her some medicine. She said he tried to talk big and tell her she was sure to get worse if she didn't let him give her a needle. But she and Alena wouldn't let him, and there wasn't a thing he could do about it.

The way they talked about it you'd have thought Jemmie LaBotte was like a little dog or something they'd taken some kind of fancy to. Alena got rid of all her men friends, and even when it made Mama Callie cough and spit up blood she burned a little basket full of dried-up willow leaves every day. Alena said, "We burn them leaves 'cause it make him get us on the brain and pretty soon he be coming right on down here all the time."

Sure enough, Jemmie LaBotte did start going down to Mama Callie's. He told Mrs. LaBotte he went down there so he could leave medicines for Mama Callie and try to make her take them. But Mrs. LaBotte noticed how much he was going down there. She even told old man LaBotte. And he used to lie in his bed and call Jemmie. "Jemmie, come tell your daddy what's going on down there at Mama Callie's. Come tell me! How come you're down to Mama Callie's so much, Jemmie?" But Jemmie stopped going in his daddy's room. Even Mrs. LaBotte couldn't make him go in any more. And that hurt Dr. LaBotte. He began to fall off a lot. You could tell because his hands and face got so thin. But still he'd lie in his bed and call in that nagging voice, like there was something he knew about Jemmie.

Mama Callie and Alena got so they bragged and said they were going to have Jemmie LaBotte pretty soon. Alena tied up her hair every day in a lot of silk rags because she wanted to look fine when he came. And Mama Callie claimed they could get him down to the Quarter whenever they wanted to. Alena was always telling everybody, "All I got to do is heat up that hog oil and start rubbing on Callie with it. That Jemmie LaBotte look like his eyes going to pop out. He know we ain't going to let him touch her, but he just keep on looking. Sometimes he look right pitiful."

I didn't think Jemmie still cared anything about his daddy. He did though. Because when old man LaBotte had that heart attack you could see it did something to Jemmie. They had a lot of fine specialists with Dr. LaBotte, but it didn't do him any good. He lingered, and he got weaker every day. They said he was "in coma" so nobody could go in there to see him. Jemmie and Mrs. LaBotte would just sit in that big living room all day long with the shades down; and two or three nurses were always coming and going and walking soft on those big thick rugs. They made me think of white rabbits, the way they were always streaking through the house. I didn't like them because they wouldn't let Jemmie LaBotte see his daddy, and he wanted to a lot. He kept saying he had something he wanted to say to his daddy.

Alena and Mama Callie told Aunt Albertine Jemmie LaBotte had stopped trying to make Mama Callie take his medicines. They said he came to their house just to see them and they called him sweet-boy-Jemmie. "He just like a baby," Mama Callie was always saying. "He come and just sit there and watch Alena swing hair-plaits around in the air. Sometime Alena hand him one of them hair-plaits and he hold it and he just laugh. Just like a young'un with a sugar-tit." Alena swore Mama Callie was telling it like it was. "Callie telling the honest-to-God truth! That Jemmie LaBotte done changed a heap."

It got around that Jemmie LaBotte had started writing prescriptions for Mama Callie to get codeine with. Somebody even said they saw him go in the drugstore to get it for her one day; but I still thought it was just meanness making them all tell lies on him. All that time Dr. LaBotte was sinking. Mrs. LaBotte couldn't understand why Jemmie was staying away more and more. She didn't think it hurt him that his daddy was dying, but she was wrong. He never did mention Dr. LaBotte much, but you could see he cared about the old man, just by some of the other things he'd say. Like one day he told me, "Mama loves this house, but I want to get out of here. I can't stand it any more."

My Aunt Albertine was there at Mama Callie's one day when Jemmie LaBotte came to see her. She said Mama Callie had a pretty bad coughing spell and her mouth started running blood, but Jemmie LaBotte didn't do a thing except just get down on his knees by Mama Callie's bed. And when she'd stopped coughing Mama Callie took a little ball of hair from under her pillow and gave it to him. Mama Callie told him that little ball had some of her and Alena's hair in it. She gave it to Jemmie LaBotte because he'd kept asking her to give him something to help his daddy in his misery. I'll tell you the truth, I didn't even believe my own flesh-and-blood aunt. For one thing I couldn't *see* Jemmie LaBotte doing all they said. I didn't even believe the willow leaves I'd found meant anything.

In the end I saw for my own self, though. One night. Dr. LaBotte had been real low all that day, and they'd put him under an oxygen tent. And Mrs. LaBotte had been calling up her friends telling them she didn't understand why Jemmie was off down in the Quarter. I think she must have known Dr. LaBotte was going to die. Anyway, that night after I'd got off I was walking up Bourbon Street on my way over to the show field to see if the carnival had come; and so I passed by Mama Callie's. Even when I was still way up the street I heard that singing. Mama Callie was singing that little French song, but it went so slow I could tell she was weak; she was so feeble her voice sounded high like a chicken squawking.

All the lights were on real bright in the room where she was. And she was sitting right up in the window with some kind of a shawl on that had long fringes that kept blowing around her arms. I couldn't help but look in there when I went by, but Mama Callie didn't see me because she had her eyes shut. Alena was sitting a little behind Mama Callie. She was in a straight chair and she had silk rags tied all through her hair: red and blue and green and yellow; all kinds of colors. Jemmie LaBotte must have been down on his knees or almost on his knees, anyway, because all I could see was his head. Alena had Jemmie LaBotte's head, holding it *tight* in her arms. Just as tight as she could. It was so queer, because it looked like she might have cut off his head from his body and was just holding nothing but that head in her arms. She had her eyes closed and he had his closed too. Only in the light I could see shining streaks on his face, like he was crying. He looked pretty: like a young girl. Maybe it was because Mama Callie and Alena were so wrinkled and ugly. His skin was so smooth, and his hair was shiny and very thick; like purple and black mixed together.

When I got back home that night I told Aunt Albertine how I saw the three of them. And she said, "I been thinking about it a while. I don't like all that funny stuff that's going on." She told me she wanted me to quit working for the LaBottes.

Only the next day when I went up there a lot of people were at the house. Women in fine clothes with feathery hats and little white handkerchiefs. They were answering the telephone and talking loud all over the house and wiping their eyes because old man LaBotte had died the night before. I didn't even get a chance to see Mrs. LaBotte, because a nurse was keeping her quiet. But everybody was whispering about Jemmie. They said they thought he must be crazy because half an hour after the old man died he went driving off down to the Quarter.

It seems like it's been longer than two years since all that was going on, but it's just been about that long. I don't know for sure, but I don't think Jemmie LaBotte even went to his daddy's funeral. I do know one thing for sure though; he doesn't stay home much. I see him every time I go past Mama Callie's house because he's always over there. He always waves his hand to me when he sees me. They say Mama Callie sleeps most of the time because she's only hanging by a thread. And when she's not sleeping she's coughing. But Jemmie LaBotte keeps her full of codeine so she doesn't feel anything. He doesn't just only get that codeine for Mama Callie, though; he lets a lot of them have it.

And they've all stopped talking mean about Jemmie LaBotte in the Quarter now. That's not something that's just happened either; they stopped *long* ago. Even Mrs. Clara and old big-head David don't put the bad-mouth on him any more. You wouldn't believe how everybody changed up. Jemmie LaBotte never has to beg to get his money out of anybody. And that goes to prove what I was just saying.

You ought to hear the way some of them call his name now whenever he comes walking up Bourbon Street. When he comes at night people lean out their windows and all you can see in the dark is fire from cigarettes, but you can hear the laughing and talking. And you can hear that laugh of his above everybody else's. Nobody can tell me all that fuss they make doesn't give him a good feeling. You can tell it makes him feel good. You ought to see the way his eyes flash, and the way he talks to everybody. Just the way he talks makes you know he'll do anything in the world for them.

The Poets

The Atlantic's *attitude toward poetry was at the beginning confident and proprietary. After Poe's death in 1849, the ranking American poets, with one exception, were New Englanders — Longfellow, Lowell, Emerson, Whittier, and Holmes — and all were charter contributors to the* Atlantic. *They all had reached their maturity before the magazine was founded; under the stress of the Civil War, they were prompted to write with depth and emotion, and at the war's end they were for a time sustained by the feeling that the nation was at last truly united. They were certainly aware that there was a need, an opportunity for a national literature, but by 1870 their poetic powers were declining, and it is doubtless this realization which prompted T. W. Higginson to write in January of that year, "The American poet of passion is yet to come. How tame and manageable are wont to be the emotions of our bards, how placid and literary their allusions."*

The one outsider in all of this was Walt Whitman, and he was not "manageable." Lowell, the first editor, accepted and published Whitman's "Bardic Symbols" in April 1860. But Lowell, who could be a stern taskmaster, asked Whitman to delete two lines, which the poet did, though grudgingly. It took some years and a new editor to restore the peace, and Whitman reappeared with his "Proud Music of the Sea-Storm" in February 1869. When Howells took over the desk in 1870, he found among the undecided manuscripts three of Whitman's poems—a long one which the poet had offered for twenty dollars and two shorter ones to be had for eight dollars each. Howells never quite approved of Whitman; he was uncertain, and when editors are uncertain they usually reject. Back went the manuscripts, and the association was at an end. Horace Scudder, the fifth editor, probably had something of this in mind when he wrote his conciliatory appraisal of Whitman the month following the poet's death.

Poetry reached its lowest ebb in the Atlantic in the 1880s under the editorship of Thomas Bailey Aldrich. The flowering of New England was over; he seemingly did not know where to turn. The standards began to rise again at the turn of the century, and we like to think that they are today as high as they ever were. But there are lacunae which are hard to explain: no Rudyard Kipling (here we may have been outbid by the New York editors); no Ezra Pound during his early and spectacular years, although surely his friend Amy Lowell must have recommended his work; no T. S. Eliot at a time when it really would have counted for him—and for us.

But with others, we think, we have been rewarded.

A Dutch Picture

by HENRY WADSWORTH LONGFELLOW

FEBRUARY 1877

Simon Danz has come home again,
　　From cruising about with his buccaneers;
He has singed the beard of the King of Spain,
And carried away the Dean of Jaen
　　And sold him in Algiers.

In his house by the Maese, with its roof of tiles,
　　And weathercocks flying aloft in air,
There are silver tankards of antique styles,
Plunder of convent and castle, and piles
　　Of carpets rich and rare.

In his tulip garden there by the town,
　　Overlooking the sluggish stream,
With his Moorish cap and dressing gown,
The old sea captain, hale and brown,
　　Walks in a waking dream.

A smile in his gray mustachio lurks
　　Whenever he thinks of the King of Spain,
And the listed tulips look like Turks,
And the silent gardener as he works
　　Is changed to the Dean of Jaen.

The windmills on the outermost
　　Verge of the landscape in the haze,
To him are towers on the Spanish coast,
With whiskered sentinels at their post,
　　Though this is the river Maese.

But when the winter rains begin,
    He sits and smokes by the blazing brands,
And old seafaring men come in,
Goat-bearded, gray, and with double chin,
    And rings upon their hands.

They sit there in the shadow and shine
    Of the flickering fire of the winter night;
Figures in color and design
Like those by Rembrandt of the Rhine,
    Half darkness and half light.

And they talk of ventures lost or won,
    And their talk is ever and ever the same,
While they drink the red wine of Tarragon,
From the cellars of some Spanish Don,
    Or convent set on flame.

Restless at times with heavy strides
    He paces his parlor to and fro;
He is like a ship that at anchor rides,
And swings with the rising and falling tides,
    And tugs at her anchor tow.

Voices mysterious far and near,
    Sound of the wind and sound of the sea,
Are calling and whispering in his ear,
"Simon Danz! Why stayest thou here?
    Come forth and follow me!"

So he thinks he shall take to the sea again
    For one more cruise with his buccaneers,
To singe the beard of the King of Spain,
And capture another Dean of Jaen
    And sell him in Algiers.

Prospice

by ROBERT BROWNING

JUNE 1864

Fear death?—to feel the fog in my throat,
    The mist in my face,
When the snows begin, and the blasts denote
    I am nearing the place,
The power of the night, the press of the storm,
    The post of the foe;
Where he stands, the Arch Fear in a visible form,
    Yet the strong man must go:
For the journey is done and the summit attained,
    And the barriers fall,
Though a battle's to fight ere the guerdon be gained,
    The reward of it all.
I was ever a fighter, so — one fight more,
    The best and the last!
I would hate that Death bandaged my eyes, and forbore,
    And bade me creep past.
No! let me taste the whole of it, fare like my peers
    The heroes of old,
Bear the brunt, in a minute pay glad life's arrears
    Of pain, darkness, and cold.
For sudden the worst turns the best to the brave,
    The black minute's at end,
And the elements' rage, the fiend-voices that rave,
    Shall dwindle, shall blend,
Shall change, shall become first a peace, then a joy,
    Then a light, then thy breast,
O thou soul of my soul! I shall clasp thee again,
    And with God be the rest!

Calverly's

by EDWIN ARLINGTON ROBINSON

MAY 1907

We go no more to Calverly's,
For there the lights are few and low;
And who are there to see by them,
Or what they see, we do not know.
Poor strangers of another tongue
May now creep in from anywhere,
And we, forgotten, be no more
Than twilight on a ruin there.

We two, the remnant. All the rest
Are cold and quiet. You nor I,
Nor fiddle now, nor flagon-lid,
May ring them back from where they lie,
No fame delays oblivion
For them, but something yet survives:
A record written fair, could we
But read the book of scattered lives.

There'll be a page for Leffingwell,
And one for Lingard, the Moon-calf;
And who knows what for Clavering,
Who died because he couldn't laugh?
Who knows or cares? No sign is here,
No face, no voice, no memory;
No Lingard with his eerie joy,
No Clavering, no Calverly.

We cannot have them here with us
To say where their light lives are gone,
Or if they be of other stuff
Than are the moons of Ilion.
So, be their place of one estate
With ashes, echoes, and old wars —
Or ever we be of the night,
Or we be lost among the stars.

The Road Not Taken

by ROBERT FROST

AUGUST 1915

Two roads diverged in a yellow wood,
And sorry I could not travel both
And be one traveler, long I stood
And looked down one as far as I could
To where it bent in the undergrowth;

Then took the other, as just as fair,
And having perhaps the better claim
Because it was grassy and wanted wear,
Though as for that the passing there
Had worn them really about the same,

And both that morning equally lay
In leaves no step had trodden black.
Oh, I marked the first for another day!
Yet knowing how way leads on to way
I doubted if I should ever come back.

I shall be telling this with a sigh
Somewhere ages and ages hence:
Two roads diverged in a wood, and I,
I took the one less traveled by,
And that has made all the difference.

Come In

by ROBERT FROST

FEBRUARY 1941

As I came to the edge of the woods,
Thrush music — hark!
Now if it was dusk outside,
Inside it was dark.

Too dark in the woods for a bird
By sleight of wing
To better its perch for the night,
Though it still could sing.

The last of the light of the sun
That had died in the west
Still lived for one song more
In a thrush's breast.

Far in the pillared dark
Thrush music went —
Almost like a call to come in
To the dark and lament.

But no, I was out for stars:
I would not come in.
I meant not even if asked;
And I hadn't been.

On Growing Old

by JOHN MASEFIELD

AUGUST 1919

Be with me, Beauty, for the fire is dying,
My dog and I are old, too old for roving;
Man, whose young passion sets the spindrift flying,
Is soon too lame to march, too cold for loving.
I take the book and gather to the fire,
Turning old yellow leaves. Minute by minute
The clock ticks to my heart; a withered wire
Moves a thin ghost of music in the spinet.
I cannot sail your seas, I cannot wander
Your mountains, nor your downlands, nor your valleys,
Ever again, nor share the battle yonder
Where your young knight the broken squadron rallies:
Only stay quiet, while my mind remembers
The beauty of fire from the beauty of embers.

Beauty, have pity; for the young have power,
The rich their wealth, the beautiful their grace,
Summer of man its fruit-time and its flower,
Springtime of man all April in a face.
Only, as in the jostling in the Strand,
Where the mob thrusts, or loiters, or is loud,
The beggar with the saucer in his hand
Asks only a penny from the passing crowd,
So, from this glittering world with all its fashion,
Its fire and play of men, its stir, its march,
Let me have wisdom, Beauty, wisdom and passion,
Bread to the soul, rain where the summers parch.
Give me but these, and though the darkness close,
Even the night will blossom as the rose.

The Wild Old Wicked Man

by WILLIAM BUTLER YEATS

APRIL 1938

"Because I am mad about women
I am mad about the hills,"
Said that wild old wicked man
Who travels where God wills.
"Not to die on the straw at home,
Those hands to close these eyes,
That is all I ask, my dear,
From the old man in the skies."
                    Daybreak and a candle end.

"Kind are all your words, my dear,
Do not the rest withhold,
Who can know the year, my dear,
When an old man's blood grows cold.
I have what no young man can have
Because he loves too much.
Words I have that can pierce the heart,
But what can he do but touch?"
                    Daybreak and a candle end.

Then said she to that wild old man,
His stout stick under his hand,
"Love to give or to withhold
Is not at my command.
I gave it all to an older man,
That old man in the skies.
Hands that are busy with His beads
Can never close those eyes."
                    Daybreak and a candle end.

"Go your ways, O go your ways,
I choose another mark,
Girls down on the seashore
Who understand the dark;
Bawdy talk for the fishermen,
A dance for the fisher lads;
When dark hangs upon the water
They turn down their beds."
                    Daybreak and a candle end.

"A young man in the dark am I
But a wild old man in the light,
That can make a cat laugh, or
Can touch by mother wit
Things hid in their marrowbones
From time long passed away,
Hid from all those warty lads
That by their bodies lay."
                    Daybreak and a candle end.

"All men live in suffering
I know as few can know
Whether they take the upper road
Or stay content on the low,
Rower bent in his rowboat
Or weaver bent at his loom,
Horseman erect upon horseback
Or child hid in the womb."
                    Daybreak and a candle end.

"That some stream of lightning
From the old man in the skies
Can burn out that suffering
No right-taught man denies.
But a coarse old man am I,
I choose the second-best,
I forget it all awhile
Upon a woman's breast."
                    Daybreak and a candle end.

Joy

by WALTER DE LA MARE

MARCH 1940

This little smiling Boy
Stretched out his hands to me,
Saying his name was Joy;
Saying all things that seem
Beautiful, wise and true
Never need fade while he
Drenches them through and through
    with witchery,
Told me that Love's clear eyes
Pools were without the sky,
Earth without Paradise
Were he not nigh;
Even that Sorrow is
Him in a dark disguise;
And tears light-bright because
Sprung from his eyes.

Then went he singing on
Just like a child, and O
All his sweet converse done,
Where could I go?
What could I do
But seek him up and down —
Thicket and thorn and fell —
Till night in gloom came on
Unpierceable?
And lo, unmoved yet pale
Stepped from the dark to me,
Voiced like the nightingale,
Masked, weeping, He.

Heart and Mind

by EDITH SITWELL

JULY 1944

Said the Lion to the Lioness, "When you are amber dust,
No more a raging fire like the heat of the Sun
(No liking but all lust) —
Remember still the flowering of the amber blood and bone,
The rippling of bright muscles like a sea;
Remember the rose-prickles of bright paws
Though we shall mate no more
Till the fire of that sun, the heart, and the moon-cold bone are one."

Said the Skeleton lying upon the sands of Time,
"The great gold planet that is the mourning heat of the Sun
Is greater than all gold, more powerful
Than the tawny body of a Lion that fire consumes
Like all that grows or leaps . . . so is the heart
More powerful than all dust. Once I was Hercules
Or Samson, strong as the pillars of the seas,
But the flames of the heart consumed me, and the mind
Is but a foolish mind."

Said the Sun to the Moon, "When you are but a lonely white crone,
And I a dead King in my golden armor somewhere in a dark wood,
Remember only this of our hopeless love:
That never till time is done
Will the fire of the heart and the fire of the mind be one."

Serenade

by W. H. AUDEN

NOVEMBER 1947

On and on and on
The forthright catadoup
Shouts at the stone-deaf stone;
Over and over again,
Singly or as a group,
Weak diplomatic men
With a small defiant light
Salute the threatening night.

With or without a mind,
Chafant or outwardly calm,
Each thing has an ax to grind
And exclaims its matter of fact;
The careful child with charm
Or a sudden opprobrious act,
The tiger, the griping fern,
Extort the world's concern.

All, all have rights to declare,
Not one is man enough
To be simply publicly there
With no private emphasis;
So my embodied love,
That like most feeling is
Half humbug and half true,
Asks neighborhood from you.

In Country Sleep

by DYLAN THOMAS

DECEMBER 1947

Never and never, my girl riding far and near
In the land of the hearthstone tales, and spelled asleep,
Fear or believe that the wolf in a sheepwhite hood
Loping and bleating roughly and blithely shall leap,
          My dear, my dear,
Out of a lair in the flocked leaves in the dew dipped year
To eat your heart in the house in the rosy wood.

Sleep, good, for ever, slow and deep, spelled rare and wise,
My girl ranging the night in the rose and shire
Of the hobnail tales: no gooseherd or swine will turn
Into a homestall king or hamlet of fire
          And prince of ice
To court the honeyed heart from your side before sunrise
In a spinney of ringed boys and ganders, spike and burn,

Nor the innocent lie in the rooting dingle wooed
And staved, and riven among plumes my rider weep.
From the broomed witch's spume you are shielded by fern
And flower of country sleep and the greenwood keep.
          Lie fast and soothed,
Safe be and smooth from the bellows of the rushy brood.
Never, my girl until tolled to sleep by the stern

Bell believe or fear that the rustic shade or spell
Shall harrow and snow the blood while you ride wide and near,
For who unmanningly haunts the mountain ravened eaves
Or skulks in the dell moon but moonshine echoing clear

From the starred well?
A hill touches an angel. Out of a saint's cell
The nightbird lauds through nunneries and domes of leaves

Her robin breasted tree, three Marys in the rays.
Sanctum sanctorum the animal eye of the wood
In the rain telling its beads, and the gravest ghost
The owl at its knelling. Fox and holt kneel before blood.
                                        Now the tales praise
The star rise at pasture and nightlong the fables graze
On the lord's-table of the bowing grass. Fear most

For ever of all not the wolf in his baaing hood
Nor the tusked prince, in the ruttish farm, at the rind
And mire of love, but the Thief as meek as the dew.
The country is holy: O bide in that country kind,
                              Know the green good,
Under the prayer wheeling moon in the rosy wood
Be shielded by chant and flower and gay may you

Lie in grace. Sleep spelled at rest in the lowly house
In the squirrel nimble grove, under linen and thatch
And star: held and blessed, though you scour the high four
Winds, from the dousing shade and the roarer at the latch,
                                        Cool in your vows.
Yet out of the beaked, web dark and the pouncing boughs
Be you sure the Thief will seek a way sly and sure

And sly as snow and meek as dew blown to the thorn,
This night and each vast night until the stern bell talks
In the tower and tolls to sleep over the stalls
Of the hearthstone tales my own, last love; and the soul walks
                                        The waters shorn.
This night and each night since the falling star you were born,
Ever and ever he finds a way, as the snow falls,

As the rain falls, hail on the fleece, as the vale mist rides
Through the haygold stalls, as the dew falls on the wind-
Milled dust of the apple tree and the pounded islands
Of the morning leaves, as the star falls, as the winged

Apple seed glides,
And falls, and flowers in the yawning wound at your side,
As the world falls, silent as the cyclone of silence.

Night and the reindeer on the clouds above the haycocks
And the wings of the great roc ribboned for the fair!
The leaping saga of prayer! And high, there, on the hare-
Heeled winds the rooks
Cawing from their black bethels soaring, the holy books
Of birds! Among the cocks like fire the red fox

Burning! Night and the vein of birds in the winged sloe wrist
Of the wood! Pastoral beat of blood through the laced leaves!
The stream from the priest black wristed spinney and sleeves
Of thistling frost
Of the nightingale's din and tale! The upgiven ghost
Of the dingle torn to singing and the surpliced

Hill of cypresses! The din and tale in the skimmed
Yard of the buttermilk rain on the pail! The sermon
Of blood! The bird loud vein! The saga from mermen
To seraphim
Leaping! The gospel rooks! All tell, this night, of him
Who comes as red as the fox and sly as the heeled wind.

Illumination of music! the lulled black backed
Gull, on the wave with sand in its eyes! and the foal moves
Through the shaken greensward lake, silent, on moonshood hooves,
In the winds' wakes.
Music of elements, that a miracle makes!
Earth, air, water, fire, singing into the white act,

The haygold haired, my love asleep, and the rift blue
Eyed, in the haloed house, in her rareness and hilly
High riding, held and blessed and true, and so stilly
Lying the sky
Might cross its planets, the bell weep, night gather her eyes,
The Thief fall on the dead like the willynilly dew,

Only for the turning of the earth in her holy
Heart! Slyly, slowly, hearing the wound in her side go
Round the sun, he comes to my love like the designed snow,
                                        And truly he
Flows to the strand of flowers like the dew's ruly sea,
And surely he sails like the ship shape clouds. Oh he

Comes designed to my love to steal not her tide raking
Wound, nor her riding high, nor her eyes, nor kindled hair,
But her faith that each vast night and the saga of prayer
                                        He comes to take
Her faith that this last night for his unsacred sake
He comes to leave her in the lawless sun awaking

Naked and forsaken to grieve he will not come.
Ever and ever by all your vows believe and fear
My dear this night he comes and night without end my dear
                                        Since you were born:
And you shall wake, from country sleep, this dawn and each first dawn,
Your faith as deathless as the outcry of the ruled sun.

The Fancy

by WILLIAM ROSE BENÉT

(With a bow to George Borrow's *Lavengro*)

JULY 1950

The bruisers of England, the men of tremendous renown,
The choice of the Fancy who tooled through the dust from the Town
With peers in their chariots all hasting toward glory and fame,
And gigs and blood horses that raced till they came to the game —

Their times and their seasons, their glory, alas, that must pass
With the turf-treading masters, to fade like the flower of the grass!

Cribb, champion of England, the lion-faced, leading the van;
And Belcher the Younger, a most scientifical man;
The savage, dark Shelton whose blow was a thunderbolt dealt,
The tiny and terrible Randall, the man-eating Celt —

The luck of the ring and the roaring of mass and of class
To the rush and the rally and shifting of feet on the grass!

Black Richmond; the Welshman; and Hudson the Bulldog, and Tom —
That tall Tom of Bedford, brown-eyed, of a thunderous calm,
That yeoman of Holborn, fit follower of Broughton and Brain
Whose portraits grinned down, in his pub, on the hubbub profane —

The clamor of backers in bars and the clinking of glass
At a name new to fame, soon to pass like a cloud from the grass!

Straight left and Long Melford; the battlers stripped down to the buff;
The blows of bare morleys, and neither to hollo enough;
The swells with their whiskers, their beavers aslant on the ear,
In greatcoat and hessians, to parley and wager and peer —

The cross and the counter, the feint and the grunt and the thud;
The down's sun and shadow; the challenger first drawing blood!

The days of the Fancy! A turbulent tale and a dream
That feats of fair field and no favor are fain to redeem
In old colored prints; the profession that Borrow extolled
As though he were Homer invoking the heroes of old —

Their life in his language; his memory never to pass
Though faded their glory as fadeth the flower of the grass!

The Renovated Temple

by ARCHIBALD MacLEISH

DECEMBER 1951

Ma'am, you should see your house!
Remember where the pillars stood, the douse
Of sea-surge smashing clean across the porches,
Everything open, the wet windy torch,
The blind man shouting things of gods and girls
Above the wave sound in the smoky swirling —
Things about Troy, the horse-trick and those troubles?

The place, Ma'am, is a private club —
Never a shout in the house or a girl either:
Only those pimply boys who breathe
Sour as cooky dough. Where once the surge,
Curtains: mirrors where the windows were.
It's a neat place, Ma'am. They've stuffed the hawk
And hung the oars up varnished and they talk:
God, how they talk! — about the members and their **stations,**
About the house rules and the regulations,
About their battles with the mice and spiders —
They talk of anything but what's outside.
The coal-fire tinkles and the tea-cup lulls.

It's not like Dante's time with all those skulls
And shrieks and pitch-pots and old putrid years
Dug up from Hell to dress the chandeliers,
Or Villon's, dragging dead men in to hang,
Or Baudelaire's when all the roof cats wrangled —
Shakespeare's of the Fierce Dispute —

It's not like that. It's neat, Ma'am, and they know their duty:
Neat as a catechism.

Still, they thumb
Their eyes and wonder why you never come.

Through the Drift of Years

by ROBERT HILLYER

FEBRUARY 1952

Never go back: if landscapes do not change
Then the familiar will but seem more strange,
Shorn of the magic cast on field and tree
By memory's and time's mendacity;
Or, if they have changed, then we join the chorus
Who now, with their own recollections, bore us.
After a lapse of decades it is folly
To trace old joys through mists of melancholy:
The brook we leaped so nimbly in our nonage
Is a mere ditch or too wide for our tonnage,
And so with the dark-flowing past: one jumps
To drown midstream or sprawl in thorny clumps.

Not for a fortune (let me reconsider
If I am tempted by a generous bidder!)
Would I return to Paris, there to chase
Through haunted streets the phantom of lost grace.
To Denmark? Even northern beauties wilt,
Their golden tresses turned to gray or gilt —
Only the Mermaid by the Sound responds
Unchanged to memory, and she is bronze.
Boston — where everyone now hopefully looks
To find himself in one of Marquand's books?
No, I should be, beneath the State House dome,
Most homesick where I once was most at home.

Only New York is safe, where late and early
The riveters outstrip life's hurly-burly,
Where nothing now recalls my childhood era
That shook in needless fear of poor Cevera
And witnessed Admiral Dewey's victory march
Pass by forever through the Dewey Arch.
I speak of childhood, but, to tell the truth,
There's nothing much remaining from my youth,
Hardly one stone upon another. Splendid!
Here all things change before they need be mended,
And mortal years, in contrast to such haste,
Move almost to immortal measures paced.

A Lonely Lotus

by LORD DUNSANY

DECEMBER 1952

A wind that wandered through Cathay
      Drifted a lotus seed aloft
And dropped it long before our day
      On to a mudbank warm and soft.
And ages turned the mud to clay.

And so a million years went by.
      And men appeared and found the seed
And underneath a western sky
      Have planted it, and the bloom freed
From earth and time rose up on high,

And opened, rivaling our rose.
      How feels it in that other clime
And other age, so far from those
      That knew it in the deeps of time
Where other vegetation grows,

I wondered. Till I chanced to find
    One day a faded photograph
Of some festivity designed
    Before this century, whereof half
Is fading out of sight and mind.

And in that group, so changed, was I.
    All in that moment I had known
How sighed that bloom, if blossoms sigh,
    To find, a flower all alone,
A million years had hurried by.

Dethronement

by ROBERT GRAVES

DECEMBER 1952

With pain pressing so close about your heart,
Stand (it behoves you), head uncovered,
To watch how she enacts her transformations —
Bitch, vixen, sow — the laughing, naked queen
Who has now dethroned you.

Hymns to her beauty or to her mercy
Would be ill-conceived. Your royal anguish
Is all that she requires. You, turned to stone,
May not speak nor groan, will stare dumbly,
Grinning dismay.

But as the play ends, or in its after-hush,
O then, deluded, flee! Her red-eared hounds
Scramble upon your track; past either cheek
Swan-feathered arrows whistle, or cruelly comb
Long furrows in your scalp.

Run, though you hope for nothing: to stay your foot
Would be ingratitude, a sour denial
That the life she bestowed was sweet.
Therefore be fleet, run gasping, draw the chase
Up the grand defile.

They will rend you to rags assuredly
With half a hundred love-bites —
Your hot blood an acceptable libation
Poured to Persephone, in whose demesne
You shall again find peace.

.

Banjo Boomer

by WALLACE STEVENS

MARCH 1955

The mulberry is a double tree.
Mulberry, shade me, shade me awhile.

A white, pink, purple berry tree,
A very dark-leaved berry tree.
Mulberry, shade me, shade me awhile.

A churchyard kind of bush as well,
A silent sort of bush, as well.
Mulberry, shade me, shade me awhile.

It is a shape of life described
By another shape without a word.
Mulberry, shade me, shade me awhile —

With nothing fixed by a single word.
Mulberry, shade me, shade me awhile.

Drone

by LEAH BODINE DRAKE

JUNE 1955

Gay burly beau, his life is summer only.
He lives in riot-time of green — jeweled summer
When golden odors rise from swamp and meadow
Of mint and clethra. O the lime's gold shadow
Falls on a world all one warm smell of honey
To this rich brummel in his banded gold!

He wings through mornings flower-sweet and gold,
Fit-as-a-fiddle velvet boy, fit only
To buzz in lazy joy and suck the honey
From honeysuckle swags — gold bells of summer
That chime so richly in the swamp's warm shadow
With clover-balls of sweetness in the meadow.

And he's the booming fop of the clover meadow,
A swaggerer in velvet, boy of gold,
Upon whose useless head there falls no shadow
Of humming work: such haunts the virgins only,
Those fierce nuns who carry off the summer
To opulent cloisters dark with thrifty honey.

The warm days hum with their brisk song of honey,
Pure, hurried maidens in the lazy meadow.
Their work will seal away the happy summer
When riotous fields are wasted of their gold.
Proud amazons, their little hearts feel only
Scorn for the drone whose riches know no shadow.

Gourmand of grapes, the wild vine wears his shadow,
Rose and raspberry tangles cup him honey.

He thinks the goldenrod's sweet waters only
Distill for his delight and jewel the meadow!
He rinses his wings in odors rich as gold,
His heart is humming a song of always-summer.

But when October cools the golden summer
On the poor clown falls the relentless shadow
Of thrifty virgin wings. O his splendid gold
Does not protect him from those nuns of honey!
He lumbers, stung to death, to the dark meadow
Where once he knew green days and riches only.

The swaggerer in gold lays on the meadow
His jeweled heart whose only song was summer;
And on him honey-dark falls the hive's shadow.

Within the Wave

by ANNE MORROW LINDBERGH

OCTOBER 1951

Within the hollow wave there lies a world,
Gleaming glass-perfect, rising to be hurled
Into a thousand fragments on the sand,
Driven by tide's inexorable hand.
Now in the instant while disaster towers,
I glimpse a land more beautiful than ours;
Another sky, more lapis lazuli,
Lit by unsetting suns; another sea,
By no horizons bound; another shore,
Glistening with shells I never saw before.
Smooth mirror of the present, poised between
The crest's "becoming" and the foam's "has been" —
How luminous the landscape seen across
The crystal lens of an impending loss!

The Dignity of Man

We who are older than the century have learned to our chagrin that the pendulum of opinion in a democracy continually swings from liberalism to reaction and back again, with results which are for a time most difficult to control. The Red-baiting under Attorney General Palmer at the end of the First World War found its parallel in McCarthyism and guilt by association after the Second. In each case it seems as if the self-sacrifice and devotion which drove people to the winning of the war left us in the aftermath exhausted and suspicious. To preserve the dignity of man calls for constant vigilance, for brave and imperturbable judges, for lawyers willing to take the unpopular, unpaid case. It calls for the Bill of Rights and most of all for the courage to stand up and be counted. These have always been the traditional checks against the surge of mobbism. And to them there has been added a new recourse — the opportunity of hearing and seeing the demagogue in his daily dealings and in his tirade. The relentless day-by-day televising of the McCarthy hearings, the televised testimony of the citizens of Clinton, Tennessee, on "You Are There," brought home to the American people truths which no amount of print could have made so clear. And as they understood, the danger diminished.

The most momentous case to be reviewed at length in the Atlantic was that of Sacco and Vanzetti, which Felix Frankfurter, professor in the Harvard Law School, subjected to a most searching analysis in March 1927. The case had then been before the Massachusetts courts for more than six years; Frankfurter was convinced that the men were innocent, and he wrote in the belief that they would be granted a new trial. He published his findings before the Superior Court of the Commonwealth had given its verdict, and for this so-called impropriety he and the magazine were bitterly assailed. Criticism was heaped upon the Harvard Law

School and eventually found voice at a meeting of the Harvard Overseers, where the blast was directed against President Lowell. "What would you have had him do?" asked President Lowell. "Wait until the men were dead?" The President's defense of Professor, now Justice, Frankfurter, was indicative of Lowell's belief in academic freedom; it has an additional point of irony when one remembers that shortly thereafter Lowell himself took a decisive part in the special commission appointed by the governor which eventually found the men guilty.

Law and Manners

by LORD MOULTON

John Fletcher Moulton, first Baron of Bank, served for many years as a Lord Justice of Appeal and, during the First World War, as Minister of Munitions. Skilled as an administrator and parliamentarian, he was above all a philosopher of the law, as these passages testify.

JULY 1924

In order to explain this extraordinary title I must ask you to follow me in examining the three great domains of human action. First comes the domain of positive law, where our actions are prescribed by laws binding upon us which must be obeyed. Next comes the domain of free choice, which includes all those actions as to which we claim and enjoy complete freedom. But between these two there is a third large and important domain in which there rules neither positive law nor absolute freedom. In that domain there is no law which inexorably determines our course of action, and yet we feel that we are not free to choose as we would. The degree of this sense of a lack of complete freedom in this domain varies in every case. It grades from a consciousness of a duty nearly as strong as positive law, to a feeling that the matter is all but a question of personal choice. Some might wish to parcel out this domain into separate countries, calling one, for instance, the domain of duty, another the domain of public spirit, another the domain of good form; but I prefer to look at it as all one domain, for it has one and the same characteristic throughout — it is the domain of obedience to the un-enforceable. The obedience is the obedience of a man to that which he cannot be forced to obey. He is the enforcer of the law upon himself.

This country which lies between law and free choice I always think of as the domain of manners. To me, manners in this broad sense signifies the doing that which you should do although you are not obliged to do it. I do not wish to call it duty, for that is too narrow to describe it, nor would I call it morals for the same reason. It might include both, but it extends beyond them. It covers all cases of right doing where there is no one to make you do it but yourself.

All these three domains are essential to the properly organized life of the individual, and one must be on one's guard against thinking that any of them can safely be encroached upon. That law must exist needs no argument. But, on the other hand, the domain of free choice should be dear to all. This is where spontaneity, originality, and energy are born. The great movements which make the history of a country start there. It covers a precious land where the actions of men are not only such as they choose, but have a right to claim freedom even from criticism. Men must keep safely guarded this right to follow the bent of their nature in proper cases and act as they would without anyone having the right to utter a word of dictation or command. This country forms the other frontier of the domain of manners and delimits it on the side farthest away from that of positive law.

The dangers that threaten the maintenance of this domain of manners arise from its situation between the region of absolute choice and the region of positive law. There are countless supporters of the movements to enlarge the sphere of positive law. In many countries — especially in the younger nations — there is a tendency to make laws to regulate everything. On the other hand, there is a growing tendency to treat matters that are not regulated by positive law as being matters of absolute choice. Both these movements are encroachments on the middle land, and to my mind the real greatness of a nation, its true civilization, is measured by the extent of this land of obedience to the unenforceable. It measures the extent to which the nation trusts its citizens, and its existence and area testify to the way they behave in response to that trust. Mere obedience to law does not measure the greatness of a nation. It can easily be obtained by a strong executive, and most easily of all from a timorous people. Nor is the license of behavior which so often accompanies the absence of law, and which is miscalled liberty, a proof of greatness. The true test is the extent to which the individuals composing the nation can be trusted to obey self-imposed law.

In the changes that are taking place in the world around us, one of those which is fraught with grave peril is the discredit into which this idea of the middle land is falling. I will give two examples. First, I will take freedom of debate in the houses of legislature such as our own House of Commons. For centuries the members had unrestricted freedom of debate, and no inconvenience was felt. But in recent times some members of this House have said to themselves: "We have unrestricted freedom of debate. We will use it so as to destroy debate. The absence of imposed restriction enables us to do it." This obstruction was developed, and it has destroyed freedom of debate, and, indeed, all useful debate in practically every legislature. Clumsy and even mischievous regulations have necessarily been introduced which fetter debate but prevent its being absolutely stifled. The old freedom cannot now be entrusted to the members, because when they possessed it they did not respond to it by the exercise of that moral sense which would have led them to treat it as a trust, and not as an absolute possession, unburdened by obligations which they should compel themselves to regard.

It is not only the conduct of individual members of the legislature that furnishes an illustration. The conduct of the legislatures themselves furnishes an equally striking one. It is the fundamental principle of democracies to bow to the decision of the majority. But in accepting this we do not surrender ourselves to the rule of the majority in all things, but only in those things which are of a kind fit to be regulated by government. We do not admit, for instance, the right of the majority to decide whom we should marry or what should be our religion. These are but types of a vast number of matters of great interest in life which we hold to be outside the decision of a majority, and which are for the individual alone to decide. But in form the power of a government has no restrictions. It has the power to do everything, and too often it forgets that this limitless power does not leave the scope of its legislation a matter of absolute choice on its part, but a choice fettered by a duty to act according to the trust reposed in it, and to abstain from legislating in matters where legislation is not truly within its province. And what is true as to the scope of legislation is also true to a great extent as to the nature of that legislation. But there is a widespread tendency to regard the fact that they can do a thing as meaning that they may do it. There can be no more fatal error than this. Between "can do" and "may do" ought to exist the whole realm which recognizes the sway of duty, fairness, sympathy, taste, and all the other things that make life beautiful and society possible. It is this confusion between "can do" and "may do" which makes me fear at times lest in the future the worst tyranny will be found in democracies. Interests which are not strongly represented in parliament may be treated as though they had no rights by governments who think that the power and the will to legislate amount to a justification of that legislation. Such a principle would be death to liberty. No part of our life would be secure from interference from without. If I were asked to define tyranny, I would say it was yielding to the lust of governing. It is only when governments feel it an honorable duty not to step beyond that which was in reality, and not only in form, put into their hands that the world will know what true freedom is.

I am not afraid to trust people — my fear is that people will not see that trust is being reposed in them. Hence I have no wish that positive law should annex this intermediate country. On the contrary, I dread it. Instead of the iron rule of law being thrown over it I would rather see it well policed by the inhabitants. I am too well acquainted with the inadequacy of the formal language of statutes to prefer them to the living action of public and private sense of duty.

The great principle of obedience to the unenforceable is no mere ideal, but in some form or other it is strong in the hearts of all except the most depraved. I have no fear of its strength, whatever be the class appealed to. Even if one takes the least educated — the so-called lower classes, of whom so many are afraid — one would find the same loyal obedience to unenforceable obligation in the relationships with which these classes are familiar. The danger lies in that by the growth of the democratic spirit they have newly come into much larger powers, and they have not yet learned that power has its duties as well as its rights. When they have become familiar with these powers, and when intercourse with those who have a wider outlook has taught them that the domain of obligation includes them in their use of them, I am satisfied that those who have been loyal to duty in the smaller lives that they have led will be loyal in the wider fields in which they are now able to exercise their power. It is this faith that makes me dread lest we should hurriedly let positive law come in and check the growth of self-reliance and lead people to feel that, if they obey the law, they have done all their duty. It is wiser to exercise patience and let them alone till increase of experience teaches them to appreciate better their true position and to see for themselves that they behave as worthy men should do.

Now I can tell you why I chose the title "Law and Manners." It must be evident to you that manners must include all things which a man should impose upon himself, from duty to good taste. I have borne in mind the great motto of William of Wykeham — *Manners makyth Man*. It is in this sense — loyalty to the rule of obedience to the unenforceable, throughout the whole realm of personal action — that we should use the word "manners" if we would truly say that "Manners makyth Man."

The Case of the Negro

by BOOKER T. WASHINGTON

*Booker T. Washington was born a slave in Franklin County,
Virginia, in 1856. At twenty-five he was chosen to establish
and head the Tuskegee Institute for the training of Negroes
in the trades and professions. Today Tuskegee has an endowment of over $7 million, a faculty of 230, and a student
body totaling more than 1600.*

NOVEMBER 1899

All attempts to settle the question of the Negro in the South by his
removal from this country have so far failed, and I think that they are
likely to fail. The next census will probably show that we have nearly
ten million black people in the United States, about eight million of
whom are in the Southern states. In fact, we have almost a nation within
a nation. When we consider that the race has doubled itself since its
freedom, and is still increasing, it hardly seems possible for anyone to
take seriously any scheme of emigration from America as a method of
solution. At most, even if the government were to provide the means,
but a few hundred thousand could be transported each year. The yearly
increase in population would more than likely overbalance the number transported. Even if it did not, the time required to get rid of the
Negro by this method would perhaps be fifty or seventy-five years.

I wish first to mention some elements of danger in the present situation, which all who desire the permanent welfare of both races in the
South should carefully take into account.

First. There is danger that a certain class of impatient extremists
among the Negroes in the North, who have little knowledge of the actual
conditions in the South, may do the entire race injury by attempting to
advise their brethren in the South to resort to armed resistance or the
use of the torch, in order to secure justice. All intelligent and well-con-
sidered discussion of any important question, or condemnation of any

wrong, whether in the North or the South, from the public platform and through the press, is to be commended and encouraged; but ill-considered and incendiary utterances from black men in the North will tend to add to the burdens of our people in the South rather than to relieve them. We must not fall into the temptation of believing that we can raise ourselves by abusing someone else.

Second. Another danger in the South which should be guarded against is that the whole white South, including the wise, conservative, law-abiding element, may find itself represented before the bar of public opinion by the mob or lawless element, which gives expression to its feelings and tendency in a manner that advertises the South throughout the world; while too often those who have no sympathy with such disregard of law are either silent, or fail to speak in a sufficiently emphatic manner to offset in any large degree the unfortunate reputation which the lawless have made for many portions of the South.

Third. No race or people ever got upon its feet without severe and constant struggle, often in the face of the greatest discouragement. While passing through the present trying period of its history, there is danger that a large and valuable element of the Negro race may become discouraged in the effort to better its condition. Every possible influence should be exerted to prevent this.

Fourth. There is a possibility that harm may be done to the South and to the Negro by exaggerated newspaper articles which are written near the scene or in the midst of specially aggravating occurrences. Often these reports are written by newspapermen, who give the impression that there is a race conflict throughout the South, and that all Southern white people are opposed to the Negro's progress; overlooking the fact that though in some sections there is trouble, in most parts of the South, if matters are not yet in all respects as we would have them, there is nevertheless a very large measure of peace, good will, and mutual helpfulness. In the same relation, much can be done to retard the progress of the Negro by a certain class of Southern white people, who in the midst of excitement speak or write in a manner that gives the impression that all Negroes are lawless, untrustworthy, and shiftless. For example, a Southern writer said, not long ago, in a communication to the New York *Independent:* "Even in small towns the husband cannot venture to leave his wife alone for an hour at night. At no time, in no place, is the white woman safe from the insults and assaults of these creatures." These statements, I presume, represented the feelings and the conditions that existed, at the time of the writing, in one community or county in the South; but thousands of Southern white men and women would be ready to testify that this is not the condition throughout the South, nor throughout any Southern state.

Fifth. Owing to the lack of school opportunities for the Negro in the rural districts of the South, there is danger that ignorance and idleness may increase to the extent of giving the Negro race a reputation for crime, and that immorality may eat its way into the fiber of the race so as to retard its progress for many years. In judging the Negro we must not be too harsh. We must remember that it has been only within the last thirty-four years that the black father and mother have had the responsibility, and consequently the experience, of training their own children. That perfection has not been reached in one generation, with the obstacles that the parents have been compelled to overcome, is not to be wondered at.

Sixth. Finally, I would mention my fear that some of the white people of the South may be led to feel that the way to settle the race problem is to repress the aspirations of the Negro by legislation of a kind that confers certain legal or political privileges upon an ignorant and poor white man, and withholds the same privileges from a black man in a similar condition. Such legislation injures and retards the progress of both races. It is an injustice to the poor white man, because it takes from him incentive to secure education and property as prerequisites for voting. He feels that because he is a white man, regardless of his possessions, a way will be found for him to vote. I would label all such measures "laws to keep the poor white man in ignorance and poverty."

To state in detail just what place the black man will come to occupy in the South as a citizen is beyond the wisdom of anyone. Much will depend upon the sense of justice of the American people; almost as much will depend upon the good sense of the Negro himself. That question, I confess, does not give me the most concern just now. The important and pressing question is, Will the Negro, with his own help and that of his friends, take advantage of the opportunities that surround him? When he has done this, I believe that he will be treated with justice, be given the protection of the law and the recognition which his usefulness and ability warrant. If, fifty years ago, one had predicted that the Negro would receive the recognition and honor which individuals have already received, he would have been laughed at as an idle dreamer. Time, patience, and constant achievement are important factors in the rise of a race

I do not believe that the world ever takes a race seriously in its desire to share in the government of a nation until a large number of individual members of that race have demonstrated beyond question their ability to control and develop their own business enterprises. Once a number of Negroes rise to the point where they own and operate the most successful farms, are among the largest taxpayers in their county, are moral and intelligent, I do not believe that in many portions of the South such men need long be denied the right of saying by their votes how they prefer their property to be taxed, and who are to make and administer the laws.

I was walking the street of a certain town in the South lately in company with the most prominent Negro there. While we were together, the mayor of the town sought out the black man, and said, "Next week we are going to vote on the question of issuing bonds to secure waterworks; you must be sure to vote on the day of election." The mayor did not suggest whether he should vote yes or no; but he knew that the very fact of this Negro's owning nearly a block of the most valuable property in the town was a guarantee that he would cast a safe, wise vote on this important proposition. The white man knew that because of this Negro's property interests he would cast his vote in the way he thought would benefit every white and black citizen in the town, and not be controlled by influences a thousand miles away. But a short time ago I read letters from nearly every prominent white man in Birmingham, Alabama, asking that the Reverend W. R. Pettiford, a Negro, be appointed to a certain important federal office. What is the explanation of this? For nine years Mr. Pettiford has been the president of the Negro bank in Birmingham. During these nine years, the white citizens have had the opportunity of seeing that Mr. Pettiford can manage successfully a private business, and that he has proved himself a conservative, thoughtful citizen, and they are willing to trust him in a public office. Such individual examples will have to be multiplied till they become more nearly the rule than the exception they now are. While we are multiplying these examples, the Negro must keep a strong and courageous heart. He cannot improve his condition by any short-cut course or by artificial methods. Above all, he must not be deluded into believing that his condition can be permanently bettered by a mere battledore and shuttlecock of words, or by any process of mere mental gymnastics or oratory. What is desired along with a logical defense of his cause are deeds, results — continued results, in the direction of building himself up, so as to leave no doubt in the mind of anyone of his ability to succeed.

My own feeling is that the South will gradually reach the point where it will see the wisdom and the justice of enacting an educational or property qualification, or both, for voting that shall be made to apply honestly to both races. The industrial development of the Negro in connection with education and Christian character will help to hasten this end. When this is done, we shall have a foundation, in my opinion, upon which to build a government that is honest, and that will be in a high degree satisfactory to both races.

The education and preparation for citizenship of nearly eight million people is a tremendous task, and every lover of humanity should count it a privilege to help in the solution of a problem for which our whole country is responsible.

His Eye Is on the Sparrow

by ETHEL WATERS

Ethel Waters is a great American artist, but few who saw the triumph that she scored as Hagar in Mamba's Daughters *realized how closely that play touched on her own life. She achieved national prominence first as a blues singer; in 1933 she starred in Irving Berlin's* As Thousands Cheer; *and five years later her song recital filled Carnegie Hall. The next year she made her unforgettable hit on the legitimate stage in* Mamba's Daughters. *This excerpt is from her autobiography,* His Eye Is on the Sparrow.

MARCH 1951

Mamba's Daughters opened at the Empire Theatre, which has the richest theatrical history of any showhouse in America. And the Empire's star dressing room was mine on that opening night. While the carriage trade was arriving outside, I sat at the dressing table where all the great actresses, past and present, had sat as they made up their faces and wondered what the first-night verdict would be — Maude Adams, Ethel Barrymore, Helen Hayes, Katharine Cornell, Lynn Fontanne, and all the others who had brought the glitter of talent and beauty and grace to that old stage.

Yes, there I was, the Ethel who had never been coddled or kissed as a child, the Ethel who was too big to fit, but big enough to be scullion and laundress and bus girl while still a kid. And I could have looked back over my shoulder and blown a kiss to all my yesterdays in show business. I had been pushed on the stage and prodded into becoming Sweet Mama Stringbean and the refined singer of risqué songs in Edmond's Cellar, and on and up to best-selling records, Broadway musicals, and being the best-paid woman in all show business.

That was *the* night of my professional life, sitting there in that old-fashioned dressing room that was a bower of flowers. The night I'd been born for, and God was in the room with me. I talked to God, shivered and cried until the callboy came to say: "Five minutes, Miss Waters."

Five minutes more to get ready to be Hagar and tell the story of my mother in front of the carriage trade. I asked God, "Oh, stay with me! Lord, keep Your hand on my shoulder! Please, God!"

Then I got up and started off on that terrifying last mile a performer has to walk every opening night. Into the wings, a pause there for a moment waiting for the cue — and then on, Ethel Waters, to glory or . . .

I was Hagar that night. Hagar and my mother Momweeze and all of us. Seventeen curtain calls on opening night for me alone. I couldn't stand it. Half collapsing with joy and humility, I pushed through the kissing mouths and the slaps on the back to my dressing room, where Elida Webb, my secretary, was waiting.

"How do you feel now, Miss Waters?" she said. "And what are you thinking?"

"Elida, if I died here and now," I told her, "it would be all right. For this is the pinnacle, and there will never be anything better or higher or bigger for me. I have fulfillment, Elida. At last, I have fulfillment."

And I burst into sobbing as I humbly thanked my God. Because even if no one else knew it, I had been no actress that night. I had only been remembering and all I had done was carry out His orders. And I had shown them all what it is to be a colored woman, dumb, ignorant, all boxed up and feeling everything with such intenseness that she is half crazy. The role gave me the sort of release I'd long needed. Being Hagar softened me, and I was able to make more allowance for the shortcomings of others. Before that I'd always been cursing outside and crying inside. Playing in *Mamba's Daughters* enabled me to rid myself of the terrible inward pressure, the flood of tears I'd been storing up ever since my childhood.

After a solid run on Broadway we took *Mamba's Daughters* out on tour.

Down through the years I'd been visiting my mother regularly. I had rented a little house for her on Catherine Street in Philadelphia, and she lived there with her sister Vi. But her nervousness kept getting worse.

One night during the week we played Indianapolis I saw a man in a gray uniform crouching behind a counter on the stage. I got angry, thinking he was a stagehand who'd been caught on stage when the curtain went up. But when I walked out he'd disappeared. Later, when I described the apparition to the backstage crew fellers, they told me that my description fitted exactly a man who had fallen to his death from the flies about a year before. He had not died immediately. He was an atheist, that man, and he lay on the stage cursing God as he died.

I knew that seeing that apparition was a bad omen. And soon I got word that on that very same evening, almost at the same hour, my mother had got into bad trouble. Some newcomers to the neighborhood had sat on her stoop. When she ordered them away they just laughed at her. Momweeze then threw some hot coffee on them. The people went to the station house and signed an arrest paper.

When we moved to Detroit I was worried sick about Momweeze. And I had another omen there. During my stage fight with Willie I fell down in a dead faint. He had to shake me to make me come to. At that very moment in Philadelphia the authorities were taking Momweeze to the hospital. I tried to get a plane to take me there the moment I heard about this. It was Christmas week, and a bad, bitter night. All passenger flights had been canceled, but I managed to get in a mail plane to New York and went on to Philadelphia by train.

The story I got from Genevieve, my half sister, shocked me. My mother had been handled very roughly by the ambulance people. She wasn't crazy, just eccentric. Yet they had forced her to go out with them — without even giving her a chance to get her coat — out into the cold and the biting wind. Vi had gone along in the ambulance to the Philadelphia General Hospital.

"Not the General!" I said. For what good was the money I was making if Momweeze could be hustled off like that, without a coat, to be thrown into some dirty, overcrowded ward?

I hurried to the hospital, where a nurse took me to the ward. It was the snake pit. Women who seemed no longer human leered and grinned and chattered all about us. Young women, old women, grimacing and making obscene gestures, women so far gone into mental decay they could no longer keep themselves clean or decently clothed.

And there sat my mother. She was in a corner, at a window, and looking out, her back straight as a rod and her head up.

"Louise," said the nurse, "here is your daughter."

Slowly Momweeze looked around at me. Her expression didn't change. "Ethel," she said. "Who am I, Ethel?"

"My mother," I said, my heart bursting.

Momweeze looked triumphantly at that nurse and said, "I told you my daughter would come and get me out of here."

I couldn't take my eyes off Momweeze. I'd never seen her looking so thin and undernourished. I learned the reason for that later on. It had been the work of Vi, my always mischievous and troublemaking aunt. She had stayed on with Momweeze in the ward. When their first meal came Vi whispered to my mother, "Don't eat nothin', Louise. The food is all doped. It puts you to sleep. If you eat any of it you'll never get out of here."

Vi had been eating all the food brought for both of them. Unable to reason with my mother, the hospital authorities had been feeding her intravenously.

I had the nurse take me to the doctor in charge of the ward. He proved to be a courteous and friendly man. "Why was my mother taken here?" I asked. "You people must know she isn't mad. Her conduct may seem a little eccentric at times, but she's far from crazy."

"That's true," he agreed, "your mother is not demented. But she is very nervous, very high-strung. I'm very sorry to have to tell you that there was no other place we could take her."

"I take good care of my mother, Doctor — "

"We know that, Miss Waters," he said. "We investigated and learned you send her three hundred dollars each month. In fact, we discovered that three hundred dollars — two semimonthly money orders for one hundred and fifty dollars each — are waiting for her right now. Nevertheless, we will have to send her to Norristown tomorrow."

"Norristown! Norristown!" Norristown is the state's mental institution. I tried to be calm. I tried not to cry. But the savage irony burned into my soul. Each night for a year many hundreds of white men and women had been acclaiming me for portraying my mother on the stage. These white people had sobbed and suffered with Hagar, who to me was the replica of my mother. I had broken their hearts and so blinded them to reality that I had stopped being Ethel Waters to them. And there was the original of my stage portrait, thin, wasted, unfed. Tomorrow they'd put her in a wagon and cart her off to the state crazy house.

"Your mother had some terrible shock early in life," the doctor was saying.

"Me!" I thought. "The shock came when she brought *me* into the world." As a child my mother was religious and at all times had Christian learning. She was always where there was a church meeting, and wanted to be an evangelist. She went to church instead of with the boys. She shut out of her mind everything worldly.

One of the boys who would come around to our rickety home in an alley was John Waters, my father. One day he forced my mother to submit to him. She tried to fight him, but he raped her, holding a knife to her throat. She was only twelve and didn't know what it was all about, but she had to give in to him. And that is how I was conceived.

My mother always hated and resented my father and never afterward would have anything to do with him. It was just that one time with them. Nobody suspicioned anything was wrong. And my mother wouldn't tell, she being so hurt and bitter and hardly understanding herself what was happening inside her body. It was Sally, my grandmother, who finally noticed the bulge that was beginning to show under her dress.

"As a young woman," the doctor was saying, "your mother withdrew from all normal living. She's always suffered from complete frustration. She's an introvert."

"I understand that, Doctor," I told him. "But you yourself say she is not crazy. I've investigated and I found that in the whole great state of Pennsylvania there is not one place I can send my mother as a patient. For one reason only: my mother is a colored woman.

"Can't I please take her home? You know she doesn't belong here, or in Norristown, or in any other institution like that. Genevieve, my half sister, would take good care of her, Doctor."

Thoughtfully he said, "I can do that, but only on one condition: someone must be with her at all times, night and day."

"That is something I can guarantee," I promised him. Then I went back into that ward.

"Are you going to get me out of here, Ethel?" my mother asked.

"Yes, but only when you can walk out on your own two feet. To do that, you must eat. You must forget what Vi told you about the food here being poisoned. It's not true, Momweeze."

My mother promised to eat the hospital's food. She was not sent to

Norristown the next day, or ever, in that locked-up wagon. Within a week I was able to get her out of the snake pit.

Some people around Philadelphia who knew my mother said she was crazy. But they were wrong. Whatever they thought, they never knew that Momweeze had endured torment, long sustained, that few human beings could have survived.

Momweeze was always as unhappy as Hagar, and as lonely. Playing that role gave me new insight into the depthless nature of her loneliness, and also the loneliness I've known ever since I was born.

Somehow or other, the things my mother wanted to do, the release in evangelism that she sought with such frenzy, were transferred to me. I think that through my plays and my pictures I have been able to get across the message she never had the chance to deliver.

That was her destiny — and my own. Our destiny, shared, lay in everything that my mother thought and felt about God in her heart being said — but not by her from a pulpit, but from me on stage and screen; me, her unwanted one, conceived in terror and violence, and against her will.

Where Equality Leads

by OSCAR HANDLIN

Oscar Handlin, who has devoted years of study to the blood streams that make up America, is the author of The Uprooted, *which won the Pulitzer Prize for History in 1952. His most recent book is* Race and Nationality in American Life.

NOVEMBER 1956

The public debate on desegregation has dealt largely with the shadow of the issue rather than with its substance. Not states' rights or federalism or the control of education, but some other, gnawing fear — rarely expressed — lies behind the violence of the protest against the Supreme Court's decision. The dread lest desegregation open the way to a contaminating race mixture is the fundamental anxiety that troubles many white Southerners; it is the nightmare that drives men to disregard the law in Tennessee and Texas and Alabama.

The haunting specter of racial amalgamation corresponds to nothing in the world of actuality. It is rather the product of three profound misconceptions. The men frightened by it mistake the meaning of the Supreme Court's decision of 1954. They misjudge the probable consequences of desegregation on both whites and blacks. And, most important, their conjectures as to what results will follow upon more intimate contact between Negroes and other Americans in the schools run counter to all the available evidence.

Segregation emerged as a defined pattern of social behavior in the 1880s. Segregation was not directed simply at the schools; it aimed to create a mode of life that would establish the distinct inferiority of the Negro by setting him apart in every important activity — in the school as elsewhere. The supporters of segregation argued that they had no intention of negating the rights of the Negro. It was possible, they insisted, to provide separate but equal facilities in education as in transportation and in the other spheres where the two races had contact. In 1896, in the famous case of *Plessy v. Ferguson,* the Supreme Court accepted that contention, assuming that the privileges guaranteed by the Fourteenth Amendment would still be assured under a segregated regime. The decision affirmed the right of the Negroes to equality, but it accepted the argument that equality could be attained through separateness.

When the Supreme Court reviewed this issue in 1954, it had almost sixty years of experience on the basis of which to test the validity of that argument. Its unanimous decision was that the pattern of separate treatment, as it had developed, had not brought equality of treatment to the Negro. This was a question of fact and not of law. No serious observer of the Southern scene has denied that the educational facilities supplied to the black citizens of the Southern states were markedly inferior to those of the whites. Indeed, in many vital respects the Negro's relative situation had actually deteriorated since 1896. Those who had affirmed the compatibility of segregation and equality had not in those decades of opportunity made it work.

The Court was therefore compelled to review the findings of *Plessy v. Ferguson.* If separateness did not bring the equality guaranteed by the Fourteenth Amendment, then the laws establishing the segregated system were unconstitutional, for they fixed the Negro in an inferior place and thus deprived him of the rights guaranteed by the Amendment.

But that was all the Court said. Its findings were purely negative. It did not go on to any positive injunction laying down a line of action to be followed. Instead, it left the various states free gradually to develop a variety of adjustments that would meet the clear constitutional obligation to provide equal treatment for all citizens regardless of race.

The Court's decision insisted only that the element of racial compulsion be removed, and it left a considerable range of alternatives available to those who wish to adapt themselves to the conditions it created. In the years to come, good sense and tolerance will undoubtedly encourage the majority of Americans to explore these alternatives. The results will vary widely according to the local conditions of each community.

Desegregation therefore does not necessarily involve the emergence of a single, all-inclusive, integrated type of school, unless the students and their parents choose to have it do so. The question then arises: what will the parents choose?

Under conditions of genuine equality, Negroes have thus shown the inclination to continue to attend schools preponderantly made up of members of their own race. In 1949, for instance, an Indiana state law prohibited the segregation which theretofore prevailed in some schools, including those of the city of Evansville. The result was not the mass rush to the white schools that some Hoosiers had anticipated. The overwhelming majority of Evansville Negroes — over 90 per cent — continued to attend their own schools. On the other hand, there is no doubt that the colored people of Clinton, Tennessee, or Clay, Kentucky, who braved obloquy, boycott, and the danger of violence to do so, preferred to send their children to integrated schools.

Integration is not an end in itself but a means to an end. Black parents, like white, hope that education will give their boys and girls the best possible preparation for life. They resent the compulsion to attend Negro schools, unequal to the white, that will forever burden their children with handicaps and label them indelibly with the stigma of inferiority. They will not resent schools that are genuinely equal and that bear no imputation of inferiority, no matter what their racial composition. Indeed, under some circumstances, they may actually find their children more comfortable in such schools with those who share a common cultural and social background.

There will necessarily be substantial regional and communal differences in adjustment. Classes in Bronzeville and Harlem are predominantly Negro, just as those in East Boston are Italian and those in Hamtramck are Polish. Only in rare instances are such schools likely to contain a completely mixed and heterogeneous student body. In smaller cities there is less scope for such adjustments. The elementary schools may reflect the neighborhood differences. But if there is only one high school in town it will have to accommodate all the students eligible to attend it.

The greatest problem will no doubt exist in rural regions which enjoy a minimum of flexibility. There the segregated school has been least convenient and most expensive; and there it most often produced the types of inferiority that the Supreme Court condemned. It may be that no solution other than integration in the general school system will do justice to the dozen Negro families of Clinton, Tennessee. But the fact that integration is sought there does not mean it will be sought everywhere.

There has been a subtle change in the attitudes of Negroes with the improvement of their status in the past thirty years. There was a time when colored people were so depressed by the sense of their own inferiority that they accepted unquestioningly all the white man's standards. Their own habits and tastes, like their blackness, were inherently degrading; and success and happiness went to those who could most closely model themselves upon the dominant race. There was a premium upon "marrying light" even though within the group, because that most closely approximated the standards of the whites.

With the Negro's achievement of some degree of stability and the restoration of his self-confidence, there has been a significant change, even since Gunnar Myrdal noticed it in 1944. Rejecting the notion of his own inferiority, the Negro has ceased to take the white as the determining model. He has come to value the standards and tastes of his own group and often actually to take pride in his color. Not a few are unwilling to "pass" even though their pigmentation is pale enough to permit them to do so. The girl who holds the cake of soap in the *Ebony* advertisement is black; and she is pretty to those who see her because she is black. The era of the hair straightener is coming to an end. The notion that Negroes are eager to marry whites is a delusion born of the white's own vanity and of his ignorance of the real sentiments of his fellow Americans of another color.

The experience of schools in which segregation has come to an end amply confirms these judgments. The circumstances vary widely according to the conditions and traditions of the communities in which the adjustment occurs. In the Southern colleges, Negroes, once admitted, have generally enjoyed a minimum of social contact with white students.

Elsewhere the relationship between the races has extended beyond the classroom to the formal social activities conducted under school auspices. But even when the boy and girl of different colors dance together at the senior prom, they do not think of dating. They hesitate, as does the Methodist with the Catholic, because courtship and marriage involve an altogether different order of considerations.

The obsession with the unreal dangers of intermarriage has unfortunately obscured the true source of race mixture in the past and in the present. The white ancestors of the mulattoes and of the Negroes of varying degrees of lightness of skin were not married to blacks. These are the progeny of relationships outside wedlock; and miscegenation, not intermarriage, has, in the United States, been the mode of infusing the black with the white strain in our society. Furthermore, miscegenation under these terms was the direct product of the inferiority of Negro women. Whatever has tended to increase that inferiority has increased the rate of miscegenation. Whatever diminishes it lowers the rate. In that sense, segregation actually is indirectly more conducive to the mixture of races than is desegregation.

Through much of the nineteenth century, white men who kept black concubines suffered no loss of social esteem thereby. Until the Civil War, the women were their property, and no control limited the treatment accorded them. In most of the Southern states miscegenation was no crime, although intermarriage was.

Concubinage began to decline after the Civil War. It hardly exists now. It was extirpated by the liberation of the Negroes, which removed their women from the absolute power of the masters.

Less formal sexual relations between white men and black women, however, were long thereafter tolerated in many parts of the South. They were facilitated by the disorganization of Negro family life and by the simple brute fact that blacks were incapable of protecting their daughters and sisters against the aggressions of those who had once been their masters. The law and the mores were alike acquiescent. There are authentic, if scarcely credible, instances of respectable white businessmen who warned off the Negro preacher who wished to strengthen the morals of the women in his flock.

Insofar as that can be measured, the incidence of interracial sexual intercourse seems also to have declined perceptibly in the last forty years. It has fallen off precisely because the Negro now sees the prospect of leading a decent family life and because he himself has grown in self-respect and in the power to resist. The transformation in the general conception of what the law and the practices of society owe him is the most important element in that change.

If we strengthen the trend toward equality of opportunity and of rights, then we strengthen also the elements of cohesion and order in the Negro's own life. If we weaken that trend and perpetuate his inferiority, then we weaken also the fabric of his family life and leave him a loose, helpless, and potentially disorderly element in our society. If we can but free ourselves of the habit of thinking in terms of the absolutes of total conformity and amalgamation on the one hand and of total separateness and segregation on the other, we shall find our institutions flexible enough to accommodate a variety of solutions among which individuals will be able to make their own personal choices. It was the virtue of the Supreme Court to have understood that, and in its decision to have laid a foundation for constructive development in the future. And it is the insistence upon thinking of the nightmare of amalgamation as the only alternative to segregation that is most likely to perpetuate the tensions that all Americans should dread.

The Freedom to Think

by ZECHARIAH CHAFEE

Professor of law at Harvard for forty years, Zechariah Chafee was a trenchant defender of civil rights. He is best known for his authoritative book, Free Speech in the United States.

JANUARY 1955

The capacity of citizens to adjust themselves wisely to changes is particularly urgent in matters of government, law, economic transactions, and other areas of the social sciences. Even if there were no new inventions, we should be foolish to expect ideas to stay as they are, however satisfactory we now find them. Sometimes it is hard for a community to see the need for new methods of conducting its affairs even though that need is great. The Industrial Revolution caused an immediate, enormous, and never-ending growth of metropolitan areas, whose problems could not possibly be handled efficiently by the old simple, overlapping governments of counties, townships, and cities in a particular region like Greater New York. And yet it was decades before men began asking what kind of government ought to replace those which had hopelessly broken down.

In the United States today institutions are not frozen, nor are they so anywhere in the free world from which we must seek allies. As the newly independent nations of Asia plan their governments, we ought not to be shocked if they decide to govern themselves in ways which are somewhat unfamiliar to us. The numerous problems the American people face at home or in their relations with other countries call for inventiveness and wisdom on the part of the few who propose solutions and of the many who decide whether to accept or modify or reject them. Devotion to tradition is useless here. The inevitability of change requires our unyielding maintenance of the principle of open discussion, not only for ideas and persons we like but also for those we detest.

This brings me to what I want to say most. The universities of the United States are taking an indispensable share in the work of continuously testing, readjusting, and improving the machinery of human relations, and nobody else can do what they do. Of course, a great deal of this work will always be carried on by the active men in the field, such as politicians, journalists, lawyers, judges, and businessmen. They have an experience, a sense of what is possible, and other qualities of mind which are rare among professors. Still, no matter how shrewd the practical men are, they are absorbed in a crowded succession of immediate tasks; and this leaves them far less time than professors have for taking long views.

In former times in England and the United States there were a considerable number of able men outside universities who had sufficient leisure to take long views of society and put them into books. Remember the influence exerted by Jeremy Bentham and Walter Bagehot. John Stuart Mill did not even go to college. Most of the great American historians of the nineteenth century held no professorships. However, with high taxes and modern pressures we can no longer count on getting the help we need from such independent men. No doubt there will still be an occasional farsighted columnist like Walter Lippmann, an occasional part-time historian like Douglas Southall Freeman. But the major contributions to comprehensive thinking about the problems of society will have to come from the universities. Think of Adam Smith at Glasgow, Blackstone at Oxford, Wythe the teacher of John Marshall at William and Mary, Thomas Cooley at Michigan, William Graham Sumner at Yale, Woodrow Wilson at Princeton, Frank Taussig at Harvard, to mention a few.

The professor in a social science performs his indispensable task in several different ways. He writes himself. He teaches the writers of the future. Still more important, he trains potential politicians and voters to deal wisely and well with the problems which they will have to face. And the classroom discussions teach him as well as his students; he discovers the weak spots in his views and puts them into print more clearly than if he wrote in isolation.

What I am saying about the indispensable task of a university applies to all universities in the United States, public or endowed, and particularly to the former. As taxes rise, endowed universities lose and state universities gain. The fact that these public universities are ultimately controlled by legislatures ought to be irrelevant to their performance of the indispensable task of supplying long views about the problems of society. The government pays judges, but it does not tell them how to decide. An independent state university is as essential to the community as an independent judiciary. Legislatures make it possible for scholars to think and teach. There the political part in education should end. When he who pays the piper insists on calling the tune, he is not likely to get much good music.

For many decades the American universities have been performing their indispensable task. All of a sudden they are gravely hampered in carrying it out by current fears of radicalism. There is no class of people more injured by repression than teachers. If you confine the teacher in his thinking, what do you leave him? That is his job, to think. Universities should not be transformed, as in Nazi Germany, into loudspeakers for the men who wield political power. If they are deprived of freedom of thought and speech, there is no other place to which citizens can confidently turn for long views about public issues. Here and there some courageous writer or speaker may still make himself known, but such men are no substitute for the present systematic creation and communication of ideas which take place in our universities.

We have come a long, long way from Thomas Jefferson, whose name is so frequently invoked by the politicians who have brought about the present laws of the United States. He invited professors from abroad to the University of Virginia, which (he wrote) "will be based on the illimitable freedom of the human mind. For here we are not afraid to follow truth wherever it may lead, nor to tolerate error so long as reason is left free to combat it." Our government is repudiating the spirit of Jefferson just at the time when it is more important than ever before that the free countries should pool their intellectual resources for the sake of preserving their freedom and increasing human welfare.

The doors of the United States are now locked on both sides. When American scholars are asked to lecture at European universities or attend important conferences, their passports may be denied by subordinate officials or delayed so long that the object of the journey is wrecked. Linus Pauling, former president of the American Chemical Society and winner of the 1954 Nobel Prize in Chemistry, was invited to take part in a discussion of the structure of proteins at the Royal Society in London on May 1, 1952. Pauling applied for a passport on January 24. Through the efforts of Senator Wayne Morse, he finally got it — on July 15. Ten weeks too late for the Royal Society meeting!

Meanwhile, some of the most distinguished thinkers in free countries have been refused visas to enter the United States and help us advance our knowledge. According to a very measured and painstaking examination of such cases in the *Bulletin of Atomic Scientists* for October 1952, none of the many excluded foreign scholars there discussed would have been dangerous to the United States if admitted, and not one had the remotest tinge of Communism. The natural sciences are the chief sufferers from this policy, but the social sciences are by no means left free. Michael Polanyi, for example, is professor of social studies at Manchester in England. Polanyi was among the distinguished scholars whom Princeton gathered at its bicentenary in 1946, but in 1951 he was not allowed to return to the United States to occupy the chair of social philosophy at the University of Chicago. The adamant American consul never looked at any of Polanyi's writings.

Visas are not always denied, only delayed without reasons. "I waited, but nothing happened." "Weeks and months elapsed without an answer." Anybody who has been shocked by Menotti's opera *The Consul* will find its scenes re-enacted in offices which fly the Stars and Stripes.

Today we, the people of the United States, are shutting out quiet thinkers who are anxious to come among us to help us treat leukemia and breast cancer, and to aid us in many different ways to develop valuable ideas for our industry and our welfare. Russia has hung an iron curtain along its frontiers and China a silken curtain. The government of the United States is doing its best to put around our shores a curtain of solid ivory.

Thirty years ago I was on the receiving end of an academic investigation for heterodox writing, and I know what a great encouragement it has been to feel absolutely assured that the authorities of Harvard will never dismiss a professor because of his honestly held opinions, whether expressed in or out of the classroom. For the sake of having a university do its special and essential work well, it is worth while to run the risk of whatever injuries may come from a few men on its faculty with objectionable ideas.

As it was declared by Justice Robert Jackson, whose death is a bitter loss:

> Our forefathers found the evils of free thinking more to be endured than the evils of inquest or suppression. This is because thoughtful, bold and independent minds are essential to wise and considered self-government.

The time has come to strike back. Individual professors can be brought under fire and easily picked off like an isolated sentry. They ought not be allowed to feel like the young State Department man in Europe who explained to me why he was resigning. "I haven't been attacked yet, but I know that if I am attacked, not a single person in Washington will raise a finger in my defense." In contrast I thought of what President Lowell told me, after he had warded off the Wall Street lawyers who sought my dismissal: "I had to protect my front."

To presidents, trustees, regents, alumni, I say, "This is your fight." Despite proper anxieties about future gifts and student enrollments, I believe a university which proclaims its devotion to freedom and lives up to it will attract farsighted givers and young men and women who are worth teaching. It is easy to underestimate the admiration which American citizens feel toward courage.

The issue is whether the unusual man shall be rigidly controlled by the usual men. No more concessions. We will not bow down in the House of Rimmon. We will not take breakfast in the Schine apartment.

The time has come for the universities of the United States to stop retreating. We ought to educate more than our students. "We must educate our masters" — the legislators and the citizens who in the end make educational institutions possible. We need to persuade them to minimize the dangers of heterodoxy and be ready, as Jefferson was, to take a calculated risk. We need to convince them of what they have forgotten — the importance of intellectual freedom, if we are to have the kind of country most loyal Americans desire. We need to make our fellow citizens realize that freedom is not safety, but opportunity.

By Slow Degrees

by CATHERINE DRINKER BOWEN

*A writing member of the famous Drinker clan of Phila-
delphia, Catherine Drinker Bowen has scored a notable success with her interpretive biographies, three of which have
dealt with eminent jurists:* Yankee from Olympus, *her study
of Justice Oliver Wendell Holmes, secondly* John Adams and
the American Revolution, *and more recently* The Lion and
the Throne: The Life and Times of Sir Edward Coke.

FEBRUARY 1955

Lawyers and writers have much in common. We are concerned with
words — how to say exactly what we mean and no more than we mean.
We are concerned also with the behavior of individuals under given circumstances. Such behavior is, indeed, our stock in trade. Nevertheless
there is between us a fundamental difference. I am not belittling my
own profession when I say that lawyers and judges have a more immediate stake in what is set down on paper. I write a biography and
perhaps it touches the emotion of my readers. I hope it does. But a lawyer's brief, a judge's rendered opinion, leads to direct action. Somebody
goes to jail, somebody pays a fine or forfeits his money or his reputation.
That irrepressibly oracular figure, Dr. Samuel Johnson (women do not
like him), said a good thing: "Lawyers know life practically. A bookish
person should always have them to converse with. Lawyers have what
the writer wants."

For fifteen years, I have been writing about lawyers. My notebooks
are filled with the characteristics of professional legal gentlemen: judges,
ready to sum up or to instruct; law school professors, ready to make
statements — and then qualify those statements; advocates, born advocates, with their wonderful, remorseless, happy courtroom voices that
go on and on! I am grateful to lawyers and I welcome a chance to say

so. Think of the material the legal profession has given me! My biography of Justice Holmes was four hundred pages and the one on John Adams was seven hundred pages. For the past four years I have been writing about that sixteenth-century legal figure, Sir Edward Coke, the man whom Maitland wrote of as "the common law made flesh." Three lawyers, then, have furnished me with superb material. The world likes to grumble because lawyers make their living from the troubles of laymen. Here is one laywoman who for fifteen years has been making quite a thing for herself out of the troubles and the triumphs of lawyers.

There is a question which lawyers often ask me about my biographies: "Why did you go backwards, in time? Holmes, John Adams, Edward Coke." To me, the natural progression is backward. Writing about a nineteenth-century legal thinker, a person becomes curious to find out where that thinker, that judge, derived certain of his ideas. So I went back to a fertile century, the eighteenth — and came upon John Adams. Then the question arose, "Where did John Adams find these practical, idealistic eighteenth-century notions about how to form governments and write state constitutions?" There was one place to look: England, in the seventeenth and sixteenth centuries. Edward Coke, for the purpose, comes in just the right place. His dates were 1552–1634, although, as I go along, I discover that Coke's story actually starts in 1215, with Magna Carta.

My three legal subjects had certain personal characteristics which impelled me to choose them in the beginning. First, a deep pride in their profession. Holmes, Adams, and Coke looked on the law historically, in a long and, to them, magnificent perspective. "This abstraction called the law," Holmes said, "where, as in a magic mirror, we see reflected, not only our own lives but the lives of all men that have been." John Adams was not capable of that kind of diction. Few people are. But he had the same outlook, coupled with a hard, earthy, practical nature. Law, to Adams, was constitutional law; it was government. Quite early in life he became absorbed in the study of comparative government, reading whatever he could find about the Italian republics of the Middle Ages, the ancient city-states, the Dutch experiments. He was surprised when people would not listen to him talk about it. "I know not how it is," he wrote plaintively to a friend, "but mankind have an aversion to the science of government. To me, no romance is more entertaining."

Sir Edward Coke compiled eleven volumes of law reports (thirteen, counting the posthumous ones) covering about six hundred cases. I know because I counted them. He wrote four volumes on the laws of

England, the first being the famous *Commentary upon Littleton*. He did this in his leisure time. He served often in Parliament, once as Speaker. He was Attorney General for thirteen years, Chief Justice of Common Pleas, then King's Bench.

Coke was forever defending the English law as against Roman or civil law, Continental law, the law ecclesiastic. Often enough he defended it where, quite palpably, at that stage of history, the English law did not deserve defense. Coke was an excellent teacher, an inveterate teacher. As Speaker of the House of Commons, he taught law to the Commons, gave them little lectures from the Chair. All his life he taught his law students at the Inns of Court in London. He said they complained because the laws of England were "dark, and hard to be understood." He had therefore, in his books, "opened such windows as make the laws lightsome and easy . . . so that any man who hath but the light of nature (which Solomon calleth the candle of Almighty God) if he add industry and diligence thereto, can easily discern the same."

Men who themselves possess great intelligence are forever demanding diligence from their students or their colleagues, when what they really look for is talent or genius equal to their own. Coke called this quality the "light of nature, candle of Almighty God." As for Holmes, do you remember his story about his teaching days at Harvard Law School? "I used to tell my students," he said, "that they could do anything they wanted, if only they wanted to hard enough. But what I did not tell them was, they must be born wanting to."

These three lawyers showed a deep, almost romantic reverence for their profession. Something else which they manifested was a consciousness of being intellectually alone and an ability to bear and to endure this loneliness. For such men the experience begins early. With Holmes I would say it began in his late twenties, when he was preparing a new edition of *Kent's Commentaries*. His friends noted his extreme absorption and it made them uneasy. Later, Holmes spoke of it as an adventure of sailing for the polar ice and letting oneself be frozen in. "No one," he said, "can cut new paths in company. A man does that alone." John Adams kept a diary, voluminous, infinitely revealing — heaven's gift to a biographer. To watch young Adams wrestle with his particular devils, you might think Martin Luther wrote that diary. At twenty-four, Adams scolds himself because he cannot spend a whole day upon one especial book, say, Justinian's *Institutes*. Why, he asks, must he stop to smoke, to write a letter, or "to think of the girls"? Is there not someone who can help him, guide him, is there not some easier way out? "It is my destiny," he writes, "to dig treasures with my own fingers. *Nobody will lend me or sell me a pickaxe.*"

There is in men of such endowment a vast, continuing impatience, a desperate persistence which for the biographer is an awesome thing to watch. Holmes believed that a man who has not arrived by forty will never arrive. He nearly broke himself in two trying to get his book, *The Common Law,* written by that strategic date. It is to be noted also that intellectual men, who live by and through books, mourn continually that they are not men of action.

They show embarrassment because they are not soldiers, stevedores, boxers. Holmes had little complaint on this score, with his record of three years' active service in the Civil War. But John Adams, bald and fortyish and making himself surely useful enough at the Continental Congress, wrote frantically to his wife, Abigail: "Oh, that I were a soldier! I will be. I am reading military books. Everybody must, and shall, and will be a soldier."

Sir Edward Coke, on the other hand, never apologized for being a bookish man. On the contrary, he defended it. In the year 1601, as Queen Elizabeth's Attorney General, Coke prosecuted the Earl of Essex for treason. The Essex Rebellion lasted only a day — one of the silliest attempts of history. In connection with it, seven men were tried. All were convicted, six were executed. At the last trial of all, Coke seized the occasion to express his satisfaction that in the entire affair, though some three hundred were in prison, not one was a lawyer. "To the honor of the City of London," Coke said in the courtroom, "not one Inns of Court man followed the Earl of Essex. Not one scholar of the law. Not one." During the rebellion, there had been an incident where Chief Justice Popham and Lord Chancellor Egerton were locked into Essex House and left there for six hours, their lives threatened by a crowd of swordsmen in the courtyard.

Around midday, one of Essex's followers offered the Chief Justice his liberty. Whereupon old John Popham said no, he would not dream of accepting freedom unless the Lord Chancellor could go too. Coke told about it in court. And then he said proudly, "To their honors I will speak it, that in some gown-men there rest as valiant minds, where the cause requires it, as in them that wear swords."

For better or for worse, most lawyers are eloquent. One finds in legal gentlemen a provision of good, healthy *ham.* (Something else which they share with writers.) Eloquent men, especially those with a tendency to be quarrelsome, a bit quick on the trigger, like to protest how silent they are under stress. Holmes of course was too truly so-phisticated to protest anything of the kind. Moreover Holmes was, as Justice Brandeis said to me, "an ivory tower man, raised in his father's library."

And Brandeis added that it was "a good thing for the Supreme Court to have an ivory tower man at least once in a generation." But John Adams was not an ivory tower man, and neither was Coke. They were hot-tempered, frequently embroiled in quarrels. John Adams, after such a fracas, listed his new enemies in his diary and then added loftily, "This storm will blow over me in silence."

No storm ever blew over John Adams or any good lawyer in silence. Take Sir Francis Bacon, who was Coke's rival straight along through their two careers, one in equity, one in the common law courts. In the year 1601, Coke and Bacon had a noisy row in Exchequer Court, on the first day of term. They slanged away at each other, and we know what they said because Bacon went immediately home and wrote a careful report to the Secretary of State, who happened to be his first cousin. (It was characteristic of Bacon to get there first with the news.) Bacon told what Coke had said to him and then added, "Mr. Attorney" — they called Coke "Mr. Attorney" in those days — "Mr. Attorney gave me a number of disgraceful words, which I answered with silence and show-ing I was not moved by them."

Holmes, John Adams, Coke were concerned with the business of government. Neck and neck with the personal story there runs therefore the history of constitutions; written constitutions and unwritten ones. Lord Brougham made a remark, which he said he got from somebody else: "All that we see about us, kings, lords and commons, the whole machinery of state, all the apparatus of the system and its varied work-ings, end in simply bringing twelve good men into a box."

Teachers of the law will want that remark qualified, at once. Pos-sibly it is a bit exaggerated. All I wish to say is that nobody could write those three biographies without finding herself frequently in the court-room or the legislature. And no layman can spend time in either of those places without perceiving the extraordinary importance of *procedure*.

Observing Edward Coke as Speaker of the House of Commons, I saw his care concerning, for instance, the matter of voting from the floor. (Those were the days when parliamentary procedure was still in the making.) When a division was called, should the Ayes get up and go out to the lobby to be counted while the Noes sat still, or the other way?

There were not nearly enough seats to go round. A man voting Aye went out and lost his seat to somebody who had been standing. Consequently it happened that members actually voted against their conviction so as not to have to stand up for the rest of the day.

Small matters of procedure can have vast repercussions on us plain people, waiting outside. I'm aware that it is not advisable to judge a nation's legal procedure by what happens in big dramatic cases which are bounded on three sides by politics. (Wasn't it Holmes who said, "Great cases make bad law"?) In such trials, everything is warped by that huge imponderable which enters the courtroom: *public opinion.* It was that way in 1600, it is that way now. Academically, these cases are not typical of customary procedure. Nevertheless, the layman, the general public, does look on such trials as, let us say, a *test* of how well customary procedure holds up under stress. Specialists in any field avoid large, fuzzy words. Judges avoid the word *justice,* preferring, quite rightly, to speak of *the law.* But we laymen use the words *justice* and *injustice.* We happen to be the ones who are caught in the machinery. "Is it fair?" we ask. "Was it fair?"

Ranging, as a layman, over nearly four centuries of courtroom procedure, legislative procedure, I was particularly impressed with one thing. If reform in law is to come at all, it must come slowly or it will not stick. When it comes fast it boomerangs, or else we laymen ignore the new law. Voltaire said something which I doubt would be said — I trust would not be said — by an American or Englishman in any century. And his context does not suggest irony. "Do you wish good laws? *Then burn the ones you have and make new ones.*" Occasionally, during a lifetime, we see the rules burned. We see a brand-new kind of tribunal set up — I won't say a court — a tribunal which burns the old rules and makes its own. We laymen watch what happens. And we do not like it.

For all my books I have a private working title, a slogan by which I operate and which has nothing to do with what publishing houses refer to as "the selling title." For Edward Coke my private title is three words, and they refer not to Coke but to public law — "By Slow Degrees."

Consider the seven centuries of Anglo-American common law, a big arc in time. Edward Coke comes in the middle, at a moment when some rather reprehensible notions were floating about the courtroom — leftovers from an earlier day when England's government was not strong enough to dispense with certain legal tyrannies. For the biographer it is distressing to watch Mr. Attorney in, say, the trial of Sir Walter Ralegh

— which actually was not a trial at all but a public inquiry into guilt already prejudged by Bench and Bar; and not only prejudged but proclaimed. Coke's brutality to Ralegh has become a byword. I see it quoted in Bar Association Journals, month after month. I wish those gentlemen would quote the context — what the Chief Justice said at that trial, his expressed reasons for not permitting Ralegh to have his one and only accuser brought to the courtroom to confront him face to face, as Ralegh requested. Should he permit *that,* Chief Justice Popham told the court, why, it would be to endanger the state! Everybody accepted the dictum. It was recognized procedure.

Right in the middle of this appalling situation, judges and prosecutor spoke proudly of the laws of England. "The law of England is a law of mercy." Coke said it in courtroom and out, and when he wished to be mysterious or especially impressive he put it, after his fashion, into Latin: *Lex Angliae est lex misericordiae.*

And yet, one has the conviction — or, rather, one hazards the guess — that Coke's very faith in English law was something of a foundation for our own future, here in the United States. His was not a complacency but a true pride upon which, as a judge and Parliament man, he acted, later, at peril of his life. Out of Coke's experience and the experience of those who followed and preceded him, there was shaped at last that system which America and England share and in which they can both take pride.

Seeing at first hand what lawyers are trying — *by slow degrees* — to achieve, I recall something Blackstone said. He referred to a specific point of law, yet what he wrote has wide application here as in England: "Legislature and judges in the course of a long, laborious process, extracted by noble alchemy, rich medicines out of poisonous ingredients."

Blackstone was not urging that two wrongs make a right; or, Do evil that good may come of it; or, The end justifies the means. I think he gave us one of those vague, perceptive distortions which sometimes carry farther than logic.

We laymen, then, watch and observe our courts, our judges, our public prosecutors, our public defenders, and our law institutes. We do not look for a millennium, for that perfect state which will need no lawyers. But we are reassured by what the legal profession is trying to do. We like to know that among men wise in the law, there is a certain vigilance, the courage of persistence, the courage of patience. We laymen feel that the gentlemen of the law are reaching for things that will come — *by slow degrees.*

The Creative Process

The Atlantic has always felt that it had an obligation to foster the fine arts, and early and quite dutifully it published articles on architecture and reviews of the more notable galleries and exhibits here and abroad. For a time there was a monthly letter covering the social, artistic, and theatrical activities of New York City, and for a mercifully brief interval under Howells it even attempted to publish sheet music, with very sentimental results.

But when in 1891 T. W. Higginson published his correspondence with Emily Dickinson, he opened up a new approach to the creative process, an approach of which we have availed ourselves with increasing interest in recent years. When Laurence Housman writes with such illumination of the art of his brother, A. E. Housman ("A Poet in the Making," July 1946), when John Masefield tells what it meant to him when as a young man he first heard Yeats speak on poetry (March 1951), and when we print W. H. Auden's splendid, candid essay on "Making and Judging Poetry" (January 1957), we are helping to remove some of the natural obstacles between poet and reader.

These obstacles have been magnified since the 1920s, as the new poets tended to become more abstract and more difficult for the layman to follow. A void opened, and the bridge across it is at best a suspension affair. We are living in an age which prides itself on its advance in communication; yet it is a curious commentary that many more people are writing verse (the Atlantic receives upward of forty thousand poems a year) than will buy it in book form.

Poets today deserve all the encouragement we can give them. So do the writers of prose; it is humbling to hear James Joyce tell of the seven years of abuse and frustration which he had to suffer before he was permitted to bring his first book, Dubliners, *into print, just as it is touching to hear William Saroyan speak of his belief in himself and of his self-imposed disciplines, as he looks back in his article "Twenty Years of Writing" (May 1955).*

Books call for time, and in this competitive age of ours the book's most serious competitor is not the television screen but the long-playing record. Every magazine must look to the undergraduate body for its coming readers, and the undergraduates today have a knowledge and love of music far keener than that of their predecessors. All of which explains why the Atlantic of late has been devoting so much space to the interpretive writing of composers like Prokofiev and Stravinsky. We encouraged Koussevitzky to write of his favorite composers, Debussy, Mendelssohn, and Brahms; Toscanini was described minutely as he recorded the Beethoven Ninth; Leonard Bernstein has told us more trenchantly than any other of the racking choice a composer must make between the rewards of musical comedy and the prestige minus cash of symphonic composition.

So too in the dance we have moved from the heavy-footed anticipatory essays by Havelock Ellis to the more impassioned accounts by Isadora Duncan, and thence to the intense and moving prose of the most articulate of choreographers, Agnes de Mille. There can be nothing perfunctory about the creative process.

A Sculptor at Work

from "*Sculptors of Today*"

by JACOB EPSTEIN

Born in New York City of Russian parents in 1880, Jacob Epstein studied as a young man under Auguste Rodin. At the age of twenty-seven he was commissioned to decorate the new building of the British Medical Association in London; his work, which has always been a storm center, established him in London, and there he has made his home.

NOVEMBER 1940

In my portraits it is assumed that I start out with a definite conception of my sitter's character. On the contrary, I have no such conception whatever in the beginning. The sitter arrives in the studio, mounts the stand, and I begin my study. My aim, to start with, is entirely constructive. With scientific precision I make a quite coldly thought-out construction of the form, giving the bony formations around the eyes, the ridge of the nose, mouth, and cheekbones, and defining the relation of the different parts of the skull to each other. As the work proceeds I note the expression and the changes of expression, and the character of the model begins to impress itself on me. In the end, by a natural process of observation, the mental and physiological characteristics of the sitter impose themselves upon the clay. This process is natural and not preconceived. With close and intensive study come subtleties and fine shades. From turning the work round so as to catch every light comes that solidity that makes the work light-proof, as it were. For in a work of sculpture the forms actually alter with the change of light, not as in a painting or drawing, where the forms only become more or less visible.

It is said that the sculptor as an artist always depicts himself in his work, even in his portraits. In only one sense is this true — that is, in the sense in which the artist's own nature colors his outlook. To illustrate what I say, take a portrait by Frans Hals. We observe that his outlook on humanity is cold and detached; he observes his models without any emotions and never warms to them. He seemed unfortunate in his sitters; as human beings they evidently aroused in him no feeling of sympathy, and he turned to their clothes with greater pleasure than he got from their faces. He obviously enjoyed his own technique and reveled in his marvelous skill.

With Rembrandt the opposite seems the case. His great heart seemed to warm toward the men and women who sat for him, and he seemed to penetrate into their inner selves and reveal their very souls — in children their lively joy, and in grownups the burden of living, their sorrow and disappointments. There is a great wisdom in him, and his people look out of his canvases, human beings whose trades and business you cannot tell, but they have deep human thoughts; they are not just tradesmen and shrews, as in Hals. A beggar in the hands of Rembrandt is some ancient philosopher, a Diogenes content in his tub; a manservant in a borrowed cloak becomes a king of the East with splendor wreathing him round. So with the portraits of Goya. His men are witty, cynical, brutal, and his women lovely, gallant, and lecherous.

Rarely have I found sitters altogether pleased with their portraits. Understanding is rare, and the sitter usually wants to be flattered. How Goya ever got away with his superb portraits of the Spanish Royal Family is still an inexplicable mystery.

I recall the naïve expression of one of my sitters who asked me if his nose was as I depicted it, and, when I assured him that it was so, cajolingly exclaimed, "Can't you cheat nature a little?"

Another will feel the bump at the back of his neck and look ruefully at my bust. On the whole, men sitters are more vain than women sitters. Shaw was terribly nervous about his bust; so was Priestley; and I have found that rarely does a wife see eye to eye with the artist. Always the artist has just missed something that she wants in or has put in something that she has never observed.

My best portraits, of course, have been those of friends and people I have asked to sit for me. The model who just sits and leaves the artist to his own thoughts is the most helpful one — not the model who imagines she is inspiring the artist. It seems to me that Mona Lisa said nothing; that enigmatic smile was quite enough for Leonardo to bother about.

Sometimes the sitter impresses his own conception of himself upon the artist. This can never result in a successful work — one that renders the character of the model. Sir Hugh Walpole was one of these sitters. He insisted on sitting to me like a Pharaoh, with head held high and chin stuck out. In reality Sir Hugh is the most genial of men, with sparkling, twinkling humor in his eye, and his mouth wreathed in a kindly smile. But with the rigidity of Sir Hugh's pose I could do nothing. I knew that the head was well modeled, but as for a portrait of my model's real self, I never thought it was that for a moment. It was Sir Hugh Walpole in the role of Benito Mussolini.

Muirhead Bone had arranged that I should do a bust of Conrad for him. I had desired ten years before to work from him, and had spoken to Richard Curle about it. I had been informed by him that Conrad could not sit for me, owing to the intervention of a painter "friend." At the time I was deeply disappointed and dropped the idea. But in 1924 the commission was finally arranged. My admiration for Conrad was immense, and he had a head that appealed to a sculptor, massive and fine at the same time, so I jumped at the idea of working from him at last. After a meeting in London it was arranged with him that I should go down to his place at St. Oswalds, near Canterbury, and at my suggestion I should live in an inn in a nearby village while working on the bust.

Conrad was an absorbing study. He took posing seriously and gave me good long sittings until one o'clock, when we lunched and talked. From the beginning he called me "Cher Maître," embarrassing me by this mode of address from a much older man who was a great master of his own craft. His manners were courtly and direct, but his neurasthenia forced him at times to outbursts of rage and irritability with his household, which quickly subsided. I already had a fairly clear notion as to how I should treat the bust. A sculptor had previously made a bust of him which represented him as an open-necked, romantic, out-of-door type of person. In appearance he was the very opposite. His clothes were immaculately conventional, and his collar enclosed his neck like an Iron Maiden's vise or a garroter's grip. He was worried if his hair and beard were not trim and neat as became a sea captain. There was nothing shaggy or bohemian about him. His glance was keen despite the drooping of one eyelid. He was the sea captain, the officer, and in our talks he emphasized the word "responsibility." Responsibility weighed on him, weighed him down. He used the word again and again, and one immediately thought of *Lord Jim* — the conscience suffering at the evasion of duty. It may have been because I met him late in life that Conrad gave me a feeling of defeat — but defeat met with courage.

He was crippled with rheumatism, crotchety, nervous, and ill. He said to me, "I am finished." There was pathos in his pulling out of a drawer his last manuscript to show me that he was still at work. There was no triumph in his manner, however; and he said that he did not know whether he would ever finish it. "I am played out," he said; "played out."

We talked after the sittings, mostly in the afternoons when we had tea together, and Conrad was full of reminiscences about himself. We were generally alone together. There in his country house he seemed to live alone, although the house was filled with servants. A few visitors came at the weekends, but he seemed a lonely, brooding man, with none too pleasant thoughts.

He was a good sitter, always strictly punctual, and he stuck to the stand, giving me plenty of opportunity for work and study. I was with him for twenty-one days. Once, while posing, he had a heart attack, and he felt faint. His manservant brought him a stiff whiskey, and he insisted on renewing the sitting. I had no hesitations while at work, owing to his very sympathetic attitude. A doubtful or critical attitude of the sitter will sometimes hang like a dark cloud over the work and retard it. Conrad's sympathy and good will were manifest. He would beam at me with a pleased expression and forget his rheumatism and the tree outside the window at which he railed. The tree was large and beautiful, but to Conrad it was a source of misery. No outdoors for him. The sea captain hated out-of-doors, and never put his nose into it.

To return to the bust; Conrad had a demon expression in the left eye, while his right eye was smothered by a drooping lid, but the eyes glowed with a great intensity of feeling. The drooping, weary lids intensified the impression of brooding thought. The whole head revealed the man who had suffered much — a head set on shoulders hunched about his ears. When he was seated, the shoulders gave the impression of a pedestal for the head. His gnarled hands were covered with woolen mittens, and his habit of tugging at his beard when in conversation or in thought gave me the idea of including the hands in the bust; but he recoiled from so human a document.

On anything connected with the plastic arts, Conrad frankly confessed ignorance, although perhaps to flatter me he attempted to draw a parallel between the process of building up a work of sculpture and that of writing a novel. Of music he said he knew nothing, nor did it interest him; but he admitted being impressed by the sound of drums coming across the waters in Africa at night.

I looked at Conrad's bookshelf. He had not many books, in no sense a library; but he had a complete edition of Turgenev in English. We talked of books, and I mentioned Melville's *Moby Dick*, expecting him to be interested. Conrad burst into a furious denunciation of it. "He knows nothing of the sea. It's fantastic, ridiculous," he said. When I mentioned that the work was symbolical and mystical: "Mystical, my eye. My old boots are mystical." Meredith? His characters are ten feet high. D. H. Lawrence had started well, but had gone wrong. "Filth. Nothing but obscenities." For Henry James he had unqualified admiration. Of his own novels he said it was a tossup at one time as to whether he would write in English or in French. He emphasized the amount of labor he gave to a novel to get it to satisfy himself.

The work on the bust was nearing completion. One day, at the end of the sittings, Mrs. Conrad appeared at the door to see it. She gave one glance and fled. Perhaps a wife, a lover, can never see what the artist sees. At any rate, the fact is that they rarely ever do. Perhaps a really mediocre artist has more chance of success in this respect. When George Bernard Shaw was sitting to me I asked him why he had given sittings to a very incompetent artist. Shaw exclaimed: "Why, he is a fine portrait painter — my wife, on entering the room where the portrait was, actually mistook it for myself."

Conrad's own opinion about my portrait of himself was conveyed in a letter he wrote to Richard Curle, his biographer and literary executor. "The bust of Ep has grown truly monumental. It is a marvelously effective piece of sculpture, with even something more than a masterly interpretation in it. It is wonderful to go down to posterity like that." Later Sir Muirhead Bone offered the bust to the National Portrait Gallery. It was refused.

At last the work was completed. I wired my molder to come and carry it away to London to be cast. I said good-by to the old Master and traveled with the bust. Five months later I opened a newspaper and read that Joseph Conrad was dead.

Shaw sat on condition that I was commissioned to do the work. He thought I ought to benefit materially and not just do his bust for its own sake. Orage arranged a commission for me from Mrs. Blanche Grant, an American. Shaw sat with exemplary patience and even eagerness. He walked to my studio every day, and was punctual and conscientious. He wisecracked, of course. In matters of art he aired definite opinions, mostly wrong; and I often had to believe that he wished to say smart, clever things to amuse me. On seeing a huge block of stone, unworked, in the studio, he asked me what I intended to do with it. Not wishing to tell him exactly what my plans were, I merely remarked that I had a plan. "What!" he exclaimed. "You have a plan? You shouldn't have a plan. I never work according to a plan. Each day I begin with new ideas totally different from the day before." As if a sculptor with a six-ton block to carve could alter his idea daily! Shaw believed that sculptors put into their portraits their own characteristics, and of a bust done of him by a prince he remarked that it contained something very aristocratic. This was amusing in view of the fact that this particular bust was peculiarly commonplace.

Shaw was puzzled by the bust of himself and often looked at it and tried to make it out. He believed that I had made a kind of primitive barbarian of him, something altogether uncivilized and really a projection of myself, rather than of him. I never tried to explain the bust to him, and I think that there are in it elements so subtle that they would be difficult to explain. Nevertheless, I believe this to be an authentic and faithful rendering of George Bernard Shaw physically and psychologically. I leave out any question of aesthetics, as that would be beyond Shaw's comprehension. When the bust was finished, we were filmed; and Shaw was wonderful as an actor, taking the filming very seriously.

In 1934, when the work in bronze was done, I offered Shaw a copy of the bust through Orage, but was told that Shaw could not think of having it in his house. This I believe was because of Mrs. Shaw's dislike of it.

Throughout my life in England, Shaw has been an outspoken champion of my work, on several occasions giving the great British public lively smacks on my behalf. I will not say that he understands what I have made. He seems deficient in all sense of the plastic, but has a lively notion of how stupid the newspapers can be. He is generous to young talent, but seems likely to be taken in by cleverness or pretense. I would say that Shaw is not really interested in the plastic arts, although he can be got to take a passing or journalistic interest in controversial work. On one occasion, on visiting an exhibition of paintings of Epping Forest, not knowing what to say, he asked me if I had done the paintings with brushes.

Rhythm in My Blood

by AGNES DE MILLE

Dancer, choreographer, and writer, Agnes de Mille has brought to the ballet an American idiom and impetus which were responsible for her first great successes, Rodeo and the dances she designed for Oklahoma! She is today recognized as one of our most original choreographers, and in this article she shows us the drives and aspirations which set a dance in motion.

FEBRUARY 1956

Artists work in the belief that what lies in their hearts is as attractive to others — great numbers of others — as to themselves. Now obviously hearts must be in some things similar or they could not communicate; but similarity of expression in art is castigated with scorn, at first sight anyway — criticism which must on consideration prove as invalid as it is futile. For artists must repeat themselves.

In all processes of life people imitate, and so must artists. They are influenced by their peers as by their antecedents because this is the way of organic development. Late Beethoven and early Schubert, for instance, are almost indistinguishable; while Brahms took certain themes, note for note, from Beethoven; and Shakespeare stole nearly all his plots — all the good ones certainly. Had they worked as contemporaries in the same studio, as do choreographers, with the same performers, the tie would have been closer yet. Furthermore, most choreographers, like the apprentice painters of the Renaissance, get their initial experience studying under the personal influence of a master, taking part in the actual creation of his works, and spending years — the formative years — under constant personal artistic domination. The wonder is that any individual expression develops at all.

But it does develop, and with it the deviations and mannerisms we call personal style. Usually the artist is unaware of the process, as he is unaware of his other spontaneous modes of expression. Few willingly believe the insistent repetition, the catch phrases, the special idioms we use in conversation. Who among us has recognized a first recording of his own voice? We prefer to think of ourselves in terms of universals shared by all mankind — by all the ways, in short, in which we resemble or possibly surpass others. Our neighbors, on the contrary, distinguish us by our oddities and crotchets, and it is just for this reason that an effective cartoon strikes everyone but the subject as revealing.

If idiosyncrasies of expression constitute a key to others' understanding, they serve the artist in much the same way, as a means of self-revelation and a technique for reaching his emotional reservoir. They determine his work habits and of course the character of his expression. But whereas each worker will develop his own combination, his own formula so to speak, he will have virtually nothing to do with its choosing and can use his critical faculties only to shape and correct. The emotional key, the kindling spark, lies beyond the reach of his mind deep in instinct. When we find these habitual patterns pleasing, we say the artist has developed style; when they appeal to our taste less, we say that he is repeating himself.

But the great repeated constantly. How do we, for instance, recognize Bach in any two measures of his music? Obviously because it sounds precisely like him and no one else. It is a question, I believe, of what is basically present and not how often the devices and tricks are employed. Indeed if variety were all, one could compose with a slide rule. There is great style and lesser style, and style altogether to be condemned; but none of it has to do either with repetition or derivation.

Every worker recognizes his own devices. I can name mine easily. I cannot always control them, but I can name them: I have an affinity for diagonal movement on the stage, with figures entering at one corner and leaving at the opposite, and unless I watch myself, this pattern recurs tiresomely. Why in one corner and out the other? I am not such a fool that I don't recognize the tendency, nor so starved for invention that I cannot think of other geometric directions. But this particular arrangement moves me and releases ideas. Could it be because the first fine choreographic design I ever saw was the *Sylphides* mazurka danced by Lydia Sokolowa with the Diaghilev ballet? And when I think of her great leap and the lines of still and waiting women leaning in a kind of architectural wonder for the next cross flight, I understand. That was the path of the first comet and it blazed a mark on my brain. That track spells ecstasy. But behind this reason, there must be more.

I use a still figure, usually female, waiting on the stage, side or center, with modifying groups revolving about, always somehow suggesting the passing of time and life experience. Why does the woman waiting seem to me so emotionally pregnant? One woman standing alone on the stage while people pass until a man enters upstage behind her? Why upstage and why always behind and why the long wait? I cannot be sure, but I remember waiting for years seemingly shut away in my mother's garden. My father was absent most of that time and I longed for him to come home to release me from the spell. Possibly the answer is somewhere here.

Why is my use of circles open or closed a constant? The avoidance of symmetrical design with the exception of the circle, my acute difficulty with all symmetrical design even including square-dance pattern which one might think was my native language? My repeated use of three female figures, a trilogy which because of plurality takes on symbolic force? And the falling patterns — the falling to earth, the swooning back, the resurrection, the running away always to return to a focal point — seem also to be insistent; and more important, more gross and unbearable, the breaking of all lyric line with a joke, as though I could not trust emotional development but must escape with a wisecrack.

It must be obvious even to people not familiar with dancing that these relations are individual, that they are to some degree sexual, and that they reflect a special personality pattern. I speak of my own work because I have a right to, but these observations apply to everyone. Consider, for instance, some of the recurring idioms of Balanchine: the single male figure embroiled with two to six females, one of whom either blinds or strangles him; the entanglement of either male or female bodies in endless ropes or chains (the lines are seldom made up of both men and women); the repetitive use of the grand reverence or imperial court bow as part of the texture of movement; the immaculate discipline of traditional gesture; the metrical, machine-like arrangement of school positions as unadorned as the use of unmodified scales in a musical composition; the insistence on two-dimensional symmetrical design; the superb but classic relation to music. One might build an interesting picture of Balanchine, the man, from these points of style. They are as natural to him as his sniff.

The characteristics of Jerome Robbins are very different. There is above all his free-limbed and virile use of the body, a complete spontaneous release as in sports, an exuberance, a total employment of all energies. Whether the gesture is gay or anguished, all resources are put into play and the strength and vigor of the movement communicates with the gusto of an athlete's. This in part may explain his enormous popularity with all audiences. The gesture is manly, it is keen and bold, and it is complete. Briefly it is exhilarating, and it brings to the spirit the satisfaction that a yawn or a stretch brings to the muscles. Women choreographers are less released, their movement often blocked or broken, or modified by reticences, not shyness of content but carefulness in physical effort. The difference is equivalent to that between a man and a woman throwing or jumping. Her gesture may be exact and serviceable; his will be total. Robbins enhances this quality by quoting literally from acrobatics or by using stunts.

His skill in rhythmic invention is the greatest in the business, according to the composer Trude Rittmann, who has worked with all of us. Robbins is besot by rhythm, visual and bodily rhythms as well as auditory, and when he gets hold of a gesture he continues inventing out of the core of the matter until he has built an entire design and must wait for the composer to catch up. His rhythms will then work in counterpoint to the musical pattern. It is thought that if he had turned his attention to music, he might have been a first-class composer. Whereas Balanchine's rhythmic sense is spatial and linked to the music, Robbins' is independent. I, on the other hand, am totally derivative and lean and grow on melody. I cannot move without melody. May there not here be revealed a subtle sexual distinction? The men work free and on their own. The woman must wait for the lead.

But Robbins' most easily recognized trait is, praise heaven, his humor. In its grossest aspects, it takes the form of straight gags — very good ones, but bald and outrageous. In its more sophisticated manifestations, he introduces surprising and impertinent conclusions into his pattern, deliberately leading one on to expect a certain resolution and then insolently offering another, untraditional and slightly rude, though always logical because he is never foolish. He jokes with rhythms, with space, with relations of bodies, with light, with silence, with sound. These are all elements of style.

The grosser emotional fixtures of theme and content are plainly manifest — fixtures such as, in the case of Robbins, a preoccupation with childhood and games, with the bewilderment of growing up, with the anguish of choice. The unexpected, the joke, in this field seems to turn back on the choreographer and sit hard; each love story splits into three or more people; each romance spells destruction or transience; all repeats over and over. There is no resolution. In short, life turns out not to be a joke.

For my part, I seem to be obsessed by an almost Henry Jamesian inability for hero and heroine to come together happily, and by that other bedeviling theme, the woman as hunter. These are easily read. But the impregnation of abstract pattern with personality adjustments is, I find, far more subtle and more interesting. A great deal has been written about the kinesthetic transference between audience and dancer in the actual muscular technique; the field of spatial aesthetics remains, however, almost unexplored.

We know much about emotional symbols. They have a history and a science, iconography. Those used by the medieval and Renaissance painters were understood by the scholars and artists of the time — but, more wonderful, they mean to us today spontaneously just what they meant then; they seem to be permanent. We dream, Jung tells us, in the terms and symbols of classic mythology. Moreover, primitives shut away from classic learning dream in the same terms. Is it not also likely then that certain space relations, rhythms, and stresses have psychological significance, that some of these patterns are universal and the key to emotional response, that their deviations and modifications can be meaningful to the artist in terms of his own life experience and that these overtones are grasped by the spectator without conscious analysis?

Doctors are aware of this and utilize the knowledge in diagnosis. The significance of children's manipulation of space in writing and drawing is carefully studied, and the insane are observed for their relation to and use of walls, floor, doorways, heights, and so forth. Obviously these matters are basic to our well-being as land and air animals. And as plants will turn to sunlight or rocks or moisture according to their nature, so we bend toward or escape from spatial arrangements according to our emotional needs. In the diseased mind, the reactions are overwhelmingly overt. But look around any restaurant and see how few sane people will sit at a center table unless the sides are filled up. Yet formerly the king always dined dead center and many times in public.

The individual as a personality then has his own code in space and rhythm. It is evolved from his life history and from his race memory or, as Jung calls it, the collective unconscious. It is just the manipulation of these suggestions through time-space that is the material of choreography.

It is the actor's art to mimic exactly with a full awareness of all the overtones and significances. The dancer, on the other hand, explodes the gesture to its components and reassembles them into a symbol that has connotations of what lies around and behind the fact, while the implications of rhythm and spatial design add further comment. Of course the choreographer is no more troubled by all this than is the businessman by the enormous anthropological heritage he puts into play every time he casually tips his hat.

Coleridge says of portraiture: "A good artist must imitate that which is within the thing, that which is active through form and figure, and discourses to us by symbols . . . the universal in the individual or the individuality itself — the glance and the exponent of the indwelling power. . . . Hence a good portrait is the abstract of the personal; it is not the likeness for actual comparison, but for recollection." Every gesture is a portrait. Behind it lie the histories of the race and the individual as well as the comment of the artist.

When I, as an artist, am moved, I must respond in my own instinctive way; and because I am a choreographer, I respond through my instinctive gestures. I may come into the pattern with conviction and the excitement of fresh experience, but this will reflect a personality habit. It cannot be otherwise. Somehow, as in the grooves in a gramophone record, the cutting edge of my emotion follows a track played deep into the subconscious.

There is a further personal identification in choreography because most choreographers compose on their own bodies. Certain recurring steps can be explained simply by the fact that the choreographer performs these steps well and has a tendency to use them when demonstrating. Martha Graham has a kick and a particular skip that have stood her in good stead for twenty years. The explanation is simply that her left leg kicks straight up in a split, 180 degrees — a very spectacular feat. The right does not; hence the single-legged pattern. (It has been very interesting to observe over the years that Graham pupils who began by imitating her mannerisms have gradually eliminated the physical idiosyncrasies and personal accent and maintained the great style unblemished. In *Diversion of Angels* and *Canticle for Innocent Comedians,* Graham's personal gesture has been purified of all subjective tricks and stands in the keeping of her disciples as impersonal and abstract as the ballet code. It is overwhelmingly beautiful.) I am right-legged and right-footed, and most of the sustaining and balancing work in my choreography is done on the left leg; many of my dancers have complained bitterly. A dancer with short legs jumps in one manner, whereas a dancer with longer ones performs the same kind of jumps in quite another. So with composing. And identical pattern problems take on the modification of the composer's physique as well as his character adjustment, for it is always the choreographer who has to start the moving, and naturally he does it his way. If there were no instrument on which a song writer could work except on his own voice, unquestionably his vocal restrictions would shape the melodic line.

The choreographer is also influenced by his performers. If I were to work, let us say, with a soloist whose arms and back were the strongest in the dance world and whose phrasing of legato lifts the most beautiful, but whose footwork, on the other hand, and allegro were weaker, quite obviously my composing style would adjust to his needs. Were I to compose with a man of enormous elevation and brilliant *batterie* but less dramatic force, my approach would then be necessarily different. And it must be noted that one works with the dancers at hand. One cannot summon from outer space a dream body capable of anything — or even exactly what one wishes. In the matter of one's own body one has obviously even less choice and must make do.

It is difficult for the individual to evaluate his own strengths and characteristics, and the theatre is strewn with lives ruined by unwarranted determinations to sing, or write, or act. No guarantee goes with desire, and there is unhappily just enough genuine talent neglected to confuse the issue. Nevertheless, granting a modicum of true ability, one must not be afraid to fail now and then. It all depends on the reason why. One may, of course, fail because one has chosen the wrong kind of work. One may fail because one has no discipline either in work or the handling of emotional problems. One may fail because one wishes to fail — a hard tendency to detect, but a history of avoidable catastrophe indicates a need for medical help. One may fail temporarily because of grief, harassment, or exhaustion and, in the theatre, from lack of time. And then one may fail in trying new and unknown ways of expression. A creative life without failure is unthinkable. All physical growth and emotional change involve discomfort and a good bit of highly unattractive transition. Consider any adolescent, for example, taken at face value and with no thought of what is to come.

This fear of defeat haunts the creative worker uncomfortably, and there are days when all of us long to be let alone. But the first moment we permit ourselves to feel safe, the first moment we save ourselves from exposure, we are in danger of retreating from the outposts. We can be quite sure that this particular job need not be done, for, in all probability, it will have been done before.

But although work will never be safe, it may happily sometimes be easy and quick. Very frequently the best work is the easiest. But the rhapsodic release comes only infrequently and the professional must learn to compose at will — to employ aesthetic aphrodisiacs. For a young artist, this is perhaps the hardest task. Each person must learn his own path through the labyrinth of escape and idleness. Anne Lindbergh speaks of a technique of "acquiring grace": "Most people are aware of periods in their lives when they seem to be 'in grace' and other periods when they feel 'out of grace.' . . . In the first happy condition, one seems to carry all one's tasks before one lightly, as if borne along on a great tide; and in the opposite state one can hardly tie a shoe-string. It is true that a large part of life consists of tying the shoe-string, whether one is in grace or not."

To translate this into terms of the working artist, the state of "grace" or inspiration occurs when an idea is both clearly perceived and deeply felt, when circumstances do not block realization, and when technique waits ready and almost unconsciously available. The last is the controllable factor, a technique ready and available at the needed moment. Behind this lies a life's ordering.

But we may be grateful that very seldom are circumstances propitious and that the work fights through hard and slow. The moment one knows how, one begins to die a little. Living is a form of not being sure, of not knowing what next or how. And the artist before all others never entirely knows. He guesses. And he may be wrong. But then how does one know whom to befriend or, for that matter, to marry? One can't go through life on hands and knees. One leaps in the dark. For this reason creative technique reduces itself basically to a recognition and befriending of one's self. "Who am I?" the artist asks, and he devotes his entire career to answering. There is one clue: what moves him is his. What amuses or frightens or pleases him becomes by virtue of his emotional participation a part of his personality and history; conversely what neither moves nor involves him, what brings him no joy, can be reckoned as spurious. An artist begins to go wrong exactly at the point where he begins to pretend. But it is difficult sometimes to accept the truth. He has to learn who he in fact is, not who he would like to be, nor even who it would be expedient or profitable to be.

He may think he cannot afford this risk, but it is equally evident he cannot afford hackneyed success. For this is no success. And everyone instantly recognizes what has happened. The breath of life has gone; the workshop has become a morgue.

The real failing, the killing off, is not in taking risks but in choosing some work beneath his capacities and in doing it in a slick and routine fashion purely for recompense. This hurts the whole field of work, dirties and dulls down the audience, and destroys the individual. In the disreputable suburbs of each art form flourish great fortunes made just this way. I do not for one moment wish to imply that first-class work does not also bring in money. God is good, and it frequently does. But let us be sure in our hearts, no first-class job was ever achieved without a good deal in view besides the check.

The folks who think only of money may cynically pretend they do not care, but their stomach ulcers and their alcoholism prove they do most dreadfully. It is not so much a matter of what work is done but how it is done. It is vital to everyone to know that work is necessary and done to the best ability whether making soap operas or washing floors, and it is only when the dust is swept under the rug that the process of disintegration sets in.

Far better than succeeding regularly is a good tough falling-short of a challenge. All work, one's own and everyone else's, benefits from this effort, successful or not, just as all science benefits from each difficult experiment — even the ones that seem not directly to bring results.

It is not for the individual to demand a certificate of quality before starting. He cannot and he may not. He has to work on faith. And he must listen only to his conscience, which will be stern enough in truth. He must listen to no other voices. For to listen is to be lost — to listen to critic, or friend, or business interest. He can pray only that his tastes and passions will be common to many. But he must suit himself first, himself before everyone else. He must, in other words, marry the girl of his heart despite the family or he will bed down for life with a wench not of his choosing.

The Writing of *Ulysses*

Letters of James Joyce

Edited by STUART GILBERT

*An Irish novelist born in 1882, James Joyce had a greater
influence upon twentieth-century literature than any other
novelist of our time. He spent his boyhood in Dublin, was
educated in Jesuit schools and colleges, and at the age of
twenty broke away from family and church to live and write
as a free lance on the Continent. By 1917, after incredible
frustrations, Joyce had published his first two books,* Dubliners *and* A Portrait of the Artist as a Young Man. *Then he
went to work on* Ulysses, *but trouble with his eyes, which had
necessitated several operations, had seriously depressed him.
In March 1918 the* Little Review *in New York began to publish* Ulysses *in serial form, and from then on he wrote regularly to Harriet Shaw Weaver, one of the editors.*

APRIL 1957

To HARRIET SHAW WEAVER   *Zurich*
18 May 1918

Dear Miss Weaver: Many thanks for your letter. As regards the
scheme of printing my novel *Ulysses* at a private press and inserting it
as a supplement I shall be glad if it is carried out. I had a card from
Mr. Courtney saying that if a copy of my novel be sent to him c/o *Daily
Telegraph* he will get it noticed but, he adds, the literary page of that
paper is much reduced. I am sorry you do not find it possible to accept
Messrs. Crès' offer and have your paper printed in Paris. I fear you
have lost a great deal of money on my wretched book and so I propose
to cede to you, in reversion from Mr. Richards, the book rights and to
consider the sums already advanced by you for serial rights as an advance of royalties to be written off, if you agree, in two or three deduc-
tions from sums eventually due to me by half yearly accounts of sales.

There is little likelihood that Mr. Richards will publish the book. I thank you for having transmitted to me the kind proposal of my New York publisher. Will you please write to him and say that I could not, for many reasons, undertake to deliver the entire typescript of *Ulysses* during the coming autumn. If the *Little Review* continues to publish it regularly he may publish as a cheap paperbound book the *Telemachia,* that is, the three first episodes — under the title, *Ulysses I.* I suggest this in case his idea be to keep the few persons who read what I write from forgetting that I still exist. The second part, the *Odyssey,* contains eleven episodes. The third part, *Nostos,* contains three episodes. In all seventeen episodes of which, including that which is now being typed and will be sent in a day or two, *Hades,* I have delivered six. It is impossible to say how much of the book is really written. Several other episodes have been drafted for the second time but that means nothing because although the third episode of the *Telemachia* has been a long time in the second draft I spent about 200 hours over it before I wrote it out finally. I fear I have little imagination. This subject I am sure must be rather tiresome to you. However, if all goes well the book should be finished by the summer of 1919. If it be set up before it could then be published at once. It is not quite clear to me from Mr. Pound's last letter whether he is transmitting my typescript to New York or not. However I am sending the next episode also through him.

I think I ought to say in conclusion that if you wish to print any other book as a serial story in the place of *Ulysses* I beg you not to consider any imaginary claims of mine. I made the proposal in this letter partly to allow you to proceed as you may think fit.

To Carlo Linati
[In Italian]   *Paris*
                                                    21 September 1920

Dear Mr. Linati: Concerning Mr. Dessy's suggestion I think that in view of the enormous bulk and the more than enormous complexity of my three times blasted novel it would be better to send you a sort of summary — key — skeleton — scheme (for your personal use only). Perhaps my idea will appear clearer to you when you have the text. Otherwise, write to Rodker and ask him to let you have the other copies. I have given only catchwords in my scheme but I think you will understand it all the same. It is an epic of two races (Israelite — Irish) and at the same time the cycle of the human body as well as a little story of a day (life). The character of Ulysses always fascinated me — even when a boy. Imagine, fifteen years ago I started writing it as a short story for *Dubliners!* For seven years I have been working at this book — blast it! It is also a sort of encyclopaedia. My intention is to transpose the myth *sub specie temporis nostri*. Each adventure (that is, every hour, every organ, every art being interconnected and interrelated in the structural scheme of the whole) should not only condition but even create its own technique. Each adventure is so to say one person although it is composed of persons — as Aquinas relates of the angelic hosts. No English printer wanted to print a word of it. In America the review was suppressed four times. Now, as I hear, a great movement is being prepared against the publication, initiated by Puritans, English Imperialists, Irish Republicans, Catholics — what an alliance! Gosh, I ought to be given the Nobel prize for peace!

To Harriet Shaw Weaver   *Paris*
                                                    24 June 1921

Dear Miss Weaver: A nice collection could be made of legends about me. Here are some. My family in Dublin believe that I enriched myself in Switzerland during the war by espionage work for one or both combatants. Triestines, seeing me emerge from my relative's house occupied by my furniture for about twenty minutes every day and walk to the same point, the G.P.O., and back (I was writing *Nausikaa* and *The Oxen of the Sun* in a dreadful atmosphere) circulated the rumour, now firmly believed, that I am a cocaine victim. The general rumour in Dublin was (till the prospectus of *Ulysses* stopped it) that I could write no more, had broken down and was dying in New York. A man from Liverpool told me he had heard that I was the owner of several cinema theatres all over Switzerland. In America there appear to be or have been two versions: one that I was an austere mixture of the Dalai Lama and sir Rabindranath Tagore. Mr. Pound described me as a dour Aberdeen minister. Mr. Lewis [Percy Wyndham Lewis] told me he was told that I was a crazy fellow who always carried four watches and rarely spoke except to ask my neighbour what o'clock it was. Mr. Yeats seemed to have described me to Mr. Pound as a kind of Dick Swiveller. What the numerous (and useless) people to whom I have been introduced here think I don't know. My habit of addressing people I have just met for the first time as 'Monsieur' earned for me the reputation of a *tout petit bourgeois* while others consider what I intend for politeness as most offensive. One woman here originated the rumour that I am extremely lazy and will never do or finish anything. (I calculate that I must have spent nearly 20,000 hours in writing *Ulysses.*) A batch of people in Zurich persuaded themselves that I was gradually going mad and actually endeavoured to induce me to enter a sanatorium where a certain Doctor Jung (the Swiss Tweedledum who is not to be confused with the Viennese Tweedledee, Dr. Freud) amuses himself at the expense (in every sense of the word) of ladies and gentlemen who are troubled with bees in their bonnets.

I mention all these views not to speak about myself but to show you how conflicting they all are. The truth probably is that I am a quite commonplace person undeserving of so much imaginative painting. There is a further opinion that I am a crafty simulating and dissimulating *Ulysses*-like type, a 'jejune jesuit,' selfish and cynical. There is some truth in this, I suppose: but it is by no means all of me (nor was it of *Ulysses*) and it has been my habit to apply this alleged quality to safeguard my poor creations.

This letter begins to remind me of a preface by Mr. George Bernard Shaw. It does not seem to be a reply to your letter after all. You have already one proof of my intense stupidity. Here now is an example of my emptiness. I have not read a work of literature for several years. My head is full of pebbles and rubbish and broken matches and lots of glass picked up 'most everywhere.' The task I set myself technically in writing a book from eighteen different points of view and in as many styles, all apparently unknown or undiscovered by my fellow tradesmen, that and the nature of the legend chosen would be enough to upset anyone's mental balance. I want to finish the book and try to settle my entangled material affairs definitely one way or the other (somebody here said of me: 'They call him a poet. He appears to be interested chiefly in mattresses'). And, in fact, I was. After that I want a good long rest in which to forget *Ulysses* completely.

To Harriet Shaw Weaver   *Paris*

                                                7 August 1921

Dear Miss Weaver: I have had five weeks of delightful vacation with my eyes — the strangest but not at all the worst attack because instead of coming to a head in three weeks it did so in three hours. The people who persisted in regarding me as a foot-in-the-grave young man would have [been] edified to see me rolling over the carpet. The good point was that the attack was shorter in the recovery stage. I am now advised to go to Aix-les-Bains but am in Ithaca instead. I write and revise and correct with one or two eyes about twelve hours a day I should say, stopping for intervals of five minutes or so when I can't see any more. My brain reels after it but that is nothing compared with the reeling of my readers' brains. I have not yet quite recovered and I am doing the worst thing possible but can't help it. It is folly also because the book will probably not repay a tithe of such labour.

I was going to take a forty-eight hour holiday somewhere but decided not to do so. If I lay down in some remote part of the country I am so tired that I should never have the energy to get up.

I have the greater part of *Ithaca* but it has to be completed, revised and rearranged above all on account of its scheme. I have also written the first sentence of *Penelope* but as this contains about 2500 words the deed is more than it seems to be. The episode consists of eight or nine sentences equally sesquipedalian and ends with a monosyllable. Bloom and all the Blooms will soon be dead, thank God. Everyone says he ought to have died long ago.

To Mrs. William Murray   *Nice*
                                                 23 *October* 1922

Dear Aunt Josephine: A few days before I left Paris I got a letter from you which seemed very wrathful. The facts are these. *Ulysses* was published on 2 February. When the edition was sold out Nora said she wanted to go to Ireland to see her mother. I did all I could to dissuade her but her friends here and in Ireland told her it was as simple as anything. Finally as my father also wished to see the children I let them go but made them promise to stay a week or so in London and watch. I managed to hold them up in London for ten days by means of express letters and telegrams. Then they suddenly left for Ireland. They stopped a night in Dublin and Lucia kindly suggested that they should visit my father whose address she remembered. This they did and went on to Galway. In Galway my son was dogged about the streets and as he told me since he could not sleep at night with the thought that the Zulus, as he calls them, would take him out of bed and shoot him. A drunken officer swaggered up to him blocking the path and asked him 'How does it feel to be a gintleman's son?' Meanwhile in Paris utterly exhausted as I was after eight years ceaseless labour I was on the verge of lunacy. Needless to say what I had foreseen took place and the next thing was that I got a telegram from London to say they wanted to come back to Paris. The warehouse opposite their lodgings in Galway was seized by rebels, free state troops invaded their bedrooms and planted machine guns in the windows. They ran through the town to the station and escaped in a train lying flat on their bellies (the two females that is) amid a fusillade which continued for an hour from right and left between troops on the train and ambushes along the line. They fled through Dublin in the dark and so came back to Paris. I then sent Lucia to a summer camp on the coast of Normandy for four months and Giorgio to the Austrian Tyrol. After which I collapsed with a furious eye attack lasting until a few weeks ago — but apparently that does not interest.

The second cause of your wrath seems to be my book. I am as innocent in this case as in the former. I presented it to you seven months ago but I never heard anything more about it beyond a few words acknowledging receipt and an allusion in your last letter. The market price of the book now in London is £40 and copies signed are worth more. I mention this because Alice [daughter of Mrs. Murray] told me you had lent it (or given?) and people in Dublin have a way of not returning books. In a few years copies of the first edition will probably be worth £100 each, so book experts say, and hence my remark. This of course has nothing to do with the contents of the book which it seems you have not read. I sent it however as I sent all my other books and at your request in a letter of a year or so ago. There is a difference between a present of a pound of chops and a present of a book like *Ulysses.* You can acknowledge receipt of the present of a pound of chops by simply nodding gratefully, supposing, that is, that you have your mouth full of as much of the chops as it will conveniently hold, but you cannot do so with a large book on account of the difficulty of fitting it into the mouth.

A second edition of *Ulysses* was published on the 12 October. The entire edition of 2000 copies at £2.2.0 a copy was sold out in four days.

Poetry and Drama

by T. S. ELIOT

Eliot's play, The Cocktail Party, *was running in New York and in London at the time he was called on to deliver the first Theodore Spencer Lecture in memory of his friend, a poet, Shakespearean scholar, and member of the Harvard faculty. His utterance has a modest, direct bearing on his own work in the theater.*

FEBRUARY 1951

Reviewing my critical output for the last thirty-odd years, I am surprised to find how constantly I have returned to the drama, whether by examining the work of the contemporaries of Shakespeare, or by reflecting on the possibilities of the future. It may even be that people are weary of hearing me on this subject. But, while I find that I have been composing variations on this theme all my life, my views have been continually modified and renewed by increasing experience; so that I am impelled to take stock of the situation afresh at every stage of my own experimentation.

As I have gradually learned more about the problems of poetic drama, and the conditions which it must fulfill if it is to justify itself, I have made a little clearer to myself, not only my own reasons for wanting to write in this form, but the more general reasons for wanting to see it restored to its place. And I think that if I say something about these problems and conditions, it should make clearer to other people whether and if so why poetic drama has anything potentially to offer the playgoer, that prose drama cannot. For I start with the assumption that if poetry is merely a decoration, an added embellishment, if it merely gives people of literary tastes the pleasure of listening to poetry at the same time that they are witnessing a play, then it is superfluous. It must justify itself dramatically, and not merely be fine poetry shaped into a dramatic form. From this it follows that no play should be written in verse for which prose is *dramatically* adequate. And from this it follows, again, that the audience, its attention held by the dramatic action, its emotions stirred by the situation between the characters, should be too intent upon the play to be wholly conscious of the medium.

Whether we use prose or verse on the stage, they are both but means to an end. The difference, from one point of view, is not so great as we might think. In those prose plays which survive, which are read and produced on the stage by later generations, the prose in which the characters speak is as remote, for the best part, from the vocabulary, syntax, and rhythm of our ordinary speech — with its fumbling for words, its constant recourse to approximation, its disorder and its unfinished sentences — as verse is. Like verse, it has been written, and rewritten. Our two greatest prose stylists in the drama — apart from Shakespeare and the other Elizabethans who mixed prose and verse in the same play — are, I believe, Congreve and Bernard Shaw. A speech by a character of Congreve or of Shaw has — however clearly the characters may be differentiated — that unmistakable personal rhythm which is the mark of a prose style, and of which only the most accomplished conversationalists — who are for that matter usually monologuists — show any trace in their talk. We have all heard (too often!) of Molière's character who expressed surprise when told that he spoke prose. But it was M. Jourdain who was right, and not his mentor or his creator: he did not speak prose — he only talked. For I mean to draw a triple distinction: between prose, and verse, and our ordinary speech which is mostly below the level of either verse or prose. So if you look at it in this way, it will appear that prose, on the stage, is as artificial as verse; or alternatively, that verse can be as natural as prose.

But while the sensitive member of the audience will appreciate, when he hears fine prose spoken in a play, that this is something better than ordinary conversation, he does not regard it as a wholly different language from that which he himself speaks, for that would interpose a barrier between himself and the imaginary characters on the stage. Too many people, on the other hand, approach a play which they know to be in verse with the consciousness of the difference. It is unfortunate when they are repelled by verse, but can also be deplorable when they are attracted by it — if that means that they are prepared to enjoy the play and the language of the play as two separate things. The chief effect of style and rhythm in dramatic speech, whether in prose or verse, should be unconscious.

From this it follows that a mixture of prose and verse in the same play is generally to be avoided; each transition makes the auditor aware, with a jolt, of the medium. It is, we may say, justifiable when the author wishes to produce this jolt: when, that is, he wishes to transport the audience violently from one plane of reality to another. I suspect that this kind of transition was easily acceptable to an Elizabethan audience, to whose ears both prose and verse came naturally; who liked highfalutin and low comedy in the same play; and to whom it seemed perhaps proper that the more humble and rustic characters should speak in a homely language, and that those of more exalted rank should rant in verse. But even in the plays of Shakespeare some of the prose passages seem to be designed for an effect of contrast which, when achieved, is something that can never become old-fashioned. The knocking at the gate in *Macbeth* is an example that comes to everyone's mind; but it has long seemed to me that the alternation of scenes in prose with scenes in verse in *Henry IV* points an ironic contrast between the world of high politics and the world of common life. The audience probably thought they were getting their accustomed chronicle play garnished with amusing scenes of low life; yet the prose scenes of both Part I and Part II provide a sardonic comment upon the bustling ambitions of the chiefs of the parties in the insurrection of the Percys.

Today, however, because of the handicap under which verse drama suffers, I believe that prose should be used very sparingly indeed; that we should aim at a form of verse in which everything can be said that has to be said; and that when we find a situation which is intractable in verse, it is merely because our form of verse is inelastic. And if there prove to be scenes which we cannot put in verse, we must either develop our verse, or avoid having to introduce such scenes. For we have to accustom our audiences to verse to the point at which they will cease to be conscious of it; and to introduce prose dialogue would only be to distract their attention from the play itself to the medium of its expression. But if our verse is to have so wide a range that it can say anything that has to be said, it follows that it will not be "poetry" all the time. It will only be "poetry" when the dramatic situation has reached such a point of intensity that poetry becomes the natural utterance, because then it is the only language in which the emotions can be expressed at all.

It is indeed necessary for any long poem, if it is to escape monotony, to be able to say homely things without bathos, as well as to take the highest flights without sounding exaggerated. And it is still more important in a play, especially if it is concerned with contemporary life.

The reason for writing even the more pedestrian parts of a verse play in verse instead of prose is, however, not only to avoid calling the audience's attention to the fact that it is at other moments listening to poetry. It is also that the verse rhythm should have its effect upon the hearers without their being conscious of it. A brief analysis of one scene of Shakespeare's may illustrate this point. The opening scene of *Hamlet* — as well constructed an opening scene as that of any play ever written — has the advantage of being one that everybody knows.

What we do not notice, when we witness this scene in the theatre, is the great variation of style. Nothing is superfluous, and there is no line of poetry which is not justified by its dramatic value. The first twenty-two lines are built of the simplest words in the most homely idiom. Shakespeare had worked for a long time in the theatre, and written a good many plays, before reaching the point at which he could write those twenty-two lines. There is nothing quite so simplified and sure in his previous work. He first developed conversational, colloquial verse in the monologue of the character part — Faulconbridge in *King John,* and later the Nurse in *Romeo and Juliet.* It was a much further step to carry it unobtrusively into the dialogue of brief replies. No poet has begun to master dramatic verse until he can write lines which, like these in *Hamlet,* are *transparent.* You are consciously attending, not to the poetry, but to the meaning of the poetry. If you were hearing *Hamlet* for the first time, without knowing anything about the play, I do not think that it would occur to you to ask whether the speakers were speaking in verse or prose. The verse is having a different effect upon us from prose; but at the moment, what we are aware of is the frosty night, the officers keeping watch on the battlements, and the foreboding of a tragic action. I do not say that there is no place for the situation in which part of one's pleasure will be the enjoyment of hearing beautiful poetry — providing that the author gives it, in that place, dramatic inevitability. When we have both seen a play several times and read it between performances, we begin to analyze the means by which the author has produced his effects. But in the immediate impact of this scene we are unconscious of the medium of its expression.

From the short, brusque ejaculations at the beginning, suitable to the situation and to the character of the guards — but not expressing more character than is required for their function in the play — the verse glides into a slower movement with the appearance of the courtiers Horatio and Marcellus.

Horatio says 'tis but our fantasy, . . .

and the movement changes again on the appearance of Royalty, the ghost of the King, into the solemn and sonorous

> What art thou, that usurp'st this time of night,

(and note, by the way, this anticipation of the plot conveyed by the use of the verb *usurp*); and majesty is suggested in a reference reminding us whose ghost this is:

> So frown'd he once, when, in an angry parle,
> He smote the sledded Polacks on the ice.

There is an abrupt change to staccato in Horatio's words to the Ghost on its second appearance; this rhythm changes again with the words

> We do it wrong, being so majestical,
> To offer it the show of violence;
> For it is, as the air, invulnerable,
> And our vain blows malicious mockery.

The scene reaches a resolution with the words of Marcellus:

> It faded on the crowing of the cock.
> Some say that ever 'gainst that season comes
> Wherein our Saviour's birth is celebrated,
> The bird of dawning singeth all night long;

and Horatio's answer:

> So have I heard and do in part believe it.
> But, look, the morn, in russet mantle clad,
> Walks o'er the dew of yon high eastern hill.
> Break we our watch up;

This is great poetry, and it is dramatic; but besides being poetic and dramatic, it is something more. There emerges, when we analyze it, a kind of musical design also which reinforces and is one with the dramatic movement. It has checked and accelerated the pulse of our emotion without our knowing it. Note that in these last words of Marcellus there is a deliberate brief emergence of the poetic into consciousness. When we hear the lines

> But, look, the morn, in russet mantle clad,
> Walks o'er the dew of yon high eastern hill

we are lifted for a moment beyond character, but with no sense of unfitness of the words coming, and at this moment, from the lips of

Horatio. The transitions in the scene obey laws of the music of dramatic poetry. Note that the two lines of Horatio which I have quoted twice are preceded by a line of the simplest speech which might be either verse or prose:

So have I heard and do in part believe it

and that he follows them abruptly with a half line which is hardly more than a stage direction:

Break we our watch up.

It would be interesting to pursue, by a similar analysis, this problem of the double pattern in great poetic drama — the pattern which may be examined from the point of view of stagecraft or from that of the music. But I think that the examination of this one scene is enough to show us that verse is not merely a formalization, or an added decoration, but that it intensifies the drama. It should indicate also the importance of the unconscious effect of the verse upon us. And lastly, I do not think that this effect is felt only by those members of an audience who "like poetry" but also by those who go for the play alone. By the people who do not like poetry, I mean those who cannot sit down with a book of poetry and enjoy reading it: these people also, when they go to a play in verse, should be affected by the poetry. And these are the audiences whom the writer of such a play ought to keep in mind.

At this point I might say a word about those plays which we call *poetic,* though they are written in prose. The plays of John Millington Synge form rather a special case, because they are based upon the idiom of a rural people whose speech is naturally poetic, both in imagery and in rhythm. I believe that he even incorporated phrases which he had heard from these country people of Ireland. The language of Synge is not available except for plays set among that same people. We can draw more general conclusions from the plays in prose (so much admired in my youth, and now hardly even read) by Maeterlinck. These plays are in a different way restricted in their subject matter; and to say that the characterization in them is dim is an understatement. I do not deny that they have some poetic quality. But in order to be poetic in prose, a dramatist has to be so consistently poetic that his scope is very limited. Synge wrote plays about characters whose originals in life talked poetically, so he could make them talk poetry and remain real people. The poetic prose dramatist who has not this advantage has to be too poetic. The poetic drama in prose is more limited by poetic convention or by our conventions as to what subject matter is poetic, than is the poetic drama in verse. A really dramatic verse can be employed, as Shakespeare employed it, to say the most matter-of-fact things.

Yeats is a very different case, from Maeterlinck or Synge. A study of his development as a dramatist would show, I think, the great distance he went, and the triumph of his last plays. In his first period, he wrote plays in verse about subjects conventionally accepted as suitable for verse, in a metric which — though even at that early stage having the personal Yeats rhythm — is not really a form of speech quite suitable for anybody except mythical kings and queens. His middle-period *Plays for Dancers* are very beautiful, but they do not solve any problem for the dramatist in verse: they are poetic prose plays with important interludes in verse. It was only in his last play *Purgatory* that he solved his problem of speech in verse, and laid all his successors under obligation to him.

Now, I am going to venture to make some observations based on my own experience, which will lead me to comment on my intentions, failures and partial successes, in my own plays. I do this in the belief that any explorer or experimenter in new territory may, by putting on record a kind of journal of his explorations, say something of use to those who follow him into the same regions and who will perhaps go farther.

The first thing of any importance that I discovered was that a writer who has worked for years, and achieved some success, in writing other kinds of verse, has to approach the writing of a verse play in a different frame of mind from that to which he has been accustomed in his previous work. In writing other verse, I think that one is writing, so to speak, in terms of one's own voice: the way it sounds when you read it to yourself is the test. For it is yourself speaking. The question of communication, of what the reader will get from it, is not paramount; if your poem is right to you, you can only hope that the readers will eventually come to accept it. The poem can wait a little while; the approval of a few sympathetic and judicious critics is enough to begin with; and it is for future readers to meet the poet more than half way. But in the theatre, the problem of communication presents itself immediately. You are deliberately writing verse for other voices, not for your own, and you do not know whose voices they will be. You are aiming to write lines which will have an immediate effect upon an unknown and unprepared audience, to be interpreted to that audience by unknown actors rehearsed by an unknown director. And the unknown audience cannot be expected to show any indulgence toward the poet. The poet cannot afford to write his play merely for his admirers, those who know his nondramatic work and are prepared to receive favorably anything he puts his name to. He must write with an audience in view which knows nothing and cares nothing about any previous success he may have had before he ventured into the theatre. Hence one finds out that many of the things one likes to do, and knows how to do, are out of place; and that every line must be judged by a new law, that of dramatic relevance.

When I wrote *Murder in the Cathedral* I had the advantage for a beginner of an occasion which called for a subject generally admitted to be suitable for verse. Verse plays, it has been generally held, should either take their subject matter from some mythology, or else should be about some remote historical period, far enough away from the present for the characters not to need to be recognizable as human beings, and therefore for them to be licensed to talk in verse. Picturesque period costume renders verse much more acceptable. Furthermore, my play was to be produced for a rather special kind of audience — an audience of those serious people who go to "festivals" and expect to have to put up with poetry — though perhaps on this occasion some of them were not quite prepared for what they got. And finally it was a religious play, and people who go deliberately to a religious play at a religious festival expect to be patiently bored and to satisfy themselves with the feeling that they have done something meritorious. So the path was made easy.

It was only when I put my mind to thinking what sort of play I wanted to do next, that I realized that in *Murder in the Cathedral* I had not solved any general problem; but that from my point of view the play was a dead end. For one thing, the problem of language which that play had presented to me was a special problem. Fortunately, I did not have to write in the idiom of the twelfth century, because that idiom, even if I knew Norman French and Anglo-Saxon, would have been unintelligible. But the vocabulary and style could not be exactly those of modern conversation — as in some modern French plays using the plot and personages of Greek drama — because I had to take my audience back to an historical event; and they could not afford to be archaic, first because archaism would only have suggested the wrong period, and second because I wanted to bring home to the audience the contemporary relevance of the situation. The style therefore had to be *neutral*, committed neither to the present nor to the past. As for the versification, I was only aware at this stage that the essential was to avoid any echo of Shakespeare, for I was persuaded that the primary failure of nineteenth-century poets when they wrote for the theatre was not in their theatrical technique, but in their dramatic language; and that this was due largely to their limitation to a strict blank verse which, after extensive use for nondramatic poetry, had lost the flexibility which blank verse must have if it is to give the effect of conversation. The rhythm of regular blank verse had become too remote from the movement of modern speech. Therefore what I kept in mind was the versification of *Everyman,* hoping that anything unusual in the sound of it would be on the whole advantageous. An avoidance of too much iambic, some use of alliteration, and occasional unexpected rhyme helped to distinguish the versification from that of the nineteenth century.

The versification of the dialogue in *Murder in the Cathedral* has therefore, in my opinion, only a *negative* merit: it succeeded in avoiding what had to be avoided, but it arrived at no positive novelty; in short, insofar as it solved the problem of speech in verse for writing today, it solved it for this play only, and provided me with no clue to the verse I should use in another kind of play. Here, then, were two problems left unsolved: that of the idiom and that of the metric, (it is really one and the same problem) for general use in any play I might want to write in future. I next became aware of my reasons for depending, in that play, so heavily upon the assistance of the chorus. There were two reasons for this, which in the circumstances justified it. The first was that the essential action of the play — both the historical facts and the matter which I invented — was somewhat limited. A man comes home, foreseeing that he will be killed, and he is killed. I did not want to increase the number of characters, I did not want to write a chronicle of twelfth-century politics, nor did I want to tamper unscrupulously with the meager records as Tennyson did (in introducing Fair Rosamund, and in suggesting that Becket had been crossed in love in early youth). I wanted to concentrate on death and martyrdom. The introduction of a chorus of excited and sometimes hysterical women, reflecting in their emotion the significance of the action, helped wonderfully. The second reason was this: a poet writing for the first time for the stage is much more at home in choral verse than in dramatic dialogue. This, I felt sure, was something I could do, and perhaps the dramatic weaknesses would be somewhat covered up by the cries of the women. The use of a chorus strengthened the power and concealed the defects of my theatrical technique. For this reason I decided that next time I would try to integrate the chorus more closely into the play.

I wanted to find out also whether I could learn to dispense altogether with the use of prose. The two prose passages in *Murder in the Cathedral* could not have been written in verse. Certainly, with the kind of dialogue verse which I used in that play, the audience would have been uncomfortably aware that it was verse they were hearing. A sermon cast in verse is too unusual an experience for even the most regular churchgoer; nobody could have responded to it as a sermon at all. And in the speeches of the knights, who are quite aware that they are addressing an audience of people living 800 years after they themselves are dead, the use of platform prose is intended of course to have a special effect: to shock the audience out of their complacency. But this is a kind of trick: that is, a device tolerable only in one play and of no use for any other. I may, for aught I know, have been slightly under the influence of *St. Joan*.

I do not wish to give you the impression that I would rule out of dramatic poetry these three things: historical or mythological subject-matter, the chorus, and traditional blank verse. I do not wish to lay down any law that the only suitable characters and situations are those of modern life, or that a verse play should consist of dialogue only, or that a wholly new versification is necessary. I am only tracing out the route of exploration of one writer, and that one myself. If the poetic drama is to reconquer its place, it must, in my opinion, enter into overt competition with prose drama. As I have said, people are prepared to put up with verse from the lips of personages dressed in the fashion of some distant age; they should be made to hear it from people dressed like ourselves, living in houses and apartments like ours, and using telephones and motorcars and radio sets. Audiences are prepared to accept poetry recited by a chorus, for that is a kind of poetry recital, which it does them credit to enjoy. And audiences (those who go to a verse play because it is in verse) expect poetry to be in rhythms which have lost touch with colloquial speech. What we have to do is to bring poetry into the world in which the audience lives and to which it returns when it leaves the theatre; not to transport the audience into some imaginary world totally unlike its own, an unreal world in which poetry is tolerated. What I should hope might be achieved, by a generation of dramatists having the benefit of our experience, is that the audience should find, at the moment of awareness that it is hearing poetry, that it is saying to itself: "I could talk in poetry too!" Then we should not be transported into an artificial world;

on the contrary, our own sordid, dreary daily world would be suddenly illuminated and transfigured.

I was determined, therefore, in my next play to take a theme of contemporary life, with characters of our own time living in our own world. *The Family Reunion* was the result. Here my first concern was the problem of the versification, to find a rhythm close to contemporary speech, in which the stresses could be made to come wherever we should naturally put them, in uttering the particular phrase on the particular occasion. What I worked out is substantially what I have continued to employ: a line of varying length and varying number of syllables, with a caesura and three stresses. The caesura and the stresses may come at different places, almost anywhere in the line; the stresses may be close together or well separated by light syllables; the only rule being that there must be one stress on one side of the caesura and two on the other. In retrospect, I soon saw that I had given my attention to versification, at the expense of plot and character. I had, indeed, made some progress in dispensing with the chorus; but the device of using four of the minor personages, representing the Family, sometimes as individual character parts and sometimes collectively as chorus, does not seem to me very satisfactory. For one thing, the immediate transition from individual, characterized part to membership of a chorus is asking too much of the actors: it is a very difficult transition to accomplish. For another thing, it seemed to me another trick, one which, even if successful, could not have been applicable in another play. Furthermore, I had in two passages used the device of a lyrical duet further isolated from the rest of the dialogue by being written in shorter lines with only two stresses. These passages are in a sense "beyond character," the speakers have to be presented as falling into a kind of trancelike state in order to speak them. But they are so remote from the necessity of the action that they are hardly more than passages of poetry which might be spoken by anybody; they are too much like operatic arias. The member of the audience, if he enjoys this sort of thing, is putting up with a suspension of the action in order to enjoy a poetic fantasia: these passages are really less related to the action than are the choruses in *Murder in the Cathedral*.

I observed that when Shakespeare, in one of his mature plays, introduces what might seem a purely poetic line or passage, it never interrupts the action or is out of character, but on the contrary, in some mysterious way supports both action and character. When Macbeth speaks his so often quoted words beginning

Tomorrow and tomorrow and tomorrow

or when Othello, confronted at night with his angry father-in-law and friends, utters the beautiful line

Keep up your bright swords, for the dew will rust them

we do not feel that Shakespeare has thought of lines which are beautiful poetry and wishes to fit them in somehow, or that he has for the moment come to the end of his dramatic inspiration and has turned to poetry to fill up with. The lines are surprising, and yet they fit in with the character; or else we are compelled to adjust our conception of the character in such a way that the lines will be appropriate to it. The lines spoken by Macbeth reveal the weariness of the weak man who had been forced by his wife to realize his own halfhearted desires and her ambitions, and who, with her death, is left without the motive to continue. The line of Othello expresses irony, dignity, and fearlessness; and incidentally reminds us of the time of night in which the scene takes place. Only poetry could do this; but it is *dramatic* poetry: that is, it does not interrupt but intensifies the dramatic situation.

It was not only because of the introduction of passages which called too much attention to themselves as poetry, and could not be dramatically justified, that I found *The Family Reunion* defective: there were two weaknesses which came to strike me as more serious still. The first was that I had taken far too much of the strictly limited time allowed to a dramatist, in presenting a situation, and not left myself enough time, or provided myself with enough material, for developing it in action. I had written what was, on the whole, a good first act; except that for a first act it was much too long. When the curtain rises again, the audience is expecting, as it has a right to expect, that something is going to happen. Instead, it finds itself treated to a further exploration of the background: in other words, to what ought to have been given much earlier if at all. The beginning of the second act presents much of the most difficult problem to director and cast: for the audience's attention is beginning to wander. And then the conclusion comes so abruptly that we are, after all, unready for it. This was an elementary fault in mechanics.

But the deepest flaw of all was in a failure of adjustment between the Greek story and the modern situation. I should either have stuck closer to Aeschylus or else taken a great deal more liberty with his myth. One evidence of this is the appearance of those ill-fated figures, the Furies. They must, in future, be omitted from the cast, and be understood to be visible only to certain of my characters, and not to the audience. We tried every possible manner of presenting them. We put them on the stage, and they looked like uninvited guests who had strayed in from a fancy dress ball. We concealed them behind gauze, and they suggested a still out of a Walt Disney film. We made them dimmer, and they looked like shrubbery just outside the window. I have seen other expedients tried: I have seen them signaling from across the garden, or swarming onto the stage like a football team, and they are never right. They never succeed in being either Greek goddesses or modern spooks. But their failure is merely a symptom of the failure to adjust the ancient with the modern.

A more serious evidence is that we are left in a divided frame of mind, not knowing whether to consider the play the tragedy of the mother or the salvation of the son. The two situations are not reconciled. I find a confirmation of this in the fact that my sympathies now have come to be all with the mother, who seems to me, except perhaps for the chauffeur, the only complete human being in the play; and my hero now strikes me as an insufferable prig.

Well, I had made some progress in learning how to write the first act of a play, and I had — the one thing of which I felt sure — made a good deal of progress in finding a form of versification and an idiom which would serve all my purposes, without recourse to prose, and be capable of unbroken transition between the most intense speech and the most relaxed dialogue. You will understand, after my making these criticisms of *The Family Reunion,* some of the errors that I endeavored to avoid in designing *The Cocktail Party.* To begin with, no chorus, and no ghosts. I was still inclined to go to a Greek dramatist for my theme, but I was determined to do so merely as a point of departure, and to conceal the origins so well that nobody would identify them until I pointed them out myself. In this at least I have been successful; for no one of my acquaintance (and no dramatic critics) recognized the source of my story in the *Alcestis* of Euripides. In fact, I have had to go into detailed explanation to convince them — I mean, of course, those who were familiar with the plot of that play — of the genuineness of the inspiration. But those who were at first disturbed by the eccentric behavior of my unknown guest, and his apparently intemperate habits and tendency to burst into song, have found consolation in having their attention called to the behavior of Heracles in Euripides' play.

In the second place, I laid down for myself the ascetic rule to avoid poetry which could not stand the test of strict dramatic utility: with such success, indeed, that it is perhaps an open question whether there is any poetry in the play at all. And finally, I tried to keep in mind that in a play, from time to time, something should happen; that the audience should be kept in the constant expectation that something is going to happen; and that, when it does happen, it should be different, but not too different, from what the audience had been led to expect.

I have not yet got to the end of my investigation of the weaknesses of this play, but I hope and expect to find more than those of which I am yet aware. I say "hope" because while one can never repeat a success, and therefore must always try to find something different, even if less popular, to do, the desire to write something which will be free of the defects of one's last work is a very powerful and useful incentive. I am aware that the last act of my play only just escapes, if indeed it does escape, the accusation of being not a last act but an epilogue; and I am determined to do something different, if I can, in this respect. I also believe that while the self-education of a poet trying to write for the theatre seems to require a long period of disciplining his poetry, and putting it, so to speak, on a very thin diet in order to adapt it to the needs of the stage, he may find that later, when (and if) the understanding of theatrical technique has become second nature, he can dare to make more liberal use of poetry and take greater liberties with ordinary colloquial speech. I base this belief on the evolution of Shakespeare, and on some study of the language in his late plays.

In devoting so much time to an examination of my own plays, I have, I believe, been animated by a better motive than egotism. It seems to me that if we are to have a poetic drama, it is more likely to come from poets learning how to write plays than from skillful prose dramatists learning to write poetry. That some poets can learn how to write plays, and write good ones, may be only a hope, but I believe a not unreasonable hope; but that a man who has started by writing successful prose plays should then learn how to write good poetry, seems to me extremely unlikely. And, under present-day conditions, and until the verse play is recognized by the larger public as a possible source of entertainment, the poet is likely to get his first opportunity to work for the stage only after making some sort of reputation for himself as the author of other kinds of verse. I have therefore wished to put on record, for what it may be worth to others, some account of the difficulties I have encountered, and the mistakes into which I have fallen, and the weaknesses I have had to try to overcome.

I should not like to close without attempting to set before you, though only in dim outline, the ideal toward which poetic drama should strive. It is an unattainable ideal; and that is why it interests me, for it provides an incentive toward further experiment and exploration beyond any goal which there is prospect of attaining. It is a function of all art to give us some perception of an order in life, by imposing an order upon it. The painter works by selection, combination, and emphasis among the elements of the visible world; the musician in the world of sound. It seems to me that beyond the namable, classifiable emotions and motives of our conscious life when directed toward action — the part of life which prose drama is wholly adequate to express — there is a fringe of indefinite extent, of feeling which we can only detect, so to speak, out of the corner of the eye and can never completely focus; of feeling of which we are only aware in a kind of temporary detachment from action. There are great prose dramatists — such as Ibsen and Chekhov — who have at times done things of which I would not otherwise have supposed prose to be capable, but who seem to me, in spite of their success, to have been hampered in expression by writing in prose. This peculiar range of sensibility can be expressed by dramatic poetry, at its moments of greatest intensity. At such moments, we touch the border of those feelings which only music can express. We can never emulate music, because to arrive at the condition of music would be the annihilation of poetry, and especially of dramatic poetry. Nevertheless, I have before my eyes a kind of mirage of the perfection of verse drama, which would be a design of human action and of words, such as to present at once the two aspects of dramatic and of musical order. It seems to me that Shakespeare achieved this at least in certain scenes — even rather early, for there is the balcony scene of *Romeo and Juliet* — and that this was what he was striving toward in his late plays. To go as far in this direction as it is possible to go, without losing that contact with the ordinary everyday world with which drama must come to terms, seems to me the proper aim of dramatic poetry. For it is ultimately the function of art, in imposing a credible order upon ordinary reality, and thereby eliciting some perception of an order *in* reality, to bring us to a condition of serenity, stillness and reconciliation; and then leave us, as Virgil left Dante, to proceed toward a region where that guide can avail us no farther.

XVII

Anglers and Others

It happens that several of the Atlantic *editors have been devotees of the fly rod. Boston's proximity to the fast streams and cool forests of Maine and New Brunswick is partly responsible for this, and the present editor can testify that there is no more beneficial rest for tired eyes than to concentrate on sunlit and shadowed water and the stirring life beneath. With the cities and suburbs pressing out, and wilderness far to seek, it was only natural that editors and readers should begin to have a kindred interest in the secret place and in those measures of conservation which will keep the woods undamaged and the white water unpolluted. The need for country, like the need for laughter, is a constant with the modern man, and this accounts for the increasing volume of nature writing in the* Atlantic *and for the inclusion of papers like Dillon Anderson's incomparable description of his friend Billingsley playing poker, a contribution which might have been thought frivolous by our founders.*

Relax, relax!

Fishing with a Worm

by BLISS PERRY

Teacher and editor who will long be remembered for his endearing book, And Gladly Teach, *Bliss Perry was the seventh editor of the* Atlantic. *He fished at every opportunity and with every form of lure, from garden hackle to the most delicate dry fly.*

MAY 1904

"The last fish I caught was with a worm." — Izaak Walton.

A defective logic is the born fisherman's portion. He is a pattern of inconsistency. He does the things which he ought not to do, and he leaves undone the things which other people think he ought to do. He observes the wind when he should be sowing, and he regards the clouds, with temptation tugging familiarly at his heartstrings, when he might be grasping the useful sickle. It is a wonder that there is so much health in him. A sorrowing political economist remarked to me in early boyhood, as a jolly red-bearded neighbor followed by an abnormally fat dog sauntered past us for his nooning: "That man is the best carpenter in town, but he will leave the most important job whenever he wants to go fishing." I stared at the sinful carpenter, who swung along leisurely in the May sunshine, keeping just ahead of his dog. To leave one's job in order to go fishing! How illogical.

Years bring the reconciling mind. The world grows big enough to include within its scheme both the instructive political economist and the truant mechanic. But that trick of truly logical behavior seems harder to the man than to the child. For example, I climbed up to my den under the eaves last night — a sour, black sea fog lying all about, and the December sleet crackling against the windowpanes — in order to varnish a certain fly rod. Now rods ought to be put in order in September, when the fishing closes, or else in April, when it opens. To varnish a rod in December proves that one possesses either a dilatory or a childishly anticipatory mind. But before uncorking the varnish bottle, it occurred to me to examine a dog-eared, water-stained fly book, to guard against the ravages of possible moths. This interlude proved fatal to the varnishing. A half hour went happily by in rearranging the flies. Then, with a fisherman's lack of sequence, as I picked out here and there a plain snell hook from the gaudy feathered ones, I said to myself with a generous glow at the heart: "Fly fishing has had enough sacred poets celebrating it already. Isn't there a good deal to be said, after all, for fishing with a worm?"

Let us face the worst at the very beginning. It shall be a shameless example of fishing under conditions that make the fly a mockery. Take the Taylor Brook, "between the roads," on the headwaters of the Lamoille. The place is a jungle. The swamp maples and cedars were felled a generation ago, and the tops were trimmed into the brook. The alders and moosewood are higher than your head; on every tiny knoll the fir balsams have gained a footing and creep down, impenetrable, to the edge of the water. In the open spaces the joe-pye weed swarms. In two minutes after leaving the upper road you have scared a mink or a rabbit, and you have probably lost the brook. Listen! It is only a gurgle here, droning along smooth and dark under the tangle of cedar tops and the shadow of the balsams. Follow the sound cautiously. There, beyond the joe-pye weed, and between the stump and the cedar top, is a hand's-breadth of black water.

Fly casting is impossible in this maze of dead and living branches. Shorten your line to two feet, or even less, bait your hook with a worm, and drop it gingerly into that gurgling crevice of water. Before it has sunk six inches, if there is not one of those black-backed, orange-bellied Taylor Brook trout fighting with it, something is wrong with your worm or with you. For the trout are always there, sheltered by the brushwood that makes this half mile of fishing "not worth while." Below the lower road the Taylor Brook becomes uncertain water. For half a mile it yields only fingerlings, for no explainable reason; then there are two miles of clean fishing through the deep woods, where the branches are so high that you can cast a fly again if you like, and there are long pools, where now and then a heavy fish will rise; then comes a final half mile through the alders, where you must wade, knee to waist deep, before you come to the bridge and the river. Glorious fishing is sometimes to be had here, especially if you work down the gorge at twilight, casting a white miller until it is too dark to see. But alas, there is a well-worn path along the brook, and often enough there are the very footprints of the fellow ahead of you, signs as disheartening to the fisherman as ever were the footprints on the sand to Robinson Crusoe.

But between the roads it is "too much trouble to fish"; and there lies the salvation of the humble fisherman who disdains not to use the crawling worm, nor, for that matter, to crawl himself, if need be, in order to sneak under the boughs of some overhanging cedar that casts a perpetual shadow upon the sleepy brook. Lying here at full length, with no elbowroom to manage the rod, you must occasionally even unjoint your tip and fish with that, using but a dozen inches of line and not letting so much as your eyebrows show above the bank. Is it a becoming attitude for a middle-aged citizen of the world? That depends upon how the fish are biting. Holing a put looks rather ridiculous also, to the mere observer, but it requires, like brook fishing with a tip only, a very delicate wrist, perfect tactile sense, and a fine disregard of appearances.

There are some fishermen who always fish as if they were being photographed. The Taylor Brook between the roads is not for them. To fish it at all is back-breaking, trouser-tearing work; to see it thoroughly fished is to learn new lessons in the art of angling. To watch R., for example, steadily filling his six-pound creel from that unlikely stream is like watching Sargent paint a portrait. R. weighs two hundred and ten. Twenty years ago he was a famous amateur pitcher, and among his present avocations are violin playing, which is good for the wrist, taxidermy, which is good for the eye, and shooting woodcock, which before the days of the new nature study used to be thought good for the whole man. R. began as a fly fisherman, but by dint of passing his summers near brooks where fly fishing is impossible, he has become a stouthearted apologist for the worm. His apparatus is most singular. It consists of a very long, cheap rod, stout enough to smash through bushes, with the stiffest tip obtainable. The lower end of the butt, below the reel, fits into the socket of a huge extra butt of bamboo, which R. carries unconcernedly. To reach a distant hole or to fish the lower end of a ripple, R. simply locks his reel, slips on the extra butt, and there is a fourteen-foot rod ready for action. He fishes with a line unbelievably short and a Kendal hook far too big, and when a trout jumps for that hook, R. wastes no time in maneuvering for position. The unlucky fish is simply "derricked," to borrow a word from Theodore, most saturnine and profane of Moosehead guides.

"Shall I play him awhile?" shouted an excited sportsman to Theodore, after hooking his first big trout.

"—— no!" growled Theodore in disgust. "Just derrick him right into the canoe!" A heroic method, surely; though it once cost me the best squaretail I ever hooked, for Theodore had forgotten the landing net and the gut broke in his fingers as he tried to swing the fish aboard. But with these lively quarter-pounders of the Taylor Brook, derricking is a safer procedure. Indeed, I have sat dejectedly on the far end of a log, after fishing the hole under it in vain, and seen the mighty R. wade downstream close behind me, adjust that comical extra butt, and jerk a couple of half-pound trout from under the very log on which I was sitting. His device on this occasion was to pass his hook but once through the middle of a big worm, let the worm sink to the bottom and crawl along it at his leisure. The trout could not resist.

Dainty, luring, beautiful toy, light as thistledown, falling where you will it to fall, holding when the leader tightens and sings like the string of a violin, the artificial fly represents the poetry of angling. But angling's honest prose, as represented by the lowly worm, has also its exalted moments. "The last fish I caught was with a worm," says the honest Walton, and so say I. It was the last evening of last August. The dusk was settling deep upon a tiny meadow, scarcely ten rods from end to end. The rank bog grass, already drenched with dew, bent over the narrow, deep little brook so closely that it could not be fished except with a double-shotted, baited hook, dropped delicately between the heads of the long grasses. Underneath this canopy the trout were feeding, taking the hook with a straight downward tug, as they made for the hidden bank. It was already twilight when I began, and before I reached the black belt of woods that separated the meadow from the lake, the swift darkness of the north country made it impossible to see the hook. A short half hour's fishing only, and behold nearly twenty good trout derricked into a basket until then sadly empty. Your rigorous fly fisherman would have passed that grass-hidden brook in disdain, but it proved a treasure for the humble.

In more open brook fishing it is always a fascinating problem to decide how to fish a favorite pool or ripple, for much depends upon the hour of the day, the light, the height of water, the precise period of the spring or summer. But after one has decided upon the best theoretical procedure, how often the stupid trout prefers some other plan. And when you have missed a fish that you counted upon landing, what solid satisfaction is still possible for you, if you are philosopher enough to sit down then and there, eat your lunch, smoke a meditative pipe, and devise a new campaign against that particular fish. To get another rise from him after lunch is a triumph of diplomacy; to land him is nothing short of statesmanship. For sometimes he will jump furiously at a fly for very devilishness without ever meaning to take it, and then, wearying suddenly of his gymnastics, he will snatch sulkily at a grasshopper, beetle, or worm. Trout feed upon an extraordinary variety of crawling things, as all fishermen know who practice the useful habit of opening the first two or three fish they catch, to see what food is that day the favorite. But here, as elsewhere in this world, the best things lie nearest, and there is no bait so killing, week in and week out, as your plain garden or golf-green angleworm.

Walton's list of possible worms is impressive, and his directions for placing them upon the hook have the placid completeness that belonged to his character. Yet in such matters a little nonconformity may be encouraged. No two men or boys dig bait in quite the same way, though all share, no doubt, the singular elation which gilds that grimy occupation with the spirit of romance. Nor do any two experienced fishermen hold quite the same theory as to the best mode of baiting the hook. There are a hundred ways, each of them good.

As to the best hook for worm fishing, you will find dicta in every catalogue of fishing tackle, but size and shape and tempering are qualities that should vary with the brook, the season, and the fisherman. Should one use a three-foot leader or none at all? Whose rods are best for bait fishing, granted that all of them should be stiff enough in the tip to lift a good fly by dead strain from a tangle of brush or logs? Such questions, like those pertaining to the boots or coat which one should wear, the style of bait box one should carry, or the brand of tobacco best suited for smoking in the wind, are topics for unending discussion among the serious minded around the campfire. Much edification is in them, and yet they are but prudential maxims after all. They are mere moralities of the Franklin or Chesterfield variety, counsels of worldly wisdom, but they leave the soul untouched. A man may have them at his fingers' ends and be no better fisherman at bottom; or he may, like R., ignore most of the admitted rules and come home with a full basket. It is a sufficient defense of fishing with a worm to pronounce the truism that no man is a *complete* angler until he has mastered all the modes of angling. Lovely streams, lonely and enticing but impossible to fish with a fly, await the fisherman who is not too proud to use, with a man's skill, the same unpretentious tackle which he began with as a boy.

Many Rivers

by FERRIS GREENSLET

Editor and biographer, and one of the most superlative fly fishermen in North America, Ferris Greenslet served as associate editor to Bliss Perry before assuming the editorial direction of Houghton Mifflin Company.

OCTOBER 1943

Perhaps the reason I have brought so eager a passion to the fishing of so many rivers is that I have never had enough of that sport. Three times in forty years I have taken a full month off just to fish — once in County Cork, once in the Cévennes, once on the far isle of Anticosti. Apart from those halcyon cycles of the moon, my fishing has always been over long weekends or, at best, two weekends with the week between; never so far away that telegrams or the telephone plus swift-footed messenger couldn't catch up and keep me in touch with work.

It was during the Dividend and Depression decades of the twenties and thirties that such escapes brought the most tingling pleasure. The truth is that in those years I seemed to have become a schizo personality, 50 per cent executive and factual, the other moiety literary and fanciful. There was a civil war in my innards for which I could negotiate no peace save when wading in the river with the fish, sharing their cold, sweet, silver life, becoming for bird and kine and native passer-by merely a harmless "feller in the creek."

Of the fourscore rivers I have fished, I remember not only the pools and runs but the best methods of approaching them and the actual lie of the fish. On nights when care-charming sleep will not be wooed to my bed, I count no silly sheep, but fish a mile or two of selected river, downstream wet or upstream dry, as suits my mood. Always I drop off and sometimes finish out the stretch in sleep. But the fish we hook in dreams rarely reach the net.

The choice of fishing companions is a deep matter. In camp, for bridge or dominoes in the evening, three are all right, but on the water one is enough, and, unless rating at least 90 on a scale of 100, too many. A wife or daughter, or what you have, who takes an intelligent interest in the proceedings, who appreciates your merit without emulation and is not bored when you expound it to her, who likes fish to eat, is an excellent fellow traveler. Of your own sex, the ideal is someone who is not only keen and competent, but curious, reflective, well-read in the literature of the subject, who considers fishing not a competitive sport but a branch of philosophy, who takes as much pleasure in your fish as you do in his.

Of my own preferred companions, a majority have been surgeons or painters — neat-handed, individualistic, free-minded fellows, like Bob Greenough, *beau joueur* at every outdoor and indoor sport, lord of the Seigneurie of Pertuis in the Laurentians, who fought the battle of public health against cancer till his own untimely death. Par excellence, I'd choose Leslie Thompson, distinguished painter and fishing philosopher, master of the useful art of camouflaging quick thinking behind slow speech. I have fished, or discoursed of fishing, with the chief angling authorities of our time — Lord Grey, Sheringham, Skues, Hewitt, La Branche — but have known no more knowledgeable head and cunning hand than Lett Thompson's, no companion who so consistently doubles stream-side joys and halves the griefs.

Of guides and gillies, a book could be written. Two would deserve a chapter apiece: Jim O'Brien of the Kennebago, guide, philosopher, naturalist, stream strategist, friend; and Jack O'Brien of the Cork Blackwater, incomparable raconteur.

One day, during a mixed party of happy memory at Castle Hyde, near Fermoy, the men went for the day to some hopeful salmon water downstream. There Jack O'Brien, octogenarian, tall, ruddy-cheeked, taciturn, took us in charge. From the stratospherical point of view, Ireland is but a green speck in the Atlantic Ocean. So it is, too, from the meteorological, and we were having that day quite a spot of Atlantic weather. We worked downstream — three casts, three steps forward, three more casts, three steps forward, and so on *da capo*. I did it in three-four time, to the melody of "Casey would waltz with the strawberry blonde." At every step the rain in the back of my neck got colder. The seely salmon hugged the bottom where it was warm. It was a blank and chilling forenoon.

At lunchtime, the ladies of the party arrived on the dripping scene with a hamper. From it appeared a roast duck, a whole ham with fixings, two bottles of Burgundy, six of Bass, and one of John Jameson.

As the last was handed out, I descried a dotted line straight to it from O'Brien's faded eye:

"Would you like a drink, O'Brien?"

"I would, sir!"

Taking a water tumbler, he filled it seven-eighths full of the creature, put it down the hatch in two gulps, and became suddenly loquacious:

"Sure and it's strange things that happen on this Blackwater River, and the strangest I ever seen was right by yon tree, in 1872, it was, in February. I was spinning for pike. I was casting it out and reeling it in, and casting it out and reeling it in, and of a sudden I heard the sound of the hunting horn. And I looked over there across the river, and round that little hill there I seen the fox coming, and after him the hounds, and the master, and the beautiful gentlemen and ladies on their big beautiful horses.

"And the fox he jumped in the river and started swimming this way, and the hounds after him, and the gentlemen and ladies wading their horses up there by the stickle.

"And the fox he got halfway across and then he sank from sight; and I said to meself, 'Alas, the fox, poor fellow, he's drowned!'

"And just then I felt a big pull on me spinning rig. A great pike it was that weighed forty-three pounds, and I played him up and I played him down, and at last I got the gaff into him, and I pulled him out on the bank and hit him three — no, 'twas four times, on the head with me priest.

"And I turned him over, and there was his belly bulging out like nothing you ever saw before. And I says to meself, 'Sure and it's funny the way that pike's belly sticks out,' and I took out me knife and slit him up the belly.

"And out jumps the fox, and he ran three miles before they killed him."

The mood of the actual fishing is the same everywhere. It is always a restrained and muted fierceness. It is in the casting of the fly, when a moment's languor is fatal — in the striking and playing of the fish. It is the source of numberless acts of unrecorded heroism, as when rheumatic old men deliberately go over their waders to cover a rising fish without drag. It is a fire in the heart that drives us on to one more pool long after we are thoroughly exhausted and reprehensibly late for supper. The Indians knew it as they cast their buck tails on virgin waters, and my great-uncle Charles, God rest him, who caught his death wading in the brook on his eightieth birthday, felt its propelling urge. In short, it is fishing. And of fishing, the fly rod is the characteristic implement and perfect symbol.

And what of the River of Life, the springs whence it comes and the sea where it goes?

An English friend, G. E. M. Skues, has written a classic fishing book, *Minor Tactics of the Chalk Stream.* Minor tactics have their place on the turbid stream of consciousness, too. It is the little things that make up the good day. The scent of a country morning, a catbird's phrase, a line of verse or a page of prose, some small mirth-making incongruity, a happily found word for a quaint conceit, the warm presence of a friend, a responsive smile, the light of sun or moon or star, or, if the weather turns sour, the dash of rain in your face.

Nor is this the supine philosophy of a new beatitude. Minor tactics are active, not passive. They succeed only at the hands of the persistent and alert. As in fishing, languor is fatal.

Ballade About Nish

by R. P. LISTER

JULY 1948

If it is true I do not know,
I heard it from a man called Jake
Who heard it from a man called Joe
Who found it graven on a plaque
Screwed to the handle of a rake,
In letters crabbed and heathenish.
These were the words, and no mistake:
　　There are no fish
　　In Nish.

Across the marshes of the Po
Glide duck with their attendant drake;
In Indian jungles brightly glow

The tiger, tiger, burning Blake;
There are ten million kittiwake
And seven terns in Vaternish;
But in all Ireland not a snake
    And not a fish
    In Nish.

Search then for bears in Bendigo,
Seek ambergris in walrus steak,
Discover diamond dust in dough
And cadmium carbonate in cake,
Go hunting shark in Grasmere lake,
Drink whiskey from an empty dish
And cure a worm of stomach-ache;
    Then find a fish
    In Nish.

Prince, you may call for cod or hake
    Or what you wish.
There are no saints in Savernake
    Or fish
    In Nish.

"Is This Your First Visit?"

by JOHN MASON BROWN

Author and critic who had chosen the theater for his special province, John Mason Brown was at the peak of his fame as a lecturer when in 1941 he wrote the series of endearing papers which first appeared in the Atlantic *and then in book form under the disarming title* Accustomed As I Am.

DECEMBER 1941

As a lecturer you never know, of course, when you are going to be "met." This means you have to drop off the train in a fair state of order — shaved, eyes open, hair brushed, wearing a suit that was once pressed, and with a simper of salutation on your face. When, on the platform or at the gate, you spot two or three people as sheepish in appearance as you feel, who clutch a photograph between them, and when you notice that they keep looking up from this photograph to scan the features of everyone who has left the train, like Federal Agents about to pick up a bank robber, you can be fairly sure the Welcoming Committee is before you.

Needless to say, it would be easier for all concerned if lecturers wore white carnations in their lapels or carried yellow tickets. They really ought to. Because the only certain thing about lecturers is that they will never bear the slightest resemblance to the photographs — off or on the circular — which their managers have sent ahead of them.

The young ones, wanting to be old as only the young do, are usually represented by scowling portraits, executed by one of those phrenologists of light who excel at making Penrod look like Von Hindenburg three days after death. The older ones, wishing to be young as only the old can, would send their baby pictures if they thought they could get away with them. Instead they forward either some misty profile à la John Barrymore or pictures taken two weeks after their graduation.

It's all very confusing, and can lead to humiliations, as well I know. Only last winter, for example, I found myself arriving in a strange town. The train was an hour late. No one was on the platform, but at the gate I did notice three people wearing that telltale look of welcome. I smiled vaguely in their direction, the kind of smile which shows itself in the eyes but does not dare to take possession of the mouth. One by one they looked intently at me. But as there was no sign of recognition, and as once I had approached just such a group and coyly whispered, "I am Mr. Brown," only to have the three good people composing this group say, "What of it? You're not H. G. Wells, are you?" I hurried on to a taxi.

At the hotel twenty minutes later there was a knock on my door. And the same three people trooped into my room. "So you *are* Mr. Brown," said the spokesman, smiling amiably. "I'm sorry we missed you. We saw you at the station, but did not recognize you. You see, your circular said you were red-headed, and though we looked hard at you, we all decided you couldn't be you because your hair was so gray."

Once they have recovered from their natural surprise at discovering how little you resemble your photographic self, and once they have come to understand the wisdom of the policy that makes this difference necessary, they can be charming, these good men and women who have had wished upon them the duty of inquiring, "Is this your first visit to ——?"

They love their towns, and want you to love them, too. You may be bewildered by the stone bridge which they assure you is the longest stone bridge in the world. Among the wonders of this structure is that, though seemingly so immutable, it is migratory. It crops up in city after city, galloping ahead of you, you finally suspect, like a courier. If you cease to react to it quite as breathlessly as your guides desire, it is because (though you dare not say so) any loyal citizen of Pennsylvania's capital will tell you that the longest four-track-stone-arch bridge in the world is the one that spans the Susquehanna. After much ardent research devoted to this subject, I have convinced myself — and been convinced — that Harrisburg is at any rate this bridge's point of departure.

Except for Huey Long's skyscraper at Baton Rouge, Nebraska's proud tower at Lincoln, and the gold-domed old structure in Boston, the state capitols may in retrospect become at times as hard to tell one from another as are the Mesdemoiselles Dionnes. Your scalp may ache as you try to keep clear the tribal distinctions of the Kiowas, the Sauks, the Onondagas, the Blackfeet, the Flatheads, the Shoshones, and the Tuscaroras. The battlefields of the French and Indian War, the Revolution, and the Civil War may merge like the Seven Cities of Troy in your itinerant mind. Your head may reel as, passing through the beautiful residential sections that fringe American cities, you try to remember who lives in the huge house behind this fence or hedge, and what it was that its owner's great-grandfather stood for when he was a defeated candidate for the Vice Presidency. State histories and local legend may at times prove more adhesive to themselves than to you, as nightly you hopscotch across state lines and daily change towns.

But you do learn. More and more you realize what a giant delusion is the self-sufficiency of those proud towers which are New York. In spite of its fascinations, Manhattan, you come to see, is no more than a man-made delta deposited at the mouth of the endless river of enterprise and hope, of energy and defiance, which is America. It is the biggest of our towns — indeed, a huge anthology of friendly villages-within-villages brought together to make the largest and seemingly most impersonal of our cities. But, great as New York is, America is its absentee landlord. And we who proudly call Manhattan our home prove ourselves to be the greatest of all provincials when New York tempts us to forget this, as it often does.

Up, down, and around the country are millions of things to see, if your curiosity is not dormant and your energies are not drained. Jostling with the strivings of the present — with gasoline stations, hot-dog stands, hideous road signs, and tourist camps where Cupid no less than motorists can rest; with eating places doing their best to look like dining cars, grounded battleships, brown derbies, or anything but restaurants; with the shacks of shanty towns, the neglect of forgotten sections of cities now pushing into wooded suburbs, the roar and smoke of factories, or the greater competition of natural wonders of the out-of-doors — are reminders of the past. Old houses, instructive plaques, charming reconstructions, historic shrines — these are the sudden spokesmen for different days, for conflicting civilizations, forgotten issues, and those arduous battlings, inch by inch, which have made possible the way of life so many of us, in our unearned softness, now take for granted.

If these places with conjuring names from a past incredibly near are neither as numerous nor as old as the ones that beckon in Europe, it is because the greatest monument of them all is the country itself: the country and its people.

As you listen at every turn to those countless accents and vocabularies that color the voice of Uncle Sam; as each morning brings a new landscape as easily before your Pullman window as a fresh backdrop is lowered on the stage; as elms turn into palms and palms into oranges; as wheat changes into cotton and race horses into cattle; as the snow by the Northern lakes melts in a few hours into spring in Texas; or as you leave behind you the East's cool, manicured green to cross the great muddy inland rivers and traverse the granaries, and the Rockies suddenly rise from the plains, you cannot help sensing the differences in race, class, and region of those millions who have either become or are becoming that new people, the Americans, and marveling at the miracle which is their country.

You cannot help thinking of the bent backs, the raised axes, and the sweat which every house and cleared space and humming railroad tie and car-filled highway and proof of ease represents. You cannot help being amazed at the patience and the impatience, the bravery and the sacrifices, the huge geyserlike burst of energy which, beautiful or hideous in its aesthetic results, the whole conquest of the continent stands for. And you cannot help having a fresh faith in America's new frontier, which is the future.

Above all, you are bound to wonder how all these diversities in nature and in man, in interest and tradition, were ever fused into a union or have been held there. But the more you see of the United States, the more you realize that the greatest reality of the American dream is the vague common hope which has enabled all of these people and all of these sections to speak of themselves as "we" and mean it.

The Welcoming Committees do not hymn America when they meet you. They are not wrapped up in bunting. Their spirit is anything but Rotarian. They are pleasant people, delegated to do a job, who in the kindness of their hearts seek to make a stranger feel at home. They want to fill your empty hours, to have you see what you should see and should want to see.

Their hospitality does not end with history or with sights. They also want to share their houses and friends with you. So genuine and warm-hearted and amusing are most of these men and women you have met shyly at the station in the early morning that for you America soon becomes people no less than places; people you look forward to seeing again because, with reason, you have come to count them among your friends. From them you learn as much as from the places, if not more. They give you the country's temperature better than any Gallup poll.

Around the Horn
by WYMAN RICHARDSON, M.D.

In an ancient Cape Cod cottage, the Farm House, the walls of which were decorated by his uncle, the artist Frank W. Benson, Dr. Wyman Richardson spent some fifty summers. Here he came to know the moods and ever-changing beauty of Nauset Beach and the great salt marsh within; here he developed his extraordinary knowledge of the shore birds; and here he guided his family and friends on happy expeditions for the striped bass or the blue crab.

SEPTEMBER 1954

The Nauset Marsh at Eastham on outer Cape Cod is a most unusual salt marsh. Most such marshes are protected to the seaward by a barrier beach through which an estuary enters. This estuary is widest at its mouth and divides into smaller and smaller branches which lead into denser and denser bodies of solid sedge.

Not so the Nauset Marsh. It contains more water than sedge and has large bays at the upper end. Even the main channel, while nearly two miles from the inlet, is a quarter of a mile wide. (The "inlet" is the passage through the barrier beach.) The sedge is divided into sections. The large ones are called "flat" or "marsh," and the small "hummock." The largest such piece, Porchy Marsh, is about a mile and a half from north to south. Its nearest, or north, edge is about a mile from the Farm House. We call the southernmost tip Cape Horn, and the shallow passageway that makes a tiny island of it, the Strait of Magellan.

One of our best expeditions is to "round the Horn" in the canoe. In order to do this, there must not be so much wind that paddling becomes a task, and the tide must serve in such a manner that we can drop down the main channel on the ebb, meet the flood at the Horn, come up with it, and get home at a comfortable hour for dinner.

The tide is right for us the ninth of one October. There is a light breeze from the northeast and the air is sparklingly clear. From the Farm House piazza the water in the marsh channels is a clear blue, while through the dips in the dunes we can see the deeper blue of the Atlantic.

As we leave the mouth of the Salt Pond Creek and begin to negotiate the twists and turns of the upper channels, we see many ducks along the edge of Tom Doane's Hummock. Most of them are black, although we note two hen mallards, one pintail, and perhaps half a dozen baldpates. As we approach, the black ducks begin to take notice. Their necks become straight, long and stiff — at least twice as long as a duck's neck should be. The nearer ones separate from one another and luff up into the wind, a sure sign that they are about to fly. And away they go, with that spectacular jump of theirs.

We soon come to that deep part of the channel south of the Cedar Bank, where we put out a bucktail fly and begin trolling. This is simply to protect ourselves; for what with the bright sun and very low water, it does not seem like a very good chance. The flats are pretty well covered with shore birds. "Winter" yellowlegs and black-bellied plover represent the larger birds, while the smaller ones are mostly red-backed sandpipers. Suddenly we hear their shrill alarm note, and at once every bird is in the air. "Must be a duck hawk around," I observe.

My wife snatches off her white hat. A day or two before, when she was sketching, a duck hawk had come along. She had taken up her binoculars and, just as she had them focused on the hawk, he had made a pass at her hat. This, as seen through her glasses, had been truly terrifying. "Leave it on," I suggest. "You may attract him."

"Here," she says, "you wear it."

"I guess I won't," I reply, lamely enough.

White hat or no white hat, a handsome full-plumaged male duck hawk comes directly over our heads. Soon he begins to soar and in an incredibly short time disappears to the northeast.

At this point five huge shore birds come low over our heads and light on the flat in front of us. A quick glance through the glasses shows that they are all godwits, four marbled and one Hudsonian. We all have a good look at these magnificent birds, the largest of our shore birds. We let the canoe drift up to within thirty feet of them. The marbled godwits show at the base of their long, upturned bills an orange tinge which we have never noticed before. The Hudsonian is considerably darker and there is a bit of the white patch at the base of his tail which is obvious when he flies. We leave them to their bickerings and their worms, as the ebb takes us slowly past.

We go by Hay Island, where some bass boil ahead of the canoe and corroborate the old adage that "a boiling bass never bites." Past the mouth of Jeremiah's Creek, where we put a night heron in a dither as to whether to fly or not to fly. Past the outermost end of Porchy Bar, which so many neophytes have tried to cheat by cutting across too soon, only to find themselves hopelessly stuck on the sand riffles. Past Broad Creek, now, at low water, almost dry except for a few deep holes here and there. Past Deep Water Point, which is no longer a point and where there is no deep water. And finally, down to the sand bar to the south of the Horn.

The sand bar is covered with herring gulls, perhaps two hundred of them, and we wonder why they are standing so still and so erect with all eyes turned in the same direction. And then the reason for this rapt attention becomes apparent. At the upper end of the bar, austerely aloof, is a large brown bird, about as big as the gulls. When we get the glasses focused on him, we realize he is a brown gyrfalcon. He seems to be eying the gulls with a malevolent expression. As we approach, he turns his baleful glance on us, as if to say: "Get to hell out of here."

But it is he at last who moves. He allows us to come within about fifty yards and finally takes off. As he does so, every gull turns and faces him. He flies directly over them and makes several dives at them. Each time, the target gull spreads his wings, opens his beak wide, and screams. And each time, the gyrfalcon swoops up, inches from the gull's head, without touching him.

The gyrfalcon does this about three times and then, off to the east, he spies a marsh hawk. He dashes away and comes down on the marsh hawk from above. But just before he gets there, the marsh hawk flips over on his back, with upraised talons, and again gyrfalcon swoops up and away. Time after time, this performance is repeated, until finally gyrfalcon tires of the sport and lazily flies to the south.

After this excitement, we go ashore at the end of the sand bar and wait for the flood tide to take a hold. We walk over the riffled sand in our bare feet, looking for items of interest, but we find nothing more interesting than that savage shellfish, *Polynices heros.* He is the common big round "snail" which makes a trail in the sand ending in a very suggestive hump. He is equipped with not only a powerful foot but also an effective rasp as well. He it is who destroys so many mollusks, and he who fashions that smooth sand collar which never meets in the middle but which nevertheless holds many thousands of Polynices eggs.

When we climb back into the canoe the tide is flooding strongly. We make our southing and turn with the tide, leaving Cape Horn to starboard. The channel takes us close to the Tonset Shore where eelgrass, five or six feet long, has come in thick. We skirt the edge of it and are just approaching the rocks, when suddenly the rod man's reel begins to screech.

I backwater sharply to stop the canoe's progress; but the fish continues to tear off line. Not only that, but he starts weaving around some lobster pot buoys which are always to be found in this region. I do my best, in the strong current, to weave the canoe around after him, and must confess to a feeling of relief when he suddenly kicks off. At this moment someone spies a large white object in the Skiff Hill pastures, a quarter of a mile ahead. "It's a mushroom," say I, making a rather poor joke.

At the foot of the pastures, we land and climb the green slope. And a mushroom it is! Nine and one-half inches across the top it measures, with a stem an inch and three-quarters thick. In the old Farm House log, my father wrote of mushrooms as big as dinner plates. Well, this pasture is full of dinner plates and we pick a mess of them.

The mushroom-picking diversion allows the tide to catch up with us and we all pile back into the canoe. Even so, the upper flats are still out. The Skiff Hill Channel is plenty deep but it shoals to nothing when we get up toward our hill. We follow a run which turns and twists through the West Cove flats. For some time it is satisfyingly deep. However, it peters out just as we approach the first bend of the main channel. When we come to a stop, there is some talk about getting out and dragging. But the hazards of wading in bare feet through soft mud are too great. We prefer to wait.

And we are repaid for our waiting. As we sit quietly, an army of sandpipers lights beside us. Each little bird begins frantically to scurry to and fro, constantly probing with his bill the soft surface and evidently getting something to his liking. We watch them through our glasses, trying to tell the difference between the semipalmated and the least sandpiper. The least is darker and has greenish legs, and the semipalmated is lighter and has black legs. They look very small beside their cousins with the down-curved bill, the redbacks. The latter, who are winter visitors, seem to specialize on a small, pink worm which they carefully dunk in the water before swallowing.

So engrossed do we become looking for darker backs and greener legs that we are surprised when the canoe suddenly begins to move. The tide is not only rising; it is flooding. We go along with it into the channel, up into the Salt Pond Creek, and back to the boathouse. We park the canoe alongside and, somewhat wearily, trudge up the hill to the Farm House.

Portrait of a Poker Player

by DILLON ANDERSON

Author of I and Claudie *and* Claudie's Kinfolks, *Dillon Anderson is a Houston lawyer who enjoys nothing so much as a relaxing game of poker. The mentor of his poker table is his friend Billingsley, and Billingsley's methods of wearing down the opposition will be relished by every reader who ever tries to bluff with a broken straight.*

DECEMBER 1954

From the vantage point of a fellow player, I have frequently witnessed the nigh invariable success of Billingsley's matchless poker — stud and draw — and have heard it described on countless occasions as defying analysis. Now, having finally mastered the subject, at the expense of many of the little luxuries that might otherwise have come to

me at this stage of life — if not, in fact, a few downright necessities —
I am setting down this analytical study for future reference.

BILLINGSLEY WILL COME TO THE GAME LATE

Billingsley has never been to a game on time yet, even when we who
always have to organize the evening attempt to trick him by naming
seven as the starting hour for games that are scheduled to start at eight.
He comes to games like that around nine-thirty. When we are honest
with him he comes by nine.

Now the obvious result of such a course of conduct is that Billingsley
will avoid having to help classify and count out the chips, and will likewise escape other growing pains that attend every game, including:

1. The argument as to "Who the hell is going to bank this game anyway?"

2. The discussion and arbitration over how the banker's mistakes
will be handled when the settling up is done. (This usually proves to
be an academic problem for reasons which will be related.)

3. Putting the beer on ice, paying for it, and pinching the first pots
to cover. This is usually over by nine or a little after.

4. The slow start when all pots are fairly small and hardly worth
the employment of much virtuosity to garner. (In describing his attitude toward these early hands Billingsley employs a Latin quotation
which escapes me just now, but the literal translation is "An eagle will
not bite at a fly.")

5. The ringing of the telephone by the wives of some of the players
who merely wish to check up on their whereabouts.

Thus it will be seen that by the time our hero arrives the coast is
clear and the quarry is ready.

BILLINGSLEY ARRIVES

He can be heard when he slams the door of his car outside. Billingsley
calls from the front door and says, good news, he has arrived; he wants
to be counted in on the very hand we are then playing. If it is winter
he has his coat and tie off by the time he enters the room. If it is summer
he has his shirt off, but he often leaves his hat on throughout the first
few rounds.

I do not wish to imply by the foregoing that Billingsley is rude, has
bad manners, or, in fact, has any manners at all except what the reader
will come to recognize as Billingsley manners. They are unique. And
in order that we may do him no injustice in this respect, let it be under-

stood that no ladies clutter up the regular site where the game is played; it is a bachelor household. It is, in fact, the home of Worthington, a really feeble player, whose aunt left it to him, along with a fine set of ivory poker chips and a cool million in tax-exempt bonds.

BILLINGSLEY WILL BADGER

This is literally true, and I stand steadfastly on every word of it. He will badger the dealer about the slowness of the deal and accuse him of holding up the game deliberately. If this should fluster the dealer — as often it does — Billingsley will be quick to notice it and step up the pace and severity of his heckling. Then, if the dealer drops a card, turns up one meant to be down, or vice versa, Billingsley announces that he has an idiot yard boy who gives dealing lessons on Thursday mornings, and suggests that the hapless dealer should enroll in the course. He adds that tuition will be free on a certified Billingsley scholarship.

He will badger a player who fails to make up his mind promptly whether he will call a bet or drop out. Of course I am no longer fooled about Billingsley's real motives here. It is not alone that he wishes to get along with the game — turnover being calculated, as a matter of elementary mathematics, to enhance the chances of winning by the superior player; Billingsley's real object is to study the demeanor of the player who is put to a decision under pressure. If such a player is possessed of a very heavy hand — I mean is really loaded — and is delaying merely for effect and in the hope of getting a call or a raise, Billingsley will thus elicit some response and a consequent show of the badgered player's emotion. In such situations where real strength has been disclosed, I have seen Billingsley throw in threes or better, advising the loaded player that his noisy heartbeat, engendered by the heavy hand, has begun to disturb the peace and tranquillity of the whole neighborhood.

On the other hand, if the hesitating player has been badgered and thereby exposed in the process of running a windy, his nervousness will be brought fully to light, and Billingsley can run him out of the hand with one high card and one moderate-sized chip.

BILLINGSLEY WILL BOOST THE ANTE

I confess that some conclusions set out elsewhere in this study may be debatable, but this one thing can be put down as fundamental and axiomatic: Billingsley will not tolerate the status quo ante. He will "up it." If the game is knocking along at a reasonable rate with a quarter ante, he will call for a half-dollar ante on his deal until I, who am sitting on his left and feeling that I have already held up normal progress of the game long enough, break over and throw in a four-bit chip. Then soon no one dares to face the Billingsley glare and comment which would attend the recession to a quarter ante. Thereafter Billingsley will ante a dollar on his deal, throwing out, in response to any complaints ventured, a rhetorical question, "It's dealer's choice, isn't it?" By morning any remaining players who should dare to name less than a dollar ante will simply be stared out of the pot.

So overweening is the desire of this great man to have the pot anted fully that he will count the antes often, and even before he has finished he will utter a general pronunciamento that someone has not come in yet. This usually garners two or three more chips from the more absentminded players. Then, to those who have thus tacitly admitted their delinquency, he says witheringly, "It will be all right for you not to ante all the time. Just don't withdraw any of my chips from our pot." Such a scolded victim naturally has his next several hands spoiled.

BILLINGSLEY WILL DRAW TWO CARDS TO A FLUSH

It is really foreign to the nature of such a conservative player as I am to execute this incomparable play; nevertheless, I shall not hesitate to point out that I know all of its basic elements as executed by Billingsley. It comes about thus: when draw poker is dealt, Billingsley is annoyed. He would prefer to play stud, he insists. I record this because his annoyance is a psychologically component part of his two-card-draw-to-a-flush-and-follow-through play. Unless several hands have been passed for want of openers, he will not employ the particular technique in question; he simply sits looking into the next room with a pained expression in his eyes. He might even get up and stroll around muttering and scratching himself. Then, say there have been three hands passed, swelling the pot to a sizable amount. Thereupon the hand, let us assume, is opened by a pair of aces. A pair of deuces calls, matched by another caller holding a straight, open at both ends. Billingsley swoops down, raises the bet the full size of the pot, and explains piously that he is doing it merely to give a little protection to the opener. Stark terror grips all the players, but Billingsley usually gets two or three customers. Honest draws are made by the others, but Billingsley, looking as contented as Walter P. Chrysler might contemplating the Chrysler Building, says that two cards will do for him. After the draw he bets the first installment on a Jaguar and launches on his campaign speech.

Anglers and Others

He insists that he hasn't a damn thing. He wants to know whether we are mice or men to let him "bull the game" like that.

Beads of perspiration pop out on the pair of aces, the openers, since the draw has produced another little pair. Similar beads cover the pair of deuces, now joined by a third. The straight is busted and flown. Finally Billingsley drags down the pot with no callers and shows his hand: three miscellaneous hearts and two orphans that look as if they belonged in a used pinochle deck. He announces in a loud tone that he would rather have three hearts in this game than three aces in any other game he ever played in. Also he sometimes laughs boisterously at this juncture and asks if there are any pitch players in the crowd.

The whole thing is simple. The two times that I called him on this particular play — once in 1938, just before I sold my car, and again last week — he wasn't using exactly the same technique that I have described. The first time he really had a big pair and a kicker; then he caught two to match the latter on the draw — a cat hop, so called, to a full house. Last week he had filled his flush. But you get the general idea anyhow, and I have the satisfaction of knowing that Billingsley wasn't bluffing either time. Successful bluffing, I have said a thousand times, is a thing that can't be allowed in a well-ordered game.

BILLINGSLEY WILL NOT BET ON A "LOCK" — MUCH

The quality of Billingsley's game, which I now describe, is really one of the refinements that we doubtless find in all truly great technicians in poker. It goes into effect in the following type of situation: in a stud game, let us say, Jones has queens back to back and has bet them so heavily that the down queen might as well be sitting on a neon throne. Naturally everybody but Billingsley is long since out of the game by the time the fifth card is dealt. Jones gets no pairs showing and no possibilities of a better hand. Billingsley's ace in the hole gets a companion on the fifth card, and if there is any way he could lose to poor old Jones under these circumstances, I have never yet been able to develop it. Armed with a real "lock," Billingsley will discount the limit moderately.

The same thing is true about four of a kind. If Billingsley bets slightly less than the limit, you can tell he has them. Here is a weak point in his game which I have pointed out to him several times, but he has only thrown back his shoulders and looked far away on each such occasion. He says it is a matter of *noblesse oblige* or, translated freely, "leaving a man carfare."

BILLINGSLEY WILL BULL THE GAME

It is not an easy undertaking to describe that hard and smooth facet of Billingsley's play to which I now address myself. Not that I do not understand it thoroughly — not at all, for I do; the difficulty, rather, is born of the realization that my description might put him in a slightly unfavorable light with readers of less than adequate appreciation of refined poker psychology. But this is an unexpurgated account, and I must reiterate my mild indictment in frankness and in candor: Billingsley will bull the game.

He will bet his chips, particularly during the early stages of a stud hand, in the same spirit of reckless abandon with which an Oriental war lord orders coolie troops into battle. The latter's action, I take it, is explicable in the cognizance that they are breeding them faster in the zone of the interior than they are being slaughtered in battle.

Now this is precisely the impression which Billingsley seeks to create on the first card that shows in stud: reckless abandon. He discloses this rash and irresponsible attitude by betting inordinate amounts on the first card that shows in several successive stud hands. Since every player will know that by the law of averages Billingsley can't have his hole card wired to a twin on every hand, he will gradually undermine the other players' faith in his good judgment.

Thus, soon his heavy bet on the first card is bringing the hopeful players along in droves. They count his empty beer bottles on the floor and decide to get a crack at this easy money. Also by staying they will each get a glimpse of their second card to show, and natural curiosity at this stage is always a factor to be reckoned with. When the second up card is dealt, Billingsley seems to go absolutely wild. He bets all the law allows — the game being, of course, pot limit — and some other players, though a little less avaricious by now, nevertheless stay because there are still two more chances to improve. Also they discover that they have a pretty substantial investment in the pot by this time.

When the third card up produces no pair showing, Billingsley's technique calls for a marked change. If he is high, he hesitates but does not check the bet. He speaks of acting against his better judgment. There is absolutely no more transparent aspect of Billingsley's game than this very one. Deception being important in poker, his feigned dubiety is calculated to stir hope in the breasts of fellow players. Now the elemental parallel of this gambit is, of course, the broken-wing act of the mother hawk, which, like Billingsley's technique, still works after all these years. The refinement, doubtless clear by now to the reader, is that Billingsley *may have a broken wing* in the form of a deuce in the hole.

In any event, whether Billingsley opens the next bet or has to be content with raising it the absolute limit, he will see to it that nobody stays in the pot at bargain basement rates.

The amount of money it will cost simply isn't worth another draw to anyone with less than a big pair or a straight or a flush draw, and many a fat pot is thus won at this very stage by Billingsley and quite irrespective of the quality of his hand. He calls this "keeping the ribbon clerks away from the gravy."

There is one other obvious contingency in this connection, and to it I shall now advert. Let us take a case where strength has shown elsewhere on the turning of the second or third card, and let us assume likewise that Billingsley's big bet is raised right back into his teeth. He looks hurt, and the wounded tragedian emerges in his whole demeanor. Unless he has an absolute lock on the player who raised him back, he will withdraw from the hand with the suggestion of a tear in his eye.

BILLINGSLEY HAS UNLIMITED ENDURANCE

Billingsley will not discuss the matter of ending the game before midnight. He will agree after that time to consider 1:30 as the time to take up the subject with a view then to setting some later hour as a time limit. By 1:30 we will have lost one or possibly two players who have reached a certain predetermined limit of loss and gone home. Along about two, if Billingsley is winner he will actually consider naming a time to quit — rather, I should say, to start the last round.

If he should be loser — I have to strain my memory to the breaking point to recall this testimony — he jumps up and down, gnashing his teeth and shouting until his veins stand out that he wants to play. "Deal!" he cries raucously. "Deal!" But the converse impression should not be gleaned from the foregoing that Billingsley will want to quit if he is winner. This is wrong. Billingsley doesn't *ever* want to quit, and the game never breaks up as long as any one player is willing to deal even one more cold hand for as much as a dollar.

Then, when Billingsley's last adversary finally folds his tents, Billingsley will stalk out alone, grumbling to himself in what has often been described as a tone of contempt blended with disgust and disappointment. His words, when they can be made out, reveal that which, to my mind, is the real secret of his bountiful success. They are that he "came to play."

XVIII

A Divided World

We came into being in an age of high tension, with the country aroused and inflamed at the thought of division; we find ourselves today a people united, of many bloods, with a common understanding, which in crises is capable of enormous exertion. We lived for the better part of a century with the belief that democracy would spread, making other people as tractable as we believe we are, and to that extent easier to live with. It has come as a shock to realize that perforce or by choice, so large a part of mankind lives under systems of government not only alien but hostile to ours. The implacable hostility of the Communist orbit, as it has come to be understood since 1946, first surprised and then angered us. And when to that we added the recognition that Russia would soon be able to match us in nuclear weapons, an element of dread — something totally new — became part of our daily thinking.

The state of the Union, the safety of the Republic, was paramount in the thinking of our first contributors. "Sometimes gunpowder smells good," wrote Emerson in 1861. Soon after the attack on Sumter he said in a public address, "We have been very homeless for some years past, say since 1850; but now we have a country again. . . . The war was an eye opener, and showed men of all parties and opinions the value of those primary forces that lie beneath all political action." And it was almost a personal pledge when he said at the Harvard Commemoration in 1865, "We shall not again disparage America, now that we have seen what men it will bear."

Today the question of safety of the Union is the vigilant concern of readers quite as much as writers, and they are almost as eager to be heard — but there is this difference: they are also thinking of the safety of the world. Never in the past has there been so much unsolicited writing on a single subject. In the win-

ter, when the number of contributions is at its peak, it would be possible, though not profitable, to fill an extra issue each month with publishable articles on war and peace. But not until the 1950s, not until the Bomb, or that imaginative version of it which many of us for a time wore on the back of our minds like an old derby — not till then did many Americans begin to wonder if there really was an alternative to war. This never occurred to men as farsighted as Brooks Adams, Theodore Roosevelt, or Walter Hines Page, partly because in the flush of the new century they were so wholly absorbed in our emergence as a world power, partly because they lived before the unleashing of annihilating weapons. William James was the only early thinker to publish his powerful premonition in our columns, and the warning he uttered at the Peace Banquet in 1904 was reinforced forty-three years later, and then by another scientist, Albert Einstein, when he spoke his mind to Raymond Swing at Princeton.

The daily dilemma, as Walter Lippmann so clearly puts it, is how to live with mounting inflammable rivalry in a divided world. "We insist on treating the rivalry of nations," he says, "as something that could not exist among right-thinking men." If education can keep pace with our refinement of missiles, perhaps man's imagination will prove a restraining force. The Atlantic used every form of persuasion to enforce Lincoln's belief in One Nation Indivisible; is it to be expected that in the century ahead the editors will exert their influence to preserve not only the nation but the world from the devastation of radioactivity?

The Influence of Sea Power Upon History

by THEODORE ROOSEVELT

Theodore Roosevelt was thirty-two years old when he first read Captain Mahan's book on sea power, and the major part of his career as Governor of New York, Vice President under McKinley, and President from 1901 to 1909 lay ahead of him. But if ever there was a formative moment in a stateman's career, this was one.

OCTOBER 1890

Captain Mahan has written distinctively the best and most important, and also by far the most interesting, book on naval history which has been produced on either side of the water for many a long year: *The Influence of Sea Power upon History* by Captain A. T. Mahan, USN. Himself an officer who has seen active service and borne himself with honor under fire, he starts with an advantage that no civilian can possess. On the other hand, he does not show the shortcomings which make the average military man an exasperatingly incompetent military historian. His work is in every respect scholarly, and has not a trace of the pedantry which invariably mars mere self-conscious striving after scholarship. He is thoroughly conversant with his subject and has prepared himself for it by exhaustive study and research, and he approaches it in, to use an old-fashioned phrase, an entirely philosophical spirit. He subordinates detail to mass effects, trying always to grasp and make evident the essentional features of a situation; and he neither loses sight of nor exaggerates the bearing which the history of past struggles has upon our present problems.

He does not fall into the mistake of trying to make forced analogies, but he does prove, for one thing, that the school which professes the melee or "never-mind-maneuvering" principles, no less than the other school, which tends to turn maneuvering into an end instead of a means and to develop mere timid tactical trifling, may study the fleet actions and naval campaigns of the last two centuries to good purpose. There are plenty of naval authorities who believe that an encounter between squadrons of modern ironclads, with their accompanying rams and torpedo boats, can be nothing but a huge bloody scramble in which each ship fights for its own hand. This belief may be true as an estimate of probabilities; but if it be, it will only show that as yet the nineteenth century does not know how to wield with proper skill the wonderful weapons it has forged.

Similarly, the early sea fights between fleets of sailing ships were mere melees; men knowing nothing more of tactics than that one-sided view of the "shock" principle, which consists in running headlong at an adversary — a system whereof the success depends entirely upon the nature of the adversary. But as time went on, a change took place, and there arose great admirals, who differed as much from the rough fleet leaders who preceded them as Alexander differed from Alaric. Sea war grew into an art, and the fleet that conquered had to pay heed to such considerations as unity of action and intelligent direction of force quite as much as to the valor of the seamen and the fighting capacity of the individual ships.

Captain Mahan's effort is to show the tremendous effect which sea power has had upon the development of certain of the great nations of the world, especially at momentous crises of their history. In his introductory chapter he gives one striking illustration, for he shows that it was the sea power of Rome, during the second Punic war, which was one of the chief determining factors in bringing about the failure of Hannibal's campaign in Italy and the consequent overthrow of Carthage. The second Punic war has been described again and again by every kind of writer for the past twenty centuries, yet Captain Mahan is the first who has given proper prominence to one of the main causes by which the result was determined.

Hitherto, historians of naval matters, at least so far as English and American writers are concerned, have completely ignored the general strategic bearing of the struggles which they chronicle; they have been for the most part mere annalists, who limited themselves to describing the actual battles and the forces on each side. On the other hand, the general historian sees but dimly how much and in what way the net outcome of a conflict has been influenced by the might of the contestants on the sea, and in consequence pays but vague and unsubstantial heed to the really vital cause by which the result was accomplished. Captain Mahan, however, never loses sight of the deep, underlying causes and of the connection between events. His discussion of the campaigns and battles, of the strategy and tactics, is full and clear and written in a perfectly scientific and dispassionate spirit. But this is not his greatest merit. He never for a moment loses sight of the relations which the struggles by sea bore to the history of the time; and for the period which he covers he shows, as no other writer has done, the exact points and the wonderful extent of the influence of the sea power of the various contending nations upon their ultimate triumph or failure and upon the futures of the mighty races to which they belonged.

In the first chapter after the introduction, he discusses the various elements which go to make up sea power, writing always, as elsewhere throughout the book, with especial heed to the circumstances of the United States at the present time. He shows how sea power is affected by the geographical position, physical conformation, extent, and density of population of a country no less than by the character of the people and of the government. He points out the need of adequate fortifications and navy yards on all the coast, and incidentally specifies the need at some point on the Gulf coast, preferably the mouth of the Mississippi; and he lays stress on the necessity of a large commercial marine, if we wish the sea population which alone furnishes a secure base for naval power. He draws one or two instructive lessons from the sudden rise and no less sudden fall of the French sea power during the reign of Louis XIV, and shows how that monarch undid the work of his great minister Colbert.

One of the most interesting points he makes is when he deals with the inherent wrongheadedness of the French policy of hostility to Holland. As he shows, Holland's greatness lay on the sea, and her real rival, the rival before whom she ultimately succumbed, was England. France also strove for development by sea, only to be steadily thwarted and finally worsted by the island kingdom; while on land Holland had no territory which France was able to gain. It was, therefore, clearly the true wisdom of both nations to make common cause against the people who, in the end, triumphed over both. A policy of steady alliance between France and Holland, from the days of De Ruyter, Tromp, Duquesne, and Tourville onward, might have changed the fate of the world; and, if so, would probably have changed it much for the worse. The spread of the mighty English-speaking race, their rise to world dominion, was greatly helped by the jealous division between its two most formidable foes during the critical years when the possession of the North American continent hinged largely on the control of the Atlantic Ocean.

In the war of the Spanish succession, England established her overwhelming preponderance at sea, which has lasted, with but one or two partial interruptions, to our own time. Until this period she has shown no such preponderance. During the seventeenth century, though on the whole she established her superiority, she did so only by a long series of desperate and doubtful struggles with the Dutch and French; and she was defeated again and again by both these rivals. She produced one or two noted admirals, like Blake and Monk, but none who stood above the sea chiefs of her adversaries.

All this was changed after the year 1700. From the time when Gibraltar was taken to the beginning of the war for American independence, England possessed the undisputed supremacy of the ocean. It was this, more than anything else, which gave her North America and India and paved the way for her taking possession of Australia and South Africa. But the very extent of her superiority prevented any serious efforts to overcome it, and the campaigns and battles of this period possess but little interest in themselves.

When, however, England, in the midst of her struggle with the revolted colonies, was struck by the combined navies of France and Spain — both of them, but especially that of France, having been sedulously cared for and built up in the interval — the fight became most interesting, for it was waged on equal terms. Captain Mahan's account of this war is excellent. Among other things, he shows clearly the harm wrought to France by the system of tactical timidity in naval warfare which her rulers adopted and instilled into the minds of their sea commanders. The English always tried to destroy their opponent's navies, and it was their cue to attack, which they always did with great courage though often with so little skill as to neutralize their efforts. The French, on the other hand, had been cowed by repeated defeat, and except when led by some born fighter, like the Bailli de Suffren, rarely took the offensive or pressed home a blow, though they fought with great skill when attacked; and their strategy was fatally defective, in that they conducted their campaigns not with the purpose of destroying the enemy's fighting power — his war fleets — but with the purpose of neutralizing or evading it while some island or outpost was secured or conquered. It must be said, nevertheless, that our author does not give sufficient weight to the military operations on land and the effect of the American privateers.

This war of the American Revolution brought to the front two great admirals, Rodney and Suffren; and two of the best chapters in Captain Mahan's book are those in which he describes the deeds of these men. The military analysis in these two chapters is really very fine; no previous writer has approached it, in dealing with either the Frenchman or the Englishman. In particular, Suffren's campaign in the Indian Ocean has never before been treated with such clearness of perception and appreciation. Indeed, to most English writers he has hitherto been little but a name; and it was hardly possible for a Frenchman to write of him as justly as Captain Mahan has done.

One or two of the points which Captain Mahan brings out have a very important bearing on our present condition, especially in view of the increased interest which is felt in the navy and coast defense. There is a popular idea that we could accomplish wonders by privateering — or rather by commerce-destroying, as Captain Mahan calls it. He shows very clearly, on the other hand, that commerce-destroying can never be more than a secondary factor — even though of very considerable importance — in bringing to a conclusion a war with a powerful foe. He shows also that for the most successful kind of commerce-destroying there must be a secure base of operations near the line of the enemy's commerce and some kind of line of battle to fall back on — and the United States possesses neither. Doubtless, in event of a war, we might cause annoyance and loss to an enemy's commerce; but we could not by this method accomplish anywhere near as much as the people at large, and not a few of our naval officers also, believe. It is beyond all comparison more important to cripple the enemy's fighting ships than to harass his merchantmen.

Again, as Captain Mahan shows, our experience in the Civil War is worthless as a test of what we could do against a foreign sea power. It is impossible to imagine a more foolish state of mind than that which accepts the belief in our capacity to improvise means of resistance against the sea power of Europe, ready equipped and armed at all points, because we were successful in overcoming with our makeshifts an enemy even more unprepared than we were ourselves. It is true that at the end of four years' warfare we had developed a formidable fleet; but in the event of a European contest, it is not likely that we should be allowed as many weeks before the fatal blow fell. There is a loose popular idea that we could defend ourselves by some kind of patent method, invented on the spur of the moment. This is sheer folly. There is no doubt that American ingenuity could do something, but not enough to prevent the enemy from ruining our coasting trade and threatening with destruction half our coast towns. Proper forts, with heavy guns, could do much; but our greatest need is the need of a fighting fleet. Forts alone could not prevent the occupation of any town or territory outside the range of their guns, or the general wasting of the seaboard; while a squadron of heavy battleships, able to sail out and attack the enemy's vessels as they approached and possessing the great advantage of being near their own base of supplies, would effectually guard a thousand miles of coast. Passive defense, giving the assailant complete choice of the time and place for attack, is always a most dangerous expedient. Our ships should be the best of their kind — this is the first desideratum; but, in addition, there should be plenty of them. We need a large navy, composed not merely of cruisers, but containing also a full proportion of powerful battleships, able to meet those of any other nation. It is not economy — it is niggardly and foolish shortsightedness — to cramp our naval expenditures while squandering money right and left on everything else, from pensions to public buildings.

The End of the War, and After

by WALTER HINES PAGE

The Spanish-American War was brought to a close with the crushing defeat of the Spaniards in the Battle of Santiago, July 1–3, 1898. On the assumption that peace would soon be signed, Walter Hines Page, the first Southerner to be editor of the Atlantic, *wrote this prophetic editorial.*

SEPTEMBER 1898

It is reason for universal congratulation that the war is ended so early and so happily — for us, for the Spanish colonies, and, in spite of her present humiliation, for Spain herself; for the result makes for civilization. There was never a doubt that it would end with an American victory; but that the victory would be so easily and so cheaply won was not foreseen. Nor were the incidental benefits foreseen; for there are incidental benefits as great as the main result itself. Unforeseen also were the new obligations that have been imposed on us.

The danger to our successful management of Cuba and Porto Rico, or even of the Philippine Islands, consists not in their distance from our shores but in their difference of population and institutions from ours. They cannot be converted into American states by any statutes, and no laws can change their character. Nor is there any need that they should now or ever be converted into American states.

We are committed to two duties: we have by conquest taken upon ourselves a solemn obligation to the people of the conquered islands to insure stable government, and the nature of our institutions forbids that we should set up any form of government except one that at the earliest possible moment shall become self-government. Even if we wished we could not shirk these responsibilities. We cannot leave the people of these islands either to their own fate, or to the mercy of the now defeated and disorganized Spanish rule, or yet to the mercy of any predatory nation that might seize them. We are responsible for their development.

We want no "colonies," can indeed have no "colonies," in the Continental sense; but we must fulfill every obligation to Spain's conquered subjects that our conduct of the war in Asiatic waters has put upon us, without regard to the colonizing ambitions of the European nations; and we shall hardly fail, moreover, to keep whatever strategic advantage our Navy has won in either ocean.

The war, then, brings within the sphere of English-speaking civilization two of the most valuable of the Antilles; incidentally the Hawaiian Islands and perhaps a part of the Philippine group; and these results can be only good. But in achieving them we have achieved other results quite as great, and no less great because they were unexpected.

We have recovered our own national feeling. Four months ago, we were a great mass of people rather than a compact nation conscious of national strength and unity. By forgetting even for this brief time our local differences, we have welded ourselves into a conscious unity such as the Republic has not felt since its early days. Not only have the North and the South forgotten that they were ever at war — for time and industry had already well-nigh brought this result — but the Pacific states are nearer to the rest of the Union than they ever were before, and the great Middle West is no longer estranged from the seaboard. We can work out our own problems and build our own future with a steadier purpose.

This consciousness is the keener because of the increased respect that other nations have for us. The United States was never before understood in official Europe, perhaps not even in official England. When the war was begun, most of the Continental nations failed to conceal their contempt of us; they now respect us as they never dreamed they should. Nor is it only our naval victories that have given the world a somewhat new conception of the United States. Quite as impressive has been the absence of the old-time barbarities of war and of warlike vindictiveness. To send home across the ocean a captured army, to parole the officers of a captured squadron, to feed not only the victims of Spanish misrule but the Spanish themselves, have laid emphasis on other reasons for war than the old reasons of the punishment of enemies and the conquest of tribute-bearing territory. In humanity to the enemy this war is without parallel. Both the power and the aims of the Republic are more clearly understood in Europe than a half century of peace could have revealed them.

It is to be hoped, too, that we have had some effect on the medieval diplomacy of Europe. We have often been called blunt and discourteous in our diplomacy, no doubt with truth; for European diplomacy is a dilatory art that has always been as courteous as it has usually been mendacious. Ministers have seldom said what they or their masters meant. Now, if the dealings of civilized governments with one another are ever to advance beyond evasion and cunning, the old diplomacy must change to republican directness and frankness. It need not take on discourtesy in manner, but it must speak the truth and keep faith. If we have even in slight measure discredited the old mendacious and dilatory methods, we have done something toward furthering political civilization.

Nor will the impulse that asserted itself in the war stop with the war. The spirit of the people once having looked outward, American enterprise will seek new fields of conquest — not by arms, but by trade and legitimate adventure. Our Navy has revealed to ourselves not less than to the rest of the world our rightful place among the nations. Modern transportation, which we have done most to develop, has changed all international political conditions. By reason of it we are already "entangled" with other peoples in ways that the fathers could not foresee and that no policy can prevent. The great outward pressure that all nations feel is the pressure of commerce for new markets; and statesmen, whether they know it or not, minister to trade and through trade to civilization. With larger and further-reaching political duties, too, which appeal to the imagination rather than to the private greed of men, our public life will once more rise to the level of statesmanship.

The Making of the Nation

by WOODROW WILSON

A statesman ahead of his time and architect of the League of Nations, Woodrow Wilson was a professor of history at Princeton University when, at the insistence of Horace Scudder, he wrote this farsighted paper on the eventual unification of the United States.

JULY 1897

The making of our own nation seems to have taken place under our very eyes, so recent and so familiar is the story. The great process was worked out in the plain and open day of the modern world, statesmen and historians standing by to superintend, criticize, make record of what was done. The stirring narrative runs quickly into the day in which we live; we can say that our grandfathers built the government which now holds so large a place in the world; the story seems of yesterday and yet seems entire, as if the making of the republic had hastened to complete itself within a single hundred years. We are elated to see so great a thing done upon so great a scale and to feel ourselves in so intimate a way actors in the moving scene.

Yet we should deceive ourselves were we to suppose the work done, the nation made. We have been told by a certain group of our historians that a nation was made when the federal Constitution was adopted; that the strong sentences of the law sufficed to transform us from a league of states into a people single and inseparable. Some tell us, however, that it was not till the War of 1812 that we grew fully conscious of a single purpose and destiny and began to form policies as if for a nation. Others see the process complete only when the Civil War struck slavery away and gave North and South a common way of life that make common ideals and common endeavors at last possible. Then, when all have had their say, there comes a great movement like the one which we call Populism, to remind us how the country still lies apart in sections: some at one stage of development, some at another; some with one hope and purpose for America, some with another. And we ask ourselves: Is the history of our making as a nation indeed over, or do we still wait upon the forces that shall at last unite us? Are we even now, in fact, a nation?

Clearly, it is not a question of sentiment, but a question of fact. If it be true that the country, taken as a whole, is at one and the same time in several stages of development — not a great commercial and manufacturing nation, with here and there its broad pastures and the quiet farms from which it draws its food; not a vast agricultural community, with here and there its ports of shipment and its necessary marts of exchange; nor yet merely a country of mines pouring their products forth into the markets of the world, to take thence whatever it may need for its comfort and convenience in living — we still wait for its economic and spiritual union. It is many things at once. Sections big enough for kingdoms live by agriculture and farm the wide stretches of a new land by the aid of money borrowed from other sections which seem almost like another nation, with their teeming cities, dark with the smoke of factories, quick with the movements of trade, as sensitive to the variations of exchange on London as to the variations in the crops raised by their distant fellow countrymen on the plains within the continent. Upon other great spaces of the vast continent, communities, millions strong, live the distinctive life of the miner, have all their fortune bound up and centered in a single group of industries, feel in their utmost concentration the power of economic forces elsewhere dispersed, and chafe under the unequal yoke that unites them with communities so unlike themselves as those which lend and trade and manufacture and those which follow the plow and reap the grain that is to feed the world.

Such contrasts are nothing new in our history, and our system of government is admirably adapted to relieve the strain and soften the antagonism they might entail. All our national history through our country has lain apart in sections, each marking a stage of settlement, a stage of wealth, a stage of development as population has advanced, as if by successive journeyings and encampments, from East to West; and always new regions have been suffered to become new states, form their own life under their own law, plan their own economy, adjust their own domestic relations, and legalize their own methods of business. States have, indeed, often been whimsically enough formed. We have left the matter of boundaries to surveyors rather than to statesmen, and have by no means managed to construct economic units in the making of states.

is a master in the House, as every member very well knows and
easygoing public are beginning to observe. The Speaker ap-
he committees; the committees practically frame all legislation;
ker, accordingly, gives or withholds legislative power and op-
y, and members are granted influence or deprived of it much
leases. He of course administers the rules, and the rules are
to prevent debate and individual initiative. He can refuse rec-
for the introduction of measures he disapproves of as party
e may make way for those he desires to see passed. He is chair-
the Committee on Rules, by which the House submits to be
l (for fear of helplessness and chaos) in the arrangement of its
and the apportionment of its time. In brief, he is not only its
or but its master.

members protest and write to the newspapers; but old members
— and indeed the Speaker's power is inevitable. You must have
n a numerous body, leaders with authority; and you cannot give
y in the House except through the rules. The man who ad-
s the rules must be master, and you must put this mastery into
ls of your best party leader. The legislature being separated from
utive branch of the government, the only rewards and punish-
which you can secure party discipline are those within the gift
les — the committee appointments and preferences. You can-
inister these by election; party government would break down
idst of personal exchanges of electoral favors. Here again you
ist the Speaker to organize and choose, and your only party
your moderator. He does not lead by debate; he explains, he
nothing to the country; you learn his will in his rulings.

with such machinery that we are to face the future, find a wise
lerate policy, and bring the nation to a common, cordial under-
, a real unity of life. The President can lead only as he can
d the ear of both Congress and the country — only as any other
al might who could secure a like general hearing and acquies-
'olicy must come always from the deliberations of the House
ees, the debates, both secret and open, of the Senate, the com-
of committee conference between the Houses; no one man, no
men, leading; no one man, no group of men, responsible for
me. Unquestionably we believe in a guardian destiny! No other
ld have accomplished so much with such a system; no other
ild have dared risk such an experiment. We shall work out a
for work it out we must. We must find or make, somewhere in

We have joined mining communities with agricultural, the mountain
with the plain, the ranch with the farm, and have left the making of
uniform rules to the sagacity and practical habit of neighbors ill at ease
with one another. But on the whole, the scheme, though a bit hap-
hazard, has worked itself out with singularly little friction and no disaster, and the strains of the great structure we have erected have been
greatly eased and dissipated.

Elastic as the system is, however, it stiffens at every point of national
policy. The federal government can make but one rule, and that a rule
for the whole country, in each act of its legislation. Its very constitution
withholds it from discrimination between state and state, section and
section; and yet its chief powers touch just those subjects of economic
interest in which the sections of the country feel themselves most unlike. Some have one interest in a principle of interstate commerce;
others, another. It would be difficult to find even a question of foreign
policy which would touch all parts of the country alike. A foreign fleet
would mean much more to the merchants of Boston and New York than
to the merchants of Illinois and the farmers of the Dakotas.

The conviction is becoming painfully distinct among us, moreover,
that these contrasts of condition and differences of interest between sections of the country are now more marked and emphasized than they
ever were before. The country has been transformed within a generation, not by any creations in a new kind, but by stupendous changes in
degree. Every interest has increased its scale and its individual significance. The East is transformed by the vast accumulation of wealth
made since the Civil War — transformed from a simple to a complex
civilization, more like the Old World than like the New. The West has
so magnified its characteristics by sheer growth, every economic interest
which its life represents has become so gigantic in its proportions, that
it seems to Eastern men, and to its own people also, more than ever a
region apart.

That there are currents of national life, both strong and definite, running in full tide through all the continent from sea to sea, no observant
person can fail to perceive — currents which have long been gathering
force and which cannot now be withstood. There need be no fear in
any sane man's mind that we shall ever again see our national government threatened with overthrow by any power which our own growth
has bred. The temporary danger is that, not being of a common mind
because not living under common conditions, the sections of the country,
which a various economic development has for the time being set apart

and contrasted, may struggle for supremacy in the control of the government, and that we may learn by some sad experience that there is not even yet any common standard, either of opinion or of policy, underlying our national life. The country is of one mind in its allegiance to the government and in its attachment to the national idea; but it is not yet of one mind in respect of that fundamental question: What policies will best serve us in giving strength and development to our life?

We have now to look more closely to internal conditions and study the means by which a various people is to be bound together in a single interest. Many differences will pass away of themselves. East and West will come together by a slow approach, as capital accumulates where now it is only borrowed, as industrial development makes its way westward in a new variety, as life gets its final elaboration and detail throughout all the great spaces of the continent, until all the scattered parts of the nation are drawn into real community of interest. Even the race problem of the South will no doubt work itself out in the slowness of time, as blacks and whites pass from generation to generation, gaining with each remove from the memories of the war a surer self-possession, an easier view of the division of labor and of social function to be arranged between them. Time is the only legislator in such a matter.

But not everything can be left to drift and slow accommodation. The nation which has grown to the proportions almost of the continent within the century lies under our eyes, unfinished, unharmonized, waiting still to have its parts adjusted, lacking its last lesson in the ways of peace and concert. It required statesmanship of no mean sort to bring us to our present growth and lusty strength. It will require leadership of a much higher order to teach us the triumphs of coöperation, the self-possession and calm choices of maturity.

Much may be brought about by a mere knowledge of the situation. It is not simply the existence of facts that governs us, but consciousness and comprehension of the facts. The whole process of statesmanship consists in bringing facts to light and shaping law to suit or, if need be, mold them. It is part of our present danger that men of the East listen only to their own public men, men of the West only to theirs. We speak of the West as out of sympathy with the East: it would be instructive once and again to reverse the terms, and admit that the East neither understands nor sympathizes with the West — and thorough nationalization depends upon mutual understandings and sympathies.

Ignorance and indifference as between section and section no man

need wonder at who knows the habitual courses o
who comprehends the essential soundness of our
trust the future of the nation. He may confiden
tionalization of interest and policy in the end, wh
ment and fitful change he may fear in the mea
wonder that we should continue to leave oursel
adequate means of formulating a national policy
has presided over our affairs with a strange indul
Providence helps only those who first seek to help
ing of a nation has never been a thing delibera
summated by the counsel and authority of lead
duct and policy of a nation which has won its pla
So far we have had the hopefulness, the readin
of youth in these matters, and have never becom
position into which our peculiar frame of goverm

We have waited a whole century to observe
provision for authoritative national leadership in
President does not always speak with authority, l
a man picked out and tested by any processes in
been participants, and has often nothing but his
fluential. Even when the country does know and
his views no further than to recommend them
gress in a written message which the Houses
subservient to give too much heed to. Within
man except the Vice President to whose choice
heed; and he is chosen, not to be a Senator, b
disability of the President and preside meanwh
he is not a member. The House of Representa
days made its Speaker its political leader as
moderator; but the country is, of course, never
forehand, and his leadership is not the open
but the undebatable leadership of the parliame

To the uninitiated, Congress is simply a mas
responsible leaders known to the system of gov
recognized by its rules are one set of individu
tion, another for another. The secretaries ca
either House as a whole; in dealing with cor
only with groups of individuals; neither par
are only influential men here and there who
caucuses and take advantage of parliamentary

our system, a group of men to lead us, who represent the nation in the origin and responsibility of their power; who shall draw the Executive, which makes choice of foreign policy and upon whose ability and good faith the honorable execution of the laws depends, into cordial coöperation with the legislature, which, under whatever form of government, must sanction law and policy.

Only under a national leadership, by a national selection of leaders, and by a method of constructive choice rather than of compromise and barter, can a various nation be peacefully led. Once more is our problem of nation-making the problem of a form of government. Shall we show the sagacity, the open-mindedness, and the moderation in our task of modification that were shown under Washington, Madison, Sherman, and Franklin in the task of construction?

Economic Conditions for Future Defense

by BROOKS ADAMS

A historian and an expert on trade routes and their influence upon the history of peoples, Brooks Adams was the younger brother of Henry (who never contributed to the Atlantic) *and the last to occupy the Adams House in Quincy.*

NOVEMBER 1903

The United States has aimed, like all empires, at being self-sufficing. She has met with unusual success because, while steadily expanding, she has reduced the cost of manufactures to a parity with the cost elsewhere. She has succeeded not by lowering the scale of living of her population but by increasing their efficiency. She has accelerated the social movement and has carried consolidation to unparalleled intensity. Perhaps the best measure of that intensity may be steel architecture. We concentrate in the steel cage of four-and-twenty stories the energy which a decade since was diffused over a short street; and through this concentration comes economy in space, in time, and in energy. By equivalent methods in railways, foundries, and farms, we cause labor to pro-

duce more here than abroad. If the scale of the modern building be
applied it would be from four- to six-fold.

The result may suffice, but it has been attained by changing our building material from wood, brick, or stone, to steel, and by this change we
have altered the conditions upon which competition has heretofore existed. Cheap steel in quantities equal to brick and stone is now the basis
of Western civilization. We may smelt approximately 20 million tons of
pig annually; should our progress last we shall consume from 80 million to 100 million tons within fifty years. No one can foretell how long
our mines will yield such an amount without a rise in the price of ore;
but, in any event, an alternative seems likely to be presented to us.
Either our mines will fail and we shall, like the Romans, have to seek
minerals beyond our borders, or our abundance will constrain Europeans to do the like. If they find cheaper beds than ours we shall be
undersold, and mines which are undersold are, practically, exhausted.
Hence the control of the most advantageous raw material is likely, in the
future, to assume the importance between nations which it now has between rival corporations in the United States. Nevertheless, as among
nations, there is but one way in which the possession of prizes of this
nature can be determined, and that is by force. Arbitration can only
serve where strength is equally balanced, and the matter in dispute is
not worth the price of the conflict. So far as we now know, the district
in which iron can be produced cheapest and in unlimited volume is
northern China. Russia is, at present, massing several thousand men in
Eastern Asia preparatory to an attempt to crush Japan and absorb this
region. Each citizen can judge for himself what attitude befits the
United States in this emergency.

Furthermore, as industries acquire momentum the necessity for a
vent grows imperative; Germany feels this necessity. Germany and Russia form together an overland economic system stretching from the Pacific to the North Sea. In the main the interests of the two empires are
identical. Meeting in Central Europe, the adjoining ends of these empires are fixed, but the extremities are free; and thus Russia expands
toward Peking, and Germany seeks to enter South America. But South
America is the last continent at once rich, vacant, in the path of exchanges, and accessible. Also South America is the only certain vent for
our surplus in the future, as Asia is the only certain base from whence
we can draw raw material. Should Russia absorb northern China, and
by means of German capital and talent establish an industrial center
there, and should Germany occupy South America and develop it with

Chinese steel, the overland economic system would girdle the world, and the United States would suffocate. Both base and vent would be closed.

Dreams of peace have always allured mankind to their undoing. Human destiny has been wrought out through war. The United States is an illustration. Little of the soil which now acknowledges the sovereignty of the Union has not been subdued by arms. The first settlers slew the Indians, or were themselves slain; next the Americans and English conquered the French; afterward the Americans turned on the English and, with the aid of France, ejected them. In 1812 we again fought the English to defend the national unity, and subsequently took California from Mexico by the sword. To consolidate a homogeneous empire we crushed the social system of the South, and lastly we cast forth Spain. The story is written in blood, and common sense teaches us that as the past has been, so will be the future. Nature has decreed that animals shall compete for life, or, in other words, destroy or be destroyed. We can hope for no exemption from the common lot.

As the economic system, of which the Union forms the heart, stretches across oceans toward other continents, in obedience to its law of being, it must encounter rivals also seeking treasure. At the points where the roads converge there will almost certainly be conflicts — as there was at Pittsburg between the French and English — and then he who recoils is lost. Victory in such cases usually means high fortune, and defeat signifies ruin. It is the lesson of Wolfe and Montcalm, or of Adams and Hutchinson.

In these crucial moments races either develop genius or sink into imbecility, and the time when the people of the United States may again be tried is uncertain. Now they can arm and be ready, or they can elect the placid life which leaves the future to chance. Inertia blasted Rome under Augustus, and an easy self-complacency fostered those delusions as to the power of England which bewildered Townsend and Lord North.

The tale of Rome is threadbare; that of England is still new. If our people would know the price which Great Britain is now paying for defeats a century old, they may learn it in Mr. Chamberlain's manifestoes, or in the report of the Inspector General of Recruiting on the degeneracy of the British army.

Remarks at the Peace Banquet

by WILLIAM JAMES

Toward the close of his career, William James, psychologist and professor of philosophy at Harvard, spoke these prophetic words at the banquet which brought to an end the World's Peace Congress in Boston, October 7, 1904.

DECEMBER 1904

I am only a philosopher, and there is only one thing that a philosopher can be relied on to do. You know that the function of statistics has been ingeniously described as being the refutation of other statistics. Well, a philosopher can always contradict other philosophers. In ancient times philosophers defined man as the rational animal; and philosophers since then have always found much more to say about the rational than about the animal part of the definition. But looked at candidly, reason is one of the very feeblest of Nature's forces, if you take it at any one spot and moment. It is only in the very long run that its effects become perceptible. Reason assumes to settle things by weighing them against one another without prejudice, partiality, or excitement; but what affairs in the concrete are settled by is and always will be just prejudices, partialities, cupidities, and excitement. Appealing to reason as we do, we are in a sort of a forlorn hope situation, like a small sandbank in the midst of a hungry sea ready to wash it out of existence. But sandbanks grow when the conditions favor; and weak as reason is, it has the unique advantage over its antagonists that its activity never lets up and that it presses always in one direction, while men's prejudices vary, their passions ebb and flow, and their excitements are intermittent. Our sandbank, I absolutely believe, is bound to grow — bit by bit it will get diked and breakwatered. But sitting as we do in this warm room, with music and lights and the flowing bowl and smiling faces, it is easy to get too sanguine about our task, and since I am called to speak, I feel as if it might not be out of place to say a word about the strength of our enemy.

Our permanent enemy is the noted bellicosity of human nature. Man, biologically considered, and whatever else he may be in the bargain, is simply the most formidable of all beasts of prey and, indeed, the only one that preys systematically on its own species. We are once for all adapted to the military status. A millennium of peace would not breed the fighting disposition out of our bone and marrow, and a function so ingrained and vital will never consent to die without resistance, and will always find impassioned apologists and idealizers.

Not only men born to be soldiers, but noncombatants by trade and nature, historians in their studies, and clergymen in their pulpits, have been war's idealizers. They have talked of war as of God's court of justice. And, indeed, if we think how many things beside the frontiers of states the wars of history have decided, we must feel some respectful awe, in spite of all the horrors. Our actual civilization, good and bad alike, has had past wars for its determining condition. Great-mindedness among the tribes of men has always meant the will to prevail, and all the more so if prevailing included slaughtering and being slaughtered. Rome, Paris, England, Brandenburg, Piedmont — soon, let us hope, Japan — along with their arms have made their traits of character and habits of thought prevail among their conquered neighbors. The blessings we actually enjoy, such as they are, have grown up in the shadow of the wars of antiquity. The various ideals were backed by fighting wills, and where neither would give way, the God of battles had to be the arbiter. A shallow view, this; for who can say what might have prevailed if man had been a reasoning and not a fighting animal?

But apart from theoretic defenders, and apart from every soldierly individual straining at the leash and clamoring for opportunity, war has an omnipotent support in the form of our imagination. Man lives *by* habits, indeed, but what he lives *for* is thrills and excitements. The only relief from habit's tediousness is periodical excitement. From time immemorial wars have been, especially for noncombatants, the supremely thrilling excitement. Heavy and dragging at its end, at its outset every war means an explosion of imaginative energy. The dams of routine burst, and boundless prospects open. The remotest spectators share the fascination. With that awful struggle now in progress on the confines of the world, there is not a man in this room, I suppose, who doesn't buy both an evening and a morning paper, and first of all pounce on the war column.

This is the constitution of human nature which we have to work against. The plain truth is that people *want* war. They want it anyhow; for itself; and apart from each and every possible consequence. It is the final bouquet of life's fireworks. The born soldiers want it hot and actual. The noncombatants want it in the background, and always as an open possibility, to feed imagination on and keep excitement going. Its clerical and historical defenders fool themselves when they talk as they do about it. What moves them is not the blessings it has won for us, but a vague religious exaltation. War, they feel, is human nature at its uttermost. We are here to do our uttermost. It is a sacrament. Society would rot, they think, without the mystical blood payment.

We do ill, I fancy, to talk much of universal peace or of a general disarmament. We must go in for preventive medicine, not for radical cure. We must cheat our foe, politically circumvent his action, not try to change his nature. In one respect war is like love, though in no other. Both leave us intervals of rest; and in the intervals life goes on perfectly well without them, though the imagination still dallies with their possibility. Equally insane when once aroused and under headway, whether they shall be aroused or not depends on accidental circumstances. How are old maids and old bachelors made? Not by deliberate vows of celibacy, but by sliding on from year to year with no sufficient matrimonial provocation. So of the nations with their wars. Let the general possibility of war be left open, in Heaven's name, for the imagination to dally with. But organize in every conceivable way the practical machinery for making each successive chance of war abortive. Put peace-men in power; educate the editors and statesmen to responsibility. Foster rival excitements and invent new outlets for heroic energy; and from one generation to another, the chances are that irritations will grow less acute and states of strain less dangerous among the nations. Armies and navies will continue, of course, and will fire the minds of populations with their potentialities of greatness. But their officers will find that somehow or other, with no deliberate intention on any one's part, each successive "incident" has managed to evaporate and to lead nowhere, and that the thought of what might have been remains their only consolation.

The last weak runnings of the war spirit will be "punitive expeditions." A country that turns its arms only against uncivilized foes is, I think, wrongly taunted as degenerate. Of course it has ceased to be heroic in the old grand style. But I verily believe that this is because it now sees something better. It has a conscience. It knows that between civilized countries a war is a crime against civilization. It will still perpetrate peccadilloes, to be sure. But it is afraid, afraid in the good sense of the word, to engage in absolute crimes against civilization.

An Appeal to Sanity

by ALFRED NORTH WHITEHEAD

Philosopher, author, and mathematician, Alfred North Whitehead was born in England in 1861, taught long full years at Cambridge University and at the University of London, and brought his career to a golden sunset at Harvard. "An Appeal to Sanity," of which this is a quarter, dealt with the question of world tensions and how they came to arise in four areas: Central Europe, Southern Asia, the British colonies, and the Arab world. The power and perception of Whitehead's thinking are shown in these pages written shortly after Munich.

MARCH 1939

Today the most universal problem is the relation of the Jews to the various countries in which they dwell. Our modern progressive civilization owes its origin mainly to the Greeks and the Jews. The progressiveness is the point to be emphasized. China and India long ago attained to types of life with more delicate aesthetic and philosophic appreciations, in some respects, than our Western type. But they reached a level and stayed there. The Greeks and the Jews, in the few centuries before and after the beginning of the Christian era, intensified an element of progressive activity which was diffused throughout the many peoples in the broad belt from Mesopotamia to Spain.

The Roman Empire was a great creation. But no Roman ever disclosed a new idea in religion, in science, in philosophy, in art, in literature, or even in the law which is called Roman. The sustained habit of progressive activity was the discovery of Greeks and Semites in the marvelous thousand years which precede and include the foundation of Christianity. The Greeks have vanished. The Jews remain.

Today we are witnessing a relapse into barbarism. The tendency touches every country. But it is centered in Europe. And in Europe Germany is the main seat of the vicious explosion. The general character is overemphasis on the notion of nationality, producing the ideal of the totalitarian state. The activity, derivative from this debased notion, is the determination to exterminate international factors which exhibit human nature as greater than any state system. The Jews are the first example of this refusal to worship the state. But religions, arts, and sciences will come next, until mankind are reduced to mean little creatures subservient to the god-state, embodied in some god-man. The worth of life is at stake.

Two problems of pressing importance are made urgent by the anti-Jewish explosion in Germany. How can the Jews in Germany be saved? How can the Jews from Germany and elsewhere be redistributed throughout the world?

It should be realized at once that war is no solution for either of these perplexing duties. An immediate war would probably lead to the massacre of hundreds of thousands of Jews, together with the slaughter of other millions throughout various nations. Europe may be forced into war by the wild lusts of dictatorial states to achieve domination. It is necessary for the democracies to be armed and watchful. But war cannot solve the Jewish question. However successful the crusade, it will leave eighty million Germans with emotions yet more remote from civilized standards.

It is obvious, therefore, that our first task is to undertake the expense of receiving the Jews and of enabling them to settle elsewhere after such training as is necessary for their new life.

The final problem is the permanent settlement. There is not one solution. There must be many settlements in diverse regions. In considering such districts we must be careful to judge them in reference to the techniques of the present and the future, and to free our imaginations of pictures derived from a vanished past. This caution especially applies to the large stretch down the East Coast of Africa. Hitherto it has been out of the way and remote. But tomorrow, when airplane traffic has developed, the whole coast line will be intimately connected with Egypt, Palestine, and India. The world is on the eve of a development as important and as revolutionary as that produced by the introduction of railways. Disastrous oversights will be committed by people whose imaginations are fettered to past history.

And yet, in other ways, the converse error of neglecting the lesson of history shows ominous signs of hindering the process of settlement.

The association of Jews with the Mahometan world is one of the great facts of history from which modern civilization is derived. The Jewish settlement in Palestine has been established with success, in respect to its immediate aims. It has been supported with ability and self-sacrifice. The result has made it evident that the country is capable of supporting yet larger numbers.

There is one exception to this satisfactory issue of the experiment. The Arabs in Palestine are dissatisfied — not all the Arabs, but large sections who are in open revolt. This serious state of things is probably in part due to lack of statesmanlike initiative on the part of British officials. Some genius was required and failed to appear; perhaps there was positive inefficiency. The situation has not been rescued by them, nor has it been improved by two committees of inquiry dispatched from England.

There is, however, another side to this question, which may produce disaster. Any fusion of Jewish and Arab interests must be produced by the Jews and Arabs themselves. This primary objective of statesmanship seems to have been largely overlooked by the Jewish controlling agencies. It would not be fair to the mass of emigrants from Central Europe to expect from them any insight into the complications of Syrian life, but the controlling agencies in England and the United States might have been asked to show some grasp of the essential objectives.

Unfortunately in public utterances, whatever may have been done behind the scenes, there has predominated the demand that Great Britain should force upon Palestine an unrestricted Jewish domination. In one instance there was even a suggestion that the Jewish agencies should refuse to attend any conference to which dissentient Arabs were to be admitted.

This attitude, if maintained, is signing the death warrant of the Jewish home in Palestine — perhaps not today, but in the near future. In the region of large political affairs, the test of success is twofold — namely, survival power and compromise.

The literary interest of historians is captured by transitory brilliance. Survival power is the basic factor for political success.

For Palestine, any immediate solution which depends on the persistent military might of Great Britain is bound to fail. Within the next century there is every prospect that in times of crisis England will be unable to transport sufficient troops. She cannot be depended on to exercise continuous military domination along the Syrian coast. She may return, but continuity is unlikely.

Any convulsion within the vast area of British influence may occupy her reserves of military strength, which merely amount to an adequate police force. When this happens, a convulsion in Palestine must go its own way. Also, in that neighborhood, convulsions do happen. Within this century, Armenians have been massacred, and the Greeks have been driven from Asia Minor, which was their homeland for nigh three thousand years.

Most British statesmen are keenly aware that they are primarily a coördinating agency, exercising police control and seeking political structures with intrinsic survival power. Some English statesmen of vigorous decisiveness forget this role; they try to decide and impose. They are the failures in modern English history, much beloved by vivid intellectuals. Cromwell in Ireland is an outstanding example in the past, and Carlyle was an admiring intellectual.

The second element in political success is compromise. The essence of freedom requires political compromise. A clash of interests arises when the social system concerned involves a divergence of aim; compromise means an endeavor to adjust these differences so that the social life shall offer the largest spread of satisfactions. Political solutions devoid of compromise are failures from the ideal of statesmanship.

The tradition of Jewish life does not include any large experience in the political management of the societies throughout which it is spread. Jewish thought naturally concentrates on specific ideals, conceived in the abstract, devoid of compromise and of the requisites for survival.

This characteristic, combined with the ability of the race, is the reason for the incalculable services of the Jews to civilization. They supplied ideals beyond conventional habits. At the same time it explains the failure of the race throughout its long history to maintain stable political structures. Jewish history, beyond all histories, is composed of tragedies.

Christianity was founded in Jerusalem, proclaiming ideals beyond the customary habits of the world. The Christian Church, which gave Europe its modern civilization, was seated in Rome, where the long habit of imperial rule adjusted ideals to immediate necessities. Christianity gained its genius from Judea and its survival power from the Roman Empire. In the result, Christianity was a Jewish creation interfused with Roman stability.

Today another tragedy is crucifying the Jewish race. The work of rescue is again vivified by a prophetic hope — the ideal of a Jewish national home in the central region of its history.

There is always a condition attached to the success of any ideal seeking embodiment in historic reality. The condition in this case is the coöperation of the Mahometan world. There is good reason to anticipate success; Jewish coöperation was a factor in the great period of Mahometan brilliance. In the present remodeling of the Mahometan world, Jewish skills give the exact assistance that the populations require: Jewish learning can mold Mahometan learning to assimilate modern knowledge; Palestine is placed exactly at the sensitive point where the Western world touches Mahometan life.

The University of Jerusalem, technological schools, modes of agriculture and of manufacture should extend their influence throughout the Near East. Also, care should be taken to avoid the indiscriminate extension of European legal ideas into a social life to which they are alien. Crude notions of personal ownership or of state dominance fail to apply to the subtleties of tribal life. A sensitive response to the real facts of the life around is required. The simplicities of abstract thought must be shunned. These warnings are commonplace. Unfortunately they are required.

In the adjustment of Jews and Arabs, one-sided bargains are to be dreaded. They spell disaster in the future. The hope of statesmen should be to elicit notions of mutual service and of the interweaving of habits so that the diversity of populations should issue in the fulfillment of the varied subconscious claims on life.

There is a new world waiting to be born, stretched along the eastern shores of the Mediterranean and the western shores of the Indian Ocean. The condition for its life is the fusion of Mahometan and Jewish populations, each with their own skills and their own memories, and their own ideals.

War can protect; it cannot create. Indeed, war adds to the brutality that frustrates creation. The protection of war should be the last resort in the slow progress of mankind toward its far-off ideals.

Atomic War or Peace

by ALBERT EINSTEIN as told to RAYMOND SWING

Winner of the Nobel Prize for Physics in 1921, Albert Einstein was driven into exile by Hitler. He sought refuge in the United States in 1933, became a life member of the Institute for Advanced Study at Princeton and an American citizen. His daring formula, E equals mc², led to the belief that atomic energy could be unlocked. We published the article which follows almost two years before Russia had the Bomb.

NOVEMBER 1947

Since the completion of the first atomic bomb nothing has been accomplished to make the world more safe from war, while much has been done to increase the destructiveness of war. I am not able to speak from any firsthand knowledge about the development of the atomic bomb, since I do not work in this field. But enough has been said by those who do to indicate that the bomb has been made more effective. Certainly the possibility can be envisaged of building a bomb of far greater size, capable of producing destruction over a larger area. It also is credible that an extensive use could be made of radioactivated gases which would spread over a wide region, causing heavy loss of life without damage to buildings.

I do not believe it is necessary to go on beyond these possibilities to contemplate a vast extension of bacteriological warfare. I am skeptical that this form presents dangers comparable with those of atomic warfare. Nor do I take into account a danger of starting a chain reaction of a scope great enough to destroy part or all of this planet. I dismiss this on the ground that if it could happen from a man-made atomic explosion it would already have happened from the action of the cosmic rays which are continually reaching the earth's surface.

But it is not necessary to imagine the earth being destroyed like a nova by a stellar explosion to understand vividly the growing scope of atomic war and to recognize that unless another war is prevented it is likely to bring destruction on a scale never before held possible and even now hardly conceived, and that little civilization would survive it.

In the first two years of the atomic era another phenomenon is to be noted. The public, having been warned of the horrible nature of atomic warfare, has done nothing about it, and to a large extent has dismissed the warning from its consciousness.

Americans may be convinced of their determination not to launch an aggressive or preventive war. So they may believe it is superfluous to announce publicly that they will not a second time be the first to use the atomic bomb. But this country has been solemnly invited to renounce the use of the bomb — that is, to outlaw it — and has declined to do so unless its terms for supranational control are accepted.

I believe this policy is a mistake. I see a certain military gain from not renouncing the use of the bomb in that this may be deemed to restrain another country from starting a war in which the United States might use it. But what is gained in one way is lost in another. For an understanding over the supranational control of atomic energy has been made more remote. That may be no military drawback so long as the United States has the exclusive use of the bomb. But the moment another country is able to make it in substantial quantities, the United States loses greatly through the absence of an international agreement, because of the vulnerability of its concentrated industries and its highly developed urban life.

I am not saying that the United States should not manufacture and stockpile the bomb, for I believe that it must do so; it must be able to deter another nation from making an atomic attack when it also has the bomb. But deterrence should be the only purpose of the stockpile of bombs. In the same way I believe that the United Nations should have the atomic bomb when it is supplied with its own armed forces and weapons. But it too should have the bomb for the sole purpose of deterring an aggressor or rebellious nations from making an atomic attack. It should not use the atomic bomb on its own initiative any more than the United States or any other power should do so. To keep a stockpile of atomic bombs without promising not to initiate its use is exploiting the possession of the bombs for political ends. It may be that the United States hopes in this way to frighten the Soviet Union into accepting supranational control of atomic energy. But the creation of fear only heightens antagonism and increases the danger of war. I am of the opinion that this policy has detracted from the very real virtue in the offer of supranational control of atomic energy.

We have emerged from a war in which we had to accept the degradingly low ethical standards of the enemy. But instead of feeling liberated from his standards, and set free to restore the sanctity of human life and the safety of noncombatants, we are in effect making the low standards of the enemy in the last war our own for the present. Thus we are starting toward another war degraded by our own choice.

It may be that the public is not fully aware that in another war atomic bombs will be available in large quantities. It may measure the dangers in the terms of the three bombs exploded before the end of the last war. The public also may not appreciate that, in relation to the damage inflicted, atomic bombs already have become the most economical form of destruction that can be used on the offensive. In another war the bombs will be plentiful and they will be comparatively cheap. Unless there is a determination not to use them that is far stronger than can be noted today among American political and military leaders, and on the part of the public itself, atomic warfare will be hard to avoid. Unless Americans come to recognize that they are not stronger in the world because they have the bomb, but weaker because of their vulnerability to atomic attack, they are not likely to conduct their relations with Russia in a spirit that furthers the arrival at an understanding.

But I do not suggest that the American failure to outlaw the use of the bomb except in retaliation is the only cause of the absence of an agreement with the Soviet Union over atomic control. The Russians have made it clear that they will do everything in their power to prevent a supranational regime from coming into existence. They not only reject it in the range of atomic energy: they reject it sharply on principle, and thus have spurned in advance any overture to join a limited world government. Their reasons quite obviously are pretexts. But what seems to be true is that the Soviet leaders believe they cannot preserve the social structure of the Soviet state in a supranational regime. The Soviet government is determined to maintain its present social structure, and the leaders of Russia, who hold their great power through the nature of that structure, will spare no effort to prevent a supranational regime from coming into existence, to control atomic energy or anything else.

The Russians may be partly right about the difficulty of retaining their present social structure in a supranational regime, though in time they may be brought to see that this is a far lesser loss than remaining isolated from a world of law. But at present they appear to be guided by their fears, and one must admit that the United States has made ample contributions to these fears, not only as to atomic energy but in many other respects. Indeed this country has conducted its Russian policy as though it were convinced that fear is the greatest of all diplomatic instruments.

That the Russians are striving to prevent the formation of a supranational security system is no reason why the rest of the world should not work to create one. It has been pointed out that the Russians have a way of resisting with all their arts what they do not wish to have happen; but once it happens, they can be flexible and accommodate themselves to it. So it would be well for the United States and other powers not to permit the Russians to veto an attempt to create supranational security. They can proceed with some hope that once the Russians see they cannot prevent such a regime they may join it. It may be that the first response would be to reject the world of law. But if from that moment it began to be clear to the Russians that such a world was coming into existence without them, and that their own security was being increased, their ideas necessarily would change.

I am in favor of inviting the Russians to join a world government authorized to provide security, and if they are unwilling to join, to proceed to establish supranational security without them. Let me admit quickly that I see great peril in such a course. If it is adopted it must be done in a way to make it utterly clear that the new regime is not a combination of power against Russia. It must be a combination that by its composite nature will greatly reduce the chances of war. It will be more diverse in its interests than any single state, thus less likely to resort to aggressive or preventive war. It will be larger, hence stronger, than any single nation. It will be geographically much more extensive, and thus more difficult to defeat by military means. It will be dedicated to supranational security, and thus escape the emphasis on national supremacy which is so strong a factor in war.

If a supranational regime is set up without Russia, its service to peace will depend on the skill and sincerity with which it is done. Emphasis should always be apparent on the desire to have Russia take part. It must be clear to Russia, and no less so to the nations comprising the organization, that no penalty is incurred or implied because a nation declines to join. If the Russians do not join at the outset, they must be sure of a welcome when they do decide to join. Those who create the

organization must understand that they are building with the final
objective of obtaining Russian adherence.

These are abstractions, and it is not easy to outline the specific lines
a partial world government must follow to induce the Russians to join.
But two conditions are clear to me: the new organization must have no
military secrets; and the Russians must be free to have observers at
every session of the organization, where its new laws are drafted, discussed, and adopted, and where its policies are decided. That would
destroy the great factory of secrecy where so many of the world's suspicions are manufactured.

It may affront the military-minded person to suggest a regime that
does not maintain any military secrets. He has been taught to believe
that secrets thus divulged would enable a war-minded nation to seek to
conquer the earth. (As to the so-called secret of the atomic bomb, I
am assuming the Russians will have this through their own efforts
within a short time.) I grant there is a risk in not maintaining military
secrets. If a sufficient number of nations have pooled their strength they
can take this risk, for their security will be greatly increased. And it
can be done with greater assurance because of the decrease of fear,
suspicion, and distrust that will result. The tensions of the increasing
likelihood of war in a world based on sovereignty would be replaced by
the relaxation of the growing confidence in peace.

Membership in a supranational security system should not, in my
opinion, be based on any arbitrary democratic standards. The one re-
quirement from all should be that the representatives to supranational
organization — assembly and council — must be elected by the people
in each member country through a secret ballot. These representatives
must represent the people rather than any government— which would
enhance the pacific nature of the organization.

To require that other democratic criteria be met is, I believe, inad-
visable. Democratic institutions and standards are the result of historic
developments to an extent not always appreciated in the lands which
enjoy them. Setting arbitrary standards sharpens the ideological differences between the Western and Soviet systems. But it is not the ideological differences which now are pushing the world in the direction of
war. Indeed, if all the Western nations were to adopt socialism, while
maintaining their national sovereignty, it is quite likely that the conflict
for power between East and West would continue.

I should wish to see all the nations forming the supranational state pool all their military forces, keeping for themselves only local police. Then I should like to see these forces commingled and distributed as were the regiments of the former Austro-Hungarian Empire. There it was appreciated that the men and officers of one region would serve the purposes of empire better by not being stationed exclusively in their own provinces, subject to local and racial pulls.

I should like to see the authority of the supranational regime restricted altogether to the field of security. Whether this would be possible I am not sure. Experience may point to the desirability of adding some authority over economic matters, since under modern conditions these are capable of causing national upsets that have in them the seeds of violent conflict. But I should prefer to see the function of the organization altogether limited to the tasks of security. I also should like to see this regime established through the strengthening of the United Nations, so as not to sacrifice continuity in the search for peace.

I do not hide from myself the great difficulties of establishing a world government, either a beginning without Russia or one with Russia. I am aware of the risks. Since I should not wish it to be permissible for any country that has joined the supranational organization to secede, one of these risks is a possible civil war. But I also believe that world government is certain to come in time, and that the question is how much it is to be permitted to cost. It will come, I believe, even if there is another world war, though after such a war, if it is won, it would be world government established by the victor, resting on the victor's military power, and thus to be maintained permanently only through the permanent militarization of the human race.

But I also believe it can come through agreement and through the force of persuasion alone, hence at low cost. But if it is to come in this way it will not be enough to appeal to reason. One strength of the Communist system of the East is that it has some of the character of a religion and inspires the emotions of a religion. Unless the cause of peace based on law gathers behind it the force and zeal of a religion, it hardly can hope to succeed. Those to whom the moral teaching of the human race is entrusted surely have a great duty and a great opportunity. The atomic scientists, I think, have become convinced that they cannot arouse the American people to the truths of the atomic era by logic alone. There must be added that deep power of emotion which is a basic ingredient of religion. It is to be hoped that not only the churches but the schools, the colleges, and the leading organs of opinion will acquit themselves well of their unique responsibility in this regard.

The Rivalry of Nations

by WALTER LIPPMANN

Nearly forty years ago, as a young assistant to President Wilson, Walter Lippmann played a formative part in drafting the Fourteen Points. Since then, as a political analyst, he has observed the American people as they pledged themselves to disarm, to outlaw war, to be neutral at all costs. After a second world war for which we were unprepared, he came to believe that an error in our philosophy prevented us from forming an effective foreign policy. The article which follows was the Phi Beta Kappa address which he gave at the College of William and Mary in 1948. A decade later, his argument is still applicable.

FEBRUARY 1948

If we study the history of American foreign relations during the past forty years, we must be struck by an extraordinary paradox. During this period the United States has emerged from its long isolation. It has become one of the leading powers of the world. Not once but twice during this period the American people have had to face the awful issues of war and peace. Can it be said that during this momentous period we have ever succeeded in forming and agreeing on a foreign policy which foresaw correctly and enabled us to deal successfully with the actual course of events? The record is, I think, clear. We have won both wars. But on the crucial issues our diplomacy has thus far always miscarried. It has been unable to prevent war. It has been unable to avoid war. It has not prepared us for war. It has not been able to settle the wars when they have been fought and won.

At no critical phase in this epoch has the actual outcome conformed with our declarations and our expectations. Never has the country been able to achieve any of the principal objectives to which again and again it has been so solemnly and fervently committed.

Thus from 1914 to 1917 the country believed and hoped that it could avoid participation in the First World War. Yet it was compelled to participate. And when it did participate, it was unprepared because it had believed that it would not have to participate. During that war the country hoped and believed that by a victory it would achieve a lasting and democratic peace. The victory was attained. But the peace which had been promised was not achieved. After the First World War the country again believed that if there were another war, it would be able to remain out of it. Again it did not prepare for war. Once again it was unable to remain out of the war when it came.

During the Second World War the country again believed that with victory over the Germans there would begin an era in which all the victorious powers would agree and be harmonious and become unanimous on the terms and conditions of a just and durable peace. We have had the victory. But we have not been able to attain that peace.

Now, after two victorious world wars, we find ourselves discussing the possibility of a third world war. And so we must ask ourselves whether we have become entangled in a degenerating cycle of wars that breed more wars, each more savage and more inconclusive than the last. It is a grim question. We must, however, face it; and I believe that we must answer it by saying that if our present estimates and calculations are no more correct than those on which we acted before, during, and immediately after the First and Second World Wars, then we shall be surprised and disappointed again. Once more we shall not know how to prevent war, or how to prepare for it correctly, or how, assuming we win it, to make peace after it. And if a second world war leads to the third — because we cannot make a settlement of the war we have just won — what ground is there to suppose that we could settle a third world war so that it did not lead to a fourth?

Is it not true that in the twentieth century we have witnessed on the one hand the rise of the United States to pre-eminence among the nations, to a position of great leadership and immense responsibility in shaping the destiny of mankind? And on the other hand, is it not also true that the course of events during the American rise to pre-eminence is strewn with the debris and wreckage of high and hopeful declarations of policy: with Wilson's neutrality, Wilson's Fourteen Points, and the Covenant of the League of Nations; with the Washington treaties of disarmament and the Kellogg Pact to outlaw war; with the Dawes Plan, the Young Plan, and the Hoover Moratorium to reconstruct the world after the First World War; with the Stimson Doctrine to prevent aggression;

with the Neutrality Act before the Second World War; with the quarantine speech of Franklin Roosevelt, and the Four Freedoms, and Hull's Seventeen Points, and the Atlantic Charter, and the Yalta Declaration, and the Truman Doctrine?

When we reflect on this series of declarations and the disappointments which followed them all, we must be struck by the contrast between our capacity as a people to develop national power, and our ability to use it and to manage it successfully. And is it not plain that our failures lie in the field of policy — that is to say, in deciding correctly when, where, how, and to what ends we shall exert the enormous power and influence which we are able to generate?

It cannot be argued that the miscarriages of American diplomacy during the past forty years are due to the weakness of the American nation. Among the powers of the world the United States is the least vulnerable to invasion, to blockade, or, with existing weapons, to decisive assault. The United States has the material resources and it has the productive capacity to develop enormous offensive power in time of war. In time of peace it produces a great export surplus — a surplus above and beyond a high standard of life at home — which renders it economically invulnerable in the outer world. Two great wars have proved the valor of American troops, the fortitude of the American people, and the military competence of American military commanders. Our institutions and our traditions are respected. And on the whole our participation in world affairs is welcomed by the great masses of mankind as promising liberty, justice, peace, and plenty.

We must seek the cause of our diplomatic failures, therefore, in our own minds. We must look for the cause of trouble not in material circumstances but in our own habits of thought when we are dealing with foreign affairs and with the formation of American policy. In the period from Woodrow Wilson to Harry S. Truman our foreign policy has miscarried so regularly because there has been interposed within our own minds, between the outer world and ourselves, a collection of stereotyped prejudices and sacred cows and wishful conceptions, which misrepresent the nature of things, which falsify our judgments of events, and which inhibit the formation of workable policies by which our available means can be devoted efficiently to realizable ends.

We have brought along with us from our age of innocence, from the nineteenth century when we were isolated and when we were sheltered from the rivalries of states and empires, an ideological picture of the world, a philosophical framework of preconceptions. We think this picture of the world is real and noble. In fact it is imaginary and false. And because our philosophy of the nature of international life is false our efforts to play an effective part in world affairs are frustrated.

What then is it in our philosophy which, instead of guiding us, misguides us continually? I think that the question can be answered. The point, as I have already indicated, where our declarations of policy have regularly miscarried is in avoiding war, in preparing for war, and in settling wars. We must ask ourselves whether there is here some common factor of error which confuses all of us on the issues of war and peace. I think there is. I think the error is a refusal to recognize, to admit, to take as the premise of our thinking, the fact that rivalry and strife and conflict among states, communities, and factions are the normal condition of mankind. The popular American philosophy of international life refuses to recognize this fact. It denies that in the world as it is, the struggle for existence is fundamental and in the nature of things. This, I believe, is the philosophical error which prevents us from forming an effective foreign policy.

In the American ideology the struggle for existence, and the rivalry of nations for advantages, are held to be wrong, abnormal, and transitory. Our foreign policy throughout this period has been dominated by the belief that the struggle does not exist, or that it can be avoided, or that it can be abolished. Because of this belief our aim has not been to regulate and to moderate and to compose the conflicts and the issues, to check and to balance the contending forces. Our aim has been either to abstain from the struggle, or to abolish the struggle immediately, or to conduct crusades against those nations that most actively continue the struggle.

Our refusal to recognize the struggle for existence as the normal state of mankind in international affairs has resulted in the repeated miscarriage of American policies. Our efforts to deal with events, as if they conformed or could be made to conform with our ideological picture of what they ought to be, has been rather like using a map of Utopia to find your way around New York City.

The American refusal to recognize the struggle for existence has in this century crystallized in three recognizable patterns of conduct: in a neutrality which assumes that the struggle can be ignored and avoided; in crusades that assume that by defeating the chief troublemaker the struggle for existence will end; in the sponsorship of a universal society which assumes that the struggle can be abolished.

Since 1914 American relations with the outer world have oscillated among these three patterns of conduct. The great debates within this country have turned upon them. But the experience of these forty years shows conclusively, I think, that if we insist on treating the conflict of states, communities, and factions as abnormal, as exceptional, as transitory, we are unable to form an efficient foreign policy. Our American ideology, which we have brought over from a time when we did not have to play a responsible part among the powers of the earth, distorts our judgment when we deal with the problems of power. It distorts our judgment when we have to calculate how a balance can be struck between our aims and our power to realize them.

In practical judgments — and diplomacy, when the stakes are life and death, calls for very practical judgments — the criteria are always relative. There is no such thing as absolute power. Whatever the wealth, the power, and the prestige of a nation may be, its means are always limited. The problem of the maker of policy is to select objectives that are limited — not the best that could be desired but the best that can be realized without committing the whole power and the whole wealth and the very existence of the nation.

But if we examine the issues of foreign policy as they are presented to our people, we find an overwhelming disposition to regard the choices before us not as relative but as absolute. We are disposed to think that the issue is either this or that, either all or nothing, either isolationism or globalism, either total peace or total war, either one world or no world, either disarmament or absolute weapons, either pious resolutions or atomic bombs, either disarmament or military supremacy, either nonintervention or a crusade, either democracy or tyranny, either the abolition of war or a preventive war, either appeasement or unconditional surrender, either nonresistance or a strategy of annihilation.

There is no place in this ideological pattern of the world for the adoption of limited ends or limited means, for the use of checks and balances among contending forces, for the demarcation of spheres of influence and of power and of interest, for accommodation and compromise and adjustment, for the stabilization of the status quo, for the restoration of an equilibrium. Yet this is the field of diplomacy. These are the substance and the matter of an efficient diplomacy.

Our ideologists, however, regard the use of power to achieve and maintain an equilibrium of power as "power politics." And they regard the recognition of spheres of influence as "appeasement." Yet in the absence of a world state, and except in a world dominated by one supreme power, there must be an equilibrium among several powers and a recognition of their spheres of influence. A diplomacy for the world as it is, which is not to expend itself in verbal declarations on the one hand, and on crusades of annihilation on the other, must deal with the balance of power and the determination of spheres of influence.

But under the spell of our ideological picture of the world, we exclude from our minds the very subject matter of diplomacy itself. We would exclude it, we would outlaw it, and we would excommunicate those who discuss it. We insist on treating the rivalry of nations as something that could not exist among right-thinking men. We do not regulate the rivalries because we hold that the rivalries ought not to exist. And so we are left with our three patterns of policy: to ignore the rivalries by proclaiming our neutrality, or to deny the rivalry and to believe it will disappear if the nations are members of a universal society, or to conduct crusades of annihilation against the lions who do not wish to lie down with the lambs.

How does what I have been saying bear upon the subject which preoccupies us all so anxiously and so profoundly — upon our relations with the Soviet Union, with which we are now engaged in a world-wide diplomatic conflict?

The beginning of wisdom on the Russian question is, I believe, to recognize the historic fact that the division between Eastern and Western Europe, the rivalry between Russia and the nations of the West, did not begin with Marx, Lenin, and Stalin, nor would it end if the Soviet regime were overthrown or defeated. The cultural and ideological division of Europe is as old as the division of Christendom between Rome and Byzantium. The imperial rivalry with Russia in the Baltic, in Eastern and Central Europe, in the Danube valley, in the Balkans, in the Middle East, and in the Far East did not begin with the Communists and will not end with Communism. It was one of the great fields of diplomacy under the Czars as it is under the Communists. Rivalry with Russia is a new problem for the United States. But the British Foreign Office has been preoccupied with it for a hundred and fifty years. We had better make up our minds that we shall now be preoccupied with it for a very long time to come.

That being the case, we must give up the notion that the choice is between one world, in which the Russians are our partners, and two worlds, in which we must annihilate the Russians or they must annihilate us. I do not believe that we must either marry the Russians or must fight them, that we must have either a perfect peace or a total war. I believe that the best policy is to recognize that the rivalry will remain, and not to expect it to disappear, and not to think it could be abolished by the United Nations, and not to think it could be abolished by a victorious war; and having recognized that the rivalry is a permanent fact, to use our whole power and influence to regulate it, to keep it within bounds, to establish spheres of influence which limit the rivalry, and a balance of power in the world which checks it.

I do not believe that we can settle the Russian problem once and for all. I do believe we have enough power and influence, if we use them efficiently, to bring about a settlement with Russia in this generation. But it will have to be a settlement which aims not at unanimity, not at ideological harmony, not at the abolition of all our differences and disagreements, but at a truce in the cold war, a *modus vivendi* during which the nations can recover from World War II, at treaties which end in the withdrawal of the armies of occupation in Europe, and the restoration of Europe to the Europeans.

This will not be easy to achieve. It will require the pressure of power — which will offend those among us who do not like power politics. It will require political and economic compromises — which will offend those who regard all compromise as appeasement. But if a truce, and a *modus vivendi,* and a treaty are hard to achieve by power and by compromise, it is certain that without power on the one hand, and compromise on the other, nothing can be achieved.

If we will not or cannot use the classic procedure of diplomacy — which is always a combination of power and compromise — then the best we can look forward to is an era of disintegration in the civilized world, followed perhaps by a war which, once it began, would be savage, universal, and indecisive.

That must not happen. And it need not happen if only our people will abjure their illusions about the nature of the world in which they have so recently become a leading power, and will permit and assist those who must form our policy to go forward on the assumption that our aim is not to marry the Russians and then to live with them happily ever after, nor to fight them and let the whole world be devastated. Our aim is to transact our necessary business with the Russians, at arm's length, coolly, shrewdly, without fear and without extravagant hope, and with as much justice as may be possible where there is as yet no agreement on first principles and where the rivals do not live in the same moral order.

Some of the Notable Books Which Have Been Serialized in the *Atlantic*

Aldrich, Thomas Bailey — *The Stillwater Tragedy*
Antin, Mary — *The Promised Land*
Bates, H. E. — *Spella Ho*
Bowen, Catherine Drinker — *Yankee from Olympus*
Brooks, Van Wyck — *The World of Washington Irving*
Cushing, Harvey — *From a Surgeon's Journal*
de la Roche, Mazo — *Jalna*
de Mille, Agnes — *Dance to the Piper*
de Roussy de Sales, Raoul — *The Making of Yesterday*
De Voto, Bernard — *The Year of Decision: 1846*
Eggleston, George Cary — *A Rebel's Recollections*
Fields, James Thomas — *Our Whispering Gallery*
Galsworthy, John — *The Patricians*
Haines, William Wister — *Command Decision*
Hall, James Norman — *My Island Home*
Hawthorne, Nathaniel — *Passages from Hawthorne's Notebooks*
Hearn, Lafcadio — *Glimpses of Unfamiliar Japan*
Helm, MacKinley — *Angel Mo' and Her Son: Roland Hayes*
Higginson, Thomas Wentworth — *Cheerful Yesterdays*
Hilton, James — *Goodbye, Mr. Chips!*
Household, Geoffrey — *Rogue Male*
Howells, William Dean — *Their Wedding Journey*
James, Henry, Jr. — *The Portrait of a Lady*
Jewett, Sarah Orne — *The Country of the Pointed Firs*
Johnston, Mary — *To Have and To Hold*
Keith, Agnes Newton — *Land Below the Wind*
Kropotkin, Peter — *The Autobiography of a Revolutionist*
Krutch, Joseph Wood — *The Modern Temper*
Lea, Tom — *The Brave Bulls*
Leonowens, Mrs. Anna Henrietta — *The English Governess at the Siamese Court* (Anna and the King of Siam)

MacDonald, Betty — *The Egg and I*
Mackenzie, Jean Kenyon — *The Trader's Wife*
Parker, Gilbert — *The Seats of the Mighty*
Rossetti, William Michael — *The Wives of Poets*
Saint-Exupéry, Antoine de — *Flight to Arras*
Simmons, Ernest J. — *Leo Tolstoy*
Sitwell, Sir Osbert — *Autobiography*
Stein, Gertrude — *The Autobiography of Alice B. Toklas*
Stevens, Vice Admiral Leslie C. — *Russian Assignment*
Stowe, Harriet Beecher — *Agnes of Sorrento*
Thoreau, Henry D. — *Journal*
Tinker, Chauncey B. — *The Young Boswell*
Twain, Mark — *Life on the Mississippi*
Waln, Nora — *The House of Exile*
Welles, Gideon — *Diary*
Welty, Eudora — *Delta Wedding*
West, Rebecca — *Black Lamb and Grey Falcon*
Woolf, Virginia — *Flush: A Biography*
Zinsser, Hans — *As I Remember Him*

Index

746 *Index*